Statistics for Empowerment and Social Engagement

Jim Ridgway

Editor

Statistics for Empowerment and Social Engagement

Teaching Civic Statistics to Develop Informed Citizens

 Springer

Editor
Jim Ridgway
School of Education
University of Durham
Durham, UK

This work was supported by University of Szeged, Hungary and University of Haifa, Israel

ISBN 978-3-031-20750-1   ISBN 978-3-031-20748-8   (eBook)
https://doi.org/10.1007/978-3-031-20748-8

This Springer imprint is published by the registered company Springer Nature Switzerland AG
The registered company address is: Gewerbestrasse 11, 6330 Cham, Switzerland

Foreword

Democracy Needs Statistical Literacy

In his beautiful essay *What is Enlightenment?* Kant spoke of people's emergence from their self-imposed nonage. Nonage is the inability to use one's own mind without another's guidance. It is self-imposed when it originates not in a lack of understanding but in a lack of courage. Dare to know: That is the message of the Enlightenment.

That was in 1784. Since then, statistical data, once a state secret, have become public and statistical thinking has emerged as one of the most powerful weapons of the Enlightenment. One might therefore presume that, by the twenty-first century, with data as the lifeblood of our societies, every citizen would be interested and skilled in understanding it. Surprisingly, that is not so. Most doctors still do not understand health statistics, most judges still do not know how to evaluate DNA evidence, and most of the public is still not even sure what a 30% probability of rain means.

In 2016, Laura Martignon approached me to ask whether I would host a round table of the *International Association for Statistical Education* (IASE) at the Max Planck Institute for Human Development in Berlin on the topic of promoting understanding of statistics about society, in collaboration with the ProCivicStat project (which was then supported by the ERASMUS+ programme of the European Commission and described later in the book). Impressed by the effort to make Civic Statistics a part of school curricula, I enthusiastically agreed. My former Center for Adaptive Behavior and Cognition, known as the ABC Group, developed teaching tools (such as natural frequencies) to foster the intuitive understanding of statistics; as a member of this group, Laura had made important contributions to research on decision-making under uncertainty. The Max Planck Institute hosted two further meetings on Civic Statistics, in the course of which the idea was born to immortalise the results of the ProCivicStats project in the form of this book.

Why, in the age of big data, is the Enlightenment dream still largely science fiction? The traditional enemies of statistical literacy have been authoritarian governments and lack of public education. In most countries we have overcome these, and pioneers such as Otto Neurath and online tools such as those created by the Harding Centre[1] and the ProCivicStat group[2] have helped to make the public risk literate. Yet, a good education in statistical thinking remains the exception rather than the rule in the majority of countries, resulting in collective statistical illiteracy (Gigerenzer, 2014). The Enlightenment dream has also met new challenges and foes. One new rival emerged in the social sciences. In the 1970s, a program known as "heuristics and biases" asserted that people's statistical intuitions are plagued with systematic flaws and that attempts to educate people out of their biases are largely doomed to fail because these biases, like visual illusions, are hardwired. That was a surprising message given that the bulk of psychological research, from Jean Piaget to Ward Edwards, had previously shown that people's statistical intuitions are quite good, albeit not perfect. Many of the celebrated biases were later found not to be biases in the first place (Gigerenzer, 2018). Nevertheless, the message spread and has fuelled a new kind of soft paternalism. Governments around the world began to "nudge" their people into better behaviour instead of teaching them risk literacy.

Paternalism is older than statistical thinking, and secret data are older than open data. Before the 1830s, statistics about citizens were largely considered state secrets and deliberately kept sealed. They were the key to recruiting taxes and soldiers and to economic success. As the saying went, if you wanted something from Napoleon, then give him statistics. Today most data are open to the public; the current problem is how to teach everyone to distinguish reliable data from fake news. The ProCivicStat project has made an important contribution to enabling future generations to make better decisions.

This book is a remarkable achievement. It synthesises much of the work of the ProCivicStat project, along with valuable contributions from fellow travellers. Contributors bring experiences from different countries and academic backgrounds. The book maps out data creators and consumers in the turbulent sea of information in which we all swim. It describes the components of knowledge needed by enlightened citizens (many of these components are absent from current school and undergraduate curricula), illustrated via examples in contexts such as COVID-19 and global warming. It describes and links to resources relevant to teaching such as data visualisation tools, sources of open data, and tools for data analysis, and—most important of all—it describes material for teachers and students developed for use in classrooms at school and university level on Civic Statistics topics such as pollution, migration, social inequalities, and racial bias. It reports on classroom experiences in a wide range of teaching contexts that include social sciences, business education, and teacher education. It discusses data science and describes teaching and activities to support the uses of data science and statistics for social good. It also makes a call

---

[1] https://www.hardingcenter.de/en

[2] http://iase-web.org/islp/pcs/

for action that advocates appropriate actions by stakeholders in different locations in the educational system that are needed if we are to bring about urgently needed curriculum reform.

Kant's vision is one of the biggest dreams of humankind. In the age of big data and fake news, it is as pressing as ever before. We need to find the courage to speak out, defend the scientific method, and make as many people statistically literate as we can. *Sapere aude*—have the courage to know.

Harding Center for Risk Literacy at the   Gerd Gigerenzer
Max Planck Institute for Human
Development, Berlin, Germany

References

Gigerenzer, G. (2014). *Risk savvy: How to make good decisions.* New York: Viking.
Gigerenzer, G. (2018). The bias in behavioral economics. *Review of Behavioral Economics, 5,* 303–336.

Contents

Editors and Contributors

About the Editors

Jim Ridgway is an emeritus professor in the School of Education at Durham University, with a background in cognitive psychology. He directed the SMART Centre which developed data visualisations and curriculum materials to engage students in reasoning with evidence in a range of curriculum areas. In a similar vein, the ProCivicStat project (a collaboration between European partners) has created materials designed to engage high school and undergraduate statistics students with data relevant to pressing social issues. Jim's past work has included the creation of materials to develop mathematical thinking on undergraduate courses in the USA, creation of computer-based materials to identify students in poorly supported communities who have a flair for STEM (subsequently used in 20+ countries), work with the House of Commons Library to provide (huge amounts of) data accessible to citizens via their phones (along with some gamification), design and delivery of the first OECD workshop for politicians and policymakers on evidence-informed decision-making, and several EU-funded projects on girls and STEM. A current project entitled "Firing up the epistemological engine" uses AI (and conventional methods) to challenge some current research practices and conclusions in science and medicine.

Rolf Biehler is an emeritus professor for mathematics education at the University of Paderborn. Earlier, he was professor for mathematics education at the University of Kassel (1999–2009), which followed on from a post as senior researcher at the University of Bielefeld. His research domains include probability and statistics education with digital tools, data science education, tertiary mathematics education, and the professional development of teachers. He was co-director of the Competence Centre for Tertiary Mathematics Education Research (khdm) situated at the universities Paderborn, Kassel, and Hannover from 2011 to 2020. He is co-directing the Project Data Science and Big Data at school level since 2018.

Pedro Campos is professor of statistics and data analysis at the University of Porto, Faculty of Economics. He holds a degree in applied mathematics and statistics, Portucalense University, and a Ph.D. in business and management studies. He is a researcher at LIAAD, the Laboratory of Artificial Intelligence and Decision Support, a unit of INESC TEC, where he coordinates the research line of agent-based modelling. He is also Director of the Post Graduate Course on Business Intelligence and Analytics, at Porto Business School (PBS). He is currently Vice-President of IASE—International Association for Statistical Education and Deputy Director of the International Statistical Literacy Project. Since January 2019, he is the Head of Methodology at Statistics Portugal.

Joachim Engel received a diploma in mathematics from the University of Bonn and a Ph.D. in applied mathematics from the University of Southern California. He was also trained as a high school teacher. Since 2004, he has been professor for mathematics and mathematics education, first at the University of Hannover and then at Ludwigsburg University of Education. He is the author of two popular textbooks on applied mathematics. His research interests are in the area of statistical literacy, mathematical modelling, nonparametric statistics, statistics and society and data science education. He served as President of the International Association for Statistical Education (2019–2021); from 2015 to 2018, he was coordinator of the strategic partnership ProCivicStat, funded by the Erasmus+ programme of the EU.

Daniel Frischemeier is a professor of mathematics education at the primary level at the University of Münster. He received a Ph.D. degree in mathematics education at the University of Paderborn in 2016. From 2009 to 2020, he has been working in the field of mathematics and statistics education at the University of Paderborn in the research group of Rolf Biehler. From 2020 to 2021, he was a member of the working group of Christoph Selter at TU Dortmund University. His major research interests concentrate on the development of statistical thinking of learners from different age levels ranging from primary school to tertiary education. Fundamental aspects in his research focus on the use of digital tools in statistics and data science education.

Iddo Gal is a professor at the Department of Human Services Management, University of Haifa, Israel. His work focuses on the development, teaching, and assessment of adult numeracy and statistical literacy skills and also on managerial issues in service organisations and empowerment of workers and clients in service organisations. He was President of the International Association for Statistics Education (IASE), was Chair of the Numeracy Expert Group of OECD's Programme for International Assessment of Adult Competencies (PIAAC), and led the Numeracy Team of the Adult Literacy and Lifeskills Survey (ALL). He has worked with UNESCO on developing the framework for assessing adult numeracy for SDG Indicator 4.6.1 and is involved in various educational initiatives and research projects in statistics and mathematics education.

Peter Kovacs received his mathematics diploma from the University of Szeged, Hungary, and has a Ph.D. and habilitation in economics. Analysis of multicollinearity was the topic of his dissertation and the habilitation concentrated on statistical and financial literacy development. He is Associate Professor and Chair of the Department of Statistics and Demography at the University of Szeged (2013–). In 2016, he was appointed Vice-President of the Hungarian Statistical Association; he is the chair of the Statistics Scientific Subcommittee of the Hungarian Academy of Science (2018–). His main research interests are in statistical and financial literacy, statistics education development, and multivariate statistical models. He leads a research group on financial literacy and takes part in several research projects—for instance, ProCivicStat.

James Nicholson has a mathematics degree from Cambridge University and an MSc in applied statistics with statistical education from Sheffield Hallam University. He trained as a high school mathematics teacher at Cambridge and taught for 25 years at Harrow School and then as Head of Mathematics at Belfast Royal Academy. He has subsequently been involved in developing data visualisations with the SMART Centre at Durham University. He is the author of four advanced-level textbooks on statistics as well as writing extensively on statistics education issues. His research interests are in statistical literacy, statistics education, and data visualisation. He is Chair of the Advisory Board for the International Statistical Literacy Project.

Susanne Podworny received her Ph.D. in mathematics education in 2018. She began her research career in the working group of mathematics and statistics education at the University of Kassel (Germany) in 2008 and moved to the University of Paderborn in 2012. She is doing research on students using technology for learning and doing statistics with a focus on probabilistic simulations with software such as TinkerPlots and Fathom. Developing learning environments to foster inferential reasoning is one of her main research interests. Another research interest is to design and implement learning environments on civic statistics for secondary and tertiary level with a focus on big and open data.

Achim Schiller is currently a doctoral student in mathematics education under the supervision of Joachim Engel, after studying mathematics, history, and political science as a teacher. His main interests are statistical literacy and the empowerment of people through statistics education. He develops and implements learning environments for students, using educational software and multivariate data.

Contributors

Karen François is Philosopher of Science at Vrije Universiteit Brussel (VUB—Brussels Free University) and full professor and director of the Centre of Logic and Philosophy of Science (CLPS) http://www.vub.ac.be/CLWF/welcome/index.shtml.

She teaches courses and seminars in BA, MA, and Research MA in Philosophy: Science and Society, Ontology, Phenomenological approach to the sciences and develops and writes research proposals in philosophy, ethics, and scientific integrity. Her research focuses on philosophy of science and mathematics, mathematics and statistics education, mathematical, statistical, and (big) data literacy, science and society, scientific integrity, methodology, phenomenology, and philosophy of mathematics education. She has published international high-impact articles in these fields.

She is the Director of the Doctoral School of Human Sciences at VUB, managing and organising multiple activities to assist Ph.D. students in extending and improving their capabilities, in succeeding in gaining a Ph.D. https://student.vub.be/phd/dsh#about-dsh.

She is the co-founder of the Flanders Training Network for Methodology and Statistics (FLAMES), an interuniversity training initiative of the Flemish universities (supported by the Flemish government). FLAMES supports young researchers in their pursuit of best-in-class training in methodology and statistics. https://www.flames-statistics.com/

Gerd Gigerenzer is Director of the Harding Center for Risk Literacy at the Max Planck Institute for Human Development in Berlin. He is Member of the Berlin-Brandenburg Academy of Sciences and the German Academy of Sciences and Honorary Member of the American Academy of Arts and Sciences and the American Philosophical Society. He has been awarded honorary doctorates from the University of Basel and the Open University of the Netherlands and is Batten Fellow at the Darden Business School, University of Virginia. Awards for his work include the AAAS Prize for the best article in the behavioural sciences, the Association of American Publishers Prize for the best book in the social and behavioural sciences, the German Psychology Award, and the Communicator Award of the German Research Foundation. His award-winning popular books *Calculated Risks*, *Gut Feelings: The Intelligence of the Unconscious* and *Risk Savvy: How to make good decisions* have been translated into 21 languages. His academic books include *Simple Heuristics That Make Us Smart*, *Rationality for Mortals, Simply Rational*, and *Bounded Rationality*. His research interest focus on bounded rationality and social intelligence; decisions under uncertainty and time restrictions; competence in risk and risk communication; and the decision-making strategies of managers, judges, and physicians.

Nuno Guimarães is currently a researcher at the Laboratory of Artificial Intelligence and Decision Support (LIAAD), a unit of INESC TEC. Previously, Nuno was part of the research team in the international project REMINDS and conducted research at CIAFEL on the AFINA-TE project. Nuno has a BSc, MSc and PhD in computer science. His areas of interest are fake news detection, social media analysis, and sentiment analysis.

Klára Kazár graduated as an economist at the University of Szeged. She received her Ph.D. degree in 2016 on the topic of examining brand communities with the help of PLS path analysis. Currently, she works as an assistant professor at the University of Szeged in the Faculty of Economics and Business Administration. Klára Kazár teaches several BA and MA statistics courses (in both Hungarian and English). Her research activities include using multivariate statistical techniques, especially in PLS (partial least squares) path analysis in the field of marketing (in the topic of loyalty and brand communities); another part of her research activities is developing statistical education. She takes part in several projects, for instance in ProCivicStat, and another one focuses on developing e-learning (MOOC) materials.

Éva Kuruczleki is an assistant lecturer at the University of Szeged, Faculty of Economics and Business Administration. She has been affiliated with the Department of Statistics and Demographics of the Faculty for the past ten years, first as a teaching assistant, then as a research fellow, and subsequently as an assistant lecturer (since August 2018) and is currently working on her doctoral studies on the topic of "Developing statistical models for measuring SME financial literacy." Her research interests are focused on three main areas: financial literacy research (focusing mainly on SME financial literacy and the application of multivariate models, PLS-SEM modelling, or cognitive mapping), statistical literacy (including the topic of network analysis), and EU integration (from a complexity perspective).

Josephine Louie is a senior research scientist with Education Development Center in Waltham, Massachusetts. She received a bachelor's degree in Social Studies from Harvard College, a master's degree in city planning from MIT, and a doctorate from the Harvard Graduate School of Education. She leads research and development of programs to improve science, mathematics, and data literacy learning in K-12 education. She is the principal investigator of the NSF-funded project "Strengthening Data Literacy across the Curriculum: Engaging Students in Statistical Thinking with Big Social Science Data."

Laura Martignon obtained a bachelor's degree and a master's degree in mathematics at Universidad Nacional de Colombia in Bogotà and a doctorate at the University of Tübingen. Since 2003, she has worked as Professor of Mathematics and Mathematical Education at the Ludwigsburg University of Education and was until 2017 an Adjunct Scientist of the Max Planck Institute for Human Development in Berlin. Her main academic contributions have been in probabilistic reasoning and decision-making. She was one of the founding members of the ABC Center for Adaptive Behaviour and Cognition, directed by Gerd Gigerenzer. She is best known for having conceptualised and defined fast-and-frugal trees for classification and decision-making, proving their fundamental properties, and creating a theoretical bridge from natural frequencies to fast-and-frugal heuristics for classification and decision-making.

Carlos Eduardo Ferreira Monteiro I am professor at the Centre of Education (CE) at the Federal University of Pernambuco (UFPE). Since 1995, I have been involved in teacher education courses mainly related to educational psychology and mathematics and statistics education. Since 2008, I have taught and supervised Ph.D. and master's students on the Post-Graduate Programme in Mathematics and Technological Education (Edumatec) https://www.ufpe.br/ppgedumatec

I have been involved in collaborative national and international research projects, including periods as visiting postdoctoral fellow at the University of Leicester UK (2007), Brussels Free University—VUB (2012), the University of Lisbon (2014–2015), and the Federal University of Rio Grande do Sul—UFRGS (2017).

My research focuses are on psychology of mathematics education, statistics education, critical sense in statistics, statistical and (big) data literacy, sociocultural aspects involved in the teaching and learning of mathematics and statistics, rural education, and mathematics and statistics teacher education, and my publications are related to these topics.

Andreas Proemmel has been a teacher of high school mathematics, geography, and computer science for more than 25 years. In 2012, he obtained a Ph.D. at the University of Kassel with a thesis in stochastics education under the supervision of Rolf Biehler. Currently, he is teaching mathematics and computer science at a German Gymnasium in Thuringia.

Sónia Teixeira has a mathematics degree and an MSc in data analytics—modelling, data analysis, and decision support systems, from the University of Porto. Since 2015, she has worked as a researcher in the Laboratory of Artificial Intelligence and Decision Support, Portugal. She is currently a Ph.D. student in engineering and public policy at the University of Porto. Her research interests are data science for social good, ethical issues of disruptive technologies, namely fairness and transparency of artificial intelligence, and sciences and technology policy.

Anna Trostianitser received an MA degree in cognitive psychology and human factors in 2021 and BA degrees in psychology and human services management in 2015 from the University of Haifa, Israel. She has finished her MA thesis work under the supervision of Prof. Iddo Gal. The name of her research is "Interpreting statistics in the media about the COVID-19 pandemic." Since 2012, she has been working as a research assistant in the field of cognitive psychology at the Institute of Information Processing and Decision Making (IIPDM), University of Haifa, Israel. Since 2015, she has been participating in the ProCivicStat project. Her major research interests are cognitive processes that influence understanding and performance, storytelling and different data representations, use of real data and data in context, statistical literacy, mathematics education, adult numeracy education, critical numeracy, civic skills, statistical attitudes, and interpretation of statistics in the media.

Kimmo Vehkalahti is a fellow of the Teachers' Academy at the University of Helsinki in Finland. He has been a part of the faculty of Social Sciences for about 30 years, currently as senior university lecturer of social statistics in the Centre for Social Data Science. He is author of a Finnish textbook on measurement and survey methods as well as an international textbook on multivariate analysis for the behavioural sciences. His research and teaching activities are related to open data science, multivariate analysis, and introductory statistics.

Christoph Wassner after graduating from the University of Erlangen-Nürnberg with a degree for teaching high school, Christoph Wassner worked as a research assistant at the Max Planck Institute for Human Development in Berlin and obtained a Ph.D. with a thesis in stochastics education under the supervision of Laura Martignon and Rolf Biehler. For the last 15 years, he has been teaching mathematics, computer science, and economics at a German Gymnasium in Bavaria.

Chris Wild did his first degrees at the University of Auckland followed by a Ph.D. at the University of Waterloo before joining the then Statistics Unit of the Auckland Department of Mathematics in 1979. He was Head of Auckland's Department of Statistics 2003–2007 and co-led the University of Auckland's first-year statistics teaching team to a national Tertiary Teaching Excellence Award in 2003. His main research interests are in statistics education with a particular emphasis on visualisation, software for data analysis and conceptual development, and statistical thinking and reasoning processes. Examples of this work include the iNZight system, visual inference tools, and bootstrap animations. Much of his career has been spent in developing methods for modelling response-selective data (e.g. case–control studies) and missing data problems and other aspects of biostatistics. Chris is Fellow of the American Statistical Association and the Royal Society of New Zealand; he is Elected Member of the International Statistical Institute, is Honorary Life Member of the NZ Statistical Association, and has received the Campbell Award the (principal award of the NZ Statistical Association).

Abbreviations

ACLED	Armed Conflict Location and Event Data Project
ACS	American Community Survey
AI	Artificial Intelligence
AIDS	Acquired Immune Deficiency Syndrome
AR	Augmented Reality
BAMS	Bulletin of the American Meteorological Society
BLI	Better Life Index
BMI	Body Mass Index
C3S	Copernicus Climate Change Service
CAST	Computer-Assisted Statistics Textbooks
CATS	The National Academies' Committee on Applied and Theoretical Statistics
CDC	Centers for Disease Control and Prevention
CDC	Climate Data Center
CEO	Chief Executive Officer
CLI	Command Line Interface
CNN	The Cable News Network
CODAP	Common Online Data Analysis Platform
CQS	Critical Questioning of Data-based Statements
CRED	Center for Research on the Epidemiology of Disasters
CS	Civic Statistics
DFDC	Deepfake Detection Challenge
DSSG	Data Science for Social Good
DST	Disruptive Socio-Technical Systems
DV	Data Visualisation
ECSAB	Contextualised Education for Coexistence with the Brazilian Semi-arid Region
EDA	Exploratory Data Analysis
EM-DAT	Emergency Events Database
EPD	Equal Pay Day
ERSST	Extended Reconstructed Sea Surface Temperature

ESCI	Exploratory Software for Confidence Intervals
ETL	Extract, Transform, and Load
FT	Financial Times
GAISE	Guidelines for Assessment and Instruction in Statistics Education
GDP	Gross Domestic Product
GHI	Global Health Security Index
GIS	Geographical Information Systems
GISS	Goddard Institute for Space Studies
GISTEMP	Goddard Institute for Space Studies Surface Temperature Analysis
GMSL	Global Mean Sea Level
GPG	Gender Pay Gap
GPS	Global Positioning Systems
GUI	Graphical User Interface
HANCI	Hunger and Nutrition Commitment Index
HDI	Human Development Index
HIV	Human Immunodeficiency Virus
IASE	International Association for Statistical Education
IBGE	Instituto Brasileiro de Geografia e Estatística
ICIJ	International Consortium of Investigative Journalists
ICT	Information and Communications Technologies
IDE	Integrated Development Environment
IDEA	Institute for Democracy and Electoral Assistance
IDS	Institute of Development Studies
IDS	Introduction to Data Science
IDSSP	International Data Science in Schools Project
IDV	Interactive Data Visualisation
IFHV	Institute for International Law of Peace and Armed Conflict
IFR	Infection Fatality Rate
IoT	Internet of Things
IPUMS	International Public Use Microdata Sample
IRI	International Research Institute
ISCCP	International Satellite Cloud Climatology Project
Isotype	International System of Typographic Picture Education
IWPR	Institute for Women's Policy Research
MEC	Ministry of Education (Brazil)
MERS	Middle East Respiratory Syndrome
ML	Machine Learning
MMR	Measles, Mumps, and Rubella
MR	Mixed Reality
NASA	National Aeronautics and Space Administration
NCTM	National Council of Teachers of Mathematics
NGO	Non-Governmental Organisation
NHANES	National Health and Nutrition Examination Survey
NHS	National Health Service

NO_2	Nitrogen Dioxide
NSO	National Statistics Office
NYT	New York Times
ODI	Open Data Institute
OECD	Organisation for Economic Co-operation and Development
OSA	Official Statistics Agencies
PCS	ProCivicStat
PES	Portuguese Public Employment Services
PIAAC	Programme for the International Assessment of Adult Competencies
PISA	Programme for International Student Assessment
PPDAC	Problem, Plan, Data, Analysis, and Conclusion
PPMV	Parts Per Million by Volume
PPP	Purchasing Power Parity
PS	Participatory Sensing
PUF	Public Use Files
QL	Quantitative Literacy
RESAB	Educational Network of the Brazilian Semi-Arid Region
RSS	Royal Statistical Society
SARS	Severe Acute Respiratory Syndrome
SBE	School of Business and Economics
SDG	Sustainable Development Goal
SEIR	Susceptible, Exposed, Infected, and Removed
SER	Susceptible, Exposed, and Removed
SRLE	Statistical Reasoning Learning Environment
TI	Transparency International
UN	United Nations
UNESCO	United Nations Educational, Scientific and Cultural Organization
UNHCR	United Nations High Commissioner for Refugees
UNICEF	United Nations Children's Fund
USGS	United States Geological Survey
VR	Virtual Reality
WHO	World Health Organization

Chapter 1
Why Engage with Civic Statistics?

Jim Ridgway (iD)

Abstract There is much to celebrate about human progress—increased life expectancy, and global collaboration on pandemics and climate change. Nevertheless, we face major barriers if we are to achieve global sustainable development, and are to avoid cataclysmic wars. Willingness and competence to engage with complex issues are, perhaps, the most difficult barriers to overcome. There are problems with education systems world-wide; engaging with complex issues requires working with diverse sets of multivariate data, and considering different moral and philosophical frameworks. However, in the humanities, too few teachers have appropriate quantitative skills; in STEM, too many teachers stay in their comfort zone and focus on the development of technical skills, at the expense of interpretation and possible action. This chapter maps out the content of the book—a book which offers practical approaches to working in a new field of knowledge—Civic Statistics. Civic Statistics sets out to address important social issues by analysing authentic, authoritative data sets (often using innovative approaches). We aim to support and enhance the work of everyone working in high schools and at tertiary level, by engaging students with important topics, and introducing them to exciting and intuitive data visualisations, rich authentic, data sets, and intellectually stimulating ideas. Part 1 begins by explaining the concept of Civic Statistics, tracing its history, and justifying its place in the curriculum. Part 2 focuses on tools and data sets. Part 3 focuses on design principles in practice, and is the heart of this book. It offers examples of Civic Statistics courses in a range of contexts (including mathematics and business education) applied to educational levels that include postgraduate, undergraduate, high school, and primary teaching. Practical examples are associated with design ideas related to both content and pedagogy, and include reflections on the successes (and less-than-successes) of different teaching approaches. Part 4 takes us beyond the traditional classrooms in which statistics has been taught, and points to some future directions for Civic Statistics. Our ambitions when writing this book have

J. Ridgway (✉)
School of Education, University of Durham, Durham, UK
e-mail: jim.ridgway@durham.ac.uk

been to foster an empowered citizenry who push for political actions to address the existential threats we all face.

Keywords Civic Statistics · Statistical literacy · Curriculum reform · Empowerment · Reasoning · Data science · Media literacy · Citizenship

1.1   Why Do We Need Another Book About Teaching Statistics? Why Now? What? And for Whom?

1.1.1   Why We Need Another Book About Teaching Statistics, and Need It Now

Humanity faces existential threats posed by global warming, pandemics and nuclear war. There are urgent problems to be solved, notably those identified by the United Nations Sustainable Development Goals (SDGs). We do have much to celebrate, such as increases in life expectancy world-wide, and international collaborations such as those associated with the Covid-19 epidemic, and on-going work on the SDGs. We have new ways to gather information, new ways to analyse information, and new ways to present information. However, there are major problems posed to social progress attributable to big gaps in public understanding (here the 'public' in 'public understanding' refers to politicians and policy makers, as well as to citizens). If action is to be taken on (for example) climate change, there needs to be a groundswell of public opinion, expressed forcefully enough for politicians to respond appropriately. This requires better public understanding of complex issues, and an empowered citizenry.

A great deal of this public inability to reason with evidence can be attributed to problems with education systems world-wide. Deriving meaning from evidence is common to all academic disciplines, and to all human pursuits, yet students in our education systems seem not to acquire appropriate skills. There is simply too little attention devoted to reasoning with evidence as the basis for decision making. Paradoxically, academic cultures themselves can present barriers to the development of empowered citizens. In high schools, few social science teachers or humanities teachers have skills in communicating statistical ideas. In the sciences and mathematics, teachers may stay within their comfort zone by emphasising statistical techniques and subject-specific methods and theories, as opposed to using statistics and mathematics as part of reasoning about broader social issues. As a result, nowhere in the curriculum is serious attention paid to the exploration of multivariate data relevant to social trends, or to analysis, interpretation, and communication about the meaning and implications of such data.

This book offers practical approaches to working in a new field of knowledge— Civic Statistics—which sets out to engage with, and overcome well documented and long-standing problems in teaching quantitative skills (see Cobb, 2015; GAISE, 2016; Ridgway, 2016). We aim to support and enhance the work of teachers and lecturers working both at the high school and tertiary levels. We describe a wide variety of teaching resources (in an easy-to-search database) that can be used both to enliven single lessons or lectures, and also to provide the basis for an entire course.

1.1.2 What Is 'Civic Statistics'?

Civic Statistics can be thought of as the big sister of (statistical) literacy. An often-quoted definition of statistical literacy highlights two interrelated components:

> ... People's ability to *interpret and critically evaluate* statistical information, data-related arguments, or stochastic phenomena, which they may encounter in diverse contexts, and when relevant their ability to *discuss or communicate* their reactions to such statistical information, such as their understanding of the meaning of the information, their opinions about the implications of this information, or their concerns regarding the acceptability of given conclusions. (Gal, 2002, p2)

In Civic Statistics, the scope of the *interpretation* and *critical evaluation* extends to meaningful contexts such as natural disasters, climate change, pollution, poverty, Covid-19, inequality, racism, migration, refugees, and the ageing society (all of which are addressed in our teaching materials, and presented in this book). In Civic Statistics, students do not 'learn statistics' to master a collection of technical skills; rather, they develop and use technical skills in order to *discuss* and *communicate* ideas about important phenomena, with a primary goal of discussing the implications of information for (and perhaps advocating) social action.

Vygotsky (1978) discusses higher- and lower- order thinking. An example of lower-order thinking is a person with a doctorate in statistics who accepts a media account of (say) the spread of Covid-19, uncritically. An example of higher-order thinking is a teenager who reads a claim that eating burnt toast increases the chances of developing a rare cancer by a factor of 5, then asks what the baseline incidence is. Higher- and lower- order thinking is not about the extent of a person's knowledge; rather it is about the degree of integration into their everyday cognitive functioning. A major goal of Civic Statistics is to cultivate habits of mind where people bring their statistical knowledge to bear whenever they encounter claims about data, whatever the state of their knowledge. A pedagogical design principle is that technical aspects of statistics are taught in context—having a problem you actually want to solve motivates your learning (another of Vygotsky's insights).

1.1.3 So Who Is This Book For?

Our primary audience is anyone involved with teaching about the use of quantitative evidence. This includes primarily teachers of statistics and applied mathematics, and social sciences. However, there is no need to exclude teachers of humanities and arts from the target audience; everyone reasons from evidence, and the topics discussed in this book are important to every sector of humanity. The sources and nature of evidence used in every academic discipline are becoming increasingly varied, and old boundaries between reasoning with qualitative and quantitative evidence are becoming increasingly blurred. We also want to reach out to everyone concerned with the planning of educational systems; this includes curriculum designers and developers, and school managers. Data science is an emerging area of interest; Civic Statistics offers many practical approaches to introducing data science across the curriculum.

1.2 Background to the Book: ProCivicStat

This book has its origins in the ProCivicStat project. ProCivicStat (PCS) was a three year collaboration between people working in the Universities of Durham, Haifa, Ludwigsburg, Paderborn, Porto, and Szeged supported with funding from the Erasmus+ Program of the European Union. The project brought together people from a wide variety of backgrounds, all committed to improving the quality of teaching and learning with and about statistics. We have received support from the International Association for Statistics Education (IASE), which hosts many of our resources, and via IASE conferences where we have run workshops and presented papers. Many of our ideas were presented and refined at conferences hosted by (and run in collaboration with) the Max Planck Institute for Human Development in Berlin.

The products of the collaboration (see ProCivicStat Partners, 2018) include:

- A conceptual framework mapping the skills and knowledge required for Civic Statistics
- CivicStatMap[1]—a database of teaching and learning materials, lesson plans and datasets geared to supporting innovative teaching practices related to Civic Statistics in high schools and universities
- A review of dynamic visualisation tools
- A review of relevant data bases
- Sample syllabuses
- Workshop materials
- A Call for Action that maps out the actions needed by different players in our education systems
- Dozens of conference papers that describe many of the above ideas and materials in more detail

We have increased the scope of this book beyond these resources. The book includes an extended account of the rationale for Civic Statistics, along with a conceptual framework that maps out the requisite component skills, and we have elaborated on

---

[1] http://iase-web.org/islp/pcs/

the PCS Call for Action and recommendations. We provide examples of a wide variety of data visualisations that can be used in class to teach about Civic Statistics, and describe some relevant sources of data in detail. We describe our approaches to the design of lesson plans; current examples may need to be refreshed over time, so we hope an explanation of the principles of lesson design will be helpful to teachers in the long run. We offer descriptions of materials that can be used in a variety of diverse contexts—high schools, adult education programs, undergraduate and graduate courses; teacher education, statistics, business studies; computer science, and social sciences, and we also offer pedagogical advice around the theme of question posing and tasks that provoke discussion. In some chapters we explore the relationships between Civic Statistics, statistics, and data science, and describe programmes that promote data science for social good, with illustrations from a wide range of cultural settings. We also offer a map of the emerging evidence ecosystem, to re-emphasize the growing importance of statistical literacy, and its big sister, Civic Statistics.

1.3 Overview of the Book's Content

Part 1 of this book (edited by Joachim Engel and James Nicholson) begins by explaining the concept of Civic Statistics, tracing its history, and justifying its place in the curriculum. Citizens see, read and hear messages in a wide variety of formats—many of which they do not see in formal education. When students encounter data in educational contexts, it has usually been carefully curated; in statistics classes, data are often artificial. Outside classrooms, data are typically messy, multivariate, and maybe relevant only to specific locations and contexts. Cobb (2015) and Ridgway (2016) argue that conventional statistics courses simply fail to prepare students to reason from anything but the simplest sorts of data (and teach just a narrow subset of analytic tools).

Chapter 2 is an invitation to rethink the purpose and nature of statistics education. We identify features of the data that citizens encounter in their everyday lives, starting with the contexts in which people encounter data: first, the focus is often on topics of social importance; statistics are embedded in rich text; causality is often attributed; and conclusions and implications of the data are discussed. The nature of the data encountered is more varied than data commonly encountered in statistics classes: phenomena are often multivariate; decisions have been made about measures and operationalisation; data are often aggregated; indicator systems are common; and data often span time and place. Citizens also come across methods and representations that are unfamiliar: for example, novel data sources (e.g., from sensors in mobile phones, or credit cards); data collection methods can be opportunistic (or simply inappropriate); and data are often presented via novel visualisations. Education should prepare citizens to engage appropriately with this data landscape. We describe and map out some resources and initiatives that will be needed to promote Civic Statistics, such as curriculum maps and educational resources, access to emerging technologies, an evolving body of pedagogic content knowledge, professional development, innovative assessment, cross-curricular initiatives, and collaborations between different stakeholders.

In Chap. 3 we offer a comprehensive model of 11 facets and tools which together describe the knowledge, skills and dispositions that (young) adults need in order to comprehend, critically evaluate, communicate about, and engage with statistics about society. We identify knowledge bases covering selected statistical and mathematical constructs and skills; core literacy and mathematical enabling skills; extensions related to official statistics and risk on the societal level; understanding models and modelling, and multivariate and textual representations; knowledge of research methods and data production methods used in official statistics; and we emphasise the importance of appropriate dispositions. We offer examples and curriculum tasks that illustrate the facets and their interconnectedness. We also describe the use of a radar plot tool to analyse the balance of prospective class activities or test items in terms of coverage of the 11 facets and tools. The chapter ends with a brief discussion of the implications of the conceptual model and its 11 facets for planning curricula, instruction, and assessments related to the promotion of teaching and learning about Civic Statistics.

In Chap. 4 we launch a Call for Action—identifying responsibilities, roles, and the actions required of key players located in different places in the education system, if statistics curricula are to be reformed. The chapter examines issues that are essential for promoting necessary changes in the teaching and learning of Civic Statistics, and which are needed for empowering citizens to engage with data-informed reasoning about burning issues in society. The chapter shows how to analyse task demands in terms of the facets and tools required (mapped out in Chap. 3). Then, general questions are raised about the alignment of the demands of Civic Statistics with curriculum intentions (the intended curriculum), classroom teaching practices (the implemented curriculum), and assessment methods (the attained curriculum). We provide some guidelines for developing assessment items relevant to Civic Statistics. Finally, the chapter presents six broad recommendations related to systemic changes that can promote attention to, and critical understanding of, Civic Statistics at the school and university levels which can improve effective instruction and assessment.

Part 2 of this book (edited by Rolf Biehler and Peter Kovacs) focuses on tools and data sets. Data visualisation has been a game-changer in communicating complex information; dynamic visualisations provide opportunities for citizens to ask (and answer) their own questions about data. Chapter 5 documents some historical landmarks in data visualisation (including examples associated with Florence Nightingale and Otto Neurath), then offers a review of modern data visualisation tools. Modern data visualisations are categorised as tools to display individual data sets, and tools to support the exploration of rich data sets. Examples are given which can be used to provide stand-alone illustrations of core statistical ideas (such as seasonal changes embedded in changes over time, variability, or stochastic processes), to illustrate predictive models such as dynamic population pyramids, and to explore complex ideas such as the Better life Index.

A plethora of open data is available, but it is not obvious how to locate, access, and work with these data. Chapter 6 points to sets of both macro and micro data we have found valuable in teaching Civic Statistics—i.e. data which are authentic and from trustworthy sources, multivariate, and which address topics of social importance, such as climate change, malnutrition, and migration. This chapter also describes *CivicStatMap*, a software tool created as part of the ProCivicStat project designed to make it easy for users to locate resources by providing links to and between data sources, statistical concepts, visualization tools and lesson plans. Some data sources are described in detail, along with illustrative analyses and visualisations.

Chapter 7 describes the approach we have taken to the design of lesson plans. Essentially, our ambitions are to empower teachers to engage students in storytelling about complex phenomena using authentic data in class. We describe the milestones that are important in the creation of a lesson plan, and offer guidance on designing teaching materials and materials for students. A sample lesson is shown, with annotations which explain the rationale underpinning each section, and which highlight important design features. Materials will need to be refreshed over time, so we hope an explanation of the principles of lesson design will be helpful to teachers who wish to create their own resources.

Chapter 8 describes the use of interactive data visualisations in action, and offers reflections on experiences using some *Gapminder* tools. The Gapminder Foundation has developed several visualization tools (using bubble charts, trend lines, ranks, maps, etc.) in order to facilitate the exploration of complex relationships between variables, to rank countries, and to explore things such as time series, age distributions and income distributions. The goals of this chapter are to show these different tools in action in the context of undergraduate and postgraduate courses in economics and business studies. Classes explored poverty and the ageing society; we describe some experiences, and the advantages and disadvantages of using different tools.

A wide variety of digital tools is available to support the analysis of large and multivariate data sets. These range from sophisticated tools designed for professional users, through to tools designed specifically for use in primary and secondary school classrooms. Chapter 9 illustrates and compares the characteristics and functionality of some tools designed specifically for use in education—notably *TinkerPlots*, F*athom* and *CODAP*. To illustrate the functionality of each tool a variety of analyses are shown (such as *income* as a function of *education level* and *race*) using data from the American Community Survey.

Chapter 10 focusses on just one software package—*iNZight*. It describes features that facilitate data exploration by both naïve users (which include both direct guidance and hooks to encourage engagement and further learning), and by advanced users (such as the automatic generation of R code for documentation and software reuse). It illustrates ways of working with multivariate data, exploring subgroups within data, using multiple representations, analysing and reanalysing, exploring changes over time and spatial patterns, and telling stories grounded in evidence, in a wide range of Civic Statistics contexts.

Climate change is an existential threat facing humanity. Climate data on a massive scale has been collected, but exploring and extracting useful knowledge from large quantities of data requires powerful software. Chapter 11 presents some possibilities for exploring these data using the statistical programming language *R* together with the computing environment *RStudio*. We present exercises for use in class along with sample solutions. We also provide *R* scripts for exploring and presenting data, along with annotated references to climate data sets.

There are few better examples than a pandemic to demonstrate the importance of, and need for, Civic Statistics. Citizens and governments need to take account of existing and emerging evidence, in order to decide on effective action. This puts high demands on skills associated with communicating statistical evidence on the side of governments and media, and requires a citizenry able to understand statistical messages. Evidence associated with Covid-19 covers the full spectrum of the features of Civic Statistics data, and citizens need to acquire the full range of skills needed to understand and act on evidence set out in Part 1 of the book. Chapter 12 illustrates these features and points to requisite skills, in the context of Covid-19, and suggests some activities for students.

Part 3 (edited by Iddo Gal and Daniel Frischemeier) focuses on design principles in practice, and is the heart of this book. It offers examples of Civic Statistics courses in a range of contexts (including mathematics and business education) applied to educational levels that include postgraduate, undergraduate, high school, and primary teaching. Practical examples are associated with design ideas related to both content and pedagogy, and include reflections on the successes (and less-than-successes) of different teaching approaches.

Chapter 13 aims to support the development of students' statistical literacy and critical understanding of Civic Statistics. For many teachers of statistics, this will be unfamiliar ground. We provide suggestions to support tutors' reflection and action. These include: decisions about meaningful and important contexts worthy of attention when teaching for statistical literacy; suggestions for questions and tasks about these contexts; and ideas about the questions we want students to have internalised (i.e. to have become 'habits of mind') by the end of a course. The chapter closes with a discussion of the implications for teaching, and in particular ideas for developing opinion questions and worry questions that will help students engage effectively with the data and arguments they encounter in their daily lives.

Chapter 14 describes hands-on experiences implementing Civic Statistics in business education. Civic Statistics is particularly important in business education because topics both cut across, and link, different areas of students' studies and the multidisciplinary nature of Civic Statistics helps students to develop complex and critical thinking. We report experiences teaching in both large and small classrooms, and highlight the differences between the techniques and topics employed in different circumstances. Topics include: the ageing society, poverty and income inequality, social and business networks and financial literacy. Student feedback is discussed in terms of increased engagement and participation, and students' overall enjoyment when working on unfamiliar topics and tools.

Chapter 15 discusses the design of a course on Civic Statistics for pre-service mathematics teachers in their teacher education program. At the beginning of the course, participants were confronted with an example of Civic Statistics; participants' statistical knowledge was then refreshed in several sessions, so that they were able to engage with further Civic Statistics activities. A structure for Civic Statistics activities is presented, intended to introduce design principles for implementing Civic Statistics content in classes, and to develop the pedagogical content knowledge of pre-service teachers. This structure also facilitates understanding of the example lesson plans that can be found at *CivicStatMap*. Detailed examples are offered of Civic Statistics activities organized both as short mini-projects and also as a longer project.

Chapter 16 describes a new type of introductory statistics course for prospective secondary school mathematics teachers which focuses on Civic Statistics. The course aims at developing statistical content knowledge with regard to Civic Statistics, critical thinking, cross-disciplinarity, and some contextual knowledge, as well as subject-matter related pedagogical competencies, and technological competencies. A specific challenge was to engage students majoring in mathematics with socio-politically sensitive and controversial issues, and to foster reflection about these topics from an instructional and educational perspective. An important element of the course focussed on critical questioning of data-based statements in the media, where students deconstructed media headlines by evaluating claims using the original data and information about the research design. As in the case of the activities described in Chap. 15, the course design is based on principles associated with the Statistical Reasoning Learning Environment (Garfield & Ben-Zvi, 2008), as well as the recommendations of the ProCivicStat Partners (2018).

A basic tenet of this book is that statistical literacy should be an integral part of general education. To achieve this, more attention at school level must be given to skills in reasoning with authentic data, with a particular emphasis on key societal issues. Chapter 17 describes work in high schools, where teachers designed, implemented and evaluated learning units. Activities included an exploration of the gender pay gap in Germany, using *Fathom*. In addition to sharing classroom experiences, the authors discuss conceptual, as well as process- and curriculum-oriented issues. They offer suggestions and recommendations for the teaching and learning of Civic Statistics at the secondary level, taking into account didactic principles and the special educational demands involved.

Civic Statistics by its nature is highly interdisciplinary. From a cross-curricular perspective, teaching and learning Civic Statistics poses specific challenges related to the preparation of teachers and the design of instruction. Chapter 18 presents examples of how Civic Statistics resources and concepts can be used in a wide variety of courses and subject areas, including biology, business and economics, citizenship and civics, geography, media studies, sociology, earth sciences and psychology. Because topical issues and current data are central to these resources, we recognise that the original ProCivicStat resources will become outdated in time, and (again) offer some guidance about how to develop new Civic Statistics resources.

Civic Statistics involves both analysis and decision making. The notion of risk is central to decision making, and estimating risks is often experienced as difficult (in the Preface, Gerd Gigerenzer points out that health professionals and others can be poor at estimating risk). Sometimes the difficulties are intrinsic and sometimes the difficulties may be inherent in the representations and formalisms used to represent them. Chapter 19 describes ways to communicate risks and uncertainties visually, using representations which foster intuition and are easily grasped. These tools have been shown to be effective when modelling risky situations and making decisions that can lead to better informed action. These tools require an understanding of conditional probabilities and the chapter illustrates how conditional probability can be introduced to primary school children in a playful way, thus helping them acquire the first elements of risk literacy.

Part 4 of this book (edited by Pedro Campos and Achim Schiller) takes us beyond the traditional classrooms in which statistics has been taught, and points to some future directions for Civic Statistics. One chapter illustrates how Civic Statistics can help people improve the quality of their lives; one describes experiences using project-based teaching to develop skills necessary for engagement in data science projects for social good; a third chapter explores the evolving relationships between data science, statistics and Civic Statistics; and a fourth chapter locates Civic Statistics in an evolving evidence ecosystem.

Chapter 20 explores the changing roles that statistics has had, and will continue to have, in people's lives. It offers an historical perspective on the origins of statistics, then discusses social aspects which can facilitate empowerment through the use of statistics. A third element considers the cognitive, socio-cultural, and affective dimensions of critical issues associated with people interpreting statistical data. A concluding element presents three examples of projects (from Brazil, and Belgium) that involve teachers, students, and communities in employing Civic Statistics to initiate social actions on environmental themes. These projects show how Civic Statistics can act as a tool to empower people to achieve important changes in their environments.

A number of pro-social groups have established themselves in response to emerging disparities between profit-driven companies and charitable and governmental organisations in their capacity to process and utilise data. To address these disparities and make a positive impact on society, the focal point of the activities of these groups has been to embark on collaborative ventures where they provide expertise in using data to inform decision making. How might educational institutions support such initiatives? In Chap. 21 we describe Data Science for Social Good, a 12-week fellowship focused on solving problems that matter, with the help of machine learning and data mining techniques using problem-based learning. We describe the logistical challenges to higher education associated with this approach (and some solutions). We hope the insights will inspire others to consider unfamiliar styles of teaching which promote new ways to engage with society through civic action and applied data science.

Chapter 22 addresses the relationship between data science, statistics, and Civic Statistics. Products of data science have transformed modern life. We outline the idea of disruptive socio-technical systems (DST)—new social practices that have been made possible by innovative technologies, and which have profound social consequences. Civic Statistics should go beyond simply addressing known problems, and should include empowering citizens to engage in discussions about our possible futures. We have a responsibility to prepare students for their roles as *spectators* (understanding the nature and potential of data science products in creating DST), and as *referees* (having a political voice about which DST are acceptable and unacceptable), and as *players* (engaging with data science for their own and others' benefit), and we elaborate on the skills needed for these roles.

Our knowledge is shaped by an ecosystem comprising a web of creators and consumers who are connected in complex ways. In Chap. 23, we identify some of the elements in this ecosystem, and map some of their relationships with Civic Statistics. Many actors in the evidence ecosystem hold Enlightenment views (i.e. that human happiness can be increased by knowledge, evidence and wise actions); other actors reject the Enlightenment view entirely. We argue that students should see the evidence they encounter in the context of this evidence ecosystem, comprising agents whose ambitions range from benign to malevolent. As educators, we should look for ways to develop student resilience—in particular to make them more resistant to polluting elements in the evidence ecosystem. We offer some practical suggestions for educational practices.

1.4 Educating for Citizenship

Consider this question: *Is access to the internet a basic human right?* Imagine posing the same question 10 years ago, or 20 years ago, or 30 years ago. At some point, the question would have had no meaning (what is 'the internet'?); later, people might ask: why would anyone want to use it?; now the question leads to discussions about social equality, governance, propaganda, and ethics. Information is being created, distributed, and used in new ways; informed citizens should have a voice in shaping these new uses. There is an apparent paradox for educators here; education should prepare students for citizenship in a world whose nature cannot be predicted. What *can* be predicted, however, is that the world will become more connected, that new ways of communication will be adopted, and that the total amount of information available will increase.

So what will be worth knowing? There is a general consensus on the importance of literacy, where literacy is conceptualised as the ability to communicate effectively using the tools in common currency. This conception of literacy carries with it the seeds of change—as communication tools change, so do the skills needed to work effectively with these tools. In societies where there are few written records, memory for events and laws, creation of epic poems and fables, and rhetorical skills are highly valued; with printing and industrialisation come demands for technical skills associated with text and mathematics; in the information era, literacy means being able to function effectively in an environment full of information of variable quality.

Civic Statistics encourages students to acquire the skills associated with accessing and reasoning with information relevant to social issues using whatever tools are available (and—when appropriate—acting on the conclusions drawn).

In an enlightened society, citizens have access to information, can express their views openly, and can contribute to governance. This works only insofar as people feel empowered, and engage with evidence and ideas. The primary aim of Civic Statistics is to facilitate this process, not simply at the level of promoting appropriate skills of analysis, but also by inculcating confidence, and a willingness to engage. In this volume, we set out to make a contribution to statistics education by focusing on issues of social concern; this fundamental idea of using authentic data to address social problems is shared with a number of agencies and actors, and we believe that engagement with organisations and communities that share these Enlightenment values will be mutually beneficial.

Throughout, we advocate the use of evidence to inform decision-making, and to lead to better actions. We argue for the use of evidence as an integral part of decision making. We argue for the need to interpret quantitative evidence in the context of broad knowledge schemas—evidence is part of a rich process of interpretation and understanding, and can support decision making.

There is an on-going battle for the soul of society, where proponents of informed democracy across the political spectrum are challenged by people (across the political spectrum) who believe in power and personal gain, no matter what the social cost. Technology offers some partial defences, but the most effective strategies for preserving things of value will always reside in shaping the ways that people interact with technologies. Citizens need to feel empowered, and need to have skills in critiquing and interpreting evidence. For educators, there is a real opportunity to make use of new and exciting resources to both educate and empower. These are not easy ideas to communicate to our students—teaching to inculcate things that are 'correct' is far easier than teaching to develop nuanced judgement. We hope this book will help educators to engage with the exciting opportunities afforded by new ideas and resources.

References

Cobb, G. (2015). Mere renovation is too little too late: we need to rethink our undergraduate curriculum from the ground up. *The American Statistician, 69*(4), 266–282. https://doi.org/10. 1080/00031305.2015.1093029

GAISE. (2016). *Guidelines for assessment and instruction in statistics education: College report.* American Statistical Association. https://www.amstat.org/asa/education/Guidelines-for-Assess ment-and-Instruction-in-Statistics-Education-Reports.aspx

Gal, I. (2002). Adults' statistical literacy: Meanings, components, responsibilities. *International Statistical Review, 70*(1), 1–25.

Garfield, J., & Ben-Zvi, D. (2008). *Developing students' statistical reasoning. connecting research and teaching practice*. Springer.

ProCivicStat Partners. (2018). *Engaging civic statistics: A call for action and recommendations. A product of the ProCivicStat project*. http://iase-web.org/islp/pcs

Ridgway, J. (2016). Implications of the data revolution for statistics education. *International Statistical Review, 84*(3), 528–549.

Vygotsky, L. S. (1978). *Mind in society: Development of higher psychological processes*. Harvard University Press.

Part I
Edited by Joachim Engel and James Nicholson

Chapter 2
Back to the Future: Rethinking the Purpose and Nature of Statistics Education

Joachim Engel ⓘ **and Jim Ridgway**

Abstract The purpose of this chapter is to explain the concept of Civic Statistics, and to justify its place in modern statistics curricula. Effective citizen engagement with social issues requires active participation and a broad range of skills, including understanding data and statistics relevant to these social issues. We set out 12 characteristics of data about society, mapping out the nature of the information relevant to Civic Statistics that citizens *see, read* or *hear* about in public discourses. Many introductory statistics courses fail to prepare students to understand and critically analyse empirical evidence in the public domain. Many courses are not designed to teach relevant skills and improve learners' statistical literacy, despite the importance of engaging learners and future citizens with data about social issues and their connections to social policy. We also describe and map out some resources and initiatives that will be needed to promote Civic Statistics, such as curriculum maps and educational resources, access to emerging technologies, an evolving body of pedagogic content knowledge, professional development, innovative assessment, cross-curricular initiatives, and collaborations between different stakeholders.

Keywords History of statistics · Civic Statistics · Statistical literacy · Curriculum · Climate change

2.1 Introduction

The discipline of statistics emerged in response to the perceived need to understand phenomena better, and to address important problems in a broad range of disciplines which involved uncertainty. Early pioneers came from a wide variety of

J. Engel (✉)
Ludwigsburg University of Education, Ludwigsburg, Germany
e-mail: engel@ph-ludwigsburg.de

J. Ridgway
University of Durham, Durham, UK
e-mail: jim.ridgway@durham.ac.uk

backgrounds and invented new mathematics and new ways to look at the world. For example, the early members of one of the earliest professional statistical organizations—the Royal Statistical Society (RSS), founded in 1834—came from diverse backgrounds that included politics, the army, law, history, physical sciences, philosophy, the church, art, journalism, medicine and philanthropy, as well as economics and mathematics. They were driven by a desire to develop and apply new methods to help understand the world around them and to act to make things better (see Pullinger, 2014). The early basis of the RSS was in social issues rather than mathematics and it lists among its founding aims the "collection and classification of all facts illustrative of the present condition and prospects of Society".[1] This desire to collect information to inform action is illustrated vividly by the work of Florence Nightingale (1820–1910), the first female elected to the RSS. In Chap. 5, Ridgway, Campos, Nicholson, and Teixeira show and describe her 'coxcomb' plots of deaths during the Crimean war attributable to battle and to diseases encountered in military hospitals. This startling data [2] was used by Nightingale to push forward major changes in hospital hygiene and sanitation in general.

The challenges faced by the modern world are at least as difficult as those faced by early pioneers, and the range of people engaged, and the variety of investigative methods and analytic tools have grown, and continue to grow in a dramatic way. A number of commentators (e.g. Cobb, 2015; Ridgway, 2016) have argued that many statistics curricula at high-school and college have both forgotten the original impetus for statistics, and have failed to keep up with new methods. Rather, they focus on teaching the mechanics of a beautiful and powerful mathematical structure invented 100 years ago, which is well suited to using well-structured numerical data for solving a certain class of problems. Addressing new classes of real-world problems, and working with new sorts of data and new classes of model have largely been ignored. Some consequences are that students are not empowered to address contemporary problems, do not understand some widely-used techniques that have a direct impact on their lives, and perceive the discipline of statistics itself to be a mathematically-challenging irrelevance.

2.2 The Need for Civic Statistics

Digital media and the ready accessibility of data are shaping personal and political discourses. Non-partisan organizations have gathered a wealth of information that anyone can use for information and debate—from the United Nations work on Sustainable Development Goals created to measure social progress, through National Statistics Offices gathering information on employment, income, and migration, to Non-Governmental Organizations monitoring climate change or

---

[1] https://rss.org.uk/about/history/

[2] https://en.wikipedia.org/wiki/Infographic#/media/File:Nightingale-mortality.jpg

citizens' health. Technology provides powerful tools for data visualisation that offer the potential for citizens to explore rich information sources for themselves. The World Wide Web facilitates public access to open data and government documents, influences the tactics and content of political campaigns, and can shape the behaviour of voters. The explosion of social media is fuelling new and unanticipated directions in e-democracy and e-participation—including increased pressure for direct democracy and new forms of engagement where citizens are actively involved in data gathering (Engel, 2017).

A countervailing trend is a growing disdain for factual knowledge in public discourse, accelerated through the proliferation of misinformation in social media, disseminated without journalistic fact-checking filters. Evidence-informed decision making is facing an existential crisis. In the USA and elsewhere, responsible journalists have been portrayed as "enemies of the people", and government agencies have been forbidden to report raw data that might contradict the political dogma (e.g. on climate change). The ready availability of resources to create deep fake videos poses yet another threat. In a climate of anxiety, confusion, and nostalgia for an imaginary idealized past, raw emotions can prevail—a rather poor way to cope with real challenges and uncertainty (Nowotny, 2016).

For democracy to function, citizens need to have a critical understanding of quantitative evidence about key issues related to social and economic well-being. For example, in a society that promises equality and fairness to all citizens, questions as to whether women, minorities, or people with disabilities are disadvantaged in their career options, wages, or access to education or to services, have to be judged on the basis of quantitative evidence, and this requires some statistical competence. Sound evidence-informed decision making in private as well as in public life requires quantitative reasoning skills, and (equally important) positive attitudes towards engaging with statistical data. In an increasingly complex world, implementing difficult decisions on controversial social topics (such as migration), or enforcing people to behave in ways which have a profound effect on their lifestyle (such as measures to mitigate disease spread) depends on citizens' consent and support. If citizens do not understand and engage in the discussions and decisions themselves, trust in political decision making can be lost (OECD, 2009). Citizen engagement can support the effective functioning of democracy, the legitimacy of government, the successful implementation of policy, and the achievement of social outcomes. Lack of engagement can lead to poor decisions, and alienation. An enlightened citizenry that is empowered to engage with evidence-informed arguments and has the ability to manage, analyse, and think critically about data should be a major educational goal. Civic Statistics aims to develop (*inter alia*) critical evaluation and reflection—essential skills for informed citizenship.

2.3 What Is Civic Statistics?

Until relatively recently (and in many parts of the world still today) information about the state of society was kept secret. Set against this is a long history of advocacy for the role of evidence to promote social justice. As early as 1792, Nicolas de Caritat, Marquis de Condorcet (1994), French mathematician and philosopher around the time of the French Revolution, argued for the importance of informing citizens about governance, and presenting evidence about the state of society in order to raise awareness of injustices and structural social inequalities. He believed in *savoir liberateur*—knowledge that would enable people to free themselves from social oppression. William Playfair's *Political and Commercial Atlas* (1786) is an early publication designed to make complex evidence accessible to a wide audience; John Snow's (1834) map of cholera deaths in London, [3] and Florence Nightingale's (1858) work on deaths in the Crimea both used powerful graphical displays to address problems associated with disease; Otto Neurath's work in the early twentieth century (see Neurath, 2010) on Isotype set out to establish a universal graphical language for communicating about social issues such as urbanization, and the relationship between overcrowding and infant mortality (More detailed examples of the Neurath's work are presented by Ridgway, Campos, Nicholson, and Teixeira in Chap. 5, by Martignon, Frischemeier, McDowell, and Till in Chap. 19 and by François and Monteiro in Chap. 20).

In this book we describe a subfield we call Civic Statistics which focuses on understanding statistical information about society. Civic Statistics involves understanding evidence about key social phenomena that permeate civic life in many areas such as migration, unemployment, social (in)equality, demographic changes, racism, crime, poverty, access to services, health, climate change, education, and human rights. Civic Statistics calls upon social sciences and politics, and requires a unique pedagogical approach. It is situated at the intersection of Statistics and Civics/Social Science and has a distinct educational mission: to empower (not only young) people to understand statistics about society in order to support their informed participation in public discourse and evidence-informed decision processes (see Fig. 2.1).

Early advocates of statistical literacy (e.g. Wallman, 1993; Gal, 2002) typically described the basic competences required to understand and assess statistical data encountered in everyday life. Early advocates promoting the linkage of statistical literacy to understanding of statistics about society include Fischer (1984) and Borovnick and Ossimitz (1987). Lesser (2007) describes statistics as grammar for social justice, and discusses ways to treat various statistical concepts in the context of social justice issues. Skovsmose (1994) argues that mathematics and statistics are a key part of moving towards more democratic, participatory and socially just structures in society. In a related approach Steen et al. (2001, p. 2) characterize mathematical and statistical knowledge within democracy as 'Quantitative Literacy' arguing "*quantitatively literate citizens need to know more than formulas and*

---

[3] https://upload.wikimedia.org/wikipedia/commons/2/27/Snow-cholera-map-1.jpg

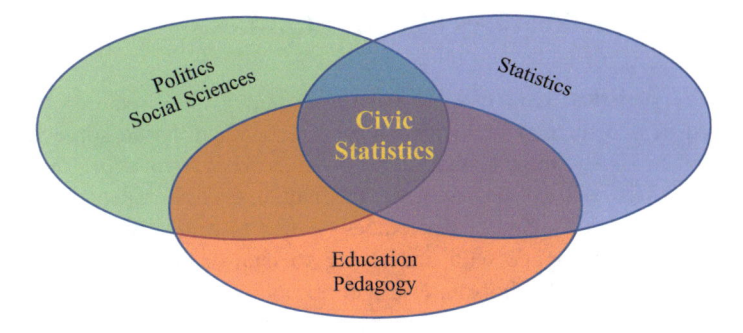

Fig. 2.1 Civic Statistics at the intersection of statistics, social and educational science

equations. They need a predisposition to look at the world through mathematical eyes, to see the benefits (and risks) of thinking quantitatively about commonplace issues, and to approach complex problems with confidence in the value of careful reasoning. Quantitative literacy empowers people by giving them tools to think for themselves, to ask intelligent questions of experts, and to confront authority confidently". Civic Statistics builds on these ideas.

Civic Statistics is related to the concepts of critical statistical literacy (Weiland, 2017) and combines them with modern teaching-learning concepts of statistics (e.g., Ben-Zvi and Garfield, 2004; Ben-Zvi et al., 2018). In teaching quantitative literacy, content is inseparable from pedagogy and context is inseparable from content (Steen et al., 2001, p. 18). Contexts are much more than a pretext for learning particular statistical procedures. The outcome of an investigation in Civic Statistics should be some socio-political reflections (and perhaps conclusions and actions), based on quantitative evidence. The ambition is to support the development of critical citizenship in which students cease to be passive observers of the world, and instead become participants and potential transformers of social crises. Literacy is more than the ability to read, to write, and do elementary computations; it should also encompass competences to interpret social life (Freire, 2014). By extension, statistical literacy means more than the ability to summarize data numerically. Civic Statistics encompasses a demand for empowerment—linked to the concept of "Mündigkeit". This German word has a double meaning. As a legal term, it refers to a person coming of age and thus acquiring an adult's rights and responsibilities in society—notably the ability to act autonomously (e.g. being able to take out a bank loan), and to be responsible for their own actions (e.g. regarding criminality). However, the term has also an informal meaning: that of having the capacity to speak for oneself. So 'the ability to act autonomously' is extended to mean engaging effectively with the world—such as participating in and investigating public policy decisions via statistical arguments. So *Mündigkeit* includes competence in investigating decisions with statistically formulated arguments.

2.4 The Unique Features of Civic Statistics

Much of the statistical data that inform social policy have features not usually encountered in introductory statistics courses. Here we describe some features of data relevant to Civic Statistics that citizens *see, read* or *hear* about in the media, private discussions or in public discourse. In Chap. 3, Gal, Nicholson, and Ridgway describe the tools, skills, and competencies needed to critically *understand* Civic Statistics in order to engage with underlying societal or economic issues, and in Chap. 4, Gal, Ridgway, Nicholson, & Engel set out a call for action.

Statistical information about society is often quite complex. Data are usually multivariate; aggregated data and indicator systems are common; variables interact; data may be time critical. There is a core set of ideas associated with literacy and numeracy that are essential to functioning in society, such as reading skills, understanding arguments, reading graphs and handling percentages. Beyond this, citizens need to do more than understand data—they need to see the implications for society and policy. This requires knowledge about the processes of knowledge generation, and ways to represent and model situations, along with ideas commonly taught in statistics courses such as sample bias and effect size. It also requires contextual knowledge about the state of society. Civic Statistics aims to empower citizens and policy makers by addressing the central issues associated with evidence-informed decision making. These include: developing a sophisticated approach to questions of data provenance and data quality; understanding the uses and abuses of a wide range of methods for presenting and analysing social data from a variety of sources; ways to represent and model situations; understanding risk; and appropriate advocacy.

Statistics about social phenomena often have a number of properties that are different from statistics encountered in other settings; data can have features not typically encountered in introductory textbooks. Some of these features are set out below (for a shorter list, see ProCivicStat Partners, 2018). We categorize the features in three groups: (I) Contexts and interpretations; (II) The nature of statistics; and (III) Rich, new, or uncommon methods and representations. Table 2.1 provides a brief overview.

I. Contexts and Interpretations

1. Societal Context Is the Focus

    Civic Statistics involve issues of importance to society at large or to large subgroups within it. Statistics about civic issues are collected because of societal needs for information about social and economic well-being, trends and changes in society. Statistical methods and concepts in Civic Statistics are taught not for their own sake, but for the purpose of gaining more thorough insight into some context. An important educational goal is to develop students' positive dispositions towards appreciating the potential value of quantitative evidence and to engage with the world. Interpreting Civic Statistics requires attention to the broader world context (e.g., one cannot understand statistics about migration into Europe without being

Table 2.1 Features of Civic Statistics data

Twelve features of Civic Statistics
I. Contexts and Interpretations
1. Societal context is the focus
2. Statistics are embedded in rich texts
3. Causality is often attributed
4. Conclusions implications, and consequences for society are discussed
II. The Nature of the Statistics
5. Phenomena are often multivariate
6. Decisions have been made about measures and operationalization
7. Data are often aggregated
8. Indicator systems are common
9. Dynamic data, spanning times and locations is common
III. Unfamiliar Methods and Representations
10. Novel data sources and analysis techniques are common
11. Varied data collection methods are used
12. Innovative visualisations have been invented

aware of the phenomenon of migration and its possible impact on different communities). Understanding the meaning or societal significance of Civic Statistics requires familiarity with and sensitivity to a network of correlates, both antecedents (including causal factors) and outcomes (consequences for individuals, communities, stakeholders, and society).

2. Statistics Are Embedded in Rich Texts

Statistics about society are presented through texts published by official statistics offices (such as press releases and short reports), and articles in print media and in digital media, and often comprise a combination of graphic, tabular and textual elements. Text is a primary medium for communicating statistics, and citizens need to work with information presented in different ways, such as the formalized language that is often used in official reports, and (sometimes polemic) journalistic texts. A special feature of such texts is their enrichment with data, evaluations and visualisations, which require special reading competence. Journalists often select specific aspects of the original publications, and sometimes present them in ways that promote particular views. Interpretation requires analytical skills to understand information presented in different ways, and critical skills in evaluating the quality of both the evidence and the conclusions drawn. The emergence of data journalism [4] to promote engagement and accurate analysis of data is a welcome development.

3. Causality Is Often Attributed

Analyses in Civic Statistics often explore theories of causality; causality is associated with difficult philosophical challenges (which extend way

---

[4] E.g. https://datajournalism.com/

beyond simple mantras such as 'correlation does not imply causality')—e.g. see Pearl and Mackenzie (2016). Civic Statistics data come mostly from observational studies, surveys or archive data, and rarely from experimental studies, and so a reliable identification of cause-and-effect relationships can be very difficult to establish. As an illustration, in Charles Dickens' *Pickwick Papers* Sam remarks to Mr. Pickwick *"It's a very remarkable circumstance, sir ... that poverty and oysters always seems to go together ... the poorer a place is, the greater call there seems to be for oysters."* Oysters are unlikely to cause poverty; poverty is (today) unlikely to lead to a desire for oysters.

Ideas about possible approaches to social problems need to anticipate possible responses from different agents in social systems—this sort of speculation goes well beyond topics typically taught in statistics classes.

4. Conclusions, Implications, and Consequences for Society Are Discussed

Often in introductory statistics classes, the overall goal is to teach mastery of statistical techniques. To engage with socio-political issues, it is important that statistical literacy goes beyond the consumption or production of statistical/data-based arguments, to include considering how such arguments shape the world around us, and how statistics can be used to better understand the reality in which we live (Weiland, 2017).

In Civic Statistics, analysis is an essential early stage, but is not a destination. The key question for Civic Statistics is 'so what?'. The 'what' might refer to plausible generalisations from the data, conclusions about what they mean, stories about causality, or recommendations for action. Extending this point, it is unusual for a single data set or a single analysis to be sufficient to answer a question in the arena of Civic Statistics. Results are often a provocation to find and analyse more information, as in the case of any scientific enquiry.

II. The Nature of the Statistics

5. Phenomena Are Often Multivariate

Real-world phenomena can be difficult to describe using simple measures. Consider gender equality. One might look at *life expectancy by sex, child care provision, pay, distribution across roles in organisations (including parliaments), dress codes,* and/or *perceptions of appropriate sexual behaviour.* None of these measures captures 'gender equality', but all are relevant. Variables may be correlated (so *pay* and *distribution across roles in an organization* will be related), may interact with each other (so women who are involved in *child care provision* may be disproportionately disadvantaged in terms of *pay* when compared with men who have the same commitment to child care), or variables may have nonlinear relationships among themselves. Similarly, if we are to explain the causes of poverty, it is likely that the measurement of poverty will involve a number of variables, many of which are correlated, and stories about causality are likely to involve multiple variables which, again, are likely to be correlated.

6. Decisions Have Been Made About Measures and Operationalization

It is easy to forget the early struggles in the physical sciences to create measures such as time, temperature, mass, and length. Measurement is a complex issue, and the holy grail is to create measures that are objective, reliable and valid in a variety of situations. Engagement with Civic Statistics needs to be based on a sophisticated approach to measurement. At the simplest level, when using data from official sources, it is essential to pay attention to the metadata—exactly how have things been measured? For example, what does it mean to be *employed*? Here is the definition from the Organization for Economic Cooperation and Development (OECD)—an intergovernmental economic organisation established to promote democracy, and economic progress: "Employed people are those aged 15 or over who report that they have worked in gainful employment for at least one hour in the previous week or who had a job but were absent from work during the reference week". So, while this internationally agreed upon definition is unambiguous, for some people there might be very little practical difference between being employed and unemployed in terms of their income.

At a more complex level, one can ask why particular measures have been chosen, by whom, and for what purposes. Measurement is always linked to some theory of the phenomenon being studied. In the example of physical sciences, mass, length, and time were not chosen as measures because they are 'obvious', but rather because when they are measured, precise predictions can be used about the physical world—for example using Newton's laws of motion to plan a lunar landing. In the case of Civic Statistics, we can point to the use of gross domestic product (GDP) as a measure of government success, and the OECD report *Beyond GDP* (Stiglitz et al., 2018) which challenges the use of this monolithic measure in favour of a collection of measures that includes the well-being of citizens. A corollary of the question about 'what has been measured and why' is the mirror image question about what has *not* been measured and why? Absence of evidence permits all sorts of self-serving stories to be told. In Victorian England, a pervasive story was that poor people are responsible for their own poverty, because of the bad choices they make. Seebohm Rowntree conducted a detailed study of poverty in York at the end of the nineteenth century, via a survey of more than 45,000 people (about two thirds of the city population). He found that almost 30% of the sample did not have enough food, clothing or fuel to keep them in good health—even if they spent their money 'wisely'. Rowntree's work (1908) led directly to major social reforms. Management of the UK's National Health Service (NHS), provides a more recent example. The NHS is free at the point of care to users. Some health care is contracted out to private providers (in 2016/17 this amounted to about 8% of health spending). Paradoxically, private providers are required to produce far less data on performance measures (such as unexpected deaths) than are state providers

(Ruane, 2019). Some websites[5] document such gaps in government data, and why they are important for understanding and policy.

7. Data Are Often Aggregated

Statistics about society often include data grouped in several ways—for example, via nominal variables (men vs. women) or ranks (e.g. level of educational qualifications). Sometimes data are reported for multiple subgroups at different levels of aggregation. Possible conclusions may be influenced by the level of aggregation—patterns in the data may change when data within subgroups are aggregated or disaggregated. For example, mortality is likely to be higher in specialist hospitals where the best surgeons operate than it is in local hospitals. However, when the nature of the surgery is taken into account (specialist hospitals are more likely to perform higher risk operations, such as those on elderly, diabetic, obese patients than are local hospitals, for example) this pattern is likely to be reversed. Specialist hospitals are likely to have lower mortality associated with both high-risk and low-risk surgery than are local hospitals, but because they perform more high-risk surgery, the overall mortality is higher.

8. Indicator Systems Are Common

Statistics providers create key messages for decision makers and the general public regarding levels or changes in hundreds of *indicators,* such as GDP, unemployment, inflation, or income inequality. These indicators are rarely raw variables, such as those encountered in introductory statistics classes, but rather are combinations of data elements that may be expressed as percentages, ratios, or numbers on arbitrary scales. For example, income inequality can be measured via the Gini coefficient—an index of the deviation of the actual distribution of salaries from the situation where everyone in the population receives the same salary—or by dividing the combined incomes of the highest earning (say) 10% of the population by the combined incomes of the lowest 10% of the population. The consumer price index (and measures of inflation) is based on the price of a notional 'basket of goods' that a 'typical' household would buy in a certain period of time. Indicators may be based on either objective data (e.g. *consumer spending*) or subjective data (e.g. *consumer confidence*) and their definitions, underlying methods or measurement methods may evolve and change over time to ensure relevance. Changes in the choice of items in the basket of goods used to calculate inflation—e.g. by including the costs of owning a mobile phone—provides an obvious example.

9. Dynamic Data Spanning Times and Locations

Civic Statistics are often not the result of a one-time data collection effort (unlike, say, a survey conducted in an introductory statistics course) but often are based on multiple data sources. These may be data collected

---

[5]E.g. https://missingnumbers.org/

periodically using the same methodology across time (e.g. an employment survey each month or year) or at different locations and reported on a comparative basis (e.g., of countries, as in statistics published by Eurostat, OECD, WHO, UNESCO, and the World Bank). Consequently, data are often reported as a trend over time, and may be updated when new data become available or old data re-evaluated. Further, different stakeholders may provide different findings and messages regarding the same social phenomena (e.g., *gender pay gap*, *crime rates* among different social groups, people under *the poverty line*), or may use different indicators or levels of aggregation to analyse and communicate their findings.

III. Rich, New or Uncommon Methods and Representations

10. Novel Data Sources and Analysis Techniques

Information is available in an increasing variety of forms, and is being analysed in novel ways. For example, text is presented via print materials, and via social media such as *Twitter* and *Facebook*. Techniques for language translation and semantic analyses have been developed. Images abound in static forms via print, and dynamically via a variety of video outlets (e.g. TV, *YouTube*, and cctv). Image interpretation (and creation) is well developed—face recognition and fake video provide examples. Data from sensors provide information on a large scale—from fitness trackers, 'internet of things' devices around the home, environmental sensors to monitor traffic and pollution, to satellite images. Web search terms are, themselves, an interesting data source. 'Surveillance capitalism' in the West, and citizen control in China are examples where information from a variety of sources is synthesized to draw conclusions about the behaviour of individuals. Rich authentic data sources are available from official sources such as statistical offices and Non-Governmental Organisations (NGO); the web is a source of large volumes of information about almost everything (for instance, *Wikipedia* and *WikiLeaks*). Ways to represent evidence—often dynamically—continue to be invented.

11. Varied Data Collection Methods

Data collection methods colour the generalisations that can be made. For example, one can conflate differences between age groups and trends over time. Consider taking a snapshot at a single point in time across people of different ages versus following the same group of people over time. Suppose one is considering the take-up of some innovative technology, and that the 'true' underlying pattern is that all age groups make equal use of the technology, but, year-on-year there is an increase in use. A snapshot across all age groups would simply show equal take-up; a longitudinal study of a single age group would show an apparent increase in take-up with age over time. Similarly, observational studies (e.g. in epidemiology) can produce different results from designed experiments; designed experiments can rule out some counter explanations by adding appropriate control conditions; however, for practical (and sometimes) ethical reasons experiments to explore many social phenomena can be impossible to conduct.

12. Innovative Visualisations

Data on social issues are often communicated via rich, novel data visualisations—some examples are shown in Chap. 5. These continue to be invented, and presented to citizens via print and video. Users need the ability to understand data presented in a novel way, and they need skills to access and manipulate computer-mediated interactive visualisations. They need to be able to critique the ways in which data are presented, and need to develop skills of effective data communication.

In Chap. 3, we take these features of Civic Statistics, and describe the tools, skills and competencies needed to critically understand data about society. The conceptual structure of tools and facets—along with a diagnostic device—paves the way to evaluating curricula and assessment systems in terms of the extent to which they support Civic Statistics. The resulting evaluation can then be used as the basis for planning curriculum reform, along with appropriate assessment systems to support these reforms. For now, we will use the topic of climate change to illustrate the characteristic features of Civic Statistics identified above.

2.5   Exemplifying Features of Civic Statistics: Understanding Evidence Related to Climate Change

First, consider features grouped as *Contexts and Interpretations*.

It is clear that *social context* is a primary focus—a rise in sea levels, and destruction of fertile land would both lead to mass migration, and associated challenges.

Statistics are embedded in rich texts—this is illustrated throughout this section. This quotation is taken from Eckstein et al. (2019, p. 5).[6]

People all over the world are facing the reality of climate change—in many parts of the world this is manifesting in an increased volatility of extreme weather events. Between 1999 and 2018, about 495,000 people died worldwide and losses of US$ 3.54 trillion (in PPP) were incurred as a direct result of more than 12,000 extreme weather events.

There is a *need to explore possible causes.* In this context, we can identify two separate questions about causality—one concerns the causes of extreme weather events (e.g. can weather events be attributed to global warming?); the other concerns global warming itself (is it attributable to human actions?). The American Meteorological Society publishes annual reports on explaining extreme events. The

---

[6] https://www.germanwatch.org/sites/germanwatch.org/files/20-2-01e%20Global%20Climate%20Risk%20Index%202020_14.pdf

following text is taken from their 2019 report[7] (Herring et al., 2021) and makes both these causal claims—students could be asked to explore the plausibility of each.

The desiccating Four Corners drought, intense heat waves on the Iberian peninsula and in northeast Asia, exceptional precipitation in the Mid-Atlantic states, and record-low sea ice in the Bering Sea were 2018 extreme weather events made more likely by human-caused climate change, according to new research published today in the Bulletin of the American Meteorological Society (BAMS).

In this context, many sources draw *conclusions*, explore the *implications* and *consequences* of further global warming, or the likely effects of different sorts of action designed to reduce warming.

Although Europe—especially France—has made progress in preventing heat fatalities by implementing better early warning systems, disruptions have still been significant. Partly because adaptation measures could not keep up with the rapid changes. As an example: While it is clear that houses must be equipped with better insulation to deal with extreme heat in Germany, less than 1% of residential buildings are being adapted annually ... Being particularly dependent on the jet stream, extreme heat during European summers is likely to occur more often and intensively in the future. In 2019, in Germany the heat record was broken yet again several times, raising it by 2.3 °C to 42.6 °C in just one summer. (Eckstein et al., 2019, p. 19).

It is hard to think of a context that better illustrates *Conclusions from data are just starting points* than global warming—statistics provides tools for analysis and evaluation, and the conclusions should provoke dramatic action—which will necessitate further data gathering, analysis and conclusion.

2.5.1 Reflecting on the Nature of the Statistics Presented

It is obvious that climate change considers *multivariate phenomena* that range across physical events such as acidification of oceans, wildfires in Alaska and Siberia, the activities of humans—such as death and migration, and ecological events such as the destruction of habitat and loss of species.

Measures and operationalization pose serious challenges—for example, how might the severity of bush fires in Australia be measured? Measures might include: the number of fires; the area destroyed by the fires; the number, or the value of the houses destroyed; the number of deaths of people and animals; decreases in economic activity, and so on.

It is important to consider the problems associated with a*ggregated data*. This is again illustrated by a quote from Eckstein et al. (2019, p. 18)—we have removed the footnotes.

---

[7] https://www.ametsoc.org/ams/index.cfm/publications/bulletin-of-the-american-meteorological-society-bams/explaining-extreme-events-from-a-climate-perspective/

A recent study by Campbell et al. (2018) found that heatwave and health impact research is not evenly distributed across the globe. They highlight that "regions most at risk from heatwaves and health impact are under-represented in the research." … These circumstances may cause countries with large data gaps to appear less affected by heatwaves than they might be in reality. We also have to note that climate change disproportionately affects the poor. Many low-income urban residents live in precariously located informal settlements, characterised by poor-quality housing that is susceptible to extreme heat and they have less access to affordable healthcare. These factors make them both more exposed to heatwaves, and less able to deal with them when they occur.

Indicator systems are common. Germanwatch have developed a *Global Climate Risk Index*, which is used to rank countries based on: *death toll, deaths per 100,000 inhabitants, absolute losses in purchasing power parity, and losses per GDP unit.* Weighted (1/6; 1/3; 1/3; 1/6) respectively. At the start of their 2020 report (Eckstein et al., 2019, p. 3), they offer this caution:

However, the index must not be mistaken for a comprehensive climate vulnerability scoring. It represents one important piece in the overall puzzle of climate-related impacts and the associated vulnerabilities. The index focuses on extreme weather events but does not take into account important slow-onset processes such as rising sea-levels, glacier melting or more acidic and warmer seas. It is based on past data and should not be used as a basis for a linear projection of future climate impacts. More specifically, not too far-reaching conclusions should be drawn for the purpose of political discussions regarding which country or region is the most vulnerable to climate change.

Dynamic data, spanning times and locations is common—again, global warming provides some splendid illustrations.

2.5.2   Unfamiliar Methods and Representations

Climate change illustrates the use of *novel data sources and analysis techniques* that students should experience. We have already referred to the wide range of data sources. Climate change in particular is an area of research which is rich in analysis techniques, and which uses a wide variety of models at different grain sizes. For example, in plants (including trees) the rate of photosynthesis depends (*inter alia*) on temperature, and is optimal at different temperatures for different plants. So, growth, carbon capture and oxygen production by plants in any area will change as temperature increases, in fairly predictable (and dramatic) ways. Eckstein et al. (2019, p. 13) illustrate the problems of understanding more complex systems, and the tentative nature of some models.

Climate change essentially affects weather in two ways: Firstly, through the thermodynamic effect, in other words the warming of the atmosphere. Warmer air can absorb more water vapour. Hence, we expect more extreme precipitation on a global average. The second effect is trickier. As we change the composition of the atmosphere, so does the atmospheric circulation and thus where weather systems are created and how they move. This effect varies by region and season, which is why we need attribution research. One example: While we can generally say that tropical cyclones will bring more intense and higher amounts of precipitation, we do not know whether and how their frequency will change.

Climate change also illustrates the *wide variety of data collection methods* used to address complex problems. Examples include satellite images, sensors on land and sea, and survey data on human activity.

Similarly, discussions on climate change are rich in *innovative visualisations*. These include video (mapping the extent and age of polar ice, or images of natural disasters), a wide range of choropleth maps, along with more conventional interactive time series.

2.6 What Are Our Ambitions for Civic Statistics?

> Most real life statistical problems have one or more nonstandard features.
> There are no routine statistical questions; only questionable statistical routines.
> (David Cox, quoted in Chatfield, 1991, p. 240).

Our grandest ambition for Civic Statistics is to create a social and political climate world-wide where evidence is considered carefully whenever decisions are made. We do not advocate blind technocracy—quantitative evidence is part of an elaborate network of elements that influence decision making, and slogans such as 'evidence-based decision making' are both naïve and dangerous. Ways to promote the health of the global information ecosystem are explored by Ridgway and Ridgway in Chap. 23. Part of our grand ambition is to improve educational provision, so that students are able to wrangle effectively with evidence, draw conclusions, and consider consequences (and perhaps recommend action).

We need to develop students' ability to address Cox's nonstandard features, sensibly and critically. Problem representation and reflecting about appropriate models is a core skill—in contrast to applying standard models. Some data will need cleaning, and the problem of missing data may need to be addressed. This requires technological tools for access to data, for visualisation and for analysis, but also a clear rationale for the whole process—from problem identification, through modelling, to drawing conclusions—geared to the social context of the analysis.

Problems addressed in Civic Statistics rarely have a simple, clear-cut right or wrong answer—contrary to problems in traditional school mathematics and introductory statistics courses. Students should consider how much evidence the data provide for the claims being made, should explore ways to triangulate the problem, and gain insights through different approaches, alternative representations, and by exploring related data sets.

When working with Civic Statistics, students need to be aware that often there is no definitive, single way to describe a social phenomenon of interest. Everyone needs to adopt a questioning attitude, and to know what questions to ask about the nature, limitations, or credibility of different data sources, statistical messages, and conclusions. They need to adopt a critical stance when assessing evidence. But that does not mean simply "blind" criticizing. There is a danger that a critical attitude degenerates in cynicism over all data sources, as it is expressed in the much quoted phrase "lies, damned lies and statistics". Rather, criticism is about adopting the attitude of a fair sceptic who is ready to accept an account, but has to be convinced by evidence (Ridgway et al., 2017).

2.7 Curricular Implications

There are serious problems with the ways that statistics is taught in most countries in high school and at the introductory undergraduate level (Cobb, 2015; for a review, see Batanero et al., 2011), and also in the content of courses in the social sciences. In essence, most statistics curricula focus on single (or perhaps two) variable problems; they focus on technical mastery of mathematical techniques developed over 100 years ago; they use artificial data; and they make little use of data visualisation techniques. Statistical techniques taught and data sets used in current curricula (at the high-school and introductory university levels) are misaligned with the needs of citizenship, and are not geared to enable learners to transfer any skills they acquire to their duties as engaged citizens—in essence, the current way statistics is taught at high school or university does not address the needs of Civic Statistics. Social science teaching often fails to engage with statistical ideas at all.

The competences and content of Civic Statistics cannot be delegated to a single, isolated discipline or field of knowledge. Making sense of data is part of teaching in geography, history, sociology, psychology, civics and economics as well as in biology and physics (this theme is explored further by Engel, Louie, and Nicholson in Chap. 18). In high schools, few teachers in mathematics or social science receive any training on how to teach statistics. As a result, mathematics teachers may stay within their comfort zone and overemphasize a narrow range of statistical techniques and computations, whilst teachers of social sciences may choose to sidestep quantitative approaches almost entirely. Across the curriculum there is too little attention to working with and understanding multivariate data that describe social trends, or to the analysis, interpretation and communication about the meaning of such data.

Central to Civic Statistics are issues of public interest concerning the social and economic well-being of all citizens and the functioning of democracy. This puts high demands on the instructors: Civics and geography teachers need more than basic knowledge of descriptive statistics—they need deeper insights and some statistical pedagogical content knowledge. Mathematics teachers need to be able to interpret the results of statistical representations and analyses against the background of the social context from whence they are derived, and to facilitate discussions on controversial issues in the classroom. Interdisciplinary teaching should emphasize interest in burning issues related to social and economic well-being and the realization of civil rights. Students need to experience the role of evidence and data in understanding these issues. To do this, it is important to use authentic data and texts of direct relevance to the social phenomena of interest.

To help young people engage in public debates on societal issues and to engage them in addressing burning issues, curriculum changes are necessary. Data analysis, interpretation of graphics and (dynamic) visualisations are not just a part of mathematical knowledge, but rather are part of the knowledge gained in many subjects and should therefore be incorporated into a range of disciplines in a systematic way. Mathematics instruction should not be confined to the teaching of techniques and formal terms with little relevance to content. Problem solving and modelling have always been key components of real-world mathematics (often ignored in school). Civic-statistical topics illustrate the usefulness and relevance of mathematical analysis in a wide range of contexts. This both serves the discipline of mathematics and can empower young people to form their own evidence-informed position and engage in public decision-making processes.

These arguments resonate with the recent Guidelines for Assessment and Instruction in Statistics Education at the college level (GAISE College Report, 2016). The guidelines build upon an extensive body of research in statistics teaching, and argue that we should teach statistics as an investigative process of problem-solving and decision-making, with an emphasis on giving students experiences with multivariable thinking, should integrate real data with a context and purpose, foster active learning, use technology to explore concepts and analyse data, and should use assessments to improve and evaluate student learning. In an otherwise excellent document, we see a weakness (from our point of view)—almost all the examples provided fall short when it comes to connecting statistics with contextualized issues—and there are no examples to engage students with civic issues. In Chap. 4, Gal, Ridgway, Nicholson and Engel offer a more detailed analysis of parts of the GAISE College Report; In Chap. 18 Engel, Louie and Nicholson explore ways to promote Civic Statistics across the whole curriculum.

2.8 A Need for New Teaching Resources

Teaching Civic Statistics requires a comprehensive set of innovative teaching materials that include lessons plans, data sets, visualisation tools and guidelines for instruction and evaluation. The ProCivicStat project has developed an integrated framework depicted in Table 2.2, which summarises the key building blocks that need to be in place in order to provoke systemic change and growth in teaching focused on Civic Statistics. The elements listed in Table 2.2 are organized in four layers, from broad publications for encouraging public discourse and awareness, to general guidelines, specific teaching resources (instructions and lesson plans or activity sheets for teachers and for students regarding datasets, visualisation and analysis tools, selected media articles, texts from official statistics producers, and more), and finally various supporting materials and other auxiliary products. Many of these resources, developed by ProCivicStat partners, can be found on the website

Table 2.2 An overview of ProCivicStat outputs and desired elements

Public discourse	Call for action and recommendations		A book about PCS and Civic Statistics	
Broad Frameworks	Conceptual Framework of needed skills (*Short*, Long)	Guidelines for task design & assessment (with examples)	Course designs • for all students • for pre-service	
Instructional Resources	CivicStatMap (task design tool)	Lesson plans	Dataset guides	Workshop and visualisation guides
	For Teachers		*For Students*	
Supporting materials	Conference proceedings	Papers by PCS partners	PCS website (at IASE)	Bibliography, links, etc.

of the International Association for Statistics Education (IASE)[8]; other resources are available through electronic resources associated with this book.

Civic Statistics requires a different teaching focus to that of traditional statistics, and so more is needed than a list of resources. The ProCivicStat resources on the IASE website offer resources and suggestions for instructional sequences that are coordinated via the overarching conceptual framework associated with Civic Statistics presented by Gal, Ridgway and Nicholson in Chap. 3. The CivicStatMap (described in Chap. 6 by Teixeira, Campos and Trostianitser) makes it easy to find lesson plans and class activities for specific age groups, Civic Statistics topics and core statistical ideas. Lesson plans (resources are described by Trostianitser, Teixeira and Campos in Chap. 7) make it clear how each is related to the facets of the ProCivicStat conceptual framework. Similarly, datasets and data-analysis activities have been chosen to engage students with specific societal issues (see Teixeira, Campos, and Trostianitser in Chap. 6 for further details).

2.9   Concluding Remarks

Civic Statistics sets out to empower students to engage with social issues, and has an important role to play in supporting the democratic process, and in improving decision making at all levels from the personal, through local, national, and international levels. The challenges we face as individuals and as global citizens continue to grow; the resources to make us more able to face these challenges also continue to grow. Describing and developing the competencies required to deal with evidence will evolve as different problems and different sorts of data emerge. Skill development in Civic Statistics is a journey to be enjoyed, not a destination to be reached.

---

[8]https://iase-web.org/islp/pcs

References

Batanero, C., Burrill, G., & Reading, C. (Eds.). (2011). Teaching statistics in school mathematics: Challenges for teaching and teacher education. *18th Study of the international commission on mathematical instruction*. Springer.

Ben-Zvi, D., & Garfield, J. (2004). Statistical literacy, reasoning, and thinking: Goals, definitions, and challenges. In D. Ben-Zvi & J. Garfield (Eds.), *The challenge of developing statistical literacy, reasoning, and thinking* (pp. 3–15). Kluwer Academic Publishers.

Ben-Zvi, D., Makar, K., & Garfield, J. (Eds.). (2018). *International handbook of research in statistics education*. Springer International Publishing. https://doi.org/10.1007/978-3-319-66195-7

Borovnick, M., & Ossimitz, G. (1987). *Materialien zur Beschreibenden Statistik und Explorativen Datenanalyse*. Hölder-Pichler-Tempsky.

Campbell, S., Remenyi, T., White, C., & Johnston, F. (2018). *Heatwave and health impact research: A global review*. https://www.sciencedirect.com/science/article/pii/S1353829218301205

Chatfield, C. (1991). Avoiding statistical pitfalls. *Statistical Science, 6*(3), 240–268.

Cobb, G. (2015). Mere renovation is too little too late: We need to rethink our undergraduate curriculum from the ground up. *The American Statistician, 69*(4), 266–282. https://doi.org/10.1080/00031305.2015.1093029

Condorcet, A. (1994). *Foundations of social choice and political theory*. Edward Elgar (Original published 1792).

Eckstein, D., Künzel, V., Schäfer, L., & Winges, M. (2019). Global climate risk index 2020: Who suffers most from extreme weather events? Weather-related loss events in 2018 and 1999 to 2018. *GermanWatch*. https://www.germanwatch.org/en/17307.

Engel, J. (2017). Statistical literacy for active citizenship: A call for data science education. *Statistics Education Research Journal, 16*(1), 44–49. https://iase-web.org/documents/SERJ/SERJ16(1)_Engel.pdf

Fischer, R. (1984). *Offene Mathematik und Visualisierung. mathematica didactica, 7*(3/4), 139–160.

Freire, P. (2014). *Pedagogy of the oppressed. 30th Anniversary Edition*. Bloomsbury Publishing.

GAISE College Report ASA Revision Committee. (2016). *Guidelines for assessment and instruction in statistics education college report 2016*. American Statistical Association. https://www.amstat.org/asa/education/Guidelines-for-Assessment-and-Instruction-in-Statistics-Education-Reports.aspx

Gal, I. (2002). Adults' statistical literacy: Meanings, components, responsibilities. *International Statistical Review, 70*(1), 1–51.

Herring, S. C., Christidis, N., Hoell, A., Hoerling, M. P., & Stott, P. A. (2021). Explaining extreme events of 2019 from a climate perspective. *Bulletin of the American Meteorological Society, 102*(1), S1–S112. https://doi.org/10.1175/BAMSExplainingExtremeEvents2019.1

Lesser, L. (2007). Critical values and transforming data: teaching statistics with social justice. *Journal of Statistics Education, 15*(1), 1–21.

Neurath, O. (2010). *From hieroglyphics to isotype: A visual autobiography*. Hyphen Press.

Nowotny, H. (2016). *A scientific outlook for a post-factual world. Project syndicate. The world's opinion page*. https://www.project-syndicate.org/commentary/science-uncertainty-post-factual-world-by-helga-nowotny-2016-11.

OECD. (2009). *Focus on citizens: Public engagement for better policy and services*. https://www.oecd.org/gov/focusoncitizenspublicengagementforbetterpolicyandservices.htm

Pearl, J., & Mackenzie, D. (2016). *The book of why; the new science of cause and effect*. Penguin.

Playfair, W. (1786, 2005). *The commercial and political Atlas and statistical breviary*. University Press.

ProCivicStat Partners. (2018). *Engaging civic statistics: A call for action and recommendations. A product of the ProCivicStat project*. https://iase-web.org/ISLP/PCS.

Pullinger, J. (2014). Statistics making an impact. *Journal of the Royal Statistical Society Series A, 176*(4), 819–839.

Ridgway, J. (2016). Implications of the data revolution for statistics education. *International Statistical Review, 84*(3), 528–549.

Ridgway, J., Nicholson, J., & Stern, D. (2017). Statistics education in a post-truth era. In A. Molnar (Ed), *Teaching statistics in a data rich world. Proceedings of the satellite conference of the International Association for Statistical Education (IASE)*, July 2017, Rabat, Morocco.

Rowntree, S. (1908). *Poverty: A study of town life.* Macmillan. https://archive.org/details/povertyastudyto00rowngoog/page/n8

Ruane, S. (2019). Access to data and NHS privatization. In J. Evans, S. Ruane, & H. Southall (Eds.), *Data in society: Challenging statistics in an age of globalization.* Policy Press.

Skovsmose, O. (1994). Towards a critical mathematics education. *Educational Studies in Mathematics, 27*(1), 35–57. https://doi.org/10.1007/BF01284527

Steen, L., Burrill, G., Ganter, S., Goroff, D., Greenleaf, F., Grubb, W., Johnson, J., & Malcom, S. (2001). The case for quantitative literacy. In L. Steen (Ed.), *Mathematics and democracy: The case for quantitative literacy.* NCED.

Stiglitz, J. E., Fitousi, J., & Durand, M. (2018). *Beyond GDP: Measuring what counts for economic and social performance.* OECD. https://www.oecd.org/social/beyond-gdp-9789264307292-en.htm

Wallman, K. (1993). Enhancing statistical literacy: Enriching our society. *Journal of the American Statistical Association, 88*(421), 1–8.

Weiland, T. (2017). Problematizing statistical literacy: An intersection of critical and statistical literacies. *Educational Studies in Mathematics, 96*, 33–47. https://doi.org/10.1007/s10649-017-9764-5

Chapter 3
A Conceptual Framework for Civic Statistics and Its Educational Applications

Iddo Gal ⓘ, James Nicholson, and Jim Ridgway

Abstract This chapter presents a comprehensive conceptual framework of 11 *facets and tools* which together describe the knowledge, skills and dispositions that (young) adults need in order to comprehend, critically evaluate, communicate about, and engage with Civic Statistics regarding 'burning' societal issues, and that may enhance citizen empowerment. The framework is organized around three key dimensions involving engagement & action, knowledge, and enabling processes. It identifies knowledge-bases covering meaning for society and policy and critical evaluation and reflection; selected statistical and mathematical constructs and skills; core literacy and mathematical skills; understanding models and modelling, multivariate ideas and textual and rich visual representations; knowledge of research and data production methods and extensions related to official statistics and risk on the societal level; and it emphasises the importance of appropriate dispositions, critical stance, and habits of mind. We offer examples and curriculum tasks that illustrate each of the 11 facets and their interconnectedness. We also describe the use of a 'radar plot' tool to support the analysis of how balanced are prospective class activities or test items in terms of covering the 11 facets and tools. The chapter ends with a brief discussion of the implications of the conceptual model and its 11 facets for planning curricula, instruction, and assessments that can promote teaching and learning about Civic Statistics within mathematics education, statistics and data science education, and related disciplines.

Keywords Conceptual framework · Critical statistical literacy · Dispositions and attitudes · Media and data literacy · Citizenship skills · Cognitive task demands

I. Gal (✉)
Department of Human Services, University of Haifa, Haifa, Israel
e-mail: iddo@research.haifa.ac.il

J. Nicholson · J. Ridgway
University of Durham, Durham, UK
e-mail: j.r.nicholson53@gmail.com; jim.ridgway@durham.ac.uk

J. Ridgway (ed.), *Statistics for Empowerment and Social Engagement*,
https://doi.org/10.1007/978-3-031-20748-8_3

3.1 Introduction

This chapter builds on Chap. 2 (Engel & Ridgway, this volume), which sketched the history and discussed the importance of Civic Statistics, and included more details about the goals, products, and educational resources of the ProCivicStat project (see ProCivicStat Partners, 2018). Chapter 2 also sketched the many *areas* which Civic Statistics encompass (e.g., climate change, employment and income, social justice, equality, diversity and inclusion, crime, education, sustainability, and many more) and described in detail *12 key features of Civic Statistics* that pertain to all these areas. The 12 features of Civic Statistics, which are summarised in Table 3.1, characterise the nature of the statistical and quantitative messages, texts and evidence related to Civic Statistics which citizens read, see or hear in the news media (e.g., magazines and newspaper articles, TV and radio broadcasts), press releases by statistics producers, blog entries, social networks, etc. Chapter 2 argued that these 12 features require sophisticated statistical reasoning, but are hardly addressed in introductory statistics courses. Hence, in line with earlier positions (Engel et al., 2016) Chap. 2 argued that teaching about Civic Statistics is both essential and urgent, if future citizens are to engage effectively with the media they encounter.

Table 3.1 Twelve features of Civic Statistics

Twelve Features of Civic Statistics
What citizens see/read/hear
I. Contexts and interpretations
1. Societal context is the focus
2. Statistics are embedded in rich texts
3. Causality is often attributed
4. Conclusions, implications, and consequences for society are discussed
II. The nature of the statistics
5. Phenomena are often multivariate
6. Decisions have been made about measures and operationalization
7. Data are often aggregated
8. Indicator systems are common
9. Dynamic data, spanning times and locations is common
III. Unfamiliar methods and representations
10. Novel data sources and analysis techniques are common
11. Varied data collection methods are used
12. Innovative visualisations have been invented

This chapter focuses on the following key question:

What *facets and tools* are needed (by students, and citizens in general) so that they can critically understand the statistical information that they see/read/ hear, and engage with the underlying societal or economic issues?

To answer this question, this chapter maps out a conceptual framework describing 11 facets and tools, i.e., knowledge bases, skills, enabling processes, and dispositions and attitudes that together are needed if we expect learners to critically understand and engage with Civic Statistics and all their underlying features. These 11 facets and tools, which are listed in Fig. 3.1, are all *learnable*, i.e., can be acquired or be 'improved' in the classroom. Thus, they are the basis for the development of teaching methods and curriculum materials that can help teaching/learning processes focused on Civic Statistics, and are the basis for the many examples in the other chapters in the book.

The conceptual framework in Fig. 3.1 argues that the ability to engage with Civic Statistics involves eleven separate but related facets and tools, organised in three groups:

- **Engagement & Action:** This group involves three facets (Meaning for society and policy; Critical evaluation and reflection; and Dispositions), and relates to the motivations for generating Civic Statistics, engaging with them, and investing in their critical evaluation.
- **Knowledge:** This group involves five facets (Statistics and risk; Models, patterns and representations; Methodology and enquiry processes; Extensions in official statistics; and Contextual civic knowledge). Together, these encompass the diverse knowledge bases and skills that pertain directly to the statistical

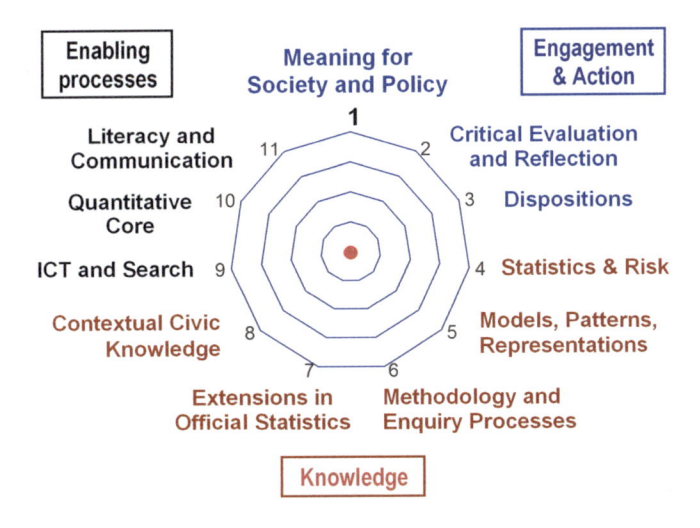

Fig. 3.1 A conceptual model for Civic Statistics

information which may be contained in messages about Civic Statistics. Note that this involves the understanding of the *context* (i.e., the social and economic settings) from which data are generated and to which the statistics refer.

- **Enabling Processes:** This group involves three facets (ICT and search; Quantitative core; and Literacy and communication)—these are general skills, not unique to the area of statistics and probability, but essential for finding, accessing and comprehending messages (textual and quantitative) with or about Civic Statistics.

The remainder of this chapter is organised in four sections. First, in order to help grasp the need for, and to better understand, the conceptual framework sketched in Fig. 3.1, Sect. 3.2 presents examples to illustrate how the 11 facets and tools in the conceptual framework are needed to understand messages about Civic Statistics. Section 3.3 sketches the theoretical background used to develop the conceptual framework. Section 3.4, which is the heart of this chapter, discusses in detail each of the 11 facets and tools, with illustrative examples. Finally, Sect. 3.5 points to some implications for teaching, and describes a simple "radar plot" tool that teachers can use to analyse how the content of instructional tasks or assessment items they may want to use relates to the 11 facets and tools.

Please note that the present chapter should be seen in the context of the whole book: Chap. 4 (Gal, Ridgway, Nicholson, & Engel, this volume), which follows, discusses more ideas, examples, and implications related to instruction, curriculum planning and assessment, based on the ideas here and in Chap. 2. The many other chapters in this book all have additional examples related to or based upon the conceptual framework in Fig. 3.1.

3.2 Opening Examples: The Facets and Tools in Action

This section presents two short examples to illustrate some of the facets and tools listed in Fig. 3.1 and show their relevance to different areas and features included in Civic Statistics. These examples are 'thinking tasks'—so please reflect about each one before moving further on.

Example 1 relates to Civic Statistics about public health, and it has two parts, first a small excerpt from one article and then a title from another article about the spread of the Coronavirus (COVID-19), both published by the USA-based news network CNN. These were just two of thousands of articles and news broadcasts that appeared around the world during the pandemic which engulfed the world in 2020. Example 2 relates to the gender pay gap (i.e., a gap between men and women in terms of wages or salaries), a thorny issue which has been getting much public attention for years and relates to social equality and employment markets.

> **Example 1: Media Excerpts About the Coronavirus (COVID-19) Pandemic**
>
> (CNN, 21 March 2020). Does Russia have Coronavirus under control? According to information released by Russian officials, Putin's strategy seems to have worked. The number of confirmed Russian coronavirus cases is surprisingly low, despite Russia sharing a lengthy border with China. The numbers are picking up, but Russia—a country of 146 million people—has fewer confirmed cases than Luxembourg, with just 253 people infected, and no deaths. Luxembourg, by contrast, has a population of just 628,000 … and by Saturday had reported 670 coronavirus cases with eight deaths …
>
> *Source*: https://edition.cnn.com/2020/03/21/europe/putin-coronavirus-russia-intl/index.html (note: the original article had much more text)
>
> (CNN, 31 March 2020) Coronavirus death rate is lower than previously reported, study says, but it's still deadlier than seasonal flu.
>
> *Source*: https://edition.cnn.com/2020/03/30/health/coronavirus-lower-death-rate/index.html

Reader—your task: before continuing, please read carefully the two excerpts in Example 1 (Note: The original articles are longer), and then reflect on this question:

What do you need to know or activate (think of the 11 facets and tools listed in Fig. 3.1) so that you can critically understand the information you encountered in the articles and engage the underlying civic issues?

Please write a list of your ideas. Only then, continue to read.

Finished? Now continue to Example 2. After doing it, you will see a short summary with a partial answer to the questions in Examples 1 and 2.

Example 2: Wage (Salary) Inequality

Assume that you want to sensitise your students to how statistics are used or reported in the real world, and decide to let them tackle statistics about the equality of income between men and women. This is a hotly debated topic; perhaps the most well-known indicator in this regard is the *Gender Pay Gap*. So, to make life easier for you and your students, you could check Wikipedia. The text there is quite detailed—so below we show only an excerpt, along with a single graph from the explanation about this concept. (Note: Wikipedia entries are edited from time to time, so when you read this book, what is listed below may not be exactly what you will actually find in Wikipedia).

Wikipedia Definition: *Gender Pay Gap*—**English** *(excerpt)*

(note: The Wikipedia entry also includes the graph shown in Fig. 3.2)

The **gender pay gap** or **gender wage gap** is the average difference between the remuneration (pay/compensation) for men and women who are working. Women are generally considered to be paid less than men.

There are two distinct numbers regarding the pay gap: *non-adjusted* versus *adjusted* pay gap. The latter typically takes into account differences in hours worked, occupations chosen, education and job experience. In the United States, for example, the ***non-adjusted*** average female's annual salary is 79% of the average male salary, compared to 95% for the ***adjusted*** average salary. The reasons link to legal, social and economic factors, and extend beyond 'equal pay for equal work'. The gender pay gap can be a problem from a public policy perspective because it reduces economic output and means that women are more likely to be dependent upon welfare payments, especially in old age . . . (More text follows)

Source: https://en.wikipedia.org/wiki/Gender_pay_gap (Retrieved June 1, 2021)

Reader—your task: As before, please read Example 2 carefully, including the text and the graph. Then, reflect on the same question:

What do you need to know or activate (think of the 11 facets and tools listed in Fig. 3.1) so that you can critically understand the information you encountered (i.e., text + graphical display) and engage with the underlying civic issues?

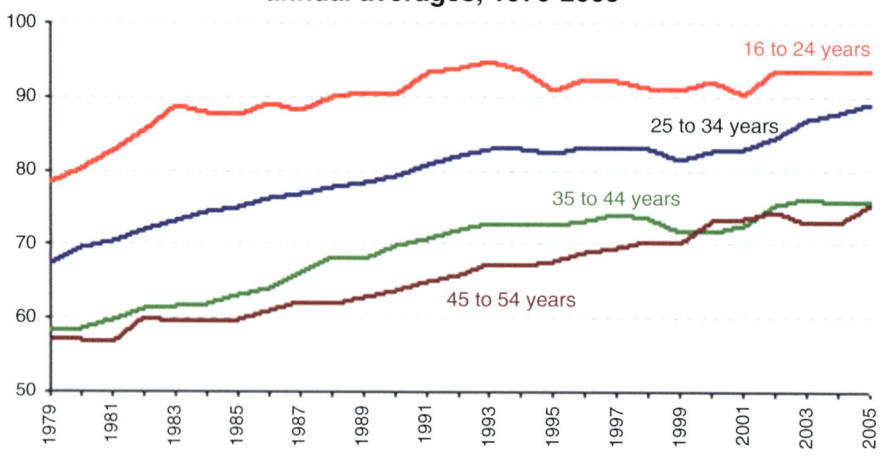

Fig. 3.2 Women's weekly earnings as a percentage of men's in the U.S. by age, 1979–2005

Please write a list of your ideas. Only then, continue to read.

Analysis of Examples 1 and 2. The two examples may not have touched on all 11 facets and tools shown in Fig. 3.1, because only short excerpts from longer sources were presented, and after all, any single example is limited. Yet, although short, even these two examples illustrated the richness of the demands on citizens when they encounter Civic Statistics. It is important to emphasise that the 11 facets and tools, which are explained in detail in Sect. 3.4, are not independent (i.e., there may be some overlap between them) and they interact together in any single task or activity. Interpreting and reacting to a media article or digital text on any important social issue, such as *health* in Example 1, or *equality* in Example 2, is likely to require the joint activation of many facets and tools.

Both examples require activation of enabling skills we have called 'literacy and communication' and 'quantitative core'. They entail knowledge about 'models, patterns and representations' (e.g., the way *gender pay gap* is calculated is one of several ways to model this phenomenon), and understanding of 'methodology and enquiry processes' or how official statistics are calculated and communication (e.g., see the 'adjusted' and 'unadjusted' rates in Example 2). The examples require a critical perspective (e.g., are the reported statistics credible enough, as in Example 1? how up to date are the graphed data, as in Example 2?). Then, 'contextual civic knowledge', 'critical evaluation' and 'meaning for society and policy' are involved, in order to link with the civic reality, and to think what might be done (if anything), in terms of policy implications. What do you think? Are other facets and tools needed or invoked in these examples?

3.3 The Conceptual Framework: Overview of the 11 Facets and Tools Needed for Understanding and Engaging with Civic Statistics

This section sketches the background of the conceptual framework of 11 facets and tools illustrated in Examples 1 and 2. This framework, which is elaborated in Sect. 3.4, was conceived by the ProCivicStat partners (2018) (see also Ridgway et al., 2018) through a multi-stage process, sketched below.

In the first stage, academic literature and conceptual frameworks related to key constructs or domains relevant to the understanding of Civic Statistics were consulted. Table 3.2 lists sample key references which were part of the literature review. The constructs and domains listed in Table 3.2 fall into two general families. Some are relatively broad and reflect generic expectations regarding general outcomes of schooling, while others are more specific to the area of statistics and probability. All of these constructs have undergone conceptual developments over the last few decades, but they have not all been integrated into a single schema, hence were the focus of much work by the ProCivicStat partners. Of course, there is

Table 3.2 Key constructs related to Civic Statistics, and sample key references

Constructs and domains	References (partial list)
Models related to adult numeracy and mathematical literacy	Geiger et al. (2015), Kilpatrick (2001), Gal et al. (2005), PIAAC Numeracy Expert Group (2009), Tout and Gal (2015)
Models related to broad quantitative reasoning (QR) competencies	Boersma et al. (2011), Madison (2014)
Heuristics related to critical reading of quantitative statements and other aspects of critical thinking	Gal (2002), Ridgway et al. (2016)
Models related to statistical literacy, probability literacy, risk literacy, data literacy, and official statistics literacy	Callingham and Watson (2017), Gal (2002, 2005), Gal and Ograjenšek (2017), Gould (2017), Watson (2013)
Models describing cognitive processes in understanding tables and graphs	Friel et al. (2001), Kemp and Kisanne (2010), Sharma (2013), Prodromou (2015), Schield (2016)
Models and perspectives describing desired behaviours of citizens and citizen engagement, as well as outcomes of statistics education or needed extensions in the twenty-first century, given trends regarding digitization, big data, data science, etc.	Ben-Zvi and Garfield (2004), Engel (2017), GAISE (2016), Gal et al. (2020), Gould (2017), OECD (2009), Ridgway (2016), Wild and Pfannkuch (1999)
Models related to dispositions and enabling processes that can support numerate behaviour and statistically literate behaviour	Gal (2002), Kilpatrick (2001), Gal et al. (2005)

some overlap between the constructs and conceptual frameworks, but each one offers additional ideas that can inform theorizing about the skills that adults (citizens) need in modern societies, hence can be of value in planning educational work on Civic Statistics.

In the second stage, the ProCivicStat partners analysed the demands of dozens of examples concerning Civic Statistics issues taken from various sources in several countries, such as articles on Civic Statistics topics in newspapers (print or digital versions), press releases from official statistics agencies, and open data sources. Just as we asked of readers in Sect. 3.2, we examined the demands of each task, i.e., what kinds of knowledge, skills, dispositions, and other enabling processes are needed to be known, used, or activated, in order to understand and engage with the diverse messages encountered on Civic Statistics topics.

In the third stage, task demands identified in the analysis were compared to the constructs and ideas included in the theoretical models. This process enabled us to identify topics that were not previously noted in the scholarly literature, expand on prior theoretical ideas, and design the conceptual framework summarized in Fig. 3.1. Section 3.4 further elaborates on the 11 facets and tools included in this framework.

3.4 The Conceptual Framework in Detail

This section elaborates each of the 11 facets and tools in the conceptual framework shown in Fig. 3.1. This elaboration is essential for understanding *why* these facets and tools are important and should be addressed in instruction and in assessment tasks. This section also includes short illustrative activities or "thinking exercises". Some can perhaps be used as classroom activities for students, but their primary intention is to help readers familiarise themselves with the 11 facets and tools, and connect them to each other, and to Civic Statistics. More tasks and ideas for classroom use appear in later chapters in this book.

Facet 1: Meaning for Society and Policy
This facet is the heart of Civic Statistics, where the focus is on the social implications of evidence. It provides the rationale for why data are needed and why statistical findings are published: societies need information about their current status, trends or changes from the past to the present, and projections to the future. Hence, statistics education classes should highlight the meaning of statistics for citizens and for social policy.

Social policy is a broad term that refers to the strategic plans, decisions about allocation of resources (i.e., in what we choose to invest public money), and other broad actions of governmental bodies or institutional agencies. Social policy aims to respond to (or pre-empt) pressing needs and gaps and improve or reform societal or economic issues. It may be enacted in many ways, such as via laws and regulations, budget allocations, and other means at the national or local levels. As Chap. 2 argued, citizens (and learners) need to be aware of key 'burning' issues regarding social and economic matters that affect society, e.g., regarding health, wages, unemployment, crime, environment, economic opportunities and equality, and access to services. (Teachers may want to discuss this topic with their students, ask them to find examples for social policy, and describe the intentions and implications of such policies).

Citizens need to know that there are social policies dealing with all these issues—and that choosing to do nothing is, by itself, a social policy. Policy is shaped by politicians & decision-makers. Decisions involve choices and risks, weighing existing evidence, options and their probabilities, costs and benefits, expected values, and subjective utilities. Evidence-informed decision making is not easy. Citizens need to worry about the quality of evidence, its timeliness and relevance. It follows that the learning of statistics should put data in context. Statistical analysis should be complemented by discussions of plausible causal factors and the likely social and policy implications of actions, both in terms of immediate impact and likely longer-term effects. Possible implications for different groups of stakeholders should be considered. It follows that education systems should produce citizens who are willing and able to provoke debate and evidence-informed action on "burning social issues" they judge to be important, and understand the connection with social policy.

Thinking Exercise/Activity #1: Aging and Public Budgets

Q1. What is the proportion of older people (65+, or 75+) in your country, and how is it projected to change or grow in the next 20–40 years? Why are these changes happening, i.e., what are the causal factors? *Most important:* What are the social or economic or business-related *consequences* or *implications*, and what changes in social policy are needed (e.g., in pensions, social security, health care plans, retirement age)?

Q2. What is the role of statistics in all of the above, i.e., in describing current trends, understanding causes and possible consequences, regarding aging and related public budgets and policies? Ask students to find relevant information sources (articles, reports, tables), discuss their social and economic implications, and support their ideas and conclusions with data. They may work with population pyramids (see Chap. 5) and various indicators from official statistics agencies.

Facet 2: Critical Evaluation and Reflection

Here we discuss issues pertaining to critical evaluation of, and reflection on, statistical messages. (Meta-cognitive and dispositional issues are also relevant, but covered in Facet 3). The core idea here is that citizens need to be able to ask critical questions to evaluate the credibility and soundness of any data, finding, or conclusion they encounter, both on technical and logical grounds—even data or reports from credible sources such as official statistics agencies.

For example, critical or reflective questions about the methods used in surveys and official statistics (see also Facet 6) could include (but are not limited to):

- Are the measures (e.g., a questionnaire) well defined? Are the measures robust and appropriate for the purposes for which they are being used? (e.g. Ridgway et al., 2018, challenge the use of a measure of 30-day mortality to judge the risks associated with hospital admissions at weekends).
- Are metadata (i.e. detailed explanations of how variables were defined, sample characteristics etc.) available?
- Were the sampling procedures appropriate? who is missing from the collected data? (e.g. measuring how citizens feel about a certain topic by analysing twitter streams fails to sample non-twitter users).

More broadly, in recent years we have seen attacks on evidence-informed policy-setting, and a proliferation of untruths labelled as 'alternative facts' or 'fake news', a term which those propagating misinformation have hijacked to describe mainstream media reporting of reality. However, most statistical findings about civic issues are released as *text* (e.g. from government agencies) and are then interpreted and re-presented for public consumption by journalists and politicians. It is important, therefore, to examine narratives and interpretations that involve statistical evidence and that touch on public policy from a critical perspective. Such criticality may involve a reflection on underlying 'power' or bias issues, such as: whose interests are served (or protected) by studying, framing, or reporting on this civic issue in this way? Are there 'political' motives behind the way the problem is being examined? Are there alternative ways to examine the social problem at hand, what correlates are considered), to improve what we know about the topic? In addition, criticality can also relate to broad methodological and interpretation issues, for example:

- What is the quality of the evidence presented in a media article or a political speech to support assertions about needed policy (e.g., regarding recycling laws, wage equality, or vaccination)?
- How sensible are the projections and how appropriate are the underlying statistical models and assumptions that have been applied to analyse data on key topics, such as regarding the progression of global warming or the rate of spread of infections such as the COVID-19 coronavirus pandemic?
- When assertions are made about a correlation between variables (e.g., smoking and risk of death), are relationships assumed to be linear, and are they really so (or perhaps curvilinear)? More important, if causal processes or cause-and-effect relationships are assumed, are there plausible rival accounts, covariates, or unexplored intervening factors which affect the findings?
- Are the conclusions consistent with other available evidence?

A more comprehensive discussion of topics for critical evaluation and reflection, including the need to be familiar with detailed "worry questions" (Gal, 2002), can be found in Chap. 13. Decisions about policy require evaluations of costs, benefits and risk. The underlying analyses and statistics can and should be examined and challenged by citizens, in terms of their quality and the soundness of the underlying statistical evidence.

> **Thinking Exercise/Activity #2: Health and Management**
> In the UK, some published statistics showed that people admitted into hospitals at the weekend were more likely to die than people admitted during the week. The Health Minister introduced major changes to staff schedules ('rotas') so more health staff are working at weekends. This triggered massive demonstrations by doctors and nurses.
>
> Q. Should the Minister have looked at more data? What data? Why?
>
> (Note: Here, students could explore relevant data for their country—including the days of the week on which people actually die in hospital. The UK data illustrated *sample bias*—patients with routine medical problems are commonly admitted on weekdays (and staffing levels are high because of all the routine treatments being conducted); weekend admissions are characterised by medical emergencies. People were actually less likely to die on Saturday and Sunday than on some other days.

Facet 3: Dispositions

Statistical knowledge and skills that might be acquired in an introductory course cover many subtopics, such as knowledge about ways to describe central tendency and spread, correlation, inference, and the like. Yet, such knowledge and skills are unlikely to be useful when engaging with Civic Statistics, unless they are supported by two further factors: *relevant disposition*s and *habits of mind* related to statistical and quantitative issues.

The term 'disposition' is an umbrella term that refers to a cluster of related but distinct concepts, including motivations, beliefs, attitudes, and emotions. Examples are attitudes to evidence, and personal sentiments regarding mathematics, uncertainty and risk. Dispositions are of particular importance if we envision citizens who actively engage with and critically reflect on Civic Statistics, since they have components (e.g., self-efficacy, self-confidence) that may affect engagement in both positive and negative ways. Dispositions have not only a personal dimension (a willingness to engage with and to devote time to understanding the information that is being presented) but also a social dimension (a willingness to share opinions and alternative interpretations with others).

A key disposition is *critical stance* (Gal, 2002), a willingness to engage with statistics and quantitative evidence related to social issues. Dispositions can be positive or negative, and can either support or disrupt engagement with statistics and other quantitative information (McLeod, 1992). Positive dispositions are exemplified by trust in fact-checking organisations (such as *Full Fact* in the UK) who offer non-partisan commentaries on statements by politicians and the media on issues of social relevance. Negative dispositions are exemplified by statements such as 'you cannot trust statistics in the news'. As well, dispositions about one's own state of knowledge are important. Ignoring evidence because of prior beliefs, accepting new information uncritically, or believing that social phenomena can only be understood by experts are all symptoms of unhealthy dispositions.

Habits of mind are specific ways of thinking that people adopt in different situations. What do citizens (and students) do when faced with an argument or statement based on (statistical) evidence? A positive disposition is exemplified by active engagement with the argument. Positive habits of mind are questions that immediately spring to mind (they are *habits!*). For example:

- What is the 'story' being told—whose story, and why are they telling it? Who is interested in the results of the study?
- Can I play with the data myself, or access additional information to confirm what is being presented?
- Do I understand the visualisations, texts, and terminologies being used?
- Do I need to boost my technical knowledge (means, medians, variance, comparing groups, boxplots, density plots, interactions)? And how?

> **Thinking Exercise/Activity #3: Public Engagement with Statistics**
> If you were to conduct a survey of 100 persons regarding the extent to which they trust government statistics, understand common terms such as 'representativeness' (of a national random sample of 500 persons), or where they stand on any of the dispositions listed above, what do you think will be the results? Now, actually choose one topic, and organise a survey among your students, and their parents or neighbours. Compare the results for such groups.

Facet 4: Statistics and Risk

Most real life statistical problems have one or more non-standard features. There are no routine statistical questions; only questionable statistical routines. (Cox, quoted in Chatfield, 1991, p. 240).

This facet encompasses much of what is commonly taught in introductory statistics college courses or in 'statistics' or 'data analysis' at the high-school level, although the emphasis for Civic Statistics is different. Every fundamental idea in 'statistics' is of relevance to understanding statistics about society—here is a partial list:

- Understanding variability and describing and comparing distributions and trends in data (e.g., via frequency tables, plots, measures of central tendency, etc.)
- Understanding association and correlation
- Informal understanding of notions of samples and populations, and of representation (as in a 'representative sample') and inference
- A sense for the notion of statistical significance or level of confidence in a statistical statement (of course, calculations of statistical significance and inferential arguments are rarely useful with large-scale data which are typical of official statistics)
- More advanced topics may include (but are not limited to): regression & associations, non-linearity, signal and noise, understanding interactions (confounding variables, Simpson's paradox), Bayesian inference, effect size, and more

In addition, this facet encompasses *risk*. Risk is a complex matter. It involves weighing evidence about the relative likelihood of different phenomena, but also about the costs and consequences associated with the results of different (in)actions. Think, for example, about global warming—what are the expected impacts of not changing current policies, as well as the results of implementing proposed policies? This requires using data, statistical methods, and models, to describe the current situation, and predict the likely impact of different (non)interventions, or making judgements about the chances of different events occurring under different scenarios (do nothing; reduce emissions; plant trees), and about causality (and indeed, about webs of causal factors). Thus, understanding risk on the *societal* level involves much more than just knowledge of the formal rules or computations of 'probability'as included in many statistics curricula.

These components of risk may also create tensions between the need to understand and think critically about current (existing) data, and the need to explore projections (with embedded causal theories) about the anticipated status and likely occurrence of hypothetical events. The notions of 'costs and consequences' noted above are also not simple, as these can be considered from both a *societal* perspective, and also from a *personal* perspective (together with points in between). Think of public discussions or media articles regarding a health epidemic. There is a need to understand the costs of some actions at a *societal level* (e.g., what happens to national death rates if there are no social restrictions?; what are the economic implications of lockdown?), and at a *personal level* (*If I don't work I don't get paid—should I hide my symptoms?*). It is clear that discussions of risk are central to facet 1: *meaning for society and policy.*

All the above demonstrates the need for citizens to develop *statistical literacy* (see Gal, 2002) and *probability literacy* (see Gal, 2005). Yet, there is also a need to understand and act upon risk hence a need to develop *risk literacy*. As Martignon, Frischemeier, McDowell, and Till explain in Chap. 19, risk literacy is a multi-faceted construct that has received much attention in recent years, in particular in connection with how people manage health or financial risks. Risk involves, among other things, some familiarity with probability and conditional probability (including an informal feeling for Bayes' theorem), but also thinking of values and expected values, costs (negative or positive) of various consequences and courses of action, and the robustness of available evidence. Overall, then, the need to engage with public dialogues about burning social issues demands that citizens understand ideas related to statistics *and* to risk, not as separate cognitive or curricular entities, but fused together.

Thinking Exercise/Activity #4: Parents, Health and Education
Herd immunity is a concept that received much public attention during the COVID-19 pandemic, but has been of longstanding interest in connection with child vaccination issues. Herd immunity arises when a sufficiently high proportion of a population becomes immune to a disease (usually through immunisation); this makes it harder for the disease to spread to unprotected persons such as infants (because immune people very rarely carry the virus, so an infant's chance of coming into contact with the disease is small). Herd immunity indirectly protects those who have not been immunised yet. However vaccination is a controversial topic in some countries, with some citizens/parents opposing mandatory vaccination, while others argue that children (or adults, such as teachers) without immunization should be prevented from entering schools.

Q. Leading doctors in a country advocate mandatory immunisation for MMR (Measles, Mumps and Rubella). What is the evidence (needed) to support such a policy? Are there credible statistics that can support parents

(continued)

> **Thinking Exercise/Activity #4: Parents, Health and Education** (continued)
> who opt *against* vaccination? Should new statistics be collected (e.g., via a survey or any other means) to help public discussions on this topic? How useful is empirical evidence in discussing the right balance between the rights of the infant, the parent, and the state?
>
> Note: This activity aims to show how statistical and risk issues are intertwined, and how understanding them is essential for engaging with certain civic issues, both at the personal level and at the societal level (and that there can be a tension between them). A discussion of such issues can also bring up ethical considerations and citizens' rights. Links to relevant data can be found in Chap. 12 by Ridgway and Ridgway, which also offers links to relevant data sets and more ideas.

Facet 5: Models, Patterns, and Representations

All models are wrong, but some are useful (Box & Draper, 1987, p 424).

The heartland of statistics is the application of mathematical and statistical models to situations of interest, e.g., in order to estimate the extent of some phenomenon or project its pattern of development over time. Recent examples which have occupied many governments are the attempts to predict the progression of disease during the COVID-19 pandemic, or to project the pace of global warming or climate change. Such predictions inform decisions on national policies in this regard.

Thus, a key component of Civic Statistics is understanding that complex social phenomena can be modelled, and that different models can be developed and used to understand the same phenomenon. For example, an economist and a sociologist might have quite different theories and methods for defining and studying *poverty* in society, and they may create different indicators to sum up different components that describe or predict poverty. Their models of the causes of, and remediation for, poverty might be quite different (they might not even agree that poverty is a problem to be solved—for example, Bishop Helder Camara is quoted[1] as saying "When I give food to the poor, they call me a saint. When I ask why they are poor, they call me a communist").

Civic Statistics requires the ability to identify and understand the use of models, and to be able to challenge the fundamental assumptions made by any model (Ridgway et al., 2016). This can be contrasted with introductory statistics courses which often teach standard procedures to model data (e.g. using linear regression) with little regard to context, underlying assumptions, or the quality of models. Facet 5 thus emphasises aspects of modelling such as making judgments about causality and about confounding or intervening variables that may help to explain the patterns seen in the data.

---

[1] https://www.theguardian.com/commentisfree/belief/2009/oct/13/brazil-helder-camara

Another aspect of this facet is the need to be able to understand rich or novel *representations*. Representing data in an effective way is essential for understanding social phenomena and showing their patterns. Simple graphs and boxplots are included in introductory statistics instruction, in part because they help to model and represent data in a concise way, e.g., a line graph to show a trend. However, the complex nature and many features of social phenomena require more sophisticated representations that highlight the non-linear features of Civic Statistics data, and that show *dynamic changes* over time or across different groups being compared. In Chap. 5, Ridgway, Campos, Nicholson, and Teixeira show how innovations in ICT and digital technology are widening the range of available multivariate (and often interactive) representations, which can enable insights into phenomena that are difficult to portray via numeric representations.

> **Thinking Exercise/Activity #5: Poverty**
> Q. Provide a method (model) for estimating the number or proportion of workers in your country who *live in poverty, even though they are working* (i.e., employed people who are nonetheless "poor"). You can submit more than one estimate or representation based on different assumptions/logics (e.g., regarding what is "employed,", "poor," etc).
>
> *Note:* There is no need to analyse raw data. The exercise is to be done by finding published sources and coming up with a *model* which defines what variables should be considered, and why (what are the underlying assumptions?). Generate a reasoned estimate, based on the figures you obtain, using any credible source that you think presents relevant data (e.g., reports with current statistics about (un)employment, wages and income, usage of public assistance, family size, etc), newspaper articles on this topic, etc.

Facet 6: Methodology and Enquiry Processes

Facet 6 refers to the statistical enquiry processes and research methods used to generate any Civic Statistics. Civic Statistics requires an understanding of the strengths and weaknesses of different discovery or data collection methods, and some procedural skills.

Facet 6 encompasses both quantitative and qualitative research and data collection methods. There is a wide range of methods involved, here are key examples:

- *Quantitative methods* include: survey research (survey types, and sampling methods; a concern is always vulnerability to bias); experiments (naturalistic, Randomised Controlled Trials; validity is always a concern), administrative records, sources of big data such as web scraping (e.g., extracting information from digital sources, such as user activity on websites), and more. Some related concepts include but are not limited to: sampling, non-response, and randomization; measurement (reliability and validity); questionnaire design; cleaning data and dealing with missing values, and more

- *Qualitative methods* include: interview techniques (e.g., as part of a pilot study); content analysis of texts (as when analysing the recorded content of calls to a service contact centre to understand typical customer complaints) and images; the use of tools for analysing posts on social media such as Twitter, Facebook, Instagram, and blogs, etc.

An understanding of *ethical issues* associated with the production of data and the use of various research methods is also an essential component of Civic Statistics. It is important by itself (i.e., related to the rights of citizens) but is also important because it can indirectly affect the results and conclusions. For example there is a need to know about issues concerning the confidentiality of data collected, and protection of the identity of respondents to surveys via anonymization; this may reduce the willingness of certain individuals to participate in a study (or not), thus affecting the sampling process and sample characteristics and representativeness.

> **Thinking Exercise/Activity #6: Migration**
> A study claims: *Recent migrants have below average intelligence.*
> Q. Identify three distinct reasons (related to methodological factors) that might invalidate these conclusions or published claims.

Facet 7: Extensions in Official Statistics
Official statistics agencies (OSA) and other statistics producers operate in virtually all countries in the world. International agencies such as Eurostat, OECD and the UN, synthesise data across countries and produce additional multinational statistics. All these OSA create and publish reports, datasets, press releases, dashboards, and other data products that are critical for understanding societies and the changes they are going through—and these information sources are critical because they are the basis for much of the statistics-based information that the media reports to the general public. However, understanding information from official statistics sources requires knowledge that goes beyond what is taught in standard introductory statistics courses.

Gal & Ograjensek (2017) have proposed a model mapping six elements that characterise 'official statistics literacy'; they argue that citizens should:

1. Know about the system of official statistics and its work principles (e.g., that OSA aim to generate statistics which are based on sound scientific principles and which are credible and trustworthy, impartial and objective, ethically sound, comparable, open and transparent, etc.).
2. Understand the nature of statistics about society, i.e., that data are often multivariate, dynamic, based on rich text and visualizations, etc. (see Chap. 2).
3. Understand the nature and use of indicators (e.g., GDP, poverty threshold) for tracking changes in key social and economic phenomena.
4. Know about the specific statistical techniques and ideas that are of relevance to official statistics.

5. Understand the research methods and data sources that are common or unique to official statistics, e.g., conducting censuses; that statistics on key topics are released and updated on a regular schedule (e.g., each month or quarter); large-scale household surveys are used.
6. Be able to access statistical reports and information products from OSA (see Facet 9).

In each of the above six areas, there are 'extensions' which go beyond the basics of descriptive and inferential statistics encountered by those who learn introductory statistics at the high school or college level. For example, statistics producers use a large array of additional techniques and ideas, such as moving averages, seasonal adjustment (see Example 2 in Sect. 3.2 on 'wage adjustment'), data smoothing, case weighting, and the like. Specific areas of official statistics may have additional important approaches, such as the use of models and assumptions for population projections, or national accounts and 'purchasing power parities' when comparing economic statistics across nations or time units (Pfeffermann, 2015). Ridgway & Smith (2013) note further topics which receive rather little attention in traditional statistics courses but are of heightened importance in understanding data from official statistics sources, such as: the perils of survey research (non-response or respondent bias); use of Geographical Information Systems (GIS) and small area estimation to provide data relevant to specific locations; and synthetic methods where data gathered by conventional survey data is combined with 'big data' (e.g. data on mobile phone traffic).

Understanding of these and related techniques may not be essential for the understanding of basic statistics reported in the media. However, knowing about their existence, even if they are treated as 'black box' techniques without understanding the underlying computations, can be important if citizens are to adopt a questioning stance and desire to understand more deeply how certain conclusions are derived. For instance, how is it possible to compare different economic, financial and social systems that have monetary systems with different characteristics, or where social or economic conditions (e.g., inflation) have changed the base against which comparisons are being made?

Thinking Exercise/Activity #7: Equality

Read again Example 2 in Sect. 3.2 (on the gender pay gap) and decide which statistical methods discussed there can be seen as "extensions in official statistics". Which important techniques or approaches are not part of *your* introductory statistics courses? Next, access the full entry about *gender pay gap* on Wikipedia, and continue your analysis for at least 4 more paragraphs. (You are not limited to English—these definitions appear in Wikipedia in multiple languages!)

Q. List the topics you found, then answer this: Do you think it is essential to understand these extensions in official statistics, in order to make sense of statistics about the gender pay gap?

Facet 8: Contextual Civic Knowledge

Statistics is about describing, comparing, projecting and modelling, but in order to do all these, one needs to have an understanding of the phenomena of interest. This requires factual knowledge about the world. For instance, knowing that absorbing one million refugees in Germany (population over 80 million) is likely to be easier than absorbing one million refugees in Hungary (population around ten million), other things being equal. Knowing that countries being compared are not necessarily equal, e.g., in terms of political climates, economic realities, or population characteristics, reflects the contextualization of civic knowledge.

Contextual civic knowledge includes, among other things:

- Factoids: sizes of populations, size of GDP, national debt and resources; demographics and population composition; history and geography of a country or region, economic sources of income
- Knowledge about institutional structures, the machinery of government, and political actors
- Knowledge about the flow of information (e.g., media and digital sources)
- Familiarity with regional and national geo-politics

A benefit of contextual civic knowledge is that one can look for alternative data analyses using knowledge of plausible covariates. For example, finding that heart disease is heritable (i.e. children of parents who suffered from heart disease are more likely to suffer from heart disease themselves) does not necessarily mean that any genetic factors are involved. Children often model their parents' behaviour in important ways, such as smoking, diet, being obese, living in the same environment, and making similar lifestyle choices about exercise. Thus, understanding 'how the world works' is also part of contextual knowledge and helps in interpretation about civic statistics. At a higher level, if one is to understand (or do) anything about social injustice, one needs to understand communication channels and governance.

It is important to understand that knowledge about the context is normally not specified within curriculum statements because it is too broad. The specific details of the contextual knowledge needed by citizens will vary depending on the tasks used (that is, depending on the civic area of interest, and the particular characteristics of the country or region or problem given). Yet such contextual knowledge is essential, because without it students and citizens cannot fully interpret and understand the importance or meaning of statistics about a social phenomenon, or its implications for social policy in a specific country or region.

Thinking Exercise/Activity #8: Demographics

In your country:

Q1. What is the annual birth rate and number of births, death rate and number of deaths? Compare these to the number of people who died from different types of transport accidents (i.e., by car, train. etc.) last year.

(continued)

Thinking Exercise/Activity #8: Demographics (continued)

Q2. What is the (approximate) total annual budget of your government? how much money was allocated during the last year to road safety (e.g., safety education, safety media campaigns, road improvement), vs. to medical or health services?

Q3. How useful are these figures for understanding and putting in perspective the number of people who died of COVID-19 (or road accidents) in your country, and associated government expenditure on medical services, payments to people who were fired (laid off from work), etc.?

Think of other questions you can pose to students that will connect different types of statistics (e.g., on demographics, employment and economic factors) and showcase the importance of contextual knowledge.

Facet 9: ICT & Search

To access and evaluate Civic Statistics, citizens need to be knowledgeable about many separate aspects of Information and Communication Technologies (ICT). At a basic technical level, students and citizens need to know how to search for information that may involve statistical evidence (using search engines effectively; locating credible information sources or relevant reports); sorting and comparing (which area has the smallest political majority?); using interactive displays effectively, e.g., choosing scales, adjusting sliders and display parameters, or using zoom functions. Some elements of Facet 9 are illustrated more fully in Chap. 5.

A different aspect of ICT and Search is knowing that citizens can access many data sources on their own. OSA and other major data providers make data publicly available. "Open data" initiatives in many countries (such as data.gov in the USA and data.gov.uk in the UK) aim to support democratic processes by giving citizens access to data that can stimulate debate and inform policy making. However, searching, accessing, and working directly with such data sets may require extra technical expertise.

Beyond traditional views of ICT or the effective use of digital tools, citizens need to be aware of the impact of digital technologies on their lives, as well as of the potential of these technologies to support Civic Statistics. 'Undoubtedly the greatest challenge and opportunity that confronts today's statisticians is the rise of Big Data' (Madigan, 2014, p4). Examples include data from wearable devices, transactional data from mobile phones, and data scraped from web pages. Civic Statistics requires an understanding of the analytic techniques suited to accessing and analysing high-volume unstructured data. As technologies have an increasing impact on many aspects of daily life, so citizens need to understand the ways data and technologies are used, in order to both protect their own direct interests, but also to engage in debates about appropriate and inappropriate uses of technologies and data. These issues are explored in detail by Ridgway, Campos and Biehler in Chap. 22, and elsewhere in Part 4.

Thinking Exercise/Activity #9: Policy Goals and International Development

The UN Sustainable Development Goals (SDGs) present many aspirations regarding desired change in 17 separate key domains related to social and economic issues, on which there is broad international agreement. To understand the role of ICT and Search enabling processes as part of understanding Civic Statistics, please:

(a) Search for basic definitions of the 17 key SDGs; choose *one* of interest to you.
(b) Find one or two repositories of data or of indicators that allow you to check on the status of your chosen SDG. Is there a single indicator or measurement model in this regard?
(c) Search for information about *your own country* and where it stands on this SDG, and compare your performance with another country you care to compare to.
(d) Reflect on the type of skills you used (this may overlap with some of the other facets and tools). What type of statistics and representations are shown? How do they relate to the regular content found in introductory statistics?

Facet 10: Quantitative Core

This facet relates to quantitative skills (many people will think of these as mathematical skills) which underpin some aspects of statistical literacy. While fluency in these topics is important, Civic Statistics needs more than simply fluency, but also numeracy (Geiger et al., 2015; PIAAC Numeracy Expert Group, 2009) because numbers are presented in contexts that require subtle understanding. Civic Statistics often involve both very large numbers (e.g. GDP measured in trillions of euros) and very small numbers (e.g. micromorts to measure the risk of death from certain activities). Conversions between measures are common; numeracy skills are needed in order to understand and compare different measures. Components of the Quantitative core include ratio, percentages, rates, fractions, and number sense. Number sense is about having a feel for numbers. In Civic Statistics, seemingly large resources may actually be small, in context. For example, a 30 million euro increase in the budget of a government department would be significant for a small department, but if the current budget is 6 billion euro, then it is likely to have little or no observable impact on department performance. There is a considerable literature on the problems associated with understanding ratio, percentages and rates—a good starting point is the StatLit webpage.[2]

---

[2] http://web.augsburg.edu/~schield/

In the context of Civic Statistics, it is easy to find examples where an author has deliberately chosen to report (accurately) data that are misleading—for example, reporting a percentage increase, where the absolute number of the starting value is very small. Civic Statistics requires an understanding of the difference between absolute and relative quantities—such as claim that the national deficit has been reduced, when what is being reported is the deficit as a proportion of GDP, in a period when the GDP denominator has increased.

> **Thinking Exercise/Activity #10: Safety in Transportation—Comparing Metrics**
> The activity below focuses on measurement issues relevant to transportation, similar activities could refer to indicators about pollution, crime, well-being, and so forth.
> Q1. How safe is it to travel by different modes of transport? Rank order the following methods of travel from most to least dangerous: car, ferry/boat, rail/ train, transit rail/metro. Find published statistics on deaths for each of them. What did you find, and how much safer is one method compared to the other?
> Q2. The most commonly used metric is *deaths per 1 billion passenger miles* (a car carrying 4 people on a journey of 100 miles = 400 passenger miles; a flight carrying 150 passengers on a journey of 400 miles = 60,000 passenger miles). However, this metric only uses *deaths* and *passenger miles* as the basis for calculating *safety*. Can you think of other models to capture other aspects of *safety* of transport modes, beyond just deaths?

Facet 11: Literacy and Communication

A great deal of information concerning Civic Statistics is presented as text, whether in printed or digital or spoken formats, and some via tables or images, charts, and graphs. Being able to read fluently and absorb the overall sense of the article or report as well as the detailed statistical information, and ask critical questions (see Facet 2) about the information, is an essential skill. Yet, reading and comprehension are not always easy since text may be dense, and difficulty increases substantially if the language of the report is not the reader's first language, a common situation in many countries.

However, in the context of Civic Statistics, both literacy and communication are moving targets. New forms of communication are emerging, that include social media, new ways to visualise data (e.g. Yau 2011; McCandless 2014, or the GapMinder resources[3]), and video (such as Hans Rosling's TED talks on YouTube). Citizens need to be able to learn how to understand and deconstruct messages conveyed in multiple or new communication forms. This requires the development of new forms of literacy—notably visual literacy (McKim, 1972), data literacy and

---

[3] www.gapminder.org

media literacy. Chapter 16 presents more examples for deconstructing newspaper reports with statistical information.

For fuller engagement in Civic Statistics, citizens also need to be able to communicate in new ways. Those wanting to communicate with others about Civic Statistics need to take care (and invest time and effort) in writing and talking in ways that the audience can absorb easily—even things like speaking slowly enough for a multilingual audience requires a conscious (and continuous) effort.

Thinking Exercise/Activity #11: 'Statistical Storytelling' About a Civic Issue

Find a recent *news story* (an article in the printed or digital media) from your own country which has some statistical information about any topic that might be called Civic Statistics (e.g., health, pollution, crime, or education). Then, find the *press release* which was published by the agency responsible (e.g., a government statistical office, a research institute). There is likely to be a number of media outlets (or social networks such as Facebook or twitter) running a story on the same topic (newspapers, TV news, etc.).

Q1. How consistent is the message from different outlets on this topic—and how compatible is it with the original press release?

Q2. From looking at the news story and the press release, what can you conclude about the *role of literacy and language skills* (and the understanding of jargon) in understanding statistical communication about civic issues?

3.5 Task Analysis: Analysing the Demands of Possible Activities via 'Radar Plots'

The prior section clarified and illustrated the nature of the 11 facets and tools included in the conceptual framework, which are needed (by students and citizens in general) so that they can critically understand Civic Statistics that they see/read/ hear, and engage with the underlying societal, political, or economic issues (Nicholson et al., 2013). Before discussing the implications of this framework for planning instruction (see Sect. 3.6 and Chap. 4), first we focus in this section on an important question: How can you analyse which of the 11 facets and tools are involved in or invoked by a certain task or activity? We advocate the use of *radar plots* (also referred to as: spider, web, star, and polar plots, or Kiviat diagrams) to support the analysis.

A radar plot analysis involves three steps:

1. **Choose a given task** (e.g., an instructional activity, class assignment, or test question that is of potential interest)
2. **Examine and reflect** on its demands, in terms of knowledge-bases, skills, dispositions, and other enabling processes—essentially thinking through the features of the resource in terms of the 11 facets of the conceptual framework.

3. **Rate on a scale** to what extent each of the 11 facets and tools are involved in or invoked by this task or activity. The rating scale can be simple and go from 1 to 3, or be more detailed, e.g., 0 to 4: "none"-"very little"-"some"-"moderate"-"a lot"; or any other labels you desire. More levels can be used, if a sensible differentiation between that many levels can be developed).

Figure 3.3 illustrates possible results from such a rating process, using a 1–8 rating scale. (Appendix A offers two empty plots for your use, with an 8-level scale and a 5-level scale, and an empty table for ratings with any number of levels). Chapter 4 shows more worked-out examples. (See Ridgway et al., 2017 for further illustrations).

Before asking you to try out such an analysis, we emphasise that a radar plot is *not* an accurate analytical tool. Different educators may vary in their interpretation of the demands of any given task across the 11 facets, especially if a very detailed scale is used. It is clear that the ratings depend on the student target group; a question where students compare means and medians may be given a high score on Statistics and Risk for young students, yet a very low score for older students. However, the radar plot is very useful because the rating process promotes a valuable intellectual analysis, and the ratings can help you to evaluate the *relative* weights or level of involvement of all facets and tools in different tasks that you are considering for a particular target group. It can also identify gaps in a curriculum if no activity engages with some of the facets in the conceptual structure.

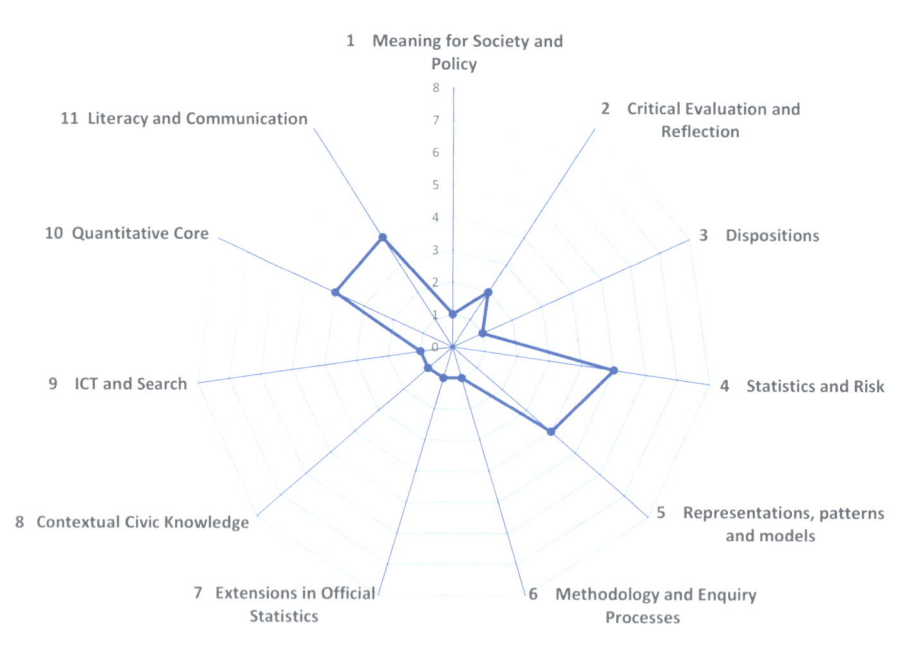

Fig. 3.3 Sample radar plot ratings for a teaching task

Further, a radar plot can be used by teams of teachers (e.g., in a workshop) to engage and bring out personal perceptions, and discuss, justify, or compare what facets and tools are demanded by different tasks or activities. All this can serve the planning of a mix of tasks that can create an effective instructional sequence covering all 11 facets and tools discussed in this chapter.

> **Example 3: Analysing the Facets and Tools Invoked by a Sample Statistics Task**
> There are ten people in an elevator, four women and six men. The average weight of the women is 120 pounds and the average weight of the men 180 pounds.
>   What is the average of the weight of the ten people in the elevator? Explain.

Reader—your task: please read the item above (from Pollatsek et al., 1981). Then, rate the extent to which this item involves or demands each of the 11 facets and tools. We suggest using the 0-4 scale described earlier by using the plot or the table in Appendix A. However, you can design your own empty plot via a simple chart in Excel, or just construct a simple table, and use any rating scale you desire.

Write your ideas in the empty plot/table as in Appendix A. **Only then, continue to read.**

Analysis of Example 3: This example illustrates a task which addresses conceptual understanding of averages. It is set in a reality which students can relate to, yet it is contrived, i.e., it does not relate to any civic context and has no social implications (see Chap. 13; and Carter & Nicholson, 2016, about contexts). It does require some understanding of statistical concepts and possibly some computation (Facets 5, 10). Some communication (Facet 11) is required by asking for an explanation, but this is not part of the task itself, which has minimal text. *What other thoughts do* you *have about the facets and tools demanded by this task?*

The example above is given only to help familiarisation with the analysis of task demands using the conceptual framework described in this chapter. What matters is to go through the reflection process, externalise your own perceptions, and be honest with yourself about the relative demands along the points of the rating scale you chose. See Chap. 4 for more examples of a radar plot analysis, using more authentic Civic Statistics tasks.

3.6   Summary and Suggestions for Planning Instruction from the Viewpoint of the 11 Facets and Tools

Civic Statistics has an important place in both statistics and social science curricula. This chapter focused on introducing a conceptual framework with three organizing dimensions (Engagement & Action, Knowledge, Enabling Processes), and 11 facets and tools that should be developed through instruction. Examples and short activities were provided for each facet and tool to highlight their nature and interconnectedness.

The 11 facets and tools discussed in this chapter have many implications for teaching/learning processes and for assessment, which are discussed in detail in Chap. 4. Here we offer two brief concluding suggestions regarding the planning of instruction on Civic Statistics, in order to sensitise you to some of the many ideas in Chap. 4:

- **Plan instruction and analyse, select, and mix examples, tasks and activities that can together cover all the 11 facets and tools, not just conventional data analysis.** A key assertion throughout this book is that just teaching traditional statistics to students is insufficient to prepare them for engagement with Civic Statistics. Instruction involves, among other things, the planning and sequencing of multiple examples and explanations, tasks and activities, and assignments and tests. While each example or activity may cover or invoke only some of the facets and tools, the idea is that over time, all 11 facets and tools discussed in this chapter will be covered, explained, and practiced, in integration. To help the planning of such instruction, a key suggestion is that teachers *analyse, select and mix in a pre-planned way* different tasks—see Sect. 3.5 for guidance on how to analyse task demands
- **Contextualise!** For instruction in Civic Statistics to be meaningful and effective, examples and activities used in the classroom have to be set in realistic social contexts. Tasks can refer to health, crime, employment, wages, equality, pollution, global warming, or any other preferred area that is of interest—but have to be contextualised. Part 3 of this book is entitled Design Principles in Practice, and provides a rich variety of starting points in this regard (e.g., see Chap. 13 on contextualization by using rich realistic texts and task design; Chap. 18 on contextualization via cross-curricular projects, or Chap. 19 for contextualization related to notions of chance and risk)

We urge you to repeat the task analysis process sketched in Sect. 3.5 with other tasks (which you may use already, or from other sources). You may find that many tasks and activities which are typically used when teaching statistics can be useful for developing procedural or conceptual understanding, but hardly touch on many important facets and tools discussed in this chapter. This is why in this section we suggest planning a mix of tasks and instructional sequences that cover all 11 facets and tools, and ensuring tasks derive from realistic social contexts. Chapter 4 discusses further examples of using radar plots and presents broader recommendations, including ideas about assessment and systemic issues. Other chapters in this book offer additional pragmatic suggestions for teachers.

Appendix A

This appendix contains two empty radar plots, with a 5-level scale (Fig. 3.A.1) or an 8-level scale (Fig. 3.A.2) and a simple table (Table 3.A.1), that can be used by teachers or researchers for rating Civic Statistics tasks. Also, see the text box for simple instructions on how to create your own radar plot in Excel.

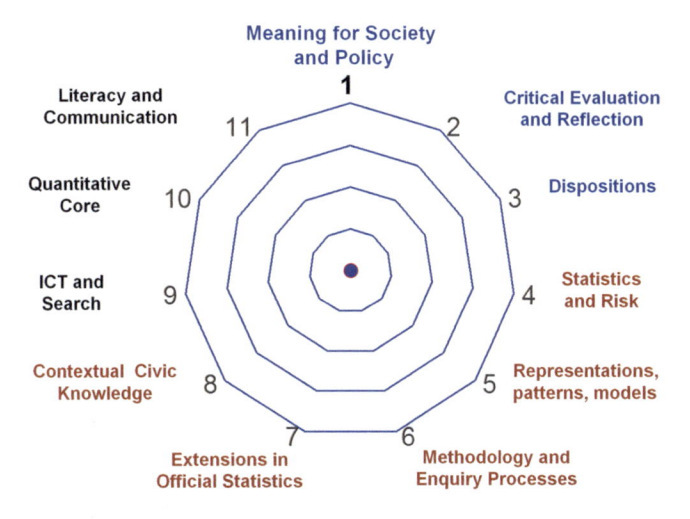

Fig. 3.A.1 Empty radar plot for an 5-level rating scale

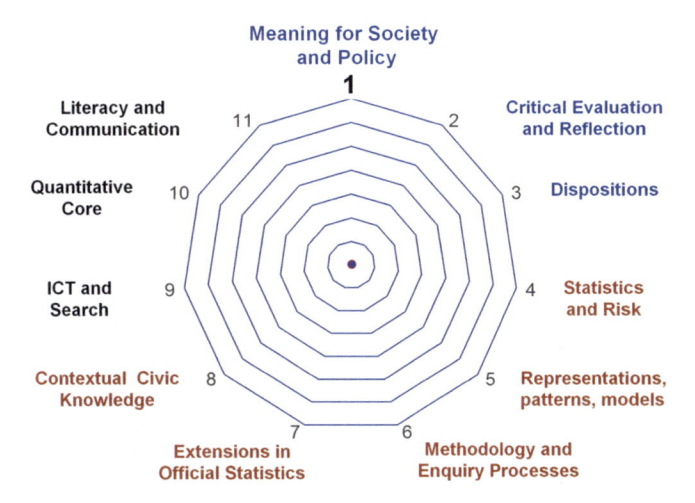

Fig. 3.A.2 Empty radar plot for an 8-level rating scale

Table 3.A.1 Empty table for rating a task

Facet	Rating	Comments
1 Meaning for Society and Policy		
2 Critical Evaluation and Reflection		
3 Dispositions		
4 Statistics and Risk		
5 Representations, patterns, models		
6 Methodology & Enquiry Processes		
7 Extensions in Official Statistics		
8 Contextual Civic Knowledge		
9 ICT and Search		
10 Quantitative Core		
11 Literacy and Communication		

The plot in Fig. 3.A.1 is suitable for a 5-level rating scale. Possible labels are: 0—none, 1—very little, 2—some, 3—moderate, 4—a lot. (Feel free to change!).

> **Do it yourself—create your own radar plot in Excel!** Enter labels from 1 to 11 as listed in Table 3.A.1 under "facet" (i.e., vertically), then click the 'chart/graph' icon and choose chart type "radar" and follow the instructions that appear. You can change the number of levels (i.e., the number of concentric circles in the radar plot) by entering the 'scale' tab and changing the value for units compared to the maximum value For example, for 5 levels, set the maximum to 1 and the unit values to 0.25. Depending on your version of Excel, some trial and error will yield the desired chart based on the ratings you enter in each cell.

References

Ben-Zvi, D., & Garfield, J. B. (Eds.). (2004). *The challenge of developing statistical literacy, reasoning and thinking* (pp. 3–16). Kluwer.

Boersma, S., Diefenderfer, C. L., Dingman, S. W., & Madison, B. L. (2011). Quantitative reasoning in the contemporary world, 3: Assessing student learning. *Numeracy, 4*(2), Article 8. https://doi.org/10.5038/1936-4660.4.2.8

Box, G., & Draper, N. (1987). *Empirical model-building and response surfaces.* Wiley.

Callingham, R., & Watson, J. M. (2017). The development of statistical literacy at school. *Statistics Education Research Journal, 17*(1), 181–201.

Carter, J., & Nicholson, J. (July 2016). Teaching statistical literacy by getting students to use real world data: 40 years worth of experience in 40 minutes. In J. Engel (Ed.), *Promoting understanding of statistics about society. Proceedings, IASE Roundtable*, Berlin. Retrieved September 10, 2020 from http://iase-web.org/Conference_Proceedings.php?p=Promoting_Understanding_of_Statistics_about_Society_2016

Chatfield, C. (1991). Avoiding statistical pitfalls. *Statistical Science, 3*, 240–268.

Engel, J. (2017). Statistical literacy for active citizenship: A call for data science education. *Statistics Education Research Journal, 16*(1), 44–49.

Engel, J., Gal, I. & Ridgway, J. (2016). Mathematical literacy and citizen engagement: The role of Civic Statistics. Paper presented at the *13th International Conference on Mathematics Education*, Hamburg. Retrieved September 10, 2018 from http://community.dur.ac.uk/procivic.stat/wp-content/uploads/2016/05/Mathematical-Literacy-and-Citizen-Engagement-The-Role-of-Civic-Statstics.pdf

Friel, S. N., Curcio, F. R., & Bright, G. W. (2001). Making sense of graphs: Critical factors influencing comprehension and instructional applications. *Journal for Research in Mathematics Education, 32*(2), 124–158.

GAISE College Report ASA Revision Committee. (2016). *Guidelines for assessment and instruction in statistics education - College report*. American Statistical Association. https://www.amstat.org/asa/education/Guidelines-for-Assessment-and-Instruction-in-Statistics-Education-Reports.aspx

Gal, I. (2002). Adults' statistical literacy: Meanings, components, responsibilities. *International Statistical Review, 70*(1), 1–25.

Gal, I. (2005). Towards 'probability literacy' for all citizens. In G. Jones (Ed.), *Exploring probability in school: Challenges for teaching and learning* (pp. 43–71). Kluwer Academic Publishers.

Gal, I., & Ograjenšek, I. (2017). Official statistics and statistics education: Bridging the gap. *Journal of Official Statistics, 33*(1), 79–100.

Gal, I., van Groenestijn, M., Manly, M., Schmitt, M. J., & Tout, D. (2005). Adult numeracy and its assessment in the ALL survey: A conceptual framework and pilot results. In T. S. Murray, Y. Clermont, & M. Binkley (Eds.), *Measuring adult literacy and life skills: New frameworks for assessment*. Statistics Canada.

Gal, I., Grotlüschen, A., Tout, D., & Kaiser, G. (2020). Numeracy, adult education, and vulnerable adults: A critical view of a neglected field. *ZDM Mathematics Education, 52*(3), 377–394.

Geiger, V., Goos, M., & Forgasz, H. (2015). A rich interpretation of numeracy for the 21st century: a survey of the state of the field. *ZDM-International Journal on Mathematics Education, 47*(4), 531–548.

Gould, R. (2017). Data literacy is statistical literacy. *Statistics Education Research Journal, 16*(1), 22–25.

Kemp, M. & Kisanne, B. (2010). A five step framework for interpreting tables and graphs in their contexts. In C. Reading (Ed.), *Data and context in statistics education: Towards an evidence-based society. Proceedings of the Eighth International Conference on Teaching Statistics* (ICOTS8, July, 2010, Ljubljana, Slovenia). International Statistical Institute/IASE. Retrieved September 10, 2018, from http://iase-web.org/documents/papers/icots8/ICOTS8_7G3_KEMP.pdf

Kilpatrick, J. (2001). Understanding mathematical literacy: The contribution of research. *Educational Studies in Mathematics, 47*(1), 101–116.

Madigan, D. (2014). *Statistics and science: A report of the London workshop on the future of the statistical sciences*. Accessed May 12, 2015, from www.worldofstatistics.org/wos/pdfs/Statistics\Science-TheLondonWorkshopReport.pdf

Madison, B. L. (2014). How does one design or evaluate a course in quantitative reasoning? *Numeracy, 7*(2), 3.

McCandless, D. (2014). *Knowledge is beautiful*. William Collins.

McKim, R. (1972). *Experiences in visual thinking*. Brooks-Cole.

McLeod, D. (1992). Research on affect in mathematics education: A reconceptualization. In D. Grouws (Ed.), *Handbook of research on mathematics teaching and learning* (pp. 575–596). Macmillan.

Nicholson, J., Ridgway, J., & McCusker, S. (2013). Health, wealth and lifestyle choices-Provoking discussion on public spending. *Teaching Citizenship, 36*, 23–27.

OECD. (2009). *Focus on citizens: Public engagement for better policy and services*. Retrieved September 10, 2018. doi: https://doi.org/10.1787/9789264048874-en

Pfeffermann, D. (2015). Methodological issues and challenges in the production of official statistics. *Journal of Survey Statistics and Methodology, 3*(4), 425–483.

PIAAC Numeracy Expert Group. (2009). PIAAC numeracy: A conceptual framework. *OECD Education Working Papers*, No. 35, OECD Publishing. Retrieved September 10, 2022. https://doi.org/10.1787/220337421165

Pollatsek, A., Lima, S., & Well, A. D. (1981). Concept or computation: Students' understanding of the mean. *Educational Studies in Mathematics, 12*(2), 191–204.

ProCivicStat Partners. (2018). *Engaging Civic Statistics: A call for action and recommendations.* (A product of the ProCivicStat project). http://iase-web.org/islp/pcs

Prodromou, T. (2015). Students' emerging reasoning about data tables of large-scale data. *International Journal of Statistics and Probability, 4*(3), 181-197/.

Ridgway, J. (2016). Implications of the data revolution for statistics education. *International Statistical Review, 84*(3), 528–549.

Ridgway, J., & Smith, A. (2013, August). Open data, official statistics and statistics education: threats, and opportunities for collaboration. In *Proceedings of the Joint IASE/IAOS Satellite Conference "Statistics Education for Progress"*, Macao.

Ridgway, J., Arnold, P., Moy, W., & Ridgway, R. (July 2016). Deriving heuristics from political speeches for understanding statistics about society. In J. Engel (Ed.), *Promoting understanding of statistics about society, Proceedings, IASE Roundtable*, Berlin. Retrieved September 10, 2018 from http://iase-web.org/Conference_Proceedings.php?p=Promoting_Understanding_of_Statistics_about_Society_2016

Ridgway, J., Nicholson, J., & Gal, I. (2017). Task analysis tool: Facets of statistical literacy. Prepared for a *ProCivicStat Workshop at the IASE Satellite Conference*, Rabat 11–13 July, 2017. http://iase-web.org/islp/pcs/documents/Rabat_Workshops_Booklet.pdf?1543033029

Ridgway, R., Nicholson, J. & Gal, I. (July 2018). Understanding statistics about society: A framework of knowledge and skills needed to engage with Civic Statistics. In M. A. Sorto, A. White, & L. Guyot (Eds.), *Proceedings of the 10th International Conference on Teaching Statistics (ICOTS10, Kyoto, Japan)*. International Statistical Institute. Retrieved Sept 10, 2018 from http://iase-web.org/icots/10/proceedings/pdfs/ICOTS10_7A1.pdf

Schield, M. (2016). GAISE 2016 promotes statistical literacy. *Statistics Education Research Journal, 16*(1), 50–54. http://iase-web.org/documents/SERJ/SERJ16(1)_Schield.pdf?1498680980

Sharma, S. (2013). Assessing students' understanding of tables and graphs: Implications for teaching and research. *International Journal of Educational Research and Technology, 4*, 51-70 Retrieved September 10, 2018 from www.soeagra.com/ijert/ijert.htm

Tout, D., & Gal, I. (2015). Perspectives on numeracy: Reflections from international assessments. *ZDM–International Journal of Mathematics Education, 47*(4), 691–706.

Watson, J. M. (2013). *Statistical literacy at school: Growth and goals*. Routledge.

Wild, C. J., & Pfannkuch, M. (1999). Statistical thinking in empirical enquiry. *International Statistical Review, Statist. Review, 67*(3), 223–248.

Yau, N. (2011). *Visualize this: The flowing data guide to design, visualization, and statistics*. Wiley.

Chapter 4
Implementing Civic Statistics: An Agenda for Action

Iddo Gal ⓘ, Jim Ridgway, James Nicholson, and Joachim Engel

Abstract The first three chapters of this book have identified societal demands for understanding Civic Statistics (Chap. 1), described specific features of the statistical and mathematical information citizens receive about civic issues (Chap. 2), and mapped out the facets and tools (skills, knowledge, mental and motivational tools) needed to critically understand such statistical and mathematical information about society (Chap. 3). The present chapter examines issues that are essential for promoting necessary changes in the teaching and learning of Civic Statistics, which are needed for empowering citizens to engage with and analyze data sources and data-informed reasoning about burning issues in society, and critically interpret messages related to Civic Statistics encountered in the news media, social networks and related digital sources. The chapter first provides further illustrations of activities or tasks pertaining to Civic Statistics and shows how to analyse task demands in terms of the facets and tools they require. Then, general questions are examined regarding the all-important alignment of the features of Civic Statistics and their demands with curriculum plans and learning goals, classroom teaching practices, and assessment methods. We provide some guidelines for developing assessment items relevant to Civic Statistics. Finally, the chapter presents six broad recommendations related to changes in systemic issues that can promote attention to and critical understanding of Civic Statistics, at the school and university levels, and which can improve effective instruction and assessment in this regard, within mathematics education, statistics and data science education, and related disciplines.

I. Gal (✉)
Department of Human Services, University of Haifa, Haifa, Israel
e-mail: iddo@research.haifa.ac.il

J. Ridgway · J. Nicholson
University of Durham, Durham, UK
e-mail: jim.ridgway@durham.ac.uk; j.r.nicholson53@gmail.com

J. Engel
Ludwigsburg University of Education, Ludwigsburg, Germany
e-mail: engel@ph-ludwigsburg.de

© The Author(s) 2022
J. Ridgway (ed.), *Statistics for Empowerment and Social Engagement*,
https://doi.org/10.1007/978-3-031-20748-8_4

Keywords Curriculum alignment · Statistics education · Media literacy · Data literacy · Statistical literacy

4.1 Introduction

This chapter presents general ideas that support the implementation of Civic Statistics in diverse teaching contexts, which are further illustrated and expanded in later parts of this book. The chapter integrates key ideas from Chaps. 2 and 3 and shows the relevance of the features and facets of Civic Statistics to the design of learning tasks and assessments in the area of Civic Statistics (and in mathematics education and statistics and data science education).

As a brief background, Chap. 2 sketched the history of Civic Statistics, and the goals, products, and educational resources of the ProCivicStat Project (PCS; see ProCivicStat partners, 2018). Chapter 2 also discussed the many *areas* which Civic Statistics encompass (e.g., climate change, employment and income, poverty, social equality and social justice, diversity and inclusion, crime, education, sustainability, and many more) and described in detail *12 key features of Civic Statistics* that pertain to all these areas, i.e., the characteristics of what citizens read, see, and hear in messages and displays related to Civic Statistics. Chapter 2 argued that these features, summarised in Table 4.1, are often not addressed in statistics and mathematics courses, and explained why teaching about Civic Statistics is both important and urgent.

Chapter 3 mapped out a conceptual framework, shown in Fig. 4.1, that describes 11 facets and tools (i.e., knowledge bases, competencies, skills, dispositions and various enabling processes) that are needed to understand and engage with the areas and features of Civic Statistics, and argued that few statistics courses address all of these facets or teach relevant enabling skills. Chapter 3 provided a dozen illustrative

Table 4.1 The 12 features of civic statistics

I. Contexts and interpretations
1. Societal context is the focus
2. Statistics are embedded in rich texts
3. Causality is often attributed
4. Conclusions, implications & consequences for society are discussed

II. The nature of the statistics
5. Phenomena are often multivariate
6. Decisions have been made about measures and operationalization
7. Data are often aggregated
8. Indicator systems are common
9. Dynamic data, spanning times and locations is common

III. Unfamiliar methods and representations
10. Novel data sources and analysis techniques are common
11. Varied data collection methods are used
12. Innovative visualisations are encountered

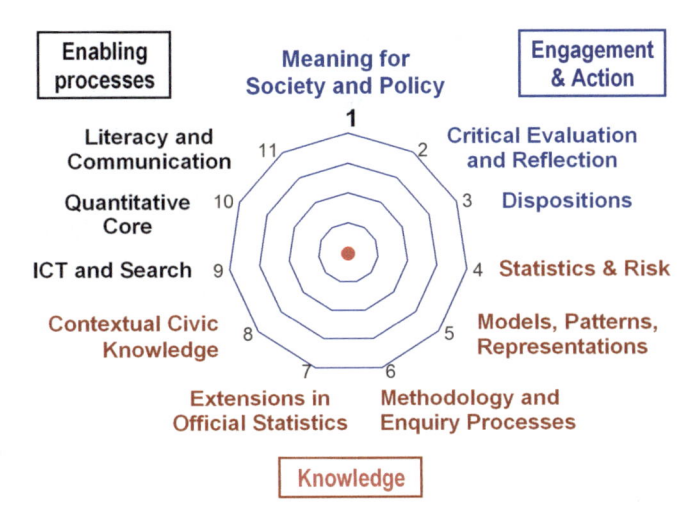

Fig. 4.1 A conceptual framework of 11 facets and tools for understanding and engaging with civic statistics

activities or 'thinking exercises' for teachers (or lecturers) and students that help to understand the importance and relevance of each facet and tool.

This chapter first provides further illustrations for activities or tasks pertaining to Civic Statistics, and shows how to analyse the facets and tools that underpin successful performance on them, in order to create a bridge to ideas introduced in Chap. 3. Then, the chapter reflects on general questions regarding the all-important alignment of curriculum intentions, classroom teaching practices, and assessment methods with the features of Civic Statistics and their demands. We provide some guidelines for developing assessment items relevant to Civic Statistics. Finally, the chapter presents six broad recommendations related to systemic changes that can promote attention to and critical understanding of Civic Statistics, at the school and university levels, and which can improve effective instruction and assessment.

4.2 Analysing the Demands of Instructional Activities Related to Civic Statistics

Instruction, when viewed broadly, involves many aspects, such as the planning and sequencing of multiple explanations and examples, tasks and activities, and assignments and tests. In Chap. 3 (Sect. 3.6) Gal, Nicholson and Ridgway defined a key goal for teachers: during a course of instruction, *all* 11 facets and tools, i.e., those listed in the conceptual framework (see Fig. 4.1) as needed for understanding Civic

Statistics, should be called upon and practiced in class by using a collection of coherent tasks or activities. Although each task or class activity will invoke only some of the 11 facets and tools, eventually *every* facet should be covered and practiced in a variety of combinations with other facets. As explained in Chap. 2 (Sect. 2.8), the materials developed in the PCS Project, including lesson plans, datasets, and many activity resources, can be useful in this regard. These materials are hosted on the website of the International Association for Statistics Education (IASE).[1]

How can you conduct a task analysis of a lesson plan or single class activity, in order to examine which of the 11 facets and tools it covers? Chapter 3 proposed the use of radar plots for task analysis, and illustrated their use with a simple task, and the Appendix of Chap. 3 offered an empty radar plot and a rating form for use. The current section aims to deepen the understanding of the 11 facets and tools and their relevance, and to familiarise readers with the process of task analysis using radar plots, by analysing the demands of two Civic Statistics tasks (see also Ridgway et al. (2017); and Chap. 12 which uses issues surrounding Covid-19 as contexts for more illustrative examples). While Chap. 3 presented a simple example of analysing the demands of a single question, in this chapter we present two much longer activities, suitable for a whole lesson or an extended home assignment. One example is elaborated below and involves the topic of poverty; another example is given in the Appendix to this chapter and deals with citizen well-being and the Human Development Index.

After each example, you are asked to evaluate it via a radar plot analysis in terms of its demands regarding the 11 facets discussed earlier. However, we re-emphasise that a radar plot is not meant to be an accurate analytical tool. In our experience, different people (e.g., teachers working with younger or older students) see different demand levels for the same task—as they do with evaluating other tasks involving mathematical and statistical skills.

The usefulness of radar plot analyses is that they help us to explore the *relative* (rather than absolute) weights of the 11 facets and tools in different tasks. Radar plots can be used as the opening step of a discussion (e.g., by a team of teachers) about the value of particular activities in teaching and assessment, and can help teachers to decide on an appropriate mixture of tasks in the curriculum, an appropriate balance of assessment tasks (illustrated later) and thus achieve an effective alignment of curricular goals, instructional activities, and assessment related to Civic Statistics.

Example 1: Analysing a Lesson Plan About 'Poverty', Using Gapminder
Please skim the whole of this section. You will see that for the activity in Example 1, we would like you to:

---

[1] http://iase-web.org/islp/pcs

- Work through a ProCivicStat lesson plan

    - Access *Gapminder*, and explore some of its functionality
    - Work through the materials (or simply work through the subset of questions, below) as if you were a student

- Reflect on the knowledge you used when working on this task
- Write down your thoughts
- Use the radar plot to focus your judgements about the likely demands of the activity for *your* students
- Compare your analysis with ours

The lesson plan (see next page) is designed to allow learners to experience how Civic Statistics enable us to understand social and economic phenomena from a comparative angle. It includes questions that aim to develop sensitivity to the multivariate and dynamic nature of Civic Statistics, understand correlations and transformations and other topics, and develop the ability to reflect critically on data and data-informed arguments.

The lesson plan is based on the use of the *Gapminder* website[2] (Kovacs, Kazar, and Kuruczleki describe classroom uses of, and experiences with *Gapminder* in Chap. 8). *Gapminder* provides access to unique visualization tools and a wealth of data on a large range of indicators across a raft of themes such as the economy, health, social progress and the environment. Users can search for topics of interest, and see data via rich and interesting dynamic graphical displays.

Searching for *poverty* on the *Gapminder* site provides a list of over 15 indicators, which can be downloaded as an Excel file or displayed in the dynamic *Gapminder* visualization interface. To illustrate, the chart in Fig. 4.2 shows *food supply* (in kcals per person per day) against the *percentage of people in extreme poverty*—defined as an income below \$3.2 per day. This chart appears static in print, but *Gapminder* itself is a dynamic visualization—pressing *Play* shows changes over time, as the bubbles (each representing a different country) move their location and expand or shrink on the graph. Different views of the phenomenon being explored can be created by choosing different variables on the *x*- and *y*- axes. The area of the bubble representing each country (e.g., India) is proportional to its population, and its colour connects it to its world region (India, in blue, is in South Asia).

The PCS Project has designed multiple activities using displays and data from *Gapminder* and other sources. Below we focus on a single extended activity called "Examining poverty and income inequalities with the help of Gapminder". (This and all the many other resources mentioned in this book can be found on the ProCivicStat webpage listed earlier, which is hosted on the website of IASE, the International Association for Statistics Education, inside the section devoted to the International Statistical Literacy Project. The *CivicStatMap* tool, also on the

---

[2]https://www.gapminder.org

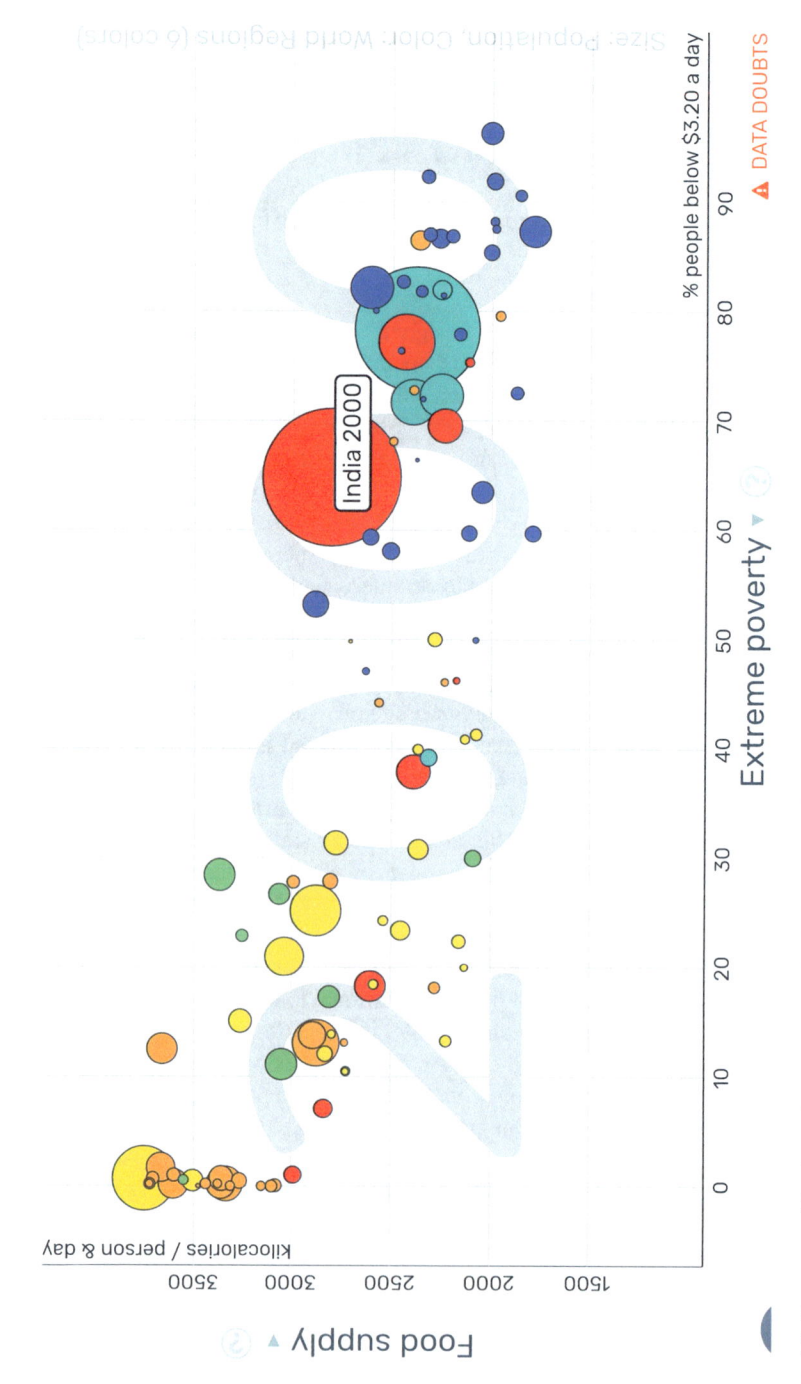

Fig. 4.2 Poverty and food supply, highlighting India for the year 2000. Gapminder is licenced under CC by 4.0

same PCS webpage, makes it easy to search for teaching resources by theme, difficulty level, tools required, etc.).

The lesson plan for the *poverty* activity (which can also be accessed directly here[3]) aims to promotes exploration and discussion about this (unfortunate) civic area and its correlates, and opens up rich opportunities for students' thinking and further learning. (An activity sheet for students appears at the end of the file).

Here are some questions that can be posed to the learners (students) in such an activity (assuming they view the dynamic visualizations within *Gapminder*, not just the static graphic shown here):

1. What is the societal issue or problem being explored in this display, and why does it matter? What are the statistical indicators that help us to describe or monitor this issue?
2. What can you say about the changes over time?
3. Are there any regional differences? (e.g., Which countries have a small (er) proportion of poor people?)
4. Are countries with large populations richer?
5. Are *poverty* or *food supply* (shown here) related to or influence other important variables, e.g., are they correlated with *life expectancy* (not shown here but available within Gapminder)
6. Overall, can you derive from these graphs any conclusions about factors which should be addressed (e.g., by public policy) in order to reduce poverty?

Reader—your task. Please work through the Poverty activity described above, using the link provided (or work on a simpler version based on questions 1, 3, and 4 and the *Gapminder* graph shown in Fig. 4.2). Then, reflect on this question:

> **Question**: What do your students need to know or utilise in terms of the 11 facets (listed in Fig. 4.1 and explained in Chap. 2) so that they can critically understand the information (i.e., the dynamic *Gapminder* graphs, and the surrounding metadata), answer the questions posed to them, and engage the underlying civic issues?

Please list your ideas.

Please rate the demands of the Poverty activity on each of the 11 facets in the conceptual framework, using an 8-point scale (1=none or very low, to 8 = very high) (An empty rating table and an empty radar plot can be found in the Appendix to this chapter or to Chap. 3)—only then continue to read.

Analysis of Example 1 Possible ratings for the poverty task are shown in Table 4.2, and in the form of a radar plot in Fig. 4.3. (Note: what matters are the *relative* values more than the absolute ratings).

This is an extended task on an important societal issue where variables are hard to define precisely and very difficult to measure directly; we have rated it highly on the first three facets. Within the knowledge group (facets 4–8) the task engages with official statistics (7), and there is also some extra contextual civic knowledge

---

[3] https://rstudio.up.pt/shiny/users/pcs/civicstatmap/5.302_TV_gapminder_level2_poverty_EN.pdf

Table 4.2 Some ratings for the poverty task in Example 1

Facet	Rating/8
1 Meaning for Society and Policy	6
2 Critical Evaluation and Reflection	5
3 Dispositions	5
4 Statistics and Risk	3
5 Representations, patterns and models	3
6 Methodology and Enquiry Processes	3
7 Extensions in Official Statistics	2
8 Contextual Civic Knowledge	3
9 ICT and Search	3
10 Quantitative Core	4
11 Literacy and Communication	5

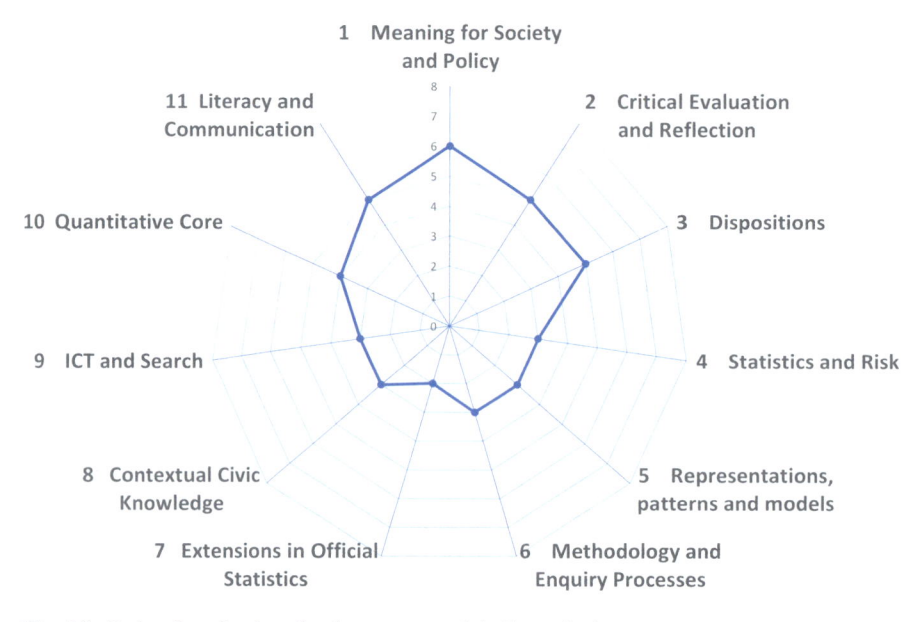

PCS Task analysis tool - Gapminder poverty

Fig. 4.3 Radar plot of ratings for the poverty task in Example 1

required (8). There is a reasonable, but not high level of demand across the content (4), modelling (5) and methodology (6) facets. The topic and data set offer scope for students to explore the data and search for other relevant information (9), using the quantitative core (10), with a relatively high demand on literacy and communication (11), partly because poverty is a complex issue (e.g. *relative poverty* is often not clearly distinguished from *absolute poverty*).

Want more examples like this? See Appendix A, for Example 2, which presents a detailed activity related to citizen well-being and to the Human Development Index. Example 2 also analyses which of the 11 facets and tools are utilised in that activity. Of course, you can analyse the demands of any other task or activity you have designed or assembled on your own, or can apply a radar plot analysis to the diverse activities offered in other chapters in this book.

4.3 Reflecting on Instruction About Civic Statistics

4.3.1 Civic Statistics and General Aspects of Teaching Statistics

The prior section showed how instructional activities can be analysed, using the conceptual framework of 11 facets and tools developed in Chap. 3, along with the radar plot tool. Task analysis is an important activity, given the need to ensure an alignment between curricular ambitions and actual teaching activities, and eventually also with assessments. The current section goes one step further and examines the relationship between the conceptual framework of 11 facets and tools and the goals mapped out in the *Guidelines for Assessment and Instruction in Statistics Education (GAISE)*, an influential set of reports[4] published by the American Statistical Association, regarding both college-level and school-level statistics education. The comparison below aims to connect our ideas about Civic Statistics with general trends in statistics education as reflected by the ideas in the *GAISE* reports.

The school-level GAISE report, which first came out in 2005, covers all grade levels from pre-Kindergarten to the end of high-school, and has been updated recently (Bargagliotti et al., 2020). Here we focus on the guidelines for students learning introductory statistics at the college level (GAISE, 2016), which are also directly relevant at the high-school level. GAISE (2016) set out nine ambitious goals for college-level statistics education, and offered some tasks that illustrate these goals. The nine GAISE (2016) goals are listed in Table 4.3.

It is useful to analyse the relationship between the nine GAISE goals listed above and the 11 facets and tools needed to understand Civic Statistics which were created by *ProCivicStat* and described earlier and in Chap. 3. This analysis is shown in Table 4.4—the shaded cells indicate where the GAISE principles appear to be aligned with the 11 tools and facets in our conceptual framework.

As shown in Table 4.4, the ProCivicStat perspective supports all of the GAISE goals for statistics education. However, the Civic Statistics conceptual framework has a much wider vision or scope than that set out in the GAISE (2016) report, as indicated by the many empty cells and whole empty rows. In particular, note that

---

[4]To find the reports, search for 'ASA GAISE assessment guidelines'.

Table 4.3 GAISE goals for students in introductory statistics college courses

	The Goal
G1	Students should become *critical consumers* of statistically-based results reported in popular media, recognising whether reported results reasonably follow from the study and analysis conducted.
G2	Students should be able to recognise questions for which the *investigative process* in statistics would be useful and should be able to answer questions using the investigative process.
G3	Students should be able to produce *graphical displays and numerical summaries* and interpret what graphs do and do not reveal.
G4	Students should recognise and be able to explain the central role of *variability* in the field of statistics.
G5	Students should recognise and be able to explain the central role of *randomness* in designing studies and drawing conclusions.
G6	Students should gain experience with how *statistical models*, including multivariable models, are used.
G7	Students should demonstrate an understanding of, and ability to use, basic ideas of *statistical inference*, both hypothesis tests and interval estimation, in a variety of settings.
G8	Students should be able to interpret and draw conclusions from standard output from *statistical software packages*.
G9	Students should demonstrate an awareness of *ethical issues* associated with sound statistical practice.

Table 4.4 A comparison of the GAISE goals for students in introductory statistics courses and the Civic Statistics facets and tools

		GAISE *Goals*								
Facets and tools		G1	G2	G3	G4	G5	G6	G7	G8	G9
1	*Meaning for Society and Policy*									
2	*Critical Evaluation and Reflection*									
3	*Dispositions*									
4	*Statistics and Risk*									
5	*Representations, Patterns and Models*									
6	*Methodology and Enquiry Processes*									
7	*Extensions in Official Statistics*									
8	*Contextual Civic Knowledge*									
9	*ICT and Search*									
10	*Quantitative Core*									
11	*Literacy and Communication*									

only one of the nine GAISE goals—G1—is directly connected to the outside world. In contrast, this is the first and most important facet in the PCS conceptual framework, because it refers to the meaning and relevance of data and statistics of any kind to societal concerns and to social policy.

In addition to these nine goals, the GAISE (2016) college-level guidelines place much emphasis on the *use of real data in the classroom*. While we fully agree with this idea as a principle for instruction in statistics, we think that a focus on 'real data' when thinking about promoting the understanding of Civic Statistics is insufficient and needs to be treated with care. 'Real data' does not mean that the data necessarily have any societal/civic meaning and purpose. Students can collect data about many 'real world' issues, e.g., conduct surveys about themselves or their peers or families, or use datasets from published studies from one of the many online repositories. However, while this would be 'real' in the sense the measurements come from the real world, there is no automatic linkage to burning societal and economic issues which are the heart of Civic Statistics.

In Table 4.1 we listed 12 features of data relevant to Civic Statistics. The first feature we emphasise is always *societal context as the focus*, and this is *not* made explicit in the GAISE guidelines. From our viewpoint, it is important that teachers design activities in such a way that students are not simply asked to crunch 'real data' and produce some statistics about them, but rather crunch data to some purpose—but also get access to ample texts and information that describe the social context. Students should be presented with questions that connect data and the real world context from which the data emerges, and should engage with the societal implications of the data. These ideas are elaborated in the next section, and illustrated in many other chapters of this book, such as in Chap. 13, which describes guidelines for creating 'opinion questions' that require students to connect statistical arguments, associated data or findings, and implications for society or for social policy.

4.3.2 Planning Instruction that Can Promote Civic Statistics

The upshot of the analysis above is that instruction in statistics, even if it uses real data, might fall short and cover only a small subset of the 11 facets and tools needed to understand and engage with Civic Statistics. To promote instruction that can enhance critical understanding of Civic Statistics, we need to go further and engage students with the wide range of issues that arise only when statistics relate to important societal issues.

Three suggestions regarding the planning of instruction about Civic Statistics emerge from Sect. 4.3.1:

1. **Plan instruction so it covers all 11 facets and tools, not just 'statistics' or 'real data'.** A key implication that emerges from our conceptual framework is that teaching data analysis to students is insufficient to prepare them to engage with Civic Statistics. Data analysis is only one of the 11 facets in the framework—and instruction should cover all of them. This means that teachers should familiarise themselves with the nature of all 11 facets, and allocate instructional time and specific activities to promote each one of them. As we argued earlier, while the use of 'real data' is crucial (as GAISE explains), tasks and activities should reflect the *questions and needs or concerns* of specific societal stakeholders (e.g., policy makers, employers, community advocates, etc.).

2. **Analyse, select, and mix examples, tasks and activities that can together cover all 11 facets and tools.** Instruction involves, among other things, the planning and sequencing of multiple examples and explanations, tasks and activities, and assignments and tests. A key suggestion is that teachers analyse, select and mix tasks in a structured way. While each example or activity may cover or invoke only some of the facets, the idea is that over time, all 11 facets discussed in the conceptual structure will be covered, explained, and practiced via exposure to coherent tasks and activities (but *not* ticked off, one-by-one!). Later we illustrate this process by offering an analysis of a complete set of assessment tasks (taken from GAISE, 2016).

3. **Contextualise!** For instruction in Civic Statistics to be meaningful and effective, statistical examples and activities used in the classroom have to be contextualised by relating them to important topics such as health, crime, employment, wages, equality, pollution, global warming, etc. In particular, as explained above, the questions posed about the texts, data or displays being analysed have to reflect a genuine "need to know" for some possible stakeholders. Examples are provided throughout this book.

In Sect. 4.5.1 we offer more general recommendations, regarding teaching, planning of information sources (texts and datasets), class atmosphere, and more. Other chapters in this book also discuss pedagogical issues and implementation principles.

4.4 Reflecting on Assessments of Knowledge, Facets and Tools Related to Civic Statistics

4.4.1 General Ideas and Approaches

The formative and summative assessments and evaluations that learners face during any course or class provide critical information both to teachers and learners about what is judged to be valuable, and what is to be learned. Assessments are arguably the strongest guide for learners about what is valued by the teacher (and the education system, in the case of high-stakes assessment) and the extent to which they are making progress. Further, useful and timely feedback is essential for teachers and can help the planning of teaching and learning processes. However, to be able to provide useful information to teachers and learners alike, assessments, in any area of education, need to be aligned with learning goals. Given the specific features of Civic Statistics, and the overarching goals of preparing learners to engage with statistics about society and to become empowered citizens, assessments in our area should be carefully planned.

Using formative and summative assessments to improve and evaluate students' learning about and engagement with Civic Statistics should include the ability to relate data analyses to *meaning for society and policy* (Facet 1). Therefore, we recommend forms of assessments which examine learners' ability, either as individuals or in teams, to: investigate and critically understand statistical texts which report findings and messages about key societal phenomena (in Chap. 13, Gal discusses the use of *opinion questions*); analyse relevant datasets; conduct project work or portfolios; use videos (exemplified by Schiller and Engel in Chap. 16); or prepare presentations or other non-traditional media.

4.4.2 Analysing the Demands of Assessment Tasks and Systems

Section 4.2 discussed the need to analyse instructional tasks and activities in terms of the 11 facets of our conceptual framework. In fact, the same type of analysis is useful (and indeed essential) when thinking of assessment tasks and assessment systems. The analysis of assessment tasks has two key goals. The first is to explore the *alignment* of assessment tasks with the *goals of instruction* and in particular the coverage of the 11 facets which should be developed during instruction. The second goal is to ensure that the content of the tasks cover all the 12 key *features* of Civic Statistics (see Table 4.1). After all, in any curriculum, there should be alignment between the intended curriculum, the implemented curriculum, and the assessments by which students are judged.

One way to start to get a feel for this is to look at a single task, and identify the extent to which it calls on each component in our conceptual framework. This can be done informally, but given that 11 facets and tools are all targets for instruction and students' growth, it is preferable to use a structured analysis using a radar plot.

To provoke readers' thinking and illustrate how an analysis of assessment items can be done, we present two short assessment items in Table 4.5 similar to tasks that teachers of traditional statistics might use as part of tests or assessments.

Reader—your task: please read (and write answers for) the two assessment items in Table 4.5, then reflect on this question:

Question: What do your students need to know or utilise (in terms of the 11 facets of the conceptual framework) in order to answer these *two* questions correctly? (Please do two radar plot analyses).

Analysis of the two items in Table 4.5 We designed item #1 to look like a typical computational item that many teachers use when teaching basic statistics. Item #2 illustrates a statistics task designed to address conceptual understanding of

Table 4.5 Two assessment items—for a radar plot analysis of task demands

---

#1. A classroom has 9 pupils. They obtained the following exam scores: 6, 3, 4, 7, 4, 13, 11, 13, 4. What is the median score on this exam? Explain.
(Source: Authors)
#2. Does everyone who scores below the median on an exam necessarily have a negative z-score for this exam? Explain.
(Source: GAISE 2016, exemplary item #4)

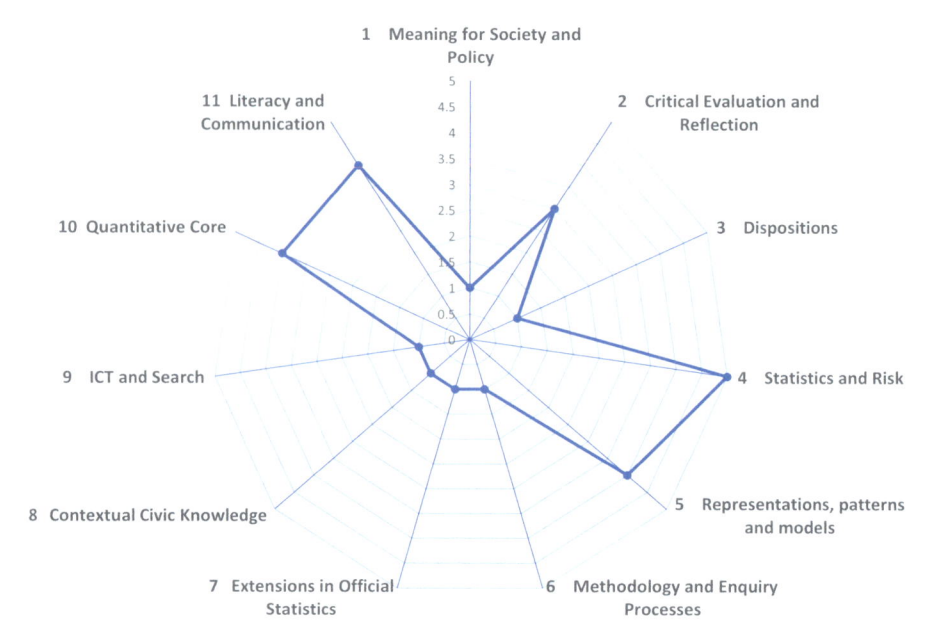

Fig. 4.4 Possible Radar Plot for Item #2 in Table 4.5 (using an 8-point scale)

arithmetic averages and medians, rather than procedural competence in calculating measures as in item #1.

Reflecting on how the 11 facets and tools are utilised or called for with items #1 and #2, we note, for example, that while both items are seemingly set in a context familiar to students (i.e., an exam) they do not relate to any *civic* context nor have any societal implications, hence these items do not address Facet 1. (In fact, both use a contrived context). Both items require some communication (Facet 11) because they ask for an explanation; however, the communication stems simply from the need to provide an answer, so the actual literacy skills required by these items are quite low. (These items do not require any reading of a real world external text such as in a newspaper article). A plausible radar plot analysis of item #2 is presented in Fig. 4.4. Item #2 requires some critical reflection (Facet 2), and an understanding of a number of statistical concepts and representations (Facets 4, 5, 10). The remaining facets 1, 3, 6, 7, 8 and 9 are not invoked at all in item #2.

Of course, you do not have to agree with the ratings in Fig. 4.4, or the analysis above. What matters is that you go through the reflection process, externalise your own perceptions, and be honest with yourself about how you see the relative demands on different dimensions. If you do that, we hope you will come to similar conclusions to us. Item #1 is a technical exercise; item #2 requires some conceptual understanding; both could be useful when teaching traditional topics in statistics. However, neither task has features related to Civic Statistics, hence would only provide a very minor component in an assessment of learning in a course aiming to promote understanding of Civic Statistics.

To help see why such a task analysis is valuable, we urge you now to re-examine the *Poverty* example you analysed in Sect. 4.2, and compare its ratings to those you gave to the two items in Table 4.5 (make sure you use the same scale). As we said earlier, what matters are not the absolute ratings, but the *relative* ratings. Having to put multiple tasks on the same rating scale helps to develop a deeper appreciation for the meaning and *breadth* of the 11 facets included in the conceptual framework (Fig. 4.1). You can also attempt the same thinking exercise by comparing such ratings to those you give (or have given) in the example about the *Human Development Index* in Appendix A.

4.4.3 Aligning Assessment Schemes with Instructional Goals in Civic Statistics

In any curriculum, there should be a good alignment between the intended curriculum, the implemented curriculum, and the *assessments* by which students are evaluated. As already argued in Sect. 4.4.1 both formative and summative assessments have a profound impact; they exemplify the curriculum for both teachers and students, and shape what is taught as well as students' focus and motivations. It is thus important that every teacher examines the alignment between the test items or assessment tasks he or she uses in teaching, and the instructional goals for Civic Statistics.

To illustrate how such an alignment analysis can be done for a *collection* of assessment items and tasks, we show here how we used a radar plot analysis to examine the alignment between assessment items set out in the GAISE (2016) report, and the instructional goals for Civic Statistics. To recap: As described earlier, GAISE (2016) sets out nine ambitious goals for statistics education at the college level (which are also relevant at the high-school level). Further, Appendix E to the GAISE 2016 Report presents 51 items (mostly short tasks) described as 'exemplary', i.e., reflecting the spirit of the GAISE instructional goals.

Our procedure was very simple: for every one of these 51 GAISE (2016) exemplary items, we made a 'one-zero' judgement on whether or not it called on each facet in our conceptual model of 11 facets and tools of Civic Statistics. Then, for each facet, we calculated a total score (between 0 to 51) based on these crude ratings. The results are tabulated in Table 4.6, and displayed in the radar plot in Fig. 4.5.

Of course, it would be unfair to describe the 51 GAISE exemplary items as an 'examination' or to argue that they necessarily reflect the complete scope of what GAISE advocates. Further, some of the items have multiple parts, and so their content cannot be fully captured by a simple 0–1 rating. Also, as we explained in Sect. 4.4.2, different teachers may see different demands in the same item, given their personal background.

Table 4.6 Number of times each facet is addressed in the 51 GAISE items

Facet	Number of items
1 Meaning for Society and Policy	1
2 Critical Evaluation and Reflection	14
3 Dispositions	1
4 Statistics and Risk	35
5 Representations, patterns and models	2
6 Methodology and Enquiry Processes	2
7 Extensions in Official Statistics	0
8 Contextual Civic Knowledge	0
9 ICT and Search	0
10 Quantitative Core	15
11 Literacy and Communication	35

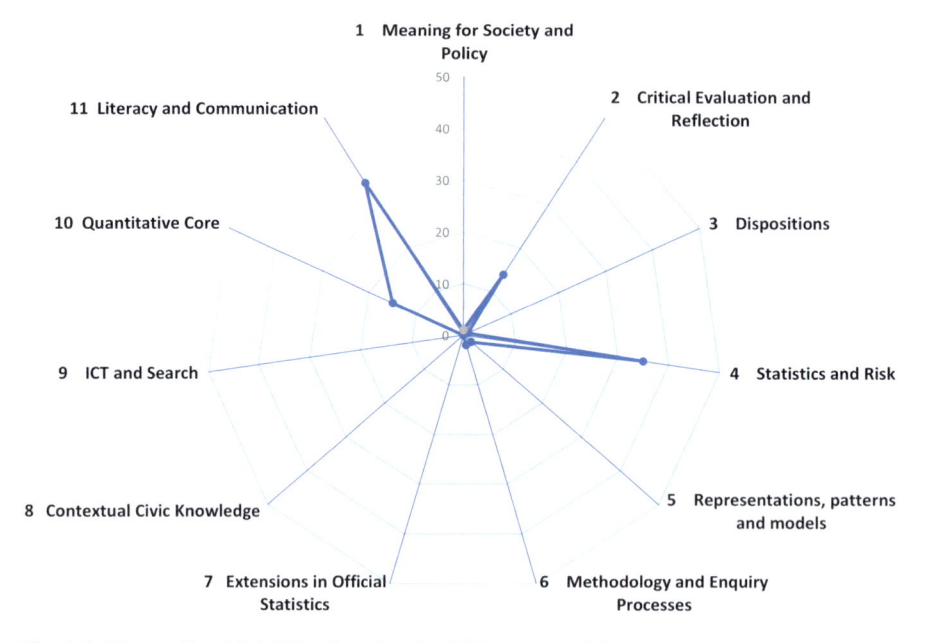

Fig. 4.5 The profile of GAISE tasks using the PCS conceptual framework

With these caveats in mind (which are important since readers may encounter them if they try to analyse their own collection of assessment items), our analysis does reveal some aspects of the GAISE framework that we believe would benefit from further exemplification. It can be seen that the GAISE items analysed are targeted primarily on statistics and risk, and literacy and communication; the quantitative core and critical evaluation are also well represented. This is perhaps unsurprising. However, from this analysis, one might suggest that more GAISE tasks be developed that address models, patterns and representations, and methodology and enquiry processes—all GAISE goals that are rather under-represented in the exemplary items offered in the GAISE 2016 report.

But the most important result of our analysis is that virtually all the exemplary GAISE items lack any explicit connection to *Meaning for Society and Policy* (Facet 1)! Advocating the use of real data is a significant improvement for statistics education, and recommendation 3 "Integrate real data with a context and a purpose" (GAISE, 2016, p. 3) is important. However, the contexts and structure of questions often do not reflect any genuine 'need to know' of a real-world stakeholder. We believe that this seriously curtails their potential for assessing knowledge of Civic Statistics.

In closing this section, we reiterate that from a Civic Statistics viewpoint, a major lesson to draw from the seemingly simple analyses presented in Fig. 4.5 is this: there is a need to reflect deeply about the demands of any single assessment (or instructional) task, as well as of a *collection* of assessment items or tasks used in combination (as in a test), *while relying on a solid conceptual framework which can guide the analysis.* Such an analysis can help with a continuing internal dialogue (among a team of teachers) about the alignment between core educational goals, curriculum activities, and assessment systems. We urge readers to re-read the opening of this section (i.e., Sect. 4.4.1) and review the broad principles and ideas that can guide the development and choice of assessment tasks in support of instruction about Civic Statistics. Further, in reading Sect. 4.5 which follows, please note Recommendation #5 which offers additional suggestions regarding assessment.

4.5 A Future Agenda and Recommendations for Action to Promote Understanding of Civic Statistics

This section builds on ideas in Chaps. 2 and 3 and in this chapter, and offers broader recommendations and suggestions that address content, pedagogy and institutional challenges needed to promote civic engagement among citizens by improving the understanding of statistics about contemporary societal issues.

Citizens need to be aware of and critically understand statistics regarding past trends, present situations, and possible future changes in key societal and economic areas such as demographics, employment, wages, migration, health, crime, poverty, access to services, education, human rights, and public expenditures. Unfortunately, traditional statistics courses do not focus on issues that are at the heart of understanding Civic Statistics, and seldom connect learners with important societal issues. Hence, there is an urgent need to rethink current educational approaches in this regard, and to create new types of resources.

Earlier chapters (and most other chapters in this book) addressed teachers and educators as the core audience, because the book focuses primarily on teaching and learning issues (along with related curriculum design and assessment issues). However, from a systemic perspective, 'education' and 'learning' involve multiple stakeholders at many different levels (e.g., at the department, school, city-wide, or national levels) whose actions may affect and contribute to teaching and learning, and if curriculum change is to happen, their goals, concerns and needs must be

Table 4.7 Six key recommendations (see ProCivicStat partners, 2018)

#1	Develop activities which promote engagement with societal issues and develop learners' critical understanding of statistics about key civic phenomena.
#2	Use relevant data and texts, and highlight the multivariate, dynamic and aggregated nature of social phenomena.
#3	Embrace technologies that enable rich visualizations and interactions with data about relevant social phenomena.
#4	Adopt teaching methods to develop skills of critical interpretation applicable to a wide variety of data and textual sources.
#5	Implement assessments which examine the ability to investigate and critically understand data, statistics findings and messages about key social phenomena.
#6	Engage stakeholders at all levels in the process of systemic change designed to promote the understanding of Civic Statistics.

considered. Thus, this section takes a broader perspective in order to address these wider issues.

Here, we present six key recommendations regarding the promotion of understanding and engagement with Civic Statistics across college and school-level systems. The recommendations, which are based on the ProCivicStat *Call for Action* (ProCivicStat Partners, 2018), are listed in Table 4.7 and amplified and explained further below.

Note that these recommendations reflect a coherent whole and should not be viewed in isolation: Recommendation 1 is about the heart and soul of Civic Statistics: the focus on societal phenomena and social policy. Recommendations 2 to 5 examine subareas related to implementation issues: information resources for teachers (i.e., datasets, articles and press releases), curricula, technology, pedagogy, assessment, etc. Recommendation 6 refers more broadly to the factors and stakeholders relevant to systemic change, beyond the focus on class-based teaching-learning processes. We emphasise that the recommendations listed below are *not* etched in stone but should be viewed as an evolving set of ideas which are open to commentary and further development. Our ultimate aim is to promote dialogue among stakeholders involved in mathematics education, statistics and data science education, and related disciplines that may also be interested in promoting aspects of data literacy and media literacy which overlap with Civic Statistics.

4.5.1   Recommendation 1: Develop Activities Which Promote Engagement with Societal Issues and Develop Learners' Critical Understanding of Statistics About Key Civic Phenomena

Statistics as a discipline is valuable because it can empower people to address real-world problems, and enable engagement with complex social phenomena. Hence, the curriculum should be revised so it introduces specific statistical ideas and techniques in a way that can empower and engage learners in addressing issues of relevance to society.

Recommendation #1 implies, among other things, that:

- A curriculum or instructional sequence has a clear rationale for content and learner activities, based on a conceptual framework that reflects a broad range of statistical skills, especially those relevant to societal issues and Civic Statistics
- The rationale should be made explicit to students via a clear conceptual framework, illustrated by tasks and activities that promote mastery of the elements of the conceptual framework
- The curriculum should go well beyond discussing specific computational techniques. It should engage directly with the *purpose* of using these techniques from a Civic Statistics perspective and on interpreting the meaning of any statistical results from a social policy perspective (e.g., what is the meaning for society or what actions or changes are needed given the findings). A particular focus should be the understanding of the role of evidence in public decision making, including concepts of uncertainty, risk, utility, and the inter-relations between them
- All this implies that tasks and activities that focus on Civic Statistics, as recommended in Sect. 4.3, must be placed in a real-world context and require learners to think of the questions that matter to different stakeholders or actors in them, along with the societal and economic implications

4.5.2 Recommendation 2: Use Socially-Relevant Data and Texts, and Highlight the Many Features of Civic Statistics (e.g., Multivariate, Dynamic and Aggregated Nature of Social Phenomena, etc.)

Understanding social phenomena, and thinking through the implications of possible policy decisions in the civic arena, requires an understanding of, and ability to work with, multivariate data and to comprehend and critique statements about multivariate phenomena. Many courses or classes make exclusive use of artificial or toy data (e.g. based on local student surveys). Such data are easy to generate, but this does students no favours, and robs them of the bigger picture! Students need to work with data in a real-world context, become aware of major data sources, the quality and the comparability of data, know how to access and manage large data files, and learn how to work with, and reason about, multivariate data. Recommendation #2 implies, among other things, that class tasks and activities will mix *three* different kinds of sources of information, listed in Table 4.8.

All of these have content related to major issues for humanity as explained in Chap. 2 (e.g., on climate change, health and epidemics, inequality, well-being, migration, and unemployment). However, a variety of contexts should be used in instruction, because each context involves different conceptual and statistical

Table 4.8 Three types of information sources for instruction on Civic Statistics

Type of source	1. Textual sources from the media, statistics providers, and social networks	2. Resources from official statistics providers	3. Raw datasets from other (open) sources
Details	Newspaper articles, TV news, podcasts, recordings from *YouTube*, press releases, websites of fact-checking organisations, social media such as *Twitter* and *Facebook*, blogs, etc.	Aggregated data such as summary tables, reports, visualizations and disaggregated data (such as public-use files and open access files). Providers include national statistics agencies, Eurostat, UN, OECD, World Bank, etc.	Open data sources with supporting metadata, e.g., big data, social media, open data repositories, 'citizen science' sources, relevant local surveys

features and may bring up different issues in terms of the argumentation encountered, quality of evidence, and the critical questions that can or should be raised by learners and by adults-at-large.

4.5.3 Recommendation 3: Embrace Technologies that Enable Rich Visualizations and Interactions with Data About Relevant Social Phenomena

If your statistics teaching is restricted to well-ordered data analysed via standard packages, students will not be well prepared for their future lives as engaged citizens. Graduates may not have skills needed for employment nor be equipped with skills in handling novelty nor be empowered to engage with civic and economic challenges of our ever-changing world.

Recommendation #3 implies, among other things, that class activities and tasks should:

- Embrace relevant current and emerging technologies, using dynamic and interactive data visualizations
- Teach students to learn to evaluate and use unfamiliar or new applications—including tools from data science and programs developed for data visualization (e.g. *R*, *Python*, *CODAP*, iNZight)
- Prepare students to become empowered citizens who can act as critical users of ICT-based resources. Students should be able to use a variety of tools to search and access diverse types of sources that pertain to Civic Statistics topics (e.g., websites, reports from different stakeholders or statistics producers, open datasets), use a variety of analytic tools such as programming languages, statistics packages, and graph plotters, and to communicate their analyses and conclusions based on comparing multiple reports or conducting their own independent analysis in a variety of media

4.5.4 Recommendation 4: Adopt Teaching Methods to Develop Skills of Critical Interpretation, Applicable to a Wide Variety of Data and Textual Sources

Teaching in classes focused on Civic Statistics should be rather different from standard courses in statistics, research methods or social statistics, because they aim to develop skills in statistical reasoning and critical appreciation of data and findings in a civic context, and to enhance skills associated with all of the 11 facets in our conceptual structure.

Recommendation #4 implies, among other things, that class activities and tasks, but also the general class atmosphere, should:

- Employ a variety of teaching strategies, with an emphasis on active learning approaches where learners formalise questions, find evidence (whether texts and reports, or data) and choose appropriate methods of analysis or reflection
- Develop skills of critical interpretation via analyses of a wide variety of sources (including newspaper articles, press releases, expert opinions, etc.)
- Encourage students and pupils to *communicate* about societal issues by creating narrative accounts of complex situations, based on multiple sources of statistical evidence, and encourage an open atmosphere in the classroom
- Introduce reasoning about non-linear and multivariate phenomena, relevant to important societal issues, early in the course
- Develop modelling skills, and sensitivity to the use of modelling in policy-related contexts (e.g. to understand and critique the models used to understand, predict, and control the progression of Covid-19—see Ridgway and Ridgway's account in Chap. 12), so that learners bring an awareness of the strengths and weaknesses of tools used to model societal and economic situations
- Engage pupils and students with the variety of ways that evidence is used to support theory or theoretical thinking in different academic disciplines. (Think of 'theory' as a set of assumptions about a system of interacting variables which have cause-and-effect relationships)

4.5.5 Recommendation 5: Implement Diverse Assessments and Evaluation Processes Which Examine and Also Promote Learners' Ability to Investigate and Critically Understand Data, Statistics Findings and Messages About Key Social Phenomena, and Communicate About Them, All Set in a Social Context

The logic for this important recommendation was explained earlier in Sect. 4.4. Please read it for more details.

Recommendation #5 implies, among other things, that class activities and tasks should:

- Embody (formative and summative) assessment systems that reflect ambitions for student outcomes relevant to Civic Statistics—in particular, assess students' ability to relate data analyses and critiques of text-based arguments to *meaning for society and policy*
- Allow learners to display mastery of the skills advocated under *R4* using the content matter and tools advocated under *R3* e.g. via project work or portfolios, using (for example) video presentations or other non-traditional media, on socially important topics
- Use a wide variety of question types, such as: Describing; Explaining; Finding resources; Posing questions; Creating multiple representations; Translating—linking multiple representations (between and within)—graphs, tables, pictures, words, functions; Combining information; Evaluating claims; Critiquing articles and reports in the media based on key 'worry questions' (see Gal's exposition in Chap. 13); Discussing implications for society, recommending actions, or proposing alternate ways to collect additional data in order to better understand a civic issue; and more

4.5.6   Recommendation 6: Engage Stakeholders at All Levels in the Process of Systemic Change Designed to Promote the Understanding of Civic Statistics and Promoting Statistical Literacy

A greater emphasis in teaching and learning related to Civic Statistics needs institutional support if it is to become a practical reality for everyone, i.e., for teachers and learners both at the high-school and university levels, as well as for learners in other formal and non-formal contexts. This requires a coherent plan for systemic change. In some contexts, this could begin by infusing Civic Statistics lessons into otherwise traditional courses: this requires support from school principals or subject-matter (department-level) coordinators. In other contexts, it might be appropriate to ask learners who study social or economic issues (e.g., in a class on sociology, history, economics, or data science) to use relevant authentic large-scale data sets or refer to official statistics from their country, or to use tables or graphs that enable international comparisons (from international sources such as Eurostat, OECD, World Bank etc.).

Such processes involve many stakeholders who can affect the shape of statistics education at tertiary or high-school levels, or who are involved or interested in fostering the statistical literacy of citizens. Further, these stakeholders include, beyond the level of school and university administrators, also education policy makers, official statistics providers, researchers, media professionals, teacher trainers, data scientists, developers of educational software or data visualization tools, and many others.

Recommendation #6 implies, among other things, that educational institutions (i.e., schools, colleges and other tertiary providers) should:

- Review individual courses and programmes of study to assess the extent to which Civic Statistics is addressed
- Ensure that Civic Statistics is a major element in courses for pre-service and in-service teachers, and that teachers experience the challenges of analyzing data and drawing conclusions for policy from information emerging from data sets about meaningful civic issues
- Encourage teachers and faculty to engage with, and provide opportunities for engagement in teaching scholarship related to Civic Statistics
- Encourage collaboration between teachers in related disciplines
- Encourage cooperation with official statistics providers (e.g., a national bureau of statistics) and with the media, in order to obtain current datasets or other materials (e.g. press releases and topical reports)

4.6 Conclusions and Future Directions

This book argues for the need to rethink conventional approaches to teaching statistics. It describes pathways for radical changes in curricula at high-schools and colleges, necessitated by the unique features of Civic Statistics, and the many facets and tools needed to understand, use, and critically interpret statistics about pressing social issues. This requires *capacity-building* and a systemic change that can support the development of the statistical literacy of future and current citizens.

We argue that in modern democracies, effective citizen engagement with societal issues requires active participation, and that this in turn requires, among other things, a broad range of skills and dispositions relevant to understanding data and statistics about societal issues. Teaching traditional statistical content in a better way does not ensure that students are familiar with the unique characteristics of Civic Statistics discussed in Chap. 2, or that they acquire the full scope of knowledge-bases, skills and dispositions described in Chap. 3. Familiarity and actual experiences with relevant, authentic texts and data relevant to meaningful societal topics are needed to foster notions of evidence-informed decision making.

Civic Statistics as portrayed in this book de-emphasises the teaching of mathematical formalisms that underpin statistics. However, Civic Statistics should not be seen as a 'simple' version of the regular statistical content encountered in introductory statistics classes. On the contrary! Given the twelve unique features of Civic Statistics reviewed in Chap. 2, Civic Statistics requires students to acquire a broader, more sophisticated intellectual tool-box, along with supporting attitudes and enabling processes depicted in Chap. 3, than those found in traditional courses. The characteristics of Civic Statistics (multivariate, dynamic, aggregated, using rich texts and rich visualizations, etc.) and the conceptual framework of 11 facets and tools needed to handle these features suggest that a much wider range of sophisticated knowledge is needed, compared to the more traditional content included in existing statistics teaching (UNECE, 2012; Ridgway, 2016; Gal & Ograjenšek, 2017).

There is an urgent need for citizens to engage with statistical messages and data-based evidence about societal issues that concern them or their communities and nations—for example, global and existential threats to humanity such as pandemics, global warming, wars or large-scale migration. Such and related issues noted earlier flood the media with Civic Statistics—and require engaged citizens to critically understand evidence if they are to provoke their governments or community leaders into appropriate action or to understand the impact of public interventions. This reality requires a rethink about the nature of statistics education in schools and universities, and how statistics are contextualized and connected to their meaning for society and policy. Civic Statistics sits at the crossroads of multiple disciplines, hence a multidisciplinary educational perspective is needed, stepping outside the comfort zone of traditional statistics education. The issues raised in this chapter require fresh and systemic thinking about approaches related to (better or more) teaching about Civic Statistics. The six Recommendations for Action provided in this chapter, which are based on the ProCivicStat *Call for Action* (ProCivicStat Partners, 2018) should be discussed widely, and (hopefully) acted upon. Later chapters in this book provide many examples and further ideas about implementing these recommendations in diverse teaching and learning contexts.

Appendix A

This Appendix includes another example for a teaching activity related to Civic Statistics, and another opportunity to practice the analysis of demands for the 11 facets and tools invoked by a Civic Statistics task or class activity. This example offers an extension of the ideas introduced in Sect. 4.2, and enables a teacher or a group of teachers to further reflect on the design of tasks and activities that can be used for instruction or assessment in the area of Civic Statistics.

> **Example 2: Analysing a task based on the Human Development Index (HDI)**

As in Example 1, we invite you to:

- Work through a ProCivicStat lesson plan
- Reflect on the knowledge you used when working on this task.
- Write down your thoughts.

- Use the radar plot to focus your judgements about the likely demands of the activity for *your* students.
- Compare your analysis with ours.

About the lesson plan: This example refers to a lesson plan (or activity guide) called "Human Development: Can you compare countries?" which you can find under the 'Lesson plans' section/button on the ProCivicStat webpage at http://iase-web.org/islp/pcs—or by using the *CivicStaMap* tool there.[5]

Explanatory notes about the HDI and the HDI task. How can we measure and compare how good the lives are of people in different countries? What variables or statistical indicators should we focus on, and why? You may want to first pose to your students this challenging question, which is also of much interest to several international bodies.

We might simply consider economic factors such as income, or wealth (measured as per capita Gross Domestic Product; GDP). However, these provide a very restricted way to summarise the well-being of individuals. Due to such concerns, the Human Development Index (HDI) was introduced by the UN as a composite index designed to measure a much broader range of issues related to the well-being in a country. The HDI summarizes a country's average achievements in three basic but multi-faceted aspects of human development: health, education, and standard of living. This index incorporates statistical measures of many specific variables, such as *life expectancy*, *literacy*, *educational attainment* and *GDP per capita*. It is a tool used by international agencies to follow changes in development levels over time, and to compare countries in terms of quality of living. Note that the HDI aims to provide a comprehensive measure for the quality of life.

This task is designed to explore the HDI and its relation to many relevant societal variables. Figure 4.A.1 illustrates some aspects of this activity. It is a scatterplot of the variables *Years in Secondary Education* versus *Life Expectancy* together with regression lines for Sub Saharan countries and East Asia & Pacific. Questions could be asked about the relative strengths of the associations in the two clusters of countries. This is a small illustration—the actual activity is much broader.

Reader—your task: please work through the lesson plan "Human Development: Can you compare countries?"

> **Question***:* What do your students need to know or utilise (in terms of the 11 facets listed in Fig. 4.1 and explained in Chap. 2) so that they can critically understand the information, answer the questions posed to them, and engage with the underlying civic issues?

Please list your ideas.

---

[5] Note: the ProCivicStat webpage is hosted on the website of IASE, the International Association for Statistics Education, inside the section for ISLP, The international Statistical Literacy project.

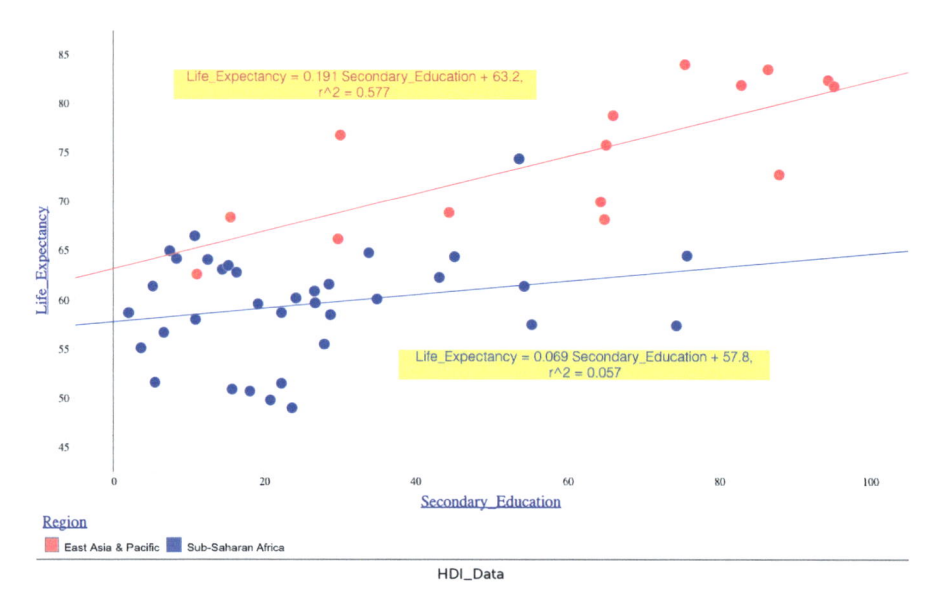

Fig. 4.A.1 Average years in Secondary Education versus average Life Expectancy, with separate regression lines for countries in Sub-Saharan Africa and East Asia & Pacific

Please rate the demand of the HDI activity on each of the facets in the conceptual framework—only then continue to read. (An empty radar plot can be found at the end of this Appendix).

Analysis of Example 2: As explained in Sect. 4.2, different readers may see different demands in the same task, given their target student cohort, personal background and perspectives. What matters is to focus on the relative weights of the different facets, not on absolute values.

With these cautionary notes, as can be seen in Fig. 4.A.2, we have rated the task high on facet 1 (meaning for society and policy) and facet 5 (representations, patterns and models). The task requires context knowledge about living conditions in different parts of the world (8), some classical statistical concepts (4) and basic computations (10) and skills in comprehending and communicating specific textual messages (11). Perhaps there are lower demands on methodology and enquiry processes, extensions in official statistics, and ICT and search—but this depends on the depth of the investigation. If the data provided are taken as given (as is the case for this lesson plan), this task may rate low on these facets. However, if you were to go deeper in questioning the research methodology, the construction of the indices involved, or if students are asked to search for additional data, then these facets would get more emphasis.

Want more examples like this? In Chap. 18, Engel, Louie, and Nicholson offer more lesson plans using the Human Development Index to compare countries. Beyond that, you might analyse the demands of any other task or activity you

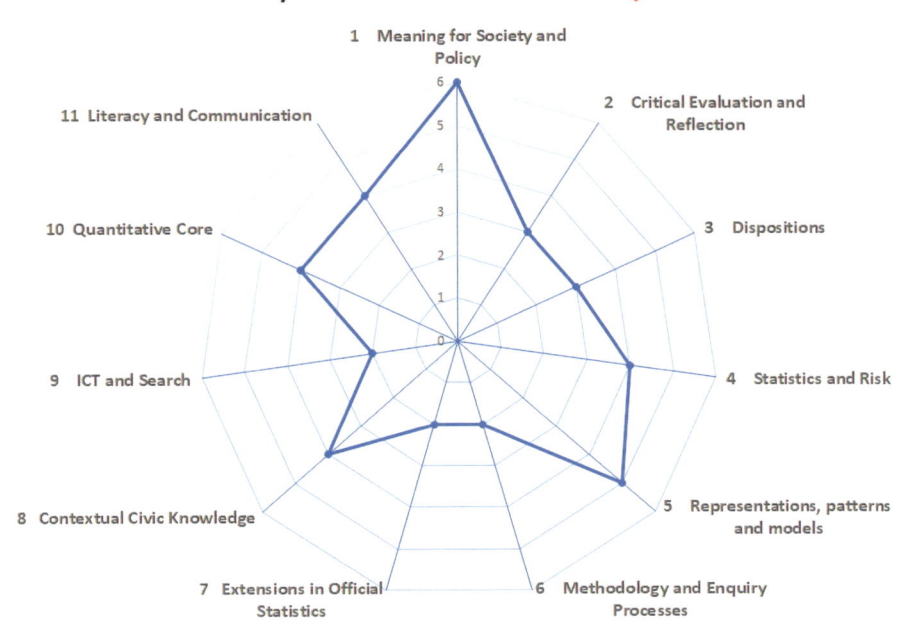

PCS Task analysis tool: **Task on Human Development Index**

Fig. 4.A.2 Possible radar plot analysis for the Human Development Index task

have designed or assembled, or apply a radar plot analysis to any of the diverse activities in other chapters of this book. Enjoy!

Below are two empty radar plots, with a 5-level scale (Fig. 4.A.3) or an 8-level scale (Fig. 4.A.4), and a simple table (Table 4.A.1), that can be used by teachers or researchers for rating Civic Statistics tasks. Also, see the text box for simple instructions on how to create your own radar plot in Excel.

The plot in Fig. 4.A.3 is suitable for a 5-level rating scale. Possible labels are: 0—none, 1—very little, 2—some, 3—moderate, 4—a lot. (Feel free to change!).

> **Do it yourself—create your own radar plot in Excel!** Enter labels from 1 to 11 as listed in Table 4.A.1 under "facet" (i.e., vertically), then click the 'chart/graph' icon and choose chart type "radar" and follow the instructions that appear. You can change the number of levels (i.e., the number of concentric circles in the radar plot) by entering the 'scale' tab and changing the value for units compared to the maximum value For example, for 5 levels, set the maximum to 1 and the unit values to 0.25. Depending on your version of Excel, some trial and error will yield the desired chart based on the ratings you enter in each cell.

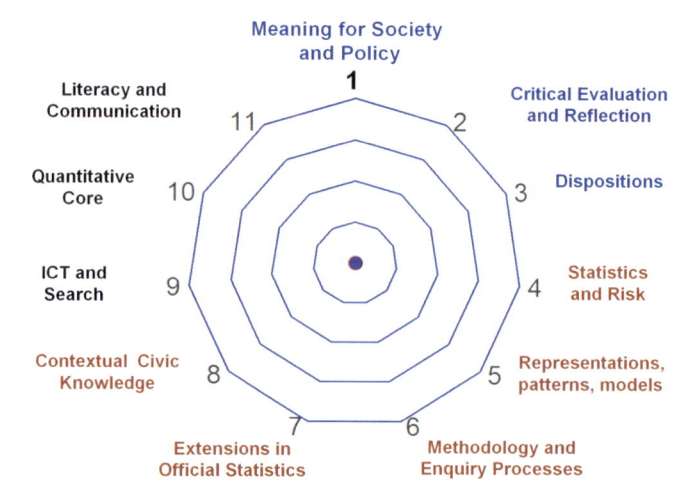

Fig. 4.A.3 Empty radar plot for a 5-level rating scale

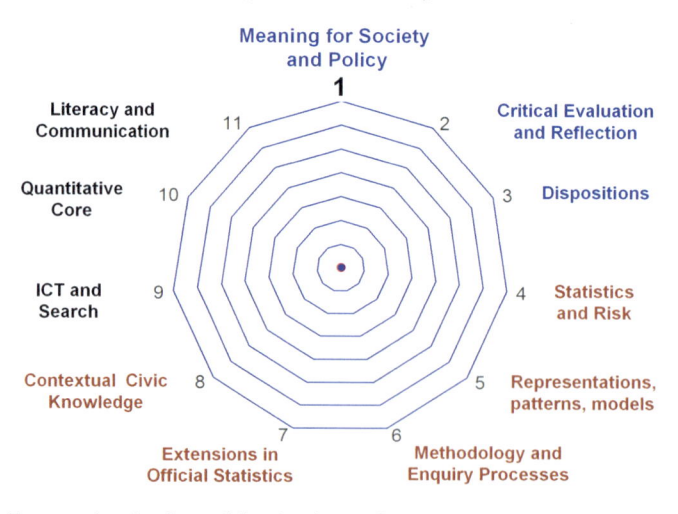

Fig. 4.A.4 Empty radar plot for an 8-level rating scale

Table 4.A.1 Empty table for rating tasks on any scale

Facet	Rating	Comments
1 Meaning for Society and Policy		
2 Critical Evaluation and Reflection		
3 Dispositions		
4 Statistics and Risk		
5 Representations, patterns and models		
6 Methodology and Enquiry Processes		
7 Extensions in Official Statistics		
8 Contextual Civic Knowledge		
9 ICT and Search		
10 Quantitative Core		
11 Literacy and Communication		

References

Bargagliotti, A., Franklin, C., Arnold, P., Gould, R., Johnson, S., Perez, L., & Spangler, D. (2020). *Pre-K-12 Guidelines for assessment and instruction in statistics education (GAISE) report II.* American Statistical Association and National Council of Teachers of Mathematics. https://www.amstat.org/asa/education/Guidelines-for-Assessment-and-Instruction-in-Statistics-Education-Reports.aspx

GAISE. (2016). *Guidelines for assessment and instruction in statistics education: College report.* American Statistical Association. https://www.amstat.org/asa/education/Guidelines-for-Assessment-and-Instruction-in-Statistics-Education-Reports.aspx

Gal, I., & Ograjenšek, I. (2017). Official statistics and statistics education: Bridging the gap. *Journal of Official Statistics, 33*(1), 79–100.

ProCivicStat Partners. (2018). *Engaging civic statistics: A call for action and recommendations. A product of the ProCivicStat project.* http://iase-web.org/islp/pcs

Ridgway, J. (2016). Implications of the data revolution for statistics education. *International Statistical Review, 84*(3), 528–549.

Ridgway, J., Nicholson, J., & Gal, I. (2017). Task analysis tool: Facets of statistical literacy. Prepared for a *ProCivicStat Workshop at the IASE Satellite Conference*, Rabat 11–13 July, 2017. http://iase-web.org/islp/pcs/documents/Rabat_Workshops_Booklet.pdf?1543033029

UNECE. (2012). *Making data meaningful: A guide to improving statistical literacy.* United Nations Economic Commission for Europe. Retrieved Sept 10, 2018 from http://www.unece.org/stats/documents/writing

Chapter 5
Interactive Data Visualizations for Teaching Civic Statistics

Jim Ridgway (iD), **Pedro Campos, James Nicholson, and Sónia Teixeira**

> *The process by which I propose to accomplish this is one essentially graphical ... by bringing in the aid of the eye and hand to guide the judgment, in a case where judgment only, and not calculation, can be of any avail. Herschel (1833, p. 178)*

Abstract How might you use data visualisation in your teaching? Here, we offer some ideas, and some provocations to review your teaching. We begin with an invitation to examine some of the historical landmarks in data visualisation (DV), to classify the data presented, and to describe the benefits of a sample of the DV to users. Early uses of DV by Nightingale and Neurath are shown, to provide examples of DV which communicated the need for action, and provoked social change. A number of modern DVs are presented, categorised as: tools to display individual data sets and tools for the exploration of specific rich data sets. We argue that students introduced to the core features of Civic Statistics can acquire skills in all of the facets of Civic Statistics set out in Chap. 3. We conclude by revisiting Herschel, to provoke thoughts about the balance of activities appropriate to statistics courses.

Keywords Data visualisation · Interaction · Simulation · Indicator systems

5.1 Introduction

In Chap. 2, Engel and Ridgway set out 12 features of Civic Statistics, under the headings of *Contexts and Interpretations* (societal context is the focus; statistics are embedded in rich texts; causality is often attributed; conclusions, implications, and

J. Ridgway (✉) · J. Nicholson
School of Education, University of Durham, Durham, UK
e-mail: jim.ridgway@durham.ac.uk; j.r.nicholson53@gmail.com

P. Campos · S. Teixeira
LIAAD-INESC TEC and University of Porto, Porto, Portugal
e-mail: pcampos@fep.up.pt; sonia.c.teixeira@inesctec.pt

consequences for society are discussed); *the Nature of Relevant Statistics* (phenomena are often multivariate; decisions are made about measures and operationalisation; data are often aggregated; indicator systems are common; dynamic data spanning times and locations are often used); and *Unfamiliar Methods and Representations* (novel data sources and techniques continue to be invented; varied data collection methods are used; innovative visualisations are presented). Chapter 3 set out 11 dimensions of knowledge, under the headings of *Engagement and Action* (meaning for society and policy; critical evaluation and reflection; dispositions); *Knowledge* (statistics and risk; models, patterns and representations; methodology and enquiry processes; extensions in official statistics; contextual civic knowledge); *Enabling Processes* (literacy and communication; quantitative core; ICT and search). In this chapter, we show how students can experience these 12 features of Civic Statistics, and can develop many of the skills relevant to the 11 dimensions of knowledge, by engaging with Data Visualisations (DV).

Any examination of media such as TV, movies, or video games demonstrates a variety of ways in which visual information (including special effects) are created and presented. There is a danger that educational resources look like (and actually are) very poor relations of the rich information resources that students encounter in everyday life. Here, we advocate the use of high-quality data visualisations which are freely available on the internet as tools to support statistics education.

We begin with a brief history of data visualisations, starting with early maps and musical notation, many of which have had a profound influence on our world (these are almost all static presentations of data). We invite the reader to analyse a few of these examples in terms of the nature of the data that is presented, and the usefulness of the presentation to users. These are questions to provoke reflections about the sorts of data we analyse in statistics classes, and the value of the analyses to our students. We offer two examples to conclude the history section to justify the role of DV in Civic Statistics: Nightingale's analysis of the causes of death in the Crimean war, that led to changes in hospital practices, and in public hygiene, which in turn had dramatic effects on public health; and Neurath's Isotype system, which has shaped the ways that information is communicated for over 100 years. We then explore computer-based DV, focusing on DV that are designed to display simple data sets, and on DV designed to support the exploration of more complex data sets.

5.2   A Brief History of Data Visualisation

A seminal paper by Funkhouser (1937) traced the historical development of graphical representation of statistical data, along with interesting information about the development of statistical ideas themselves. Friendly and Denis[1] offer a review of milestones in the history of thematic cartography, statistical graphs and data

---

[1] http://datavis.ca/milestones/

visualisation that covers a timespan from 6200 BCE to 2009 CE. Their review offers an interactive chart shown in Fig. 5.1. We have chosen to show the period 1970-2000. Each button in the display links to a description of the DV to which it refers. Many of these representations were highly significant for human development.

Table 5.1 shows some of the milestones from Friendly and Denis, with some additional elements. To this list, one might add the drawings of Leonardo da Vinci[2] which show the power of diagrams to illustrate mechanics and dynamics.

5.2.1 Reflecting on Data Visualisation

We invite you to reflect on the nature of the data that are presented, and the benefits to the user from each representation. Further, ask yourself about the value of these representations for citizens—which of these visualisations should people be able to use fluently? Further, which of the DVs deserve a place in a modern statistics curriculum? As an illustration, consider the first two examples. Early maps externalise spatial knowledge (and 'here be dragons' knowledge) from different sources, in a permanent form [*the data*], and facilitate travel for trade (and warfare); travellers no longer depend on verbal reports, personal experience, and a robust memory [*the benefits*]. Should citizens be able to use this representation fluently? In our view, *yes*. Do maps have a place in the statistics curriculum? *Yes*. Musical notation (again) externalises knowledge, this time about sound (pitch, rhythm, intensity) [*the data*] and facilitates technical mastery, and collaborative performance [*the benefits*]. Should citizens be able to use this representation fluently? We (the authors) don't agree amongst ourselves. Does musical notation have a place in the statistics curriculum? Not as a compulsory element.

For this exercise, we suggest you choose a small number of visualisations that include some you are familiar with and not familiar with; and some which are generic (e.g. Venn diagrams) and some which are specific (e.g. Minard on Napoleon).

Now-classical illustrations of good (and bad) data visualisations have been created by Tufte (e.g. 1997, 2006). Documenting the explosion of exciting data visualisations facilitated by modern computers is a task beyond the scope of this chapter (but see Ridgway et al. 2017). An illustration of the scale of recent graphical innovations can be found at Selva Prabhakan's website,[3] which offers 50 'top' visualisations in *ggplot2*, along with the *R* code.

Next, we present two examples to illustrate early uses of DV in Civic Statistics.

Florence Nightingale brought about considerable social change by her use of impressive graphics, and her petitioning of the government. One of her 'coxcomb'

---

[2] http://codex-atlanticus.it/#/

[3] http://r-statistics.co/Top50-Ggplot2-Visualizations-MasterList-R-Code.html

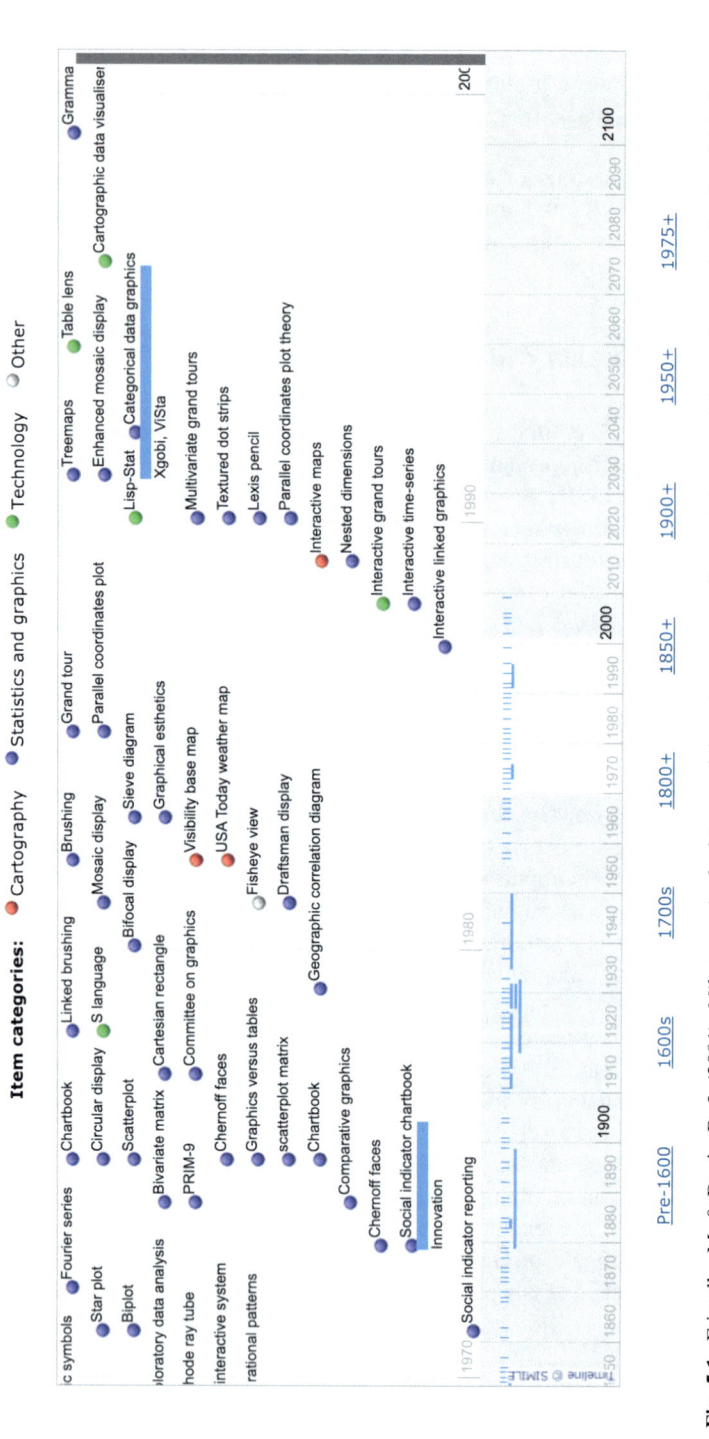

Fig. 5.1 Friendly, M. & Denis, D. J. (2001). *Milestones in the history of thematic cartography, statistical graphics, and data visualization.* Web document, http://www.datavis.ca/milestones/. Accessed: March 25, 2021. Copyright © 2001–2018 Michael Friendly

Table 5.1 Milestones in data visualisation. Adapted from Friendly and Denis

6200 BCE–1865	1865–2020
• Early maps (6200 BCE); • Musical notation (700 BCE) • Diagrams of planetary movements (950); • Cartesian graphs (1637); • Wren's (1663) weather clock, that produced graphs of wind direction and temperature; • Contour maps (1701); • The Normal distribution (1733); • Polar coordinates (1736); • Geological maps (1778); • Analysis of periodic variation (1779); • Playfair's (1786) line graphs and bar charts of economic data and his (1801) pie charts and circle graphs; • Maps of disease incidence (1798); • Weather maps (1816); • Choropleth maps (1819); • Quetelet's (1828) mortality curves; • Polar-area charts (1829); • Faraday's (1830) diagrams of magnetic lines of force; • Snow's (1855) exploration of a cholera epidemic; • Nightingale's (1857) coxcomb plots of deaths attributable to battle and to infectious disease; • Galton's (1861) 'modern' weather maps of barometric pressure and his (1875) illustration of the idea of correlation; • Minard's (1869) flow diagram of Napoleon's march on Moscow;	• Mendeleev's (1869) periodic table; • Muybridge's (1872) recordings of a galloping horse; • Gibb's (1873) trilinear coordinates; • Walker's (1874) population pyramid; • Venn's (1880) diagrams; • Booth's (1889) spatial mapping of poverty in London; • Lorenz's (1905) curve; • Gantt's (1917) chart; • Wright's (1920) path diagrams; • Neurath's (1924) Isotype system; • Beck's (1933) map of the London Tube system; • Moreno's (1934) sociogram; • Kruskal's (1962) multidimensional scaling; • Tukey's (1965, 1969) stem and leaf plots and box plots; • Radar plots (1971); • Chernoff's (1973) human face cartoons to represent multivariate data; • Shneiderman's (1991) treemaps; • Flanagan's (2002) word clouds; • Rosling's (2005) Gapminder; • Krzywinski's (2009) chord diagrams.

plots is shown below (Nightingale, 1858). Friendly and Denis (*op. cit.*) credit Balbi & Guerry (1829) with the invention of polar area charts, which show the frequency of events for cyclical phenomena. Nightingale is often credited with this invention; however, her most important contribution has been the transformation of data into evidence, and her powers of persuasion. Figure 5.2 shows causes of mortality during the Crimean war. Deaths are represented by *areas* (not by the length of the wedge). The blue wedges show relative deaths from 'preventible (*sic*) or mitigable zymotic diseases'; the red wedges represent deaths from wounds, and the black areas represent deaths from other causes. The accompanying text explains how the graphic is adapted when there are fewer deaths from 'other causes' than from wounds.

It is easy to see that far more British soldiers died from disease (blue wedges) than from wounds (pink wedges) during the Crimean war.

These diagrams were used to convince politicians and administrators about the need for reform in military hospitals - and to improve sanitation in England and India. Nightingale had the drive to change policy, and had an impact on society that is almost unimaginable today. Life expectancy in England rose by 20 years over a 60 year period, with no major advances in medical science, and there were dramatic decreases in deaths (despite some serious problems) in army hospitals in the Crimea.

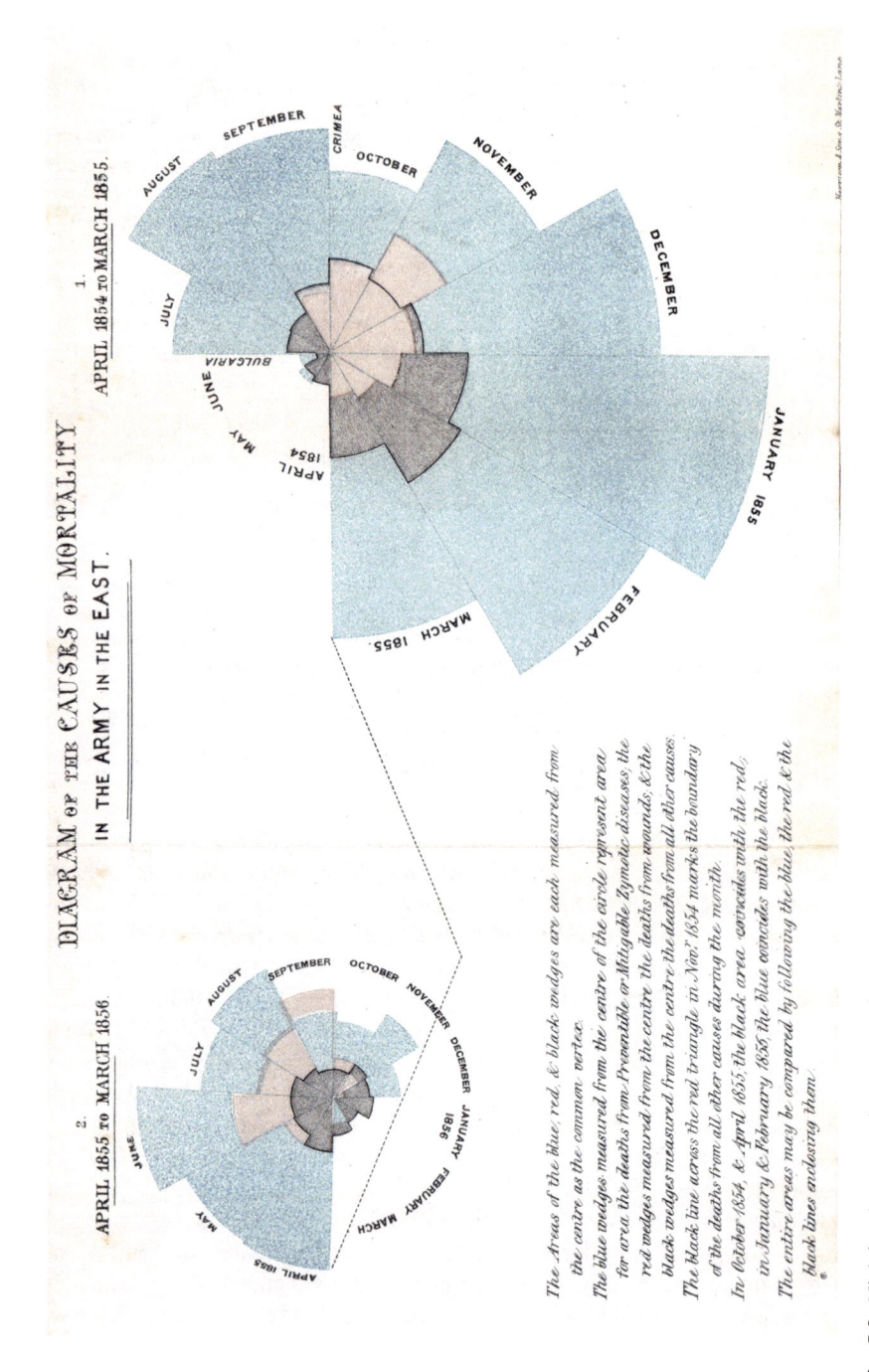

Fig. 5.2 Nightingale: comparing causes of mortality in the Army of the East

Isotype (International System of Typographic Picture Education) provides the second example. Everyone who has navigated their way to a public toilet is familiar with Isotype icons. Isotype was designed in Vienna as a universal visual language, created in the 1920s by Otto Neurath's group to promote Civic Statistics, and is grounded in a rich philosophy about the nature of knowledge, and social justice. (Neurath was one of the leading figures in the Vienna Circle, which, itself, had a huge influence on twentieth century philosophy—adopting an Enlightenment worldview, and setting out to synthesise philosophy, science and mathematics). At that time, the Austrian economy had been broken by war; food was scarce, and Europe had experienced epidemics of influenza and syphilis. Politics were in turmoil, with a conservative countryside clashing with a left-wing capital city.[4] Isotype was designed to present Civic Statistics pictorially, in order to communicate important information to the largest possible audience. A very wide range of topics was addressed—initially related to Civic Statistics in Vienna, but later (after the Neuraths' escape to England in 1940) to global trade, food production and social justice in the UK.

Pictograms are the basic elements of Isotype; pictograms are repeated (rather than being re-scaled) to demonstrate quantity. Figure 5.3 shows an example, using data from England (where Isotype was used extensively in the 1940s by government agencies, and in the media).

As well as static displays, Isotype was used in film clips to illuminate key issues[5]—in this case patterns of global food production and consumption.

It is difficult to overstate the influence of Isotype on modern visual literacy. At the most obvious level, pictograms are used very widely for signage; images from the large library of Isotype pictograms are easily recognised. For communicating more complex information, the idea of using repeated pictograms with (say) different colours to illustrate proportions and percentages is widely used in computer graphics to aid understanding - see Martignon, Frischemeier, McDowell, and Till in Chap. 19. *Realrisk*[6] from the Winton Centre is a tool to convert some measures commonly used in academic papers such as relative risk, hazard ratio, or odds ratio into icon displays.

5.3   Interacting with Civic Statistics

Books from a number of authors (e.g. Cleveland, 1985; Tufte, 1997, 2006; McCandless, 2012; Wainer, 2000, 2013) illustrate the variety of ways in which information can be presented effectively in print. Tukey's (1977) advocacy of Exploratory Data Analysis was an important development encouraging data analysts to stay close to their data. Here, we focus on data visualisation (DV) via computer,

---

[4] https://en.wikipedia.org/wiki/Red_Vienna

[5] https://www.youtube.com/watch?v=5tDOcUb4KFk

[6] https://realrisk.wintoncentre.uk/

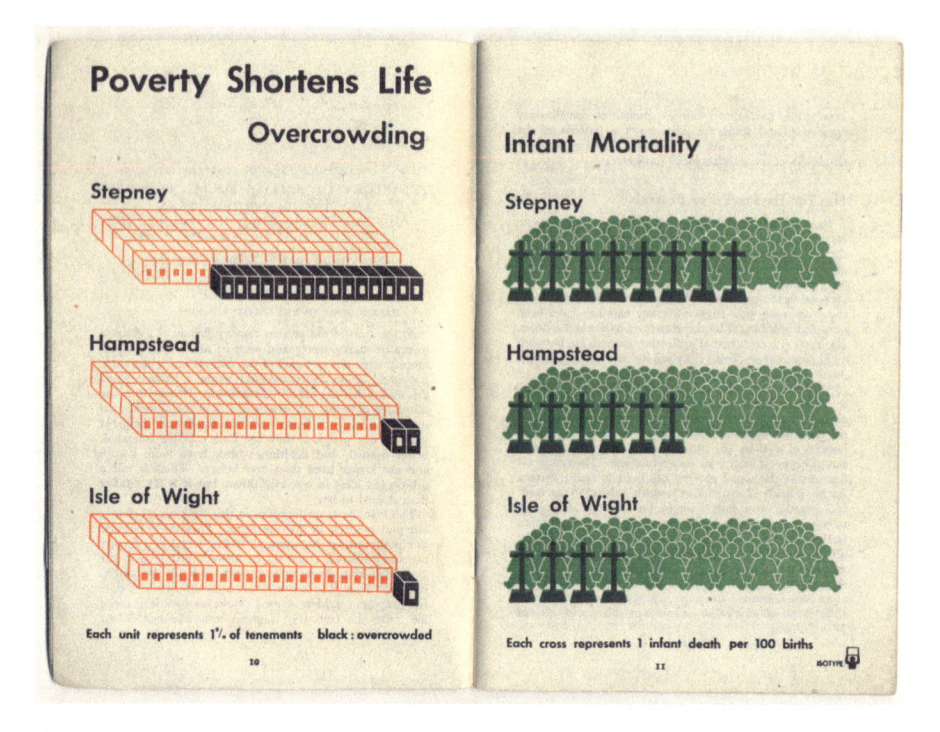

Fig. 5.3 Overcrowding and infant mortality illuminated via isotype. Isotype Institute, 'Poverty shortens life', in Ronald Davison, Social security, London: George G. Harrap & Co., 1943. Otto and Marie Neurath Isotype Collection, University of Reading

with an emphasis on interactive data visualisation (IDV) of specific data sets. First, we will make clear that we are *not* going to discuss IDV specifically designed to teach statistics. Excellent examples of the uses of DV in statistics education can be found, such as Cumming's *Exploratory Software for Confidence Intervals (ESCI)*[7]; Sterling's *Computer-assisted Statistics Textbooks (CAST)*[8]; and Wild's *iNZight*[9] (*iNZight* is described in detail in Chap. 10 by Wild and Ridgway). A variety of tools have been designed to facilitate data visualisation. These can be classified as:

- Tools for displaying specific data sets—examples (shown below) include *Arctic Ice* and *When will you Die?* These tools offer opportunities for incorporating short excursions into Civic Statistics into regular classes, and for introducing key statistical concepts without using algebra.
- Tools for facilitating the exploration of specific data sets - examples include: *Gapminder*[10] (described by Kovacs, Kazar, and Kuruczleki in Chap. 8, along

---

[7] https://www.esci.thenewstatistics.com/

[8] https://cast.idems.international/

[9] https://www.stat.auckland.ac.nz/~wild/iNZight/

[10] https://www.gapminder.org/

with lesson plans), and *OECD's Better Life Index.*[11] These can facilitate statistical thinking in constrained domains.

- Software packages with good functionality for visualising data - examples include, *RAW*,[12] *Datawrapper*[13]; *Tableau*[14]; *JMP*[15]; Google Charts[16]; *CODAP*[17]; *Tinkerplots*[18]; and *Fathom.*[19] These tools underpin much of the work of the PCS project, and activities which make use of some of these tools can be found elsewhere in this book; they are not discussed in this chapter.
- Programming tools that can be used to create visualisations—a key libraries include *plotly*[20] and *D3.js.*[21] These can support statistics classes where computing is an important element. Figure 5.4 shows some of the topics for which D3 modules are available[22]—larger circles contain more statistical routines. Again, these are beyond the scope of this chapter.

Ridgway et al. (2017) offer a review of data visualisation tools.[23] DV tools are described in terms of: tool type (as above); cost (free, free to educational users, pay); accessibility (open source, free trial, online, cloud-based); ease of use; display functionality (a tick list for lines, tables, scatter graphs etc.); available data sources (pre-loaded with data, facilities to upload data); data types handled (macrodata, microdata); and notes on interesting features (e.g. availability of tutorial material). A sample of the relevant spreadsheet is shown in Fig. 5.5; the spreadsheet itself provides links to electronic supplementary material (see Lopes et al., 2018).

The next sections offer examples from the first two tool groups—tools for displaying specific data sets, and tools for facilitating the exploration of specific data sets.

[11] http://www.oecdbetterlifeindex.org/#

[12] https://rawgraphs.io/

[13] https://www.datawrapper.de/

[14] https://www.tableau.com/en-gb

[15] https://www.jmp.com/en_us/software/data-analysis-software.html

[16] https://developers.google.com/chart/interactive/docs

[17] https://codap.concord.org/

[18] https://www.tinkerplots.com/

[19] https://fathom.concord.org/

[20] https://plotly.com/python/

[21] https://d3js.org/

[22] https://wattenberger.com/blog/d3

[23] See https://iase-web.org/islp/pcs/documents/Dynamic-Visualisation-Tools.pdf?1543033028

Fig. 5.4 A map of modules available in *D3.js* from Amelia Wattenberger (https://wattenberger.com/blog/d3)

5.3.1 Tools for Displaying Specific Data Sets

Here, we show how free-standing DVs taken from the web can be used both as starting points for explorations of substantive issues, and as the focus for the introduction of important statistical ideas.

5.3.1.1 Arctic Sea Ice Volume

Global warming is perhaps the greatest threat facing humanity. Figure 5.6 comes from the Polar Science Center at the University of Washington;[24] the observations

---

[24] http://www.climate-lab-book.ac.uk/spirals

Co-funded by the Erasmus+ Programme of the European Union

Promoting Civic Engagement via Exploration of Evidence: Challenges for Statistics Education

Pro Civic Stat

Tool	Open source/ Trial/Free/ Online/Cloud/ Educational/ Pay	Ease of use	Lines	Tables	Scatter Graphs	Bar Charts	Maps	Combined Charts	Relational Diagrams	Boxplot	Others (not mentioned before)	Data: UD=upload/ D=existing data	Micro/ Macro data	Connect with apps
BIRT	OS/T		✓	✓	✓	✓					Pie/Stock/Bubble	UD	Ma	✓
Chart.js	OS/F		✓			✓					Pie/Polar/Radar/ Bubbles	UD	MI/Ma	
Chartblocks	F/O		✓		✓	✓					Pie	UD	Ma	✓
ChartFX	F/T		✓		✓	✓	✓	✓		✓	Pie/Bubble/ Candlestick	UD	MI/Ma	✓
Chartistls	OS/F		✓	✓	✓	✓					Pie	UD	MI/Ma	
CODAP	OS/F		✓	✓	✓	✓	✓	✓		✓	simulation, restruct-ering data , extensible	D/ DU	MI/Ma	
D3.js	OS/F		✓	✓	✓	✓	✓	✓	✓	✓	Many other types	UD	MI/Ma	✓
datamatic	T/F		✓	✓	✓	✓	✓	✓	✓	✓	Pie/Rose/Bubbles/ Punch	UD	Ma	✓
datavisual	T		✓	✓	✓	✓	✓	✓			Pie/Bubble	UD	Ma	✓
Datawrapper	F/O		✓	✓	✓	✓	✓				Pie/Donnut	UD	Ma	✓
DevInfo	F/O		✓	✓	✓	✓	✓	✓		▲	Pie/Radar	D/UD	Ma	
Dygraphs	OS		✓	✓	✓	✓						UD	MI/ Ma	
Fathom	E / P		✓	✓	✓	✓	▲	▲	✓	✓	Simulations	D/ UD	MI/Ma	✓
Flare	OS/F		✓	✓	✓	✓		✓			Pie/Bubbles/Donnut	UD	MI/Ma	
FusionCharts	OS/T/F		✓	✓	✓	✓	✓	✓	✓	✓	Pie	UD	MI/Ma	✓
Gapminder	O							✓	✓	▲	Bubble	D	Ma	
Gephi														
GGobi	F				✓	✓						UD	Ma	
Google Charts	F/O		✓	✓	✓	✓	✓	✓			Pie/Bubble/Donnut/Can dlestick	UD	MI/Ma	✓
Highcharts	T/F/C		✓	✓	✓	✓	✓	✓		✓	Pie/Bubble/Funnel	UD	Ma	✓

Fig. 5.5 Part of Ridgway et al.'s (2017) Review of Data Visualisation Tools

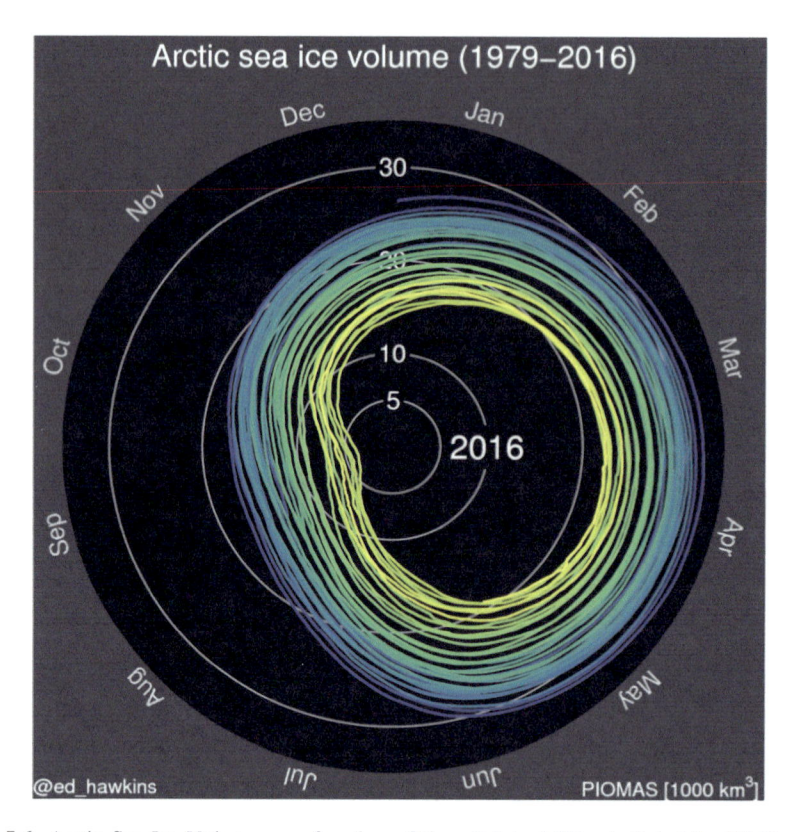

Fig. 5.6 Arctic Sea Ice Volume as a function of time Original Climate Spiral by Ed Hawkins (Climate Lab Book)

are from the Unified Sea Ice Thickness Climate Data Record. Ice volume is plotted dynamically.

The display offers an opportunity for students to interpret graphical information presented in a way they might not have seen before. Plotting data using a circular display (ice thickness is measured from the centre of the circle, and time is shown on the perimeter) reduces the problem of separating seasonal changes from long-term changes. The line is plotted in different colours as time advances, to make it easy to compare more recent estimates of ice volume with earlier ones.

The graphic can support the development of some key statistical ideas. Students can simply be asked what they see: there are marked seasonal trends, a good deal of variability in year-on-year data, and a decline in the volume of arctic sea ice over time. Is the world getting warmer? Students can be provoked to look for other evidence—is the Antarctic ice volume decreasing? What about glaciers around the globe? Or sea temperatures in different locations? These questions all provoke reflections about sampling and representativeness.

Students can also be asked about their predictions for the future—when will there be little or no Arctic ice in summer months? Can they offer a confidence interval?

This takes them into the realms of modelling, which can be addressed at different levels of sophistication. Is a simple linear model likely to apply? (probably not). What factors are likely to accelerate the change? To what extent do they believe that the phenomenon can be predicted with any degree of accuracy (past estimates have almost always under-estimated the speed of change)? Are there likely to be 'unknown unknowns' in the modelling process? (large scale fires in Australia, Alaska, and Siberia, releasing carbon dioxide into the atmosphere, is one contender that illustrates both 'unknown unknowns' and the use of positive feedback loops in models). There is a great deal of 'rich text' (see Chap. 13) on this topic; here we offer just one example. A *Guardian* article by Watts (2019)[25] explores themes such as the impact of warmer water on ecology; implications for tourism and mineral extraction; and hydrology, amongst other topics. So a powerful DV can support cross-curricular and interdisciplinary work. Civic Statistics is not 'owned' by the statistics community—a virtue of this position is that Civic Statistics can be a Trojan Horse for introducing important statistical ideas into a range of curriculum areas (see Engel, Louie, and Nicholson in Chap. 18). What are the implications if Arctic sea ice disappears? This question is likely to be beyond the remit of a statistics class, but is an interesting provocation for biologists, physicists and people concerned with population dynamics.

Causality is an important issue in statistics and science. Almost all climate scientists believe human activity to be a major contributor to global warming. However, geological evidence shows that the Earth has undergone major changes in temperature over the past million years—these changes have been modelled by the Milankovitch cycle.[26] Students can be asked if the Milankovitch cycle is a plausible counter-explanation (spoiler alert—the Milankovitch cycle predicts that the Earth should be cooling, right now). In Chap. 11, Guimarães, Vehkalahti, Campos, and Engel explore climate change in some detail.

5.3.1.2 Predicting Mortality

Figure 5.7 is a screenshot of a simulation that can be found on Nathan Yau's *Flowingdata* website.[27] The original data is taken from the Actuarial Life Table of the Social Security Administration (USA).[28] Students know that older adults are more likely to die than are younger adults; and that females (on average) live longer than males. At any age, the probability of dying can be determined from the appropriate actuarial tables (these probabilities are shown by the coloured curve in

---

[25] https://www.theguardian.com/environment/2019/jun/07/oceans-demise-the-end-of-the-arctic-as-we-know-it

[26] https://www.nature.com/scitable/knowledge/library/milankovitch-cycles-paleoclimatic-change-and-hominin-evolution-68244581/

[27] http://flowingdata.com/2015/09/23/years-you-have-left-to-live-probably

[28] https://www.ssa.gov/oact/STATS/table4c6.html

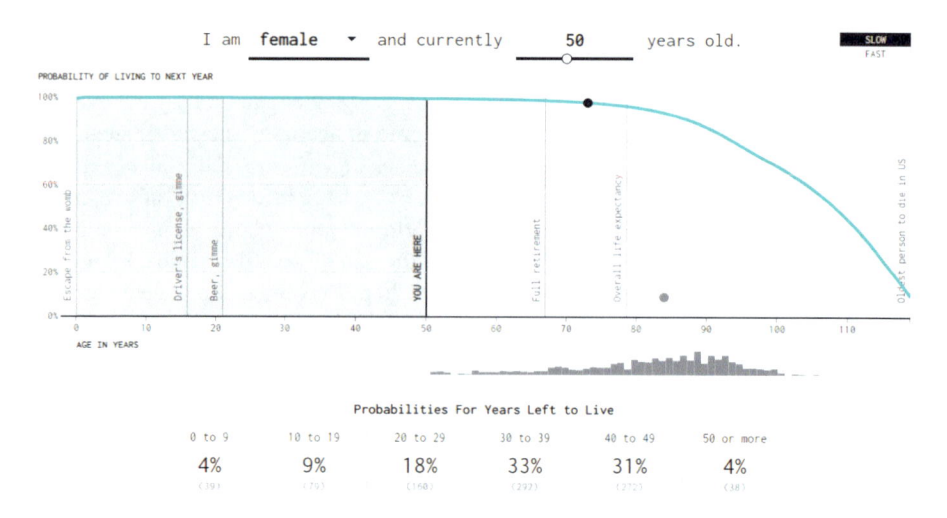

Fig. 5.7 An interactive Markov model: when will you die?

Fig. 5.7). Users of Yau's graphic can select sex and age. When the simulation is run, the 'person' either 'dies' by dropping off the curve (and their death is added to the bar graph below the display), or lives by continuing along the curve for another year. This cycle is repeated until the 'person' 'dies'. A fast version of the simulation is available, so that the probability density function for different combinations of age and sex can be obtained quickly.

The simulation offers an interactive introduction to stochastic processes in a familiar context, where multiple expected distributions of lifetime for a male or female of differing ages can be visualised (here the distribution of the observations (the histogram in the display) is for a female aged 50 years). A provocative starting point can be to ask students how old they need to be before their chances of surviving the following year are the same as their chances of not surviving. The answer (over 100 years) can be read directly from the graph, and is counter-intuitive; students can be asked to explain why this number is so high. Students can also be asked to explain how the graphic works—to offer a broad-brush description of how the probability density function is created (doing this, they will have 'invented' the idea of a Markov process and the concept of probability density for themselves).

The display paves the way to discussing properties of distributions. Students can be asked to compare the distributions of life expectancy for a young child, and for an old person. At birth, the distribution of life expectancy has a high variance, and is negatively skewed. At age 100, variance is relatively small, and the distribution is positively skewed. As in the previous example, issues of the accuracy of predictions, and confidence intervals can be introduced.

Students can be asked how they would improve the model's prediction (for example, adjusting for locality, smoking status, height and weight, or health status). This can lead to a discussion of the principles of actuarial work, and the implicit modelling assumptions (life expectancy won't increase dramatically; there will be no major epidemics such as coronavirus, or wars, or famine etc. leading to large numbers of premature deaths; governments won't legislate that differential insurance premiums for men and women are discriminatory). The graphic illustrates the profound idea that underpins the edifice of statistics: individual events (when will *you* die?) can only be predicted with very limited accuracy, but events aggregated across individuals (distributions of mortality) can be predicted with great accuracy.

In developing countries, infant mortality is often much higher than in developed countries. So conditional probabilities can be introduced—the probability of reaching age 60 years can be much higher for a 1-year old, or a 5-year old, than for a neonate.

5.3.1.3 Predicting Demographic Change

A third example is relevant to governments' responsibilities to care for their citizens. Many National Statistics Offices produce population pyramids to document trends and make predictions about future demographics that are used for planning in education and health services. Figure 5.8 shows a population pyramid from the UK Office for National Statistics.[29] This graphic uses data from 2014 to make predictions about future demographics—in this case, Fig. 5.8 shows the predictions for 2024. How is this done? The death rate of people in different age groups is known, so the numbers of people in different age groups who are likely to die each year can be calculated (as in the *Predicting Mortality* graphic, earlier). Similarly, the different fertility rates of women in different age groups is also known, so births can be predicted. The display has opportunities for students to learn about novel displays—exploring pull-down menus, turning options on and off, highlighting different parts of the display to determine the proportion of people in different age categories, comparing the demographics of different regions, and so on. Population pyramids facilitate different sorts of analysis such as comparing the demographics of countries, or of sub-populations within the same country (e.g. by ethnicity).

At a national level, future planning of resources is made easier if the likely number of births, the size of the school population and its distribution across different age groups, and number of dependent elderly people can be estimated with some degree of accuracy. Estimates are important for both planning services, and for managing the finances of a country. Of particular interest is the dependency ratio—the number of people who depend on the state (notably the very young and old) related to the number of people who are working (and paying tax).

Models make assumptions—for example, about emigration and immigration. Clearly, the scale and nature of migration is important for determining population demographics. The DV shown in Fig. 5.8 offers the facility to change some assumptions (such as assumptions about fertility or migration) and to see the consequences. Students can be asked to decide and explain which factors

---

[29] https://www.ons.gov.uk/visualisations/nesscontent/dvc219/pyramids/index.html

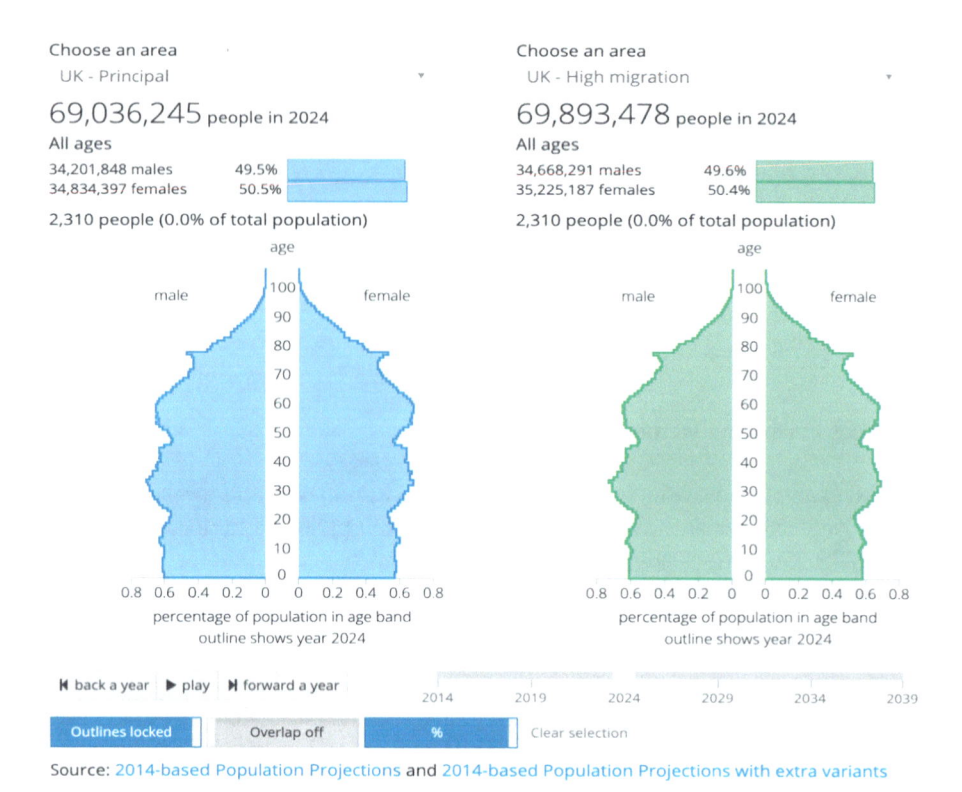

Fig. 5.8 Dynamic modelling for prediction: UK population pyramids: Source: Office for National Statistics licensed under the Open Government Licence v.1.0

(e.g. migration, fertility, life expectancy) have the largest impact on demographics. They can be asked what percentage of the population are over 65 years old in 2019 and will be over 65 years old in 2039, and to discuss the implications. In Chap. 3, the key facet relevant to Civic Statistics was identified as *Meaning for Society and Policy*. Exploring population pyramids can introduce students to the power and limits of statistics in this domain. Changes in demographics have direct implications for social policy—but the policy decisions will be embedded in values, philosophies and politics. To give a provocative example; in most European countries, populations are characterized by increasing proportions of elderly people. In many African countries, the populations are characterized by high proportions of very young people.[30] The situation could be resolved by encouraging elderly people to move from Europe to some African states, or by increasing migration of young people from Africa to Europe. These two courses of action reflect different world views, and have rather different implications for the societies and individuals involved.

---

[30] https://www.worldlifeexpectancy.com/world-population-pyramid

5.3.2 Tools to Support Exploration of Large Data Sets

5.3.2.1 Better Life Index

'Quality of Life' is an important but problematic concept. The idea is simple—poverty, disease, and awful neighbours all detract from quality of life; good health, a clean environment, and safe community all add to quality of life. Measurement is more difficult—some concepts are hard to measure ('disease'; 'environment' and so on) and people will value different things, and will probably change their ideas about quality of life over their life course. The OECD have created a tool[31] to compare different countries in terms of the quality of life offered from *your* point of view (see Fig. 5.9). You are invited to move sliders to reflect the importance of different factors relevant to your quality of life—these sliders are in the right-hand panel, and include *housing, income, education, environment, health, safety*, and *work-life balance*. The software then works out the relative importance to you of different factors. A display is then created that shows rank countries in terms of how well they score against your criteria—the *y*-axis shows the BLI, and countries are presented in alphabetical order. Each 'petal' on each 'flower' in the display shows how well each country scores on each factor. The website allows users to compare their own region to their own country in terms of every factor, and to make comparisons between countries. All the data can be downloaded.

This software offers an excellent place to start discussions about the politics and pragmatics of measurement. OECD commissioned a report by some leading economists into the over-use of Gross Domestic Product (GDP) as a measure of the success of a country. Stiglitz et al. (2018) show that GDP cannot tell us everything we need to know about economic performance (they claim that over-dependence on GDP as a measure was a major contributing factor to the global economic crisis of 2008), and that it is woefully inadequate as a measure of social progress. They argue that more sophisticated indicators are needed, such as a dashboard that gives information on who is benefiting from economic growth, perceptions of quality of life, and the environmental impact of growth in different economic sectors. These are all key messages for Civic Statistics. Designing measures is beyond the scope of this chapter (but see Ridgway et al., 2001) for a discussion, and Swan and Ridgway (2001)[32] for teaching materials). Students can be asked how sensible it is to assess the progress of developing economies by using standard international measures designed to measure the economic progress in developed countries. This links to a number of the facets in the conceptual model described in Chap. 3, notably: critical evaluation and reflection; meaning for social policy; methodology and enquiry processes; along with extensions in official statistics.

After some initial explorations, students can be asked to weight the dimensions in such a way as to push their own country as high as possible, then as low as possible.

---

[31] http://www.oecdbetterlifeindex.org/

[32] http://archive.wceruw.org/cl1/flag/cat/math/math/math1.htm

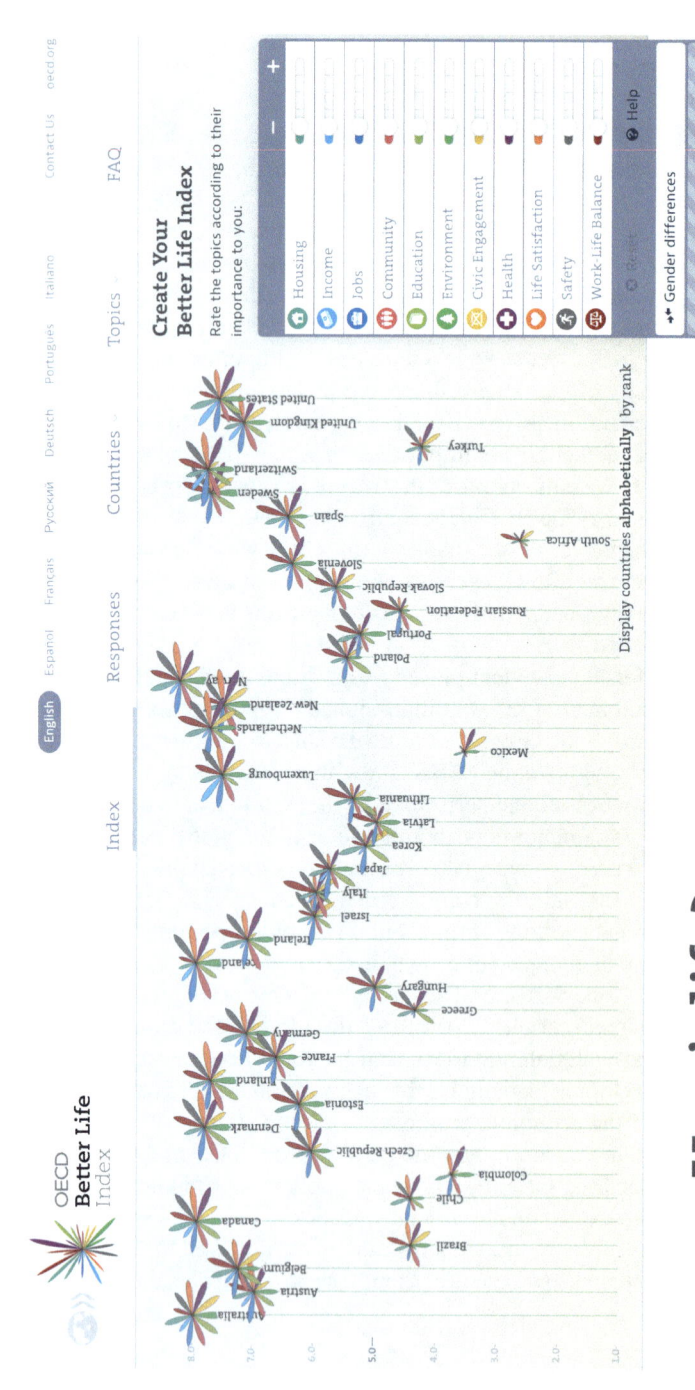

Fig. 5.9 Values and indicator systems: OECD's better life index

This can lead to a discussion about the vices and virtues of indicator systems—in particular the choices of measures to be included, and the ways that they are weighted.

5.3.2.2 The World Inequality Database

Inequality is an important issue for Civic Statistics. Some authors (e.g. Piketty, 2013) argue that inequality poses a major threat to democracy. Figure 5.10 is taken from the World Inequality database.[33] The display has two components: a map and a graph. The map shows the percentage share of national wealth held by the poorest 50% of the population in each country for the latest year for which data are available. Colour is used to show different bands—so in South Africa, the poorest 50% of the population own between −2.5% and 2.5% of the wealth; in France and India, the poorest 50% of the population own between 3.5% and 6.6% of the wealth.

The lower graph can be used to show changes in the wealth of the poorest 50% of people in selected countries over time. Here we have chosen to compare the percentage share of national wealth held by the poorest 50% of the population in China and the USA over time. There are two striking features of these data. In China, there has been a dramatic rise in inequality over a relatively short time period (at the same time as total wealth is increasing). In the USA, there was a period around 2010 when half of the population was in debt. The display allows users to explore average income, average wealth, income inequality and wealth inequality around the world, over time. Students can be asked to explore the impact of using different measures (for example, income vs wealth; top 1% share, top 10% share, bottom 50% share etc.) when drawing conclusions about inequality.

Students can also be asked to explore the relationships between measures of inequality and indicators of democracy using an infographic from *The Economist*[34] (see Chap. 23). This requires students to explore and understand both DVs, then to download data from these two different sources in order to create a single data file. After analysis, there is an opportunity to explore the plausibility of causal links, deduced from correlational data.

5.3.2.3 United Nations Sustainable Development Goals (SDG) Programme

The UN SDGs programme[35] has set 17 very ambitious goals designed to address critical issues facing humanity, such as *end poverty in all its forms everywhere*;

---

[33] https://wid.world/world/#shweal_p0p50_z/US;CN/last/eu/k/p/yearly/s/false/-2.4595/20/curve/false/country

[34] https://infographics.economist.com/2018/DemocracyIndex/

[35] https://sdgs.un.org/

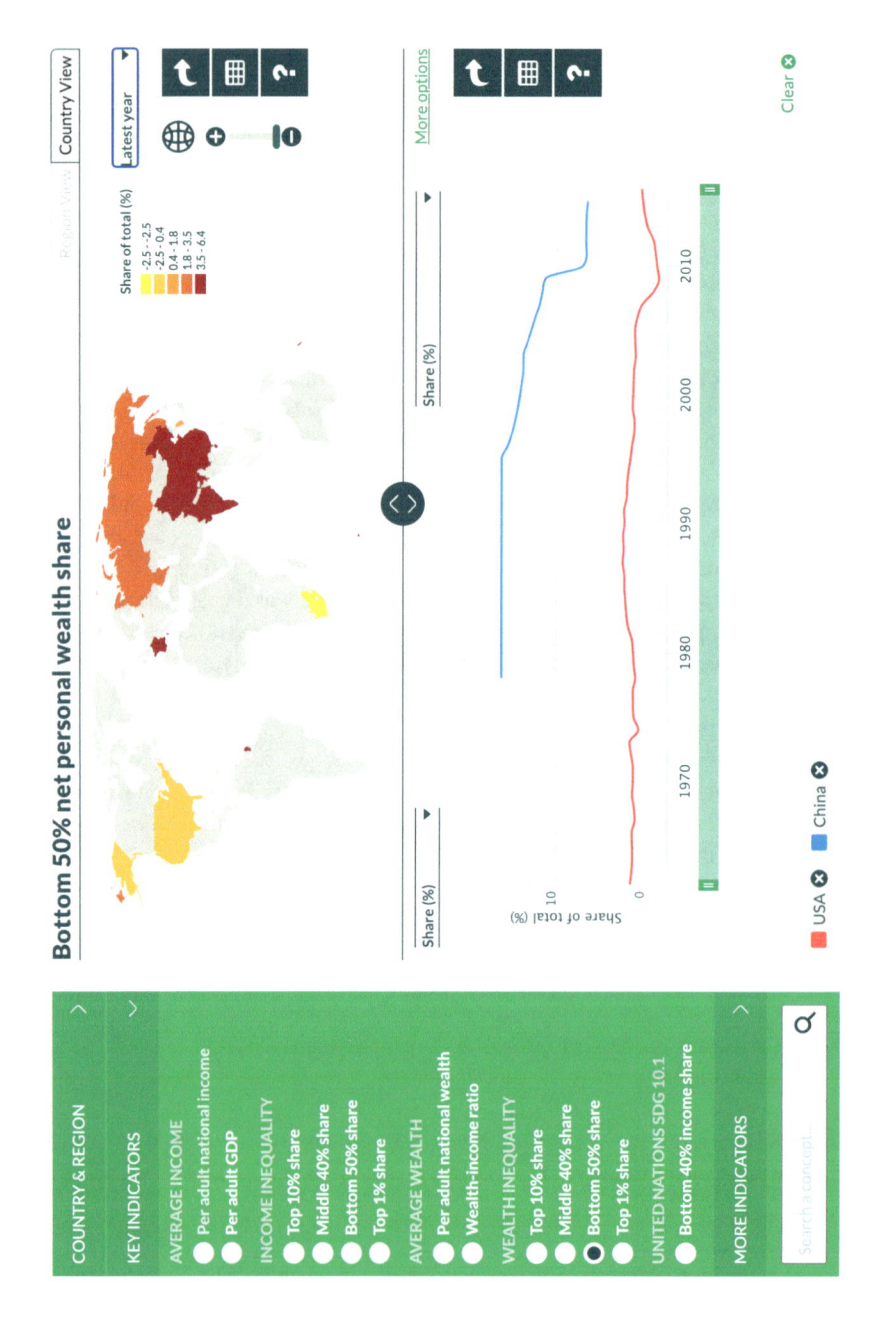

Fig. 5.10 The wealth of the bottom 50% of the population in the USA and China. The World Inequality Database is licenced under CC by 4.0

achieve gender equality and empower all women and girls; take urgent action to combat climate change and its impacts. Each goal has its own set of indicators—for example *end poverty* has 7 targets, each with a number of indicators. For example, Target 1.5

> By 2030, build the resilience of the poor and those in vulnerable situations and reduce their exposure and vulnerability to climate-related extreme events and other economic, social and environmental shocks and disasters

is assessed via, *inter alia*

- 1.5.1 Number of deaths, missing persons and persons affected by disaster per 100,000 people
- 1.5.2 Direct disaster economic loss in relation to global gross domestic product (GDP)
- 1.5.3 Number of countries with national and local disaster risk reduction strategies

The large number of organisations working on different themes (gender equity, food and agriculture, development, and so on) can be viewed,[36] and data on SDGs can be downloaded.[37]

A huge amount of effort is being devoted to the SDGs, and data visualisations continue to be created. These include choropleth maps and bubble graphs of SDGs.[38]

Figure 5.11 shows a Eurostat graphic.[39] Users can choose a country, and a Sustainable Development Goal (SDG) of interest. The DV shows the part of the graph to the left of the red dot. Users are invited to guess about future trends, and can draw their prediction on-screen (the red dotted line). They can then compare their prediction with the actual data for following years. Figure 5.11 shows the trend over time for SDG 1 (end poverty) for Germany (in blue); this was revealed *after* the user had made their own estimate (the dotted red line). This can provide an easy and engaging introduction for students to the SDGs.

Addressing SDGs is an exemplary context for Civic Statistics, and is deeply problematic. Displays of dashboards and interlinkages[40] introduce students to the complexities of addressing complex problems. Students can choose a country, and choose a subset of SDGs. The software then offers a model of the positive linkages (synergies) between SDGs, and negative linkages (trade offs).

---

[36] https://sustainabledevelopment.un.org/content/unsurvey/index.html

[37] https://unstats.un.org/sdgs/indicators/database/

[38] http://www.sdgsdashboard.org/

[39] https://ec.europa.eu/eurostat/cache/digpub/sdgs/index.html

[40] https://sdginterlinkages.iges.jp/visualisationtool.html

Fig. 5.11 Guessing Trends in SDGs. Eurostat resources are licenced by Creative Commons Attribution 4.0 International (CC BY 4.0) licence

5.4 Discussion

Civic Statistics is concerned with citizen engagement on topics that influence everyone's lives. Increasingly, information is presented in visual forms, often via interactive displays. It follows that an important aspect of statistical literacy concerns the ability to work with, critique, and learn from visual displays. Novel IDV continue to be created; learning to read and critique unfamiliar IDV has become an important life skill. IDV promote active engagement with evidence—users can explore their own conjectures and hypotheses—they are not passive recipients of others' stories. Disposition to engage is a key educational goal for Civic Statistics, and IDV provide a vehicle for inculcating the thrill of data exploration in students.

Let us return to the claims in the introduction that DV can provide ways to expose students to many of the 12 features of Civic Statistics set out in Chap. 2, and can develop skills in many of the 11 dimensions of Civic Statistics knowledge set out in Chap. 3. Table 5.2 shows how the DV described in earlier sections illustrate some key features of Civic Statistics.

In terms of the 12 features of Civic Statistics, it is clear that: societal context can be the focus (e.g. Nightingale on deaths); statistics are embedded in rich texts (e.g. the Better Life Index); causality is often attributed (e.g. discussions on global warming—see *Arctic Ice*); conclusions, implications, and consequences for society are discussed (e.g. UN SDGs). Using such tools, students immediately face data that may be unfamiliar in statistics classes: phenomena are often multivariate (e.g. UN SDGs); decisions about measures and operationalisation can be made, data are aggregated, indicator systems are used, dynamic data spanning times and locations is presented (e.g. Better Life Index and the UN SGDs). DV and IDV thrive on novel

Table 5.2 Key features of civic statistics

What citizens see/read/hear:	

I. Contexts and interpretations

1. Social (societal) context is the focus: Nightingale; Neurath; *Arctic Ice; Predicting Demographic Change; Better Life Index; World Inequality Database; UN SDGs*

2. Statistics are embedded in rich texts: Nightingale; Neurath; *Arctic Ice; Better Life Index; World Inequality Database; UN SDGs*

3. Causality is often attributed: Nightingale; Neurath; *Arctic Ice; Predicting Demographic Change; World Inequality Database; UN SDGs*

4. Conclusions, implications & consequences for society are discussed: Nightingale; Neurath; *Arctic Ice; Predicting Demographic Change; World Inequality Database; UN SDGs*

II. The nature of the statistics

5. Phenomena are often multivariate: Nightingale; Neurath; *Arctic Ice; Predicting Demographic Change; Better Life Index; World Inequality Database; UN SDGs*

6. Decisions have been made about measures and operationalization: Nightingale; Neurath; *Arctic Ice; Better Life Index; World Inequality Database; UN SDGs*

7. Data are often aggregated: Predicting Demographic Change; Better Life Index; World Inequality Database; UN SDGs

8. Indicator systems are common: Better Life Index; World Inequality Database; UN SDGs

9. Dynamic data, spanning times and locations is common: Nightingale; *Arctic Ice; When Will You Die?; Predicting Demographic Change; Better Life Index; World Inequality Database; UN SDGs*

III. Unfamiliar methods and representations

10. Novel data sources and analysis techniques: Nightingale; Neurath; *Arctic Ice; When Will You Die; Better Life Index; World Inequality Database; UN SDGs*

11. Varied data collection methods: Nightingale; Neurath; *Arctic Ice; Better Life Index; World Inequality Database; UN SDGs*

12. Innovative visualisations: Nightingale; Neurath; *Arctic Ice; When Will You Die?; Predicting Demographic Change; Better Life Index; World Inequality Database; UN SDGs*

data sources and data gathering techniques and are characterised by innovation, thus presenting engaging and novel contexts for statistics teachers and learners to explore.

What of supporting student development in key aspects of Civic Statistics knowledge? Table 5.3 shows how the DV in earlier sections can foster relevant knowledge.

Under *Engagement and Action* it is clear that DV can be used to engage students with the *meaning of data for society and policy* (e.g. *Arctic Ice*); and *critical evaluation and reflection* (e.g. UN SDGs). We believe that interactive DV (in particular) support the development of appropriate student *dispositions*. Critically, students can ask their own questions and can explore rich data sets, easily.

In terms of *Knowledge*, DV offer easy entry points to some core *statistical ideas* - for example *When Will You Die* introduces the idea of Markov processes, probability density functions, conditional probability, and modelling (as in actuarial science). The uses of communicating risk via DV is the topic of Chap. 19. Population pyramids provide a good entry to point to *modelling*; *patterns and representations*. *Methodology and enquiry processes* are illustrated by the sheer variety of topics and methods used (contrast *Arctic Ice* with *Better Life Index*); *extensions in official*

Table 5.3 How DV can develop key components of civic statistics knowledge

	Engagement and action
Meaning for society and policy	Nightingale: changing hospital practices, and public sanitation Neurath: a very wide range of social issues are addressed *Arctic Ice*: global warming is an existential threat to humanity *Predicting Demographic Change*: planning provisions for health, education, housing, etc.; informing decisions about migration *Better Life Index*: politics and pragmatics of measurement in the social domain; provokes discussion about social need and the responsibilities of governments; provokes discussions about personal value systems; measuring social progress *World Inequality Database*: addressing inequality; exploring inequality as a threat to democracy *UN SDGs*: hugely important for Civic Statistics
Critical evaluation and reflection	Nightingale Neurath *Arctic Ice* *Better Life Index* *World Inequality Database*
Dispositions	Nightingale: illustrates the potential of fierce advocacy to bring about change Neurath: strong on political advocacy We believe that all of the DV presented here engage student interest, and encourage a disposition to understand complex phenomena
	Knowledge
Statistics and risk	Nightingale: time series; seasonal variation; comparing death rates Neurath: understanding risk *Arctic Ice*: time series; seasonal variation; bounded estimates; sampling *When Will You Die?*: stochastic processes; probability; probability density; conditional probability; distributions; bounded estimates *Predicting Demographic Change*: time series; comparing distributions; *Better Life Index*: indicator systems; measurement *World Inequality Database*: indicator systems; measurement; correlation; time series
Models, patterns and representations	Nightingale: coxcomb plots; deducing causality Neurath: Isotype; deducing causality *Arctic Ice*: prediction and modelling; deducing causality *When Will You Die?*: modelling; prediction *Predicting Demographic Change*: modelling; prediction *Better Life Index*; embedding values into models *World Inequality Database*: exploration of causality
Methodology and enquiry processes	Nightingale: gathering and synthesising data Neurath: Isotype; synthesising data *Arctic Ice*: inventing measures; monitoring physical processes *When Will You Die?*: using official data *Predicting Demographic Change*: using official data *Better Life Index*; measuring; synthesising data; assessing change *World Inequality Database*: measuring; data gathering

(continued)

Table 5.3 (continued)

Extensions in official statistics	Nightingale: hospital records and military records Neurath: uses public data *When Will You Die*: uses actuarial life tables *Better Life Index*: uses official data extensively *World Inequality Database*: uses official data extensively
Contextual civic knowledge	Nightingale: disease spread Neurath: a wide range of topics are addressed *Arctic Ice*: global warming and its implications *When Will You Die?*: living and dying *World Inequality Database*: inequality
	Enabling processes
Literacy and communication	Nightingale: advocacy Neurath: Isotype to inform the illiterate
Quantitative core	Nightingale: areas; rates; comparing sizes Neurath: proportions; ratios; percentages *Predicting Demographic Change*: ratios *Better Life Index*: averages; weighting; ranking *World Inequality Database*: percentages; averages;
ICT and search	*Arctic Ice*: web searches to triangulate evidence; exploring the Milankovitch cycle *Predicting Demographic Change*: using IDV *Better Life Index*: using interactive IDV *World Inequality Database*: using IDV; downloading and synthesising data

statistics arise by using appropriate data sets (e.g. Population Pyramids); *contextual civic knowledge* is needed to discuss many of the DV.

Under *Enabling Processes*, DV are designed to communicate to people with very different levels of *literacy* (e.g. Neurath, 2010); student *communication skills* can be developed by asking them to use a DV to create products in different genres (such as: a press release; an article for a populist newspaper; a Youtube video). DV provoke mastery of *quantitative skills*; for example, *the Financial Times* chart plotting the progress of Covid[41] allows users to choose between: deaths and cases; new and cumulative; raw numbers or per million; logarithmic or linear; dates adjusted to outbreak start or not. Different choices produce displays of the same data that look radically different, and students can be asked to explain why these apparent differences occur. *ICT and search* are at the heart of DV.

---

[41] https://ig.ft.com/coronavirus-chart/

5.4.1 Criticality Not Nihilism

Critical evaluation and reflection are core life skills, and are central to Civic Statistics. It is easy to find examples of misleading graphics, and to use these to develop 'critical reflection'. Sensitivity to errors is important, but is not as important as critiquing grander stories about measurement, modelling and action. By analogy, *How to Lie With Statistics* is not as important as *How to Tell Truth to Power With Statistics*. Tim Harford (2020) expands this argument elsewhere. So we *do not* recommend devoting much curriculum time to the exploration of poor graphical displays. *The Financial Times*[42] (behind a pay wall) offers guidance on the science behind good data visualisation, common mistakes, and how to lie with maps. *The Economist*,[43] in an article entitled *Mistakes, We've Made a Few* illustrates design principles by presenting graphics published in the *Economist* that are misleading, alongside improved versions. Data can be downloaded, so these examples can form the basis for student activities. A rich source for stimulating discussion about graph interpretation is provided by the *New York Times*. In collaboration with the American Statistical Association. They publish *What's Going On in This Graph*[44] on a weekly basis. There is a facility for students to discuss these graphs in a public forum, moderated by statisticians.

Students do need to be aware of ways in which data visualisations can be misleading, and can be shown (or encouraged) how to do things better. Tufte (1997) and Wainer (2000) expose the perils of poor (or deliberately misleading) DV, and show how things can be done better. When poor and misleading DVs are encountered, we believe they should be used as opportunities for redesign, not resignation.

5.5 Herschel Revisited

DV can communicate information effectively in ways that calculations cannot: complex interactions between variables provide an example. It is interesting to speculate about the impact of algebra on the development of statistics, in the context of Herschel's ambition *to perform that which no system of calculation can possibly do, by bringing in the aid of the eye and hand to guide the judgment.* One might argue that mathematical formalisms actually mask phenomena that can be readily understood if raw data is presented in appropriate ways, and that the discipline of statistics has evolved in ways that make it harder for the majority of citizens to engage with Civic Statistics. The strongest form of our argument is that statistical education has been led astray by a focus on developing the technical skills of

[42] https://www.ft.com/content/4743ce96-e4bf-11e7-97e2-916d4fbac0da

[43] https://medium.economist.com/mistakes-weve-drawn-a-few-8cdd8a42d368

[44] https://www.nytimes.com/column/whats-going-on-in-this-graph

applying (powerful and beautiful) elementary mathematical models (using toy data) which are limited in the variety of data that can be analysed, and in the situations to which they can be applied. We should focus on the development of statistical thinking via visualisations and text based on rich contexts. 'Mathematising' should come at a later stage, and then, only when it has demonstrable virtues. The weak form of our argument is that many core statistical ideas can be made accessible to students via data visualisations, and that students should acquire a broad spectrum of statistical ideas, even at the expense of technical mastery. We offer these two versions of the argument to provoke you to reflect on your current teaching practises—are you making enough use of Data Visualisation?

References

Balbi, A., & Guerry, A.-M. (1829). *Statistique comparé de l'état de l'instruction et du nombre des crimes dans les divers arrondissements des Académies et des Cours Royales de France*. Jules Renouard.

Cleveland, W. (1985). *The elements of graphing data*. Wadsworth Advanced Books and Software.

Davison, R. (1943). *Social security: The story of British social progress and the Beveridge plan*. Harrap. Figure 15 reproduced in Neurath (2010).

Friendly, M. & Denis, D. J. (2001). *Milestones in the history of thematic cartography, statistical graphics, and data visualization*.

Funkhouser, H. G. (1937). Historical development of the graphical representation of statistical data. *Osiris, 3*, 269–404. http://www.jstor.org/stable/301591

Harford, T. (2020). *How to make the world add up*. The Bridge Street Press.

Herschel, J. (1833). *On the investigation of the orbits of revolving double stars. Memoirs of the Royal Astronomical Society*. Priestley and Wea.

Lopes, P., Teixeira, S., Campos, P., Ridgway, J., Nicholson, J. (2018) Civic.Stat.Map - Mapping datasets, viz tools, statistical concepts and social themes, In M. A. Sorto, A. White, & L. Guyot (Eds.), *Looking back, looking forward. Proceedings of the Tenth International Conference on Teaching Statistics (ICOTS10, July, 2018)*. International Statistical Institute. iase-web.org [© 2018 ISI/IASE].

McCandless, D. (2012). *Information is beautiful*. Collins.

Neurath, O. (2010). *From hieroglyphics to isotype*. Hyphen Press.

Nightingale, F. (1858). *Notes on matters affecting the health, efficiency, and hospital administration of the British Army*.

Piketty, T. (2013). *The economics of inequality*. Harvard University Press.

Ridgway, J., Swan, M., & Burkhardt, H. (2001). Assessing mathematical thinking via FLAG. In D. Holton & M. Niss (Eds.), *Teaching and learning mathematics at university level - An ICMI study* (pp. 423–430). Kluwer Academic.

Ridgway, J., Nicholson, J., Campos, P., & Teixeira, S. (2017). Tools for visualising data: A review. In: A. Molnar (Ed.), *Teaching statistics in a data rich world Proceedings of the satellite conference of the International Association for Statistical Education (IASE)*, July 2017, Rabat. http://iase-web.org/documents/papers/sat2017/IASE2017%20Satellite%20R16_RIDGWAY.pdf

Stiglitz, J., Fitousi, J.-P., & Durand, M. (2018). *Beyond GDP: Measuring what counts for economic and social performance*. OECD. https://www.oecd.org/social/beyond-gdp-9789264307292-en.htm

Swan, M., & Ridgway, J. (2001). *Assessing mathematical thinking: Field-tested learning assessment guide*. National Institute for Science Education, University of Wisconsin-Madison. http://www.wcer.wisc.edu/nise/cl1/flag/

Tufte, E. R. (1997). *Visual explanations: Images and quantities, evidence and narrative*. Graphics Press.

Tufte, E. R. (2006). *The visual display of quantitative information*. Graphics Press.

Tukey, J. W. (1977). *Exploratory data Analysis*. Pearson.

Wainer, H. (2000). *Visual revelations: Graphical tales of fate and deception from Napoleon Bonaparte to Ross Perot*. Erlbaum.

Wainer, H. (2013). *Medical illuminations: Using evidence, visualization and statistical thinking to improve healthcare*. Oxford University Press.

Watts, J. (2019). The end of the Arctic as we know it. *Guardian*, 7 June 2019. https://www.theguardian.com/environment/2019/jun/07/oceans-demise-the-end-of-the-arctic-as-we-know-it

Chapter 6
Data Sets: Examples and Access for Civic Statistics

Sónia Teixeira, Pedro Campos, and Anna Trostianitser

Abstract Citizens are more and more encouraged to participate in public policy decision processes and, therefore, critical questions regarding our lives are asked every day. Informed citizens need access to data, and knowledge in order to explore, understand, and reason about information of a multivariate nature; it is not obvious how to access such data, or how to work with them. Educators face the challenge of adopting new approaches, and grasping new opportunities in order to support the development of students into informed citizens as adults. Educators often do not have time to locate information sources; moreover, it is a challenge to exploit the possibilities of open data wisely.

This chapter points to data sets we have found valuable in teaching Civic Statistics; data must be authentic, and reflect the complexities of data used to inform decision making about social issues (whose features are explained in Chap. 2). Topics include refugees, malnutrition, and climate change. We provide enough details so teachers can locate and employ these data sets, or similar ones, as part of regular instruction. Information is made accessible using the innovative tool CivicStatMap, developed to provide access to teaching materials, along with data and analysis tools, including tools to support data visualisation.

Keywords Data sources · Data sets · Real data · Adult literacy · Migrants · Natural disasters · Climate change · Refugees

S. Teixeira (✉) · P. Campos
LIAAD-INESC TEC and University of Porto, Porto, Portugal
e-mail: sonia.c.teixeira@inesctec.pt; pcampos@fep.up.pt

A. Trostianitser
The Institute of Information Processing and Decision Making (IIPDM) and University of Haifa, Haifa, Israel
e-mail: anna.trostianitser@gmail.com

6.1   Introduction: The Importance of Real Data

The ability to find, use, and interpret data critically, demonstrating statistical literacy, is a highly desired graduate attribute (Carter et al., 2017). This is also true for other levels of education. Reasoning with data is a complex process and requires fostering students' imagination and producing a web of connections between contextual and statistical knowledge (Pfannkuch & Rubick, 2002). Prior contextual and statistical knowledge, and thinking at higher levels than constructed representations, are some of the most important aspects that have been considered for determining how students construct meanings from data (Pfannkuch & Rubick, 2002).

Civic Statistics requires a wide variety of data sources and associated techniques of analysis, notably those used for detecting patterns. In Chap. 3 we saw that in order to access and evaluate Civic Statistics, citizens need to be knowledgeable about many separate aspects of Information and Communication Technologies. At a basic technical level, students and citizens need to know how to search for information regarding real-life data that may involve statistical evidence. Such and other elements are explored more fully in Chap. 5.

However, the practice and capacity to deal with real-life data is not always developed in school. Further, negative attitudes and anxiety towards statistics can be side effects of learning this subject (Onwuegbuzie & Wilson, 2003; Tremblay et al., 2000). Many students feel fear and anguish, regarding statistics as a necessary evil and unavoidable obstacle (Willett & Singer, 1992). Therefore, Willett and Singer (1992) proposed that the focus should be shifted from the computational burden, to improving ways of teaching to analyze data and address real world problems.

Moreover, Willett and Singer (1992) recommend that instructors and textbook authors use real-world data, as it will give students an opportunity to learn skills in a realistic and relevant context (see Chap. 13). In the past, basic, secondary and university statistics courses have been criticized for being overly rigid and abstract, and that is why many teachers of statistics recommend the use of real-life data during class lessons (Neumann et al., 2013). By using real-life data when teaching statistics, Neumann et al. (2013), identify important outputs, such as relevant perspectives in learning, interest, learning and remembering material, motivation, engagement, and better understanding of statistics. Furthermore, there are indeed courses in which it is suggested that the students read the texts before the lessons, during which only questions regarding the data sets to analyse are discussed. In this context, the students are asked to analyse and use authentic data, some gleaned from available sources and other data gathered through class surveys or experiments (Campos, 2008; Neumann et al., 2013).

Increasing integration among course content, pedagogy and technology are techniques for improving the teaching of statistics (Moore, 1997). This approach can include interactive multimedia (e.g., González & Birch, 2000) and computer-based activities (e.g., Morris et al., 2002). Real data enables teachers to create a data analytic practice, so students are more empowered, as statistics is more palatable for them presented in this way (Willett & Singer, 1992). This research-paradigm pedagogic approach gives students the role of a researcher, who explores data that addresses real research questions (Willett & Singer, 1992). For example, Willett and Singer (1992) present students with newspaper articles, papers from journals, research reports etc., knowing that contextual framing will spark interest.

Clearly, not all real data are equally effective when teaching applied statistics. Firstly, using raw data instead of summarized data is essential, as rich information can be lost when raw data is replaced with means and variances. Willett and Singer (1992) argue that the data sets must be authentic not fabricated, and background information should be provided, giving students a role of a researcher. In addition, case identifiers should exist, allowing students to use their own knowledge while examining individual cases in detail. Data should be interesting, relevant and even controversial to promote intrinsic interest in students. Finally, by analyzing real world data, especially by performing multiple analyses, students might learn something of substance, about their surroundings or points of interest. The interrogative cycle matches the investigative cycle suggesting habits of mind: generate, seek, interpret, criticise, and judge. Two contrasting methods of data collection were introduced and all students participated in both methods and were asked later to decide which was more appropriate for the study of the variable of interest: the reaction time.

The collection of data should also be an important task in statistics classes. Indeed, data collection and analysis is the heart of statistical thinking (Wild & Pfannkuch, 1999), since it promotes learning by experience and links the learning process to reality (Snee, 1993). For example, Watson and English (2017) introduce two methods of collecting data as part of expanding students' experiences. They conclude that although more reinforcement is needed in the future, the students appear to develop realistic intuitions about the practice of statistics across the school years.

Students need to collect and analyse real data, and have contextual knowledge based on social issues. These are exciting times for active citizen participation in data gathering and public decision processes (Chap. 21 provides some examples). A growing disdain for factual knowledge in public discourse has been observed lately, accelerated through the proliferation of misleading information in social media, which are often disseminated without journalistic fact-checking filters (Engel, 2017). In order to re-root public debate in facts instead of emotions, and to promote evidence-based policy decisions, Engel (2017) states that statistics education needs to embrace two areas widely neglected in secondary and tertiary education: understanding of multivariate phenomena and the thinking with and learning from complex data. For more information about the use of real data in classrooms, please see the Recommendations from ProCivicStat Partners (2018).

In this Chapter we explore several data sets containing microdata (individual records) relevant to Civic Statistics—statistics about key phenomena in society (Engel et al., 2016). The structure of this chapter is the following: we introduce CivicStatMap (Sect. 6.2), a tool created to assist teachers and students to access resources after that we address the uses of micro and macrodata (Sect. 6.3); in Sect.

6.4 we talk about the importance of data cleaning and data management; then we describe the sources from which we selected the data sets used (Sect. 6.5). In Sect. 6.6 we present some of the selected data sets and their characteristics, followed by a diagram of the connection between statistical concepts, data visualization tools, type of graphs and data sets (Sect. 6.7), and finally draw some Conclusions.

6.2 CivicStatMap

CivicStatMap[1] is a software tool created in the scope of the ProCivicStat project in order to link data sources, statistical concepts, visualization tools and lesson plans (see Fig. 6.1). Teachers and students can search for real data of civic interest to explore, in order to contribute to student understanding of quantitative evidence related to social phenomena. The number of data sets available for the general public is increasing every day. However, it is important that these data sources are also trustworthy if they are to be used in class. CivicStatMap was built with this need in mind, for teachers to find data sets, allowing them to search according to their needs and according to data sets characteristics. For each data set there is a visualization tool that can facilitate statistical analysis (Lopes et al., 2018). CivicStatMap is a guide for finding a topic to be taught, the corresponding sources and data sets and for deciding what to do with the data, including software, statistical concepts, visualization tools and data analysis techniques.

It is possible to search CivicStatMap in a variety of ways—notably by Statistical Topic, Tool, Theme, Level of difficulty, Material type—as shown in the left-hand panel in Fig. 6.1. Under 'Theme' for example, we can find data sets or topics of social interest such as migration, climate and environment, demographic changes, crime, health and nutrition, education, refugees, and many others. CivicStatMap can help teachers and their students map resources. It is also possible to select the language of the lesson plans, among English, German, Hungarian and Portuguese.

6.3 Micro and Macrodata

Data sets are available mainly in *microdata* and *macrodata* formats. *Microdata* is data at the level of the individual respondent (households, persons, cities, businesses), and is also known as raw data (Campos, 2016). Users can do more in-depth analyses using microdata, such as regression, correlation, factor analysis, as well as other types of multivariate data analysis. On the other hand, *macrodata* is aggregated or summarized data, usually existing in count or magnitude tables. An example of a macrodata table is the count of COVID-19 infected individuals per world region:

---

[1] Available at: https://rstudio.up.pt/shiny/users/pcs/civicstatmap/

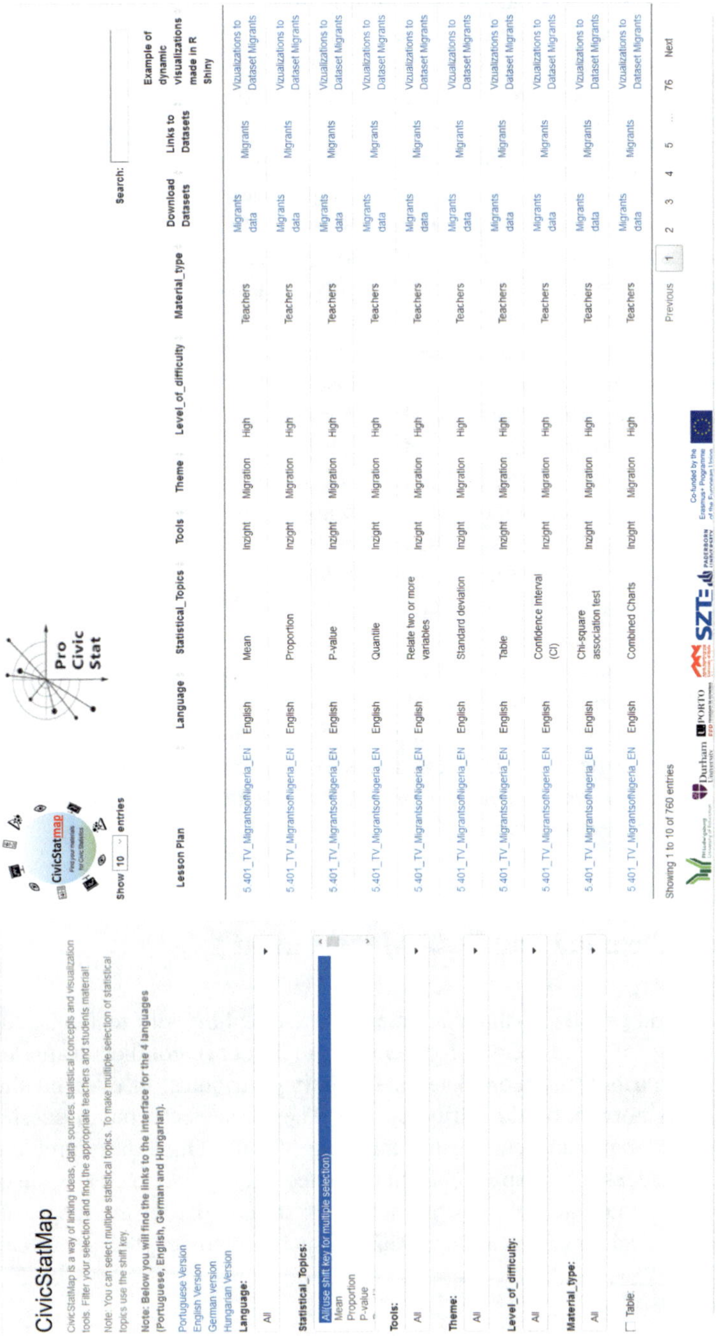

Fig. 6.1 The CivicStatMap Interface

America, Europe, Africa, Asia and Oceania. In macrodata, analyses can only be based on the summarized or aggregated information available and not with the detail afforded by microdata. In an experiment where students were asked to use both microdata and macrodata to draw conclusions based on a World Data Bank data set, Campos (2016) observed some obstacles when working with microdata; students were not able to suggest appropriate statistical techniques (such as Factor and Regression Analysis), that could help to better understand the phenomena. As a result students came to conclusions based solely on descriptive statistics, and could not explore the reasons for associations they found. It is not our intention here to discuss the best statistical techniques to apply to micro and to macrodata, although we believe that micro data encourages students to think about the best way to deal with measurement errors, draw up data summaries, plan experiments and explore the ideas suggested by their discoveries about associations between variables.

One specific type of microdata is Public Use Files (PUF) which contain individual records that preserve the privacy of the respondents. Records for dissemination are edited by suppressing information from direct and indirect identifiers to protect the anonymity of respondents. PUF are mostly disseminated for free and are often available on-line. Several methods have been appearing in the literature for producing Public Use Files, such as synthetic data production methods, sampling methods, top and bottom coding, variable suppression, and others (Viana & Campos, 2015). Many National Statistical Offices create PUF as a strategy to disseminate their information and give the users a first view of their data sets. PUF are not exclusive to National Statistical Offices. Other institutions, such as IPUMS-International[2] integrate, and disseminate samples of census microdata. IPUMS—supported by major funding from the National Science Foundation and the National Institutes of Health (USA)—has become the largest repository of census microdata in the world.

In this chapter, we will use mainly microdata (raw data) files, as they allow us to conduct more detailed analyses.

6.4   Data Cleaning and Data Management

There are several problems[3] that can emerge when dealing with real data, such as: duplication (two or more records for the same individual), conflicts (same records with different attributes), incomplete data (missing attributes) or even invalid data (the standard is not met by the attribute data). These issues can put in question the information extracted, and change the meaning of data. Once these problems are identified, it is necessary to apply data cleaning techniques and to ensure the quality of the data. The existence of missing values constitutes one of the most common concerns when dealing with real data. Authors such as Schafer (Schafer & Graham,

---

[2] https://international.ipums.org/international/

[3] https://research.aimultiple.com/data-cleaning/#what-are-the-root-causes-of-data-issues

2002) and Bennett (2001) state that the existence of values greater than, respectively, 5% and 10% of missing values is sufficient for creating bias in the results. This reinforces how important it is to pay attention to data quality, clean the data, manage the data and be careful with other aspects (other aspects that are not the focus of this book).

6.5 Data Sources

In this chapter, a group of sources and selected data sets have been identified, taking into account the topic, data availability, and their statistical potentialities. The choice of the data sets has taken into consideration the importance of the topic for Civic Statistics (for example, natural disasters, refugees, malnutrition, and literacy, etc.). We believe these data sets will promote civic interest and engagement. Additionally the statistical concepts involved have also been part of the inclusion decision. Data sets have been explored with different visualization tools. Most of the selected data sets are available in CivicStatMap and explored in lesson plans. However, these are often only samples from larger data sets (and a reduced number of data sets when compared to the number of data sets these organizations have created); variables, but not cases, have sometimes been removed. In general, datasets in CivicStatMap are free, open source, multivariate data, related to socially important issues. Since some statistical packages have limits on the number of records and variables that can be analysed, it has been important to reduce the size and complexity of data sets. The selection of variables, as already mentioned, aims to maintain the diversity of social and civic discoveries made possible through analyzes of a multivariate nature. In addition to these data sets, other data sources and resources were identified throughout the project, including 80 websites where data can be found, 56 projects which explore social data, and 26 websites presenting news (https://iase-web.org/islp/pcs/).

Sources cover several topics and are available through CivicStatMap. We will highlight the following topics:

- *Education* (from P*ISA 2012*[4] and *PIAAC 2015*[5] funded by the OECD[6]—the organization is committed to providing knowledge to formulate public policies for further improvement in the lives and well-being of citizens); the United Nations' Sustainable Development Goal SDG 4, focuses on measuring youth and adult literacy and numeracy. As this chapter aims to contribute to the use of data in the teaching of statistics, the subject of education is also of great importance for the selection of data sets. In addition to the PISA data set, another education related data set was selected, namely the program for assessment and

[4] http://www.oecd.org/pisa/

[5] http://www.oecd.org/skills/piaac/

[6] http://www.oecd.org/about/

analysis of adult skills called the Program for the International Assessment of
Adult Competencies (PIAAC).

- *Migration* (from the *World Bank*[7]—which provides funding, technical assistance
  and policy advice to developing countries in order to reduce poverty and support
  development); migration has been addressed by ProCivicStat as one social key
  phenomenon. Being a cross-cutting issue, the 2030 Agenda for Sustainable
  Development recognizes for the first time the contribution of migration to sustainable development. It is important to pay attention to studies that explore the
  causes and the consequences of flows, the choices of destination, the gender, age
  and jobs of the migrants. The corresponding Microdata library[8] gives access,
  generally, to open data, microdata for people living in the different countries
  supported by the World Bank.
- *Natural Disasters* (from the *Center for Research on the Epidemiology of
  Disasters*—CRED,[9] with the EM-DAT Emergency Events Data set); today,
  there is near universal consensus among the world's scientists that human activity
  is causing climate change. Natural disasters, wildfires and floods are intensified
  by climate change, making them increasingly devastating. Data about climate
  change on a massive scale have been collected by numerous scientific groups
  around the world, as this is often referred to as one of humanity's most complex
  problems. In Chap. 22 we present some possibilities of exploring and visualizing
  climate change data in connection with statistics education using *R*. There, data[10]
  are compiled from various sources to assist decision-making in disaster preparedness and prioritization.
- *Refugees* [United Nations data —*UNdata*[11]—from the United Nations High
  Commissioner for Refugees (UNHCR[12])]; every day we are confronted with
  news about refugees and the resulting social challenges, which highlights their
  social importance today and also in the future. War, underdevelopment and
  hunger trigger economic asymmetries among different countries, as people run
  away from their origins in the pursuit of a better life. UNHCR provides vital aid to
  refugees, saving lives, protecting rights and finding a better future for them in
  134 countries around the world, and at the same time contributes to decision
  support and public debate through its statistics. The UNHCR *Refugees* data set
  has also been transformed for network analysis. Another organization providing
  data on children and women over the past 20 years is UNICEF.
- *Malnutrition*; provided by the *Hunger and Nutrition Commitment Index*
  (HANCI). The HANCI project,[13] from the Institute of Development Studies

---

[7]https://databank.worldbank.org/source/global-bilateral-migration

[8]https://microdata.worldbank.org/index.php/%20about

[9]https://www.cred.be/

[10]https://www.emdat.be/about

[11]http://data.un.org/Data.aspx?d=UNHCR&f=indID%3AType-Ref

[12]https://www.unhcr.org/data.html

[13]http://www.hancindex.org/the-index/

(IDS), has the purpose of measuring and evaluating the goals of governments and their commitment to reducing hunger and malnutrition. In addition, UNICEF[14] also collects and disseminates similar data to improve the lives of children around the world.[15]

- *Risk of Poverty and Social Exclusion;* (from *EUROSTAT*[16]—funded by the European Commission—created to define, implement and analyze Community policies related to several topics about daily life which is useful, for example, for the work of governments, educators, and journalists).
- *Sex and Race Discrimination* (from The *Institute for Women's Policy Research*[17]—IWPR—which conducts and communicates research that supports policymaking, and promotes public dialogue to improve the lives of women from diverse backgrounds.
- *Conflict* [from the *Armed Conflict Location and Event Data Project*[18] (ACLED)]; initially, ACLED was affiliated with the University of Sussex, but since 2014 is an independent, non-governmental organization, which collects and analyzes data on political violence and protest in Africa, Asia, Europe and America.
- *Child Health* data (from the *World Health Organization*—WHO); the WHO[19] has a preventative role, and also provides help in health emergencies, and promotes universal health coverage and well-being.
- Other data sets related to Health, such as the data set about *Cardiovascular Disease*, was selected from the United States Federal agency *Centers for Disease Control and Prevention* (CDC). The CDC[20] focus is to control and prevent disease, in the United States and in other countries.

6.6 Data Sets

The selected data sets focus on social topics of civic interest, and match some of the 2030 Sustainable Development Goals (SDGs). It is important to note that the agencies that collect the data have different motivations. The Sustainable Development Goals are distributed across three areas: Economy, Society and Biosphere (to discover more about SDGs, visit Chap. 5, Sect. 5.3.2.3). In the context of Civic Statistics, 18 relevant multivariate data sets related to SDGs have been identified, along with 8 data sets relevant to other subjects (*Refugees, Student Alcohol*

---

[14] https://data.unicef.org/about-us/

[15] https://data.unicef.org/resources/resource-type/datasets/

[16] https://ec.europa.eu/eurostat/about/who-we-are

[17] https://iwpr.org/

[18] https://acleddata.com/#/dashboard

[19] https://www.who.int/about/what-we-do

[20] https://www.cdc.gov/

Consumption, Happiness, Air Quality, Ecological Footprint and Biocapacity, Mental Health in Tech and *Conflicts* data sets).

Using these data sets in class also requires judgements about the education level, syllabus, and what other types of resources are to be used. In this sense, the selected data sets are suitable for different levels, and the complexity of the statistical concepts needs to be taken into account. CivicStatMap provides the possibility to parametrize these aspects in order to select a useful resource for each teaching situation.

In most cases it has been necessary to make a selection of the variables from the original data set. As stated before, depending on the data visualization tool, it was sometimes necessary to reduce the number of records because some tools have limits on the dimensions of records and variables (for example: *iNZight*[21] deals with a limited number of rows). Even if the software does not have these limits, reading a big amount of data can be impractical or very time consuming for the data visualization tool. These challenges bring unintended barriers, irrelevant to the use of interesting and authentic data sets in a teaching context.

In this section we focus on five data sets that we describe with some detail, providing information about the variables and examples of what we can do with the data. We introduce and describe several data sets used for the experiments with several data visualization tools. For each data set, we define the Name, Source, Year (s)/time scope, Unit of analysis, Number of registers, and Number of variables. In addition, information concerning the main variables and the corresponding data types used for analysis is also provided, as well as possible cross tabulations and further activities related to teaching statistics.

6.6.1 Migration Data Set

The selected World Data Bank's 2009 Migration data set[22] (Zibah Consults Limited, 2011) includes Nigeria's Migration data containing 3344 records and 82 variables. From these, we selected ten variables. Only one of the ten variables is quantitative, all the others are qualitative. Among the qualitative variables only one is ordinal, and the other are nominal (see Table 6.1).

This data set can be explored using various software tools, such as *R*, *Plotly*, *Raw*, *Tableau*, *JMP* and *iNZight*. Lesson plans available on this topic in CivicStatMap use *iNZight* and *Tableau*. Contingency tables with two or more variables are very useful for exploring patterns in the data, and to teach statistical concepts such as average, median, quantiles, standard deviation, proportion, Chi-square test, the test of equality of proportions, confidence intervals, *p*-value, and to make bar charts, and

---

[21] iNZight is a free and easy-to-use software for statistical analysis available at: https://inzight.nz/

[22] Go to https://iase-web.org/islp/pcs/ and search for "migration" in CivicStatMap link to browse the data.

Table 6.1 Variables in the migration data set

Variable name	Meaning	Type	
HHType	Type of migrant	Qualitative	Nominal
Sex	Sex	Qualitative	Nominal
Age	Age	Quantitative	Discrete
Reasonforleaving	Reason for leaving the state of residence	Qualitative	Nominal
Howlong	How long has the individual lived in his/her current location?	Qualitative and Quantitative	
Sendmoney	Does the individual send any money to your household?	Qualitative	Nominal
Migrantgroup	Type of migrant group	Qualitative	Nominal
State	State of residence	Qualitative	Nominal
Educationgroup	Education Group (concluded level)	Qualitative	Ordinal
MaritalState	Marital State	Qualitative	Nominal

combined graphs. For example, using *iNZight*, median and quantile concepts can be learned on lesson plan 5.401[23] to answer the question:

> 1) What can we say about migrants in different age groups?

CivicStatMap offers interactive visualizations that can be used to illustrate the concepts explored in the dataset. Boxplots of *age* grouped by the variable *sent money* (amount of money sent back to the origin country by migrants), are already available interactively in CivicStatMap, or can be created using *R Shiny*[24] (Chang et al., 2021) to show that older people are more likely to send money home than are younger people (see Fig. 6.2).

We can see that the median age of people that send money back is higher than the median age of those who do not. Important insights can be gained with elementary methods, such as box plots, that are simple to create. This provides students with knowledge about migrants' behaviour, and can promote critical thinking about other real life situations. This is the type of learning that students can extract from authentic contexts.

6.6.2 Natural Disasters, Ecological Footprint and Biocapacity, and Air Quality Data Sets

Lesson plans are available in CivicStatMap[25] containing data and resources related to Natural disasters. These datasets have been explored by us using *CODAP*, *iNZight*

---

[23] https://rstudio.up.pt/shiny/users/pcs/civicstatmap/5.401_TV_MigrantsofNigeria_EN.pdf

[24] R Shiny is a *R* package that makes it easy to build interactive web apps straight from *R*.

[25] https://rstudio.up.pt/shiny/users/pcs/civicstatmap/

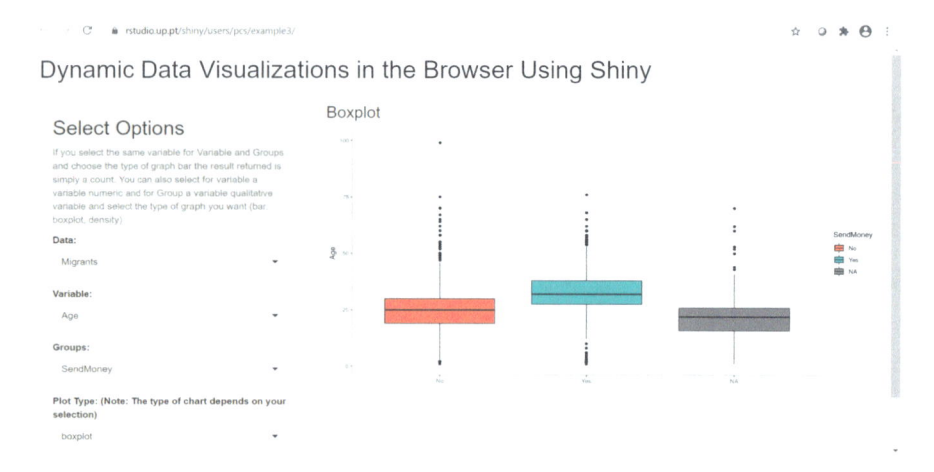

Fig. 6.2 CivicStatMap visualizations in migration dataset

Table 6.2 Variables in the natural disasters data set

Variable name	Meaning	Type	
Year	Year	Qualitative	Ordinal
Region	Region	Qualitative	Nominal
Disaster Type	Disaster Type	Qualitative	Nominal
Occurrence	Occurrence	Quantitative	Discrete
Total of deaths	Total of deaths	Quantitative	Discrete
Affected	Affected	Quantitative	Discrete
Injured	Injured	Quantitative	Discrete
Homeless	Homeless as a consequence of the disaster	Quantitative	Discrete
Total affected	Total affected (affected + injured + homeless)	Quantitative	Discrete
Total damage	Total damage ('000$)	Quantitative	Discrete

and *Tableau* (see CivicStatMap for lesson plans related to the topic of Climate and Environment). Natural Disasters data, from EM-DAT Emergency Events Data set (Guha-Sapir, 2017), include disasters between 1900 and 2015, containing 4254 records and 10 variables. Each row corresponds to a region. This data set has one ordinal qualitative variable, two nominal qualitative variables and the rest are discrete quantitative ones. The Natural Disasters data set variables are shown in Table 6.2.

It is possible, for example, to produce bar charts to answer the question (as presented at lesson plan 5.402[26]):

---

[26]https://rstudio.up.pt/shiny/users/pcs/civicstatmap/5.402_TV_NaturalDisaster_EN.pdf

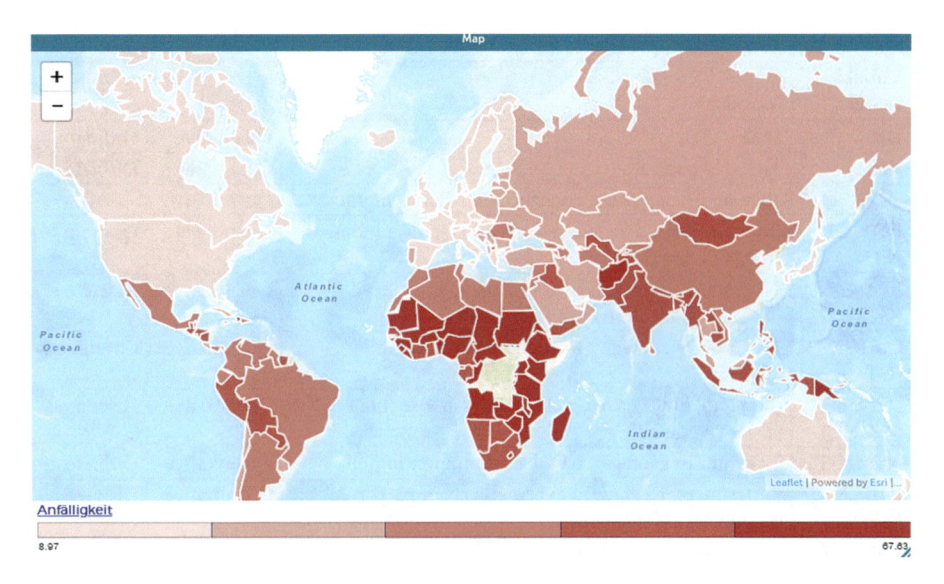

Fig. 6.3 CivicStatMap visualizations in Natural Disasters dataset

5) A friend of yours says that the natural disasters will never end and they occur in different places every year at the same rate. But you think that thanks to technology, some disasters could be prevented therefore, there should be less disasters as time goes on. To investigate this, run the following test: Year x Region x Disaster type. What are your conclusions? Please explain your answer.

In the previous example we suggest that students run a test to investigate to what extent Natural Disasters are dependent on Year and Region. This is a Chi-square test for the independence of variables. If we reject the null hypothesis (that variables are independent), it means that in some years and regions disasters are more likely to happen.

Other dataset related to natural disasters is the World Risk Index (from the Institute for International Law of Peace and Armed Conflict (IFHV)[27] of the Ruhr-University Bochum), and are used in lesson plan 5.111.[28] This data set contains information about the risk of hazard from Natural Disasters.

Figure 6.3 shows a map of risk susceptibility produced with *CODAP* (CODAP, 2014). The countries are coloured according to risk, with risk scores divided into quintiles for the map. The darker a country, the higher its susceptibility to a natural catastrophe. It is noticeable that the countries that lie near the equator tend to be darker colored, which means a higher susceptibility.

---

[27] http://www.ifhv.de/

[28] https://rstudio.up.pt/shiny/users/pcs/civicstatmap/5.111_TV_Worldrisk_EN.pdf

Table 6.3 Variables in the air quality data set

Variable name	Meaning	Type	
Date	Date	Qualitative	Ordinal
Time	Time (in hours)	Quantitative	Discrete
CO (GT)	True hourly averaged concentration CO in mg/m^3	Quantitative	
PT08.S1 (CO)	(tin oxide) hourly averaged sensor response (nominally CO targeted)	Quantitative	Discrete
NMHC (GT)	True hourly averaged overall Non Metanic Hydro-Carbons concentration in microg/m^3	Quantitative	Discrete
C6H6 (GT)	True hourly averaged Benzene concentration in mg/m^3	Quantitative	Continuous
PT08.S2 (NMHC)	(titanium) hourly averaged sensor response (nominally NMHC targeted)	Quantitative	Discrete
NOx (GT)	True hourly averaged NOx concentration in ppb	Quantitative	Discrete
PT08.S3 (NOx)	(tungsten oxide) hourly averaged sensor response (nominally NOx targeted)	Quantitative	Discrete
NO2(GT)	True hourly averaged NO2 concentration in mg/m^3	Quantitative	Discrete
PT08.S4 (NO2)	(tungsten oxide) hourly averaged sensor response (nominally NO2 targeted)	Quantitative	Discrete
PT08.S5 (O3)	(indium oxide) hourly averaged sensor response (nominally O3 targeted)	Quantitative	Discrete
T	Temperature	Quantitative	Continuous
RH	Relative Humidity	Quantitative	Continuous
AH	Absolute Humidity	Quantitative	Continuous

The Ecological Footprint and Biocapacity data set were explored by us with *Tableau*. This data set refers to the year 2015, has 188 records and 21 variables, its unit of analysis is country level. Of the 21 variables, 13 were selected, one qualitative nominal and all others quantitative continuous. Exploring the Natural Disasters and Ecological Footprint data sets identified the possibility of constructing tables that relate two or more variables, and introducing statistical concepts such as mean, quantiles, standard deviation. Possible visualizations include line graphs, scatter graphs, bar charts, maps, and combined charts. Both the Natural Disasters and the Ecological Footprint and Biocapacity data sets are appropriate for use at the pre-university level. Urban atmospheric pollutants are responsible for increasing the incidence of respiratory diseases in citizens, and some pollutants (e.g. benzene) are known to induce cancer in the case of prolonged exposure. The increase in air pollution causes climate change that brings serious consequences to health (these issues are explored in lesson plan 5.408[29]). The Air Quality data set (De Vito et al., 2008) refers to the period between March 2004 and April 2005, in an Italian city. It comprises 9357 records and 15 variables, shown in Table 6.3.

---

[29]https://rstudio.up.pt/shiny/users/pcs/civicstatmap/5.408_TV_AirQuality_EN.pdf

The data set was explored with *Tableau*[30] and *R* (R Core Team, 2021), namely with R Shiny (Chang et al., 2021). Exploration identified the possibility of constructing tables with two or more variables, and introducing statistical concepts such as mean, quantiles, standard deviation, correlation and correlation test, regression, intervals, reliability, *p*-value, time series and forecasting. Visualizations could include line graphs, scatter graphs, and combined charts. A sample question using this data set is posed in lesson plan 5.408 in Q3c:

> c. It is true that the temperature and relative humidity vary in the inverse direction and that the temperature and the absolute humidity varies in the same direction. Use graphical exploitation to answer that question.

The upper portion of Fig. 6.4 shows the relation between Relative Humidity and Temperature; the lower portion shows the relation between Absolute Humidity and Temperature. The visualizations presented in Fig. 6.4 were made using CivicStatMap. So, it is hard to draw final conclusions from the display. But the main goal of this lesson plan (as well as other lesson plans) is to stimulate critical thinking using statistical arguments for specific issues, such as air quality. This data allows the students to speculate about the relation between the variables and the reasons behind them in the real world.

6.6.3 Refugees Data Sets

Every day we are confronted with news about refugees and the resulting social challenges, which highlights their social importance today and also in the future. War, underdevelopment, natural disasters, and hunger trigger economic asymmetries among different countries, as people run away from their origins in the pursuit of a better life. By the end of 2019, 79.5 million individuals were forcibly displaced worldwide as a result of persecution, conflict, violence or human rights violations. That was an increase of 8.7 million people over the previous year, and the world's forcibly displaced population remained at a record high.

To explore this important topic, three data sets were selected from the United Nations Refugee Agency. The Refugee data set3[31] has been edited to facilitate graphical visualization and network analysis. In the case of Refugee data set1 (designated also by Refugee_UNDATA, (UNdata, 2017)) and Refugee data set2 (or Refugee_UNHCR) the tools used to explore them were *Tableau* and *Power BI*.[32] Both data sets have quantitative and qualitative variables, although Refugee data

---

[30]Tableau is a visualization software available at: https://www.tableau.com/

[31]Go to https://rstudio.up.pt/shiny/users/pcs/civicstatmap/ and search for "refugees" to browse the data.

[32]Power BI is a business analytics service by Microsoft. It is available at: https://powerbi.microsoft.com

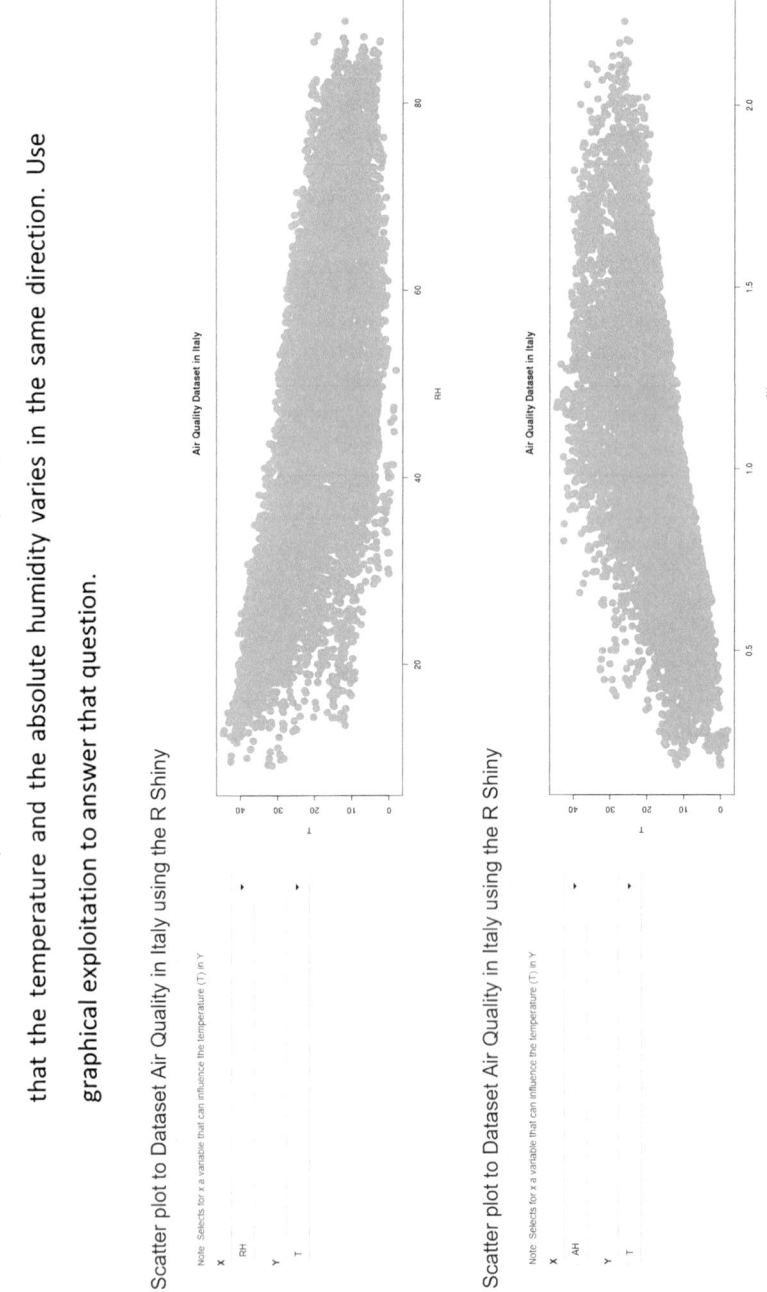

c. It is true that the temperature and relative humidity vary in the inverse direction and that the temperature and the absolute humidity varies in the same direction. Use graphical exploitation to answer that question.

Fig. 6.4 A Scatter plot for air quality in Italy using *R Shiny*

Table 6.4 Variables included in the Refugees Data Set

Variable name	Meaning	Type	
Year	Year	Qualitative	Ordinal
CountryAsylum	Country or territory of asylum or residence	Qualitative	Nominal
CountryOrigin	Country or territory of origin	Qualitative	Nominal
Refugees	Refugees	Quantitative	Discrete
RefugeesA	Refugees assisted by UNHCR	Quantitative	Discrete
TotalRefugees	Total refugees and people in refugee	Quantitative	Discrete
TRefugeesUNHCR	Total refugees and people in refugee, like situations assisted by UNHCR	Quantitative	Discrete

set2 has an ordinal qualitative variable (Table 6.4), which does not occur in Refugee data set1. Possible analyzes with these data sets involve tables that relate two or more variables, mean, quantiles, standard deviation, along with graphical representations such as line graphs, scatter graphs, bar charts, maps, and combined charts. The Refugee data set1 data set for 2013 has 80,428 records and six variables. Refugee data set2 includes data from 2013 to 2015, has 30,349 records and 14 variables. Refugee data set3, curated to support graph exercises, has 3600 records, 5 variables and refers to the year 2015.

A question related to this topic is posed in lesson plan 5.412:[33]

> 3. See the number of refugees per continent of origin, and continent of asylum. What can you conclude from this analysis?
>
> *Suggestion: Use the following variables:* **Refugees, CountryOrigin** *and* **CountryAsylum**. *Make a map of* **Refugees** x **CountryOrigin** *and* **Refugees** x **CountryAsylum** *in Power BI.*

> 3.1. Is it true that most refugees are of African or Asian origin? And that the country of origin with the largest number of refugees is in Asia?

In order to answer these questions we used *Tableau* (Chabot et al., 2003) and produced a colored map of destination. The darker the color, the more migrants applied to go to that territory (see Fig. 6.5). We used a tree map (not shown here) to plot the flow of refugees according to the country of origin to answer question 3.1. In that tree map, below the name of each (destination) country, we can read the country that contributes the greatest number of refugees. For example, we know that Germany is the country with most refugees in the world, and that the largest proportion of refugees in Germany come from Serbia and Kosovo and the Syrian Arab Republic.

---

[33] https://rstudio.up.pt/shiny/users/pcs/civicstatmap/5.412_TV_RefugeesUNdata_EN.pdf

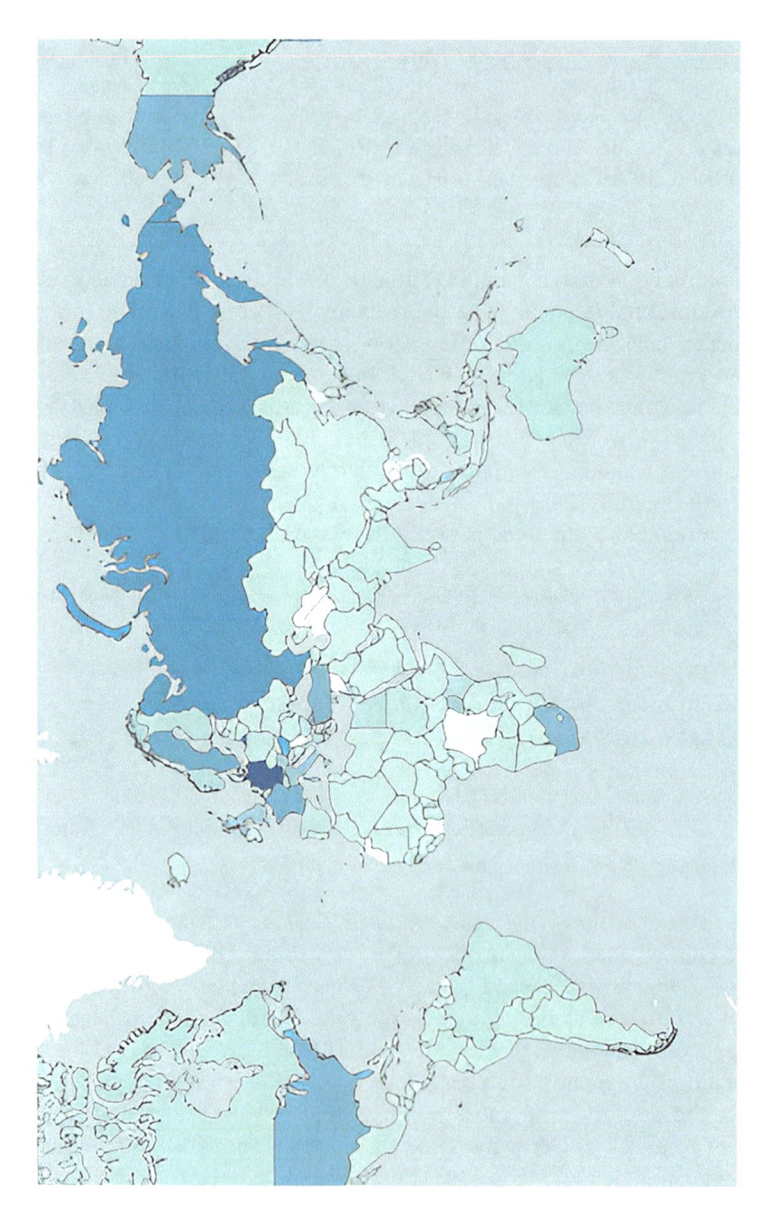

Fig. 6.5 A Tableau Visualization of Refugees per Country of Asylum

In Fig. 6.5 the most contributing countries of refugees are depicted. The darker the colour, the higher the number of refugees in each country.

6.7 Connection Between Statistical Concepts, Data Visualization Tools, Type of Graphs and Data Sets

In addition to the data sets described here, other data sets have been curated relevant to topics such as Poverty, Conflict, Happiness, Crime and Health (accessible via the CivicStatMap tool). In the Health theme, data sets were selected referring to cardiovascular disease, respiratory infections and mental health. In all these data sets it is possible to build tables that relate two or more variables, and to study statistical concepts such as mean, quantiles, standard deviation, and to create visualizations with scatter graphs, bar charts, and combined maps. In these data sets, only the mental health data set facilitates teaching about proportions, Chi-Square association test, proportion equality test, confidence intervals, and p-value.

Figures 6.6 and 6.8 show, respectively, the type of statistical concepts that can be addressed through the data set, and the type of chart that can be made by exploring each data set. The tools we suggest using in each data set are present at Fig. 6.6. All the visualizations in this section (Figs. 6.6, 6.7 and 6.8) were created using RAW^{34} (Mauri et al., 2017).

The circular dendrogram shown in Fig. 6.6 is a diagram which has a tree structure and is useful for visualising non-weighted hierarchical structures. Each depth node represents a different level. In this case, the nodes in the interior represent a statistical concept and the nodes on the exterior represent the data sets. For example, Regression can be taught using any of the Crime dataset, Cardiovascular Disease, Air Quality, Student Alcohol Consumption_MathG, Student Alchool Consumption_PortugueseG, and Sex and Race Discriminaton in Worksplace datasets.

During the development of CivicStatMap, data sets were (almost always) explored with several data visualization tools. CivicStatMap now makes recommendations about the tools we believe to be most suitable for analyzing each data sets (see Fig. 6.7).

In the Alluvial diagram shown in Fig. 6.7, on the left side you can find data visualization tools; the middle section lists some topics; and the right side gives the names of data sets. This visualization allows us to visually link elements. For example, with *Tableau* we can explore the topic of poverty through the *Risk of Poverty* data set. However, *Tableau* is a very powerful analytic tool that can also be

---

[34] *Raw* is available at https://rawgraphs.io/

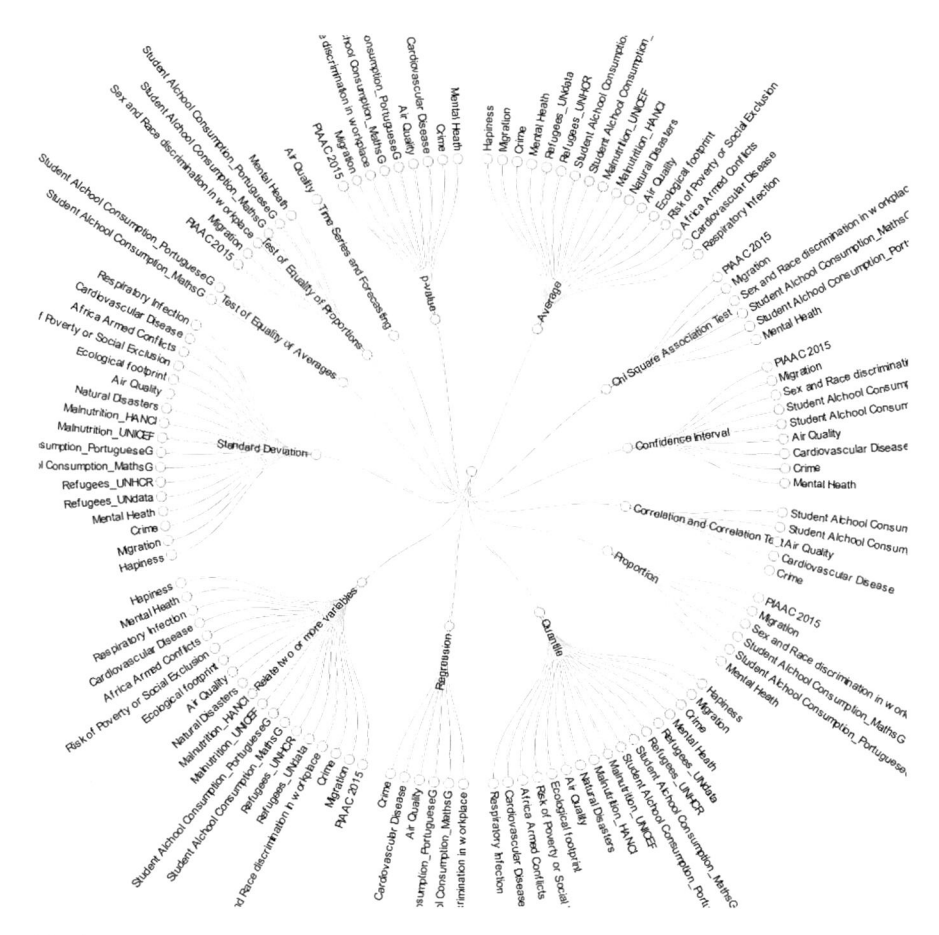

Fig. 6.6 Connection between statistical concepts and data sets

used to explore (for example) gender equity via the Sex and Race Discrimination in Workplace dataset.

Figure 6.8 presents a tree diagram, that facilitates horizontal reading. Each vertical group of nodes represents a different topic. The first vertical group of nodes, identifies different types of graphs that can be applied to the data sets, and in the second level shows the data sets themselves. In Fig. 6.8 we can observe, for example, that *Lines* can be introduced with data sets such as: Air Quality, Cardiovascular Disease, Conflits, Crime, Ecological Footprint, Happiness, Malnutrition, Natural Disasters, Refugees, Respiratory Infection, and Risk of Poverty.

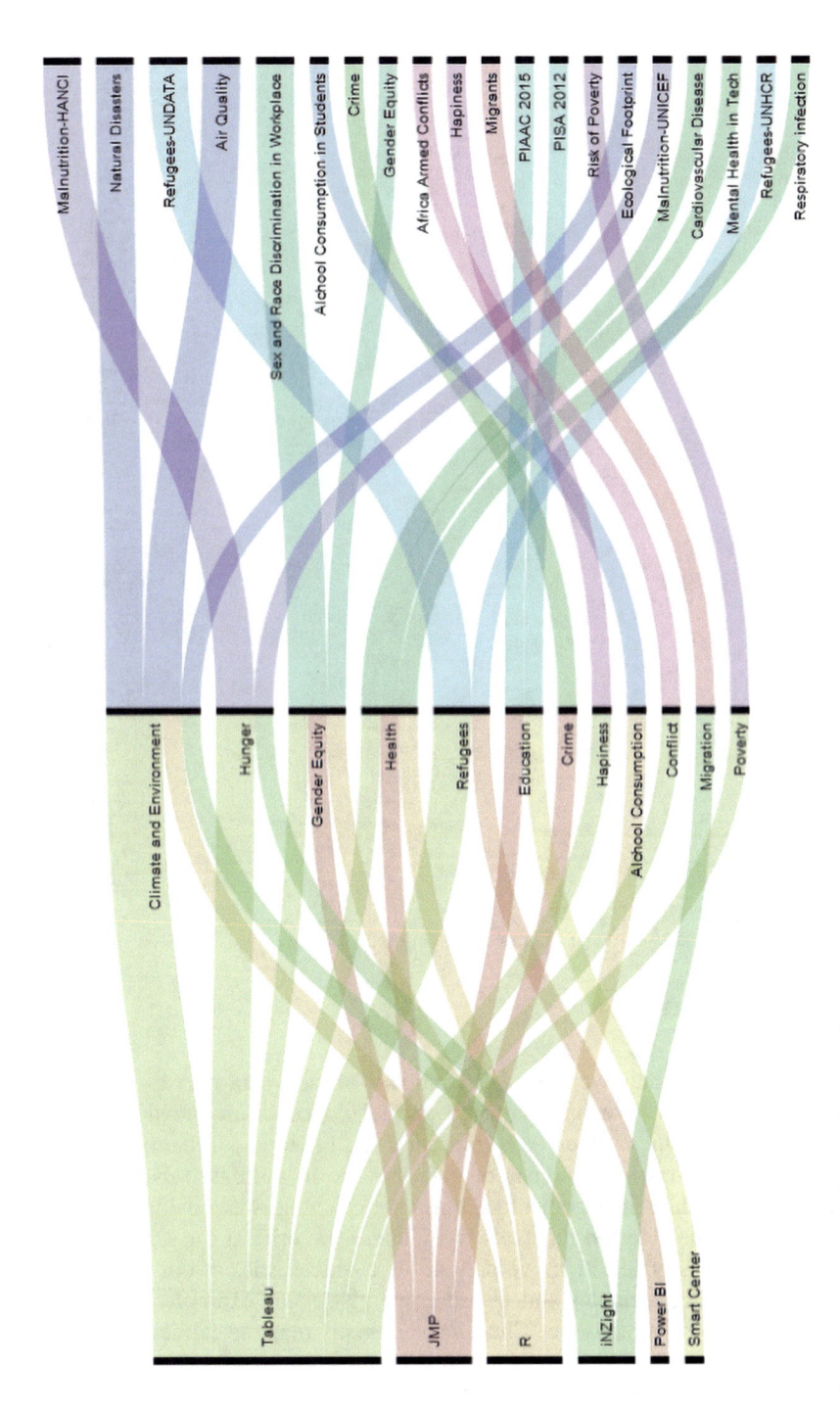

Fig. 6.7 Connections between data visualization tools, social topics and data sets

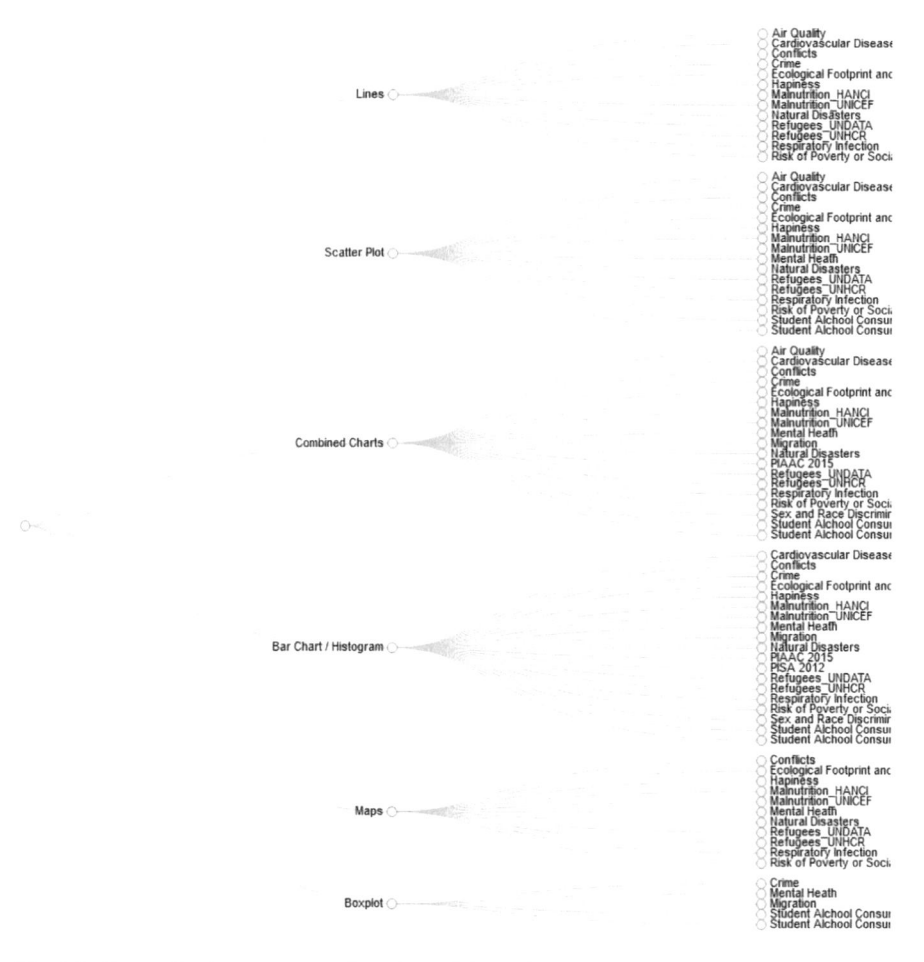

Fig. 6.8 Connection between type of graphs and data sets

6.8 Conclusion

Throughout this chapter we describe a number of rich data sets to support the teaching of statistics. We have covered several concepts around data sets and about the data sets themselves. We emphasise the importance of using real data, and offer descriptions of the types of data that are in the data sets, we address essential tasks in data management such as data cleaning, we provide links to the data sources of the selected data sets, we address the criteria for selecting social topics in our data sets selection, we present the characteristics of our data (and the reason for selecting variables and records), we give some examples of questions presented in the lesson plans (see Chap. 7), and finally map the connection between statistical concepts, data visualization tools, type of graphs and data sets. Lesson plans, as well as datasets, can be located via the innovative CivicStatMap tool. In this tool, teachers and students can search for resources using a variety of criteria mentioned in this chapter.

In the past, the teaching of statistics has been focused on the development of technical skills, often without using real data or data visualization tools. This approach has led to a gap in teaching statistics, which Civic Statistics offers to remediate. However, when using real data, other challenges arise, for example, knowing exactly what type of data we are dealing with, and the consequences of mismanaging them. The complexity of the real world is reflected in real data. Data have particularities specific to each context, and as such, offer potential for learning different aspects of statistics. These different statistical 'affordances' can be made use of in teaching by judicious choice of concepts, and by explorations of a wide variety of data sets, exploring a number of possible views. 'Views' has multiple meanings; data visualization tools continue to be invented, facilitating different sorts of insights; students should be encouraged to use a variety of tools, and to develop an understanding of the virtues of different ways to present data.

We argue that teaching should be enriched via the development of statistical thinking through visualizations, using real data, and that students should learn to tell rich stories about socially important themes, using authentic data.

References

Bennett, D. A. (2001). How can I deal with missing data in my study? *Australian and New Zealand Journal of Public Health Public Health Association of Australia, 25*(5), 464–469.

Campos, P. (2008). Thinking with data: The role of ALEA in promoting statistical literacy in Portugal. In J. Sanchez (Coord.), *Government statistical offices and statistical literacy*. International Statistical Literacy Project. www.stat.auckland.ac.nz/~iase/islp/

Campos, P. (2016). *The use of microdata versus aggregated data in teaching and learning migration statistics*. International Association for Statistical Education, IASE Round Table. http://iase-web.org/documents/papers/rt2016/Campos.pdf

Carter, J., Brown, M., & Simpson, K. (2017). From the classroom to the workplace: How social science students are learning to do data analysis for real. *Statistics Education Research Journal, 16*(1), 80–101.

Engel, J. (2017). Statistical literacy for active citizenship: A call for data science education. *Statistics Education Research Journal, 16*(1), 44–49.

Engel, J., Gal, I. & Ridgway, J. (2016). Mathematical literacy and citizen engagement: The role of Civic Statistics. *13th International Conference on Mathematics Education*, Hamburg.

González, G. M., & Birch, M. A. (2000). Evaluating the instructional efficacy of computer-mediated interactive multimedia: Comparing three elementary statistics tutorial modules. *Journal of Educational Computing Research, 22*(4), 411–436.

Lopes, P., Teixeira, S., Campos, P., Ridgway, J., & Nicholson, J. (2018). Civic.Stat.Map - Mapping datasets, viz tools, statistical concepts and social themes. In M. A. Sorto, A. White, & L. Guyot (Eds.), *Looking back, looking forward. Proceedings of the Tenth International Conference on Teaching Statistics* (ICOTS10), International Statistical Institute, Kyoto, Voorburg. iase-web. org [© 2018 ISI/IASE].

Moore, D. S. (1997). New pedagogy and new content: The case of statistics. *International Statistical Review, 65*(2), 123–137.

Morris, E. J., Joiner, R., & Scanlon, E. (2002). The contribution of computer-based activities to understanding statistics. *Journal of Computer Assisted Learning, 18*(2), 116–126.

Neumann, D. L., Hood, M. M., & Neumann, M. (2013). Using real-life data when teaching statistics: Student perception of this strategy in an introductory statistics course. *Statistical Education Research Journal, 12*(2), 59–70.

Onwuegbuzie, A. J., & Wilson, V. A. (2003). Statistics anxiety: Nature, etiology, antecedents, effects, and treatments – A comprehensive review of the literature. *Teaching in Higher Education, 8*(2), 195–209.

Pfannkuch, M., & Rubick, A. (2002). An exploration of students' statistical thinking with given data. *Statistics Education Research Journal, 1*(2), 4–21.

ProCivicStat Partners. (2018). *Engaging Civic Statistics: A call for action and recommendations. A product of the ProCivicStat project.* http://iase-web.org/islp/pcs

Schafer, J. L., & Graham, J. W. (2002). Missing data: Our view of the state of the art. *Psychological Methods, 7*(2), 147–177.

Snee, R. (1993). What's missing in statistical education? *The American Statistician, 47*(2), 149–154.

Tremblay, P. F., Gardner, R. C., & Heipel, G. (2000). A model of the relationships among measures of affect, aptitude, and performance in introductory statistics. *Canadian Journal of Behavioural Science, 32*(1), 40–48.

Viana, I., Campos, P. (2015). A new method of generating synthetic data for public use files. *Proceedings of ISI 2015, World Statistics Congress*, 26–31 July 2015, Rio de Janeiro.

Watson, J., & English, L. (2017). Reaction time in grade 5: Data collection within the practice of statistics. *Statistics Education Research Journal, 16*(1), 262–293.

Wild, C., & Pfannkuch, M. (1999). Statistical thinking in empirical enquiry: Response. *International Statistical Review, 67*(3), 263–265.

Willett, J. B., & Singer, J. D. (1992). Providing a statistical 'model': Teaching applied statistics using real-world data. In F. Gordon, & S. Gordon (eds.) *Statistics for the twenty-first century*: Mathematical Association of America, MAA Notes, 26, 83–98.

Software, Packages and Platforms Bibliography

Chabot, C., Stolte, C. & Hanrahan, P. (2003). *Tableau Software, California.* https://www.tableau.com/.

Chang, W., Cheng, J., Allaire, J. J., Sievert, C., Schloerke, B., Xie, Y., Allen, J., McPherson, J., Dipert, A., & Borges, B. (2021). shiny: Web Application Framework for R. *R package version, 1*(7), 1. https://CRAN.R-project.org/package=shiny

CODAP, Common Online Data Analysis Platform [Computer software]. (2014). *The Concord Consortium.* https://codap.concord.org/

Mauri, M., Elli, T., Caviglia, G., Uboldi, G., & Azzi, M. (2017). RAWGraphs: A visualisation platform to create open outputs. In *Proceedings of the 12th Biannual Conference on Italian SIGCHI Chapter* (pp. 28:1–28:5). ACM. https://doi.org/10.1145/3125571.3125585

R Core Team (2021). *R: A language and environment for statistical computing.* R Foundation for Statistical Computing, Vienna. Retrieved from https://www.R-project.org/

Data Sets Bibliography

S. De Vito, E. Massera, M. Piga, L. Martinotto, & G. Di Francia (2008) On field calibration of an electronic nose for benzene estimation in an urban pollution monitoring scenario, Sensors and Actuators B: Chemical, 129, 2, 750-757, ISSN 0925-4005. https://archive.ics.uci.edu/ml/datasets/Air+Quality

Guha-Sapir, D. (2017). *EM-DAT: The emergency events database–Université catholique de Louvain (UCL)–CRED*, Brussels. https://www.emdat.be/index.php

UNdata. (2017). *UNdata: Refugees - United Nations.* http://data.un.org/Data.aspx?q=refugees&d=UNHCR&f=indID%3aType-Ref

Zibah Consults Limited. (2011). *Migration Household Survey 2009.* https://microdata.worldbank.org/index.php/%20about

Chapter 7
Lesson Plan Approaches: Tasks That Motivate Students to Think

Anna Trostianitser, Sónia Teixeira, and Pedro Campos

Abstract In recent years, it has been increasingly necessary for citizens to understand real life statistical data—an ability that is rarely taught in schools, where the majority of tasks in statistics classes contain fictional data without context and make no demands on students to explore or explain. Since most real-world phenomena are multivariate (See Chap. 2), there is a need to develop students' abilities dealing with complex data and stories they encounter in the media, in order to help prepare them for informed citizenship.

The ProCivicStat project has developed materials to support teaching and learning, in the form of detailed lesson plans; a large repository of resources (http://iase-web.org/islp/pcs/) (in several languages) is freely available. This chapter describes our approach to the development of teaching resources. It introduces our storytelling approach in lesson plans, where we use real data in context to encourage students to explore and understand complex data, produce narrative accounts, and often make recommendations about appropriate social actions. The structure of this chapter is as follows: we start with a brief introduction on problems in most tasks commonly encountered in statistics education, and the need for real data in statistics teaching (Sect. 7.1), followed by the presentation of the milestones that are important for creation of lesson plans (Sect. 7.2), and after that we address the use of real data and our storytelling approach (Sect. 7.3). In Sect. 7.4 we talk briefly about empowering teachers (Sect. 7.4) and describe the teachers' version of the lesson plan (Sect. 7.5). In Sect. 7.6 we present the guidelines for designing student activities, then proceed with an excerpt of a lesson plan to exemplify products of the proposed guidelines (Sect. 7.7). We then highlight the visualization tools that help promote the data exploration step (Sect. 7.8), and finish with a conclusion (Sect. 7.9).

A. Trostianitser (✉)
The Institute of Information Processing and Decision Making (IIPDM) and University of Haifa, Haifa, Israel
e-mail: anna.trostianitser@gmail.com

S. Teixeira · P. Campos
LIAAD-INESC TEC and University of Porto, Porto, Portugal
e-mail: sonia.c.teixeira@inesctec.pt; pcampos@fep.up.pt

© Springer Nature Switzerland AG 2022   153
J. Ridgway (ed.), *Statistics for Empowerment and Social Engagement*,
https://doi.org/10.1007/978-3-031-20748-8_7

Keywords Storytelling · Data in context · Design principles · Real data · Lesson plan · Teaching statistics · Designing lesson plans

7.1   Introduction

There have been more and more projects integrating real data into introductory statistics courses, but we know that for decades, the most common approach in teaching was presenting students with closed questions about artificial data and requiring answers from them. Most of the questions were direct demands to define, explain, find a solution in the data, or to process given data in a particular way. Because the data were fictional, and the context was missing, students were trying to pinpoint answers without any requirement to think about the meaning of the analysis in context. This approach offers no opportunity to understand real data or draw meaningful conclusions. As a result, students could successfully complete courses in statistics whilst lacking the knowledge of how to cope with real data. Considering that most of the phenomena in real life are multivariate (See Sect. 2.4) students need to be taught to engage with authentic data as early as high school. With that in mind, new approaches and opportunities must be developed for students to learn and practice this crucial ability.

This chapter will introduce an approach of presenting students with a task, strongly emphasizing the importance of context for students' performance. Lesson plans, shown in this chapter, provide examples of the storytelling approach that we used to enhance students' motivation to explore and promote statistical literacy. Each lesson plan uses real data (sometimes aggregated and other times not) instead of made-up examples that are commonly used. Moreover, this chapter refers to several data visualization tools used in lesson plans, explaining the advantages and disadvantages of their use. Although working with authentic data requires much more preparation on the teachers' part, the significance of the task in students' eyes increases, as they know that they are addressing problems of real concern, using authentic data (Dear reader: you may wish to scan ahead to Sect. 7.7 to read the excerpt from the lesson plan *Natural Disasters in the World*[1]).

A particular difficulty to be addressed is students' lack of knowledge of how to approach real data. There are several references to storytelling with data. Knaflic (2015), has found that many participants (typically around 80–90% based on a show of hands) are able to remember some high-level stories. In the United Nations Commission for Europe (2005) Report *Making Data Meaningful*, authors recall that a statistical story is one that does not just recite data in words, rather, it requires telling a story about the data. The main idea is that readers tend to recall ideas more easily than they do data. If you provide a message that tells readers the what, the who, the when and the where (and additionally the why and how it happened) a statistical story will have a more meaningful and memorable message. Thus, for our

---

[1] https://rstudio.up.pt/shiny/users/pcs/civicstatmap/5.402_SV_NaturalDisasters_EN.pdf

lesson plans, we created stories, which serve as a context for the data that students are presented with that precede the questions in the tasks. Students are encouraged to take an active part in a story by presenting them with roles such as 'adviser' or 'decision maker'. This approach promotes better understanding of the material because the task feels authentic—students can see that people in the world really do have to conduct the type of analyses and make the sorts of decisions that they are being asked to do in class. As a result, the activities seem to be more captivating, realistic and provide opportunities to develop students' critical thinking. For more information about the use of real data in classrooms, please see the Call for Action by the ProCivicStat Partners (2018).

7.2 Motivation and Its Properties

Official statistics agencies and several open data sources present data products, aiming at the general public, mostly containing graphs and tables combined with descriptive statistics (Gal & Trostianitser, 2016). While information regarding trends and patterns in society is part of these data products, traditional approaches to teaching statistics rarely require students to draw conclusions about the implications of their analyses, since the focus is not on the context of the data or their societal implications, but only on statistical procedures (Gal & Trostianitser, 2016). Consequently, although schools and universities teach statistics, most students still feel unprepared when it comes to using statistics and critical thinking in matters of real-life concern.

According to Budé et al. (2007), study behavior that enhances understanding can be achieved by enhancing student motivation. Budé et al. (2007) set out to explore the dimensions of motivation in the context of statistics education. The study focused on causal explanations of events about effects on learning statistics and the relation to the exam outcomes (Budé et al., 2007). Results show that students will not profit from studying statistics if they feel a lack of control and may start disliking the subject if they invest time in studying but continue to constantly fail their exams (Budé et al., 2007).

Gal and Trostianitser (2016), show it is possible to create a task addressing important social phenomena, which requires multivariate data analysis. Most of the students will work on a task that they consider interesting even if it is difficult and demanding (Gal & Trostianitser, 2016). Finally, making statistical courses more attractive and enjoyable is a way of making statistical education more interesting and captivating (Budé et al., 2007).

Below are presented the milestones that we followed in the process of creating the ProCivicStat lesson plans, based on the results of previous studies (Budé et al., 2007; Malone & Lepper, 1987; Gal & Trostianitser, 2016):

- Choose tasks that are inherently interesting and important, such as those related to social phenomena, triggering students' motivation to engage

- Show students the material in a way whereby they easily comprehend the demands
- Present the task in an entertaining way to increase intrinsic motivation
- Promote students' control over learning outcomes
- Use real data instead of made-up examples
- Show the data in context
- Promote critical thinking

We want teachers to modify the ways they teach, and so we need to provide them with appropriate support. Teachers are busy people and need an explanation of the benefits of the changes we are advocating, and direct help with teaching ideas and classroom resources. There are several aspects to be addressed that are crucial, if teachers are to use a ProCivicStat lesson plan:

- Why should the teacher use real data in class at all?
- What topics might students engage with if the teacher uses a particular lesson plan?
- Are the activities and likely outcomes appropriate for their students (and the teacher's personal pedagogical comfort zone)?
- What software should teachers use? (Teachers need a rationale (including a discussion of the advantages and disadvantages for using the proposed program), links to resources, and guidance on (for example) downloading, installing and driving software)
- How to get started

7.3 Use of Real Data and Storytelling Approach

The creation of a lesson plan that aims to develop statistical literacy faces various challenges when students are asked to analyze raw data. The use of real-world datasets can complicate the task further, as challenges arise for both teachers and students regarding different aspects or stages of the teaching and learning processes (Chick & Pierce, 2012).

For students, there is the challenge of understanding metadata—definitions of concepts such as *poverty* or *employment* can be counter-intuitive. Students who focus on mastery of statistical technique might be unaware of the assumptions made in order to use that technique (such as linearity assumptions when using correlation) that might invalidate its use in a real-world context.

For teachers, an even bigger challenge derives from the tradition of presenting statistics topics via fictional examples and well-behaved datasets. Real data rarely leads to simple conclusions. This can be a problem, pedagogically; without proper guidance and motivating questions, students might feel helpless while approaching a large dataset, if the task posed is 'too open'.

In general, processing real data can be a complicated task, as the format and the amount of data make it difficult to understand the meaning behind the numbers. One of the biggest challenges when working with real data is the knowledge of how to approach it and to interpret it correctly. Moreover, seeing the relationships and tendencies are even greater challenges because the analysis of authentic multivariate data requires skills in exploration, and a tolerance for ambiguity, which are rarely taught (See Chap. 2).

Therefore, we think that there is an urgent need to provide teachers and students with routes into understanding real world data, which can prepare students to be empowered citizens in the future. Here, we emphasize the importance of setting the data in its context, so it is easier to understand the meaning behind the numbers. Following this idea, we use an approach of using storytelling to help understand the data.

To ease students' understanding of real-world data without being overwhelmed, we created our lesson plans based on the following principles (following Chaps. 2 and 3):

- Realistic challenges and real data are used to show the value of statistics, enhancing motivation and student engagement, to encourage better learning
- Multivariate phenomena are introduced, exposing students to interactions and non-linear relationships
- Real data are presented in raw or aggregated way to increase motivation and the ability of students to address issues in real life
- Students are assigned roles to increase interest and simulate real-life situations
- Multiple methods of analysis are available for data interpretation, so students can deploy whatever skills they have acquired
- Texts are written in a simple and understandable manner—though the challenges can be complex
- Visualizations are used to facilitate exploration and to promote better understanding of the subject
- Throughout, statistics are relevant to social contexts

Following these principles, we based all our lesson plans on clear storylines. Each storyline represents a situation in which students are actors or decision-makers who may need to use the dataset. This way, storylines make a logical connection between the student, the dataset comprising real data, which is about a real-world issue, and the actual social context in which questions emerge.

In each storyline, we put students in active positions (i.e., in "someone's shoes") to encourage them to explore, understand, use critical thinking, and come to conclusions about possible meanings, challenges and consequences. This approach draws attention to the importance of data definitions, especially in the real-world contexts in which they are used.

In this chapter, we will present several options and approaches to teaching tasks that contain real data. All the lesson plans can be found in the CivicStatMap tool[2] and can be searched using a variety of criteria to ensure easy accessibility and an

---

[2] https://rstudio.up.pt/shiny/users/pcs/civicstatmap/

Introduction:

Suppose that you are a worker at the Ministry of Education in Portugal. Recently, media has shown more and more cases of abusive alcohol consumption amongst the young people, especially secondary school students. Therefore, you were entrusted by your boss with the topic of alcohol consumption amongst students in two Portuguese secondary schools (Gabriel Pereira and Mousinho da Silveira), in which the ranks of these occurrences are the highest of all. Analyze the dataset and see if the media was right.

Fig. 7.1 From the lesson *Alcohol consumption in students of the Portuguese course in secondary school in Portugal*

Introduction:

You have recently been promoted to be the assistant to a manager at the Ministry of Welfare. The first task you've been given is to analyze the status of migrant households.
Your mentor, a manager with 15 years of experience, advices you to start from the basics and use data from the last survey.
This worksheet contains the highlights and questions that your mentor advised you to ask yourself while analyzing the currently available data.

Fig. 7.2 From the lesson plan *Migrants of Nigeria*

appropriate choice of lesson plan. For example, in the following excerpt from the lesson plan *Alcohol consumption in students of the Portuguese course in secondary school in Portugal*,[3] students are asked to adopt the role of a Ministry worker (See Fig. 7.1).

Another example is provided from the lesson plan *Migrants of Nigeria*,[4] where students are allocated the role of manager (See Fig. 7.2).

All the data used in lesson plans is accessible for public use and can be easily reached by navigating via the sorting option in CivicStatMap.[5] Navigation can be done by lesson name, language, difficulty, topics and more. In addition, users can regulate the number of options displayed on the screen. For more information, see Chap. 6: Data sets—examples and access, Chap. 5 on Data visualization, or visit the CivicStatMap site.[6] A full set of resources relevant to the ProCivicStat project can be found via the International Statistics Literacy Project.[7]

---

[3] https://rstudio.up.pt/shiny/users/pcs/civicstatmap/5.406_SV_Alcohol%20Consumption_EN.pdf

[4] https://rstudio.up.pt/shiny/users/pcs/civicstatmap/5.401_SV_MigrantsofNigeria_EN.pdf

[5] https://rstudio.up.pt/shiny/users/pcs/civicstatmap/

[6] https://rstudio.up.pt/shiny/users/pcs/civicstatmap/

[7] http://iase-web.org/islp/pcs/

7.4 Empowering Teachers

Skills in navigating real data, making decisions and use of critical thinking are crucial abilities for every citizen in everyday life. Therefore, we should ask why these skills are rarely taught. Institutions and teachers face several barriers: in schools, curriculum changes can be restricted by external pressures (such as examinations), or by teacher conservatism. In addition, at school and college, there are issues of teachers' willingness and ability to change their practices. There are also practical problems in finding resources—these can add considerably to teacher workloads.

There are multiple reasons for teachers' inability to teach students how to navigate real data. First, it can be a complicated process to adjust the common curriculum of basic courses by introducing new topics, especially if some of the teaching staff have been presenting learning material in a certain way for years. In addition, in some schools and universities, such adjustments might evoke negative responses if it requires reauthorization of the educational program. Moreover, as we discussed in Chap. 6, finding the data, raw or aggregated, for educational use is a challenge in itself. Thus, teachers might see this transition as too demanding and may want to continue using the known and established curriculum instead. Keeping these challenges in mind, we developed self-contained lesson plans that teacher can use and implement in class simply by downloading them from the PCS site.

Therefore, what is in the lesson plan? There are two versions of each lesson plan; a teachers' version (marked as TV in the filename) and students' version (marked as SV in the filename).

Students receive a worksheet, which introduces the storyline, explains the variables in the dataset, and poses selected questions that stem from the social context. It drives the analysis of the dataset and requires the students to engage in some modelling activities (An excerpt from the students' version of the lesson plan *Natural Disasters in the World*[8] is provided in Sect. 7.7).

Teachers receive more guidance. The teacher version provides essential information such as the resources needed, the anticipated length of the lesson, and so on (Please see Sect. 7.5).

The Teacher Version offers an overview of the lesson—starting by giving teachers the information they need to decide whether to use this lesson.

7.5 Teachers' Version of the Lesson Plan

The Teacher's version starts with basic information about the lesson plan. It describes the theme of interest, statistical topics that can be learned using this lesson plan, level of difficulty, topics that need to be learned beforehand (prerequisites),

---

[8] https://rstudio.up.pt/shiny/users/pcs/civicstatmap/5.402_SV_NaturalDisasters_EN.pdf

What?	Teaching Material for learning statistics about society: Analyzing data on natural disasters at the global level
Why?	Learning statistics with real data and motivating topics of high relevance for informed citizenship and civic engagement
Statistics topics	Students will be able to investigate basic notion of statistics: different types of variables, measures of location and dispersion, descriptive statistics, statistical inference
Level	High school and College
Prerequisites	Knowledge of descriptive statistics, bar charts and line graphs in *Tableau*[10] and boxplots and histograms in *iNZight*[11]
Digital tools	*Tableau* and *iNZight*
Resources needed	*Tableau* and *iNZight* need to be installed on PCs
Lesson time	6-8 hours**: This lesson plan is suitable for 2 sessions**
Further remarks	Suitable for individual/group work during class or homework assignments. Introduction to the software should be provided previously

Fig. 7.3 Sample summary at the beginning of the lesson plan—an excerpt from *Natural Disasters in the World* (https://rstudio.up.pt/shiny/users/pcs/civicstatmap/5.402_TV_NaturalDisaster_EN. pdf)

digital tools and resources that might be needed, approximate lesson time etc. This summary provides teachers with enough information to enable them to see if, and in which part of the course, it is appropriate to use this lesson plan (See Fig. 7.3).

Before the lesson can take place, there is a lot of background work for teachers. A lesson involves far more than students working through intellectual challenges. The role of the teacher is critical, especially in helping students develop competencies in Civic Statistics. We set out to provide teachers with explicit guidance, which they can use in designing and maintaining a new lesson plan.

We estimated the time teachers would have to spend in preparing a lesson. As a result, we concluded that preparing only Students' versions of lesson plans would place an unreasonable burden on teachers—especially considering the sorts of classroom activities we are advocating. As a result, we decided to always develop a version of each lesson plan as a guide/manual prepared especially for teachers' use.

The teachers' version of the lesson plan is fuller and more enriched, compared to the Students' version. Moreover, it explains and guides teachers on the key features of the lesson, prerequisites, and intended outcomes. It contains all the necessary information on steps that are needed from the point of intention to use real data in class and to the very end of running the actual activity. For example, all the main properties like the topic of the lesson, which statistical topics are covered, what is the level of difficulty, etc. are listed on the first pages of each lesson plan. Another critical point is to specify the topics and statistical definitions that should be studied beforehand, so students will understand the current lesson. In addition, we recommend digital tools to support teaching, and we provide a link to the video manual for them. We also include remarks about needed time for exploration of this lesson plan.

Moreover, the Teachers' version also contains appendices with software tutorials for those who are not familiar with the recommended program (these tutorials include links and screenshots). In addition to the appendices that enrich the knowledge of the teaching staff, there is an additional appendix, which presents answers to the questions posed in the Students' version of the lesson plan. Remarks and other recommendations for further tasks and activities are also provided.

What?	Teaching material for learning statistics about society: Analyzing data on natural disasters at the global level
Why?	Learning statistics with real data and motivating topics of high relevance for informed citizenship and civic engagement
Statistics topics	Students will be able to investigate basic notion of statistics: different types of variables, measures of location and dispersion, descriptive statistics, statistical inference
Level	High school and college
Prerequisites	Knowledge of descriptive statistics, bar charts and line graphs in *Tableau* (Tableau is a visualization software available at: https://www.tableau.com/) and boxplots and histograms in *iNZight* (iNZight is a free and easy-to-use software for statistical analysis available at: https://inzight.nz/)
Digital tools	*Tableau* and *iNZight*
Resources needed	*Tableau* and *iNZight* need to be installed on PCs
Lesson time	6–8 h**: This lesson plan is suitable for two sessions**
Further remarks	Suitable for individual/group work during class or homework assignments. Introduction to the software should be provided previously

7.6   Designing Student Activities

The student version of the lesson plan can be printed or sent digitally. The questions and tasks are sorted from the easiest ones to the most challenging, to offer a gradual increase in level of difficulty. As students proceed, questions become broader, requiring deeper understanding and higher levels of critical thinking. We set out to engage and interest students from the outset. For example, each lesson plan starts with a picture, relevant to the specific topic of the lesson, to stimulate interest and promote motivation. The goal is to give students a way in, and knowledge to engage in critical thinking and problem solving with real data, not just to pinpoint 'the answer' and receive a good grade.

The Introduction contains the story, presented to students as part of the storytelling approach. This story creates a shell for the entire lesson, inviting students to take an active role, to make decisions and answer the questions. After the instructions, students are presented with basic information about variables and the phenomena in general for better understanding. In this way, students dive into the data in a more controlled and systematic way, that will help them to think in context and use critical thinking in the very way that is needed in everyday life. Thus, after only the explanation of the storyline, several facts about the issue in the real world, and the set of variables used in this dataset, the questions start. In addition, a web link enables students to access the full dataset.

We wanted to encourage curiosity and reduce the fear of large data sets. Therefore, we provide students with options to see not only the aggregated data but also full datasets, as might be provided by government organizations and thus to prepare students as much as possible for real life. For students who use the digital version of the lesson plan, there are links to the datasets as well as links to download recommended programs. Further, the student version tasks have associated empty fields for answers, so students can key answers directly on-screen instead of dividing their attention between the task page and the notebook. Below, we show some examples of the questions posed to students in the *Natural Disasters* lesson plan.[9]

- **Question 5:** A friend of yours says that the natural disasters will never end, and they occur in different places every year at the same rate. But you think that thanks to technology, some disasters could be prevented therefore, there should be less disasters as time goes on. To investigate this, run the following test: Year × Region × Disaster type. What are your conclusions? Please explain your answer.
- **Question 11:** A magazine that focuses on climate change mentions South America as one of the regions that experiences extreme temperatures. Run a statistical analysis to check if it is true and explain your answer.
- **Question 12:** If the proposition in the previous question is true, what do you think the governments of countries in this region need to do to help people to deal with

---

[9]https://rstudio.up.pt/shiny/users/pcs/civicstatmap/5.402_TV_NaturalDisaster_EN.pdf

this kind of disaster? If the proposition is not true, how might the government maintain the current status?

- **Question 15:** As part of your presentation in class, what questions would you ask your students to check their understanding? List at least two questions and explain your choice.

7.7   Lesson Plan Demonstration

This section shows the full Students' version of the lesson plan *Natural Disasters in the World*.[10] We provide screenshots and annotations that illustrate and explain our approach, and provide some descriptions of the sorts of cognitive (and affective) activities we intend students to engage in.

7.7.1   Setting the Scene

Figure 7.4 shows the first page of the lesson plan. The vivid picture of a wildfire is designed to remind students of the human and environmental costs of natural disasters.

7.7.2   Introducing the Theme

Figure 7.5 illustrates the way we present background information and specify variables. The main purpose of this page is to explain the phenomena and their importance in the real world, list and elaborate on the variables, sources of information, and other important parameters students are going to work with. The aim is to make it clear to students that understanding statistics, and having the ability to analyze, compare and explain data are abilities crucial for everyday life. We also make students aware of some of the databases that can be interrogated to explore social phenomena.

7.7.3   Getting Down to Detail

The point of the exercise is to use real data in classrooms. It is important for students to see the source for the material used. In this page of the lesson plan, we ensure that

---

[10] https://rstudio.up.pt/shiny/users/pcs/civicstatmap/5.402_SV_NaturalDisasters_EN.pdf

Promoting Civic Engagement via Exploration of Evidence:
Challenges for Statistics Education

Co-funded by the
Erasmus+ Programme
of the European Union

ProCivicStat © - Student's Worksheet, 5.402

Natural Disasters in the World

Anna Trostianitser | Iddo Gal
Anna.Trostianitser@gmail.com | iddo@research.haifa.ac.il
Haifa University, Israel

Pedro Campos | Sónia Teixeira | Paula Lopes
pcampos@fep.up.pt | soniaacteixeira@gmail.com | rosyfogo09@gmail.com
Porto University, Portugal

Source: https://www.pexels.com/photo/backlit-breathing-apparatus-danger-dangerous-279979/

1

Fig. 7.4 The *Natural Disasters* lesson plan (https://rstudio.up.pt/shiny/users/pcs/civicstatmap/5.402_SV_NaturalDisasters_EN.pdf)—scene setting

Promoting Civic Engagement via Exploration of Evidence: Challenges for Statistics Education

Co-funded by the Erasmus+ Programme of the European Union

Introduction: gives student a role for the task, a shell to the lesson.

Introduction:
As part of the class about environment and climate change, you were presented with the task to interrogate the following dataset and run a presentation about it to the class. This worksheet contains questions to help guide you while working on this dataset.

Background:
Natural disasters can be triggered by several phenomena such as floods, landslides, erosion, earthquakes, hurricanes, storms, among others. In addition, several studies indicate that current climate variability, with a tendency towards global warming, is associated with an increase in climatic extremes. Considering all of this, the intensity of natural phenomena and the accelerated urbanization process in recent decades through the world has led to the growth of cities in areas that are sometimes not suitable for occupation, contributing to increased risk of natural disasters.

Variables and further information:

Name	Natural Disaster
Source	Center for Research on the Epidemiology of Disasters - Emergency Events Database (EM-DAT) Available in: http://www.emdat.be/advanced_search/index.html
Year	1900-2015
Unity of analysis	Region
Number of registers	4254
Number of variables	10

The data file that is enclosed with this worksheet represents the rate of natural disasters provided by the Center for Research in the Epidemiology of Disasters – Emergency Events Database (EM-DAT). It contains the analysis of last 115 years (1900-2015) of disasters throughout the globe according to specific regions and contains more than 4200 places. Although, for this task, only 10 the most important variables were selected, involving region, disaster type, occurrence, number of homeless people, total of deaths, people affected, injured and etc., as presented in the table below.

Background: elaborates about the topic in real world to provide general understanding and basis for critical thinking.

Variables and other information: source of data, year, region, number of variables and other properties, about the source of real data that students are going to work with.

2

Fig. 7.5 The *Natural Disasters* lesson plan—introduction, background, variables, and further information

there is an option for students to see data in its original form (Chap. 6 describes the ways we edit large data sets for educational uses) if the interest arises. For this lesson plan, we propose using *iNZight*[11] or *Tableau*[12] as programs suitable for performing the necessary statistical analyses (Fig. 7.6).

---

[11] iNZight is a free and easy-to-use software for statistical analysis available at: https://inzight.nz/

[12] Tableau is a visualization software available at: https://www.tableau.com/

Promoting Civic Engagement via Exploration of Evidence:
Challenges for Statistics Education

Co-funded by the
Erasmus+ Programme
of the European Union

Pro
Civic
Stat

Variables:

Name	Meaning	Type	Type
Year	Year	Qualitative	Ordinal
Region	Region	Qualitative	Nominal
Disaster Type	Disaster Type	Qualitative	Nominal
Occurrence	Occurrence	Quantitative	Discrete
Total of deaths	Total of deaths	Quantitative	Discrete
Affected	Affected	Quantitative	Discrete
Injured	Injured	Quantitative	Discrete
Homeless	Homeless as a consequence of the disa	Quantitative	Discrete
Total affected	Total affected(affected + injured + hor less)	Quantitative	Discrete
Total damage	Total damage ('000$)	Quantitative	Discrete

"Homeless" represents the "Number of people whose house is destroyed or heavily damaged and therefore need shelter after an event". In this document, the variable of "Homeless" refers to people who lost their homes because of the disaster.

"Total affected" represents the "sum of the injured, affected and left homeless after a disaster".

For more information, go to the following link: http://www.emdat.be/Glossary

You may browse to the link below and see the way real data is presented. Inquire it a bit before proceeding further.
Center for Research on the Epidemiology of Disasters - Emergency Events Database (EM-DAT)
Available in: http://www.emdat.be/advanced_search/index.html)
*In order to see the data, you may need to register.

Please use the program iNZight and Tableau to understand the data and answer the questions.
Link to download Tableau: https://www.tableau.com/academic/students
Link to download iNZight: https://www.stat.auckland.ac.nz/~wild/iNZight/getinzight.php

Variables:
List of all the variables that students are going to work with, including the types of variables and their meaning.

In addition, explanation to the definitions, critical to understanding the context.

Links:
The students are encouraged to inquire more deeply by clicking the links for more information and for options to download the programs.

Fig. 7.6 The *Natural Disasters* lesson plan—list of variables, some definitions, links, and programs used

7.7.4 Student Activities

Questions are sorted from the easiest ones to the hardest and most theoretical ones, so this set of questions shown in Fig. 7.7 starts with the most basic statistical analysis. It includes frequencies and descriptive statistics for the key variables. In addition, analysis for correlations might be required considering Natural Disaster × Region × Time.

The next set of questions is a step up from basic analysis and contains comparisons of data analyzed related to sources found via the Internet, debate about the possible causes, and further critical thinking. These are shown in Fig. 7.8.

Fig. 7.7 The *Natural Disasters* lesson plan—questions 1–4a

The next set of questions (shown in Fig. 7.9) again requires different levels of analysis: from the simplest of frequencies and distributions, to distributions and graphs, experiencing the multivariate nature of data, and engaging in some critical thinking. Students are asked to tell stories about data, and to justify their reasoning.

The final set of questions requires critical thinking, drawing conclusions, and making conjectures about possible cause and effect relations. Students are asked to draw conclusions about possible courses of action by governments. Again, story-telling, explanation and justification are essential aspects of the work. Finally, they are asked to reflect on issues around understanding multivariate data (Fig. 7.10).

For more lesson plans, please visit the CivicStatMap site[13] or the International Statistics Literacy Project[14] website.

---

[13] https://rstudio.up.pt/shiny/users/pcs/civicstatmap/
[14] http://iase-web.org/islp/pcs/

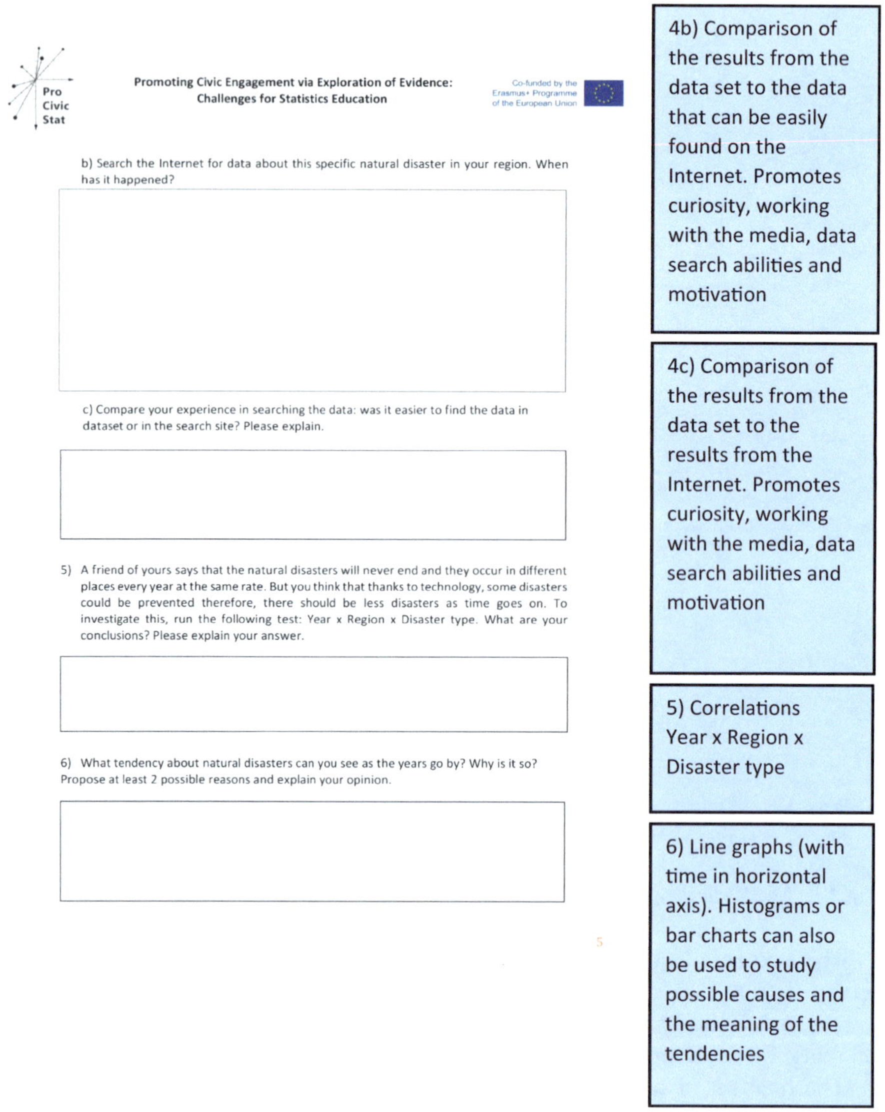

Pro
Civic
Stat

Promoting Civic Engagement via Exploration of Evidence:
Challenges for Statistics Education

Co-funded by the
Erasmus+ Programme
of the European Union

b) Search the Internet for data about this specific natural disaster in your region. When has it happened?

c) Compare your experience in searching the data: was it easier to find the data in dataset or in the search site? Please explain.

5) A friend of yours says that the natural disasters will never end and they occur in different places every year at the same rate. But you think that thanks to technology, some disasters could be prevented therefore, there should be less disasters as time goes on. To investigate this, run the following test: Year x Region x Disaster type. What are your conclusions? Please explain your answer.

6) What tendency about natural disasters can you see as the years go by? Why is it so? Propose at least 2 possible reasons and explain your opinion.

4b) Comparison of the results from the data set to the data that can be easily found on the Internet. Promotes curiosity, working with the media, data search abilities and motivation

4c) Comparison of the results from the data set to the results from the Internet. Promotes curiosity, working with the media, data search abilities and motivation

5) Correlations Year x Region x Disaster type

6) Line graphs (with time in horizontal axis). Histograms or bar charts can also be used to study possible causes and the meaning of the tendencies

Fig. 7.8 The *Natural Disasters* lesson plan—questions 4b–6

7.8 Visualization Tools to Promote Data Understanding

Chapter 5 presents four classifications of recent approaches to seeing statistics ("tools for displaying specific data sets", "tools for facilitating the exploration of specific data sets", "software packages with good functionality for visualizing data" and "programming tools that can be used to create visualizations"). In this section we

Pro Civic Stat (logo)	**Promoting Civic Engagement via Exploration of Evidence: Challenges for Statistics Education** Co-funded by the Erasmus+ Programme of the European Union	**7) Bar charts, Correlation and Association, Descriptive statistics, Frequencies, Distribution**

7) According to news reports, Western Europe suffered a lot of damage because of wildfire, especially in Portugal and Spain. In which region did wildfire leave people homeless the most in the past decade?

8) What is the distribution of the variable "Year"? What was the worst year in the sense of natural disasters?

8) Bar charts, Correlation and Association, Descriptive statistics, Frequencies, Distribution

9) Add the variable "Occurrence". How does the distribution change? Try changing the axes to see the picture more clearly.

9) Distribution, dynamic learning via graphs and representations

10) Add another variable – "Disaster Type". Which natural disaster becomes more frequent over time? Explain your answer.

10) Multivariate nature of data. Explaining the data observed

11) A magazine that focuses on climate change mentions South America as one of the regions that experiences extreme temperatures. Run a statistical analysis to check if it is true and explain your answer.

11) Evaluating the reliability of sources, comparing data and critical thinking

Fig. 7.9 The *Natural Disasters* lesson plan—questions 7–11

focus on four of the most commonly used tools in the category "software packages with good functionality for visualizing data".

Visualizations add to the technological and motivational interest of the students. In general, throughout our teaching materials, datasets have been explored with a variety of visualization tools (a review of visualization tools and their characteristics is described in Chap. 5) in order to identify which tools maximize the statistical insights that can be gained from different datasets (To learn more about uses of some data visualization packages in classrooms, see Chaps. 8, 9 and 19). Another reason

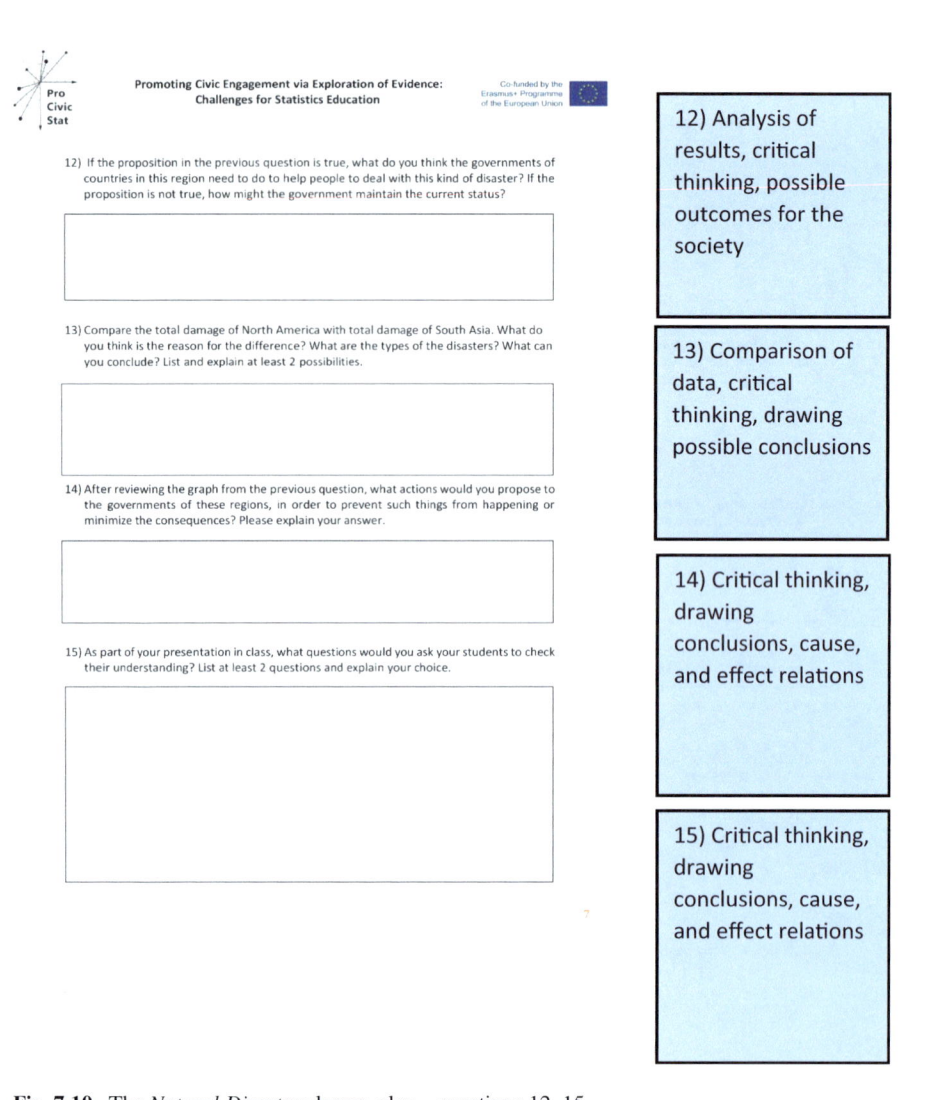

Fig. 7.10 The *Natural Disasters* lesson plan—questions 12–15

for explorations based on multiple tools is to allow students, and teachers, to have flexibility with some of the different visualization packages used to exploit datasets. In that way we aim to develop skills associated with acquiring an aesthetic for data visualizations. This section covers four general-purpose tools most commonly used in the PCS materials for data visualization. These tools are *R* (R Core Team, 2021) (see also Chap. 11), *iNZight* (Elliott et al., 2022). (see also Chap. 10), *Tableau* (Chabot et al., 2003), and *JMP* (JMP®, Version <13>. SAS Institute Inc., Cary, NC, 1989–2021. https://www.jmp.com/en_us/home.html).

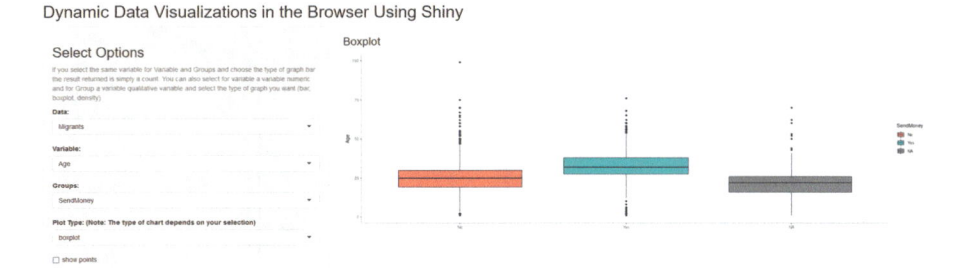

Fig. 7.11 Visualization in R: distributions of *Send Money* by *Age* for different categories of sender

7.8.1 Freely Available, Commonly Used Tools

- **Visualization features in *RStudio***

RStudio is one of the most popular visualization tools. Although *R* (R Core Team, 2021) requires some programming skills, it provides many options for analysis and visualization (such as the extensive *ggplot2* library). An example for the use of *R* can be seen in the lesson plan *Migrants of Nigeria*:[15] Fig. 7.11 shows some distributions of *Send Money by Age*. In this graph, we can see three different boxplots for the age of migrants who sent money back to Nigeria, according to different categories (No, Yes, NA). This plot has been developed with *Shiny* (Chang et al., 2021), an *R* package that makes it easy to build interactive web apps straight from *R*. The graph is interactive, and the user can choose what variables to plot and what filters to apply.

We can see that the median age of people that send money back is higher than the median age of those who do not send. These important insights can be gained with elementary methods, such as box plot graphs, that are easy to create. This provides students with hints about the real life situation, since the data they work with is real and promotes critical thinking for other real life situations. Chapter 11 focuses on the use of *R* to investigate Climate Change and provides a number of data visualizations.

- **Visualization features in *iNZight***

iNZight (Elliott et al., 2022) is an easy-to-use tool because it detects the type of the variable (numeric or categorical) and makes suggestions to the user about appropriate displays and analyses; it allows dragging and dropping the variables and presents the graphs according to the selection of variables. Chapter 10 offers an extensive discussion of the use of *iNZight* in teaching Civic Statistics. An example of its application in the lesson plan on *Migrants of Nigeria*[16] is shown in Fig. 7.12.

---

[15] https://rstudio.up.pt/shiny/users/pcs/civicstatmap/5.401_TV_MigrantsofNigeria_EN.pdf

[16] https://rstudio.up.pt/shiny/users/pcs/civicstatmap/5.401_TV_MigrantsofNigeria_EN.pdf

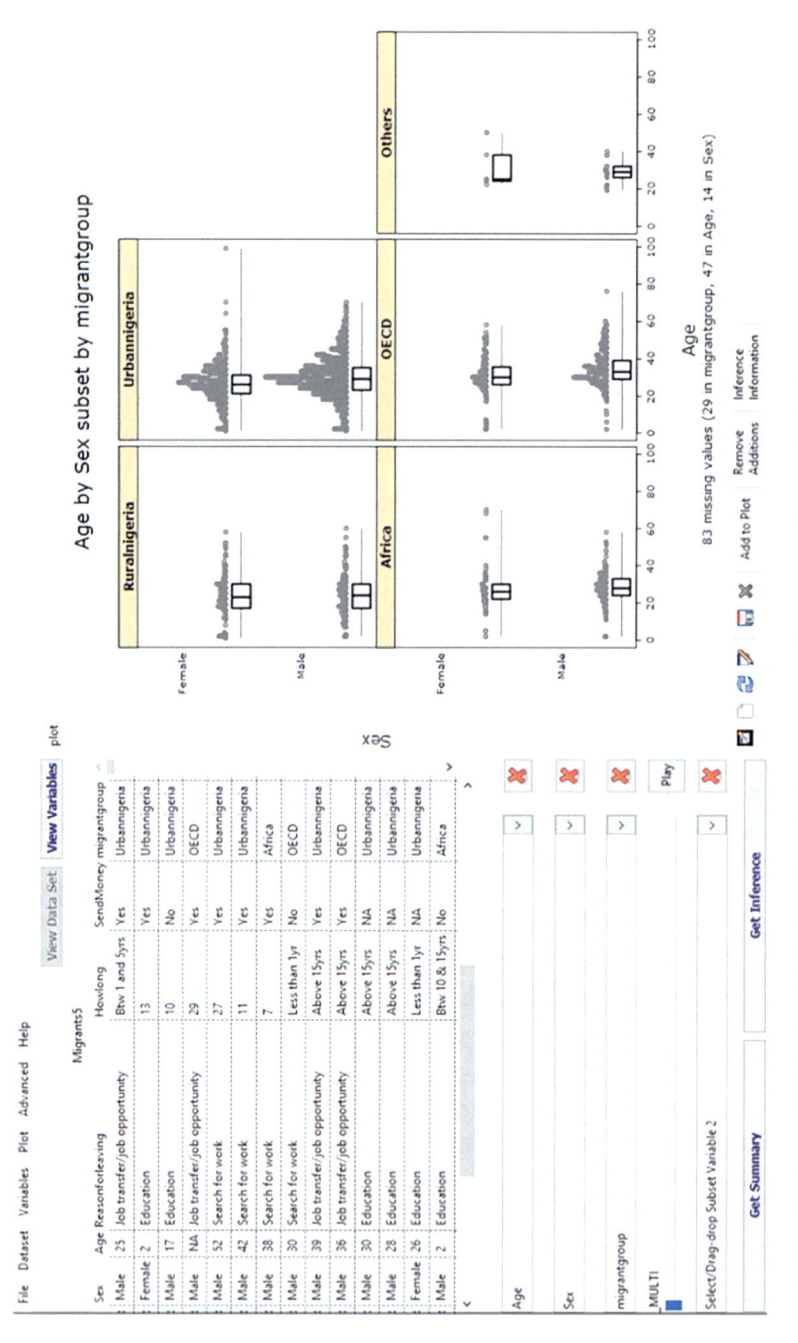

Fig. 7.12 Visualization in *iNZight*: the distribution of *Age* by *Sex* for migrant Nigerians to different destinations

Figure 7.12 shows the age distribution by sex, for each type of migrant group. There are some interesting differences to explore—for example, male migrants to urban Nigeria appear to be older than female migrants.

7.8.2 Commercially Available Commonly Used Tools

- **Visualization features using *Tableau*:**

With *Tableau* (Chabot et al., 2003), it is easy to access the datasets included in the software and also those imported by the user. *Tableau* also offers a rich data visualization menu. It allows the use of microdata and macro data, and no programming skills are required for its use, although users do have the option to program (more details about *Tableau* are presented in Chap. 5). An example of its use can be seen in the lesson *Natural Disasters in the World.*[17]

Figure 7.13 shows the total number of deaths attributable to different natural disasters for a number of regions. Stacked bars can give us important insights; each bar in the chart represents a whole (i.e. total deaths), and segments in the bar represent different parts or categories of that whole (i.e. deaths attributable to specific disasters). Here, different colors are used to illustrate the different causes of death in the bar.

Figure 7.13 shows that natural disasters are more frequent in specific regions of the globe (Southern Asia, South-Eastern Asia, Eastern Asia, South America, Northern America and Eastern Africa). However, Southern Asia, Eastern Asia and the Russian Federation are the areas where natural disasters have been most fatal. Although the Russian Federation is a region in which natural disasters are associated with a large number of deaths, their occurrence is the second smallest among all regions. This provokes reflection (and further analysis) about the reasons for low occurrence and high total deaths in the Russian Federation. Was it the intensity of some natural disaster? Was it the type of a natural disaster?

- **Visualization features using *JMP*:**

JMP (JMP®, Version <13>. SAS Institute Inc., Cary, NC, 1989–2021. https://www.jmp.com/en_us/home.html) is another example of an interactive exploratory data and statistical analysis tool (a free trial version is available). This tool is easy to use; however, it is not as intuitive as, for example, *iNZight*. An example of its use can be found in the *Migrants of Nigeria*[18] lesson plan Fig. 7.14 shows the age of migrants, and the reason why the migrants leave the place where they live, for each of several destinations.

---

[17] https://rstudio.up.pt/shiny/users/pcs/civicstatmap/5.402_TV_NaturalDisaster_EN.pdf

[18] https://rstudio.up.pt/shiny/users/pcs/civicstatmap/5.401_TV_MigrantsofNigeria_EN.pdf

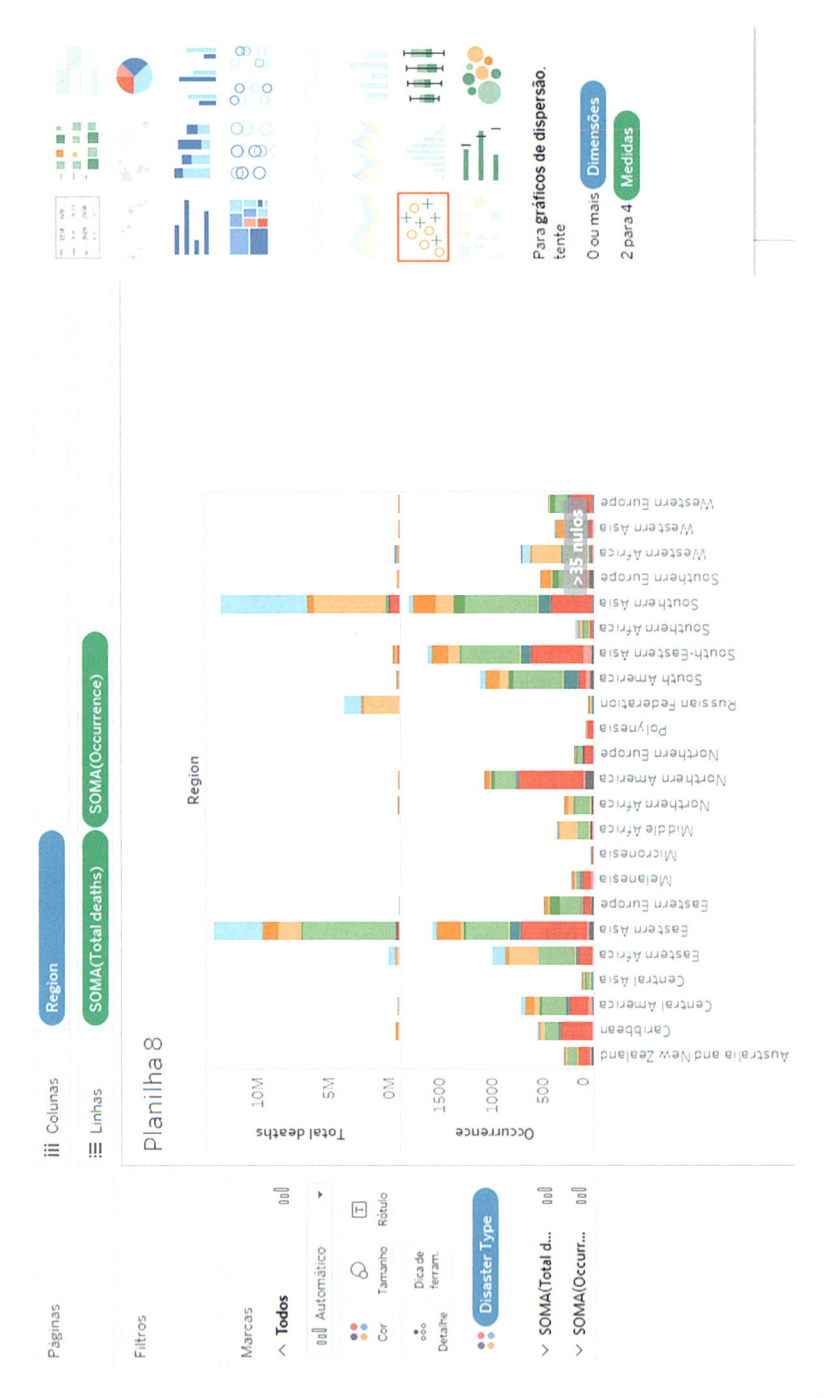

Fig. 7.13 Visualization in *Tableau*: total deaths and occurrence by disaster for different regions

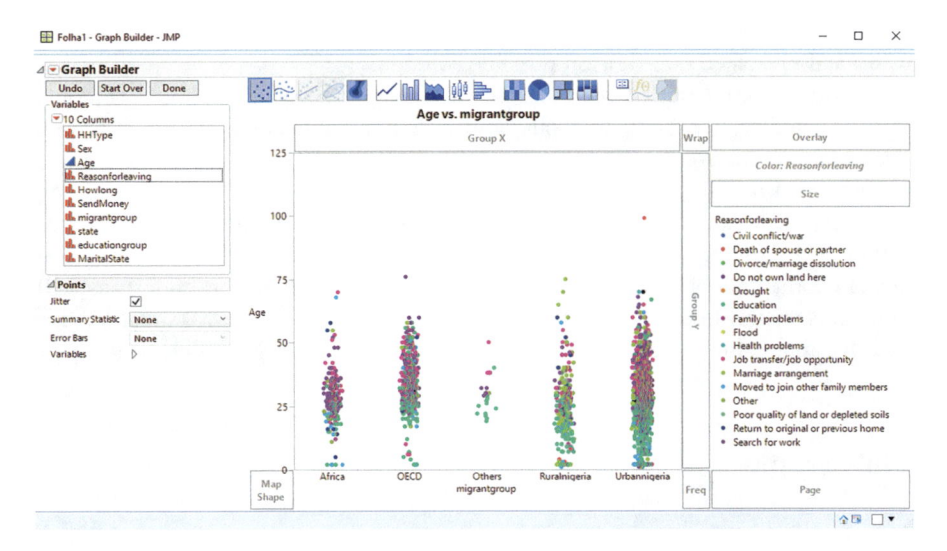

Fig. 7.14 Visualization in *JMP*: age and reason for leaving to different destinations

In Fig. 7.14, it is possible to observe that, regardless of the type of migrant group, there are reasons for leaving that are more common to migrants younger than 25 years of age than to migrants above that age. In this case, the reason is a *job transfer/job opportunity*. The pink color identifies migrants above 25 years old in the Africa, OECD and UrbanNigeria migrant groups. *Arranging marriage* is an important reason why people migrate to rural Nigeria, which occurs across most of the age distribution. Similar reflections can be drawn for the remaining reasons for *migrating* given by different age groups.

7.9   Conclusion

In this chapter, we discussed the design of lesson plans and tasks that will motivate students to engage with Civic Statistics, become statistically literate, and to think like statisticians about important topics. Our approach to more successful learning is to use real data about motivating topics. We designed our tasks using a storytelling approach that challenges students and invites them to act and think critically, as they should do in situations that might happen in the real world. We think that a more user-friendly approach where students have an active role, along with the use of authentic contexts, will trigger deeper interest and help students understand better and thus, uncover their potential as empowered citizens. A discursive approach, dynamic exploration, careful explanation, critical thinking, and reflection are all central to this process. In addition, we addressed major challenges that students and teachers face (notably in accessing appropriate teaching materials, data, and software) and presented our view on possible solutions.

Statistics should not be unnecessarily difficult or bring anxiety into students' lives. Therefore, we hope that our approach will motivate students to acquire important statistical concepts and increase their sense of empowerment. Moreover, we hope that it will give teachers ideas that will permeate their teaching and help them prepare lessons by approaching the challenge from a point of student interest and critical thinking. Options and opportunities that statistics education brings are most important not only for educational attainment, but for everyday choices as well. Thus, it is critical to promote statistical literacy in students using tasks that are user friendly, motivating, interesting and which develop the ability to think critically.

Bibliography

Budé, L., Van De Wiel, M., Imbos, T., Candel, M., Broers, N., & Berger, M. (2007). Students' achievements in a statistics course in relation to motivational aspects and study behaviour. *Statistics Education Research Journal, 6*(1), 5–21. https://doi.org/10.52041/serj.v6i1.491

Chick, H. L., & Pierce, R. (2012). Teaching for statistical literacy: Utilising affordances in real-world data. *International Journal of Science and Mathematics Education, 10*(2). https://doi.org/10.1007/s10763-011-9303-2

Gal, I., & Trostianitser, A. (2016). Understanding basic demographic trends: Connecting table reading, task design, and context. In *Promoting understanding of statistics about society. Proceedings of the IASE Roundtable conference*. http://community.dur.ac.uk/procivic.stat.

Knaflic, C. N. (2015). Storytelling with data: A data visualization guide for business professionals. In *Storytelling with data: A data visualization guide for business professionals*.

Malone, T. W., & Lepper, M. R. (1987). Making learning fun: A taxonomy of intrinsic motivations for learning. In *Aptitude learning and instruction* (Vol. 3).

ProCivicStat Partners. (2018). *Engaging civic statistics: A call for action and recommendations*. A product of the ProCivicStat project. http://iase-web.org/islp/pcs

UNECE, United Nations Commission for Europe. (2005). Making data meaningful: A guide to writing stories about numbers, .

Software, Packages and Platforms Bibliography

Chabot, C., Stolte, C., & Hanrahan, P. (2003). *Tableau software*, California, United States. https://www.tableau.com/

Chang, W., Cheng, J., Allaire, J. J., Sievert, C., Schloerke, B., Xie, Y., Allen, J., McPherson, J., Dipert, A., & Borges, B. (2021). *shiny: Web application framework for R*. R package version 1.7.1. https://CRAN.R-project.org/package=shiny

Elliott, T., Kuper, M., & Barnett, D. (2022). *iNZight: A GUI for data exploration and visualisation*. Version 3.1.1. https://www.stat.auckland.ac.nz/~wild/iNZight/

JMP®, Version <13>. SAS Institute Inc., Cary, NC, 1989–2021. https://www.jmp.com/en_us/home.html.

R Core Team. (2021). *R: A language and environment for statistical computing*. R Foundation for Statistical Computing. https://www.R-project.org/

Data Sets Bibliography

Dua, D., & Graff, C. (2019). *UCI machine learning repository* [http://archive.ics.uci.edu/ ml]. University of California, School of Information and Computer Science.

EM-DAT. (2018). In D. Guha-Sapir (Ed.), *The emergency events database – Universite catholique de Louvain (UCL) – CRED*. The International Disaster Database. www.emdat.be

World Bank. (2009). *The world bank annual report 2009: Year in review*. The World Bank.

Chapter 8
Seeing Dynamic Data Visualizations in Action: Gapminder Tools

Peter Kovacs ⓘ, **Klara Kazar, and Eva Kuruczleki**

Abstract Citizens need sophisticated ways of thinking in order to understand complex, real social and economic phenomena and to interpret relationships among social and business data correctly. Huge amounts of data, data sources and visualization tools provide an opportunity to illustrate complex relations within real data. At the same time, the misuse of these tools can lead to misinterpretations and in turn perhaps to poor decision making. The Gapminder Foundation has developed several visualization tools (using bubble charts, trend lines, ranks, maps, etc.) in order to facilitate the exploration of complex relationships between variables, to rank countries, and to explore things such as time series, age distributions and income distributions. The goals of this chapter are to: show these different tools in action in classes exploring poverty and the ageing society; to describe their advantages and disadvantages; and to compare.

Keywords Gapminder · Ageing Society · Poverty · Gapminder offline · Nonlinear relationship · Population pyramids

8.1 Introduction

When we analyze civic, social, or economic data, data visualization has a unique role to play in exploring relationships and trends. With the help of visualization, we can tell a story, teach about, and demonstrate complex phenomena relatively simply. Elaboration of civic problems contributes to an understanding of these real problems and can improve civic engagement whether in statistical or non-statistical classes. There is a wealth of online and offline databases, tools and apps which can support the analysis and visualization of real data, that can be used alone, or in combination with others (for examples, see Chaps. 5 and 6). Gapminder is a free, online

P. Kovacs (✉) · K. Kazar · E. Kuruczleki
University of Szeged, Szeged, Hungary
e-mail: kovacs.peter@eco.u-szeged.hu; kazar.klara@eco.u-szeged.hu;
kuruczleki.eva@eco.u-szeged.hu

J. Ridgway (ed.), *Statistics for Empowerment and Social Engagement*,
https://doi.org/10.1007/978-3-031-20748-8_8

visualization package. After a short summary of Gapminder tools, this chapter shows Gapminder in action, embedded in lesson plans developed by the ProCivicStat project. The first two applications use Gapminder's Bubble chart; in the third application we used Gapminder tools (to show trends, ranks, age profiles) in combination with other providers' population pyramids.

8.2 About Gapminder

The Gapminder Foundation was established in Sweden by Hans Rosling, Ola Rosling and Anna Rosling Rönnlund in 2005. Gapminder's mission is "Fighting devastating ignorance with fact-based worldviews everyone can understand". They identify misconceptions about facts, compare what people believe to what the real data show and develop course materials, visualization tools, and courses, which are available freely. Their famous book is *Factfulness*, which was published in 2018. The Gapminder webpage (www.gapminder.org) offers a collection of tools for visualizing data. As Hans Rosling said at ICOTS8 in 2010, "by serendipity Gapminder Foundation found that the beauty of a statistical database can be unveiled to a broad audience if the data set can be animated in newly developed software." On the Gapminder YouTube channel,[1] several videos are available on various topics, which can be useful in classes to illustrate a social issue. For instance, Don't Panic, The truth about population with Hans Rosling, which also was a 1-h length TV program on BBC, presents Rosling and the Gapminder philosophy.

Gapminder has a menu of over 500 indicators that can be explored via online visualization tools. From the website, all of the data are downloadable in csv or xlsx formats; metadata is provided, along with links to the original data source and provider.

There are several visualization tools at Gapminder website: Bubbles, Income Mountains, Maps, Ranks, Trends, Ages, and Dollar Street:

- The best-known tool is the **Bubble Chart**, which is a dynamic scatter plot. We can visualize five variables at the same time with the help of the two axes, the color and the size of bubbles, and a timeline. The axis can be changed to show linear or logarithmic scales. This chart is described in detail below in Sect. 8.3.
- Gapminder **Trends** is a tool to present simple line charts, used to visualize time series for the countries of interest, on the variable chosen.
- On Gapminder **Maps** sizes of bubbles represent values of a selected indicator at the country level on a map. Time is on the x-axis, and changes over time can be animated.
- Gapminder **Ranks** is a tool to prepare a horizontal bar chart if we want to show the order of countries by a selected variable. We can see not only the ranks of the

---

[1] https://www.youtube.com/c/gapminder/featured

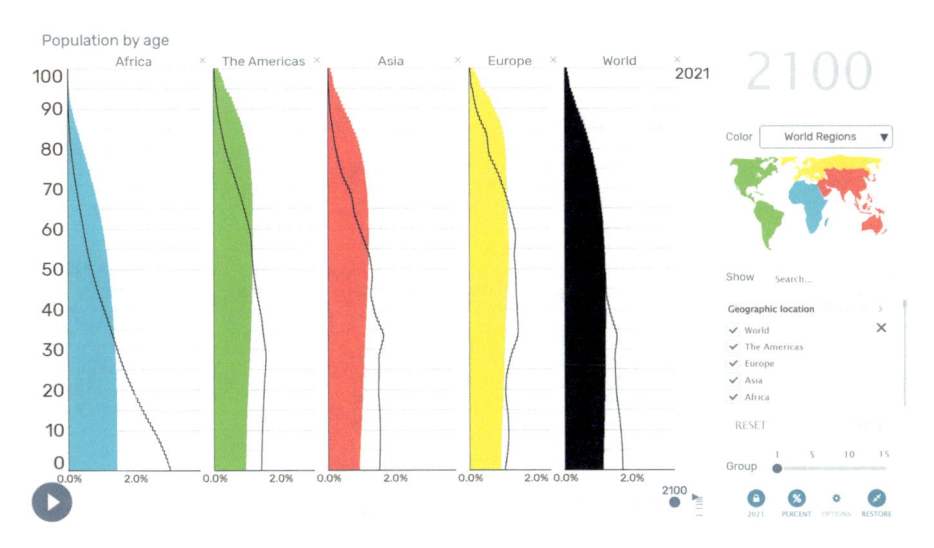

Fig. 8.1 Gapminder ages: populations' age distribution in different world regions, in 2020, represented by the black line, and projected to 2100 (colored graph). Showing a free visualization from Gapminder.org, CC-by license

countries but also the absolute value of their data, represented by the length of the relevant stack. This tool also contains a timeline, which gives an opportunity to compare rank orders between different years.

- **Income Mountain** shows the distribution of people by income in different countries, regions, and at the world level. With the help of the timeline, changes in the distributions can be animated.
- **Ages** is illustrated in Fig. 8.1. It can show the age-distribution of selected countries, or groups in different years, which gives the opportunity to compare distributions of groups, or temporal changes of the age-structures. A forecast for the future until 2100 is built into this tool. The horizontal axis can present either raw frequencies or relative frequencies of the different age groups. It is possible to lock a pyramid of a year, which is represented by a black line as a reference line, and compare the different years' age distributions to the reference year.
- **Dollar Street** is a rather different sort of visualization. It is based on a large collection of photographs in different countries of the domestic circumstances of families at different levels of wealth. Users can see the tools used for cleaning teeth, or sleeping accommodation, or toilet facilities for people at different income levels around the world. Hence, the pictures are not exact statistical data, but rather are illustrations of living conditions worldwide at different wealth levels. The measurement of wealth levels is available in FAQ on the Dollar Street website. This tool is based on a non-representative sample of images but can be used to stimulate student discussions about poverty, relative poverty, and the transitions most likely to move people out of poverty.

There is also a facility for using Gapminder offline. This enables not only the use of Gapminder without the Internet, but it also offers the opportunity to use Bubble Charts, Lines and Ranks with our own data. It is possible to import data in .xls and .

Step 2: Choose how your data is arranged:

○ Time goes down

Column 1: entities, Column 2: time values, Column 3 and on: indicators (see example)

	A	B	C	D	E	F	G	H
1	Country	Year	Region	Population	Child mortality	Child Survival	GDP per capita	Gini
2	Afghanistan	1800	Asia	3280000	468.58	531.42	603	30.51
3	Albania	1800	Europe	410445	375.2	624.8	667	41.24
4	Algeria	1800	Africa	2503218	460.21	539.79	716	57.71
5	Angola	1800	Africa	1567028	485.68	514.32	618	48.93
6	Antigua and Barbuda	1800	America	37000	473.6	526.4	757	40
7	Argentina	1800	America	534000	402.19	597.81	1507	47.1
8	Armenia	1800	Europe	413326	371.2	628.8	514	29.12
9	Australia	1800	Asia	351014	390.99	609.01	815	41.31
10	Austria	1800	Europe	3205587	387.32	612.68	1848	53.35
11	Azerbaijan	1800	Europe	879960	384	616	775	40
12	Bahamas	1800	America	27350	471.04	528.96	1445	40
13	Bahrain	1800	Asia	64474	439.79	560.21	1235	40
14	Bangladesh	1800	Asia	19227358	507.88	492.12	876	41.83
15	Barbados	1800	America	81729	469.76	530.24	913	40
16	Belarus	1800	Europe	2355081	365.67	634.33	608	57.85
17	Belgium	1800	Europe	3138137	322.4	677.6	2412	62.44
18	Belize	1800	America	25526	467.2	532.8	579	40
19	Benin	1800	Africa	636559	430.46	569.54	597	47.95
20	Bhutan	1800	Asia	89989	463.36	536.64	629	40
21	Bolivia	1800	America	1100000	404.69	595.31	854	40

○ Time goes right

Column 1: entities, Column 2: indicators, Column 3 and on: time values (see example)

	A	B	C	D	E	F	G	H	I	J	K
1	country	indicator	2005	2006	2007	2008	2009	2010	2011	2012	2013
2	United States	CO2 emissions (metric tor	19.61	19.12	19.24	18.49	17.19	17.48	17.02	16.29	16.39
3	Uzbekistan	CO2 emissions (metric tor	4.31	4.36	4.30	4.36	3.86	3.65	3.87	3.89	3.41
4	St. Vincent and the	CO2 emissions (metric tor	2.02	2.02	2.08	2.08	2.85	2.01	1.81	2.31	1.91
5	Vietnam	CO2 emissions (metric tor	1.19	1.23	1.25	1.39	1.57	1.69	1.84	1.78	1.70
6	West Bank and Ga	CO2 emissions (metric tor	0.83	0.67	0.67	0.57	0.56	0.53	0.57	0.54	0.58
7	World	CO2 emissions (metric tor	4.52	4.62	4.66	4.74	4.63	4.84	4.98	5.00	5.00
8	Samoa	CO2 emissions (metric tor	0.94	0.97	1.03	1.04	1.07	1.10	1.25	1.34	1.25
9	Yemen	CO2 emissions (metric tor	0.98	0.99	0.97	1.00	1.07	0.99	0.81	0.74	0.99
10	South Africa	CO2 emissions (metric tor	8.82	9.35	9.62	10.09	10.06	9.34	9.22	9.02	8.86
11	Congo	CO2 emissions (metric tor	0.03	0.03	0.03	0.03	0.03	0.03	0.04	0.04	0.04
12	Zambia	CO2 emissions (metric tor	0.19	0.17	0.14	0.17	0.19	0.19	0.20	0.24	0.25
13	United States	Renewable energy consur	1.86	1.93	1.35	2.32	2.21	2.64	2.24	2.37	
14	Uzbekistan	Renewable energy consur	5.81	5.59	5.45	5.34	5.36	5.24	5.13		
15	St. Vincent and the	Renewable energy consur	13.69	12.52	14.45	15.70	12.32	12.68	10.32	12.36	11.20
16	Vietnam	Renewable energy consur	67.52	73.40	43.56	47.35	39.68	39.14	34.18		
17	West Bank and Ga	Renewable energy consur	17.04	17.12	17.08	17.34	17.97	17.78	17.87	18.12	
18	World	Renewable energy consur	29.62	29.20	28.88	27.66	26.14	26.46	23.15		
19	Samoa	Renewable energy consur	0.91	0.89	0.93	0.89	0.86	0.86	0.84	0.99	1.00
20	Yemen	Renewable energy consur	17.00	15.92	16.29	16.65	16.88	17.11	16.93		
21	South Africa	Renewable energy consur	97.88	97.42	97.34	97.19	96.98	97.04	96.84	96.26	95.96

Fig. 8.2 Importable data structures to Gapminder. Based on free material from Gapminder.org, CC-by license

csv formats as well. Data can be arranged in two ways. In one structure time goes down and in the other time goes right. In the import window, several examples are available on how to handle data structures, use the correct forms of time values, etc. (Fig. 8.2). Results can be saved or exported—for instance as a picture.

group	indicator	2010	2011	2012	2013	2014	2015	2016	2017	2018	2019
Employed	At-risk-of-poverty rate, %	6,2	5,7	7	6,7	9,3	9,6	10,2	8,4	8,4	7,8
Unemployed	At-risk-of-poverty rate, %	47,1	49,6	53,2	54	54,4	48,5	51	53,6	55,9	45,1
Pensioner	At-risk-of-poverty rate, %	4,6	5,5	5,6	4,5	5	7,1	9,1	10	10,9	14,3
Other inactive	At-risk-of-poverty rate, %	22	22,6	23,3	23,6	24,5	23,5	19,5	19,6	21,2	21,7

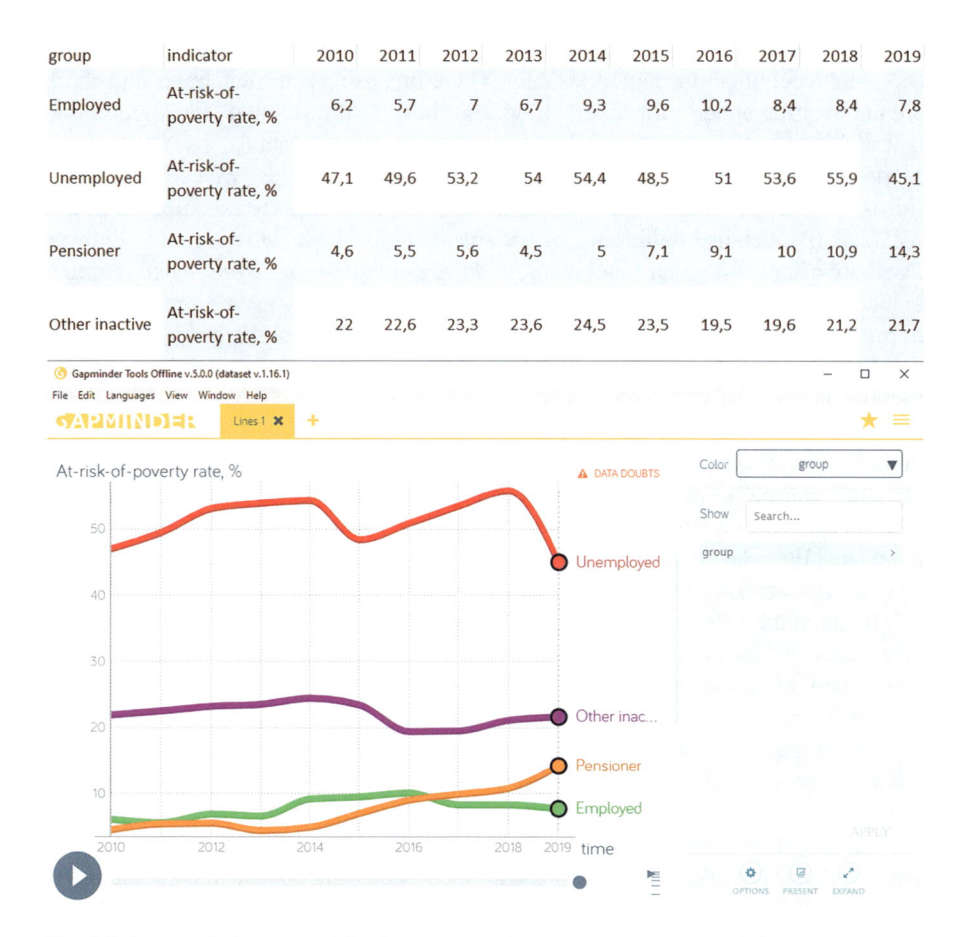

Fig. 8.3 Imported data on at-risk-of-poverty rate by the most frequent activity. Based on free material from Gapminder.org, CC-by license

The Gapminder offline tool also can visualize group data also without geo data. For instance, Fig. 8.3 shows the data structure (yearly data) and the graphical representation of the Hungarian at-risk-of-poverty rate values (half-yearly) amongst the most frequent activity groups between 2010 and 2019.

Why Is It Worth Using Gapminder?

Official statistical databases and associated visualizations, and Gapminder have different advantages and disadvantages. We recommended using them together (see for example in Chap. 10). From the point of view of teaching, we must consider the needs of students when we use databases. Based on generation theories in education (Eckleberry-Hunt & Tucciarone, 2011; Reilly, 2012), people in the same generation have common characteristics from the point of view of expectations of teaching and learning (e.g., in relation to electronic devices, and the importance of team working). Our students are members of Generations Y, Z or Alpha (Ramadlani & Wibisono, 2017). Common traits of these generations are that during lessons these young people have a need for technology, team working, dealing with entertaining tasks and receiving information visually. Therefore, using static databases and charts are not exciting enough for them—however, those "old fashioned" tools are important and necessary parts of teaching, collecting, and using data.

If we take into account some databases (see more in Chap. 6), we can say that the Eurostat Database[2] includes a wide range of indicators; data are downloadable, and metadata (i.e. detailed definitions of variables) are available. However, the Eurostat Database offers only graphs and maps, and there are no dynamic (animated) features embedded in these graphs and maps. This lack of interactivity makes it more difficult to provide enjoyable tasks for students. (As noted earlier, if we download data from those databases, then we can embed them into other interactive tools; however, this requires more steps.)

A different part of the Eurostat website hosts the Visualization Tools section.[3] It includes some spectacular and dynamic elements (such as "You in the EU" or "Quality of Life"); therefore, they are more attractive and enjoyable for students. Most of the visualization tools include the source of data (which directs the visitor to the related Eurostat Database). However, the number of available indicators included in visualizations is modest compared to the Eurostat Databases.

OECD.Stats[4] offers a wide range of downloadable indicators with directly available metadata. However, OECD.Stats offers only graphs, and its dynamic feature shows only temporal changes.

A different part of the OECD website contains the Data Visualization Lab[5] that includes dynamic charts. We can access downloadable data and metadata via more clicks (there is no direct option for downloading data or reading data); however, the number of available data sets is modest compared to OECD.Stats.

Gapminder is a spectacular dynamic visualization tool, and it is easy to find delightful and stimulating tasks for students. It is possible to download data and to access the definitions of the indicators. There is only one drawback: the number of available indicators is modest compared to Eurostat Databases or to OECD.Stats. Table 8.1 offers a comparison of the databases discussed so far.

Based on the comparison of positive and negative features of the databases examined, it may be concluded that Gapminder has the greatest potential from the point of view of teaching Generation Y, Z or Alpha. There are good reasons to make use of other databases (e.g., Eurostat Database, OECD.Stat) as well; however, the usage of Gapminder can make lectures particularly engaging and entertaining for students. Summarizing the main advantages of using Gapminder in classes we can mention the following:

- Gapminder is a free, browser-based, open-source web application.
- Gapminder was designed to be accessible to non-technical audiences; it has a user-friendly interface.

---

[2]https://ec.europa.eu/eurostat/data/database

[3]https://ec.europa.eu/eurostat/help/first-visit/tools

[4]https://stats.oecd.org/

[5]https://www.oecd.org/dac/financing-sustainable-development/datavisualisations/

Table 8.1 Comparison of statistical databases (after Kazár, 2016)

Database		Potential for downloading data	Number of available indicators	Availability of metadata	Potential for enjoyable tasks	Potential for applying visualization tools
Eurostat	Database (Database and tables by themes)	Yes	Wide	Yes	Lower	Only graphs and maps
	Visualization tools (e.g. You in the EU, Quality of life)	Yes	Narrower	Through Eurostat Database	Higher	Some, dynamic; less options
OECD	OECD.Stat	Yes	Wide	Yes	Lower	Only graphs
	OECD Data Visualization Lab	Not directly	Narrower	Not directly	Higher	Dynamic; few options
Gapminder		Yes	Narrower	Yes	Higher	Dynamic; more options

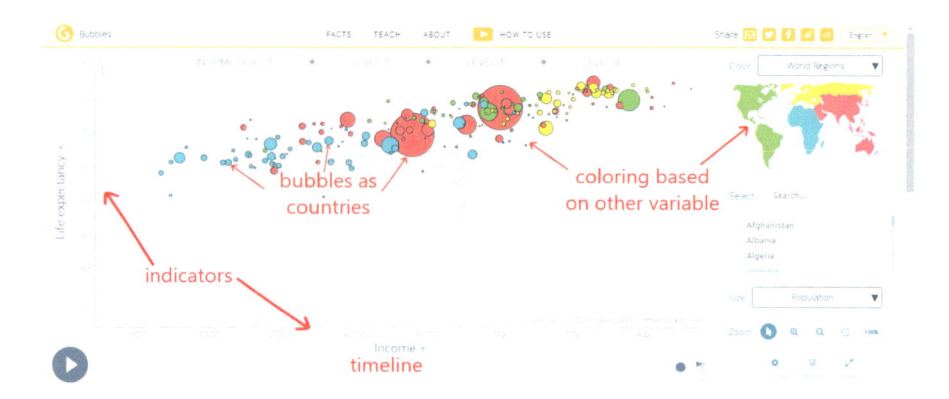

Fig. 8.4 Displaying multiple dimensions on the Bubble Chart. Showing a free vizualization from Gapminder.org, CC-by license

- It is obviously 'educational', and its dynamic visualizations (often revealing spectacular counter-intuitive insights) are very attractive to students with high expectations of the properties of visual displays.
- It is easy to use for students with no background in statistical analysis, and encourages questioning, investigation, and exploration of statistical concepts.
- The data sets are downloadable for further analysis.
- There is an option for importing data in the offline version.

There are, however, some disadvantages:

- Gapminder is limited in terms of the kinds of graphical representations and analyses it offers compared to commercial statistical software packages; however, the restricted menu avoids students being overwhelmed with choices between options they do not understand.
- Gapminder presents a narrower range of indicators than (say) Eurostat or OECD.
- It is not possible to download the visualizations created as video files.

8.3   The Gapminder Bubble Chart in Action

This section introduces the use of the Gapminder Bubble Chart in class. The Bubble Chart is a dynamic visualization tool that can be used when we want to visualize temporal changes in relationships between two variables (indicators) country by country (Fig. 8.4).

How Might the Gapminder Bubble Chart Be Used in Teaching?
From the point of view of teaching, we can use the Bubble Chart for a variety of purposes:

- Visualizing a wide variety of relationships: Gapminder has a long list of indicators on several themes. If we discuss a topic (e.g. social, economic or environmental issues) in a lesson, we can visualize some selected indicators in a spectacular way (e.g. for examining *poverty*, we can visualize and describe the relationship between the *income per capita* and *life expectancy*).
- Visualizing correlation: if we want to make the concept of bivariate correlation or regression more understandable for the students, a scatter plot is a useful tool. However, the Gapminder Bubble Chart is much more than a simple scatter plot; it presents a great deal of data in an accessible way. Instead of a simple scatter of same-size, monochrome dots, there are bubbles with different sizes (here representing population) and colors (indicating region). Temporal changes can be explored using the sliding timeline. If we consider a Civic Statistics topic (e.g. *poverty*), we can visualize a positive correlation between the *income per capita* (log) and *life expectancy*; moreover we can see how this relationship has changed over time.
- Making comparisons: in Fig. 8.4 the bubbles represent countries, so it is possible to make territorial comparisons with the help of a Bubble Chart. There is a color option that helps us to make comparisons among world regions as well as between individual countries. For instance, on the topic of *poverty*, we can highlight that the *income per capita* was lower in African countries than in European countries in 2018.
- Comparing groups: again, with the help of color option mentioned above it is possible to create groups based on other grouping variables (e.g. religion or OECD membership). If we highlight the topic of *poverty* again, we can see that in OECD countries the *income per capita* and *life expectancy* were also higher in 2018 than in the rest of the countries.

Configuring the Gapminder Bubble Chart
There are built-in visualizations (e.g. Wealth and Health of Nations) in the Bubble Chart; however, users can change all the main options when creating the content of the visualization:

- Axes: users can select two indicators, one for the horizontal and one for the vertical axes. The indicators are grouped in topics and subtopics, but they are also listed in the Data menu. It is possible to display the selected indicator on a logarithmic scale (a log scale can make it easier to see trends, and a log scale expands the scale at low values and compresses the scale at high values. Students need to be careful to read the scales of variables that are displayed. To illustrate: the opening visualization (Wealth and Health of Nations) displays income on a log scale—this can be seen (and changed) when one clicks on the indicator (Fig. 8.5).
- Size of bubbles: each bubble represents a country, and the size of a bubble shows the size of the population of the country as a default setting. However, it is possible to represent other indicators using the size of the bubble; or using no indicators (i.e making each bubble the same size).

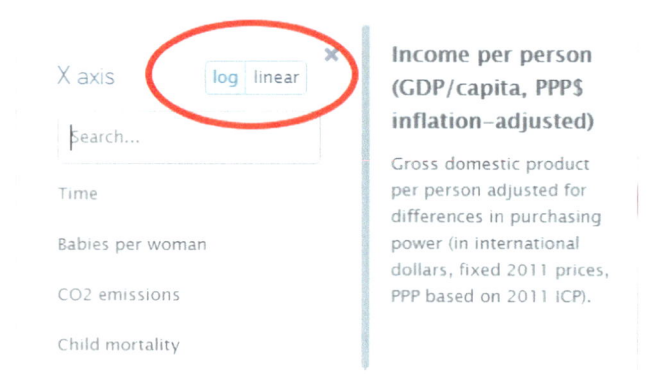

Fig. 8.5 Rescaling the *x*-axis. Based on free material from Gapminder.org, CC-by license

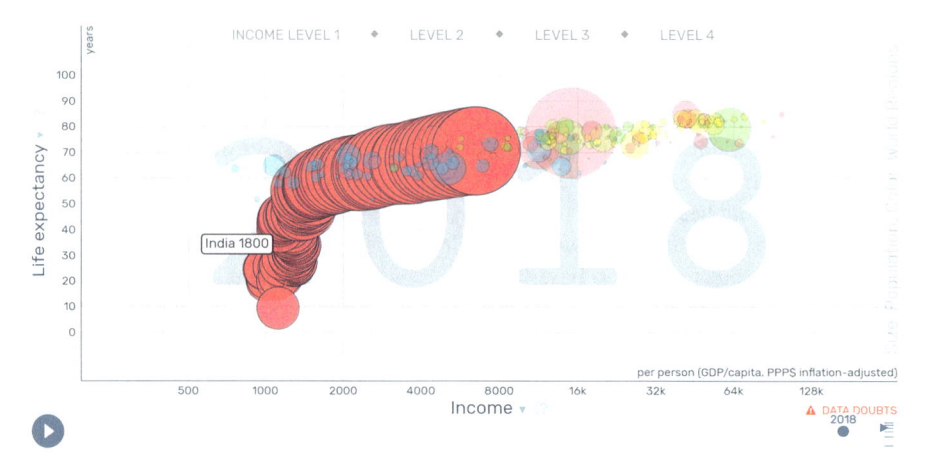

Fig. 8.6 Tracing the trajectory of a country over time. Showing a free vizualization from Gapminder.org, CC-by license

- Color of bubbles: users can select the color based on several grouping variables (e.g. country properties such as *region*, *landlocked*, *G77 and OECD countries*, *income*, or *main religion*) or based on some other metric indicator (also listed in topics). It is also possible to use no coloring in the visualization.
- Selecting a country: users can select one or just a few countries in a visualization. Selecting the *trail* button causes Gapminder to draw the path of the selected country over time (see Fig. 8.6).
- Time: can show the temporal change of the selected indicators. One can set the speed of visualization; and can pause the visualization at any time (e.g., when it shows outliers or sharp increases/decreases); one can pause the display in class and ask students to make forecasts.

Besides the content, there are other options connected to the appearance of the visualization. The opacity of the bubbles, the size of labels, the look of visualization and the position of the options menu can all be set. One can zoom in and zoom out, use a presentation mode (which enlarges the labels), or expand the visualization to full screen.

Besides the options available on the Bubble chart, it is worth mentioning other options in Gapminder that are connected to the usage of any visualization tools in Gapminder:

- Data: there are two main reasons why the data menu is important. First, metadata for each indicator are available. Gapminder uses other databases (e.g. OECD data), so we can find the source of the indicator in the data menu, as well. In addition, we can download data from this menu. This is important if we want to do further calculations or analysis with data visualized in Gapminder.
- Offline usage: it is possible to use Gapminder offline; versions can be downloaded for Windows, for Mac and for Linux. Using the offline version, students can use Gapminder without an internet connection.
- The offline version can also be used for visualizing your own data sets.
- Tutorial videos are available explaining the usage, and for the data structure specification.[6]
- Sharing charts: to show a visualization you have created, you can create a link and share it via several platforms (e.g. Facebook, Twitter, e-mail); or the link can be embedded into a presentation.

How Can I Use the Gapminder Bubble Chart in My Teaching?
Several teaching resources (e.g. videos, lesson plans, quizzes, answers, presentations) can be found on the Gapminder Website. Examples of how we have used Gapminder in our undergraduate classes can be found in ProCivicStat lesson plans via the CivicStatMap[7] (see more description about CivicStatMap in Chap. 6). These lesson plans set out tasks for students, and detailed plans for teachers (which include additional information such as some background to the theme is discussed, what statistical topics are included, level of the lesson plan, prerequisite knowledge, and possible answers). We have used these tasks with both BA and Master level students in the University of Szeged Faculty of Economics and Business Administration since 2017. In the following, we share some experiences concerning the applications of parts of the lesson plans.

Application 1
The lesson plan called **"Introduction to the usage of Gapminder—Level 1"** shows how the Gapminder Bubble Chart works via a built-in visualization. With the help of the questions and tasks of this lesson plan, students learn the functions of the Bubble Chart. This lesson plan is valuable if we want to explore or introduce how

---

[6]https://vizabi.org/tutorials/2017/04/03/show-your-data/
[7]https://rstudio.up.pt/shiny/users/pcs/CivicStatMap_English/

Gapminder works; therefore, the usage of it is important when students use Gapminder for the first time. In the frame of required preliminary knowledge, it is worth ensuring that students know about different chart types (e.g. line charts, bar charts) and about different functions (e.g. linear and log functions). You can access the lesson plan with sample activities solutions via CivicStatMap here.[8]

We introduced these tasks with a variety of undergraduate students (BA level) in the University of Szeged Faculty of Economics and Business Administration as part of an introductory statistics course in 2017. The topic of the given class was the use of official statistical databases. We wanted to collect their first impressions and experiences; therefore, we surveyed the students' opinions about the class via open-ended questions (and collected qualitative data). Based on our experiences and the students' opinions about the application, we can highlight the following:

- It was difficult for the students to answer questions because they found it hard to interpret what they saw. With the help of some additional questions (e.g. "What are the axes?"; "What do the bubbles indicate?"), students were able to better understand the meaning of the visualization. (See more detailed questions in the teacher version of the lesson plan here.[9]
- If students are not familiar with the usage of Gapminder, it is difficult for them to understand how the platform works (technical details) and to understand the message from the specific topic (content) together. It is important to understand how to handle the platform (which highlights the importance of this lesson plan), then they can focus on the message of the applied topic.
- In conventional classes, it can be difficult to grab a student's attention; however, during the Gapminder application they paid great attention to the tasks. Moreover, students said they liked the application and in particular the dynamic visualization tools in Gapminder.
- Based on our experiences, Gapminder works very well in class. However, BA students needed some extra questions and discussions to understand the meaning of the visualization; open-ended questions were too challenging at the outset.

Application 2
The lesson plan (Application 1) described above focused on technical aspects of the Bubble Chart. However, another lesson plan (called **Examining poverty and income inequalities with the help of Gapminder—Level 2**[10] shows how to use Bubble Chart to examine a specific topic and how to explore specific statistical methods (e.g. correlation or log transformation) via visualization. In terms of prerequisite knowledge for this lesson plan, it is worth having information about:

---

[8] https://rstudio.up.pt/shiny/users/pcs/civicstatmap/5.301_TV_gapminder_level1_EN.pdf

[9] https://rstudio.up.pt/shiny/users/pcs/civicstatmap/5.301_TV_gapminder_level1_EN.pdf

[10] https://rstudio.up.pt/shiny/users/pcs/civicstatmap/5.302_TV_gapminder_level2_poverty_EN.pdf

- the usage of the Gapminder Bubble Chart (see Application 1).
- poverty and income inequality indicators.
- log/linear transformations, the coefficient of correlation.

Sample activities of this lesson plan can be seen below:

Introduction

Watch the Wealth and Health of Nations in Gapminder World and answer the following questions!

1. *What is being explored in this display? (What are the indicators?)*
2. *What can you state about the changes in time?*
3. *Are there any regional differences? Which countries are rich?*
4. *Are big (large population) countries rich?*
5. *What is the relation between life expectancy and income per person?*

(Students can answer these questions by making presentations, or they can have an oral discussion about the questions; you can collect ideas for other sorts of assessment tasks from Chaps. 14–16).

Examine the relationship between extreme poverty (economy—poverty—ratio of people below 3.20$ a day) and food supply (health—nutrition)!

6. *What can you see in the visualization? Create an analysis in a few sentences!*
7. *Use the urban poverty indicator instead of (% urban people below national urban poverty line) instead of extreme poverty (ratio of people below 3.20$ a day)! What can you state about India's position in 2000 compared to Task 6)?*

We have used these tasks with Master level students in the University of Szeged Faculty of Economics and Business Administration since 2018, in the context of a multivariate statistics course. The topic of the given lesson was correlation and regression analysis; and the aim of this lesson was to understand the concepts of correlation and regression analysis by using them for analyzing indicators from the topic of *poverty*. As a sample activity from this lesson, we watched the visualization called "Wealth and Health of Nations" in Gapminder, and addressed Task 1–4 above (as "warming up" questions). Then Task 5 (What is the relation between life expectancy and income per person?) to explore the concept of correlation; and we discussed the situation from 2020 (see Fig. 8.7).

There is a positive linear relationship between *life expectancy* and the *(log) income per capita* (there is a nonlinear relationship between *life expectancy* and *income per capita*; the *income per capita* is expressed in a log scale in Gapminder as a default setting). This is true over time; however the relationship seemed to be stronger sometimes (e.g. in 2020). If a country has higher *(log) income per capita*, there is higher *life expectancy* (and vice versa).

You can access the entire list of tasks with solutions via CivicStatMap.[11]

---

[11] https://rstudio.up.pt/shiny/users/pcs/civicstatmap/5.302_TV_gapminder_level2_poverty_EN.pdf

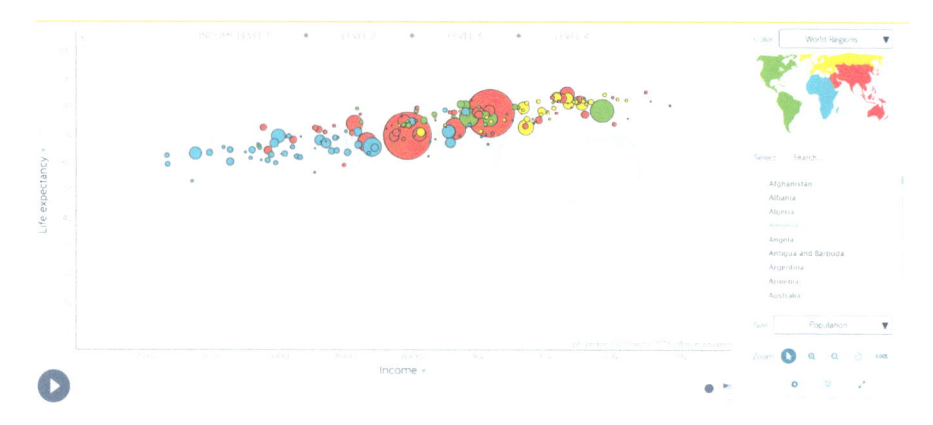

Fig. 8.7 Visualizing positive correlation in Gapminder. Showing a free vizualization from Gapminder.org, CC-by license

With the help of the questions and tasks of this lesson plan, students gained knowledge via:

- Understanding statistical concepts (e.g. correlation, log transformation) better with the help of poverty indicators.
- Understanding *poverty* better by getting to know the situation of several countries via the visualizations (e.g. Task 3, Task 4, Task 6).
- Understanding that *poverty* is a multi-dimensional concept. Students use several indicators (e.g. *income per person*, *extreme poverty*, or *urban poverty*) during the tasks for describing poverty; and poverty can show different pictures depending on the selected indicators. Therefore, students can see that there is no "one and the best" indicator for describing poverty. Students need to realize that they have to describe poverty using a variety of indicators if they are to have a better picture of (or a more nuanced approach to) the concept.

We wanted to collect the students' first impressions and experiences; therefore, we interviewed the students' after the class in open ended questions (and also collected qualitative data). Based on our experiences and the students' opinions about the application, we can highlight the following:

- Initially, students required time to recognize what they see; however, it was easier for them (MA students) to understand what they saw than BA students. We needed fewer additional questions to facilitate understanding around the meaning of the visualization.
- Students were able to recognize the positive correlation between some variables; however, they needed some explanation of possible problems interpreting the visualization because the *GDP/capita* in the "Wealth and Health" visualization is shown on a log scale.
- Similar to BA students, MA students also liked using Gapminder; this visualization tool was able to grab their attention.

- Based on our experiences, Gapminder helped students to visualize correlation and regression. However, MA students also needed some probing questions to encourage them to explore all of the options of menus in Gapminder.

Summarizing all of our experiences of using the Gapminder Bubble Chart, we note that Gapminder is a useful tool to grab students' attention; and it can help to understand and visualize statistical methods (e.g. correlation and regression) better. However, students watching the Gapminder Bubble Chart for the first time can find it difficult to understand what they see. However, if sufficient time is allocated for introducing the Bubble Chart, this problem is easily overcome.

Bubble charts can only visualize relationships between variables. If more analysis is needed, for instance, via regression models, or calculating correlations between variables, we need to combine Gapminder with other software, for instance with Excel. An example of this is the analysis of the relationship between *income* and *life expectancy*. To conduct appropriate analyses, we need to download the data from Gapminder. Data tables can be downloaded from the Facts/Data menu, which is situated under the Facts menu, or by clicking on the question mark on either axis. This gives access to details such as the source of the data and about the used indicator. The original value of the indicator can be downloaded independently of the fact that a linear or logarithmic axis is used in the visualisation. After downloading the data, we have separate Excel files for the different variables. To analyze the relationship, it is required to merge the tables. We must pay attention to this step. Different tables do not contain each country or territory, so the number of rows can be different in the case of the different tables even though the data structures are the same.

After preparing a merged Excel file we can examine the original questions. We suggest preparing a Scatter plot in Excel and selecting and fitting a regression curve on the data and showing the model equation and the predictive power of the model with the help of the fit via a trendline option (Fig. 8.8).

Throughout the book we have emphasised the importance of showing and discussing nonlinear relations on societal issues (see more in Chap. 4). With this example we can describe the nonlinear relationship between the variables. The logarithmic model has the best fit to the data ($R^2 = 0.7034$); the correlation index (square root of R^2) is 0.84 so shows a strong relationship between *life expectancy* and *income/capita*. This exercise also can show that the linear model has lower predictive power ($R^2 = 0.4655$).

As an interesting supplement, this application can highlight dangers encountered when interpreting visualizations. If we ask which country had the largest GDP/capita in 2020, the answer is Qatar according to the Excel sheet. But, if we use the online Bubble Chart tool, the answer could be Luxemburg (Fig. 8.7). The correct answer is Qatar. The basis of this misperception is that, when variables are selected in Gapminder, we think that we can see all the countries, but this is definitely not true. In this example the visible part of axis X does not show the maximum value of the variable. If we modify the zoom to 100%, the data of Qatar will be perceptible on the chart.

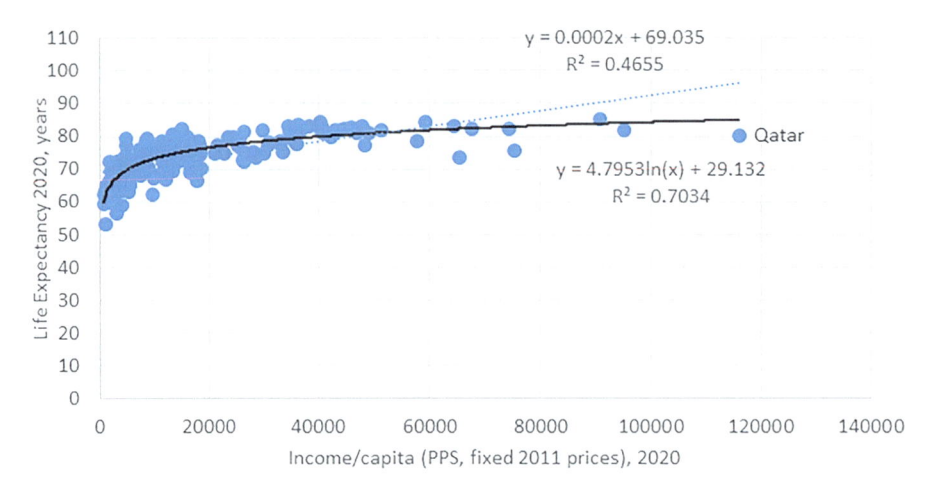

Fig. 8.8 Additional regression analysis to Gapminder in Excel. Based on free material from Gapminder.org, CC-by license

8.4 Other Gapminder Tools in Action: Ageing Society

The Ageing Society is a societal challenge with social and economic impacts in the developed world. There are several online visualization tools, population pyramids, and datasets that can be used to explore aging societies from a statistical perspective, for instance via population pyramids, census data, and the websites of National Statistical Agencies. These resources are used in the ProCivicStat Ageing Society module.[12] The first part of this module concentrates on the definition of age distributions, and the interpretation of population pyramids with the help of visualization tools. The second part focuses on the challenges of an ageing society *per se*. The exploration of ageing societies can start with a warm up question, for instance, *which country has the oldest population?* We think that asking this question as a starting point, is in line with the Gapminder's logic: firstly, we collect information on how students view this phenomenon, and explore any misconceptions that emerge.

After that in a group discussion, we can focus on what the term 'ageing society' means, exploring the likely causes, and consequences. We need indicators to analyze the ageing of a society, so we need to understand how official statistics can measure and examine the ageing society. We can focus on different indicators such as the *Old age dependency ratio*, the *Ageing index*, the *Growth rate of population*, the *Median age*, the *ratio of elderly people, population growth, fertility rate, mortality rate, life expectancy*, etc. For instance, the old age dependency ratio compares the number of elderly people (aged 65 and over) to the number of people of working age (15–64 years old). The *ageing index* is the ratio of the *number of elderly people (65–X years)* and the *child population (0–14 years)*.

---

[12] https://rstudio.up.pt/shiny/users/pcs/civicstatmap/5.303_TV_AgeingSociety_EN.pdf

After the discussion phase, we suggest turning to statistical databases and visualization tools to analyze the phenomenon. Ageing is a process, so we need time series or data from different years to describe this phenomenon, and understand what data are showing. The selection of the data source and visualization tools is based on our goals. We also can use National Statistical Agencies' websites and reports if we want to analyze national data only, without Gapminder. We suggest starting at the national level and compare different years. For instance, asking students to collect data to calculate the *ageing index*, and *old age dependency ratio* for: the most recent year for which data are available; 50 years ago; and in projections for 2100; It means data collection, calculation and interpretation of ratios and visualisation via population pyramids. With the help of this exercise, we can estimate (for instance) how big is the proportion of elderly people whose needs have to be supported by economically active people in 50 years time. Based on this result we can provoke newer questions. What kind of social and economic challenges does this result lead to?— for instance, challenges in the labour market, the sustainability of pension- and health care systems. What kind of political decisions should we make to solve these issues, to stop the ageing trend, etc.

In the next phase, if we want to do international comparisons or international forecasts, we can use (for instance) online population pyramids or international data sources. Gapminder also can be used to analyze ageing patterns in different countries over time; Fig. 8.9 provides some illustrative visualizations and can answer the warmup question if we analyze it based on the *old age dependency ratio*. Students can be set a variety of interesting challenges, for instance:

1. Analyze the order of countries by old age dependency ratio. Which countries occupy the first three places? What is the rank of your own country?
2. What was the order 50 years ago?
3. Visualize time series for the last 50 years in the case of the countries in the first three positions.
4. What answers can we give to the previous two questions if we analyze the ratio of population years 65 and above?
5. Compare your country's age distribution to the continent's age distribution.
6. Compare the different continents' age distributions to the world's age distribution.
7. How can you interpret your results?
8. What kind of thoughts are implied by the results?

We ask the students to document their work. They prepare different charts, which can illustrate answers to the questions with the help of these questions. They interpret and compare data and present their results orally. This activity can show the territorial differences and similarities in ageing and temporal changes in the values of the indicators. We can ask other questions about the phenomenon: is there any relationship between social and economic differences and differences in ageing? Or between temporal changes in ageing indicators and the changes in the social and economic situation?

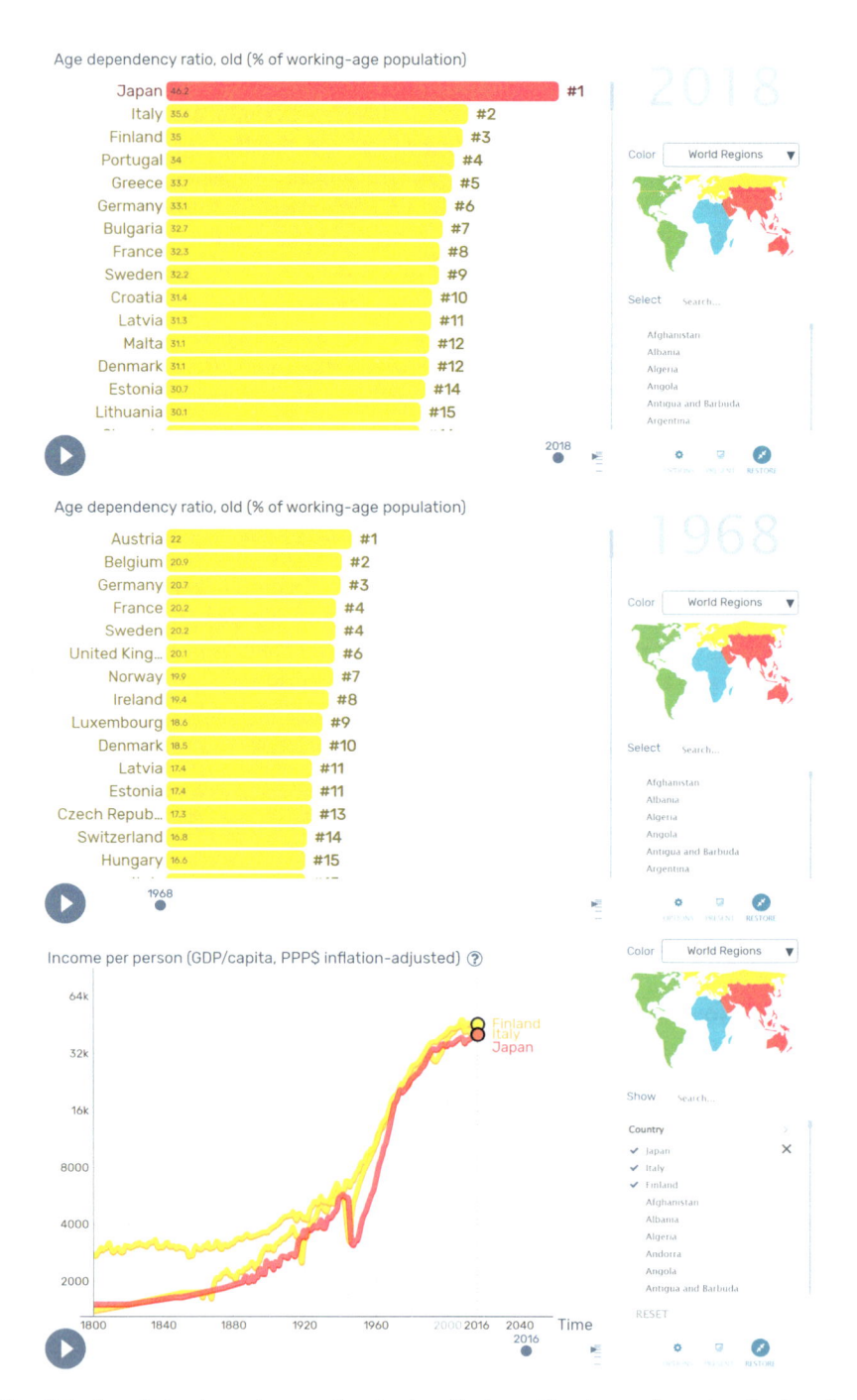

Fig. 8.9 Gapminder in action on the Ageing Society. Showing a free vizualization from Gapminder.org, CC-by license

Engaging in these activities should result in several important take-home messages for students from different points of view: data sources, definition and methodology associated with the indicators, interpretations, software functionalities, and the likely robustness of projection methodology. For example:

- Data sources do not necessarily have the indicators we might want, or the indicators can be found in different menus. For example, In Gapminder, the proportion of the population years 60 and above are available in the group of population indicators. Other indicators are situated in More data/wdi/Health/Population/Dynamics and More data/wdi/Health/Population/Structure groups. We must be careful about the indicators, and knowledgeable about sources of data. When we prepare a lesson plan, we suggest selecting indicators which we want to use in classes in advance, and after that, search for a visualization tool or database, which contains the selected indicator.
- 'The answer' can depend on the choice (and definition) of the indicator used. For example, if we compare the ranks by the different variables in the same year, Japan is situated in the first place in both cases in 2018, but we can see different orders for other countries.
- An improvement in the rankings does not necessarily mean that the underlying situation has improved. For instance, 50 years ago Hungary was situated in 15th place, improving to 21st place in 2018. So now more countries have a higher old-age dependency ratio than Hungary. Nevertheless, the Hungarian old-age dependency ratio increased from 16.6 to 28.8% during this period.
- The different charts allow us to see if something is a local or a global problem; here, it is clear that ageing is a problem across the developed world.
- The combination of different Gapminder tools can highlight different aspects of a complex phenomenon.
- Software tools have different merits, and students can develop an aesthetic for data visualization (here, it is clear that Gapminder is not a good choice if our purpose is to create a dynamic population pyramid).
- comparing distributions between groups is not a straightforward process (here we illustrated the use of relative frequencies).
- Modelling is a complex process. Different developers built population projections into their visualization tools, based on different models, and assumptions. It is essential to understand the models, and the assumptions being made. Comparing projections from different models (say for different countries) is deeply problematic and should be avoided.

8.5   Conclusion

Gapminder offers several visualization tools, which can help to visualize complex problems, trends, and relationships between variables from different points of view. These user-friendly apps are engaging for students and encourage exploration and problem-based learning. Gapminder has some limitations regarding the available data and tools available for statistical analysis. However, lessons with Gapminder provide a strong base for further statistical education and a springboard to other analytical and visualization tools, to which we can import Gapminder data and do more data analysis.

Gapminder can be used not only from primary school education to tertiary education, but also in the case of adult education to discover the World, to analyze social and economic problems with the help of data and visualization, and to develop statistical thinking and reasoning. The combined use of the different Gapminder applications for instance (Bubble chart and Ranks) can help to illustrate complex problems from different points of views.

References

Eckleberry-Hunt, J., & Tucciarone, J. (2011). The challenges and opportunities of teaching "generation Y". *Journal of Graduate Medical Education, 3*(4), 458–461.

Kazár, K. (2016). Using statistical datasets for describing poverty and income inequality. In J. Engel (Ed.), *Promoting understanding of statistics about society proceedings of the Roundtable conference of the International Association of Statistics Education (IASE)*. International Statistical Institute. http://iase-web.org/documents/papers/rt2016/Kazar.pdf

Ramadlani, A. K., & Wibisono, M. (2017). Visual literacy and character for alpha generation. In A. M. Al-Ma'youf et al. (Eds.), *Proceedings international seminar on language, education and culture* (pp. 1–7). University Press. Accessed October 26, 2019, from http://sastra.um.ac.id/wp-content/uploads/2017/12/0-cover-depan.pdf

Reilly, P. (2012). Understanding and teaching generation Y. *English Teaching Forum, 50*(1), 2–11.

Chapter 9
Data Visualization Packages for Non-inferential Civic Statistics in High School Classrooms

Daniel Frischemeier (iD), **Susanne Podworny** (iD), **and Rolf Biehler** (iD)

Abstract For a decent exploration of Civic Statistics data, the use of digital data analysis tools is essential. Digital tools enable learners and teachers to analyze large and multivariate data sets and to explore them with regard to statistical investigative questions and to look and search for patterns in the data. However, the range of digital data analysis tools is large, ranging from educational to professional data analysis tools. Whereas educational tools provide a low entrance hurdle, they are limited in their features for data analysis; professional tools offer a broad range of data analysis packages and methods but often require programming prerequisites. This chapter concentrates on educational data analysis tools and illustrates the application of tools like TinkerPlots, Fathom and CODAP in their capacity to visualize and explore Civic Statistics data—here a random sample of data from the American Community Survey.

Keywords Civic Statistics · Digital tools · American Community Survey · *TinkerPlots · Fathom · CODAP*

9.1 Introduction

Civic Statistics are statistics about health, migration, poverty, society, etc. and the availability of big and open data in these areas, and open publicly accessible data archives (by, e.g., National Statistics Offices, Eurostat, United Nations, World Bank or National Government Organizations), offers significant opportunities to advance learning, economic growth, public policy decision making and general social well-being, with profound implications for statistics education (see Cobb, 2015;

D. Frischemeier (✉)
University of Münster, Münster, Germany
e-mail: dafr@math.upb.de

S. Podworny · R. Biehler
Institute of Mathematics, Paderborn University, Paderborn, Germany
e-mail: podworny@math.upb.de; biehler@math.upb.de

© Springer Nature Switzerland AG 2022
J. Ridgway (ed.), *Statistics for Empowerment and Social Engagement*,
https://doi.org/10.1007/978-3-031-20748-8_9

Ridgway, 2016; Engel, 2017). The use of digital data analysis tools is essential for extracting information from these big and open data sets.

Over the last decades, a wide range of software tools and apps for statistics emerged. Most of them aim at professionals, for instance programs such as *Python*, *R*, *SAS*, or *SPSS* were developed for doing statistics (as opposed to learning statistics). These packages have a high entry hurdle and offer little support for learning processes (McNamara, 2015, p. 75). They often require deep knowledge of statistics as well as programming skills. Fortunately, user-friendly software tools for learning statistics have been developed too, addressing different user target groups, from primary school to tertiary level. An overview of different tools for data analysis from an educational perspective can be found in Biehler et al. (2013), Frischemeier et al. (2016) and Biehler (2019). Software that supports both the learning of statistics and the doing statistics on an elementary level are, for example, *Fathom, TinkerPlots, CODAP*, and *iNZight*.

The aim of this chapter is to illustrate and highlight the application of these different data analysis tools that were developed with a view towards education, notably *TinkerPlots*,[1] *Fathom*[2] and *CODAP*[3] in terms of their capacity to visualize and explore Civic Statistics data. The educational use of the software *iNZight*[4] is described in Chap. 10 of this book. The target groups we have in mind range from students in the early years of high school through to college and university students, and also the general public. We focus on *TinkerPlots, Fathom* and *CODAP* because our specific target group in this chapter is high school teachers and we want to provide them with tools which can be used for instruction and for supporting students' explorations and engagement with data in high school classrooms. We will point out advantages and limitations of these tools for civic statistical activities in the data exploration process, for instance, when analyzing relationships between variables and for visualizing high-dimensional data. Based on a dataset that we consider as typical for Civic Statistics data—a random subsample of participants from the 2013 American Community Survey (ACS) collected by the US Census Bureau—we illustrate *TinkerPlots, Fathom* and *CODAP* in action. Our main goal is to show the capacity to visualize and explore trends and patterns and relationships between variables such as age, education, sex, race and income from a descriptive point of view. We will concentrate on highlighting challenges and obstacles for learners on different levels when exploring these types of data with these software packages. We will focus on explorations of relationships between variables in the sample as they unfold.

---

[1] http://tinkerplots.com/

[2] https://Fathom.concord.org/

[3] https://CODAP.concord.org/

[4] https://www.stat.auckland.ac.nz/~wild/iNZight/

9.2   Requirements for Software for Learning About Civic Statistics

An overview and an early work on requirements for software tools for learning and doing statistics can be found in Biehler (1997). Biehler (1997) states that it is important that there is

- a low entry cost for learners to use a software tool
- a connection between the fields "data analysis", "simulation" and "probability theory"
- the opportunity to use different visualizations
- good interactivity

McNamara (2018) elaborated the analysis of statistical software tools from an educational and a professional perspective, distinguishing several key attributes such as accessibility, flexible plot creation, interactivity and easy entry for novice users. The key attributes identify features relevant for different software tools from a broader statistical perspective. But what about the affordances of statistical tools and activities for exploring Civic Statistics? Engel et al. (2016) identify ideas and fundamental activities for statistical issues involved in understanding civic data. From these ideas the following requirements can be extracted for exploring Civic Statistics data with software tools: comparing groups; investigating subgroups; exploring relationships between variables; multivariate thinking; and creating several types of diagrams. For instance, for group comparisons one could use stacked dotplots, boxplots and histograms. Furthermore, software should support the creation of new variables and also to switch between the disaggregation and the aggregation of data. These are features for exploratory and descriptive statistics.

TinkerPlots, Fathom and *CODAP* are easy-to-use tools that can be used to introduce the analysis of Civic Statistics data. These tools have—naturally—some restrictions compared to professional tools. For example there are limitations on the size of the datasets, and of course on functionality. But for teaching and learning purposes these tools also offer a broad list of advantages: no coding is required (apart from some simple formula editing in *Fathom* and *CODAP*), and for Civic Statistics purposes these software packages allow users to create standard statistical displays like bar graphs, stacked dot plots, box plots, histograms and scatter plots and to conduct data explorations by drag-and-drop. In addition, *TinkerPlots, Fathom* and *CODAP* offer multi-window displays; displays are dynamically linked and thus exploratory data analysis is supported. Furthermore, *CODAP* allows users to make sense of multi-level data and to switch between the disaggregation and the aggregation of data—essential when exploring Civic Statistics.

With the perspective on exploring Civic Statistics datasets with these tools in high school we want to concentrate on the exploration of relationships between two or more variables. Biehler et al. (2018) argue that three types of relationships can be explored when two variables are involved (for examples see also Konold et al., 1997).

- A relationship between two categorical variables (relevant to a question like "Are males or females more likely to have a driver's license?", Konold et al., 1997, p. 7).
- A relationship between one numerical and one categorical variable (relevant to a question like "Do those with a curfew tend to study more hours than those without a curfew?", Konold et al., 1997, p. 7).
- A relationship between two numerical variables (relevant to a question like "Is there a relation between hours spent watching TV and school grades?", Konold et al., 1997, p. 7).

These specific data exploration activities will lead us through our analysis and evaluation of the potential of the three different software tools (*TinkerPlots, Fathom, CODAP*) to explore Civic Statistics data.

9.3   *TinkerPlots, Fathom* and *CODAP* as Software for Learning About Civic Statistics

As educational software tools for learning and doing statistics, Biehler et al. (2013) illustrate the use of *TinkerPlots* as a tool for primary and secondary classrooms, and *Fathom* as a tool for secondary and tertiary classrooms. *TinkerPlots* is an educational software tool designed to develop the data competence of young learners. *TinkerPlots*

> is designed for creating many simulation models without the necessity of using symbolic input. In addition, *TinkerPlots* meets the third requirement of Biehler's (1997) framework by making students participate in the construction and evaluation of methods by providing a graph construction tool for young students who can invent their own elementary graphs, whereas most other tools provide only a readymade selection of standard graphs (Biehler et al., 2013, p. 658).

In *TinkerPlots,* the philosophy (Konold, 2007) is that data are stored in the form of data cards. Graphs can be created via the data operations *stack*, *separate* and *order* (which can also be done physically with data cards as hands-on activities). For a more detailed view on how to introduce learners to data analysis with *TinkerPlots,* and how to stepwise develop conventional graphs like bar graphs with data cards and *TinkerPlots,* see Frischemeier (2018). In addition to that, learners can also create conventional, ready-made displays like box plots or histograms.

As the "big sister" of *TinkerPlots, Fathom* is a data analysis and simulation package for learning and doing statistics at secondary and tertiary level. *Fathom* offers more formal methods especially for the exploration of the relationship between two variables and

> [*Fathom*] enables students to explore and analyze data both visually and computationally. It has a menu-driven and drag-and-drop computational environment with a general formula editor incorporated in a central place. [. . .] Its strengths are in the opportunities it provides students to:

- Quickly drag-and-drop variables into a graph to visualize distributions and relationships between variables;
- Through dragging, visualize how dynamically changing data and parameters affect related measures and representations in real time;
- Link multiple representations of data to informally observe statistical tendencies;
- Create simulations to investigate and test relationships in the data. (Biehler et al., 2013, p. 653)

As a further development, *CODAP* is a web-based and free of charge application which also allows learners to get a fast start in exploring multivariate data. Statistical graphs in *CODAP* can be created via a drag-and-drop function, so boxplots and stacked dotplots for visualizing the distribution of a numerical variable can be created by one or two single clicks. In addition to that *CODAP* allows users to aggregate and disaggregate the data; an example of how to make sense of multi-level data can be seen in Haldar et al. (2018).

Biehler (2019) used the key attributes for software specified by McNamara (2018) to summarize the features of *TinkerPlots, Fathom* and *CODAP*; his analysis is shown in Table 9.1.

Table 9.1 can be extended by the feature *availability*. *TinkerPlots* and *Fathom* are available for Windows™ and MAC™; *CODAP* is platform-independent because it is browser-based, but needs to be accessed online. According to the list in Table 9.1 all three software tools are appropriate for learning and doing statistics. Next, we illustrate the extent to which specific data exploration activities for analyzing Civic Statistics data can be realized with *TinkerPlots, CODAP* and *Fathom*.

9.4   The American Community Survey Dataset

For demonstrating how statistical explorations can be facilitated with different educational software tools at high school level, we will use the American Community Survey (ACS). Of course, the explorations we present can be carried out with any dataset similar to the structure of the ACS data. The ACS data is given in "rectangular" form—tidy data in the sense that every case is displayed as a row in a table. The ACS provides information on a yearly basis about the citizens of the United States. It collects information on citizenship, educational attainment, income, language proficiency, migration, disability, employment, and housing characteristics in the US. The ACS data are used by many public and private-sectors and the surveys are distributed to approximately 3.5 million addresses per year.[5] The survey includes 12 variables including age, marital status, education, sex, total earnings, Hispanic, race, worker type, employment status, SOCP (Standard Occupational Classification), hours worked per week and weeks worked per year. This is a good example of a Civic Statistics dataset. In our case, we will not work with the complete dataset, because this would overload the capacity of all the packages; rather,

---

[5] https://www.census.gov/programs-surveys/acs/about/information-guide.html

Table 9.1 Comparison of *TinkerPlots, Fathom* and *CODAP* with regard to specific key attributes taken from Biehler (2019, p. 7)

Key attributes	*TinkerPlots*	*Fathom*	*CODAP*
1. Accessibility	Free trial-version	Generally not free of charge except for the German version	Free of charge
2. Easy entry for novice users	Yes	Yes	Yes
3. Data as a first-order persistent object	Yes	Yes	Yes
4. Support for a cycle of exploratory and confirmatory analysis	Yes	Yes	Yes
5. Flexible plot creation	Yes	Yes	Yes
6. Support for randomization throughout	Yes	Yes	
7. Interactivity at every level	Yes	Yes	Yes
8. Inherent documentation	For formula editor	For formula editor	On website
9. Simple support for narrative, publishing, and reproducibility	Using text boxes for commenting	Using text boxes for commenting	Using text boxes for commenting: publishing interactive graphs and states of analysis on the web
10. Flexibility to build extensions	Interactive worksheets in a multiple linked window system	Interactive worksheets in a multiple linked window system	Only for expert programmers

TinkerPlots, Fathom and *CODAP* we will explore a sample of 3000 cases from the Californian ACS data set, to demonstrate the use, potential and challenges of using different tools when exploring Civic Statistics data. Specifically, we work with the ACS data downloaded from IPUMS (Integrated Public Use Microdata Series (Ruggles et al., 2019); the sample was generated with a *CODAP*-plug-in). All the records for the ACS California data (~30,000 cases) were retrieved. We then took a random sample of 3000 cases without replacement from this subset. This sample is used for demonstration purposes; and we will focus on the exploration of the data of the sample rather than going a step further and making inferences about the population. This of course could and should be a next step when exploring civic statistics data, but is not part of this chapter since we want to concentrate on the evaluation of the three data analysis tools on the level of descriptive data analysis. However, as the data are representative for the group of Californians in the ACS data, it allows to generate hypotheses and context-related interpretations in the sense of informal inferential reasoning (see Makar & Rubin, 2009).

We see the ACS data as a typical Civic Statistics dataset, because it provides data on topics such as *income* across different groups (e.g. disaggregated by sex, race, education, ...). For this sample of the ACS data we want to demonstrate how to carry out different types of explorations with regard to relationships between two variables (categorical and numeric, in different combinations) and how to explore relationships between more than two variables.[6]

9.5 Getting Started with the Exploration of ACS Data

In Table 9.2 we compare the software tools *TinkerPlots, Fathom* and *CODAP* with regard to different general characteristics to get an impression on the different features of the three tools. We address the following five issues. (1) Data Storage: How are the data stored in the software tool? (2) What sorts of data files can be imported in the software? (3) Which statistical displays does the tool offer to plot the distribution of a categorical variable? (4) Which statistical displays does the tool offer to plot the distribution of a numerical variable? (5) What is the maximum number of cases the software can handle, and still function smoothly?

Having a look at Table 9.2 we can say that the software tools *TinkerPlots, CODAP* and *Fathom* have most of the general characteristics (1)–(5) in common. They store the data in spreadsheet tables and allow users to import csv- and txt- data format; *CODAP* can also import GPS data.

Table 9.2 General characteristics of *TinkerPlots, Fathom* and *CODAP*

General characteristics	TinkerPlots	Fathom	CODAP
Data storage	Data cards Spreadsheet table	Spreadsheet table	Spreadsheet table
Import data	csv, txt, data from URLs	csv, txt, data from URLs	csv, txt, data from URLs, geographic data
Displays of distributions of categorical variables	Pie chart Bar graph	Bar graph Percentage graph	Bar graph
Displays of distributions of numerical variables	Stacked dotplot Histogram (with absolute frequencies) Boxplot	Stacked dotplot Histogram (with absolute and relative frequencies) Boxplot	Stacked dotplot Histogram Boxplot
Handling large datasets	Max. 50,000 cases	Max. 50,000 cases	Max. 5000 cases

---

[6]The sample of the Californian ACS dataset we use to illustrate the potential and the limitations of the tools *TinkerPlots, Fathom* and *CODAP* can be found here: https://iase-web.org/islp/pcs/

9.5.1 Storage of Data in **TinkerPlots, Fathom** and **CODAP**

In *TinkerPlots* the data are also represented in the form of data cards. Figure 9.1 shows a data card stack with data cards from the ACS sample; the card on top of this stack shows the data for a male aged 44 years. He has never been married, holds a bachelor's degree and has no TotalEarnings (TotalEarnings = 0) and is not a Hispanic (further values of the variable Hispanic are e.g. Bolivian, Mexican, Honduran, etc.).[7]

In addition to the data stored in the form of data cards, the data can also be stored in the form of a spreadsheet (like in Excel) as we see in Fig. 9.2. This screenshot in Fig. 9.2 is taken from *Fathom*. Spreadsheet representation in *TinkerPlots* and *CODAP* is similar to *Fathom*.

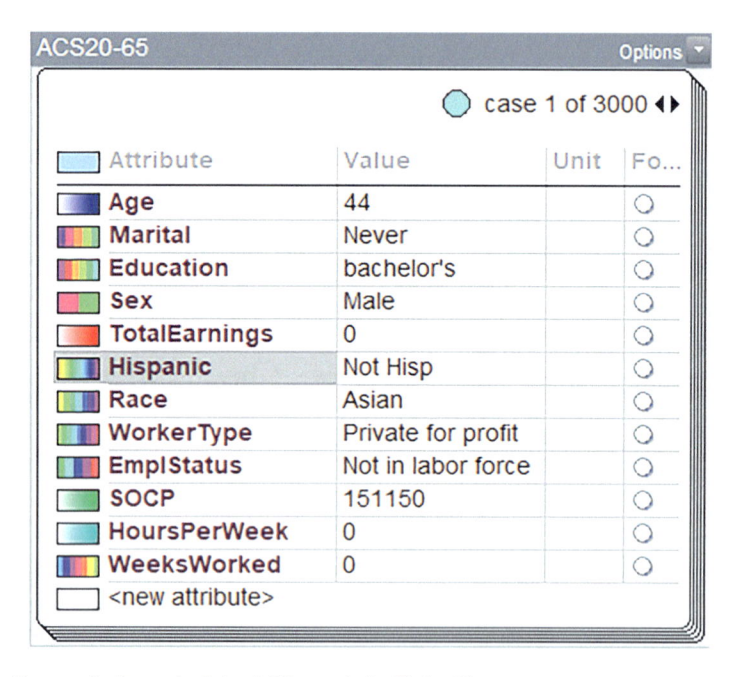

Fig. 9.1 Data card of case 1 of the ACS sample in *TinkerPlots*

Fig. 9.2 Data (snapshot of the first row of the table which contains the variables) stored in form of a spreadsheet in *Fathom*

---

[7]The meta data for the ACS dataset can be found on https://iase-web.org/islp/pcs/

9.5.2 Distribution of a Single Variable

A first overview of the distribution of a single categorical variable can be found quickly in *TinkerPlots, Fathom* and *CODAP*. For instance, the philosophy of *TinkerPlots* is that graphs are created via the data operations *stack, separate* and *order* as we can see in the preliminary stage of a bar graph in *TinkerPlots* in Fig. 9.3. Here, we have simply dropped the attribute *Sex* onto the x-axis. So we get the first impression of our data that the number of male and female interviewees in the dataset is nearly equal (1486:1514). This can be done in *Fathom* and *CODAP* accordingly.

Figure 9.4 shows the distribution of another categorical variable—education—in the form of a bar graph created in *Fathom*, again via drag-and-drop ("8 or less" means the person completed no year in school past grade 8 (typically age 13); "some HS" means the person was at a High School but did not finish with a High School degree; "HS Grad" means person with HS degree; "some" college means the person was at a college but did not finish with a college degree; "bachelor's" means the person has a bachelor degree; "graduate" means the person is graduated.).

This visual representation of the distribution of relative frequencies can only be realized in *Fathom*. In *CODAP* and *TinkerPlots* relative frequencies can be judged visually via a plot of absolute frequencies and relative frequencies can only be calculated for specific bins. The variables Sex and Education are categorical variables; a further step is the visualization of the distribution of a numerical variable, e.g. of the variable TotalEarnings. This variable contains information about the total earnings in dollars of a single person per year. *TinkerPlots, Fathom* and *CODAP*

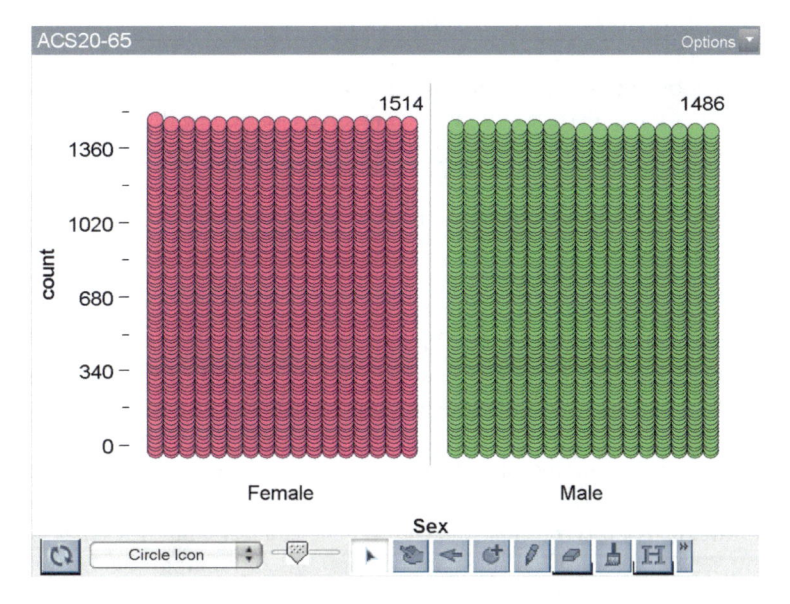

Fig. 9.3 Preliminary stage of a bar graph (stacked dots) for the distribution of the variable Sex in *TinkerPlots*

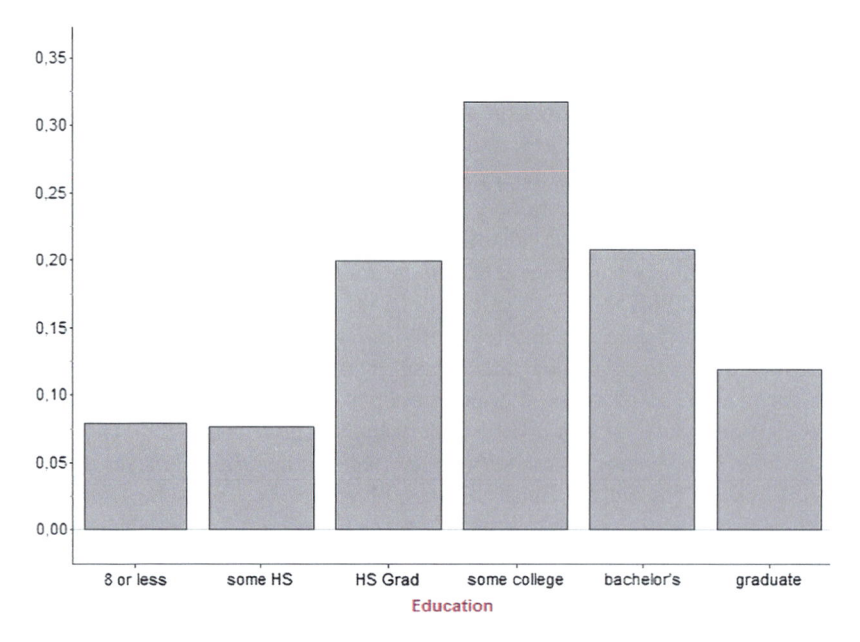

Fig. 9.4 Relative frequency distribution of the variable education in form of a bar graph in *Fathom*

offer stacked dot plots, boxplots and histograms. The technical implementation is quite similar in all three tools. In the following we will therefore only show how to display the distribution of TotalEarnings using *TinkerPlots*. Figure 9.5 presents a stacked dotplot.

Having a look at Fig. 9.5, much of the information is hidden, because the x-axis is scaled to fit all the data. Showing the incomes of a few high earners masks information about the large set of low earners. Therefore, it can be helpful to concentrate on the interviewees who earn $100,000 or less and to summarize the data into classes in a histogram (see Fig. 9.6). Here we can see that approximately half of the interviewees (48%) in the sample earn less than $20,000 and about two-third earn less than $40,000.

A further insight, especially with regard to the spread of, and outliers from, the distribution can be provided by the display of a boxplot in *TinkerPlots*. The boxplot is a standard option in *TinkerPlots* (and also in *Fathom* and *CODAP*) and with one click, it can be superposed on the distribution, here in the form of stacked dot plots (see Fig. 9.7).

The data explorations presented in this section only refer to the analysis of a single variable and show possible exploration activities of one-dimensional distributions with *TinkerPlots, Fathom* and *CODAP* using a Civic Statistics dataset. In the following section, we want to illustrate explorations of relationships between variables that are facilitated by *TinkerPlots, CODAP* and *Fathom*.

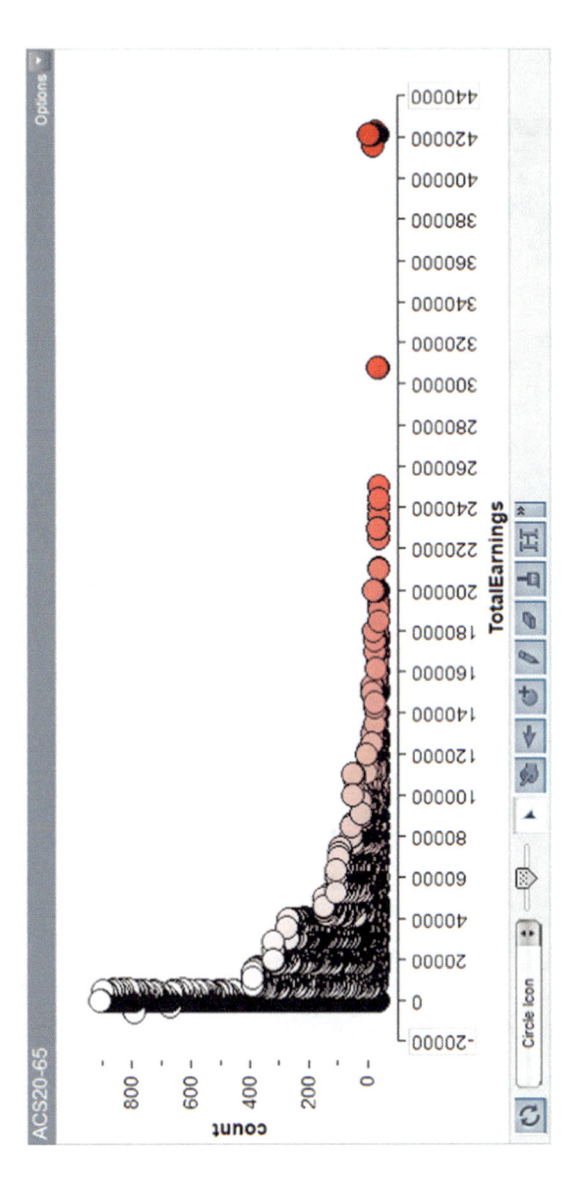

Fig. 9.5 Stacked dotplot of the distribution of the variable TotalEarnings in $/per year in the ACS sample with *TinkerPlots*

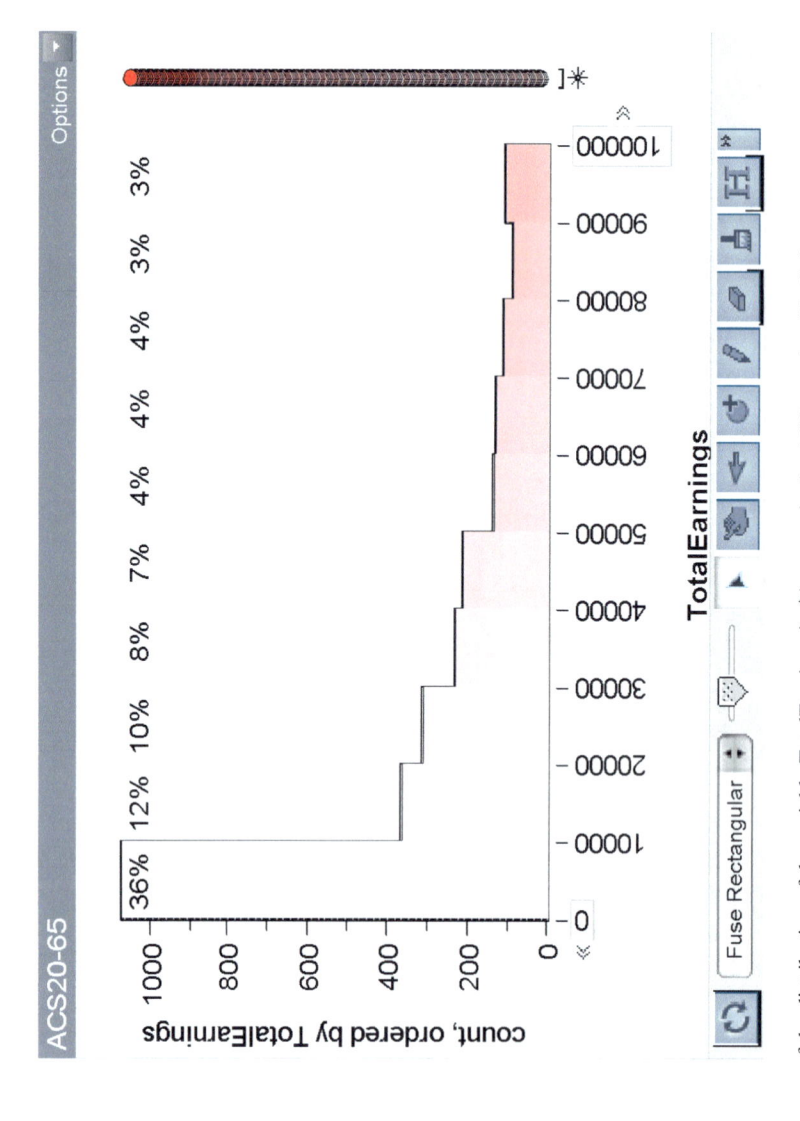

Fig. 9.6 Histogram of the distribution of the variable TotalEarnings in $/per year in the ACS sample with *Fathom*

Fig. 9.7 Stacked dotplot and boxplot of the distribution of the variable Totalearnings in the ACS sample in *TinkerPlots*

9.6   Exploring Relationships in ACS Data with *TinkerPlots, Fathom* and *CODAP*

With regard to the ACS dataset we will investigate some relationships between different sorts of variables, following Konold et al. (1997), notably relationships between:

- two categorical variables, e.g. What is the relationship between the variables Race and Education in the ACS sample?
- a numerical and a categorical variable, e.g., In how do male and female interviewees differ with regard to their total earnings in the ACS sample?
- two numerical variables, e.g. What is the relationship between total earnings and age in the ACS sample?

With these categories we cover typical questions that arise when exploring Civic Statistics data.

9.6.1   Exploring the Relationship Between Two Categorical Variables with TinkerPlots, CODAP and Fathom

When exploring the relationship between two categorical variables, a display in the form of a multi-bin plot or contingency table is helpful for a first visual impression of the relationship. To compare groups of unequal sizes, it is important to use relative frequencies or percentages instead of absolute frequencies. Moreover, it is also useful to choose different denominators when calculating percentages in order to explore the relationship of both categorical variables from different perspectives (e.g., 'the percentage of females who are graduates is not the same as the percentage of graduates who are female'). These percentages can be presented as numbers, but they can also be shown in the form of plots having bars whose heights are scaled to these percentages (as in Fig. 9.7). In Table 9.3 we see ways in which these three facilities can be realized with *TinkerPlots, CODAP* and *Fathom*.

All three tools offer a multi-bin display or a contingency table to visualize the relationship between two categorical variables. As an illustrative investigation, we explore differences between the educational attainment of male and female participants in the ACS sample. All three tools offer an easy way (via drag-and-drop and

Table 9.3 Overview of how different activities with regard to the exploration of a relationship between two categorical variables can be realized with *TinkerPlots, CODAP* and *Fathom*

	TinkerPlots	*CODAP*	*Fathom*
Multi-bin graphs (m × n contingency tables) via drag & drop	Yes	Yes	Yes
Percentages calculated in a variety of ways (row, column, cell)	Yes	Yes	Yes
Distribution of percentages displayed visually			Yes

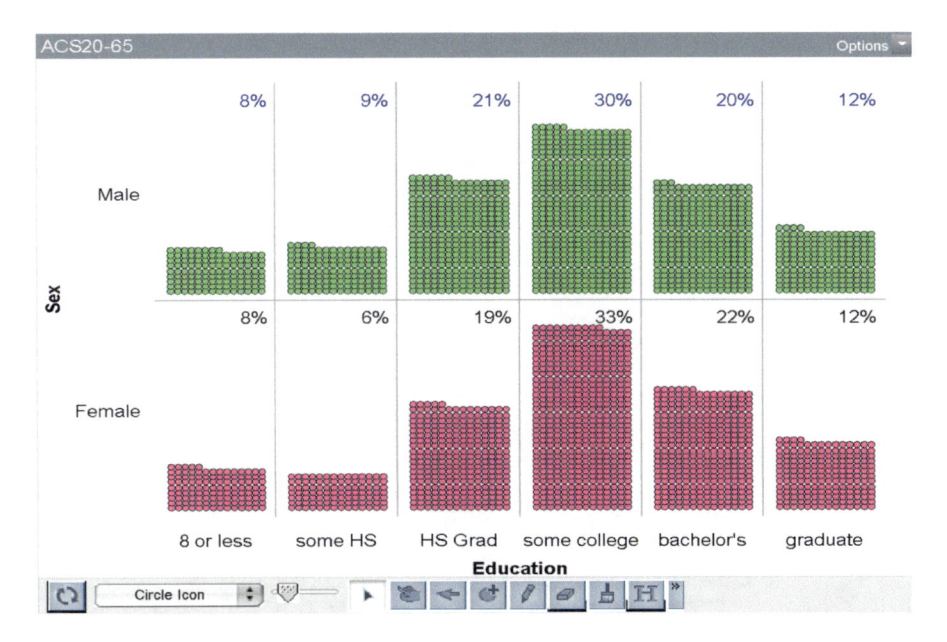

Fig. 9.8 *TinkerPlots* display with row percentages on the question of whether men or the women have a higher degree of education in this sample

mainly without using formulas) to create a multiple bin plot which also shows cell, row or column percentages—only *Fathom* requires a command/formula to choose the kind of percentages (row, column, cell). In Fig. 9.8 we see a multi bin plot with row percentages created in *TinkerPlots*.

In Fig. 9.8 we use row percentages to show that 32% of the men have a bachelor's degree or are graduates and 34% of the women have a bachelor's degree or are graduates. From another perspective we can also say that the proportion of people with few formal educational qualifications ("8 or less" or "some HS") is 14% in the group of the female and 17% in the group of the male interviewees in the ACS sample. So the female interviewees tend to have higher education levels than do the male interviewees in this sample. A very similar display—not shown here—can be created in *CODAP*.

However, *TinkerPlots* and *CODAP* do not allow users to create a multi-bin display in which the heights of the bins are adjusted to the corresponding relative frequencies. Here *Fathom* offers a better opportunity to visualize this situation as we can see in Fig. 9.9.

In Fig. 9.9 the height of the bins are adjusted to the relative frequencies and therefore allow a reader to compare the proportions in different groups not only based on numbers but also visually. In addition to and beyond the graphical display (like in Fig. 9.9) *Fathom* also allows one to use a table to display and Figure out the relevant percentages (see Fig. 9.10). The order of the educational categories is done (unhelpfully) in alphabetical order in *Fathom* by default. In *Fathom* however, there

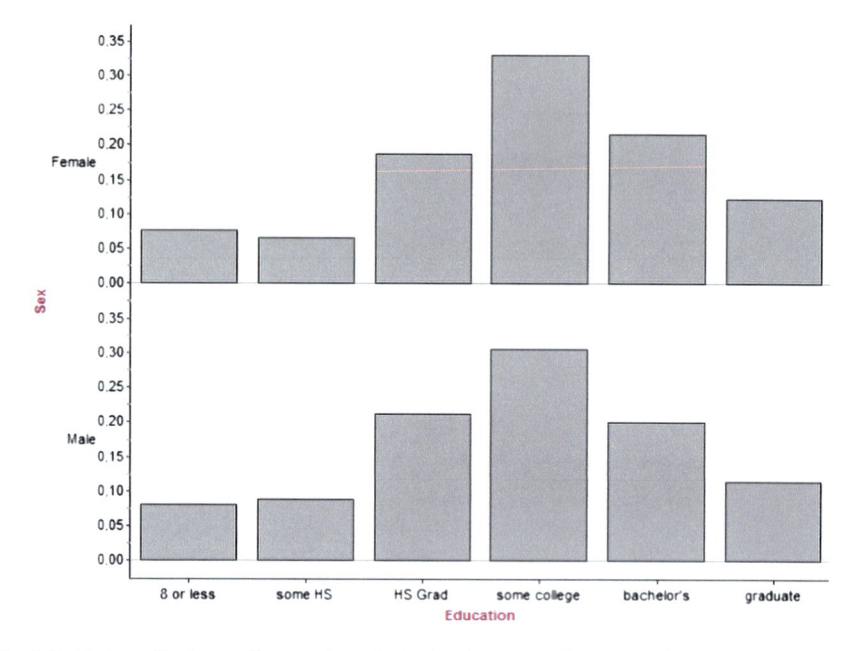

Fig. 9.9 *Fathom* display on the question of whether the men or the women have a higher degree of education in this sample

ACS20-65		Education						Row
		8 or less	bachelor's	graduate	HS Grad	some college	some HS	Summary
Sex	Female	8	22	12	19	33	6	100
	Male	8	20	12	21	30	9	100
Column Summary		8	21	12	20	32	8	100

S1 = round (rowproportion • 100)

Fig. 9.10 *Fathom* table illustrating the unhelpful alphabetical ordering of categories

is a feature that allows users to define the order of categories as a property of an attribute. If this is done, the categories are displayed in this order in tables and displays. In *TinkerPlots* and *CODAP* a work-around is to rename attributes in such a way that the alphabetic order reflects the natural order of the attributes.

We can further investigate the relationship between categorical variables which have more than two values, e.g. the extent to which Asian or black people in this ACS sample hold at least a bachelor's degree (this means bachelor or postgraduate degree). As we can see in the *TinkerPlots* display in Fig. 9.11, 18% of the Black people and 53% of the Asian people in this ACS sample have a Bachelor degree or are (post)graduates. A more open question is to ask about the ordering of the ethnic groups with regard to their education status. In the *TinkerPlots* display in Fig. 9.11,

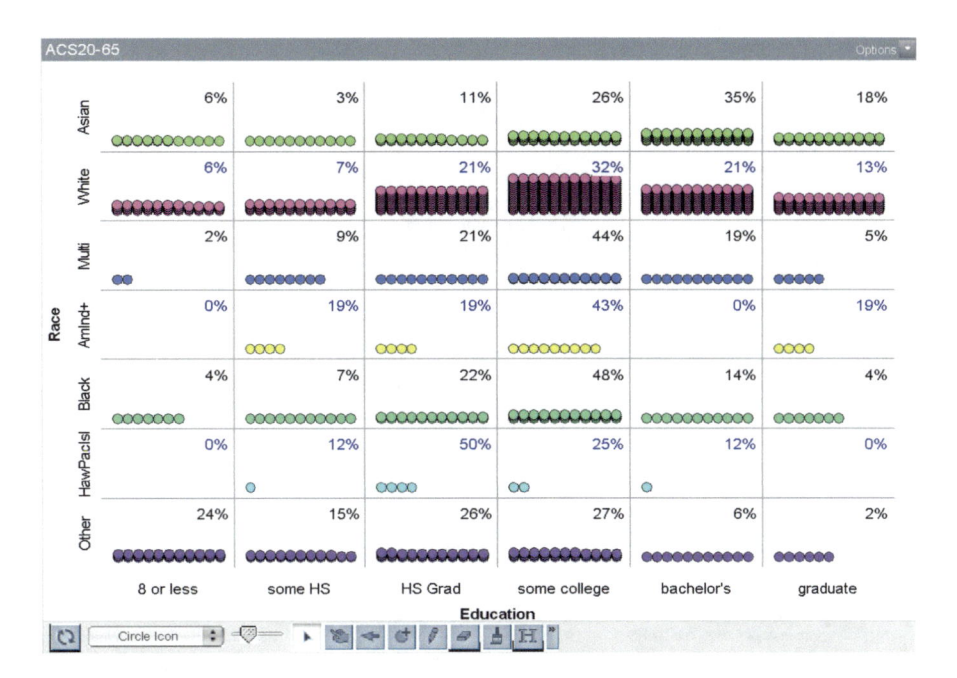

Fig. 9.11 *TinkerPlots* multi bin plot investigating the relationship between the variables Education and Race—ordered by percentages of having at least a bachelor's degree

in the *CODAP* display in Fig. 9.12 and in the *Fathom* graph in Fig. 9.13 we have ordered the ethnic groups by their education status—using the percentage of respondents having at least a bachelor degree. Note that in the *Fathom* graph the heights of the bars are adjusted to the relative frequencies, a setting which cannot be realized with *TinkerPlots* or *CODAP*. For example it is misleading in *TinkerPlots* and *CODAP* to use the height of the bars to compare the Asian group (35%) with the White group (21%), because the heights of the bars do not correspond to the related relative frequencies. In addition we can see that in this ACS sample, 53% of the Asians have at least a bachelor's degree, 34% of the white, 23% of the multi, 18% of the black, and only 8% of the "other" ethnic groups have at least a bachelor's degree. Data from groups "AmInd+" (American Indians) and "HawPacIsl" (Hawaiian or Pacific Islander) should be treated with extreme caution because of the small number of cases in this sample. However we can state that the Asian and White interviewees in this sample have higher academic attainment when compared to the other groups (Black, Multi or Other).

Figure 9.12 shows a *CODAP* display without the "HawPacIsl" and without the "AmInd+" people; with *CODAP* cases can be easily hidden by selecting and hiding them.

Comparing Fig. 9.11 (*TinkerPlots* display) and Fig. 9.12 (*CODAP* display) we have to state that the heights of the bars are displayed in a proportional manner (with regard to the frequencies in each bin) in *CODAP* better than in *TinkerPlots* .

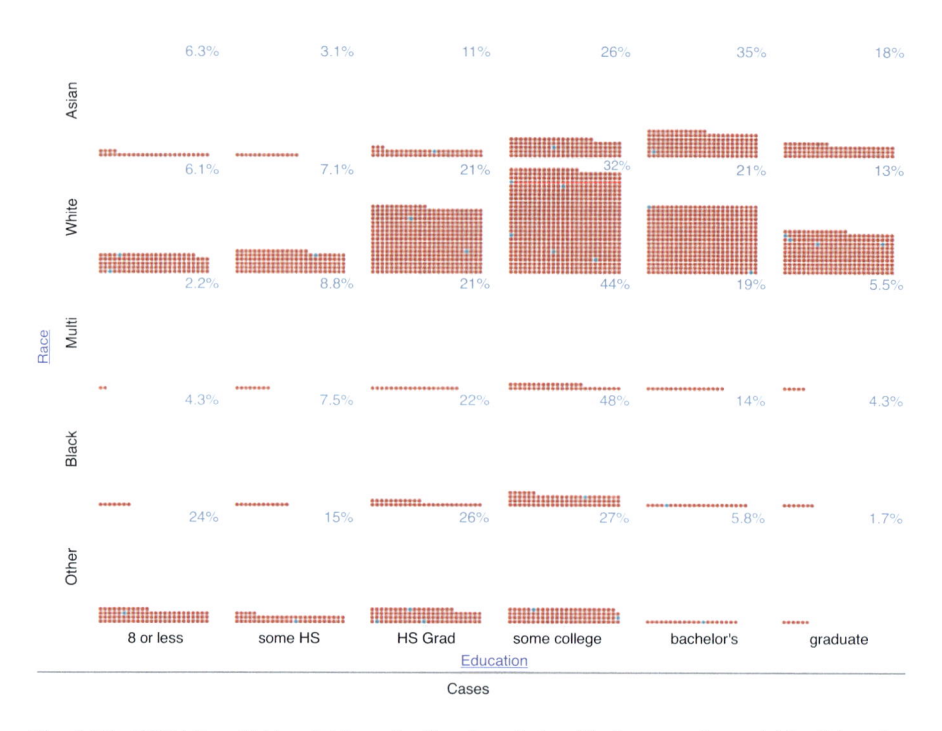

Fig. 9.12 *CODAP* multi bin plot investigating the relationship between the variables Education and Race without the categories "AmInd+" and "HawPacIsl"—ordered by percentages of having at least a bachelor's degree

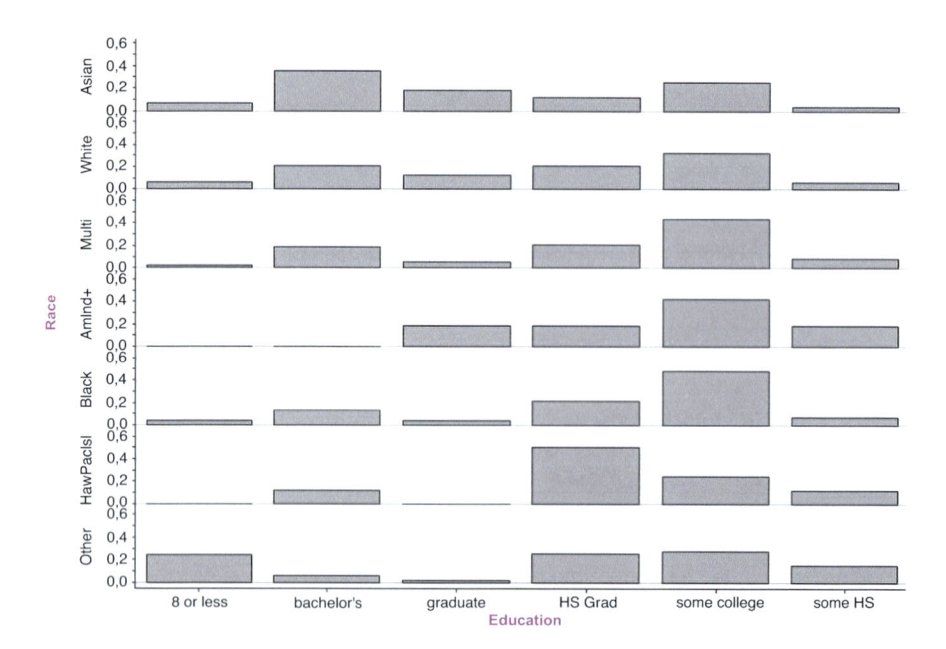

Fig. 9.13 *Fathom* display (with heights of the relative frequencies of cases in each bin and the heights of the bars adjusted) investigating the relationship between the variables Education and Race

In conclusion, we can see that all three tools facilitate the investigation of relationships between two categorical variables by creating multiple bin plots and calculating relevant percentages (cell, row, column). The user does not need to learn specific commands or formulas—apart from a very few commands for calculating the different percentages in the formula editor of *Fathom*. In addition (and superior to *TinkerPlots* and *CODAP*), *Fathom* allows users to create specific tables which present just numbers and percentages; moreover *Fathom* also allows users to create statistical displays in which the height of the bars are adjusted to the relative frequency, thus facilitating a visual comparison of the groups, when they have unequal size. *TinkerPlots* and *CODAP* display each case with a symbol of equal size. This unfortunately leads to a fundamental shortcoming of these tools for visual group comparisons of two categorical variables.

9.6.2 Comparing Groups Via TinkerPlots, CODAP and Fathom

The next step is to investigate the relationship between a numerical and a categorical variable—a common group comparison. Biehler (2001), Pfannkuch (2007) and Frischemeier (2019) report on the variety of methods that have been used at the high school level to compare groups. So for example, according to Frischemeier (2019), typical displays in descriptive statistics for comparing groups include stacked dotplots, boxplots and histograms. Especially when comparing stacked dotplots or histograms visually, important tool features include automatic scaling on the frequency-axis and a user-controlled flexible change of the bin width when working with histograms. Table 9.4 shows six key ways to compare distributions commonly used in high school classes.

Let us now have a look at Table 9.5 and consider which comparison features (visual and numerical) can be realized with which tool.

Groups and distributions can be compared using the different ways mentioned in Table 9.4. We start the comparison process by investigating differences in the centres and spreads between the distributions using appropriate visualizations. This can be realized, for example, by boxplots. In Fig. 9.14 we see a group comparison using boxplots in *TinkerPlots*. The distributions in *TinkerPlots* are displayed as stacked dotplots, boxplots and values like means. Please note that *TinkerPlots* also allows hiding the stacked dots so that one can concentrate on the boxplots when comparing groups, if wanted. This can be especially useful when comparing several boxplot distributions at once.

Additionally, dividers facilitate *p*-based comparisons (as we also see in Fig. 9.14). It appears that male interviewees in this sample have higher incomes than do the female interviewees in this sample. More specifically, the average male interviewees' income is $18,327.5 greater than the average of the female interviewees. Notice that the mean for this group comparison may be an unsuitable measure for

Table 9.4 Overview of different group comparison elements taken from Frischemeier (2019), definitions for p-based and q-based comparisons taken from Biehler (2001)

Comparison element	Definition
Comparison of centre	Two distributions of a numerical variable are compared by examining the differences between their arithmetic means or medians
Comparison of spread	Distributions are compared by examining the differences between their interquartile range or range
Comparison of skewness	Distributions are compared by examining the differences between their skewnesses/symmetries
Comparison of shift	Distributions are compared with regard to their shift—e.g. an additive or multiplicative difference of the summary statistics Q1, median, mean, and Q3 of the two distributions of the variable X (Q1 of distribution 1 of variable X and Q1 of distribution 2 of variable X, etc.)
p-based comparison	To conduct a p-based comparison between the distribution of two groups named by the variables V and W, the relative frequencies h with a given argument x of the two groups V and W, e.g. $h(V{\geq}x)$ and $h(W{\geq}x)$ are compared. A specific argument x can be given (for example: 10 h), and the proportions of cases that are equal to or larger than 10 h are compared (Biehler, 2001, p. 110).
q-based comparison	Comparisons of two distributions are called q-based if, for some proportion p between 0 and 1, the matching quantiles are compared. For $p = 0.5$ this is a comparison of medians (Biehler, 2001, p. 110).

Table 9.5 Overview of different activities with regard to the comparison of groups that can be realized with *TinkerPlots*, *CODAP* and *Fathom*

	TinkerPlots	*CODAP*	*Fathom*
Comparison displays	Stacked dotplots Histograms Boxplots	Stacked dotplots Histograms Boxplots	Stacked dotplots Histograms Boxplots
Adjusting scale of diagrams (auto control)			Yes
Flexible change of bin width (user control)	Yes		Yes
Comparing centre, spread, skewness, shift, p-based, q-based	Yes	Yes	Yes

comparison, because both distributions are highly skewed, and there are many outliers in both distributions. Having a look at the differences between the boxplots one might again conclude that the male interviewees earn more than the female interviewees based on the observation that the median in the distribution of male interviewees is higher than the median in the distribution of female interviewees, and the box representing the distribution of the male interviewees is shifted more to the right compared to the box of the female interviewees. The wider box of the male interviewees also shows that the distribution of male interviewees is more heterogeneous than of the female interviewees in this sample. Furthermore—with regard to p-based comparisons—we can say, for example, that 14% of the male interviewees

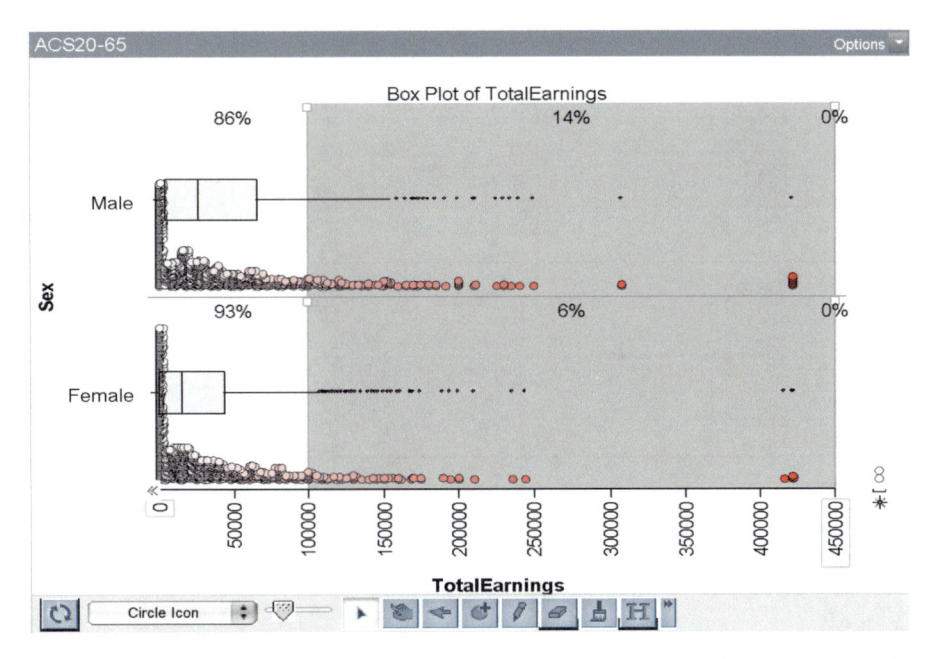

Fig. 9.14 Group comparison display in *TinkerPlots*: stacked dotplots, boxplots and means of the distribution of the variable TotalEarnings for male and female interviewees in the ACS dataset

in this sample earn a great deal of money ($100,000 or more), but only 6% of the female interviewees earn that much.

Fathom offers similar ways to compare two distributions. As we see in Fig. 9.15 (left) we can also display a boxplot of both distributions. In addition, *Fathom* can present the data as a Table (see Fig. 9.15 right) which contains relevant summary statistics (like median, Q1, Q3, mean)—very useful for using shift as comparison element (see Table 9.4). Furthermore—as we know—in the case of comparing distributions in the form of histograms, the selection of the bin width is crucial if you want to compare distributions with regard to their skewness or with regard to their shapes. In this case, *Fathom* offers users an easy way to adjust the bin width of histograms. In Fig. 9.16 we see three histograms for the group comparison setting (TotalEarnings vs. Sex) with different bin widths ($20,000; $10,000; $5000).

The automatic adjustment to the frequency-axis and the facility to change the bin width offers flexible interpretations and comparisons of the distributions with regard to the shape and the skewness of the distributions. Let us go one step further in group comparisons. We will show this in *CODAP*, by investigating differences in TotalEarnings across the different ethnic groups. *CODAP* (as do *TinkerPlots* and *Fathom*) makes it easy to display the number of cases (or the percentage of cases) in specific subgroups. So, in Fig. 9.17 we see that white people comprise the majority of this sample; nearly two-thirds of the participants in this sample are white. Some other groups, notably American Indians and Hawaiian or Pacific Islanders should be excluded from the data analysis process because these groups are too small in the

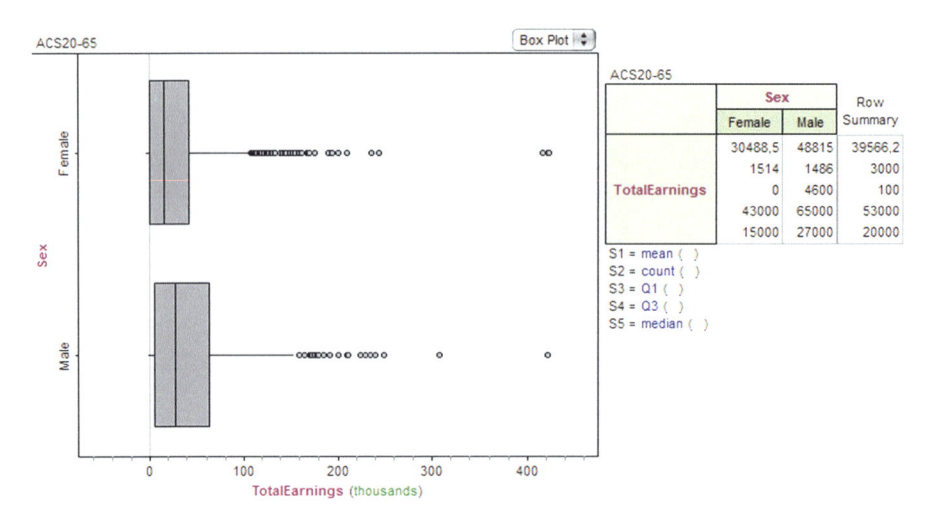

Fig. 9.15 Group comparison display in *Fathom* (left) and table with summary stats (right)

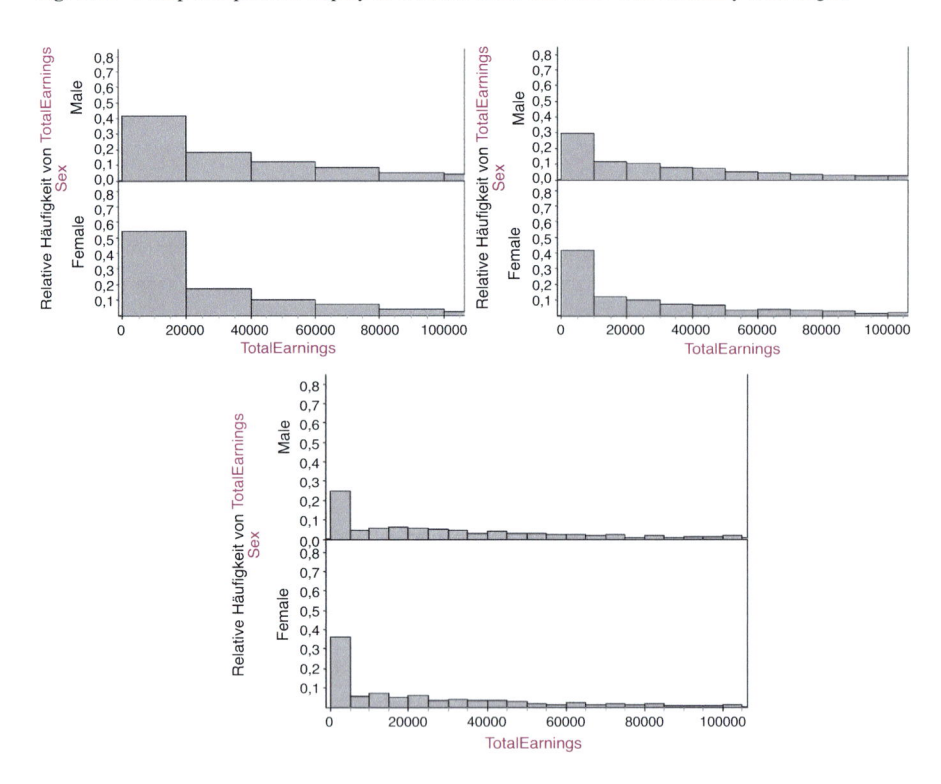

Fig. 9.16 Histograms for the group comparison setting (TotalEarnings vs. Sex) in *Fathom* with different bin widths: bin width = $20,000 (upper left); bin width = $10,000 (upper right); bin width = $5000 (lower centered)

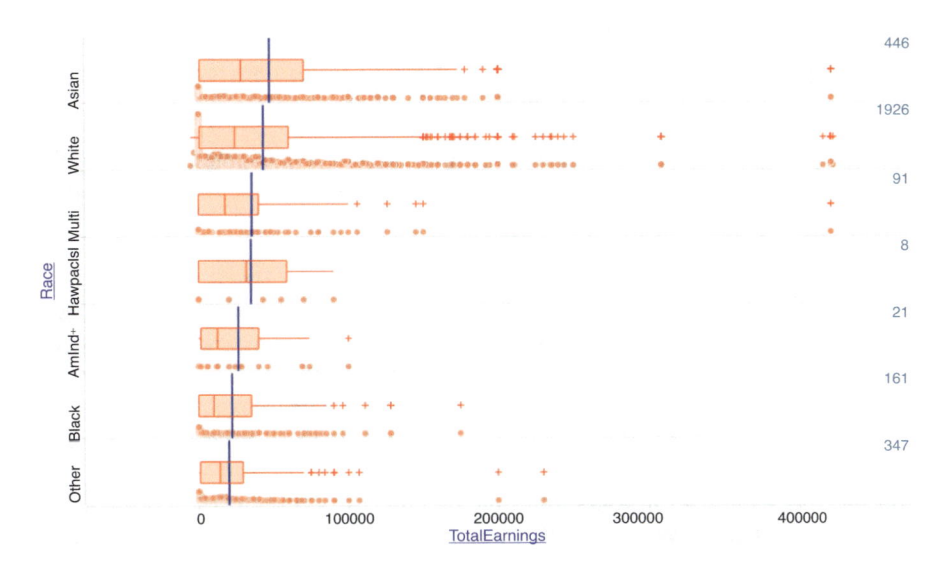

Fig. 9.17 Distribution of the variable TotalEarnings with regard to the variable Race in *CODAP* (groups of race ordered ascending by means of TotalEarnings, "AmInd+" are American Indians and "HawPacIsl" are Hawaiian or Pacific Islanders). The blue lines represent the arithmetic means of each distribution of the variable TotalEarnings

sample (and in the population). *TinkerPlots* and *CODAP* offer easy methods to exclude these cases. We see that the group of Asian interviewees and the group of White interviewees are quite similarly distributed. The Asian group is a little bit more spread. The centre is shifted a little bit more to the right, so the Asian interviewees have higher average earnings than the White interviewees. The other relevant population groups are the Blacks and the Other. They earn considerably less than the Asian or the White interviewees in this sample. In addition, the Blacks and the Other groups show a more homogenous distribution of Total Earnings because the middle 50% of the distributions (the width of the boxes) are smaller than the middle 50% of the distributions of the White and the Asian interviewees.

Overall, we can say that all three tools offer good visual features and facilitate comparisons between distributions. With all three tools the data exploration activities to create group comparison displays can be realized easily. *Fathom*, in addition to the features in *TinkerPlots* and *CODAP*, offers some more sophisticated elements such as the automatic adjustment with regard to the scales of the frequency axis when comparing multiple plots, and flexible handling of the bin width of histograms to facilitate interpretation and comparison of the shape and the skewness of distributions.

9.6.3 Exploring the Relationship Between Two Numerical Variables with TinkerPlots, CODAP and Fathom

In the following section, we want to see how the relationship between two numerical variables can be explored with *TinkerPlots, CODAP* and *Fathom*. Multi-bin plots and scatterplots can be generated easily. Furthermore, to help learners to get an understanding of scatterplots, Konold (2002) suggests referring the display of a scatterplot back to a group comparison situation as an approach to help learners understand and interpret scatterplots (see for example in Fig. 9.18). From a more formal perspective—when exploring linear relationships—one can calculate regression parameters like r and r^2 and can also calculate a least—squares regression line. Additionally *Fathom* offers a facility to plot a function and to adjust parameters of the function. The residue diagram in *Fathom* can help the learner to find the best possible function to model the equation "Data = (linear) function + residuals." The Residual Diagram helps users position the function. The residuals should be minimised and randomly distributed and approximately balanced between over- and under-estimating the data. *TinkerPlots* with its ColorMeter facilitates exploring the relationship between two variables. With the ColorMeter it is possible to calculate the average (mean, median) in a selected interval of the graph and to see the development of the parameter (mean, median) from interval to interval. In this chapter we will not elaborate on either function in any more detail.

An overview of how different features for exploring the relationship between two numerical variables can be realized with *TinkerPlots, CODAP* and *Fathom* is displayed in Table 9.6.

As we saw in Sect. 9.6.1 *TinkerPlots, CODAP* and *Fathom* allow the creation of multi-bin plots, which can be a first approach to visualizing the relationship between two numerical variables. In addition to that, all three tools enable learners to get

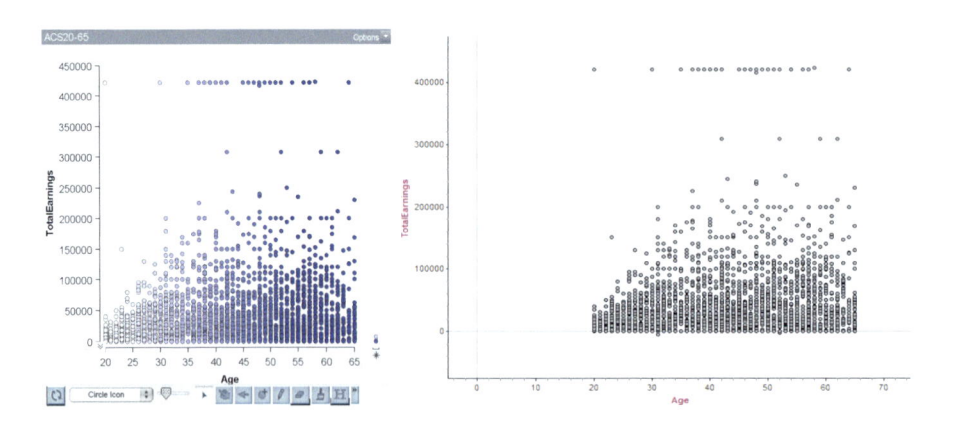

Fig. 9.18 Scatterplot to display the relationship between the variables TotalEarnings and Age in *TinkerPlots* (left) and *Fathom* (right). The colors represent the intensity of the numerical variable age. The intensity of the color is proportional to the value of the numerical variable age

Table 9.6 Overview how different options with regard to the exploration of a relationship between two numerical variables can be realized with *TinkerPlots*, *CODAP* and *Fathom*

	TinkerPlots	*CODAP*	*Fathom*
Slicing	Yes	Yes	Yes
Displaying the relationship in scatterplot	Yes	Yes	Yes
Calculating parameters like r, r^2		Yes	Yes
Calculating regression line, applying methods like the sum of least squares		Yes	Yes
Exploring the relationship between two numerical variables via the analysis of residuals			Yes
Smoothing with Loess	Yes (ColorMeter Function)		
Using non-linear models			Option to super-impose functions on scatter plots and calculate and display residuals in a second window

deeper insights into the data and they allow users to refer to a scatterplot display to facilitate the comparison of different groups (Konold, 2002). For instance all three tools provide the possibility to refer the situation of a relationship between two numerical variables to a group comparison situation. For example, one can explore the relationship between the numerical variables Age and Total Earnings. A scatterplot like in Fig. 9.18 is a first basic display to plot the relationship between both variables. In Fig. 9.18 we see the scatterplot with the variables Age (x-axis) and TotalEarnings (y-axis) in *TinkerPlots* (left) and *Fathom* (right). The colors represent the intensity of the numerical variable age. The intensity of the color is proportional to the value of the numerical variable age. The relation in this case is difficult to depict as it is not a curvilinear trend with some variation around a curvilinear line. An elementary idea is to draw students' attention to the question of how the distribution of the y-variable varies when the x-variable changes. A simple idea is to slice the x-variable into a finite number of classes and display the y-variable's distribution in these classes. After this slicing, the methods for group comparison can be applied. Loess (Locally Weighted Scatterplot Smoothing) as a method can be later explained as using a dynamic slice wandering across the x-axis and calculating a measure of centre in every window. To prepare for this idea, discrete and static slicing is an elementary method for depicting non-linear relationships taking into account not only how the measure of centre changes but the whole distribution.

To take up the idea of Konold (2002), we have created five groups of the variable age 20–29, 30–39, 40–49, 50–59 and 60–69 in a *TinkerPlots* display. In *Fathom* and *CODAP* this has to be realized in a more complex and difficult way—the transformation process e.g. in *Fathom* is more sophisticated and requires the use of formulas

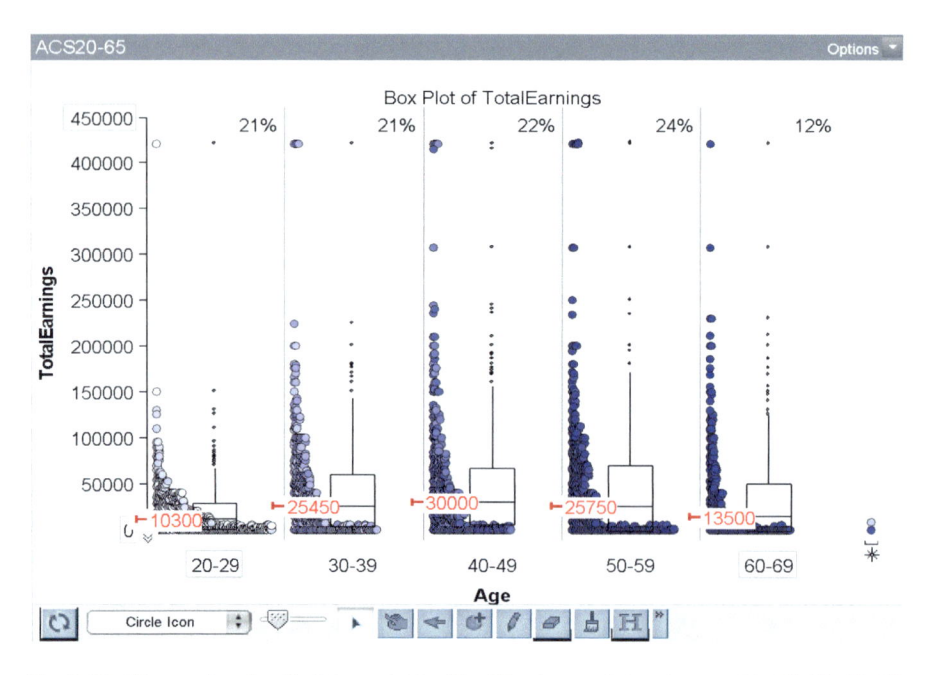

Fig. 9.19 "Scatterplot slices" of the variables TotalEarnings and Age (grouped in 20–29, 30–39, 40–49, etc.) in *TinkerPlots*

and specific *transform*-commands. The relationship between Age and TotalEarnings might not be linear—as we see in Fig. 9.19. Following Konold's (2002) suggestion, we have transformed the numerical variable *Age* into categories. This enables us to compare distributions (e.g., visualized as boxplots) along the categories. Looking at the distributions and the boxplots in Fig. 9.19, we see that the median of TotalEarnings increases with age until 40–49 and then decreases. The data follows the pattern of an increase of TotalEarnings with age followed by a decrease of TotalEarnings due to retirement.

The idea of the ColorMeter is to dynamically generate a median or mean trace and to apply this analysis method by graphical operations on the data (which is of course more flexible with R, since in R the window size and also other parameters can be adapted—see Figs. 9.20 and 9.21).

All in all we can say that *TinkerPlots, CODAP* and *Fathom* enable users to create basic statistical displays for the exploration of two numerical variables. In addition to that, all three tools also facilitate a transition from group comparisons to a conventional scatterplot as suggested by Konold (2002). *TinkerPlots* in contrast to *CODAP* and *Fathom* does not allow a formal approach to investigate the relationship between two numerical variables like calculating parameters r or r^2 or applying the method of the sum of least squares. In addition to that—although *Fathom* allows users to plot arbitrary functions—none of the three tools offer the possibility to handle nonlinear models in a formal way.

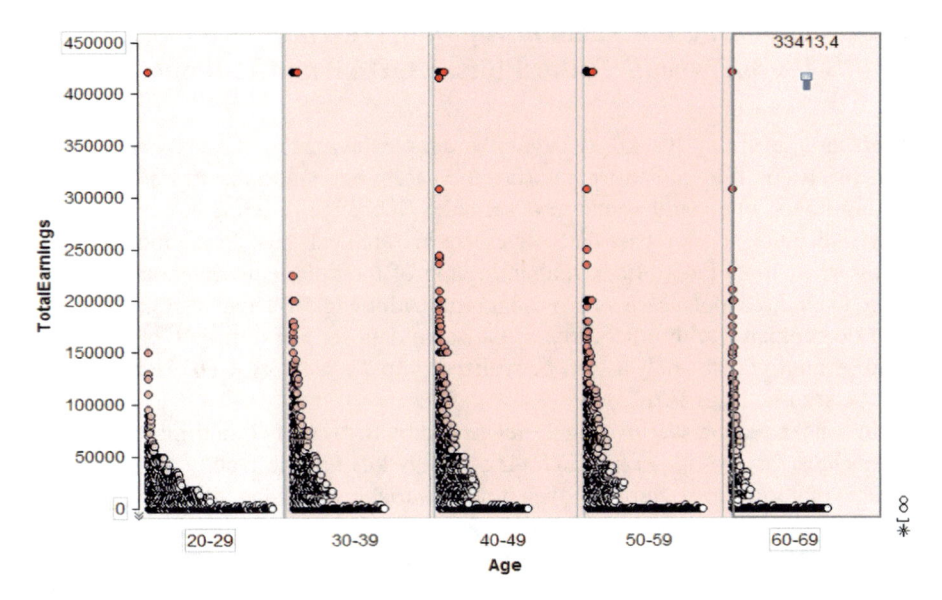

Fig. 9.20 "Scatterplot slices" of the variables TotalEarnings and Age (grouped in 20–29, 30–39, 40–49, etc.) in *TinkerPlots* and color snapshots with the *TinkerPlots* color meter

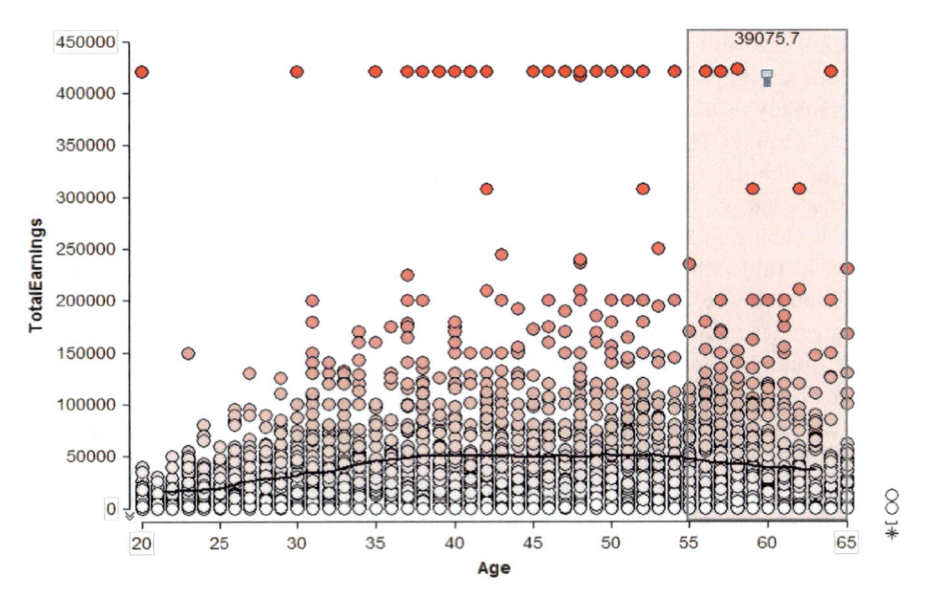

Fig. 9.21 Scatterplot of the variables TotalEarnings and Age in *TinkerPlots* and line trace of the development of the median of TotalEarnings

9.6.4 Exploring the Relationship of More Than Two Variables with TinkerPlots, CODAP and Fathom

There are several ways to go beyond a simple bivariate data analysis. A third dimension could be added by coloring the cases; one could disaggregate data by setting filters; one could define new variables to change or refine measures, create new indicators or aggregate data; or create hierarchical data. In addition to these features, all three tools offer dynamic linking of multiple representations. Furthermore in all three tools learners can use multiple plot windows, thus various plots can also be compared with other plots of the same data set. An overview of how far a kind of multivariate analysis can be realized with *TinkerPlots, CODAP* or *Fathom* can be seen in Table 9.7.

In a next section we investigate relationships between two and more variables with *TinkerPlots, Fathom* and *CODAP. TinkerPlots* has the facility to expand the data exploration to a third or even fourth variable by using the color gradient function and the label function. So let us assume that we want to investigate the ways in which male and female interviewees differ in this sample with regard to the variable TotalEarnings in different ethnic groups. The filter function (also available in *Fathom* and *CODAP*) allows one to create separate boxplots for the male and the female participants—this requires multiple graphs in *TinkerPlots, Fathom* or *CODAP* (see Figs. 9.22 and 9.23)—the *TinkerPlots* graphs (Figs. 9.22 and 9.23) can be realized in *CODAP* and *Fathom* in a similar way to *TinkerPlots* .

A direct comparison of the displays in Figs. 9.22 and 9.23 is very difficult. Unfortunately, *TinkerPlots* does not allow a direct comparison of the subgroups in a single display. Therefore the only possibility in *TinkerPlots* and *CODAP* is to aggregate the data—e.g. extract the median of the variable TotalEarnings of male and female interviewees and calculate the differences or the quotients of the medians for each subgroup by hand (see Table 9.8)—*TinkerPlots* does not offer this as a feature. In Table 9.8 we see that there are huge income differences between male and female interviewees in the subgroup of white interviewees. In this ACS sample, the white men have a median income which is two times higher than the median income of the white female interviewees. The same (from a multiplicative point of view) applies also for the group Other. Here we see that the median income in general is lower in this male group ($18,600) and in this female group ($9000) compared to the

Table 9.7 Overview of different activities relevant to the exploration of relationships between more than two variables with *TinkerPlots, CODAP* and *Fathom*

	TinkerPlots	CODAP	Fathom
Coloring	Yes	Yes	Yes
Filtering across subgroups	Yes	Yes	Yes
Multiple linked displays			Yes
Multi-window environment	Yes	Yes	Yes
Defining new variables, aggregation of data	Yes	Yes	Yes
Analyzing hierarchical data		Yes	

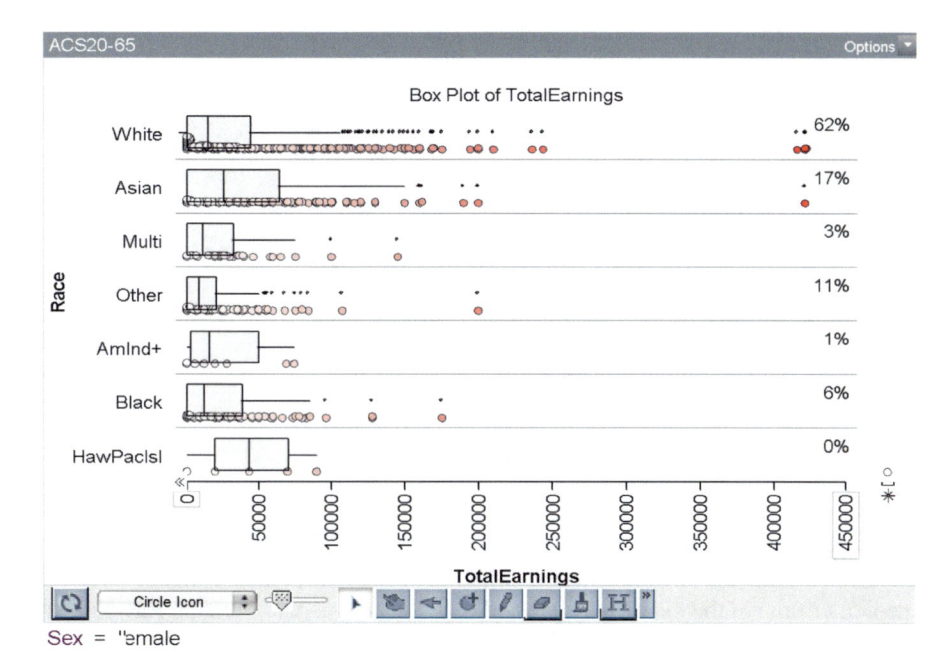

Fig. 9.22 Distribution of the variable TotalEarnings with regard to the variable Race in *TinkerPlots* in the subgroup of female interviewees

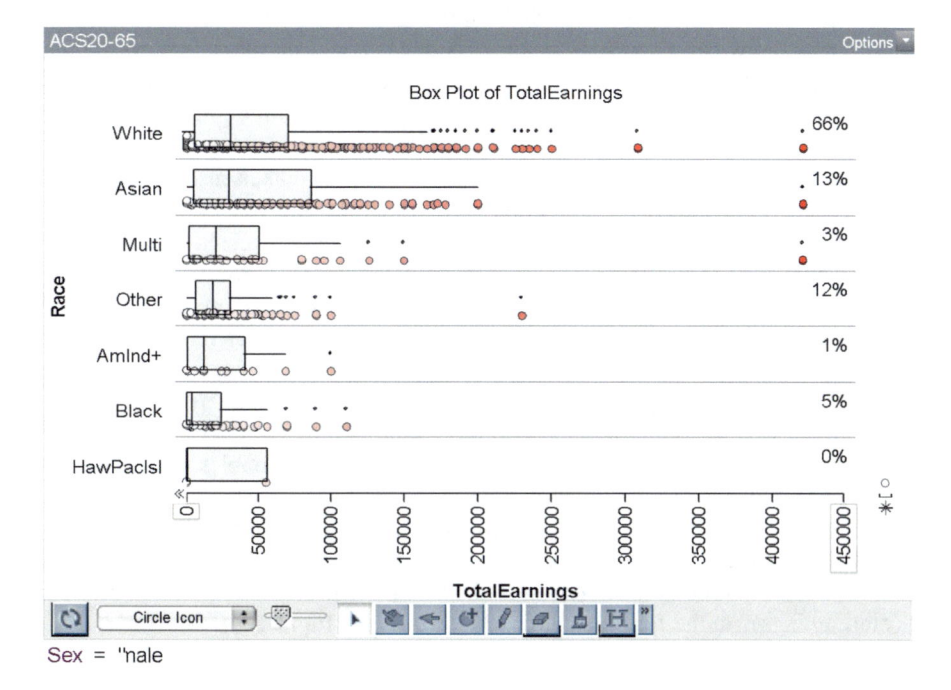

Fig. 9.23 Distribution of the variable TotalEarnings with regard to the variable Race in *TinkerPlots* in the subgroup of male interviewees

Table 9.8 Overview of the median of TotalEarnings of male and female interviewees and the differences and quotients of medians of TotalEarnings of male and female interviewees across different race groups

	Group size	Median of TotalEarnings (male) in \$	Median of TotalEarnings (female) in \$	Differences of medians of TotalEarnings (male−female) in \$	Quotient of medians of TotalEarnings (male−female) in \$
White	1926	30,750	15,050	15,700	2.04
Asian	446	30,000	25,700	4300	1.17
Multi	91	20,700	11,200	9500	1.85
Other	347	18,600	9000	9600	2.07
AmInd+	21	12,000	16,250	−4250	0.74
Black	161	4400	12,500	−8100	0.35
HawPacIsl	8	0	43,000	−43,000	0

group with all interviewees. In the group of the black interviewees, the female interviewees have a median income which is nearly three times higher than the median income of the male black interviewees. As above, data from the Hawaiian or Pacific Islanders and American Indians need to be treated also with extreme caution because only very few cases of this sample belong to these subgroups.

In *Fathom* we can use the multiple-linked window feature to study the relationship between three variables (TotalEarnings, Race, Education). The group comparison display in Fig. 9.24 shows the distribution of TotalEarnings across the variable Race. If we now also consider a third variable, e.g. Education, and select the interviewees with an education level of "8 or less" in the bar graph on the right side (Fig. 9.24 right), the "8 or less" are also highlighted in the group comparison display (Fig. 9.24 left).

Let us now focus on *CODAP*. *CODAP* allows users to make sense of multi-level data (Haldar et al., 2018) by defining new variables and aggregating data. So *CODAP* enables users to perform data moves which can be realized in *TinkerPlots* and *Fathom* only by using sophisticated commands and formulas. Now using *CODAP* we show how to discover whether the gender income differences are related to the variables Education or Race. Let us first explore the way male and female interviewees differ with regard to their TotalEarnings in different ethnic groups. *CODAP* allows users to group the data by the variable Race (see left column of the data table in Fig. 9.25) and Sex (second left column of the data table in Fig. 9.25). We choose both variables via drag and drop, and drop both variables at the left hand of the data table to get to the situation seen in Fig. 9.25. A next step to aggregate the data for our purposes is to calculate the median (MedianIncome) of the TotalEarnings via a formula for each ethnic group (see Fig. 9.26). To do this we add an extra column by clicking on "+" and then entering the formula "median (TotalEarnings)" in the formula editor of *CODAP* (see Fig. 9.26).

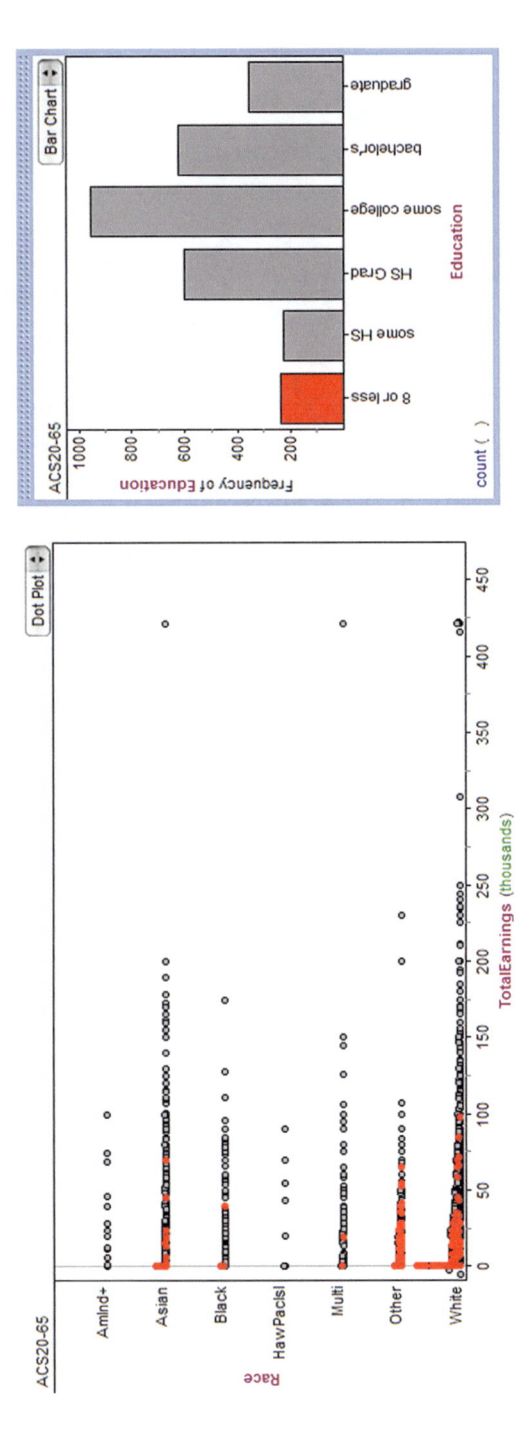

Fig. 9.24 Distribution of the variable TotalEarnings with regard to the variable Race in *Fathom* with Education level "8 or less" highlighted

Races (14 Fälle)

Index	Race	Sex
1	Asian	Male
2	White	Male
3	Other	Male
4	Asian	Fe...
5	Black	Male
6	White	Fe...
7	Other	Fe...
8	Multi	Male
9	Black	Fe...
10	AmInd-	Fe...
11	Multi	Fe...
12	HawPac...	Fe...
13	AmInd-	Male
14	HawPac...	Male

ACS_Codap — Fälle (3000 Fälle)

Index	Age	Marital	Education	TotalEarnings	Hispanic	WorkerType	EmplStatus	SOCP	HoursPerWeek	Weekorked
1	44	Never	bachelo...	0	Not Hisp	Private f...	Not in l...	151150	0	
2	42	Married	8 or less	6000	Not Hisp	Private f...	Unempl...	352010	40	14 to
3	34	Never	graduate	1900	Not Hisp	Self-Em...	Civ Em...	132051	40	50 to
4	56	Married	some c...	74000	Not Hisp	Private f...	Civ Em...	511011	40	50 to
5	51	Married	graduate	110000	Not Hisp	Private f...	Civ Em...	1721	40	50 to
6	49	Married	some c...	65000	Not Hisp	State C...	Civ Em...	499071	40	50 to
7	36	Married	graduate	50000	Not Hisp	Private ...	Civ Em...	1910	32	40 to
8	61	Married	graduate	200000	Not Hisp	Private f...	Civ Em...	291060	40	50 to
9	65	Married	some c...	0	Not Hisp	Private f...	Not in l...	512090	0	
10	39	Married	some c...	0	Not Hisp	Private f...	Unempl...	492011	0	
11	44	Married	bachelo...	65000	Not Hisp	Private f...	Civ Em...	151142	48	50 to
12	47	Married	bachelo...	28000	Not Hisp	Private f...	Civ Em...	514	40	50 to
13	59	Married	graduate	101000	Not Hisp	Private f...	Civ Em...	113071	40	50 to
14	39	Never	HS Grad	0	Not Hisp	Unempl...	Unempl...	999920	0	
15	27	Married	bachelo...	60000	Not Hisp	Private f...	Civ Em...	271020	40	50 to

Fig. 9.25 Data table in *CODAP* to aggregate the ACS data with regard to the variables Race and Sex

Fig. 9.26 Data table (and formula editor) in *CODAP* used to aggregate the ACS data with regard to the variables Race and Sex

Fig. 9.27 Comparison of the median incomes of male and female interviewees with regard to the different subgroups defined by the categories of the variable Race in *CODAP*

The dependance of the aggregated variable "MedianIncome" from the variable Race can be displayed in a graph in *CODAP* (see Fig. 9.27) in which we can observe the difference of median incomes of the male (yellow dots) and the female (purple dots) interviewees in different race groups. We see that the female interviewees have a larger median income in the groups Amind+, Black and HawPacISl in this ACS sample.

In this ACS sample it is only in the Black group where the female interviewees have a larger median income than the male interviewees. In the groups Multi, Other, and White, the median income of the male interviewees is much higher than the median income of the female interviewees; for the Asian group this difference is not so large. We can investigate the relationship between sex and total income for different levels of educational attainment in the same way. In Fig. 9.28 we see the differences between male and female interviewees in their median income of TotalEarnings for different education groups in our ACS sample. In all education groups the male interviewees have a larger median income than the female interviewees. The gap between the male and the female interviewees is extremely large in higher education groups like bachelor's or graduate in this ACS sample.

These data moves are only possible in *CODAP* and not in *TinkerPlots* nor in *Fathom*. So for some explorations in Civic Statistics that rely on at least three variables, *CODAP* supports the analysis in a better way than *TinkerPlots* or *Fathom*. Nevertheless also *CODAP*—compared to *iNZight* (see Chap. 10 of this book) or R (see Chap. 11 of this book)—has some limitations when exploring multivariate data.

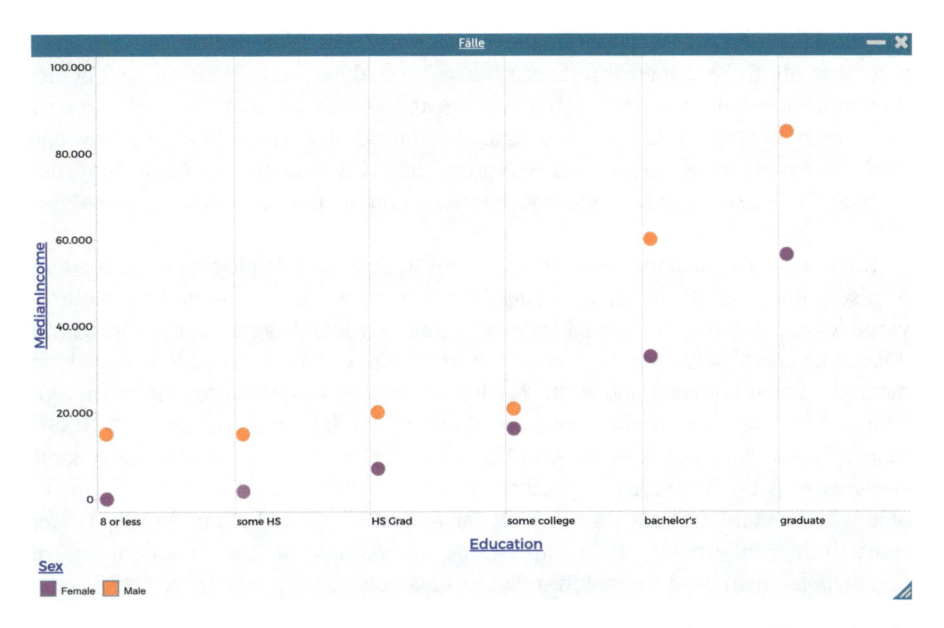

Fig. 9.28 Comparison of the median incomes of male and female interviewees with regard to the different subgroups of the variable Education in *CODAP*

9.7 Summary

TinkerPlots, Fathom and *CODAP* can serve as valuable tools to analyze and explore Civic Statistics data, exemplified here via an exploration of this ACS sample. We used *TinkerPlots, Fathom* and *CODAP* to create standard statistical displays like bar graphs, stacked dotplots, histograms and boxplots to get first impressions about the distributions of several variables in the dataset. Furthermore these tools helped us to identify differences in the educational attainment of the male and the female interviewees (female interviewees tend to have a higher degree of education than the male interviewees in this sample) and to identify also differences in educational attainment with regard to race (the Asian and the White interviewees in this sample have higher academic attainment overall compared to the Black, Multi or Other groups). With regard to explorations of the Gender Pay Gap we found that the male interviewees have a higher median income (earning $18,327.5 more on average) than the female interviewees in this sample, and also that the income distribution of male interviewees is more heterogeneous than that of the female interviewees. *CODAP* facilitated some more fine-grained analyses; investigating the Gender Pay Gap not only from a gender but also from an ethnic group perspective we found large differences in the size of the pay gap in different ethnic groups. *CODAP* was also used to discover a strong relationship between educational attainment and income, and clear gender pay gaps at all levels in this ACS sample. All these analyses could have also been done with more (technical) effort in *TinkerPlots* or *Fathom*. Again we note that all these data explorations have been done on a descriptive but not inferential level because our focus was on the evaluation of our three software tools for analyzing Civic Statistics data. We can say that *TinkerPlots, Fathom* and *CODAP* were very helpful when exploring the ACS data from a Civic Statistics perspective, when we stay in the non-inferential mode and do multivariate analyses only in a rudimentary way.

Routine statistical activities for high school students like displaying visualizations of distributions, exploring relationships between two variables, exploring multiple variables and defining new variables and aggregating and disaggregating data can be done in a general way with *TinkerPlots, Fathom* and *CODAP* and with data analysis methods which are easy and (with hardly any use of formulae) to implement. Of course there are some limitations to mention: if the dataset is too large ($>10,000$ cases) *TinkerPlots, Fathom* or *CODAP* may not be able to handle these large amounts of data. Software designed for professional use, such as *R* (see Chap. 11 of this book) and *iNZight* that is built on *R* (see Chap. 10 of this book), is less restrictive. Furthermore, there are some limitations in the functionality of *TinkerPlots* when used to explore relationships between three or more variables in the case of a too large dataset. *CODAP* with its hierarchy function allows users to disaggregate data and to analyze the relationship between more than two variables as we learned in Sect. 9.6.4. Although there are some limitations of tools like *CODAP*, *Fathom* and *TinkerPlots* when analyzing and exploring Civic Statistics data, these tools allow learners to make a quick start in the analysis of Civic Statistics data without needing to know about specific formulas or computational techniques.

TinkerPlots connects to enactive activities (like the data analysis with data cards) and serves as a data analysis tool for learners in high school and also as a demonstration tool for high school teachers. With its data card philosophy and the idea of creating diagrams based on the data operations *separate*, *stack* and *order*, *TinkerPlots* makes data analysis accessible even to young learners, and with the divider feature for *p*-based comparisons or the option to easily group data (such as the scatterplot slices) *TinkerPlots* provides learners with some powerful data analysis tools.

Fathom—which can be seen as the big sister of *TinkerPlots*—serves also as a valuable tool for high school students and teachers, providing a wider range of data analysis techniques (like regression analysis, and defining and plotting functions to fit given data) in comparison to *TinkerPlots*. In addition, *Fathom* allows a better visual interpretation of the relationship between two categorical variables, because *Fathom* offers multi-bin plot displays in which the heights of the bars of the plots are adjusted to the corresponding relative frequency. Also in group comparison processes *Fathom* offers additional features like the automatic adjustment of frequency axes when having multiple graphs, and a flexible change of bin width when comparing distributions in the form of histograms. Doing calculations in an analysis table is only possible in *Fathom* and extends the analyses that can be done with that tool.

CODAP offers valuable ready-made graphs like stacked dotplots and boxplots, is web based, free, and gives the opportunity for a quick start in the classroom— students need only an URL to a specific dataset (maybe pre-analyzed by the teacher). In addition, *CODAP* allows users to make specific data moves and define hierarchies in the data—which is very useful when exploring multivariate Civic Statistics data (Haldar et al., 2018).

TinkerPlots, Fathom and *CODAP* can serve as tools for learning and doing statistics. An introduction in the exploration of Civic Statistics data can also support the learning processes of young and high school students within the data exploration process. All three tools are useful as demonstration media for teachers. For more sophisticated explorations and also for handling larger amounts of data in Civic Statistics, users are recommended to use tools like *iNZight* (see Chap. 10) or professional tools like *SPSS* or *R* (see Chap. 11).

References

Biehler, R. (1997). Software for learning and for doing statistics. *International Statistical Review, 65*(2), 167–189. https://doi.org/10.1111/j.1751-5823.1997.tb00399.x

Biehler, R. (2001). Statistische Kompetenz von Schülerinnen und Schülern - Konzepte und Ergebnisse empirischer Studien am Beispiel des Vergleichens mpirischer Verteilungen. In M. Borovcnik, J. Engel, & D. Wickmann (Eds.), *Anregungen zum Stochastikunterricht* (pp. 97–114). Franz Becker.

Biehler, R. (2019). Software for learning and for doing statistics and probability – Looking back and looking forward from a personal perspective. In J. M. Contreras, M. M. Gea, M. M. López-Martín, & E. Molina-Portillo (Eds.), *Proceedings of the third international virtual congress of statistical education*. University of Granada. www.ugr.es/local/fqm126/civeest.html

Biehler, R., Ben-Zvi, D., Bakker, A., & Makar, K. (2013). Technology for enhancing statistical reasoning at the school level. In M. A. Clements, A. J. Bishop, C. Keitel-Kreidt, J. Kilpatrick, & F. K.-S. Leung (Eds.), *Third international handbook of mathematics education* (pp. 643–689). Springer. https://doi.org/10.1007/978-1-4614-4684-2_21

Biehler, R., Frischemeier, D., Reading, C., & Shaughnessy, M. (2018). Reasoning about data. In D. Ben-Zvi, K. Makar, & J. Garfield (Eds.), *International handbook of research in statistics education* (pp. 139–192). Springer. https://doi.org/10.1007/978-3-319-66195-7_5

Cobb, G. (2015). Mere renovation is too little too late: We need to rethink our undergraduate curriculum from the ground up. *The American Statistician, 69*(4), 266–282. https://doi.org/10.1080/00031305.2015.1093029

Engel, J. (2017). Statistical literacy for active citizenship: A call for data science education. *Statistics Education Research Journal, 16*(1), 44–49. https://doi.org/10.52041/serj.v16i1.213

Engel, J., Gal, I., & Ridgway, J. (2016). *Mathematical literacy and citizen engagement: The role of civic statistics*. Paper presented at the 13th International Congress on Mathematics Education (ICME13). Hamburg, Germany, July, 2016.

Frischemeier, D. (2018). Design, implementation, and evaluation of an instructional sequence to lead primary school students to comparing groups in statistical projects. In A. Leavy, M. Meletiou-Mavrotheris, & E. Paparistodemou (Eds.), *Statistics in early childhood and primary education* (pp. 217–238). Springer. https://doi.org/10.1007/978-981-13-1044-7_13

Frischemeier, D. (2019). Statistical reasoning when comparing groups with software—Frameworks and their application to qualitative video data. In D. Ben-Zvi & G. Burrill (Eds.), *Topics and trends in current statistics education research* (pp. 283–305). Springer. https://doi.org/10.1007/978-3-030-03472-6_13

Frischemeier, D., Biehler, R., & Engel, J. (2016). Competencies and dispositions for exploring micro data with digital tools. In: J. Engel (Ed.), *Promoting understanding of statistics about society*. Proceedings of the Roundtable Conference of the International Association of Statistics Education (IASE), July 2016, Berlin, Germany. https://doi.org/10.52041/SRAP.16504

Haldar, L. C., Wong, N., Heller, J. I., & Konold, C. (2018). Students making sense of multi-level data. *Technology Innovations in Statistics Education, 11*(1). https://doi.org/10.5070/T5111031358

Konold, C. (2002). Alternatives to scatterplots. In B. Phillips (Ed.), *Proceedings of the Sixth International Conference on Teaching Statistics*. Voorburg: International Statistical Institute.

Konold, C. (2007). Designing a data tool for learners. In M. Lovett & P. Shah (Eds.), *Thinking with data: The 33rd annual Carnegie symposium on cognition* (pp. 267–292). Lawrence Erlbaum Associates.

Konold, C., Pollatsek, A., Well, A., & Gagnon, A. (1997). Students analyzing data: Research of critical barriers. In J. Garfield & G. Burrill (Eds.), *Research on the role of technology in teaching and learning statistics: Proceedings of the 1996 IASE round table conference* (pp. 151–167). International Statistical Institute. https://doi.org/10.52041/SRAP.96302

Makar, K., & Rubin, A. (2009). A framework for thinking about informal statistical inference. *Statistics Education Research Journal, 8*(1), 82–105. https://doi.org/10.52041/serj.v8i1.457

McNamara, A. (2015). *Bridging the gap between tools for learning and for doing statistics*. PhD thesis, University of California, Los Angeles.

McNamara, A. (2018). Key attributes of a modern statistical computing tool. *The American Statistician*, 1–30. https://doi.org/10.1080/00031305.2018.1482784

Pfannkuch, M. (2007). Year 11 students' informal inferential reasoning: A case study about the interpretation of box plots. *International Electronic Journal of Mathematics Education, 2*(3), 149–167. https://doi.org/10.29333/iejme/181

Ridgway, J. (2016). Implications of the data revolution for statistics education. *International Statistical Review, 84*(3), 528–549. https://doi.org/10.1111/insr.12110

Ruggles, S., Flood, S., Goeken, R., Grover, J., Meyer, E., Pacas, E., & Sobek, M. (2019). *IPUMS USA: Version 9.0 [dataset]*. IPUMS. https://doi.org/10.18128/D010.V9.0

Chapter 10
Civic Statistics and *iNZight*: Illustrations of Some Design Principles for Educational Software

Chris J. Wild and Jim Ridgway

Abstract The PCS project has made good use of *iNZight* in exploring topics such as migration, gender inequality, childhood malnutrition, and natural disasters. Further examples of Civic Statistics topics that have been addressed using iNZight are provided here, along with a range of examples of creative ways to display data. The chapter outlines the advantages of technology enhanced statistics education and software requirements; maps some analyses which are central to Civic Statistics and shows how these can be conducted using iNZight. Examples include working with multivariate data, exploring subgroups within data, using multiple representations, analysing and reanalysing, and telling stories grounded in evidence. Often with complex social/civic datasets it is necessary to explore changes over time, and to explore spatial patterns. Here, we describe software features that facilitate data exploration for naïve users that include both direct guidance and hooks to encourage engagement and further learning, and also features for advanced users, such as the automatic generation of R code for documentation and software reuse. Software for analysing data is evolving rapidly to accommodate new sorts of data, new techniques for analysis, and new methods to present data. Therefore, the chapter concludes by describing developments to iNZight that are in progress.

Keywords Software design · Multivariate data · Multiple representations · Disaggregation · Complexity reduction · Complex survey designs

C. J. Wild (✉)
The University of Auckland, Auckland, New Zealand
e-mail: c.wild@auckland.ac.nz

J. Ridgway
The University of Durham, Durham, UK
e-mail: jim.ridgway@durham.ac.uk

© Springer Nature Switzerland AG 2022
J. Ridgway (ed.), *Statistics for Empowerment and Social Engagement*,
https://doi.org/10.1007/978-3-031-20748-8_10

10.1 Introduction

Readers of this book will already be aware of the explosive growth in the availability and importance of data in understanding and managing almost all aspects of our society. The buzz words come in and fade away, e.g., the data deluge, big data, open data. Some (like open data) have lasting value because they describe something unique. Others just convey a sense of progress, urgency, opportunity, and sometimes alarm and dread.

Things we never knew could be considered as data are now very successfully being mined for insights and predictive value—sources such as text, images, sound files, and network data. The International Data Science in Schools Project[1] is proposing that much of this should be part of the high school curriculum.

Different data types and structures demand different ways of thinking and looking. Accompanying the rapid expansion of the data universe has been an explosion of new and improved ways to visualize and analyse data. The barriers to participation are becoming ever lower. There is a steady stream of wonderful new visualization functions and packages becoming available in *R*, *Python* and *JavaScript* doing away with the need for low-level programming.

While technology is making it easier to perform specific tasks, it is also rapidly expanding the spectrum of things that non-specialists can do. Because each new data-type or graphic-type demands new ways of conceptualising data and interacting with software, the universe of possibilities that are accessible to non-specialists is rapidly expanding in size and complexity.

While this stream of new opportunities is exciting, users can become overloaded cognitively—"It is all just too much. I just can't get my head around it". Strategies are needed which enable everyone to ride the wave of progress while managing individual expanding mental universes.

An important complexity-reducing factor comes from the advance of technology. Many of the mechanical procedures underpinning important concepts are no longer worth mastering. Any particular mechanical skill tends to be death-dated because software is continually automating these procedures. Creating histograms by hand offers an obvious example; one can argue that some hand-crafting is useful pedagogically, but not that this is an essential process for exploratory data analysis. The most important capabilities for the long term are an awareness of what is possible, thinking skills (such as imagining/question posing/interpreting/critiquing/concluding) and communication skills; in contrast to the mechanical procedures that were such a focus in the past. There are clear advantages to learners from not having to master so many technical procedures. However, these gains are insufficient to compensate for the explosive growth in the data world. We need more complexity-reduction strategies to enable representative citizens to engage effectively with evidence.

---

[1] http://www.idssp.org/

In Chap. 7, Trostianitser, Teixeira and Campos outline some uses of *iNZight* contained in lesson plans accessible via CivicStatMap,[2] namely, the use of *iNZight* for exploring:

- The migration data for Nigeria taken from the UN 2015 Millennium Development Goals.
- The IPUMS Gender Equity data set for 2000 and 2005 for Brazil and the USA.
- Data on malnutrition in children from the Hunger and Commitment Index (HANCI).
- Data on natural disasters from the Center for Research on the Epidemiology of Disasters—Emergency Events Database (EM-DAT).
- Data from the OECD Program for the International Assessment of Adult Competencies (PIAAC).

In this chapter, further examples are given, which illustrate ways in which software can be used to support the sorts of analysis essential for wrangling with evidence relevant to Civic Statistics. The intention is not to provide a tutorial on the use of a particular package (tutorials can be found embedded in PCS lesson plans); rather it is to point to some principles of software design and implementation that are of general interest.

10.1.1 Design Principles for Educational Software

A seminal paper by Biehler (1997, see also 2019) discussed the criteria by which software to support learning statistics and doing statistics should be judged. Implicitly, this sort of analysis serves as a guide for future software developments. McNamara (2019) built on Biehler's (1997) work, and set out eight desirable features of educational software, which have been built into *iNZight*. These are:

- **Accessibility**—software should be affordable, work with a variety of operating systems, and should be easy to install.
- **Easy entry for novice users**—novice users should be able to see how to use the software, and what it does; using the software, users should receive immediate gratification i.e. an intelligible and immediate response to commands.
- **Data as a first-order persistent object**—Software should be able to access data presented in common formats (e.g. flat files, hierarchically ordered data, using APIs). There should be a good and transparent workflow for cleaning data. Users should always be able to view their raw data.
- **Support for a cycle of *exploratory and confirmatory analysis***—to use Tukey's (1977) words. Biehler (1997) referred to *draft results*. Essentially, software

---

[2] https://iase-web.org/islp/pcs/

should support activities such as question posing, critique, interpreting, concluding, and imagining.

- **Flexible plot creation**—there should be a facility to plot data in a variety of ways.
- **Support for randomisation**—software should support tools such as randomisation tests, and visual representations of uncertainty e.g. via bootstrap.
- **Interactivity at every level**—Biehler (1997) argued the case for direct manipulation rather than modifying a script, and that software tools should support graphs as an interface to the data. Another desirable aspect of interactivity is access to multiple coordinated views—so (say) highlighting an element in one display leads to relevant changes in every display.
- **Inherent documentation**—there is a need to show the pathway of any analysis, and also the logic of what has transpired—*Jupyter notebooks* (Toomey, 2017) provides an example. Biehler (1997) criticised the absence of inherent documentation in Velleman's (1989) *DataDesk*—the latest version generates *R* code from user actions.
- **Simple support for narrative publishing, and reproducibility**—communication is an essential aspect of any analysis. Users need to be able to share code and analyses, to say what was done, and to be able to use the same analysis on a new data set. Tools for exporting graphics and analyses should be provided.

Implicit in McNamara's and Biehler's analyses is the need to provide sophisticated tools for experienced users (and that this collection of tools will be extensible). Both authors comment that there are few if any examples of packages that satisfy all the design criteria, and support both learners and practitioners, although some—such as *Fathom*[3]—fulfilled many of these essential criteria.

iNZight satisfies all these criteria; in addition, *iNZight* sets out to entice users to learn more about data exploration and analysis. Users might not know quite what they want to do, or the opportunities available to facilitate exploration and analysis; *iNZight* suggests relevant data visualisations and analyses. *iNZight* has many interesting features, and is free to use; we think it is legitimate to devote a whole chapter of this book to this tool, to demonstrate software design principles and their implementation. Moreover, the features that *iNZight* shows can also be seen as necessary and valuable for many data explorations in Civic Statistics—so these features can also be seen as illustrations of norms and requirements for future software that combines easy access for beginners with substantial data analytic capacities. In our examples we also use data from *Gapminder*, to show that *Gapminder* analyses can be supported by *iNZight* and expanded because of the richer data analytical environment.

---

[3] https://fathom.concord.org

10.1.2 What Is iNZight?

iNZight[4] (Elliott et al., 2021; Wild et al., 2021) is a free, open-source,[5] data visualization and analysis tool that can be used by people at any stage of statistical development. It is a tool for beginners in the sense that it makes simple things very easy to do—it started off life as a tool for school children. However, it is also possible to do sophisticated things very rapidly, such as creating dynamic and interactive displays, wrangling with data, and doing complicated statistical modelling. Some capabilities are directly relevant to Civic Statistics, such as the ability to represent data from complex sample-surveys properly, and to deal with multiple response data (i.e. data from surveys where respondents can select as many answer-options to a question as they please).

iNZight comes in two versions, a desktop version that needs to be installed on a computer and an online version (called *iNZight Lite*[6]) that runs in a web browser when users are connected to the internet. Many parts of *iNZight* also make the underlying *R* code available. This has three major advantages: first, as an audit trail—audit trails are particularly important for seeing if, when and how the data itself has been modified (e.g. by removing outliers); second as a reproducibility, sharing and work-efficiency aid—a sequence of analysis steps can be shared or repurposed and re-implemented almost instantly simply by running the code; and third as a useful tool for those learning to program in *R*—viewing system-generated code can be a useful productivity-aid enabling people to find out quickly how to do things in *R*.

10.2 Key Software Functionality for Civic Statistics

In this section, we describe some of the functionality essential for working with Civic Statistics.

10.2.1 Easy Exploration of Multivariate Data

It is important for users to engage in multivariate data exploration easily, and to experience "Aha" moments. In *iNZight*, as soon as you choose to look at a variable, or a relationship between variables, *iNZight* will offer a graph. Users can refine the choices made to create new displays.

---

[4] https://inzight.nz/

[5] https://github.com/iNZightVIT

[6] https://lite.docker.stat.auckland.ac.nz/

10.2.2 Minimizing Cognitive Load

Most statistics packages are driven via a graphical user interface (GUI). GUI-based tools typically assume that users know the names of the desired graphics and forms of analysis they want to use. This can be a significant barrier to participation and access for novices; they cannot explore data unless they know and remember the name of a procedure and how it is used. *iNZight* takes account of the data being explored, and offers default presentations and analyses (and, of course, provides the ability to look at alternatives and make changes).

10.2.3 Provoking Learning

An advantage of a GUI-based system is that when the system recognizes it is in a particular situation, the interface can then change to offer up choices corresponding to useful things that can be done, or looked at, in that situation. When confronted with controls it is a natural human impulse to ask, "I wonder what that does?" So a good interface can act as a prompt for doing more, or finding out what more can be done, to draw the user into learning more. Linking "I wonder what that does?" to a good help system facilitates discovery and just-in-time learning.

10.2.4 Offering R-Code: Reproducibility and a Bridge from GUIs to Coding

GUI systems often fail to create audit trails of what has been done during an analysis. It is especially important to have records of where data has been changed for some reason (e.g., by deleting outliers) and what predates or follows such changes. GUI systems can also be bad at enabling others to reproduce an analysis that has been done, or allowing users to quickly re-run all the steps of an analysis, for example because the data has been updated or corrected since the original analysis. Saving the underlying *R*-code solves these problems. It also offers a useful aid to learning *R*, and a useful productivity-aid for people to find out quickly how to do things in *R* when they want to write *R* code (at the time of writing this is limited to all of the basic *iNZight* operations including data wrangling, and amongst the advanced modules, to the statistical-modelling module—but extensions are underway). For a fuller discussion of many of these issues, and in particular of the comparative strengths of GUIs and coding; see Wild (2018), Burr et al. (2021).

When the *show editable code boxes* feature is switched on in *iNZight*, the graphics, summary and inferential statistics features in basic *iNZight* show the code that created the current display and allow this code to be stored or modified and rerun. In addition to changing the output, the interface choices are also instantly repopulated to match the code instructions. The learning strategies being implemented include: "the code that makes it": code is always in view to foster learning by osmosis; and the mappings between GUI settings, argument values of the function calls and output are direct and immediate in order to foster seeing the relationships between them.

10.2.5 Specific Support for Civic Statistics

Civic Statistics often engages with survey data. Survey data from authoritative sources is collected using complex survey designs involving features such as the oversampling of some (usually small but important) subgroups, stratified sampling and cluster sampling. Graphics and analyses that do not take these sample-design factors into account should always raise credibility red-flags, as they can be very misleading. With *iNZight*, the program will take account of any sample-design information provided (Elliott et al., 2021).

10.3 Illustrating *iNZight*

This section provides examples of the functionality of *iNZight* as a tool for engaging with Civic Statistics.

10.3.1 Making Simple Things Really Simple

Here, a small set of workforce data is explored. In its basic mode, *iNZight* requires data with a standard, rectangular, cases/units (rows) by variables (columns) structure. Initially, only the left-hand window in Fig. 10.1 is populated (the lower right-hand window has not yet been created). The display shows the data and various command capabilities. These command actions are initiated by the variables that have been selected in the boxes at the lower left of Fig. 10.1 and determined by variable type (either numeric or categorical).

As soon as we select *Qualification* (a categorical variable) in the first box, a bar chart of the *Qualification* distribution appears. When we also select *Gender* (another categorical variable) in the second box the display changes to the side-by-side bar chart at the upper right to display the relationship between *Qualification* and *Gender*.

Pressing the **Get Summary** button at the bottom left creates a window of summary statistics (here the cross-classification between these two categorical variables presented both in terms of counts and proportions). Similarly, clicking **Get Inference** pops up a window of inferential information. For two categorical variables, the latter gives things like Chi-square test results and confidence intervals for

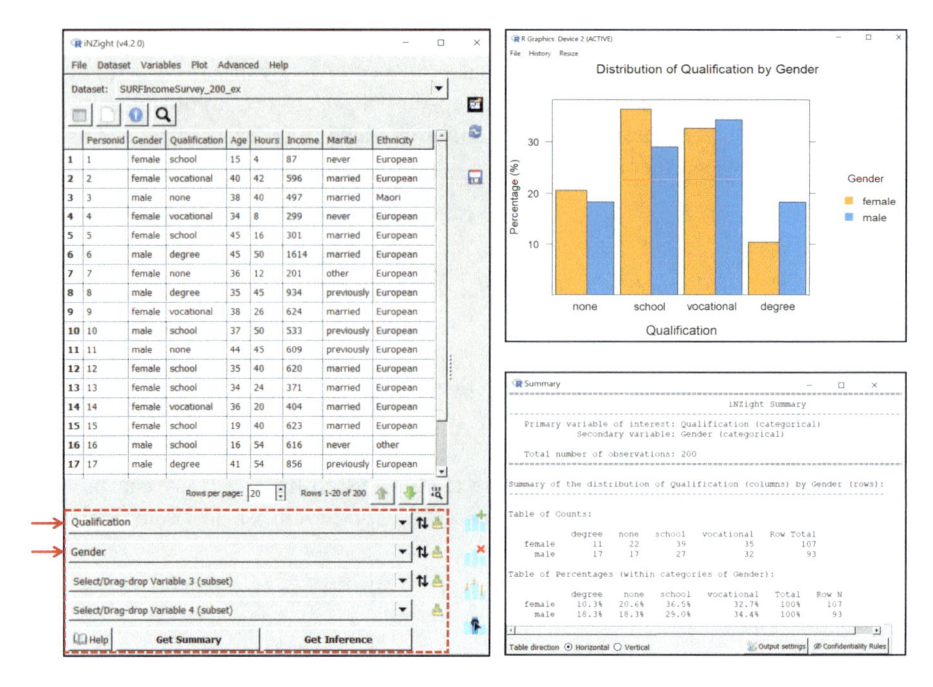

Fig. 10.1 Basic operation of *iNZight*

differences in proportions. This epitomizes the cycle of exploration for *iNZight* at its most basic. When variables are selected, a relevant graph is created. **Get Summary** and **Get Inference** deliver just what they say.

If the variable chosen had been numeric (e.g. *Income*), then a different type of plot and different types of information would have been given (e.g., extremes, quartiles, medians, means, and standard deviations as summary information; and as inferential information: *t*-tests or an analysis of variance, tests and confidence intervals for differences between group means or medians). There are options for changing default behaviour. In general, *iNZight* decides what to deliver instantly using the variable-types of the combination of variables selected—however, it also gives users options for changing the default behaviour.

Users have to know enough to be able to read and interpret the computer output, and to know whether what has been produced is sensible. However, users' efforts are focused on making meaning—in contrast to fighting software to get output.

10.3.2 Facilitating Exploration

In this Section, we illustrate ways in which software can facilitate exploration by offering a variety of ways to display data, and via the creation of interactive displays.

The **Add to Plot** facility (see Fig. 10.2) allows users to scroll through the types of graph applicable for the currently-chosen variables via the *Plot type* box. The options offered are taken from the relevant graphs from the *Financial Times* Visual Vocabulary[7] with some additions.

To illustrate, we explore the relationship between *Income* and *Gender* in the Workforce data set. For this small data set (up to about 3000 observations) the default is side-by-side dot plots with boxplot summaries underneath them, as in Fig. 10.2. If we ask for **Add to Plot** the left-hand control panel is replaced by the right-most panel in Fig. 10.2. We can use the *Plot type* selection box to choose the name of a plot type we know we want, or we can scroll through all the alternative representations (here, those in Fig. 10.3); graphs can be oriented either horizontally or vertically.

Interactive plots are particularly useful because of the ability they give the viewer to query or relate features in a plot or set of plots. Such plots can be both more engaging and more informative than static plots. Figure 10.4 is a static image from the interactive version of the graph shown in Fig. 10.1. It shows the graph and the two-way table it was produced from. In the interactive plot, hovering the mouse over a bar gives information about the bar (as shown). But there is also interactivity between the graph and the table. For example, clicking on the legend colour-square for females fades the data for males, thus highlighting the female distribution, and also highlights the corresponding percentages in the female row in the table. This shows, among other things, that the female percentages add to 100%, which is important for understanding the plot.

Figure 10.5 shows something a little more sophisticated—an interactive graph from *iNZight*'s maps module. The data is 4-yearly, country-level data from *Gapminder*.[8] The left-hand graph shows the life expectancies over time for the countries as little time-series positioned on each country. The right-hand graph shows all of the time series for all of the countries in detail. Clicking on a country on the map highlights its time series on the right-hand plot. Clicking on an interesting looking time series, such as the one for Rwanda (blue) which shows a big dip in life expectancies in the 1990s, highlights the country it came from on the map. In this case, the dip in life expectancy reflects deaths in the Rwandan civil war and the genocide against the Tutsi. Hovering over a series shows the country name, year and the life expectancy value at the mouse-pointer location.

Here, the interactive graphics work entirely independently of the system that produced them, and so can be saved as html files and embedded in webpages (or given to someone else).

---

[7] https://www.vizwiz.com/2018/07/visual-vocabulary.html

[8] https://www.gapminder.org/data/

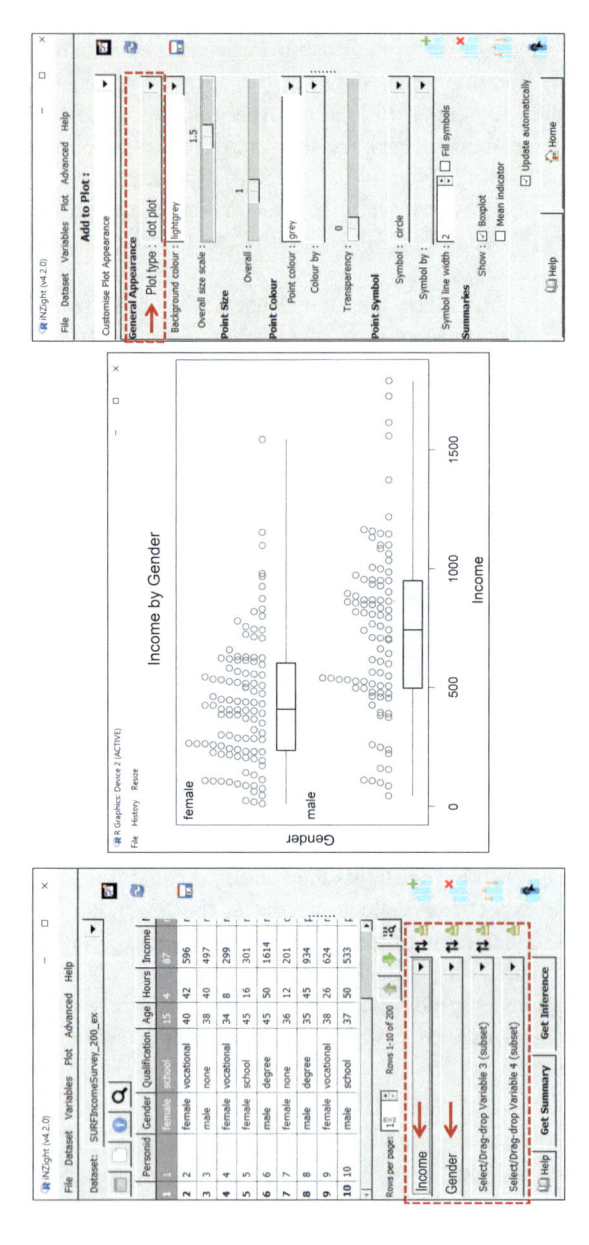

Fig. 10.2 Default plot for *Income* by *Gender* plus the **Add to Plot** control panel

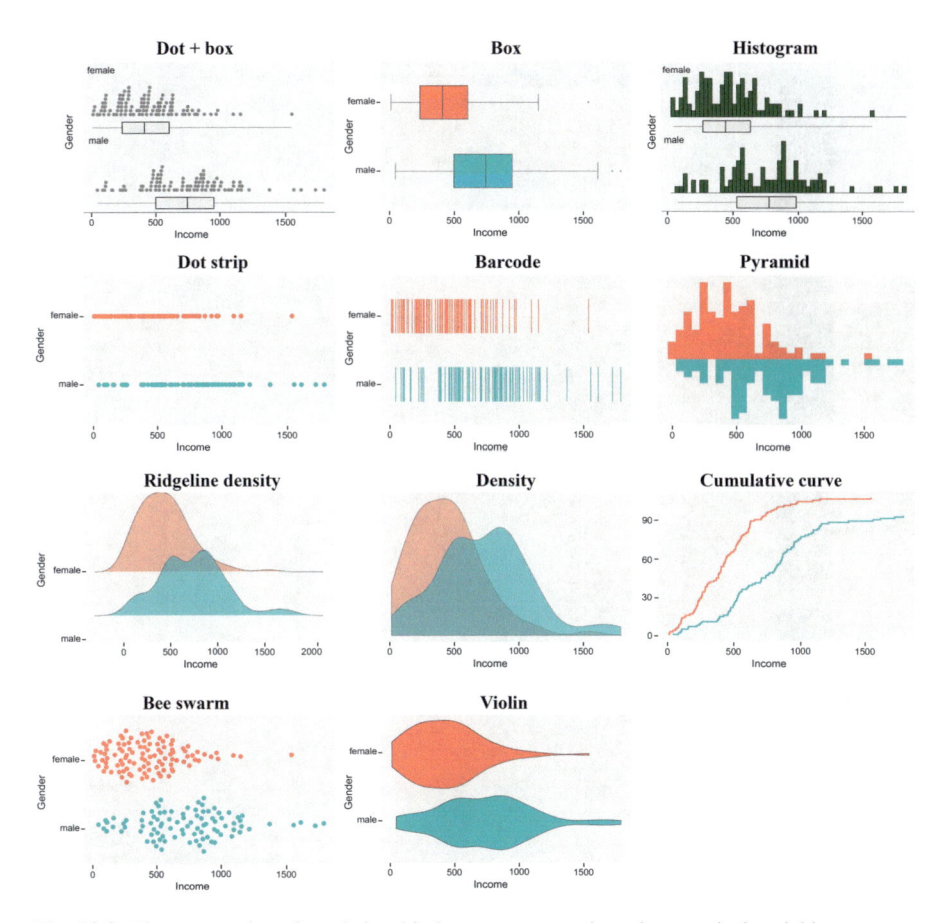

Fig. 10.3 Plot type options for relationship between a numeric and categorical variable

10.3.3 Disaggregation: Exploring Subgroups with Static and Dynamic Graphs

Here we will use a data set of about 10,000 cases from the NHANES[9] survey of the US population. Figure 10.6 shows the relationship between having smoked marijuana regularly at some point and having smoked cigarettes seriously (*has smoked over 100 cigarettes*) for everyone in the data set who answered the questions. It can be seen that cigarette smokers are much more likely to have smoked marijuana than nonsmokers. But is this relationship true for different subgroups?

Selecting *AgeDecade* in the third variable slot in the lower left panel produced Fig. 10.7—the same sort of graph, but for each age-decade group separately. The

---

[9]https://www.cdc.gov/nchs/nhanes/index.htm

Fig. 10.4 Static image from the interactive version of the graph in Fig. 10.1

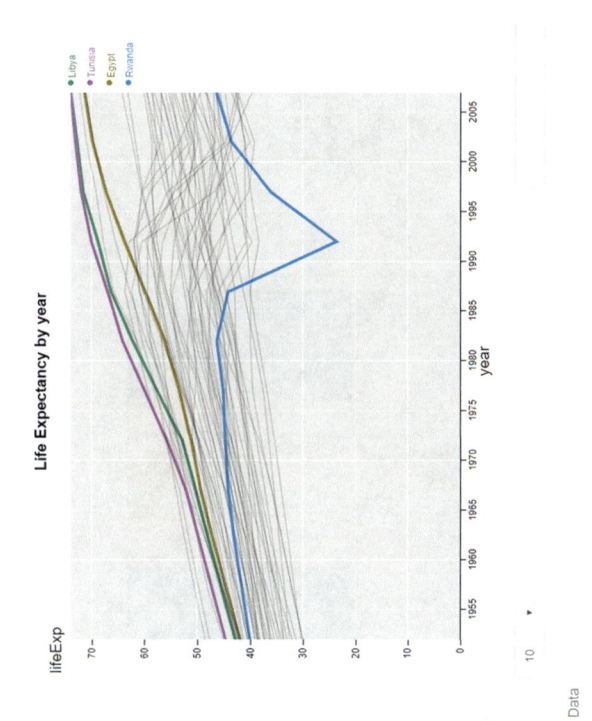

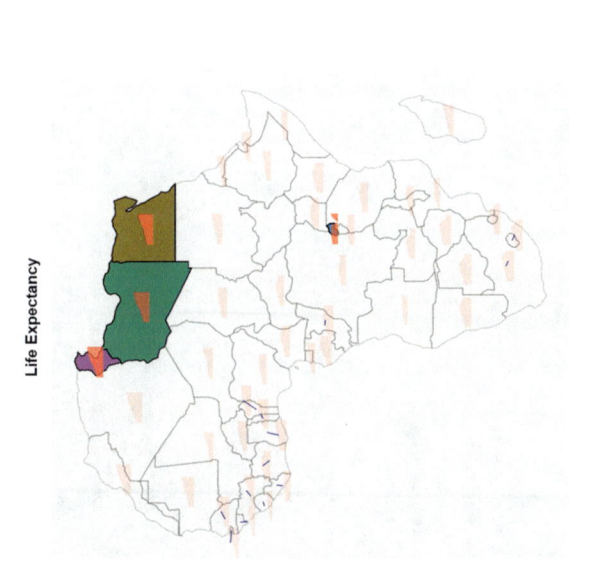

Fig. 10.5 Interactive graphs showing changes in average life expectancy over time for African countries

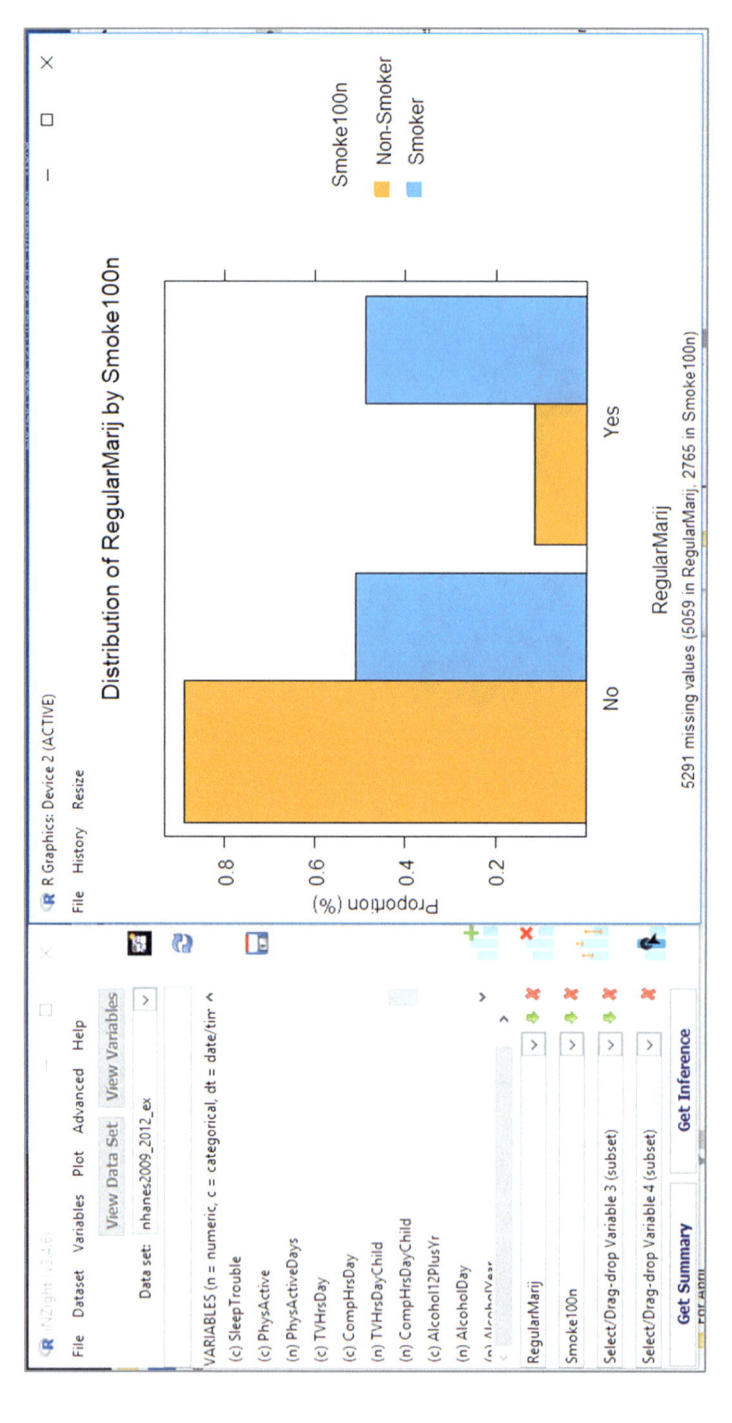

Fig. 10.6 Marijuana smoking by cigarette smoking (whole data set)

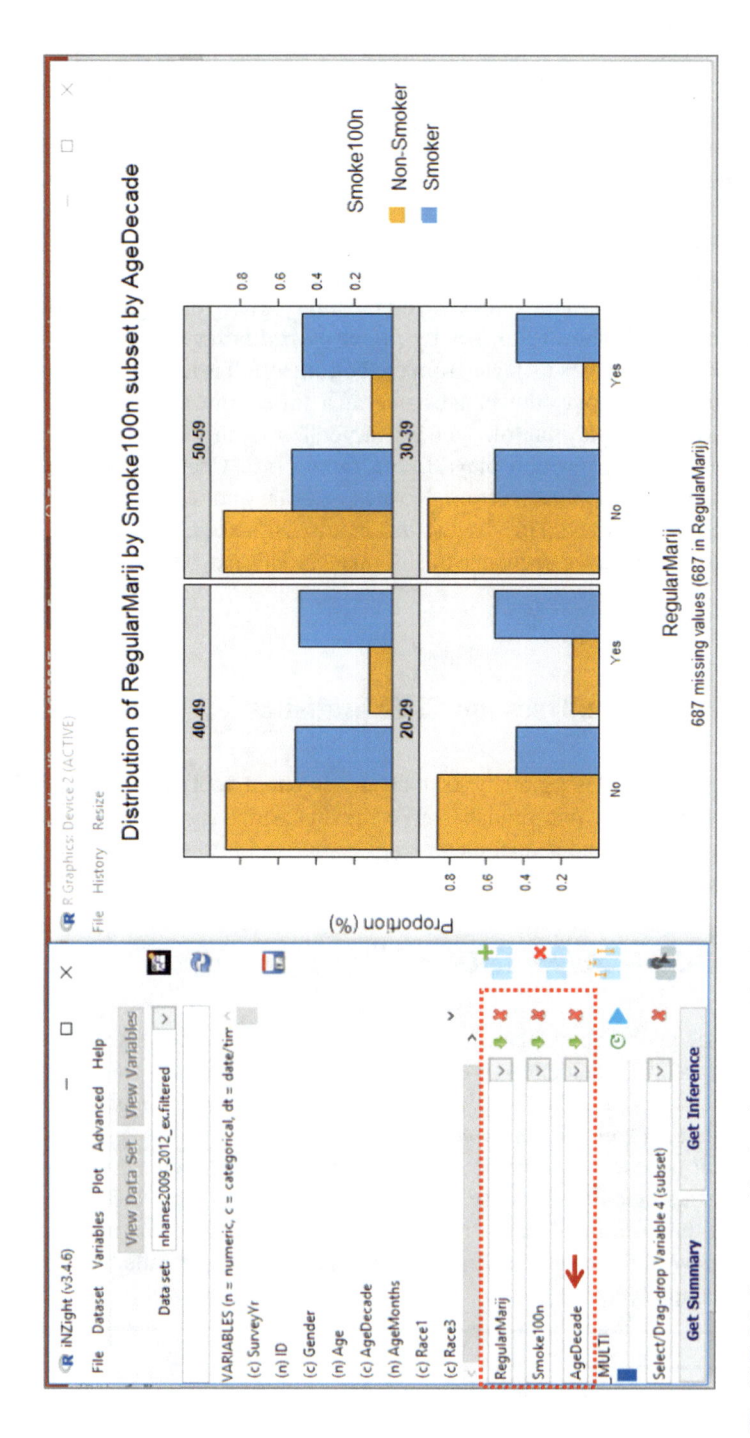

Fig. 10.7 Marijuana smoking by cigarette smoking faceted by *AgeDecade*

operation of disaggregation is sometimes called facetting (here we have "facetted by the variable *AgeDecade*"). This allows us to see that the marijuana-cigarette relationship is very similar regardless of age group. In general, facetting is good for investigating whether, or in what way, a pattern changes over subgroups determined by some variable such as ethnicity, education level, or sex (here *AgeDecade*).

Figure 10.8 goes a step further and also facets by *Race* (American for *Ethnicity*). Mostly the relationship looks similar regardless of age or race. However, having chopped up the data set into 20 subgroups, some of the sample sizes are small and so one would not be surprised to see differences attributable to random variation.

Figure 10.9 shows a more sophisticated example, where disaggregation leads to important insights. It shows *Fertility* by *Infant mortality* for the world's countries facetted by *Year*. The years increase from the bottom left. It is hard to see the changes over time, but if you play the images one at a time from oldest to most recent (e.g. using *iNZight*'s play button) you get a version of the famous Hans Rosling bubbles motion chart,[10] which plays like a movie (see Chap. 8 for examples of classroom uses of *Gapminder* from Kovacs, Kazar, and Kuruczleki). Here the changes become obvious. This is just the cartoonist's-sketchbook effect, or any regular movie, i.e. a played sequence of still images. This can be done for any type of plot.

10.4   Essential Analyses for Civic Statistics

Here, we give examples of analyses that are essential tools in the repertoire of anyone engaged with Civic Statistics. We illustrate analysis of multiple response data, time series data, and spatial data.

10.4.1   Multiple Response Data

How do young people spend their time online? Figure 10.10 shows a small segment of data from a 2011 student survey.[11] Highlighted is the data from a multiple-response question that asked *In the last 7 days, which of these online activities have you done? (You may tick more than one)*. This 'single question' elicits responses that need to be coded on many variables, one for each activity chosen. It was asked as a single item because these are a set of things that "belong together". The fact that the resulting data has multiple variables, however, can make it hard to get an overview of the results. *iNZight*'s Multiple Response module was developed to address this problem.

---

[10]https://www.gapminder.org/tools/#$chart-type=bubbles & url=v1

[11]https://new.censusatschool.org.nz/

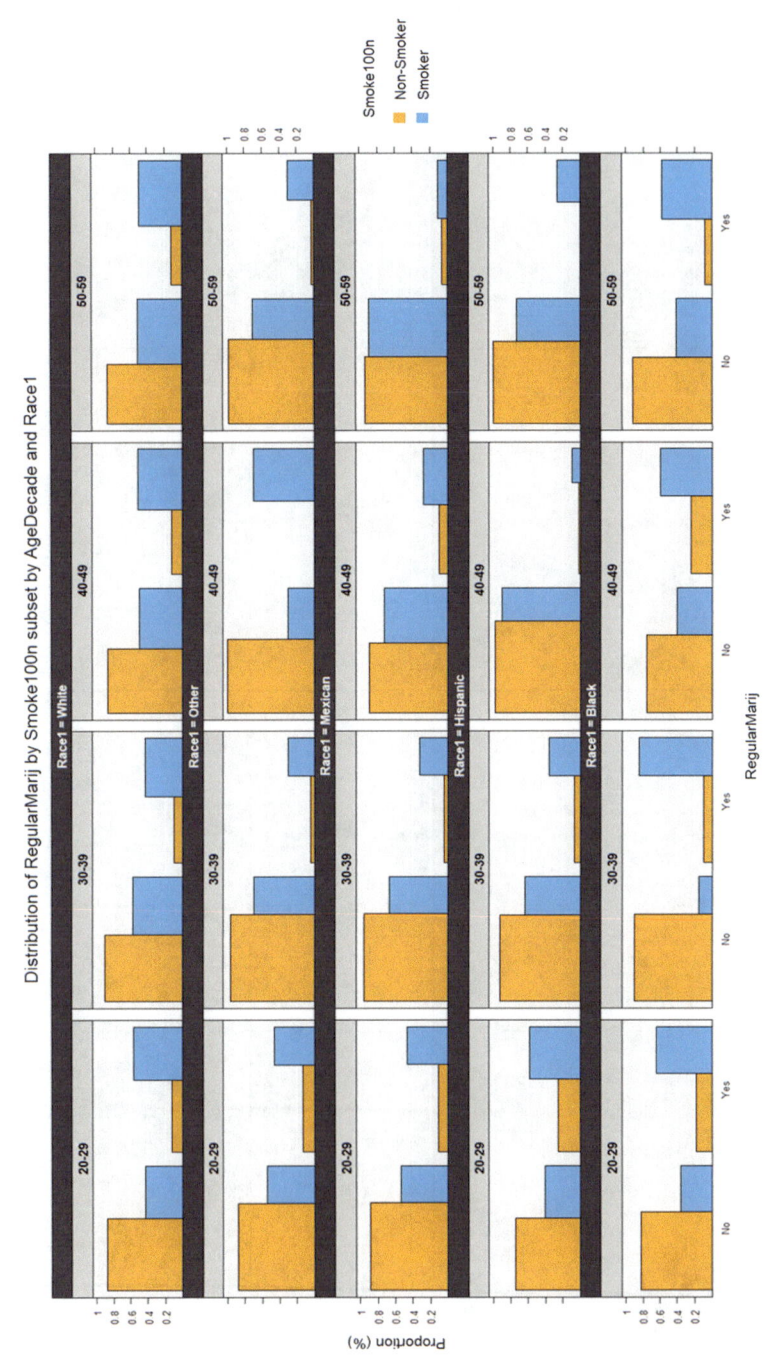

Fig. 10.8 Marijuana smoking by cigarette smoking facetted by *AgeDecade* and *Race*

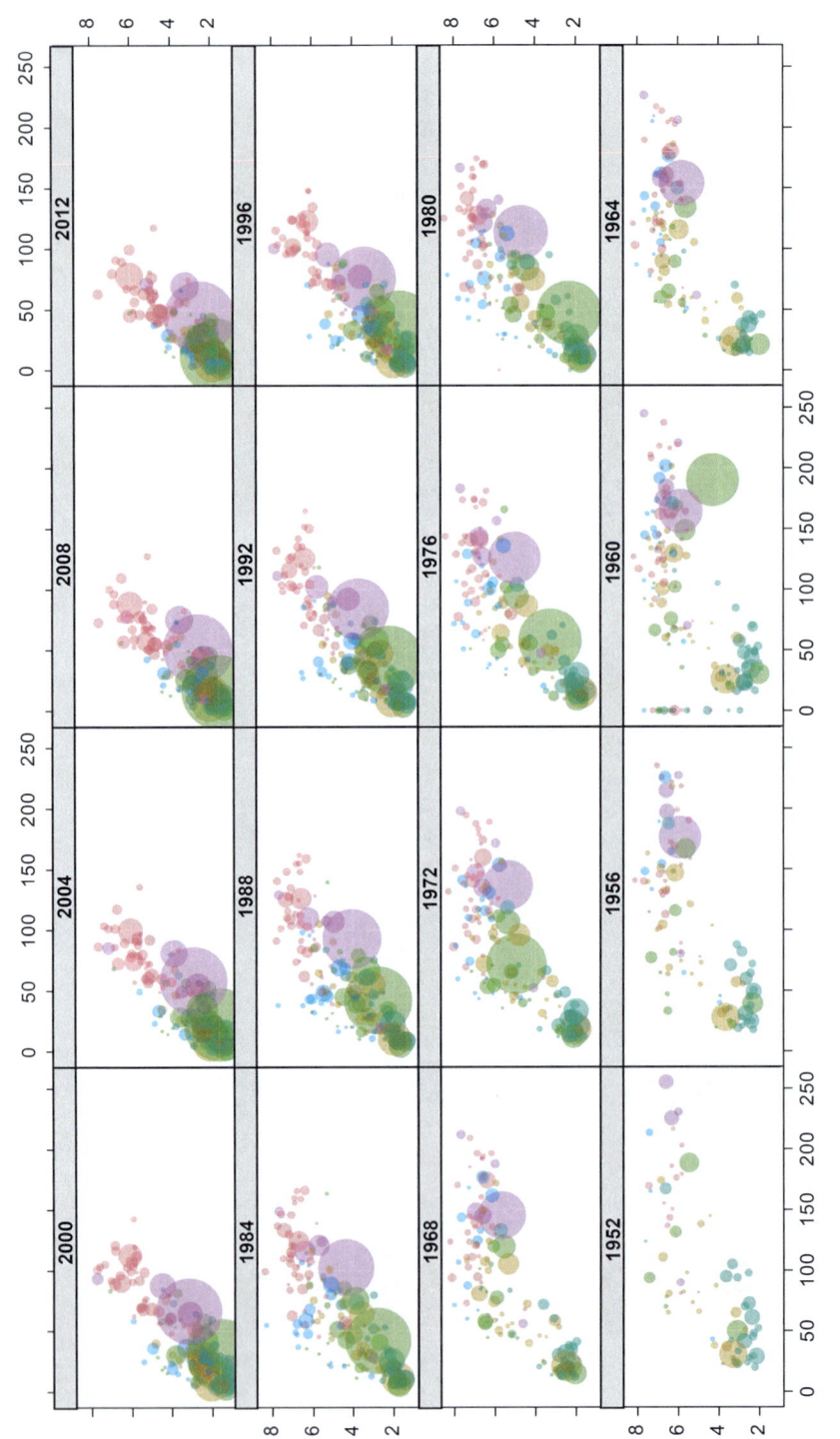

Fig. 10.9 *Fertility* by *Infant mortality* for the world's countries facetted by Year

	AW	AX	AY	AZ	BA	BB	BC	BD	BE	BF	BG
1	techconsc	technone	cellmonth	onlinemusic	onlinevideo	onlinegame	onlinefriend	onlineschool	onlineother	onlinenone	bedtime
2	yes	no	12	yes	yes	no	yes	yes	no	no	11:45:00
3	yes	no	1	yes	yes	no	yes	no	no	no	12:30:00
4	yes	no	NA	yes	yes	yes	yes	yes	no	no	10:00:00
5	yes	no	36	yes	yes	no	yes	no	no	no	10:00:00
6	no	no	10	no	no	no	no	no	no	no	11:30:00
7	yes	no	12	no	no	yes	yes	yes	no	no	10:00:00
8	yes	no	1	no	yes	yes	yes	no	no	no	9:00:00

Fig. 10.10 Some multiple-response data

In Fig. 10.11 we have told the program to treat a set of these variables together by selecting them jointly in the control panel. A graph pops up at the right giving all the proportions of positive responses for each variable in one picture.

As argued earlier, disaggregation is an essential activity if data are to be understood. Here, the data get a lot more interesting when facetted by *age* and *gender* as in Fig. 10.12. We see interesting (apparent) age trends such as the dropping off in participation in playing games online by older students, with the fall being steeper and further for girls than boys. Girls appear to take to music and socializing more than, and earlier than, boys. There is an important statistical issue for the software to address, namely that with multiple-response data, tests and confidence intervals for differences in proportions need to take account of the (differing) correlations between them.

10.4.2 Time Series

Figure 10.13 shows time series graphs of quarterly data on the average visitor numbers in New Zealand from Australia, the UK and the US in the period 1998–2014.[12] *iNZight*'s time-series module takes data from a single series or compares several series and supports additive and multiplicative methods for seasonal series, including forecasts. Visitor numbers are clearly very heavily seasonal with considerably larger numbers in the January–March quarter and lower in July–September—except for Australian visitors for whom the lowest numbers are in April–June. For the UK, there are over twice as many visitors in the southern summer than the southern winter. There are also some very noticeable differences in the time trends—with Australia climbing relatively steadily but the UK and the US numbers tipping into a decline—probably attributable to the global financial crisis (though the US numbers show recovery towards the end of the time period). Again, these displays show the importance of being able to represent data in different ways, and that disaggregated data does not always show the same patterns as aggregated data.

---

[12] http://infoshare.stats.govt.nz/infoshare/

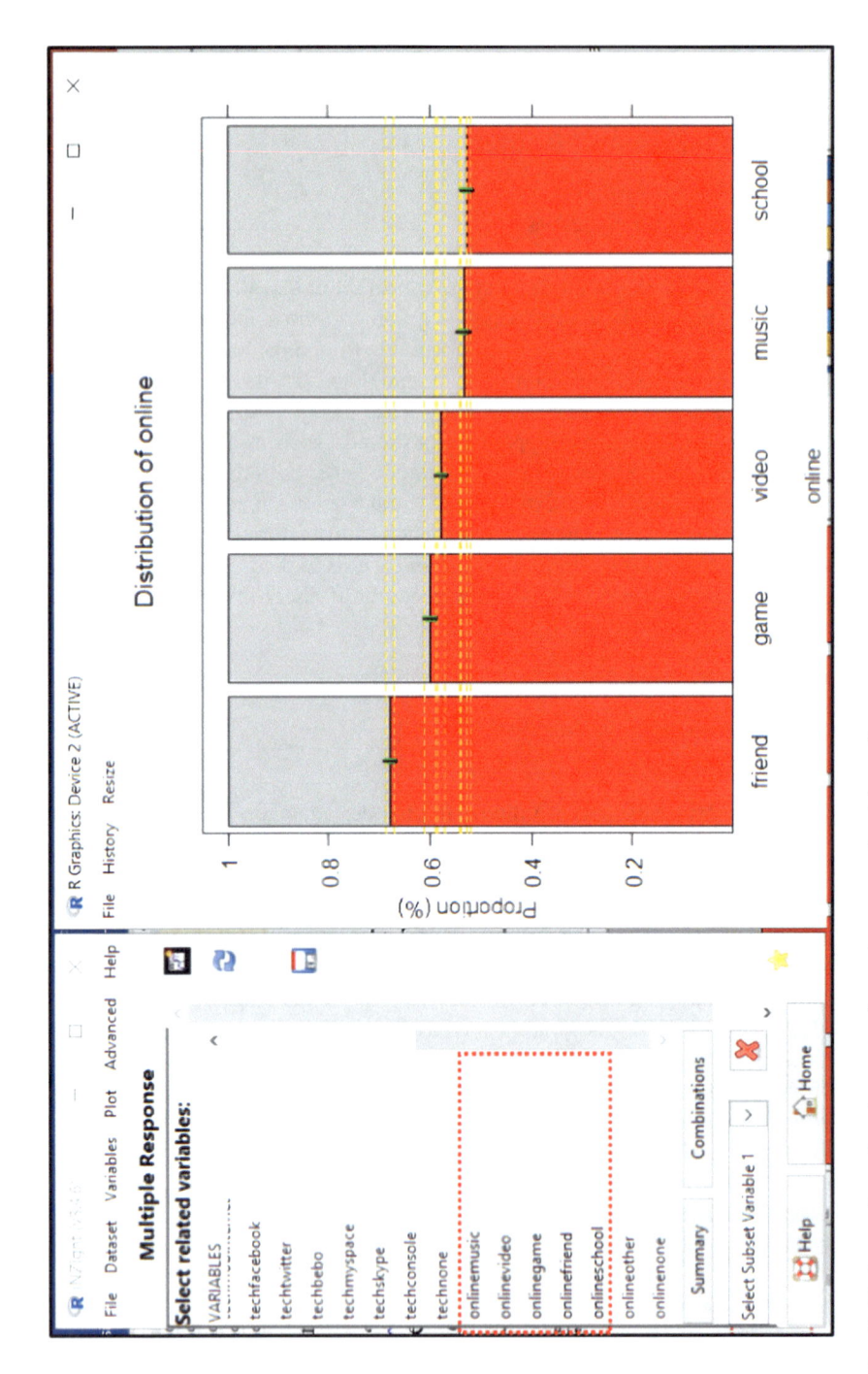

Fig. 10.11 Proportions of students reporting various sorts of activity online

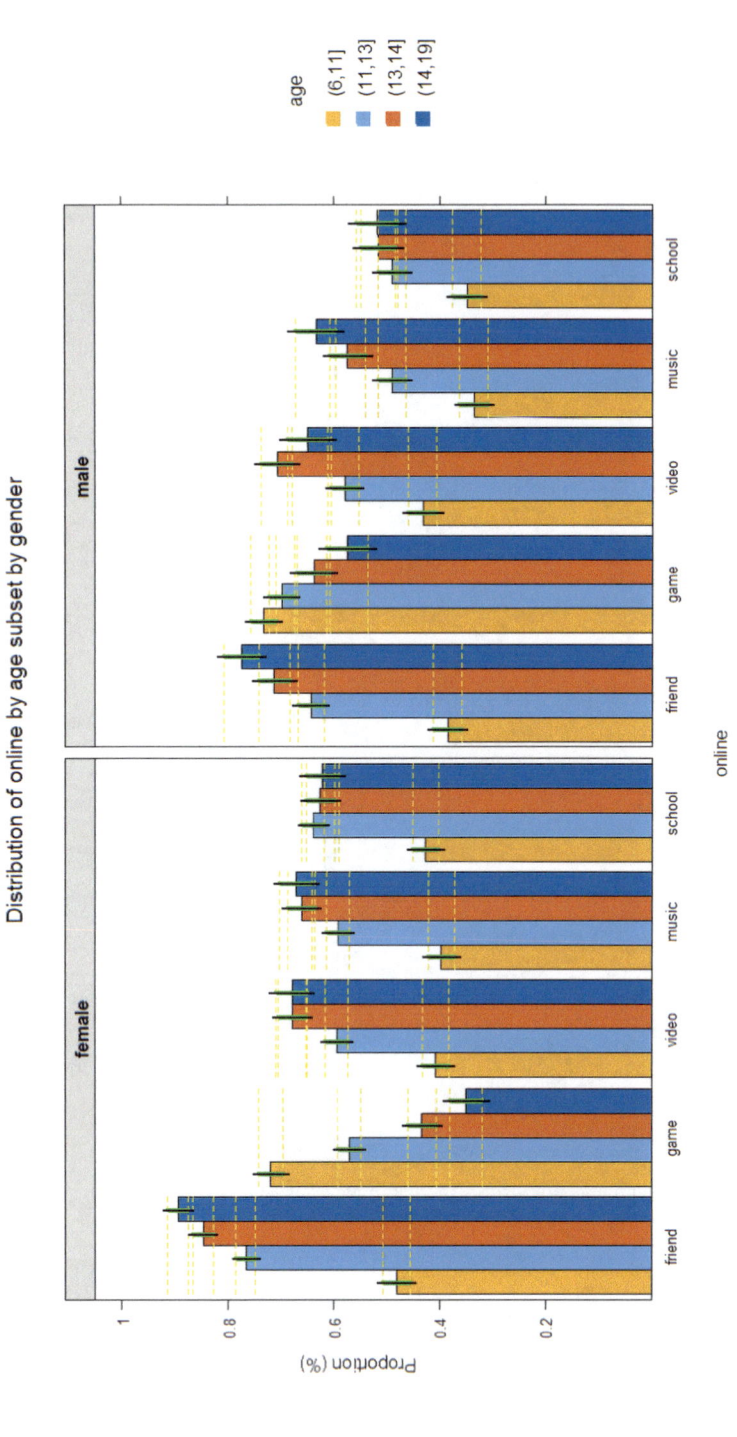

Fig. 10.12 Online-activity responses facetted by *age* and *gender*

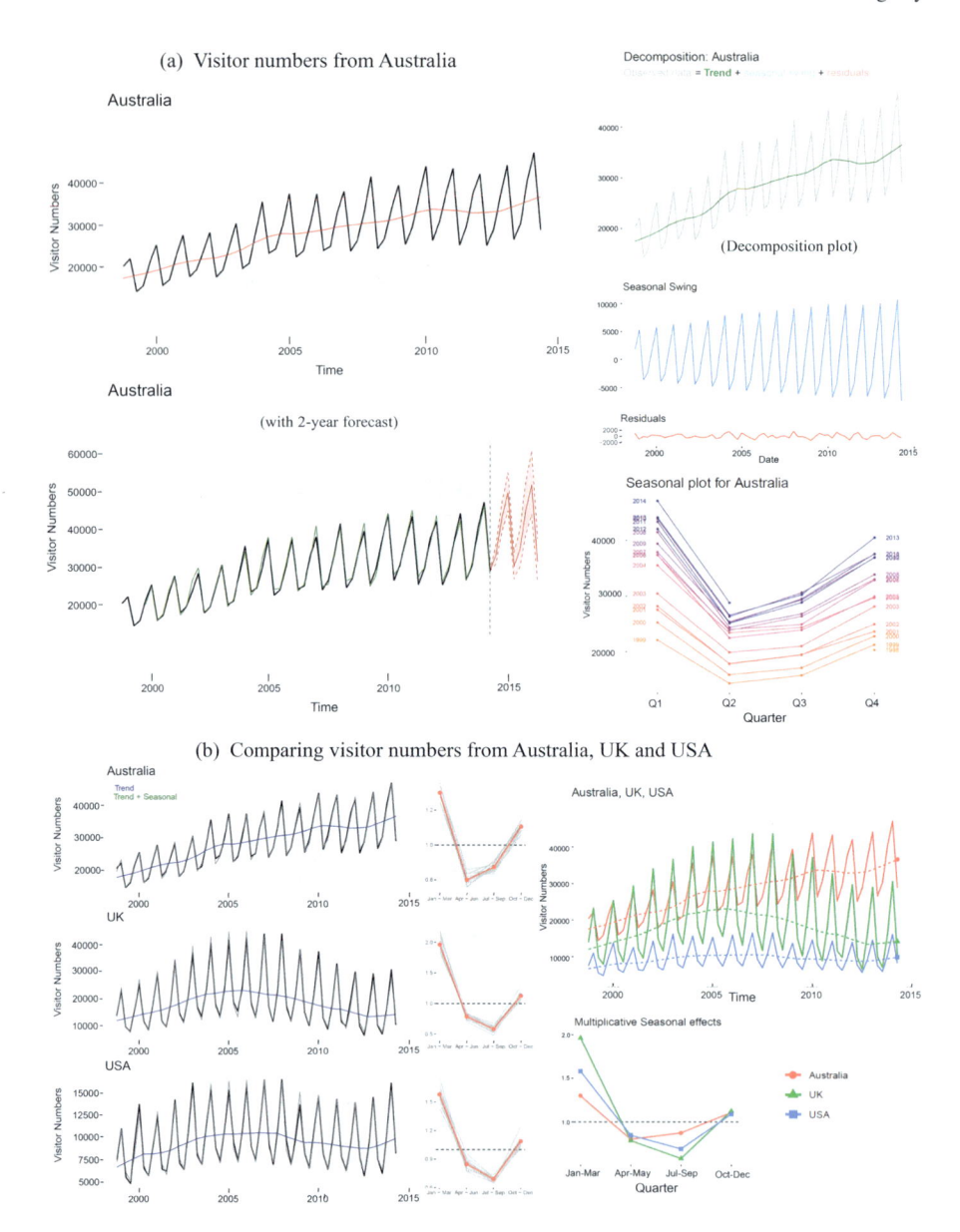

Fig. 10.13 Average numbers of visitors present in New Zealand, 1998–2014

Order	Latitude	Longitude	Depth	Felt	Magnitude	RMS	NorMidSth	Month	Day	Hour	Minute
1	-39.14347	174.8942	-218	N	4.289	0.19	North	1	3	11	53
2	-37.70441	177.2514	-65	Y	4.454	0.21	North	1	4	18	44
3	-40.25043	173.57	-196	N	4.035	0.247	North	1	6	19	19
4	-38.14048	176.3235	-158	N	4.479	0.205	North	1	7	12	30
5	-36.96741	177.0199	-212	N	4.049	0.183	North	1	7	15	30

Fig. 10.14 An example of location data: earthquakes in New Zealand in 2000

10.4.3 Maps

Data most commonly plotted on maps relates to either location or region. Here, we give an example of the use of each, starting with *location*. The commonest way of specifying a location is by its latitude and longitude. Additional variables give information about what happened there. Figure 10.14 shows a fragment of data on earthquakes in New Zealand in the year 2000;[13] we have information about where the epicenter of the quake was (latitude and longitude), how deep underground it was, how strong it was, when it occurred, and several other variables.

As is typical for location data, we start by plotting the locations of the earthquakes onto a suitable map—but that just tells us where things were, nothing else about them. There are many ways of coding more information on to these points. Figure 10.15 codes the intensity of the earthquake to point-size, and the depth to a colour scale.

In New Zealand, there are about 15,000 earthquakes each year, all are related to the movement of tectonic plates. In Fig. 10.15 we see a strong, roughly 45 degree pattern of quake locations—unsurprising, given that associated volcanoes created the islands. The deepest epicentres occurred in the South Island (a subduction zone) and the shallowest epicentres occur in the North Island, where the opposite flow of plates occurs.

Our second example illustrates the use of data plotted by region. By 'region' we mean entities such as countries of the world or states/counties/electoral districts within a country. The associated variables usually give summary measures for each region.

Figure 10.16 shows a fragment of data from *Gapminder*[14] on different countries of the world which includes: the year the data relates to, average life expectancy, population size, and GDP per capita. Figure 10.17 offers so-called "choropleth plots" of the average fertility levels (*children per woman*) and average life expectancies for the countries in Africa in 2012. This is the most commonly used plot-type

---

[13] https://www.gns.cri.nz/

[14] https://www.gapminder.org/data/

Fig. 10.15 Earthquakes in New Zealand in 2000

country	continent	year	lifeExp	pop	gdpPercap
Algeria	Africa	2007	72.301	33333216	6223.367
Angola	Africa	2007	42.731	12420476	4797.231
Argentina	Americas	2007	75.32	40301927	12779.38
Australia	Oceania	2007	81.235	20434176	34435.37
Austria	Europe	2007	79.829	8199783	36126.49
Bahrain	Asia	2007	75.635	708573	29796.05

Fig. 10.16 A fragment of data on the world's countries from *Gapminder*

for regional data. Values of the variable are coded by a colour scale which is then used to colour the regions on the map. In Fig. 10.17 the most obvious feature is the very low fertility rates in the north and the south of Africa compared with the central regions. This is pattern is partially reversed for the life expectancies with higher life expectancies in the north.

With choropleth plots, large regions are visually prominent. This is problematic when large (rural) regions with small populations are presented alongside small (urban) regions with large populations. This is less pronounced with African countries than with American (US) states, where choropleth plots of election results give a very misleading impression (dominated by large, sparsely-populated states in the

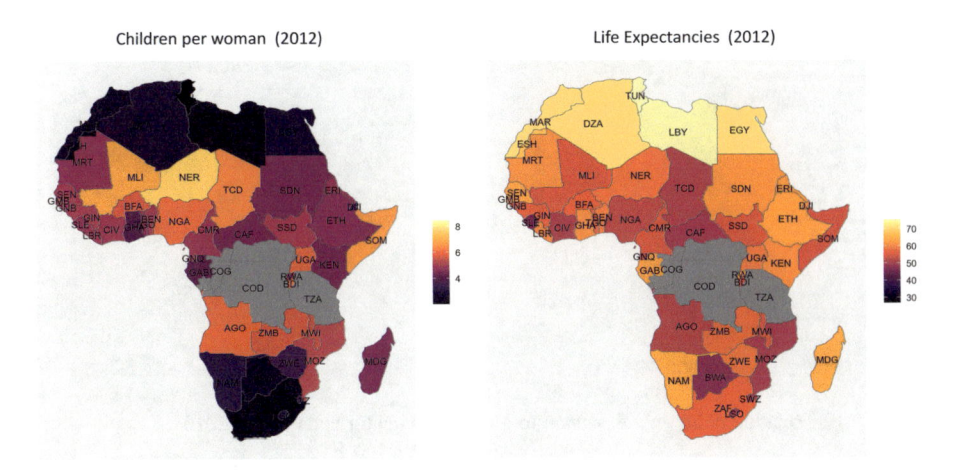

Fig. 10.17 Fertilities and life expectancies in Africa in 2012

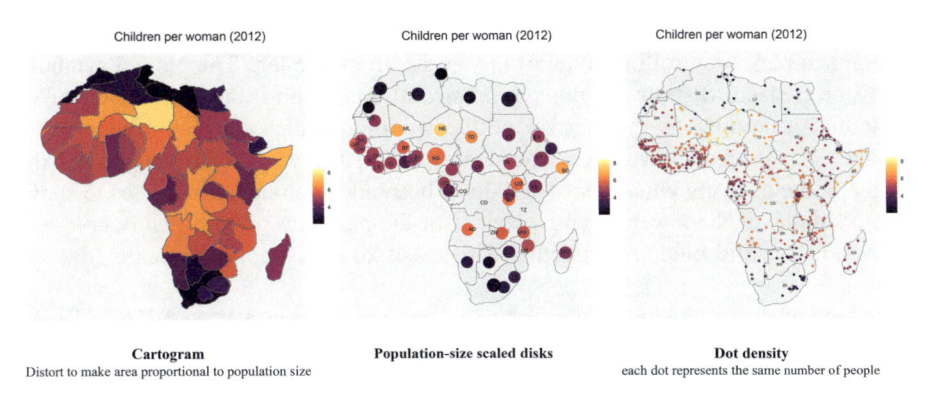

Fig. 10.18 Three methods that attempt to overcome conflations of area with number

middle of the country). Figure 10.18 shows some of the methods people have devised to try to get around this problem.

10.4.4 Communicating by Customizing: Making Aesthetic Changes and Adding Information to Plots

An essential aspect of Civic Statistics is the ability to communicate effectively. Here, we show how a standard output can be customized so that findings can be interpreted more readily by others. Country-level data has been downloaded from *Gapminder* for 2016; we are exploring the relationship between the average number of children each woman in a country has, and the life expectancy of the population in that

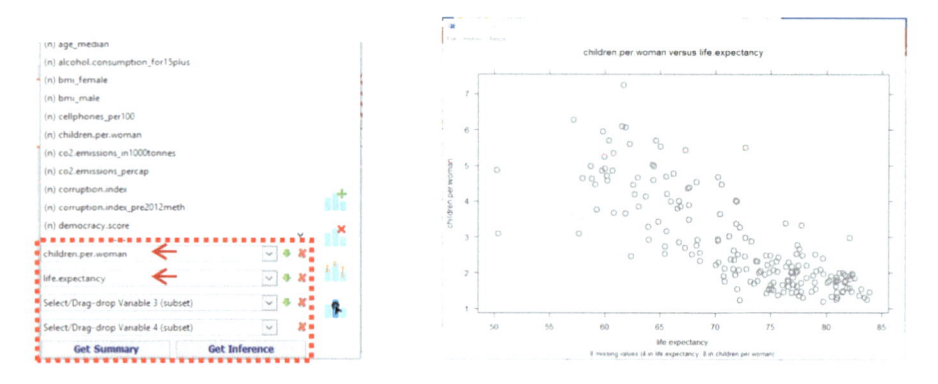

Fig. 10.19 Relating *children per woman* to *life expectancy* for countries in 2016

country. Once relevant variables have been chosen, *iNZight* creates a scatterplot (Fig. 10.19)—the default for a relationship between two numeric variables.

Figure 10.20 shows the results of using some of the facilities of **Add to Plot**—the command panel controlling some of this is shown on the left. The plotted symbols have been sized to show the *population size* of the country; the points have been coloured according to the *Region* of the world to which the country belongs; country-name labels have been placed by some of the very big countries and by some of the outlying countries; "rugs" have been added alongside the axes to show the positions of the *X*-values and *Y*-values of the points; a smooth trend-curve has been added (solid blue line) together with about 20 bootstrapped smooths (dashed lines).

Some of the aesthetic changes are as follows: the title and *X*- and *Y*-axis labels have been changed from the default (which simply picks up the variable names from the data set) into something that reads better; the background has been lightened; the points (disks) have been made semi-transparent and colored according to a chosen palette; and the overall sizes of things have been reduced somewhat.

10.4.5   Give Me the R *Code for That*

It is important that analyses of data can be reproduced, and (if necessary) re-used on other data sets. This is problematic if data are modified during the processes of exploration and analysis—for example, if outliers are removed, or some values are interpolated. In *iNZight*, the *R* code that implements user actions is automatically stored, and the stored code is made available to the user—both to provide an audit trail of changes made to the data and for possible use in *R* programs to automate such changes in the future. (To give more internal detail, when a user asks for a data-wrangling operation to be performed, the system first constructs the *R* code to do it, and then both executes and stores that code).

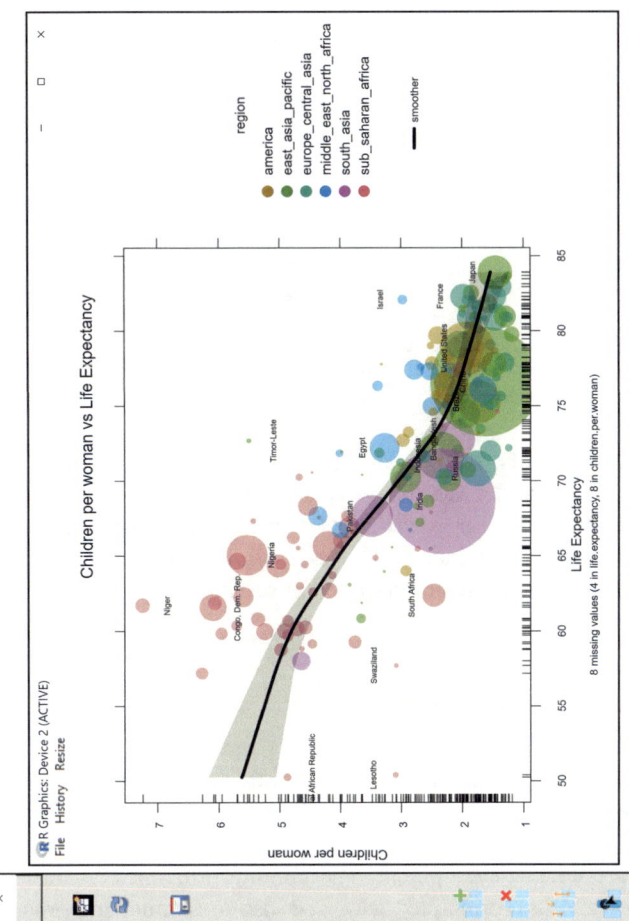

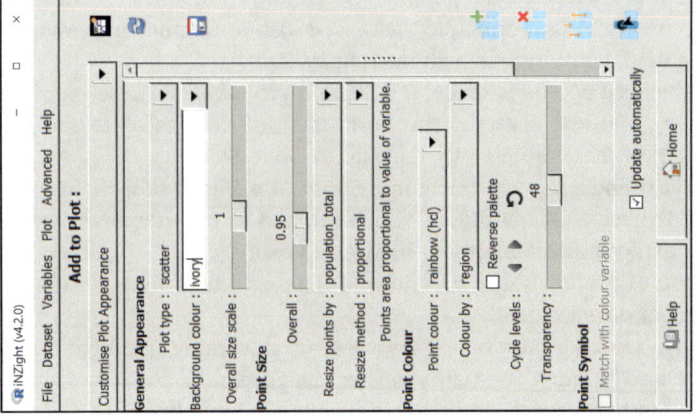

Fig. 10.20 Augmenting the scatterplot in Fig. 10.19

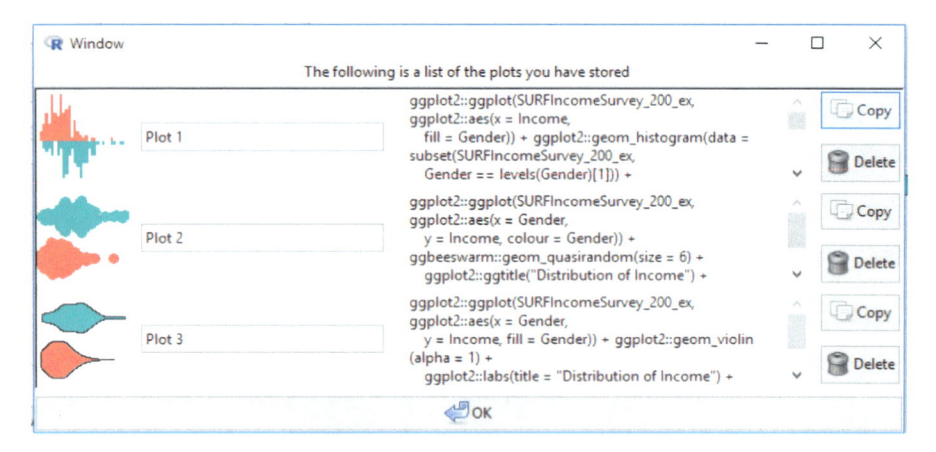

Fig. 10.21 Stored *R*-code displayed for three plots

In addition, the controls for the plot types shown in Fig. 10.3 have buttons for storing and displaying the *R*-code that produced them. Figure 10.21 shows a stored-code display window containing saved plots. Clicking on a plot thumbnail regenerates the plot in the graphics window. The code can be copied for external use and even modified and re-run in the current *iNZight* session.

10.5 Future-Proofing Software

A book chapter is a snapshot in time whereas a software project is always a work in progress. By the time you read this, whatever you gleaned about the capabilities of *iNZight* will now be out of date. So we will conclude by briefly describing some of the things that are under development. The guiding principles are to develop the software environment in a principled way, and also to monitor important developments in the field, and to implement them in *iNZight*.

In the Advanced Modules space, the *iNZight* project is working on modules for text harvesting and text analytics, network data, longitudinal data and small-area estimation. All of these are directly relevant to Civic Statistics.

Work is also underway on extending graphical displays to include multivariate graphics (in the sense of multiple *Y*-variables), and to provide much greater functionality for exploring and analysing time series data.

New modules for analysing hierarchical data, and data from designed experiments are under development.

We are also working on modules for supervised learning (predictive modelling) and unsupervised learning (primarily cluster analysis).

In the code-writing space we intend to increase the number of *iNZight* functions that write *R* code. We have prototypes of parts of *iNZight Lite* writing shell *R*-Markdown documents, which combine text and executable *R*-code and are a good way to write documents that combine discussion and analysis. The shell document delivered by *iNZight* can then be further refined independently of *iNZight* (but in conjunction with *R*). We hope also to close the loop between *iNZight Lite* and coding using cloud implementations of *R*.

The *iNZight* project's source code can be found in the Github repository.[15] We welcome collaborators.

10.6 Conclusions

We began by describing some desirable features of software to support learning and doing statistics, then set out to show how these features have been implemented in *iNZight*. A key message is the importance of engaging users and fostering their skills in statistical enquiry skills whatever their level of statistical knowledge. *iNZight* is particularly well suited to the analysis of data relevant to Civic Statistics, by facilitating multiple representations, handling multivariate data that can be dynamic, spanning time and places, collected in a variety of ways. Wrangling with Civic Statistics data requires analysis, reanalysis and reflection; tools to record analyses and data moves are essential for successful analysis. We are living in interesting times, and face new challenges in understanding an increasingly connected and complex world characterised by new artefacts, events, new sorts of data, new kinds of analysis, and new ways of communicating with each other. Tools to support our intellectual development must continue to evolve, and to be accessible to both naïve and sophisticated users.

References

Biehler, R. (1997). Software for learning and doing statistics. *International Statistical Review, 65*(2), 167–189.

Biehler, R. (2019). In J. M. Contreras, M. M. Gea, M. M. López-Martín, & E. MolinaPortillo (Eds.), *Software for learning and for doing statistics and probability – Looking back and looking forward from a personal perspective*. University of Granada. https://digibug.ugr.es/handle/104 81/55033

Burr, W., Chevalier, F., Collins, C., Gibbs, A. L., Ng, R., & Wild, C. J. (2021). Computational skills by stealth in introductory data science teaching. *Teaching Statistics, 43*, S34–S51. Special issue on teaching data science and statistics: foundation and introductory. https://doi.org/10.1111/test. 12277

Elliott, T., Wild, C., Barnett, D., & Sporle, A. (2021). *iNZight: A graphical user interface for data visualisation and analysis through R*. https://inzight.nz/papers/?paper=inzight

McNamara, A. (2019). Key attributes of a modern statistical computing tool. *The American Statistician, 73*(4), 375–384. https://doi.org/10.1080/00031305.2018.1482784

---

[15] https://github.com/iNZightVIT

Toomey, D. (2017). *Jupyter for data science – Exploratory analysis, statistical modelling, machine learning, and data visualization with Jupyter*. Packt Publishing.

Tukey, J. W. (1977). *Exploratory data analysis*. Addison-Wesley.

Velleman, P. F. (1989). *Learning data analysis with data desk*. W.H. Freeman.

Wild, C. J. (2018). Gaining iNZights from data. (Invited paper). In M. AlejandraSorto (Ed.), *Proceedings of the 10th international conference on the teaching of statistics*. International Statistical Institute. https://iase-web.org/icots/10/proceedings/pdfs/ICOTS10_9A3.pdf?15313 64299

Wild, C. J., Elliott, T., & Sporle, A. (2021). On democratizing data science: Some iNZights into empowering the many. *Harvard Data Science Review, 3*(2). https://hdsr.mitpress.mit.edu/pub/ 8fxt1zop/release/2

Chapter 11
Exploring Climate Change Data with R

Nuno Guimarães ⓘ**, Kimmo Vehkalahti, Pedro Campos, and Joachim Engel**

Abstract Climate change is an existential threat facing humanity and the future of our planet. The signs of global warming are everywhere, and they are more complex than just the climbing temperatures. Climate data on a massive scale has been collected by various scientific groups around the globe. Exploring and extracting useful knowledge from large quantities of data requires powerful software. In this chapter we present some possibilities for exploring and visualising climate change data in connection with statistics education using the freely accessible statistical programming language *R* together with the computing environment *RStudio*. In addition to the visualisations, we provide annotated references to climate data repositories and extracts of our openly published R scripts for encouraging teachers and students to reproduce and enhance the visualisations.

Keywords R · Coding · Climate data · Data visualisation · Multivariate data

11.1 Introduction

We live in a world awash with data and freely available software. Skills to use information technology, search for information, and explore data are of increasing importance. Digital literacy is a central goal for preparing students for the digital age and providing them with twenty-first century skills (OECD, 2019). Chapter 9 of this book presents various data visualisation packages designed for learning statistics and

N. Guimarães (✉) · P. Campos
LIAAD-INESC TEC and University of Porto, Porto, Portugal
e-mail: nuno.r.guimaraes@inesctec.pt; pcampos@fep.up.pt

K. Vehkalahti
University of Helsinki, Helsinki, Finland
e-mail: kimmo.vehkalahti@helsinki.fi

J. Engel
Ludwigsburg University of Education, Ludwigsburg, Germany
e-mail: engel@ph-ludwigsburg.de

© Springer Nature Switzerland AG 2022
J. Ridgway (ed.), *Statistics for Empowerment and Social Engagement*,
https://doi.org/10.1007/978-3-031-20748-8_11

data analysis, suitable for high school. Chapter 10 discusses design principles for educational software and introduces the data analysis tool iNZight for visualizing Civic Statistics data. iNZight is based on a graphical user interface (GUI), allowing its use without any knowledge of programming code—a great advantage, especially for learners, because it avoids the additional cognitive load of handling a programming language. However, GUI-based systems do not have the same level of functionality and granular control as command line interface systems (CLI) which provide greater flexibility and can be used to easily do things that are difficult or even impossible to do with a GUI.

For some burning problems facing the world today, such as global warming, the analysis involves massive complex datasets, and hence requires flexible use of professional software.

Therefore, in this chapter we go beyond GUI and illustrate how students with increasing digital skills can be encouraged to explore and visualise complex data on climate change using the command-based professional software R. Although visualisation is a great place to start with R programming, data visualisation by itself is typically not enough (Wickham & Grolemund, 2017). Data transformation and modelling is an important part of the exploratory process, since users get involved with selecting important variables, filtering out key observations, creating new variables, and computing summaries. This is a clear advantage of using R for data analysis.

We provide annotated references to climate data repositories and extracts of our openly published programming scripts for encouraging teachers and students to reproduce and enhance the visualisations. The challenge to provide students with computational tools and to enhance their data-related capacities has been emphasized by various statistics educators (e.g., Horton et al., 2014; Nolan & Temple Lang, 2010).

The purpose of this chapter is to provide an accessible entry to exploring climate change data for learners who have little previous experience with professional environments meant for statistical modelling and programming. This includes addressing some technical issues concerning coding and handling of software. Annotated references to climate data repositories and extracts of openly published programming code are provided. The reader can replicate all the visualisations presented here and may create additional representations that may look at the data from different perspectives.

> Some burning problems facing the world today such as global warming require the analysis of massive complex datasets and the flexible use of professional software

In the recent *Future of Humanity* survey of over 10,000 young people in 22 countries aged 18–25 years (also called *Generation Z)*, climate change was the most commonly cited issue facing the world.[1] From Prince Charles[2] and Pope Francis[3] to Antonio Guterres,[4] and many other prominent figures or world leaders, there is a consensus that climate change is the biggest threat to this planet. Indeed, scientists have warned for decades of the global threat that global warming and climate changes pose to planet Earth. Effects on the environment, such as loss of sea ice, accelerated sea level rise and longer and more intense heat waves are already being observed. Extreme weather events are observed in higher frequency. In addition, glaciers have shrunk, ice on rivers and lakes is breaking up earlier, plant and animal ranges have shifted, and trees are flowering sooner.

For many people, however, climate change still seems an abstract and faraway phenomenon. One way of raising students' awareness and engagement in the climate change topic is to let them explore and analyse climate change datasets by themselves, with support from their teachers. We approach this option by illustrating possibilities of exploring and visualising openly available climate data, by working with the powerful statistical programming language R (R Core Team, 2020) using the freely accessible computing environment *RStudio*.

> To raise students' awareness and engagement about climate change we encourage them to explore and analyse climate change datasets by themselves

Einstein is reported to have said that *Everything should be made as simple as possible, but no simpler.* We believe in learning by doing and following ready-made examples, but there are also challenges to our approach. As weather changes rapidly in time and with local fluctuations while climate comprises long-range patterns, the study of climate requires the exploration of complex spatial time series data. Climate change data not only have a massive scale but also high dimensionality and complicated dependency structures, making the analysis task challenging. However, using a script-based programming language, such as R, offers certain advantages: users can learn the functions and code fragments step-by-step, and the whole analysis is under full user control with all the results easily reproduced. The students can play around with the data, ask new questions and modify the code to get new representations. Another advantage of using the provided R script is the fact that by running the code, the freshest data sets are retrieved (e.g., most recent data on CO_2 concentration in the atmosphere) and made available for the analysis. Our aim is to encourage both teachers and students in using a hands-on approach that assumes no specific prior knowledge of R (Shah, 2020).

---

[1] https://www.amnesty.org/en/latest/news/2019/12/climate-change-ranks-highest-as-vital-issue-of-our-time/

[2] https://www.reuters.com/article/us-davos-meeting-prince-charles/uks-prince-charles-says-climate-change-is-humanitys-greatest-threat-idUSKBN1ZL26F

[3] https://catholicclimatecovenant.org/encyclical

[4] https://www.un.org/sg/en/content/sg/statement/2018-09-10/secretary-generals-remarks-climate-change-delivered

Why R? During its early years (around year 2000), R was mainly used in the (Mathematical) Statistics community (where it originated in the early 1990s), but nowadays R has become one of the most popular programming languages at large. Indeed, R is the *primary tool reported in data analysis* (Lai et al., 2019, p. 1). Theobold and Hancock (2019) conclude in their review of R and other computing possibilities in the environmental sciences: *Statistical computing has become a foundational aspect of research.* In many other fields there is similar evidence of the fact that R has begun to take over the role from traditional commercial software packages, such as *SAS* or *SPSS*.

An introduction to R—even for the specific area of climate change—is beyond the scope of this chapter—huge number of excellent introductory materials (e.g., slides, books, websites, blogs, and interactive courses) are freely available. It is generally wise to consult quite recent materials, because R is under constant development and it has gone through several major changes and updates during the 2010s. One example of a modern textbook is *R for Data Science* (Wickham & Grolemund, 2017) that helps users to learn the most important data science tools in R: importing, cleaning, transforming, and visualising data. The book is fully accessible online.[5] Another example of a useful resource is an online textbook on Open Data Science[6] that covers the basics of R and *RStudio* as well as the state-of-the-art tools for reproducibility and version control, namely, *Git* and *GitHub* (see also Lowndes et al., 2017). We may also mention DataCamp[7] (a commercial company) that offers a popular, free interactive course *Introduction to R*. Since 2016, almost 2 million people worldwide have taken the course.

In our examples, we focus on illustrating the potential of R for visualising climate change data. For further details, we refer the interested reader to Shen (2017) and Shen and Somerville (2019). See also the hands-on YouTube videos related to Shen and Somerville's (2019) book.[8]

The structure of the chapter is as follows. Section 11.2 provides guidance to trustworthy data repositories with visualisations to retrieve up-to-date climate data and sources for deeper background information. Section 11.3 illustrates selected visualisations of climate data supported with technical hints and activities related to the R language. Section 11.4 presents some ideas and suggestions of how to alleviate the technical challenges in implementing the R code for learners, and Sect. 11.5 concludes.

---

[5] https://r4ds.had.co.nz/

[6] https://ohi-science.org/data-science-training/

[7] https://www.datacamp.com

[8] https://www.youtube.com/channel/UC92gEJfTpsVcE92fCeSRbJg/videos

11.2   Sources for Climate Data and Visualisations

There are many comprehensive sources for climate data and their visualisation, collected and compiled by top research institutions, international organisations and government agencies. In this section, we provide a brief guidance to some of these sources with a summary provided in Table 11.1.

The "Five Most Important" Datasets of Climate Science
These datasets are based on the presentation made by Stefan Rahmstorf to the Arctic Expedition for Climate Action. [9] They include the Vostok Ice Core (Antarctica), Rise of CO_2 ("Keeling curve"), the Global Average Temperature, Sea Level Rise and Sea Ice Retreat. Despite the potential subjectivity of the selection, those datasets represent undeniably important climate science phenomena, such as temperature, atmospheric carbon dioxide (CO_2), sea level, and sea ice. These datasets are explored using R in the next section.

weatherData R Package
The *weatherData* R package[10] is a library of functions that helps in fetching weather data from websites. Given a location and a date range, these functions help fetch weather data (temperature, pressure, humidity, wind speed etc.) for any weather related analysis. Examples of the different types of data are: underground stations data, data of US weather stations, daily minimum (maximum) temperatures for a given weather station, and data from international weather stations.

Copernicus Climate Change Service
The Copernicus Climate Change Service (C3S), powered by Copernicus, the European Union's Earth Observation Programme, provides information about the past, present and future climate, as well as tools to enable modelling climate change mitigation and adaptation strategies by policy makers and businesses.[11] Here, it is possible to find extensive information (including didactic material) and illustrations in the form of explanations, tables, graphics, animations and videos. The Climate Data Store delivers many datasets, ranging from monthly data on pressure levels to data on glacier elevation and mass change data from 1850 to the present from the Fluctuations of Glaciers Database. It is freely available and functions as a one-stop shop for exploring climate data.

NASA Global Climate Change and GISS Data
NASA offers many different resources, such as educational videos, charts, tables and many explanations about climate change.[12] In particular, the Goddard Institute for Space Studies (GISS) provides some datasets and images[13] such as the one from the

---

[9] https://tamino.wordpress.com/2018/11/01/the-5-most-important-data-sets-of-climate-science/

[10] https://ram-n.github.io/weatherData/

[11] https://climate.copernicus.eu

[12] https://climate.nasa.gov/

[13] https://data.giss.nasa.gov/

Table 11.1 Summary of sources for climate change data and visualisations

Resource name and type	Data sources	Data/variables available	link
The "Five Most Important" Datasets of Climate Science (by Stefan Rahmstorf)	Stefan Rahmstorf, based on agencies, such as NASA/GISS, ERSST, etc.	Vostok Ice Core (Antarctica), Rise of CO_2 ("Keeling curve"), the Global Average Temperature, Sea Level Rise and Sea Ice Retreat.	https://tamino.wordpress.com/2018/11/01/the-5-most-important-data-sets-of-climate-science/
***weatherData* R package** (a library of functions that helps in fetching weather data from websites)	Weather underground (https://www.wunderground.com/) and others	Weather data (temperature, pressure, humidity, wind speed etc.) for any weather related analysis	https://ram-n.github.io/weatherData/
Copernicus Climate Change Service (Copernicus—the European Union's Earth Observation Programme)	Copernicus	The Climate Data Store delivers many datasets, from monthly data on pressure levels, through to data of glaciers' elevation and mass change data from 1850 to present from the Fluctuations of Glaciers Database.	https://climate.copernicus.eu
NASA Global Climate Change and GISS Data	NASA and the Goddard Institute for Space Studies (GISS)	Datasets and images where you can find data from the ISCCP (International Satellite Cloud Climatology Project) with 3-hourly weather state data at 1-degree horizontal resolution, covering the period from July 1983 to June 2015.	https://climate.nasa.gov/
Deutscher Wetterdienst	Climate Data Center	Explore "bad weather days", i.e. days when the weather makes work on construction sites difficult or impossible, and wind climatology (wind turbines in Germany).	https://cdc.dwd.de/portal/
National Geographic Climate Hub	National Geographic	Many data visualisations, such as the shrinking of Arctic Sea ice, the vanishing of some animals and plants, etc.	https://www.nationalgeographic.com/magazine/2017/04/seven-things-to-know-about-climate-change
International Research Institute (IRI) for		Datasets are available that facilitate creating	http://iridl.ldeo.columbia.edu

(continued)

Table 11.1 (continued)

Resource name and type	Data sources	Data/variables available	link
Climate & Society Data Library	University of Columbia, NY, USA	analyses and maps. Examples of datasets include Climate and Agriculture Data, Fires, El niño, Food Security, etc.	
WorldClim Database	WorldClim	Maps, graphs, tables, and data on global climate such as historical monthly weather data, global climate and weather data, bioclimatic variables, future climate data, Paleoclimate, etc.	www.worldclim.org/
RClimate (a blog from D. Kelly O'Day)	United States Geological Survey (USGS) and others including flood data	Variables such as temperature, water, discharge, suspended sediment concentration, suspended sediment discharge etc.	https://rclimate.wordpress.com/

ISCCP (International Satellite Cloud Climatology Project) with 3-hourly weather state data at 1-degree horizontal resolution, covering the period from July 1983 to June 2015.

Deutscher Wetterdienst

Here you can find the CDC (Climate Data Center)[14] and explore "bad weather days", i.e. days when the weather makes work on construction sites difficult or impossible. Another new product is the wind climatology "QuWind100", which leads to a comprehensive improvement in the accuracy of the yield estimation of wind turbines in Germany.

National Geographic

"Seven things to know about climate change"[15] is a climate hub created by National Geographic to let us know about diverse changes occurring in climate related topics, such as global warming, the shrinking of ice in the Arctic Sea and the vanishing of some animals and plants.

---

[14] https://cdc.dwd.de/portal/

[15] https://www.nationalgeographic.com/magazine/2017/04/seven-things-to-know-about-climate-change/

International Research Institute (IRI) for Climate & Society Data Library

The IRI Data Library[16] is a powerful and freely accessible online data repository and analysis tool that allows users to view, analyse, and download hundreds of terabytes of climate-related data through a standard web browser.

Datasets are available which offer the opportunity to create analyses of data, ranging from simple averaging to more advanced analyses using the Ingrid Data Analysis Language. In addition, there is a climate and society map room, a collection of maps and other figures that monitor climate and societal conditions at present and in the recent past. The maps and figures can be manipulated and are linked to the original data. Examples of datasets include Climate and Agriculture Data, Fires, El niño, Food Security, etc.

WorldClim Database

The WorldClim Database (www.worldclim.org) provides current, future, and past data in a 1 × 1 km grid format (and other resolutions). Data is formatted to be easily accessible and adapted to be used in *ArcGIS* and other standard formats. It contains maps, graphs, tables, and data on the global climate such as the historical monthly weather data, global climate and weather data, bioclimatic variables, future climate data, Paleo-climate, etc.

RClimate

RClimate[17] provides a set of problems to be solved with R related to the analysis of flash floods based on the United States Geological Survey (USGS). The National Water Information System provides data on the Schuylkill River at Philadelphia[18] regarding several variables, such as water temperature, discharge (in cubic feet per second), suspended sediment concentration, suspended sediment discharge, etc. D. Kelly O'Day, the author of this blog, provides several charts and data that allows the use of these data and R to understand climate change.

11.3 Using R in Exploring Climate Change Data

In this section, we present some impressive visualisations together with data and code for creating them in R. We will use the *Five Most Important Datasets for Climate Change* by Stefan Rahmstorf (see Table 11.1). Our R code for visualising the five datasets is adapted with modifications from a blog[19] published in 2018. The graphs of the blog were created using R and its *ggplot2* graphing package,[20] making the process reproducible and thus easier to share and study. In addition to those five

---

[16] http://iridl.ldeo.columbia.edu/

[17] https://rclimate.wordpress.com/

[18] https://waterdata.usgs.gov/nwis/inventory/?site_no=01474500

[19] https://rethinking.rbind.io/2018/11/16/the-top-five-climate-charts-using-ggplot2/

[20] https://ggplot2.tidyverse.org/

datasets, we show how to generate interactive geographical maps with R to illustrate rising temperatures in different geographical regions of the earth.

We shall present the visualisations in dynamic form using the *plotly* package of R (Sievert, 2020), that provides several advantages when compared to traditional static plots. For example, visualisations created in *plotly* allow interactive manipulations, such as zoom in/out, range selection, and trace removal with axis adjustment. In addition, *plotly* is easy to use and thus serves as a good introductory tool for visualising data in R. Of course, the graphs here are displayed only in static form, but the dynamic versions can be reproduced using the R code provided in our *GitHub* repository.[21] We encourage interested readers to do so. For working with R code, we recommend installing and using the free *RStudio*[22] software available in the *GitHub* repository. Additional recommendations on how to involve students in using the R language follow in Sect. 11.4.

The five datasets are:

1. Vostok Ice Core (Antarctica)
2. Rise of CO_2 ("Keeling curve")
3. Global Average Temperature
4. Sea Level Rise
5. Sea Ice Retreat

In the following, we shall walk through each of the five datasets summarizing the phenomena behind them, displaying views of the data and R code, plotting the graphs, and discussing key points related to the R code.

Our aim is to show and discuss the possibilities of exploring and visualising climate change data with R. We emphasize reproducibility by providing the complete R scripts online. Although our views of R code may look quite technical, we think that the views and the online R scripts will help the interested reader to get to grips with R. Those readers who are not interested in the programming issues can largely ignore the R codes and the more technical sections of the text and instead concentrate on the visualisations to help them understand the practical implications of exploring the climate change data with R. The visualisations are also directly accessible through an app with the link https://nrguimaraes.shinyapps.io/climateChanger/.

11.3.1 Vostok Ice Core (Antarctica)

The first dataset is entitled the Vostok Ice Core. Vostok is a research station in Antarctica and one of the coldest places on this planet. Snow accumulates very slowly there, and an ice core contains a long, accurate record of the temperature at

---

[21] https://github.com/nrguimaraes/climateChangeR

[22] https://rstudio.com/

Vostok, and of the atmospheric composition, because air bubbles trapped in the ice are little samples of the old atmosphere. In the 1970s and 1980s, a French-Russian team drilled a 2083-m-long ice core at the Vostok station, revealing the CO_2 concentration in the atmosphere and temperature at Vostok for about the past 400,000 years. The Vostok Ice Core data (Barnola et al., 2003) consists of two time series: *vostok_co2* and *temperature*. They are measured from the ice core so that the CO_2 concentration measurements are best estimates from each depth level of the ice core (Barnola et al., 1987) and the temperatures refer to the variation of the Vostok isotope temperature records as differences from the Vostok's modern surface-temperature mean value of $-55.5°$ in Celsius (Jouzel et al., 1987). Both time-series are included in an R list object *datasets* that contains all the datasets (as R *data frames*) needed in producing the five graphs of this section. In the R code, the Vostok Ice Core datasets are referred to with their specific names as *datasets $vostok_co2* and *datasets$temperature*, respectively. Calling those names in the R script gives brief views of so-called *tibbles*[23] containing the datasets: the dimensions, the names of the variables, and the first ten records (see Dataview 11.1).

```
> datasets$vostok_co2
# A tibble: 363 x 4
   depth age_ice age_air   co2
   <dbl>   <dbl>   <dbl> <dbl>
 1  149.    5679    2342  285.
 2  173.    6828    3634  273.
 3  177.    7043    3833  268.
 4  229.    9523    6220  262.
 5  250.   10579    7327  255.
 6  266    11334    8113  260.
 7  303.   13449   10123  262.
 8  321.   14538   11013  264.
 9  332.   15208   11326  245.
10  342.   15922   11719  238.
# ... with 353 more rows

> datasets$vostok_temperature
# A tibble: 3,311 x 4
   depth age_ice deuterium  temp
   <dbl>   <dbl>     <dbl> <dbl>
 1     0       0      -438     0
 2     1      17      -438     0
 3     2      35      -438     0
 4     3      53      -438     0
 5     4      72      -438     0
 6     5      91      -438     0
 7     6     110      -438     0
 8     7     129      -438     0
 9     8     149     -443. -0.81
10     9     170     -438.  0.02
# ... with 3,301 more rows
```

Dataview 11.1 First records of the Vostok Ice Core data sets

---

[23] https://r4ds.had.co.nz/tibbles.html

Figure 11.1 shows the graph plotted using the two datasets. The graph is a combination of two time-series plots, the CO_2 concentration and temperature variation, with a shared time scale of 400,000 years. It clearly reveals the last four, so-called *glacial cycles*, each lasting about 100,000 years. Details of the phenomenon and how it is linked to the variations in Earth's orbit, are explained in Rahmstorf's presentation.[24] Put in perspective, compare these graphs with the Keeling curve (Fig. 11.2), indicating today's CO_2 value above 410 ppm. Never in the past 400,000 years has the CO_2 concentration been nearly as high as it is now.

```
# Build the first plot with respect to co2
fig1a <- plot_ly(datasets$vostok_co2, x = ~age_ice, y = ~co2,
type = 'scatter', mode = 'lines', name = ~"Co2") %>%
  layout(xaxis = list(autorange = 'reversed',
range = c(420000, 0), showticklabels = FALSE, title = ""),
yaxis = list(title = 'CO2 concentration'))

# Build the second plot with respect to temperature
fig1b <- plot_ly(datasets$vostok_temperature, x = ~age_ice,
y = rollmean(datasets$vostok_temperature$temp, 8, na.pad = TRUE),
type = 'scatter', mode = 'lines', name = ~"Temperature") %>%
  layout(xaxis = list(title='Years before present',
autorange = 'reversed', range=c(420000, 0),
showticklabels = TRUE), yaxis = list(title = 'Temperature (C)'))

# Aggregate both with a shared X value (for better visualisation interaction)
fig1 <- subplot(nrows=2, fig1a, fig1b, shareX = TRUE, shareY = FALSE) %>%
  layout(title = "Paleoclimate: The Link Between CO2 and Temperature")

# Display the plot
fig1
```

Codeview 11.1 R code for the Vostok Ice Core graphs

Activity 11.1: Exploring the Relationship Between CO_2 Level and Temperature

1. Looking at Fig. 11.1: What kind of relationship do you expect between CO_2 level and temperature?
2. Imagine the two time series for CO_2 and temperature in one plot by overlaying the two curves. What do you observe? For creating such a plot with R, go to *GitHub* and download the file *activities.R* for help.
3. Paleoclimatologists—these are scientists who study the climate during Earth's different geologic ages—see the cause for the variation in temperature and CO_2 as being initiated by different orbital changes. Search the Internet to find out more about the interaction between temperature, CO_2 level and orbital changes. What questions come to your mind? What are your conclusions?

(continued)

---

[24] http://www.pik-potsdam.de/~stefan/5datasets_rahmstorf.pdf

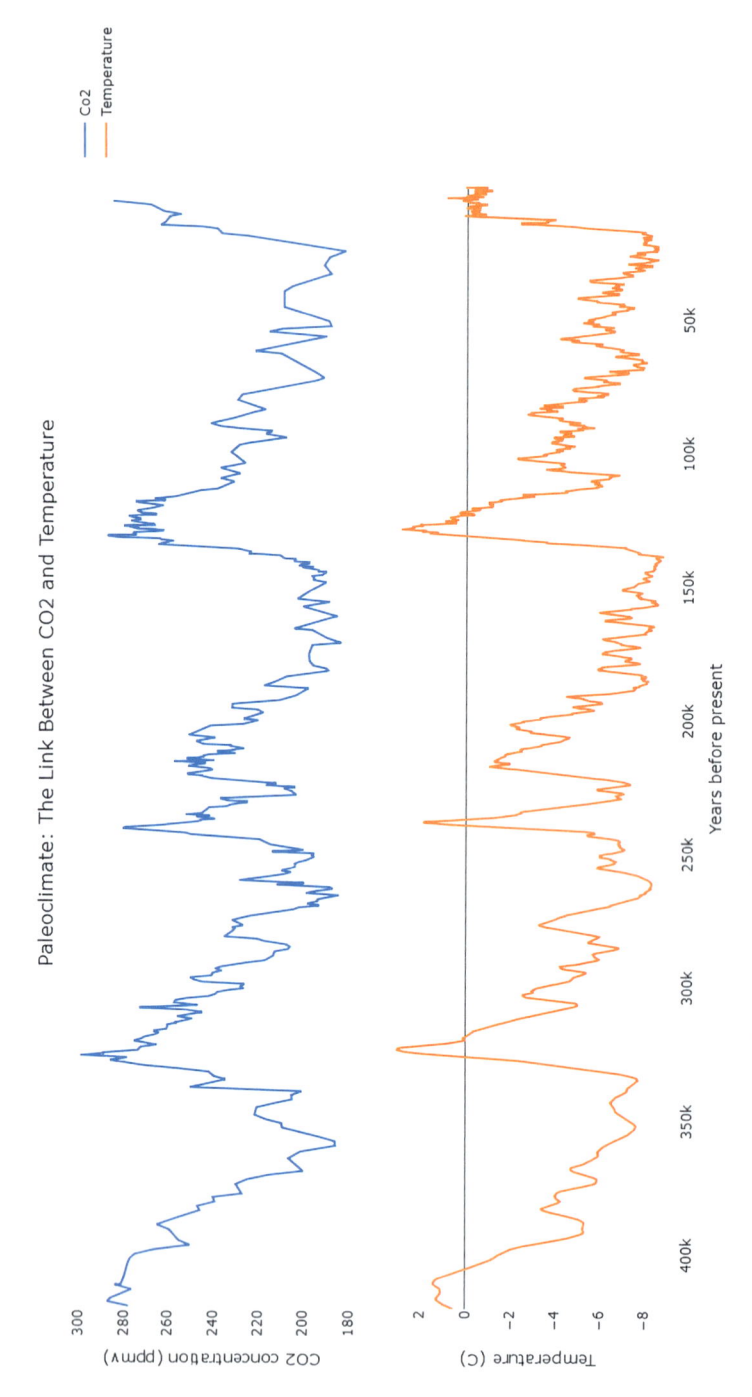

Fig. 11.1 The Vostok Ice Core graphs, displaying time series for atmospheric CO_2 concentration (above, 11.1a) and for temperature variation (below, 11.1b). Codeview 11.1 shows the R code used to create the plot in Fig. 11.1. The plot is built from two R objects that are both results of plotting a scatter diagram of two variables from the two datasets using the *plot_ly* function with various graphical parameters. As the next step, the two objects are combined in one (Fig. 11.1) using the *subplot* function that also gives a common header for the resulting plot. Finally, the plot is displayed simply by calling its name

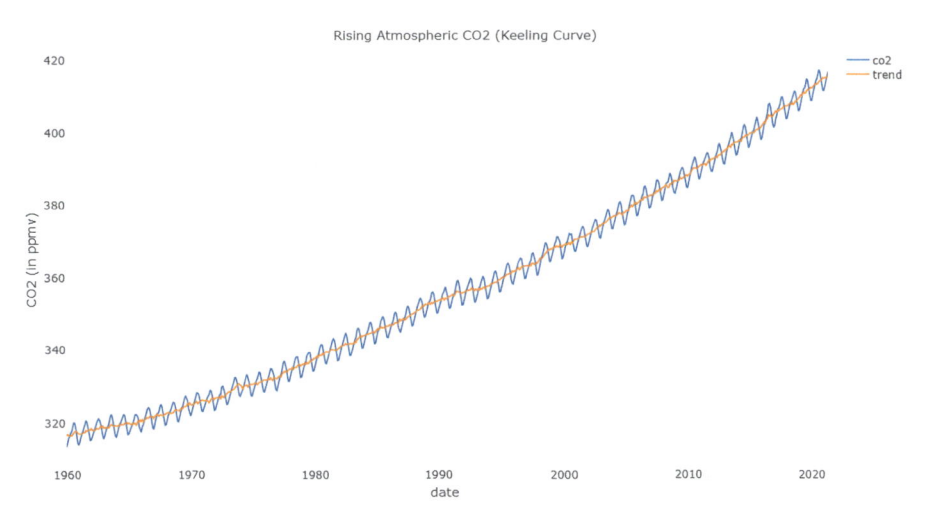

Fig. 11.2 The "Keeling curve" from 1958 to 2020

Activity 11.1 (continued)
4. Compare the variation in CO_2 and temperature in years before present with today's changes (see the CO_2 curve in Sect. 11.3.2 and temperatures in Sect. 11.3.4).

11.3.2 Rise of CO_2 ("Keeling Curve")

The second dataset is another well-known one, related to the CO_2 concentration in the atmosphere (measured in parts per million by volume, ppmv). In 1958, Charles David Keeling began the measurements on Mauna Loa, Hawaii, and they have been continued on a regular basis. Mauna Loa Observatory is located at an elevation of 3397 m above sea level and it is one of the most important atmospheric research facilities due to the strong marine inversion layer presented in that location. This allows not only a minimum interference of vegetation and human activity in the measurements but also a clearer separation between the polluted lower portions of the atmosphere and the much cleaner troposphere.[25] Dataview 11.2 displays the first ten records of monthly CO_2 averages.

---

[25] https://www.esrl.noaa.gov/gmd/obop/mlo/

```
> datasets$co2
# A tibble: 756 x 8
    year month date         average de_seasonalized  days st.devofdays unc_of_mon_mean
   <dbl> <dbl> <date>         <dbl>           <dbl> <dbl>        <dbl>           <dbl>
 1  1958     3 1958-03-01      316.            314.    -1        -9.99           -0.99
 2  1958     4 1958-04-01      317.            315.    -1        -9.99           -0.99
 3  1958     5 1958-05-01      318.            315.    -1        -9.99           -0.99
 4  1958     6 1958-06-01      317.            315.    -1        -9.99           -0.99
 5  1958     7 1958-07-01      316.            315.    -1        -9.99           -0.99
 6  1958     8 1958-08-01      315.            316.    -1        -9.99           -0.99
 7  1958     9 1958-09-01      313.            316.    -1        -9.99           -0.99
 8  1958    10 1958-10-01      312.            315.    -1        -9.99           -0.99
 9  1958    11 1958-11-01      313.            315.    -1        -9.99           -0.99
10  1958    12 1958-12-01      315.            315.    -1        -9.99           -0.99
# ... with 746 more rows
```

Dataview 11.2 First records of the "Keeling curve" dataset

Figure 11.2 displays the famous "Keeling curve" for the past 60 years (Tans & Keeling, 2020) that shows the increasing upward trend and the seasonal cycle in atmospheric CO_2. The figure shows the data with their seasonal variation and a trend curve, as provided in the data. More details are available in Rahmstorf's presentation.[26]

With the dataset embedded into an R environment (e.g., *RStudio*), there are multiple possibilities to visualise the data and explore more of the data interactively (see Cleveland, 1993). For example, the function used to aggregate data (currently the *mean* function), could easily be changed. Some common examples are the maximum, minimum, or median (depending on what type of studies the user is conducting). In addition, the function can be displayed side by side in the current visualisation by using the *add_trace* function. We encourage the readers to modify the script to enhance the visualisation by adding a trace to show, for example, the maximum CO_2 value for each year.

Codeview 11.2 shows the R code used to create the plot in Fig. 11.2. First, outliers (denoted by "−99.99") are removed and then the data is aggregated by year and month, computing the means. Finally, the scatter plot is constructed using the time on the horizontal axis and adding the trend (one of the variables) with graphical details.

---

[26]http://www.pik-potsdam.de/~stefan/5datasets_rahmstorf.pdf

```
# Remove outliers
datasets$co2 <- datasets$co2[datasets$co2$average != -99.99, ]

# Aggregate data
agg <-aggregate(x = datasets$co2,
    by = list(datasets$co2$year, datasets$co2$month),
    FUN = mean)
agg <- agg[order(agg$year), ]

# Build plot with respect to co2 in atmosphere
fig2 <- plot_ly(agg, x =  ~ date, y =  ~ average, type = 'scatter',
    mode = 'lines', name = "co2") %>%
  add_trace(y =  ~ de_seasonalized, name = "trend") %>%
  layout(title = 'Rising Atmospheric CO2 (Keeling Curve)')
# Display the plot
fig2
```

Codeview 11.2 R code for the "Keeling curve"

The notation %>% in Codeview 11.2 refers to a "pipe" that takes the result (output) from a previous function as the input of the next function. In this case, the result of the *plot_ly* function is taken via the pipe to the *add_trace* function and further to the *layout* function, hence constructing the graph step-by-step. After that, the result (the final graph) is saved in the object *fig2*. It could be given similarly with a pipe, but it is a conventional style in R to use the left arrow. The pipe represents a more recent and straight-forward style of writing R code. The new style has become popular due to *tidyverse*, a versatile collection of R packages designed for data science, standardising common data structures, and an underlying design philosophy, and grammar.[27]

> **Activity 11.2: Exploring the Keeling Curve**
> 1. Fit a linear regression line to the data and predict the atmospheric CO_2 level for the year 2030 (help for implementation in R is on GitHub in file *activities.R*).
> 2. Draw a residual plot with respect to the linear fit (help on *GitHub*).
> 3. Explore the seasonal variations. What are they caused by? (Note: This requires exploring plant physiology.)
> 4. Is a linear model an appropriate description for the data? Explain!

11.3.3 Global Average Temperature

The next dataset provides information on the global land-ocean mean temperature, measured by weather stations and ships around the world for each year from 1880 to the present (NASA GISTEMP Team, 2020). The data represents so called *temperature anomalies* or deviations that indicate how much warmer or colder it is than

---

[27] https://www.tidyverse.org/

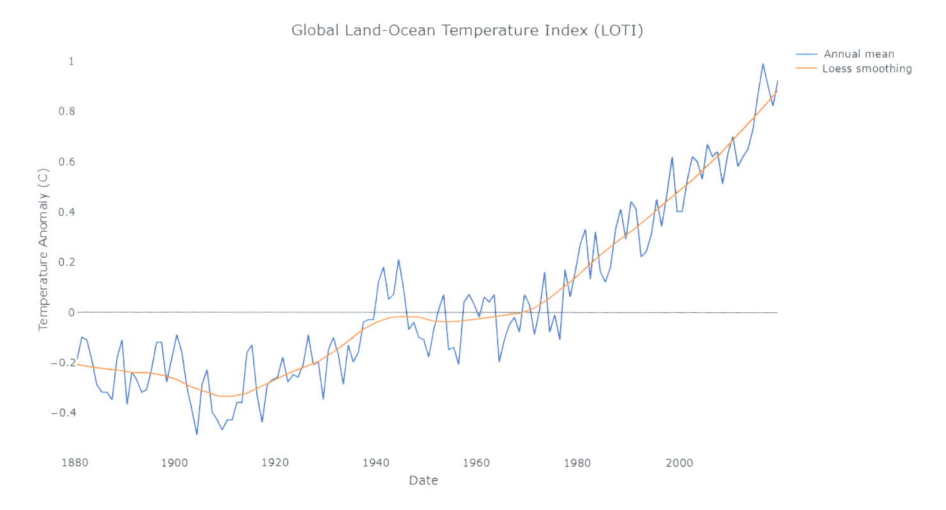

Fig. 11.3 The global average temperature rise

normal for a particular place and time. For the provider of the data, *normal* always means the average over the 30-year period 1951–1980 for that place and time of year.

The first ten records of the dataset are displayed in Dataview 11.3.

```
> datasets$land_ocean_temp
# A tibble: 141 x 2
    date        annmean
    <date>        <dbl>
 1 1880-01-01    -0.16
 2 1881-01-01    -0.08
 3 1882-01-01    -0.1
 4 1883-01-01    -0.16
 5 1884-01-01    -0.28
 6 1885-01-01    -0.32
 7 1886-01-01    -0.3
 8 1887-01-01    -0.35
 9 1888-01-01    -0.16
10 1889-01-01    -0.1
# ... with 131 more rows
```

Dataview 11.3 First records of the global temperature data set

The data visualised in Fig. 11.3 includes both the curve for the annual mean temperature anomaly (deviation from the 1951 to 1980 means) and a non-linear trend. Since the 1970s, the anomalies are positive, which shows that the warming has been strong and ongoing, and even accelerating faster in recent years.

Codeview 11.3 shows the R code used to create the plot in Fig. 11.3. First, the data is smoothed using a suitable span (found by experimenting visually with some typical smoother like *loess*, a locally estimated scatterplot smoother) and then the means are plotted as a time-series, adding the smoothed values as a non-linear trend line with some graphical details. Here, this trend is computed using the *loess.smooth* function which receives the x and y data and computes the loess smoothing. The output of this function is a *data frame* with the respective x and y for the trend, which makes it easy to add it to an existing plot (using the *add_trace* function), as we have done in Fig. 11.3.

```
# Create smoothing data
loess_smooth <- loess.smooth(y = datasets$land_ocean_temp$annmean,
                             x = datasets$land_ocean_temp$date, span = 0.2)

# Build plot of the global land-ocean temperature as well as the smooth line
fig3 <- plot_ly(data = datasets$land_ocean_temp, x =  ~ date, y =  ~ annmean,
                type = 'scatter', mode = 'lines', name = "Annual mean") %>%
        add_trace(data = loess_smooth, x = loess_smooth$x, y = loess_smooth$y,
                  name = "Loess smoothing") %>%
        layout(title = 'Global Land-Ocean Temperature Index (LOTI)',
               yaxis = list(title = 'Temperature Anomaly (C)'),
               xaxis = list(title = 'Date'))


# Display the plot
fig3
```

Codeview 11.3 R code for the temperature rise graph

Activity 11.3: Can the Number of Record Temperatures Be Explained as Random Fluctuations?

1. First, we have to define what we mean by a record in a time series: given a sequence of numbers $x_1, x_2, \ldots, x_k, \ldots$, we call x_k a record, if x_k is bigger than all of its predecessors, i.e. if $x_k > x_v$ for $v < k$. For example, in the sequence 5, 3, 4, 7, 5, 11, 13, the number 7 is a new record because 7 is larger than the three preceding figures. For the same reason, 11 and 13 are records. The initial figure, here 5, is always a record. The above sequence contains four records. If we notice in a time series too many records, we doubt that the sequence is completely random. Too many records are indicative of an upward trend, too few records let us suspect a downward trend.

2. Now download the R code from *GitHub* and reproduce Fig. 11.3. The *plotly* implementation allows you to zoom in on specific areas of the graph. Look at the temperature values between the years 1980 and 2019 and count the number of records. Could you identify 11 records?

3. Assume for a moment that the temperature data between 1980 and 2019 were completely random, without any trend over time. How likely is it to observe 11 records in a random sequence of length 40? To figure that out you could resort to somewhat sophisticated combinatorial mathematics, or you can address the problem via simulations. The file *activities.R* on *GitHub* gives you the code for finding the probability of 11 records in a random sequence of length 40 via simulation.

11.3.4   Sea Level Rise

The fourth data set concerns the rise of the sea level (Nerem et al., 2018). It consists of two distinct parts. The older part is based on tide gauge records at coastal stations,[28] and it offers the reconstructed data from 1880 to 2009 as described in Church and White (2011). The newer records (since 1993) are accurate satellite measurements.[29] The unit here is GMSL (global mean sea level). The data are reported as changes relative to January 1, 1993 and are 2-month averages.[30] The first six and last six records of the combined dataset are displayed in Dataview 11.4, using R functions head and tail, respectively.

```
> head(datasets$sea_level)
# A tibble: 6 x 3
  date                method                    gmsl
  <dttm>              <chr>                    <dbl>
1 1880-01-16 00:00:00 Coastal tide gauge records -181.
2 1880-02-16 00:00:00 Coastal tide gauge records -170.
3 1880-03-17 00:00:00 Coastal tide gauge records -163.
4 1880-04-17 00:00:00 Coastal tide gauge records -157.
5 1880-05-17 00:00:00 Coastal tide gauge records -157.
6 1880-06-17 00:00:00 Coastal tide gauge records -158


> tail(datasets$sea_level)
# A tibble: 6 x 3
  date                method                    gmsl
  <dttm>              <chr>                    <dbl>
1 2017-11-18 00:00:00 Satellite observations  83.4
2 2017-11-28 00:00:00 Satellite observations  84.8
3 2017-12-08 00:00:00 Satellite observations  83.3
4 2017-12-18 00:00:00 Satellite observations  83.9
5 2017-12-28 00:00:00 Satellite observations  81.7
6 2018-01-06 00:00:00 Satellite observations  82.0
```

Dataview 11.4 First and last records of the sea level data set

Figure 11.4 shows the data combined in one time-series plot. The sea rise since 1880 is over 200 mm (or 20 cm) and it has accelerated in the 2000s.

Codeview 11.4 shows the R code used to create the plot in Fig. 11.4. First, the variable name of the series is updated to reflect the measurement type (tide gauge records vs satellite observations). Then the data is plotted as a time-series, where the colour depends on the measurement type.

---

[28] http://www.cmar.csiro.au/sealevel/downloads/church_white_gmsl_2011.zip

[29] http://sealevel.colorado.edu/files/2018_rel1/sl_ns_global.txt

[30] https://sealevel.nasa.gov/understanding-sea-level/key-indicators/global-mean-sea-level/

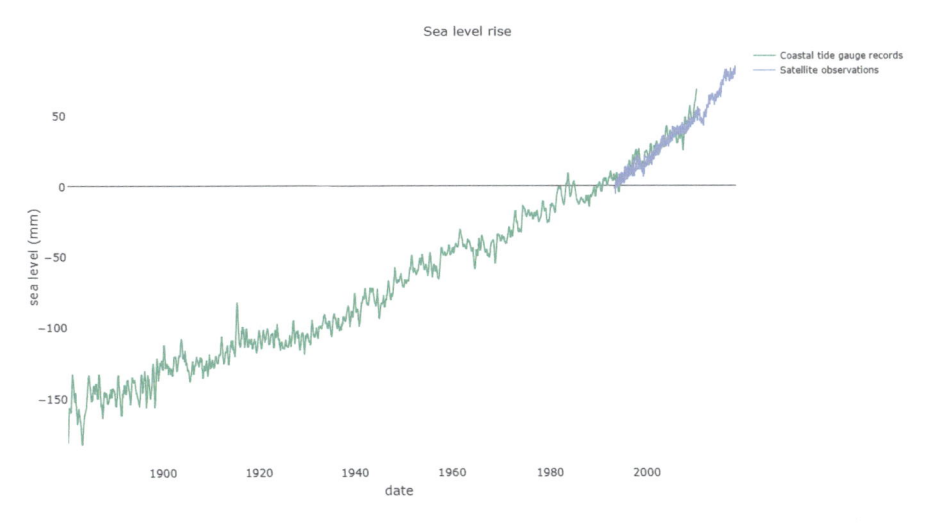

Fig. 11.4 Sea level rise from 1880 to 2018

```
# Replace the method values for a more comprehensive visualisation
datasets$sea_level <- datasets$sea_level %>%
mutate(method = replace(method, method == 'gmsl_tide',
"Coastal tide gauge records")) %>%
mutate(method = replace(method, method == 'gmsl_sat',
"Satellite observations"))

# Build the plot for sea_level data
fig4 <- plot_ly(datasets$sea_level, x = ~date, y = ~gmsl,
                color = ~method, type = 'scatter', mode = 'lines')

# Display the plot
fig4
```

Codeview 11.4 R code for the sea level rise graph

11.3.5 Sea Ice Retreat

The last one of *The Five Most Important Data Sets of Climate Science* concerns the sea ice and its retreat, with the focus on the polar region (Fetterer et al., 2017). It is a known fact that the ice extent is shrinking faster than predicted by climate models. Global warming is amplified, as the white ice (that reflects about 90% of the incident solar energy back into space) will be replaced by the dark ocean (that in turn absorbs about 90% of the solar energy). Dataview 11.5 shows the first ten records of the dataset.

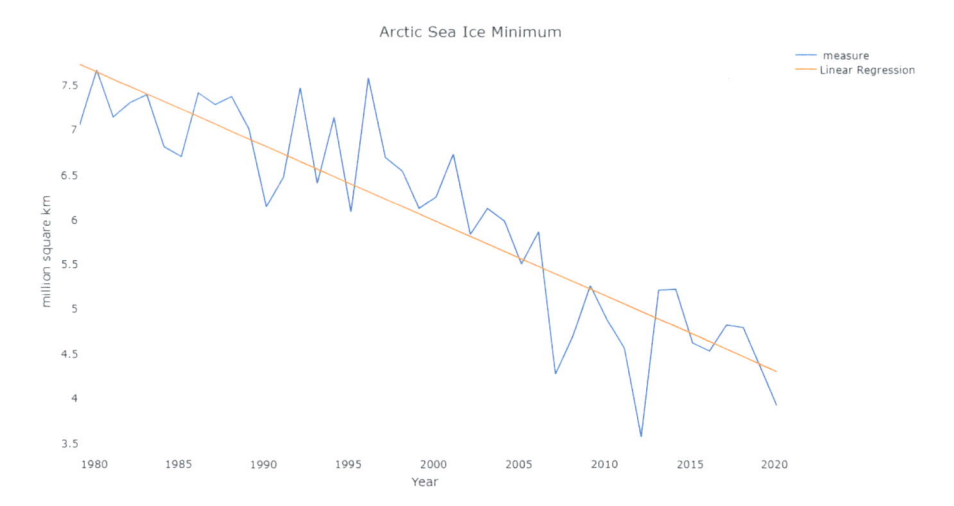

Fig. 11.5 Sea ice retreat from 1979 to 2019

```
> datasets$polar_ice
# A tibble: 41 x 6
    year                  mo `data-type` region extent  area
    <dttm>               <dbl> <chr>       <chr>   <dbl> <dbl>
 1 1979-01-01 00:00:00     9 Goddard     N        7.05  4.58
 2 1980-01-01 00:00:00     9 Goddard     N        7.67  4.87
 3 1981-01-01 00:00:00     9 Goddard     N        7.14  4.44
 4 1982-01-01 00:00:00     9 Goddard     N        7.3   4.43
 5 1983-01-01 00:00:00     9 Goddard     N        7.39  4.7
 6 1984-01-01 00:00:00     9 Goddard     N        6.81  4.11
 7 1985-01-01 00:00:00     9 Goddard     N        6.7   4.23
 8 1986-01-01 00:00:00     9 Goddard     N        7.41  4.72
 9 1987-01-01 00:00:00     9 Goddard     N        7.28  5.64
10 1988-01-01 00:00:00     9 Goddard     N        7.37  5.36
# ... with 31 more rows
```

Dataview 11.5 First ten records of the sea level data set

Figure 11.5 displays the time-series (the measurements connected by a line) with a linear trend from the end of the 1970s to present. One might ask, whether fitting a linear trend is reasonable as there is quite much variation around the regression line. It is also good to remember that the dataset includes only 41 observations, one per each year. The higher variability in some periods might be caused by chance, or there could be another factor explaining it. The linear trend is probably oversimplified, at least for a predictive model.

Codeview 11.5 shows the R code used to create the plot in Fig. 11.5. First, a linear model is fitted to find the linear trend based on years. Then, the data is plotted as a time-series, adding the trend and fine-tuning some of the graphical parameters.

```
# Fitting with linear model
lm_e <- lm(datasets$polar_ice$extent ~ datasets$polar_ice$year)

# Build the plot for the arctic sea ice minimum with the fitted values
fig5 <- plot_ly(datasets$polar_ice, x = ~year, y = ~extent,
                type = 'scatter', mode = 'lines', name = "measure") %>%
        add_trace(x = datasets$polar_ice$year, y = lm_e$fitted.values,
                  name = "Linear Regression") %>%
        layout(title = 'Arctic Sea Ice Minimum',
               yaxis = list(title = 'million square km'),
               xaxis = list(title = 'Year'))
```

Codeview 11.5 R code for the sea ice retreat graph

Activity 11.4: Exploring the Trend
1. Determine by eyeball analysis the slope of the fitted linear function describing the decline in arctic sea ice over the last 40 years.
2. Based on this trend, make a prediction of the ice volume for the year 2030.
3. In Sect. 5.3.1 you encountered a different graphical representation of the loss in arctic sea ice over time. Compare the two visualizations and assess their pros and cons.
4. To investigate the quality of the fit, it is helpful to investigate the residual plot, i.e. the plot of time versus the difference between data and fitted values. Draw a residual plot. The file *activities.R* on *GitHub* provides you with technical details. Can you discern a pattern in the residuals?
5. Another possibility to check if the trend is linear is by adding a smooth curve to the graph (again, see the file *activities.R* on *GitHub* for help). The span is a smoothing parameter, governing how closely the resulting curve follows the data. By default, we have set *span = 0.3*. Change the value of the smoothing parameter, observe the resulting curve and describe what you see.

11.3.6   Using Geographical Maps

Recent developments in computer graphics and animation have shaped the way in which data are presented in the media as images or as animated simulations. Visual representations play a central role in public communication and aim to represent the relevant dynamics and content in an easily understandable way. Choropleth maps are coloured maps which are a popular method to display spatially distributed data: the colour makes it easy to see the differences between areas. Many types of data can be placed in one picture in a comprehensible way. This is true in particular for animated maps which illustrate changes over time.

We provide the reader with resources and demonstrations of the R language to represent data through animated interactive maps, by adding a component that visualises the change over time. We continue using *plotly* as the visualisation tool, as it allows the mapping and visualisation of geospatial data while also providing an animation component that is easily integrated in the visualisations.

To facilitate the replicability without exposing the reader to a detailed explanation of the syntax and functionality of the R language, we provide a complete, well-documented R script (*utils_map.R*) in our *GitHub* repository.[31] The repository also contains the data files for the visualisations in csv format. In the following, we provide some guidelines on how the R script can be used, modified and customized.

There are three variables in the script that allow different visualisation outputs:

- *YEAR*—restrains the data to a user-specific interval of time
- *TYPE*—refers to the type of function to be used in the aggregation process of the variable *temperature*. Possible values are the average or maximum temperature. Additional aggregation functions can be implemented by the user.
- *REGION*—allows the user to define which regions of the maps will be shown. There are three different values that the user can input referring to the totality of the world, a set of specific countries, or the states of the USA.

Changing the combination of these variables will result in different outcomes. Figure 11.6 presents some of the possible visualisation examples.

The script starts by loading the necessary libraries to perform operations such as reading the data and plotting the map. It also loads additional information that may be required to work with data from the states of the USA. Then, we introduce the three variables that can be modified by the user (*YEAR, TYPE, REGION*). The data will be transformed based on their values. For example, if the reader intends to plot the temperature in the states of the USA, the data must be loaded and the names of the states must be converted to their abbreviated codes. All this will happen by running the ready-made R code presented in Codeview 11.6.

```
clim_data <- read.csv("GlobalLandTemperaturesByState.csv")

#Allow only the complete cases
clim_data <- clim_data[complete.cases(clim_data),]

#Conversion from date to different columns
clim_data  %>%separate(col = dt, into = c("Year", "Month", "Day"), convert = TRUE)
-> clim_data

#Apply the function getCode to the "States" column in dataset
codes <- unlist(lapply(clim_data$State,getCode))

#Create a new column (named variable) with the codes
clim_data$variable <- codes

#Set the location type of the map to USA-states (so the function know how to
#interpret the data we are passing it)
location_mode <- 'USA-states'
```

Codeview 11.6 R code for loading and transforming the data from the states of the USA

---

[31] https://github.com/nrguimaraes/climateChangeR

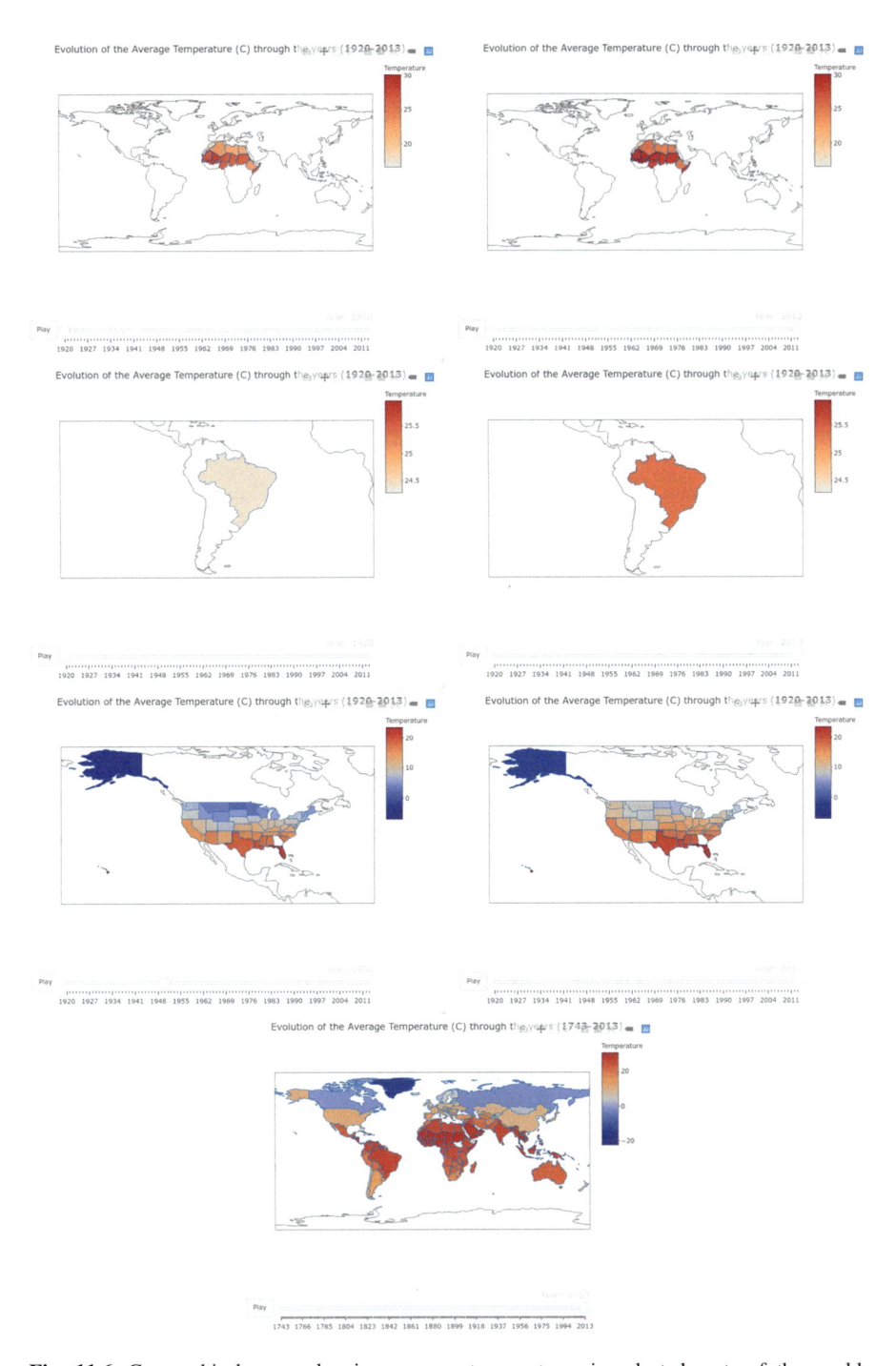

Fig. 11.6 Geographical maps showing average temperatures in selected parts of the world; snapshots from the animated displays

After reading the file with the information from the states of the USA, we ensure using the *complete.cases* function that we only want to use those entries in the dataset where there is information in all columns. Next, we use the *separate* function to decompose the collection date into three separate columns, containing the day, month, and year for better reading.

The function *getCode* is responsible for ensuring the conversion between state names and abbreviations. This conversion is necessary for the *plotly* package to be able to map the states to their respective positions. Finally, we set our *location_mode* variable to "*USA-states*" so that the *plotly* library knows how to interpret the data.

The *YEAR* and *TYPE* variables are handled next in the script. The *YEAR* variable allows us to filter the data frame if the type of information provided on the variable is an interval of years. When the *TYPE* is set to "*average*", the code in Codeview 11.7 will be executed.

```
clim_data %>%
    select(Year, AverageTemperature, variable) %>%
    group_by(Year, variable) %>%
    summarise(value = mean(AverageTemperature))-> clim_dataf
```

Codeview 11.7 R code for aggregating the data by average

The code again makes use of pipes (% > %) for better comprehension. The data frame is passed on to the *select* function, which will only use the *Year*, *AverageTemperature*, and *variable* (representing the US state codes). It is important to highlight that this *AverageTemperature* is the measure provided in the dataset while TYPE="*average*" refers to the function used for aggregation of the data (since there are multiple measurements in each year). The *group_by* function will group identical values in the *Year* and *variable* column and *summarise* will apply the mean (i.e. the average) to those grouped values. Finally, everything is stored in a new R data frame (*clim_dataf*). We opt to use a new name for the data so the reader can have a better perception on the transformations that occur in the data.

The code is very similar when the *TYPE* variable is set to "*max*", the only difference being the function used to summarise the data. With that in mind, the reader can easily add conditions to work with other functions, e.g., minimum temperature. The only requirement would be to copy the *else if* condition, change the condition to *TYPE*=="*min*" and set the *value* argument of the *summarise* function to *value=min(AverageTemperature)*.

Due to space constraints and since it is not the goal of this chapter to provide a complete introduction to R, we will conclude this section by focusing on the part of the script responsible for the visualisation of the data. Codeview 11.8 presents the code that uses *plotly* functions to present the transformed dataset in map format.

```
fig <- clim_dataf %>%
  plot_ly(
    locationmode=location_mode,
    z = ~Temperature,
    locations=~variable,
    frame = ~Year,
    type = 'choropleth',
    showlegend = TRUE,
    colorscale='bluered',
    zmax=max_value,
    zmin=min_value
    )

fig <- fig %>% layout(
  title= plot_title<-paste0("Evolution of the Average Temperature (C) through the
years (",clim_dataf$Year[1],"-",clim_dataf$Year[nrow(clim_dataf)],")"),
  geo=g
)
fig <- fig %>%
  animation_opts(
    frame=100
  )
fig
```

Codeview 11.8 R code for the visualisation of the map

The code is quite straightforward. The transformed data frame (*clim_dataf*) is passed down to the *plot_ly* function responsible for displaying the map. In this function, certain arguments must be provided. We shall briefly explain our choices of arguments to help the user in understanding how to build such visualisations.

The *z* argument corresponds to the variable we want to fill the map with (in this case the temperature column), with the *locations* argument referring to the location of that data. The *showlegend*, *colorscale*, *zmax* and *zmin* refer to the visibility of the legend, its colour scheme and the maximum and minimum value of it. Some of these arguments can be omitted with *plotly* adjusting to the default values. However, in the case of *zmax* and *zmin* it is important to maintain the same values in the animation so that the visualisation does not lead to misinterpretations (the default value of these arguments adjust the scale according to the data in each year). Finally, to add animation to the visualisation, we simply have to define what is the variable we want to change with each frame (in our case the years). This is achieved using the *frame* argument.

Optional configurations are then added to achieve a cleaner and easy-to-interpret visualisation. We use the *layout* function to define the title and configure some geographic settings. The *animation_opts* is used to slow the default duration of each frame to 100 ms. Please refer to the comments on the script and the official *plotly* documentation in R for additional information in these functions and arguments.

With the provided script and the information on this section, we do hope that readers will gain some appreciation of the flexibility and ease of use of the R language for visualising geospatial and time-dependent climate data.

> **Activity 11.5: Creating an Animated Map**
> Create an animated map for your country (or any land of your dreams) and its neighbours to explore trends in the maximum temperatures across a chosen time period. See the file *activities.R* on GitHub for help.

11.4 Recommendations for Implementation in a Classroom Environment

The primary aim of this chapter has been to facilitate the use of sophisticated software and engage students in exploring and visualising data about global warming and climate change. In this final section, we provide some technical guidelines for instructors to introduce the subject and replicate the visualisations provided in a classroom context.

The first requirement is to install R. It is very easy, because R is freely downloadable from the official R project website.[32] R has a simple command-based interface, but in order to facilitate the visualisations and code comprehension, we highly recommend also downloading and installing *RStudio*[33] software. It provides an integrated development environment (IDE) that allows an easier interaction between the R code, data, and visualisations.

As we have stated earlier, all the R code and data presented in this chapter are available for download from our *GitHub* repository.[34] *GitHub* is a huge platform that allows development teams to store and share their code as well as update and manage version control on the code. It also allows advanced functionalities such as methods for code merging and development trees.

With R and *RStudio* installed, the user may download the code from the *GitHub* repository, by finding the "Code" button and selecting "Download as Zip" (in the current layout of GitHub). When the download is complete, the user should extract the files to a folder of their preference and launch *RStudio*.

The next thing to do is to open one of the scripts that build the visualisations. To do that, just select *File → Open File* and then select the preferred script. When the script is loaded and since some external datasets are required it is necessary to "tell" R what the current working directory is. In our case, we want our working directory to be the same as the script (since it is where the datasets are also located). Thus, we select *Session → Set working directory → To source file location*. This way we set the R environment ready to run the scripts. The first time each script is loaded, the necessary libraries are installed (it may take some minutes). After that, everything should work exactly as described in the previous sections.

---

[32] https://www.r-project.org/

[33] https://rstudio.com/

[34] https://github.com/nrguimaraes/climateChangeR

The scripts provided in this chapter are highly customisable. This allows students to adapt the script to better comprehend the data and the R language itself. Let us begin by focusing on the script *utils.R* that is responsible for several visualisations presented in Sect. 11.3. The first suggestion we present to readers is to visualise the plots themselves in *RStudio*. To do that, users should study the code to see the parts of the code associated with each plot and correctly call the *plot_ly* function. For example, to create the plot presented in Fig. 11.1, the user should execute all the code until the variable *"fig"* is created. To do this, one can select all the code to this point and use the key combination Ctrl+R (Cmd + R in Mac) or select *Code → Run Selected Line(s)*. After that, the plot will appear by simply typing the name of the variable (that is, *fig*) below the selected code and running it.

The process is similar in the rest of the script. Readers can also run the full script and then type the different plot variables (*fig*, *fig2*, ...) to visualise the corresponding plot.

The plots are displayed in the plot window (usually located in the bottom right of *RStudio*). It is where users can see the advantages of using the *plotly* library since the embedded manipulation tools of the library allow a more fine-grained analysis of each visualisation. Also, *RStudio* allows (through the "*Zoom*" button in the top of the plot window) users to visualise each plot in a separate window.

We encourage instructors and students to modify the current script to explore several different advantages of manipulating and visualising climate change data with the R language. For example, when building the plot in Fig. 11.1b, we use the rolling mean function (*rollmean*) to smooth the temperature values in the dataset. Some parameters of this function can be changed, allowing a more fine-tuned visualisation. To find the possible options of this function, one can type *?rollmean* on the console and select the *zoo::rollmean* function from the help window. This can be done with any function used in this script and we encourage lecturers and readers to use the help option (by writing the name of the function preceded by a question mark) anytime they feel it necessary to better understand the code. In the help window of the *rollmean* function, each parameter of the function is explained, thus allowing users to customize how to fill the missing values or the type of alignment that they wish to do. We encourage users to understand these parameters and change the function to modify the plot in Fig. 11.1b.

Similarly, in Fig. 11.3 the Keeling curve consists of a trend plus a superimposed seasonal component, the latter reflecting the absorption of CO_2 by plants. The seasonal component is caused by the CO_2 being absorbed into plants via photosynthesis in spring and summer, leading to a decrease in the atmospheric CO_2 level during these seasons. In winter, some plants are deciduous (so do not photosynthesise at all); in regions where winter is associated with low temperatures, photosynthesis is reduced even in non-deciduous plants. The trend is modelled via data smoothing, and in this case the seasonal component can be described well through trigonometric functions.

As was mentioned in Sect. 11.3.6, the script *utils_map.R* provides a more high-end customisation where the user can change the predefined variables to plot different geographical visualisations and animations concerning countries, time intervals, and function aggregation types (mean, max, …). We encourage lecturers to use this script in a classroom environment and challenge the student to enhance the script by providing new ways to visualise the data or transform the data to provide new visualisations.

We mentioned the addition of a function *min* (minimum temperature) in the *TYPE* variable by introducing a new *if* condition. Moreover, new data transformations can be added to visualise filtered parts of the dataset. For example, it can be interesting to study the effect of climate change in a particular season. Therefore, users can filter the data before the visualisation to only contemplate spring or winter (by using the month column). We encourage lecturers to propose this challenge in the classroom and require that the modifications made in the script must be additions and thus, the current functionalities must be kept. In this way, students will better understand the base script and how the global variables *TYPE*, *YEAR*, and *REGION* work, instead of just coding by a trial-and-error approach. We do believe that the current base script *utils_map.R* provides a good skeleton for a large number of additional exercises and challenges to transform and visualise climate data and thus we encourage lecturers to create such activities and use them in a classroom context.

11.5   Conclusions

Studying climate change requires the exploration of complex spatial time series datasets, often with special tools and advanced methods. However, the basic knowledge of climate change can be understood from a few visualisations obtained with freely available data and software.

In this chapter we have given a general view on exploring climate change data, including ready-made online visualisations (such as images, maps, and animations). We have also shown a couple of examples of how to access and use climate change data from different data sources and repositories with R, the freely accessible statistical programming language and computing environment (R Core Team, 2020).

We encourage the reader to actually run our examples and to display and explore the dynamic versions of the graphs and maps. All that is required is to install R and *RStudio*, then download and use the R code shown in Sect. 11.3, available in complete form in our *GitHub* repository.[35] We note that a beginner of R does not need to understand every detail of the code. It is satisfying to see the results, especially the graphs, appearing in the *RStudio* window and to make some small modifications. Indeed, learning more R typically happens best as a process of trial-and-error, by working with ready-made examples and trying to repeat them, possibly modifying some details with the help of freely available materials, such as books and websites.

---

[35] https://github.com/nrguimaraes/climateChangeR

References

Barnola, J. M., Raynaud, D., Korotkevich, Y. S., & Lorius, C. (1987). Vostok ice core provides 160,000-year record of atmospheric CO_2. *Nature, 329*, 408–414. https://www.nature.com/articles/329408a0.pdf

Barnola, J.-M., Raynaud, D., Lorius, C., & Barkov, N. I. (2003). Historical carbon dioxide record from the Vostok Ice Core (417,160–2,342 years BP). In *Trends: A compendium of data on global change. Carbon dioxide information analysis center.* Oak Ridge National Laboratory, U.S. Department of Energy. http://cdiac.ess-dive.lbl.gov/trends/co2/vostok.html

Church, J. A., & White, N. J. (2011). Sea-level rise from the late 19th to the early 21st century. *Surveys in Geophysics*, (32), 585–602. https://doi.org/10.1007/s10712-011-9119-1

Cleveland, W. S. (1993). *Visualizing data.* AT & T Bell Laboratories.

Fetterer, F., Knowles, K., Meier, W. N., Savoie, M., & Windnagel, A. K. (2017). *Sea ice index, version 3.0.* NSIDC: National Snow and Ice Data Center. https://doi.org/10.7265/N5K072F8

Horton, N. J., Baumer, B. S., & Wickham, H. (2014). *Teaching precursors to data science in introductory and second courses in statistics.* https://arxiv.org/pdf/1401.3269.pdf

Jouzel, J., Lorius, C., Petit, J. R., Genthon, C., Barkov, N. I., Kotlyakov, V. M., & Petrov, V. M. (1987). Vostok ice core: A continuous isotope temperature record over the last climatic cycle (160,000 years). *Nature, 329*, 403–408. https://www.nature.com/articles/329403a0.pdf

Lai, J., Lortie, C., Muenchen, R., Yang, J., & Ma, K. (2019). Evaluating the popularity of R in ecology. *Ecosphere, 10*(1). https://doi.org/10.1002/ecs2.2567

Lowndes, J. S. S., Best, B. D., Scarborough, C., Afflerbach, J. C., Frazier, M. R., O'Hara, C. C., Jiang, N., & Halpern, B. S. (2017). Our path to better science in less time using open data science tools. *Nature Ecology and Evolution, 1*, 0160. https://doi.org/10.1038/s41559-017-0160

NASA GISTEMP Team. (2020). *GISS Surface Temperature Analysis (GISTEMP), version 4.* NASA Goddard Institute for Space Studies. Combined Land-Surface Air and Sea-Surface Water Temperature Anomalies (Land-Ocean Temperature Index, LOTI). Global-mean monthly, seasonal, and annual means (1880–present). https://data.giss.nasa.gov/gistemp/tabledata_v4/GLB.Ts+dSST.csv

Nerem, R. S., Beckley, B. D., Fasullo, J. T., Hamlington, B., Masters, D., & Mitchum, G. T. (2018). Climate-change–driven accelerated sea-level rise detected in the altimeter era. *Proceedings of the National Academy of Science.* https://doi.org/10.1073/pnas.1717312115

Nolan, D., & Temple Lang, D. (2010). Computing in the statistics curricula. *The American Statistician, 64*(2), 97–107. https://doi.org/10.1198/tast.2010.09132

OECD. (2019). *OECD skills outlook: Thriving in a digital world.* OECD Publishing. https://doi.org/10.1787/df80bc12-en

R Core Team. (2020). *R: A language and environment for statistical computing.* R Foundation for Statistical Computing. https://www.R-project.org/

Shah, C. (2020). *A hands-on introduction to data science.* Cambridge University Press.

Shen, S. S. P. (2017). *R programming for climate data analysis and visualization: Computing and plotting for NOAA data applications* (The first revised edition). San Diego State University. https://shen.sdsu.edu/pdf/R-TextBySamShen2017.pdf

Shen, S. S. P., & Somerville, R. C. J. (2019). *Climate mathematics: Theory and applications.* Cambridge University Press.

Sievert, C. (2020). *Interactive web-based data visualization with R, plotly, and shiny*. Chapman and Hall/CRC. https://plotly-r.com

Tans, P., & Keeling, R. (2020). *Trends in atmospheric carbon dioxide*. NOAA/ESRL and Scripps Institution of Oceanography (https://scrippsco2.ucsd.edu/). Mauna Loa CO_2 monthly mean data. https://www.esrl.noaa.gov/gmd/ccgg/trends/data.html

Theobold, A., & Hancock, S. (2019). How environmental science graduate students acquire statistical computing skills. *Statistics Education Research Journal, 18*(2), 65–85. https://iase-web.org/documents/SERJ/SERJ18(2)_Theobold.pdf?1575083627

Wickham, H., & Grolemund, G. (2017). *R for data science: Import, tidy, transform, visualize, and model data*. O'Reilly. https://r4ds.had.co.nz/

Chapter 12
Covid-19 Shows Why We Need Civic Statistics: Illustrations and Classroom Activities

Jim Ridgway ⓘ **and Rosie Ridgway**

Abstract There are few better examples than a pandemic to demonstrate the importance of, and need for, Civic Statistics. Every country affected by Covid-19 faces the threat of widespread deaths, economic damage, and social disruption. Citizens and governments need to take account of existing and emerging evidence, in order to decide on effective action. In most cases, governments need to create mechanisms to gather more evidence relevant to decision making, such as the incidence, rate of growth, and nature of the disease. For measures to be effective in democratic societies, governments need to give transparent and convincing explanations for their decisions. This puts high demands on skills associated with communicating statistical evidence on the side of governments and media, and a citizenry able to understand statistical messages. Evidence associated with Covid-19 covers the full spectrum of the features of Civic Statistics described by Engel and Ridgway in Chap. 2. Skills needed to understand and act on evidence cover the complete set of skills set out by Gal, Nicholson and Ridgway in Chap. 3. Here, we illustrate these features, point to requisite skills, and suggest some activities for students.

Keywords Covid-19 · Modelling · Risk · Causality · Plausible estimation · SEIR

12.1 Introduction

Every single avoidable death is a personal tragedy; many deaths are associated with family distress and hardship. At the time of writing (June 2021) there were 3.9 million deaths recorded world wide from Covid-19. Governments have taken actions (or not) that affect citizens in profound ways—sometimes failing in a duty of care to their citizens, in other cases by curtailing activities, causing massive social disruption, and sometimes causing economic hardship. All of these decisions were made

J. Ridgway (✉) · R. Ridgway
University of Durham, Durham, UK
e-mail: jim.ridgway@durham.ac.uk; r.a.ridgway@durham.ac.uk

on the basis of imperfect information, imperfect theories, and imperfect models. Making good decisions on the basis of imperfect data is the heartland of statistics.

A tenet of epidemiology is that disease outbreaks are inevitable, but that epidemics are optional (e.g. Brilliant, 2020). The World Health Organisation[1] provides information on deaths from pandemics, reproduced below

- 2009–2010 Swine flu (H1N1)—110–400,000 deaths
- Hong Kong Flu 1968 A(H3N2)—1–4 million deaths
- Asian flu 1957–58 A(H2N2)—1–4 million deaths
- 1918–1919 A(H1N1) Spanish Flu—20–50 million deaths

We can conclude that events such as the emergence of Covid-19 will continue to occur regularly. If we are to choose the option of 'no pandemic', lessons learned from successes and errors dealing with Covid-19 should be remembered and deployed when the global community faces similar threats in the future.

In March 2020 WHO[1] declared Covid-19 to be a pandemic—an epidemic that had spread across countries and continents. Their intention was to encourage governments world-wide to take preventative measures immediately in order to reduce the dangers posed to humanity by the disease. Examples of action would include clear communication about the dangers of the virus to citizens, development of a coherent national response that might include contact tracing, banning public gatherings, and restricting international travel. Other measures could include protecting front-line workers, and ensuring robust supply chains for food and protective equipment. Some countries followed WHO advice, some did not.

An epidemic provides a vivid example of the need to use evidence to inform policy. However, this is rarely a straightforward process. For example, a dramatic increase in cases of a disease calls for some sort of action, but different agencies will have different ideas about the best course of action to take. In the case of Covid-19, initial actions across the world included: lockdown, and border controls (e.g. New Zealand); extensive Track and Trace (e.g. Germany); allowing the disease to spread in order to develop herd immunity (Sweden); rejecting evidence and taking no action (USA).

Belief systems—including attitudes to evidence—influence decision making. For example, a politician who believes that Covid-19 is like influenza, and that influenza is not very dangerous in Western societies, is likely to be unsympathetic to calls to restrict citizens' activities. A contrast to belief-led decision making is evidence informed decision making. Dr. Angela Merkel, when German Chancellor, was quoted[2] as saying "Before I do anything, I have to understand what is going on here". It is important that politicians make decisions informed by evidence, and informed by their political judgements about actions that will be acceptable to their electorate rather than purely on the basis of belief. The lack of Civic Statistics skills in some politicians is matched by lack of skills in part of the electorate. For example, an IPSOS-mori report (2020) summarised the results of their surveys in the UK on Conspiracy theories[3] regarding Covid-19. 30% of Britons thought that Covid was probably created in a laboratory; 7% thought the whole pandemic is a hoax; 13% thought it was a secret scheme to force the world to accept mass vaccinations.

Our ambition here is not to offer either a Survival Guide to the Epidemic, nor a critique of relevant scientific evidence. Rather, we use Covid as an illustration of the importance of Civic Statistics in understanding events that influence all our lives, and in guiding appropriate civic action. A range of classroom activities have been sketched, applicable across a range of classrooms, from high school to graduate classes. Activities suitable for use in high school are presented in more detail in Ridgway (2021).

12.2 Features of Civic Statistics

In Chap. 2, Engel and Ridgway described a number of features of Civic Statistics not commonly encountered in introductory statistics courses. All of them can be exemplified using Covid-19 as a context. Table 12.1 reproduces Table 2.1. The following notes exemplify the features of Civic Statistics in the context of Covid-19; in Sect. 12.3 we relate these features to some components of statistical knowledge that students should acquire.

Table 12.1 Features of Civic Statistics data

Twelve features of Civic Statistics
What citizens see/read/hear
I. Contexts and interpretations
1. Societal context is the focus
2. Statistics are embedded in rich texts
3. Causality is often attributed
4. Conclusions, implications, and consequences for society are discussed
II. The nature of the statistics
5. Phenomena are often multivariate
6. Decisions have been made about measures and operationalization
7. Data are often aggregated
8. Indicator systems are common
9. Dynamic data, spanning times and locations is common
III. Unfamiliar methods and representations
10. Novel data sources and analysis techniques are common
11. Varied data collection methods are used
12. Innovative visualisations have been invented

---

[3] https://almanac.ipsos-mori.com/project/conspiracy-theories/

12.2.1   Contexts and Interpretations

Societal context is the focus: this is self-evident in the case of Covid-19; a pandemic has brought dramatic changes to social functioning worldwide.

Statistics are embedded in rich texts: from the start of the spread of Covid-19, there have been daily media accounts addressing different aspects of Covid-19. Data are embedded in rich texts, TV and radio, social media, and cartoons. Everyone is exposed to a great flow of data—and these data are of variable quality. The World Health Organisation refers to the Covid-19 'infodemic', and offers advice about how it might be managed.[4]

Causal claims are often made: a great variety of causal stories can be found, that use different kinds of evidence, and which have different implications for action, including:

- biological stories—for example ideas about the ways that viruses are transmitted, and the likelihood of transmission via contact with surfaces, or water droplets
- behavioural stories—for example the likely effect on transmission of social distancing, mask wearing, and hand washing
- social stories—for example the likelihood that people will follow social distancing rules in bars or at large social gatherings
- political stories—for example the likely impact of different government initiatives such as closing schools, or imposing lockdown on the short- and long-term well being of citizens
- economic stories—for example the likely impact of Covid-19 on sectors such as travel and tourism, and e-commerce, as well on individuals

Conclusions, implications, and consequences for society are discussed: deciding that Covid-19 is, indeed, a pandemic is a starting point for action, and leads directly to gathering data likely to guide future decisions. All of the themes alluded to under *causality* are relevant here.

12.2.2   The Nature of the Statistics

Phenomena are often multivariate: phenomena include: Covid-19 disease symptoms; disease incidence and geographical spread, impact on social life, impact on mental health, government actions, economic outcomes, and environmental outcomes such as reduced pollution and fewer deaths attributable to road traffic accidents.

---

[4]https://www.who.int/news/item/23-09-2020-managing-the-covid-19-infodemic-promoting-healthy-behaviours-and-mitigating-the-harm-from-misinformation-and-disinformation

Decisions have been made about measures and operationalization: these are deeply problematic—how can *cases* or *deaths* be measured accurately enough for decision making?

Data are often aggregated: when is it appropriate to add deaths from different regions? Or from different groups such as school children and people in care homes? Obese and underweight? Vulnerable and not?

Indicator systems are common: Consider the 2019 Global Health Security Index (GHI)[5]—a measure designed to *illuminate preparedness and capacity gaps. . . at the national and international levels.* It combines a number of measures (prevention of the emergence of pathogens; detection and reporting; rapid response; robustness of the health system; compliance with international norms and overall vulnerability to biological threats) to create a GHI for each of 195 countries. The two highest scoring countries (so best prepared according to GHI's creators) are the USA and the UK. At the time of writing, these two countries had some of the highest Covid-19 mortality rates, worldwide. Students can be asked to explore this paradox; details of measures, performance on subscales (prevention, detection etc), all the data, an interactive map, and a full report can be accessed and downloaded.

Dynamic data, spanning times and locations is common: Spatial data analysed over time are clearly important for understanding disease spread and planning. Disease modelling requires estimates of the number of *susceptible* people in the population, and the *chance of recovery* for those who have contracted the disease. Both of these parameters will change over time, as more people become immune, and as treatment methods improve.

12.2.3   Unfamiliar Methods and Representations

Novel data sources and analysis techniques are common: data are available from medical, social, and economic sources, amongst others. Vaccine trials range from randomized controlled trials in natural settings to controlled exposure to Covid-19 of vaccinated people (with associated ethical dilemmas).

Varied data collection methods are used: these include well designed surveys to ascertain key data such as the size of the *immune* population, and opportunistic sampling; mapping mobility patterns via records of air travel, credit card transactions and cell phone locations.

Innovative visualisations have been invented: Covid-19 has led to the design of some excellent novel ways to present data via simulations, heat maps, and icon arrays—for example, Vuorinen and Kahila's simulation of virus spread indoors via aerosols.[6] Links and some descriptions to other visualisations are provided later in this chapter.

---

[5] https://www.ghsindex.org/
[6] https://www.youtube.com/watch?v=EcpQBxBdr5g

12.3 Covid-19 and Some Components of Civic Statistics Knowledge

In Chap. 3, Gal, Nicholson and Ridgway offered a conceptual framework for Civic Statistics and its educational applications. Figure 12.1 reproduces their Fig. 3.1. Here, we show how each of these is important for citizen (and policy maker) engagement with Civic Statistics.

12.3.1 Enabling Processes

In this Section, we illustrate the importance of mastering Enabling Processes (ICT and Search, Quantitative Core, and Literacy and Communication) in order to function as informed citizens in the face of Covid-19.

12.3.1.1 ICT and Search

There are a number of authoritative sources of information about Covid-19. At the time of writing, these included the World Health Organisation Dashboard,[7] The

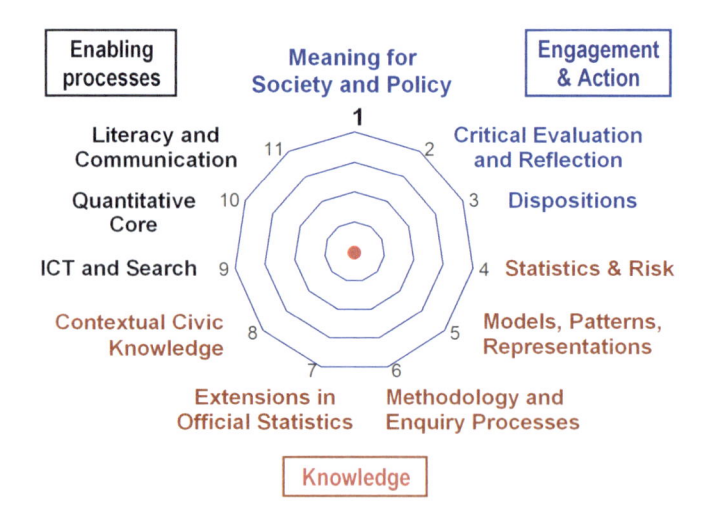

Fig. 12.1 A conceptual model for Civic Statistics

---

[7] https://covid19.who.int/?gclid=CjwKCAjwr7X4BRA4EiwAUXjbtwzv0iZu-e%2D%2
DyVoyYbPOkG5HOO6JY61AVwfqql0MAEzGWdXsX68TyBoChUoQAvD_BwE

United Nations,[8] Worldometer,[9] Our World in Data,[10] the Financial Times,[11] and the Johns Hopkins Coronavirus Resource Center,[12] along with sources of national data such as the Centres for Disease Control and Prevention in the USA[13] the Robert Koch Institute in Germany,[14] and Public Health[15] in the UK.

However, citizens need to be able to both locate and navigate these sites, as well as to be able to understand the information they contain. A picture may be worth a 1000 words, but sometimes the 'picture' needs a few hundred words of explanation, and a sophisticated recipient. ICT and search skills are particularly important in the context of Covid-19. People face two major problems when looking for information about Covid-19: one is associated with dis- and mis-information; the other is information overload (or the 'infodemic'). Citizens need skills in identifying trustworthy sources (as opposed to conspiracy theorists or the mis-informed), and in finding sites that provide succinct summaries, and clear advice.

A more fundamental question relates to access. According to the United Nations,[16] 3.6 billion people remain off-line. There are dramatic divides in access to digital learning; worldwide, half of all learners (about 830 million students) do not have access to a computer. Additionally, 40% have no internet access at home.[17] Presumably these inequalities in access play out between rich and poor families in developed countries, with obvious implications for home-based education and life chances. The UN argues strongly for universal access to the internet (and discusses some associated problems).[18]

12.3.1.2   Quantitative Core

Arithmetic Toby Young is a journalist on a major-circulation daily newspaper in the UK who regularly argues that there is no need for lockdowns or other restrictions on movement to reduce the spread of Covid-19, because Covid-19 is no more dangerous than flu. Here is a transcript of one of his tweets.

New study suggests more than five million Britons have had the coronavirus. Given that ~50,000 people have died from it, that means it has an IFR of <0.1%.

---

[8] https://www.un.org/en/coronavirus

[9] https://www.worldometers.info/coronavirus/

[10] https://ourworldindata.org/coronavirus-testing

[11] https://www.ft.com/content/a2901ce8-5eb7-4633-b89c-cbdf5b386938

[12] https://coronavirus.jhu.edu/

[13] https://covid.cdc.gov/covid-data-tracker/#cases_casesper100klast7days

[14] https://www.rki.de/EN

[15] https://coronavirus.data.gov.uk/

[16] https://www.un.org/en/coronavirus

[17] https://news.un.org/en/story/2020/04/1062232

[18] https://news.un.org/en/story/2020/05/1063272

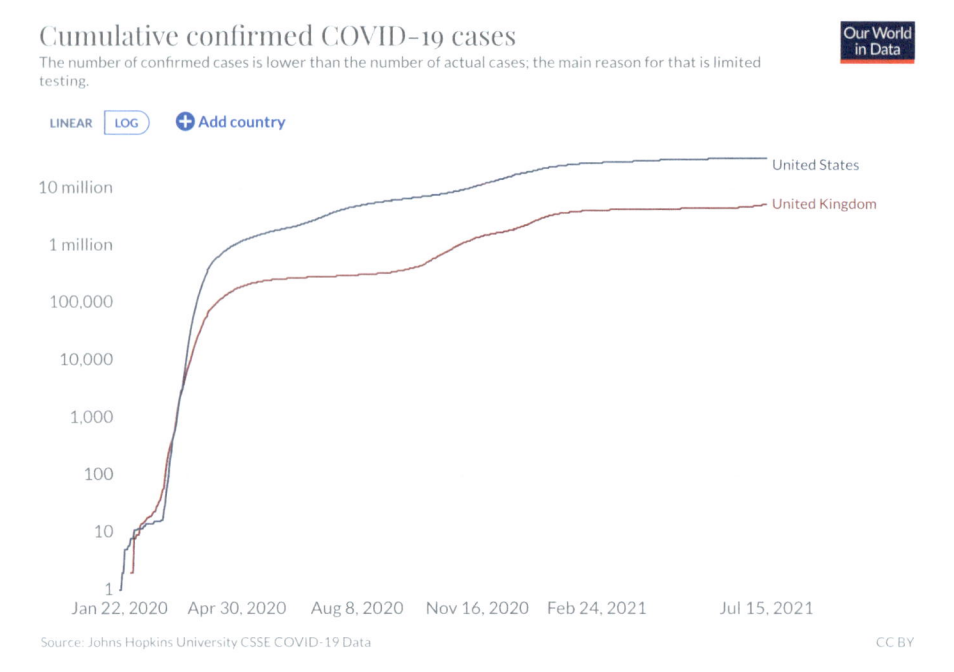

Fig. 12.2 Covid-19 cumulative confirmed cases in two countries

That's roughly the same as seasonal flu. (posted 18th November 2020, then taken down shortly after).

Assuming these data are correct, the Infection Fatality Rate (IFR) should be reported as 1% (50 thousand divided by 5 million)—so Covid-19 has ten times the Infection Fatality Rate of flu.

Interpreting Graphs Figures 12.2 and 12.3 show data from the Our World in Data data set.[19] Groups of students can be asked to explain each graph to each other, then to explain why the graphs look different. Do they believe the graphs show data from the same data set? Figure 12.2 shows cumulative confirmed Covid-19 cases in the UK and the USA, using a logarithmic scale. Figure 12.3 shows daily confirmed cases per million people.

The graphs are useful for making different sorts of decisions. For example, the number of new confirmed cases each day can be used to predict demand on hospital resources in (about) 2 weeks time. Students can be asked to say under what circumstances (and for what sorts of decisions) is it useful:

- to use a log scale
- to use a linear scale
- to know about rates rather than raw numbers

---

[19] https://ourworldindata.org/coronavirus

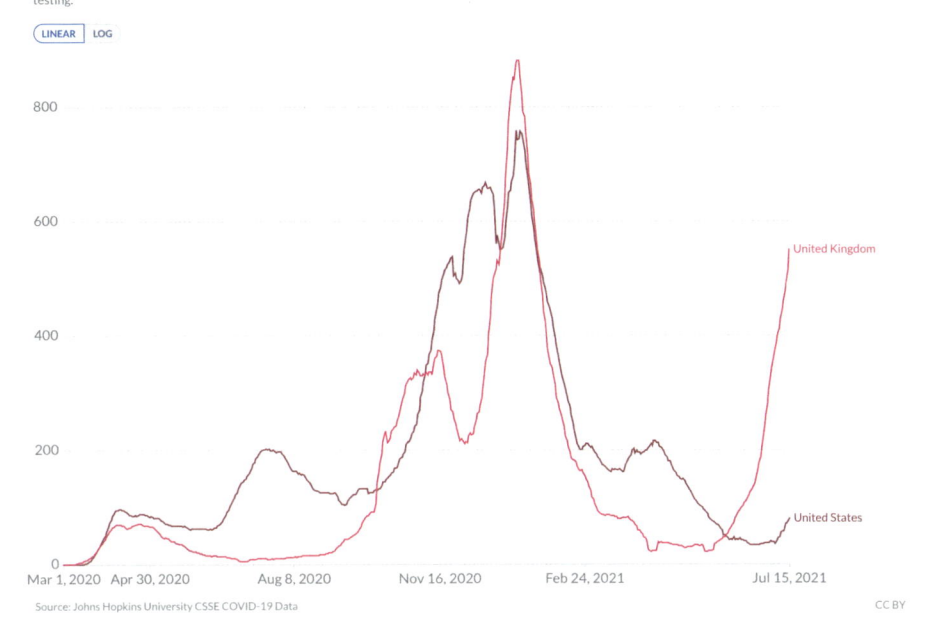

Daily new confirmed COVID-19 cases per million people
Shown is the rolling 7-day average. The number of confirmed cases is lower than the number of actual cases; the main reason for that is limited testing.

Source: Johns Hopkins University CSSE COVID-19 Data

Fig. 12.3 Covid-19 daily confirmed cases in two countries

- to know about raw numbers rather than rates
- to know about deaths rather than cases
- to know about cases rather than deaths
- To use new events
- To use cumulative events

Students can be asked to choose a graph which makes it easiest to see the success of combating an epidemic, by deciding on: log vs linear scales; rates vs raw numbers; deaths vs cases; new events vs cumulative events.

An obvious advantage of log scales is that the slope of the curve at any point gives a direct indication of the speed of spread of the disease; epidemics at an early stage can be compared with those at a later stage. Even though there are big differences in the numbers of new cases. However, log scales can be hard to understand, and can be visually misleading—for example, a change of one unit on the y-axis in Fig. 12.2 corresponds to both a rise from 10 to 100 cases, and for a rise from 1 million to 10 million cases. A linear scale gives a clearer impression of the size of the epidemic.

Planning needs to be based on raw numbers. Scaling numbers by the size of the population makes little sense at the start of an epidemic, but later gives some indication of the success of eradication programmes across different countries, and the load on a country's resources. Covid data illustrate a statistical Big Idea—estimates based on small samples are usually less stable than those based on larger samples. Countries with small populations often have very high *cases per million* (e.g. Montenegro and Andorra), and also have very low *cases per million* (e.g. Fiji, Mauritius).[20]

Exponential Growth Exponential growth is another Big Idea, relevant to the growth of populations or malignant tumours, compound interest, and inflation. Exponential growth is a key feature of epidemics. If each infected person infects two more people each day (then ceases to be infectious), the sequence of daily new cases is 1, 2, 4, 8, 16, 32. . . Students can be asked to suppose this pattern is followed worldwide (a foolish assumption), then to calculate how many days it would take for the global population (about 8 billion people) to be infected. The answer is 36 days. Students can be encouraged to use a spreadsheet to solve the problem, and can also explore the effects of different exponents (critically, above and below 1) to population growth,[21] inflation, resource extraction, consumption of goods, compound interest, or the volume of malignant tumours. Exponential growth presents decision makers with a dilemma. Can they *really* introduce measures to restrict personal liberty on the basis of a few thousand cases and a few hundred deaths? If students understand exponential growth, they will be able to explain why it is *not* correct to argue that, in the early phases of an epidemic, Covid-19 deaths are not really a cause for concern because they are small compared with (say) deaths attributable to road traffic accidents.

Plausible Estimation Plausible estimation is sometimes called a 'back of an envelope calculation' or a 'Fermi problem'. It is essential to be able to judge the order of magnitude of relevant quantities when making decisions. For example:

If every care worker changes their face mask just once every day, how many masks will be needed each week? What is the weight and volume of the waste?

How long would it take to inoculate everyone in your region?

For both questions, students can be encouraged to start with simplifying assumptions—for example: in the case of inoculations: that enough vaccine is available; that everyone can attend for vaccination; that current staff will be available throughout; and so on. Then more realistic assumptions can be made—for example about the ability of everyone in the population to attend for vaccination, and about staff illness and care responsibilities. Swan and Ridgway (2001)[22] have created materials to support teaching about plausible estimation.

---

[20] https://ig.ft.com/coronavirus-chart/?areas=eur&areas=usa&areas=bra&areas=gbr&areas= ind&areas=hun&areasRegional=usny&areasRegional=usnj&areasRegional=usca& areasRegional=usnd&areasRegional=ussd&areasRegional=usmi&cumulative=0&logScale=0& per100K=1&startDate=2020-09-01&values=deaths

[21] https://en.wikipedia.org/wiki/Population_growth

[22] http://archive.wceruw.org/cl1/flag/cat/math/estimation/estimation1.htm

12.3.1.3 Literacy and Communication

Since the outbreak of the epidemic, the media have been awash with accounts of all manner of issues regarding Covid-19. Statistical messages are embedded in text; statistics are used to inform, and as a warrant to justify political action. It is self-evident that citizens need literary and communication skills in order to use such information effectively.

12.3.2 Knowledge

In this section, we illustrate the importance of mastering Knowledge (Statistics and Risk, Models, Patterns and Representations, Methodology and Enquiry Processes, Extensions in Official Statistics, and Contextual Civic Knowledge) in order to function as informed citizens in the face of Covid-19.

12.3.2.1 Statistics and Risk

The context of Covid-19 offers many opportunities to discuss fundamental ideas around statistics and risk, of direct relevance to individual, collective, and political action. Here, we take a single but important idea about judging the reliability of a Covid-19 test, that makes use of Bayes' theorem.

Diagnostic tests can lead to errors of interpretation for a variety of reasons, some medical, some psychological, and some statistical. Medically: a test may be administered before antibodies have developed; it may detect antibodies that are ineffective against the disease; and tests do not necessarily show if a person is still infectious. If data are sparse, it is hard to estimate how accurate the test is.

There is a considerable body of evidence (building on pioneering work by Tversky and Kahneman (1974)) that illustrates the problems that people have interpreting statistical information. Gigerenzer et al. (2007), in a paper which describes ways to help doctors and patients make sense of health statistics, offer useful (research based) advice on ways to present statistical information that leads to better understanding, such as: use frequency statements rather than single-event probabilities; use absolute risk rather than relative risk; mortality rates rather than survival rates; and use natural frequencies not conditional probabilities.

However, there is also a 'statistical' problem with all screening tests—even very accurate ones. The fewer the people in the population who have some condition (a disease, or antibodies against a disease) the more likely it is that a positive test leads to the wrong conclusion. This could be dangerous if a person believes they have antibodies (and so thinks they are immune) and behaves accordingly.

Try this example with students:

Suppose 10 in 1000 people have Covid-19 antibodies (so are believed to be immune).

Suppose that, for people who have Covid-19 antibodies, a test will detect it correctly 90% of the time.

Suppose that, for people who do not have Covid-19 antibodies, the test will diagnose this correctly 90% of the time.

Now, suppose a person gets a test result that shows they have positive antibodies against Covid-19—what is the probability they actually have the antibodies?

Begin by asking for a 'ball-park' figure (perhaps via a show of hands for: p about 0.9; p about 0.75; p about 0.5; p about 0.25; p less than 0.25).

Solution:

If the incidence is 10 in 1000 people, then 990 won't have antibodies.

The test on these 990 people will be 90% accurate—so 99 people will be identified as having antibodies.

The test on the ten people who do have antibodies will correctly identify 90% of them—so nine positives.

Therefore, in the pool of positive results, we have 99 false positives and 9 true positives, in a total of 108 positives.

So, if someone tests positive, their chance of actually having Covid-19 antibodies is 9/108—less than 10%.

You can ask students to create a generalisation of this. As a starting point, ask them to repeat the calculations, using the incidence of antibodies as ten in a million people (to illustrate the increase in false positive rates as a function of the incidence of antibodies in the population). Students can then be asked to express the false positive rate as a function of: disease incidence in the population; test *sensitivity* (the ability to correctly identify those with the disease—the true positive rate); and test *specificity* (the ability to correctly identify those who do not have the disease—the true negative rate).

Quartz[23] offer an interactive visualisation on the accuracy of tests that allows students to see the effect of changing test specificity and sensitivity, using icon arrays. A model from Kennis Research[24] allows students to explore the effects of sliding disease incidence in the population, sensitivity, and specificity, on the predictive value (for positive and negative results) of the test. These visualisations (of course) are directly relevant to the Covid-19 epidemic. For clinicians and patients, it is important to know the actual probability that someone identified as having the antibodies actually has them (and so is assumed to be protected against the disease)—and that this probability will change as the incidence in the population changes.

---

[23] https://qz.com/1848674/how-to-interpret-the-specificity-sensitivity-of-antibody-tests/

[24] https://kennis-research.shinyapps.io/Bayes-App/

12.3.2.2 Models, Patterns and Representations

In this Section, we will focus mainly on modelling—often a Cinderella in introductory courses. We will point to some interesting patterns that illustrate the effectiveness of some vaccines, to show how data visualisation can be used to provide evidence supporting causal stories. There are also links to a variety of Covid-19-related representations.

Modelling
Modelling is rarely taught explicitly in introductory statistics courses, where regression is the dominant model ('this phenomenon arises as a direct result of a linear combination of these variables (and nothing is going to change over time)'). More generally, modelling is a wallflower in mathematics courses, despite its central role in understanding the world. The Covid-19 crisis provided an excellent illustration of the cyclical and iterative nature of real-world problem solving; in particular, that while the overall problem can be described simply, the nature of the problems to be solved on a day-to-day basis changes radically. For example, in the early phases of an epidemic, core tasks are to map the extent, severity, and rate of spread of the disease; middle phases involve resource allocation, researching treatments and implementing monitoring systems; in later phases, core tasks are associated with monitoring the effectiveness of treatments, and creating a plan for release of citizens from lockdown. Whilst the Covid-19 epidemic is easily labelled as 'a problem', it must be addressed as a large collection of interlinked problems, for example: reducing the infection rate; managing hospital resources; protecting supply chains for food and other essentials; and developing then distributing vaccines. Each of these problems has its own system dynamics, and a specific problem definition.

Modelling is the act of expressing a theory in a concrete form. The essence of modelling is to find some (usually mathematical) formalism that represents an important aspect of a situation, and tuning the formalism to fit with existing evidence. Next to work with that formalism to derive some conclusions, and then to act on the world by applying these conclusions. Familiar situations in statistics education include analysing games of chance, and fitting observed data to distributions. Sometimes, questions are posed in class as 'modelling' which are simply exercises in arithmetic, with a minor twist. For example:

101 people work on the 20th floor of an office block. The elevator can hold ten people. How many elevator trips are needed each morning?

If a student's answer is *11 trips* then they have made some implausible assumptions: only people on the 20th floor use this elevator; people arrive at work in groups of (at least) 10; no-one is a wheel-chair user; no-one used the stairs; and so on. Modelling in Civic Statistics requires criticality and a tolerance for ambiguity.

We all carry around models about the world that guide our actions—how a computer works, how to navigate the world, behave towards other people (especially those superficially different to us), manage our finances, and about our rights and responsibilities. These models are usually implicit. Box and Draper (1987) argued "all models are wrong, but some are useful"; we might add "and some are dangerous". An example is a politician who believes that Covid-19 is not a fatal disease, is likely to be unsympathetic to calls for compulsory mask-wearing.

Modelling Disease Spread
How might the spread of Covid-19 be understood? First, a reminder about the (current theories about) nature of viral infections such as colds, influenza, Severe Acute Respiratory Syndrome (SARS), Middle East Respiratory Syndrome (MERS), and Human Immunodeficiency Virus (HIV). A virus is a microscopic organism that needs a host in order to survive and reproduce. Different viruses can survive outside a host (e.g. on a door handle) for different amounts of time. Different methods of transmission are possible—droplet infection is common (i.e. being carried on tiny particles of water—for example face touching after contact with a door handle, or aerosol transmission (tiny water particles that hang in still air—for example in offices). Some viruses mutate rapidly (such as flu) others do not (such as polio). Some viruses have been eradicated largely via vaccination (such as smallpox); some have been contained by isolating infected people (such as SARS and MERS). The 1918 flu pandemic is thought to have killed 20–50 million people—with a high death rate in people aged 15–34 years. Factors contributing to the 'success' of the virus include: little or no immunity in the population; absence of vaccines; and the absence of antibiotics to treat associated infections such as pneumonia (penicillin was not discovered until 1928). In the case of the 1918 flu pandemic, the Western world was at war, and so there was extensive movement of people (mobilisation of troops), and large numbers of people living in very crowded conditions; health services were limited; there were no diagnostic tests (and a common belief that the disease was actually a bacterial infection); absence of intensive care wards, and no respirators; and no coordinated pandemic plans (but some cities closed schools and banned public meetings).

The SEIR model is commonly used to model epidemics. The acronym (sometimes just SIR) unpacks as Susceptible, Exposed, Infected and Removed. Everyone in the population is in one of four 'states', and there are rules for the movement between states. *Susceptible* means that a person can contract the disease. So a newborn is 'susceptible' to measles; it is very rare for someone who has had measles to get it again—so they are not *susceptible*. In the case of Covid-19, it is assumed that, initially, the entire population is *susceptible*; but it may be the case that some individuals will not contract the disease, no matter how much they are exposed to it. *Exposed* means just that—a person comes into contact with the virus. So what determines your *exposure*? The size of the infected population (i.e. the number of people who could infect you), the number of encounters you have with people, the nature of the encounter (e.g. touching elbows vs shaking hands) and the density of live viruses on surfaces you touch or the air you breathe. Obviously, lockdown, social distancing, and wearing masks influence the probability of infection. *Infected* refers to the number of people with the disease. People are infectious (i.e. can pass the disease onto others) for some of the time they are infected. The length of time a person stays infectious is important. A disease which is infectious in the absence of symptoms (such as Covid-19) is particularly problematic. The longer the infectious period, the more people there will be in the *infected* population, and the higher the rate of infection, other things being equal. *Removed* refers to people who have had the disease, and no longer have it (including those who are dead). For many viruses, *removed* individuals are no longer *susceptible*—medics talk about antibodies that destroy the virus in future encounters. You can catch a cold repeatedly; you can catch flu every year; you are most unlikely to catch chickenpox if you have had it once. What about Covid-19? It is difficult to say—current evidence is that the virus has produced fewer mutations than flu (but the more people with Covid-19, the more likely it is that new variants will arise—so epidemics and Brazil and India pose threats to countries which appear to have Covid-19 under control); we don't yet know the extent to which infection confers immunity.

To work with the SEIR model, we need to know a number of parameters. First, for the simplest model, we need to estimate the rate of contagion R_0—if someone has Covid-19, how many people will they pass it on to? This number will reflect a particular context—R_0 will be different in a densely populated city compared with a sparse rural area. If R_0 is above 1, the number of infected people will increase; if it R_0 is below 1, the number of infected people will decrease.

How lethal is the virus? Suppose someone has the virus, how likely are they to die? (i.e the *infection fatality rate*) This question is difficult to answer because of uncertainties about both the number of people infected, and the number of Covid-19 deaths. Most population estimates for Covid-19 lie between 0.5 and 2.0% (flu is about 0.1%). These numbers are elevated by *comorbidities* such as age, poverty, diabetes, hypertension, obesity, and smoking status.

SEIR is a dynamic model, because parameters change over time. For example, in later stages of a pandemic, a large number of people are *removed*, so the number of *susceptible* people is lower, as is the probability of *exposure*. The *infection rate* will change depending on behaviour changes. The *case fatality rate* is likely to reduce as treatments improve. A visualisation that lets students explore the effects of parameter changes (R_0; proportion requiring hospitalisation; and case fatality rate) has been created by the New York Times[25] (NYT).

An obvious problem arises when people try to apply this model to the population of a country. R_0 will be dramatically different in different places; Covid-19 will spread most rapidly (high R_0) in densely populated cities where large numbers of people use public transport, and socialise in bars and clubs. The case fatality rate is approximately a linear function of age,[26] so Covid-19 is likely to be far more lethal in a care home than in a nursery. This is important for planning action; people in rural areas where there is a low incidence of Covid-19, and little social mixing, may well feel aggrieved about blanket rules to restrict their mobility.

---

[25] https://www.nytimes.com/interactive/2020/03/25/opinion/coronavirus-trump-reopen-america. html

[26] https://panopto.lshtm.ac.uk/Panopto/Pages/Viewer.aspx?id=e9845ac4-d2f3-4698-aa05-ac79011322d8

To help students understand the SEIR model better, they can explore the model via the NYT visualisation, then be set this task.

Write a specification for a disease which is:

- ideal from the human point of view
- disastrous from the human point of view.

You might refer students to the Influenza Risk Assessment Tool[27] created by the US Centers for Disease Control. Paradoxically, diseases with very high *case fatality rates* (such as ebola) seem easier to control than diseases with lower rates—in part because citizens are far more scared of contracting the disease, and are more willing to change their behaviour, so R_0 is reduced dramatically.

In terms of Civic Statistics, understanding (and using) the SEIR model illustrates the need for citizens (and politicians) to understand a much wider range of ideas than those typically encountered in statistics classes—including the whole notion of modelling complex phenomena.

Patterns

In Sect. 12.3.1.1 we pointed to a number of interactive displays that make it easy to explore patterns in Covid-19 incidence over space and time. Here we offer two further examples.

Does Vaccination Reduce Disease Incidence? A Wall Street Journal[28] visualisation shows the incidence of infectious diseases over a 70-year period in a number of States in the USA for measles, hepatitis A, mumps, whooping cough, polio, rubella, and smallpox, along with a line denoting the introduction of vaccination. The graphics for measles, polio, and rubella are consistent with claims that vaccination led to a major reduction in these diseases; the graphics for hepatitis A, whooping cough and smallpox provide less clear evidence about the impact of the virus (but other evidence can be found).

These graphics can be used to explore notions of causation with students—there are different patterns of incidence with different diseases, different patterns across states, and a good deal of variability over time. Students can be asked about the nature of convincing evidence, and the links between convincing evidence and action—what else would need to be taken into account before a decision is made to introduce widespread vaccination for each of these diseases?

How Does Covid-19 Spread? The New York Times has posted a dynamic graphic that maps the spread of Covid-19 cases from February to June 2020 in the USA entitled *How the Virus Won*.[29] It shows how an analysis of the associations between different strains of Covid-19 and travel patterns can help understand the spread of the disease. It also records the decisions made by politicians to contain the disease

---

[27] https://www.cdc.gov/flu/pandemic-resources/national-strategy/risk-assessment.htm

[28] http://graphics.wsj.com/infectious-diseases-and-vaccines/

[29] https://www.nytimes.com/interactive/2020/us/coronavirus-spread.html

(or not). Starting with the first 15 recorded cases, which all had links with China, and the political response—*we could be at just one or two people over the next short period of time* (Donald Trump, in a document that is no longer accessible[30]). As well as illustrating the follies of inaction, the graphic shows that shutdowns in March 2020 stopped exponential growth in many places.

12.3.2.3   Methodology and Enquiry Processes

Measurement Fundamentals
On March 3rd 2020 the WHO estimated the *case fatality rate* (i.e of all the people diagnosed with Covid-19, how many die?) worldwide to be around 3.4%. This number is difficult to determine, because it depends critically on two things that are hard to measure; the number of people who have died as a result of Covid-19, and the number of people who have actually contracted the disease.

Measuring cases can be problematic; the more people you test, the more cases will be found. If subclinical infection is common, and if you only test people with Covid-19-like symptoms, the case fatality rate will be overestimated. It follows that there is a clear case for using careful sampling strategies to estimate the occurrence of the disease in the population, rather than opportunistic sampling.

Measuring deaths is also problematic. In hospital settings, measures of Covid-19 deaths are likely to be reliable, because it is essential to know who has, and who has not, contracted Covid-19. If someone dies at home as a result of the virus, their death might not be recorded as a Covid-19 death, unless they were tested after death. Measures can change (China and France provide examples[31]); for example, from measuring just hospital deaths, to including deaths in care homes and prisons. There are many considerations here, we might ask questions like: How do we classify a patient with a pre-existing heart condition who contacts Covid-19 and then dies of a heart attack? Or a very old person who contracts Covid-19 and dies after they have recovered? Measurement methods will be different in different countries—so comparisons need to be done with care (this challenge reinforces an idea oft-repeated in this book—namely, the importance of paying attention to metadata).

Death rates show seasonal variation, and there are considerable year-on-year differences—one approach to estimating the impact of the Covid-19 epidemic is to calculate excess deaths—that is to say, the number of deaths in excess of the 5 year average for that time of year. This makes comparisons between countries more straightforward. However, this measure is not without its problems; for example, if social distancing leads to fewer deaths in diseases such as flu, then Covid-19 deaths will be underestimated. These issues are explored further by Ridgway (2021).

---

[30] https://www.whitehouse.gov/briefings-statements/remarks-president-trump-vice-president-pence-members-coronavirus-task-force-press-conference/

[31] https://www.worldometers.info/coronavirus/worldwide-graphs/#page-top

Multiple Agents, Multiple Methods, Multiple Enquiry Processes
In Chap. 2, we located Civic Statistics at the intersection of politics and social science, education and pedagogy, and statistics. Covid-19 makes it clear that almost every dimension of human knowledge is needed for co-ordinated action to tackle an epidemic. One can make the same case for other threats to humanity, such as global warming, and for large scale initiatives such as the United Nations Sustainable Development Goals. The range of disciplines involved, and the methodologies used, can illustrated by considering the methodology and enquiry processes that were called on to create *How the Virus Won*,[32] described in Sect. 12.3.2.2.

- Recognising and diagnosing symptoms
- Mapping the location of individuals; discovering their travel history
- Modelling undetected infections (because there had to be a lot more than the 15 known cases to explain the spread of the disease)
- Using airline data to model the number and location of infected travellers from abroad
- Clinical testing; evaluating the quality of the tests (not good enough)
- Political analysis, ethics; disrupting the economy vs saving lives
- Using cellphone data to map travel patterns and travel volumes, and to estimate the number of contagious travellers
- Using genetic analysis to track the transmission of different strains of Covid-19
- Evaluating the effectiveness of a travel ban to Europe, when the epidemic was already spreading fast in the USA
- Evidence that single travellers could cause infections across entire cities
- Politics of States restricting citizens' movements
- Using cellphone data to show that, initially, mobility patterns were essentially unchanged, but that there was less travel after a presidential announcement
- Using Covid-19 test data to show the slowdown in the exponential growth of the disease
- Comparing the impact of restrictions in different part of the country (e.g. school closures; stay-at-home orders) on disease spread
- Estimating avoidable deaths if actions had been taken earlier
- Estimating the capacity to Track and Trace, using data on testing capacity

Learning from Other Countries All of these methods were used to explore the spread of Covid-19 in a single country. We can cast the net wider, and enquire about other sources of information—notably by looking at practices and methods used in different countries.

In Europe, there were dramatic warning signs from Italy about the severity of the threat—high death rates, and rapid transmission. Some European countries used this evidence as a basis for rapid action; others did not (for example Spain exempted EU citizens from travel bans). Hong Kong, Singapore and New Zealand introduced tight

---

[32] https://www.nytimes.com/interactive/2020/us/coronavirus-spread.html

border controls; Asian countries have had experience in dealing with epidemics such as SARS and MERS, and citizens are willing to accept restrictions on their actions.

If one is to learn lessons from another country, one needs to be confident that there are essential similarities with that country. For example, suppose developing herd immunity by allowing citizens to infect each other (at a rate that is manageable by the health system) proves effective in Sweden. When the next epidemic arrives, should your country adopt this approach? (Sweden has a low population density, and a young demographic).

12.3.2.4   Extensions Into Official Statistics

Official statistics agencies worldwide, and international organisations such as the United Nations (see the UN Statistics Division[33]) and the World Health Organisation[34] (WHO) have played a vital role in understanding and combating Covid-19. WHO have assembled data and advice based on excellent practice. They (unsurprisingly) offer guidance for the public, country and technical guidance, travel advice, and the latest findings (such as: Covid-19 does not transmit through water when swimming (or via house flies or mosquito bites); most people who get Covid-19 recover; etc.) as well as mythbusting (drinking bleach is not a good idea; G5 masts are not to blame for Covid-19 etc.). Websites such as Worldometer[35] compile and consolidate data from statistics agencies. Media outlets such as the Financial Times, the New York Times and the Washington Post often base articles and resources (such as their own interactive displays) on these data.

12.3.2.5   Contextual Civic Knowledge

Track and Trace provides a vivid example of the need for contextual civic knowledge. In the UK, the National Health Service had, at one time, a system of Track and Trace that had proved to be effective in combating HIV/AIDS, tuberculosis, and other socially transmitted diseases. This was operated at a local level. Health professionals working in the community were aware of high-risk individuals and areas, visited them in their homes, had medical knowledge and appropriate skills communicating about sensitive matters (e.g. HIV infections) and in changing behaviour. As a result of financial cuts, this system was massively curtailed. In response to the Covid-19 epidemic, the UK government paid billions of pounds to companies with no track record in medical matters to set up a national system for Track and Trace

---

[33] https://unstats.un.org/home/

[34] https://www.who.int/

[35] https://www.worldometers.info/about/

(in context, the total NHS budget was £160 billion).[36] This system was centralised, operated by people with little or no medical knowledge, and was based on telephone contact. According to the British Medical Association,[37] the system has identified only a small proportion of infected people, and there have been long delays in contacting people who had been exposed to infected people. A simple exercise for students is to ask them to critique this approach from the perspective of *methodology and enquiry processes.* There are vivid issues around sampling and access to be explored here.

Some countries implemented far more effective Track and Trace systems, with extensive local autonomy, notably Germany. However, as the number of infections rises, all such systems can be overwhelmed. The WHO noted that the rate of infection reported in Germany by 23 June 2020 (230 cases per 100,000 population) was about half the rate reported in the UK (451 per 100,000), and the reported mortality from Covid-19 was a sixth of that in the UK. Care needs to be taken when comparing country data (see Sect. 12.3.2.3), but these differences are stark.

For a more abstract example of the need for contextual civic knowledge, we can explore differences between sub-populations in their perceptions of the appropriate balance between citizen rights and citizen responsibilities. These assumptions underpin laws and behaviours. Political action needs to take account of both the evidence showing that action is required, and the willingness of citizens to conform to the recommended actions. Here are some aphorisms, some of which are contradictory, and some which can be endorsed together:

1. Government has a responsibility for the well-being of all its citizens
2. Government has the right (and responsibility) to restrict the actions of citizens, in pursuit of the public good
3. Individuals have a responsibility for their own well being
4. Individuals have a responsibility for the well-being of those around them
5. Individuals have liberties that should not be curtailed by any agency (including government)

These aphorisms are not mutually exclusive; each will be endorsed to a different extent by different individuals. There are some potential conflicts; aphorism 1 can be in conflict with aphorism 5; some would argue that aphorism 4 does not apply to them; on 3—some individuals (the elderly and the very young) are not able to take responsibility for their own well-being; and so on. There are marked cultural differences; Sarah Zheng,[38] writing in the South China Morning Post claimed: *In East Asia, wearing face masks is often seen as a collective responsibility to reduce disease transmission and can symbolise solidarity*: the New York Times ran a

---

[36] https://www.theguardian.com/politics/2022/sep/07/government-admits-50-firms-were-in-vip-lane-for-test-and-trace-contracts

[37] https://www.bma.org.uk/news-and-opinion/a-hidden-threat-test-and-trace-failure-edges-closer

[38] https://today.line.me/hk/v2/article/Face+masks+and+coronavirus+how+culture+affects+your+decision+to+wear+one-57qjvV

headline: *Fighting Over Masks in Public* [i.e wearing or not wearing them] *Is the New American Pastime.*[39]

12.3.3 Engagement and Action

It is self-evident that all the component skills of Engagement and Action (Meaning for Social Policy, Critical Evaluation and Reflection, and Dispositions) are essential for understanding and action at personal, local and national levels in the case of Covid-19. Here we simply sketch the argument.

12.3.3.1 Meaning for Society and Policy

An epidemic provides a vivid example of the need to use evidence to inform policy. However, this is rarely a straightforward process. A dramatic increase in cases of a disease calls for some sort of action, but different agencies will have different ideas about the best course of action to take. In the case of Covid-19, as we noted in the Introduction, initial actions across the world have included: lockdown, and border controls (e.g. New Zealand); extensive track and trace (e.g. Germany); allowing the disease to spread in order to develop herd immunity (Sweden); and rejecting the evidence and taking no action to address the pandemic (USA). Different courses of action are driven by two major interacting forces: most obviously, by theories about the nature of the disease itself and diseases like it, including mechanisms of transmission, likely severity and so on; and less obviously by beliefs about the relative roles of government and individuals in maintaining individual health, and about the value of human life relative to the economic well-being of a country. A mantra in wide circulation is 'evidence-based policy'—this should be resisted. Evidence is never neutral. Decisions are made about what to measure, and how things can be operationalised. These decisions are based on some theory about the phenomenon, how to define crucial ideas, and to analyse them. Data do not speak for themselves. We speak for them, and confer meaning based on our knowledge, beliefs and value systems.

Consider a simple example where the same evidence can lead to different actions, depending on one's view of fairness and efficiency.

A vaccine will save lives, and is to be given to the population as quickly as possible. However, the question arises: who should be vaccinated first? The decision could be based on a number of different principles, such as:

- Maximise the resilience of the system (so inoculate medical professionals and people essential to the functioning of the economy (such as bus drivers) first

---

[39] https://www.nytimes.com/2020/06/30/style/mask-america-freedom-coronavirus.html

- Protect the most vulnerable people first (so inoculate people with compromised health (e.g. diabetics and older people) first). But what about other people who may be at risk, such as the clinically obese?
- Reduce the disease as quickly as possible (so inoculate people in areas with the highest incidence of the disease, first)

From the viewpoint of teaching, students can be asked what actions would be taken, based on each of these principles. They can then be asked to compare the likely different impact on different groups of citizens.

12.3.3.2   Critical Evaluation and Reflection

Our beliefs are important in shaping behaviour; these beliefs are guided by the information we receive—and there are a large number of sources of information, misinformation, and disinformation. An important goal of education is to develop criticality—the ability to evaluate the plausibility of information, to analyse arguments, and to judge the extent to which evidence supports an argument, to triangulate evidence, and to think of different explanations. Criticality does not depend on deep knowledge of a domain—teachers can use 'worry questions' (see Gal in Chap. 13) to ask about the provenance and quality of the evidence being used, and about the conclusions being drawn. In the situations created by Covid-19, critical evaluation and reflection is a matter of life and death (and not simply the life or death of the individual making the decision). Politifact[40] chose the downplaying and disinformation surrounding Covid-19 as their Lie of the Year, 2020.They do not attribute the lie to an individual, but rather to a large cast of actors, and offer illuminating (and disturbing) commentary.

12.3.3.3   Dispositions

On their own, skills in critical evaluation and reflection are useless. For them to be effective, there has to be a willingness to engage actively in the process of understanding phenomena, and learning what is likely to be effective. Evidence-informed action should follow. One aspect of populism in politics is the emphasis on opinion and tribal affiliation at the expense of considered analysis of evidence. Ridgway and Ridgway explore these ideas further in Chap. 23.

---

[40]https://www.politifact.com/article/2020/dec/16/lie-year-coronavirus-downplay-and-denial/

12.4   Conclusions

Covid-19 provides a dramatic example of the need for Civic Statistics skills at all levels, from the individual through communities to policy makers. Death and disease can be difficult topics to manage in class. However, epidemics will continue to occur; and epidemics are not the only source of existential threat to societies. Covid-19 offers many opportunities for teaching using realistic contexts, authentic data, and real problems. Teachers who feel that Covid-19 is a topic that would cause distress to their students are encouraged to explore the ideas here, but in the context of earlier epidemics (Spanish flu, MERS, SARS, ebola) for which data are available.

Education should be more than inculcating and certifying knowledge; our primary goal is to create empowered citizens who can call out the rank stupidity of political leaders when they see it. The Covid-19 epidemic provides a deep pool for reflecting on curriculums in schools and colleges.

References

Box, G. E., & Draper, N. R. (1987). *Empirical model-building and response surfaces.* Wiley.

Brilliant, L. (2020). *Outbreaks are inevitable, but pandemics are optional.* https://www.youtube.com/watch?v=nVWoHmURDTQ

Gigerenzer, G., Gaissmaier, W., Kurz-Milcke, E., Schwartz, L. M., & Woloshin, S. (2007). Helping doctors and patients make sense of health statistics. *Psychological Science in the Public Interest, Supplement, 8*(2), 53–96. https://doi.org/10.1111/j.1539-6053.2008.00033.x

Our world in data coronavirus pandemic (COVID_19). https://ourworldindata.org/coronavirus.

Ridgway, J. (2021). Covid and data science: Understanding R0 could change your life. *Teaching Statistics, 43*(1), 84–92.

Swan, M., & Ridgway, J. (2001). *Classroom assessment techniques: 'Plausible estimation' tasks.* Accessed July 20, 2020, from http://archive.wceruw.org/cl1/flag/cat/math/estimation/estimation1.htm

Tversky, A., & Kahneman, D. (1974). Judgment under uncertainty: Heuristics and biases. *Science, 185*(4157), 1124–1131.

Part III

Edited by Iddo Gal and Daniel Frischemeier

Chapter 13
Critical Understanding of Civic Statistics: Engaging with Important Contexts, Texts, and Opinion Questions

Iddo Gal ⓘ

Abstract This chapter aims to support teachers and lecturers interested in developing students' statistical literacy in general and critical understanding of Civic Statistics in particular. The chapter provides practical advice regarding task design and development of activities that encourage critical analysis of statistical texts (such as in the news media or publications of official statistics agencies). Key topics include: analysis of the nature of 'context knowledge' and what are 'meaningful and important' contexts that are worthy of attention when teaching for understanding of Civic Statistics; ways to bring 'meaningful and important' contexts and texts about them (e.g., from newspapers or digital media) into the classroom and to make sure students understand them; ideas about question-posing and designing suitable tasks about these meaningful and important contexts, in particular how to shape 'opinion questions' that can elicit students' critical reading, reflective thinking, and communication of thoughtful opinions; and ideas about the dispositions and habits of mind (e.g., critical stance, ability to ask 'worry questions') and skills (e.g., reading comprehension, critical interpretation) we want students to internalized and be able to activate when engaging statistical messages. Based on the guidelines and examples regarding these topics, the chapter discusses implications and recommendations for curriculum design and for teaching and teachers working both at the high-school, college, and adult education contexts, in mathematics education, statistics and data science education, and related STEM disciplines.

Keywords Statistical literacy · Contextualization · Critical numeracy · Data literacy · Task design · Official statistics

I. Gal (✉)
Department of Human Services, University of Haifa, Haifa, Israel
e-mail: iddo@research.haifa.ac.il

© The Author(s) 2022
J. Ridgway (ed.), *Statistics for Empowerment and Social Engagement*,
https://doi.org/10.1007/978-3-031-20748-8_13

13.1 Introduction

This chapter aims to help educators who want to develop their students' knowledge and critical understanding of *Civic Statistics* in diverse teaching contexts, e.g., a high-school class, a college-level course, or an adult education program. As Chap. 2 of this book argues, learners need to develop their ability to engage with Civic Statistics that are generated or collected in real world contexts, and that pertain to 'burning topics' (i.e., the areas of Civic Statistics) which matter to modern societies because they affect social or economic well-being (Engel et al. 2016). Developing the ability to engage with and critically understand Civic Statistics requires attention to numerous facets and tools, and to knowledge bases and dispositions, which were discussed in Chap. 3, in connection with a conceptual framework developed by the ProCivicStat project (Nicholson et al. 2017). The richness of the demands on adults in terms of critical understanding of statistical and mathematical products in media items was recently documented by Gal & Geiger (2022), who analysed a large purposive sample of 300 diverse media items related to the COVID-19 (Coronavirus) pandemic, selected from digital news sources based in four countries. Gal & Geiger's (2022) results provide empirical support for the conceptual framework proposed by ProCivicStat Partners (2018) regarding the capabilities needed for engaging with Civic Statistics topics.

Based on the foundations in Part I of this book, the present chapter focuses on educational issues associated with two fundamental knowledge bases described in Chap. 3: 'Contextual Civic Knowledge' and 'Critical Evaluation and Reflection'. Contextual knowledge is fundamental for the development of understanding of Civic Statistics, since learners (and citizens) need to be able to read and reflect about statistics 'in context', i.e., understand the social or economic importance of any statistics they engage with, and its implications for society. 'Critical evaluation and reflection' is fundamental because it involves ways of thinking about, interrogating, being skeptic, or asking 'worry questions' about statistical findings and statistics-based or quantitative claims which are common in public life (Gal, 2002; West & Bergstrom, 2020). Both of these knowledge bases can challenge many teachers because they are not normally included, or only superficially addressed, in standard instruction and in textbooks related to statistics which are used in mathematics, science, or statistics education.

As a brief scholarly background, we note that attention to context knowledge and to critical evaluation has been a part of past discussions regarding statistical and mathematical literacy (e.g., Budgett & Rose, 2017; Haack, 1979; Watson, 2013), as well as (adult) numeracy (Gal et al., 2020) and data and media literacy. One often-quoted definition (Gal, 2002) views statistical literacy as referring broadly to two interrelated components:

> ...People's ability to *interpret and critically evaluate* statistical information, data-related arguments, or stochastic phenomena, which they may encounter in diverse contexts, and when relevant their ability to *discuss or communicate* their reactions to such statistical information, such as their understanding of the meaning of the information, their opinions

Table 13.1 Three key questions about context knowledge and critical evaluation

Questions/topics	Brief rationale
1. What are 'meaningful and important' contexts, and why do they matter for Civic Statistics?	Such contexts are mentioned in Chaps. 2 and 3 and are discussed in detail here, because they underlie the generation of Civic Statistics and their interpretation
2. How do we bring 'meaningful and important' contexts into the classroom? (The answer: use meaningful texts!)	Texts are at focus for two reasons: They are the key source through which learners can be introduced to information about key social and economic issues or dilemmas central to Civic Statistics, and because texts are the prime medium for communicating statistical findings and messages (i.e., telling data stories) to citizens and decision makers
3. What critical or reflective questions about meaningful and important contexts in Civic Statistics are worth posing in class?	Educators need to know how to design sequences of questions that take students from literal reading of simple texts to the expression of opinions with reasoned justifications about complex texts. Teachers need a repertoire of critical questions about Civic Statistics that students can then internalise - and hopefully apply in their future life as empowered adults and citizens

about the implications of this information, or their concerns regarding the acceptability of given conclusions. [page 2]

Defined in this way, statistical literacy is not a watered-down version or simple subset of formal statistics, but a stand-alone complex competency which is related to adult numeracy (Gal, 1997; Gal et al., 2020) and mathematical literacy (Kilpatrick, 2001), but goes beyond them, since statistics and risk include many unique issues (see Chap. 3). Notions of contextualization and of critical questioning are subsumed in these and other sources referenced in all chapters in Part I of this book, hence will not be repeated here.

With the above in mind, the remainder of this chapter focuses on three broad questions listed in Table 13.1 together with their underlying rationale. Please study Table 13.1 as it motivates this entire chapter, which aims to provide both a scholarly background and practical advice for educators who seek ideas on how to develop and implement in their classrooms critical understanding of context-rich statistics and data-based stories about issues of importance to society.

Accordingly, the chapter is organized in nine sections. Following this introduction, Sect. 13.2 elaborates on the key notion of 'context knowledge' and Sect. 13.3 on the first issue listed in Table 13.1, i.e., the nature of meaningful and important contexts. Section 13.4 considers the second issue listed in Table 13.1, i.e., ways to bring such contexts into the classroom. Sections 13.5–13.7 discuss the third issue of question posing, and provide guidelines and illustrations for creating 'opinion questions' that can elicit students' reflection and expression of opinions when teaching about Civic Statistics. Section 13.8 examines additional critical questions which students should internalise and skills that they should activate when engaging with Civic Statistics and statistics-based messages. Finally, Sect. 13.9 summarizes key messages and poses some questions to support reflections about pedagogy related to Civic Statistics.

13.2   The Centrality of 'Context' for Statistical Literacy and for Understanding Civic Statistics in Particular

'Context' seems to be a simple idea. After all, we all live our lives in context, not in a vacuum. And as educators, we hope that what we have taught our learners will help them to function effectively as engaged and empowered adults and citizens in multiple life contexts. However, within the classroom or lecture hall, 'context' is far from being a simple notion. This is because 'context' is not automatically present in the classroom—we need to bring it in. But on this, there is a difference between mathematics education (which is where much of statistics education happens in schools) and statistics education (which covers the school level as well as tertiary levels and many other teaching contexts, but at the tertiary level occurs mainly on its own, not under mathematics education).

In mathematics education (at the k-12 and adult levels) there are many discussions about contexts, authenticity, or realism of tasks and problems, and debates about the extent to which mathematics educators should worry about or relate to contexts as part of either teaching/learning or assessment processes. A succinct review of various views on contexts and contextualization can be found in Greatorex (2014). For example, as du Feu (2001) argues, there are five types of contexts (or lack thereof) for tasks and activities used in the mathematics classroom: *context-free, real, cleaned, parable* (fictitious but possibly real), and *contrived* (invented to drive a mathematical problem, but usually not realistic). It follows that when learning mathematics, a real context is not always seen as needed, and sometimes is even perceived as a distraction that hurts the learning of abstract ideas in mathematics.

In contrast, when teaching statistics, *context is supposed to be a foundation of all activities*. After all, the history of statistics shows that the discipline was invented in large part to serve practical needs of states and to enable administrators to understand the demographics and living conditions of their citizens and economies. Cobb and Moore (1997) have argued that statistics are 'numbers in context', and that hence, in statistics, context is the source of meaning and basis for application of statistical procedures and for the interpretation of obtained results.

Let us now reconnect with the statistical literacy point of view, which emphasizes the importance of developing citizenship-related competencies. From this perspective, it can be argued that our overarching goal in teaching statistics is that when students graduate, they are both able *and* willing to engage effectively and make sense of the statistics and statistical messages that flow to them as citizens or smart consumers of statistical messages. If so, it is critical to ask—how are the *context*s in which real-world 'Civic Statistics'—those related to social, economic, or environmental life topics—chosen by teachers and brought into the statistics classroom?

Questioning the place of 'context' in statistics education is where I believe we face a problem, or misunderstanding. There are many calls to improve conceptual understanding of 'big ideas' in statistics and to put less emphasis on procedural knowledge (Chance & Rossman, 2001; Cobb, 2007; Malone et al., 2012; Ograjenšek & Gal, 2016). The *Guidelines for Assessment and Instruction in Statistics Education* (GAISE, 2016) emphasize in particular the importance of using 'real data' in the classroom, and there are claims that this can lead to the development of statistical literacy (Schield, 2016). However, there is a big difference between using 'real' *data* and linking instruction to *meaningful and important contexts*. What matters is *not* the data per se, but the *answers and insights* we seek in the data (see also Watson, 2000).

It follows that the context (and the 'need to know' of different stakeholders) should be *the* motivator for teaching anything about statistics. After all, regular data are collected *because* somebody out there in the real world has specific information needs and specific questions for which they seek answers. Context is central to Civic Statistics—as it directly connects with *'meaning for society and policy'*, i.e., the most important facet (facet 1) in the conceptual model (see Chap. 3, Fig. 3.1).

13.3 About Meaningful and Important Contexts

Section 13.2 argued that 'context' is a fundamental aspect of Civic Statistics. A question then emerges: What are *'meaningful and important'* contexts, worthy of attention when teaching for statistical literacy in general and understanding of Civic Statistics in particular? This chapter proposes two conditions in this regard. First, *the context should be authentic*, i.e. naturally occurring in the outside world, not contrived or fictitious. Thus, if teachers conduct a local survey (or create fictitious data) simply so students have data to work on—e.g., by eliciting students' political opinions, body measurements, career plans, etc.—the data would be 'real', i.e., pertain to a phenomenon in the world which can be described statistically, but this does not serve as an authentic meaningful and authentic *Civic* context, as explained below.

The second condition is that *the context should invoke a genuine 'need to know'*, *i.e., be of interest to an outside actor or stakeholder who operates in the public sphere (broadly viewed)*. Key examples of such actors are: politicians; policy-makers and managers in a government ministry (department), a public agency or a business organization; leaders or activists in a community-based or non-profit organization; or concerned and empowered citizens who want to monitor processes in their country or region, and perhaps consider some action. The notion of 'Need to know' has been promoted by Ograjenšek and Gal (2016), who argue that a critical challenge in statistics education involves issues of students' acceptance of *purpose* and of motivation for the whole activity of generating and interpreting a statistical message or data.

As explained earlier and in Chap. 2, Civic Statistics may involve contexts related to diverse topics such as health, demographics, employment, wages, migration, crime, poverty, access to services, education, human rights, public expenditures, pollution and 'green' topics. Such topics are seen as 'burning issues' because they affect social and economic progress, and impact upon the well-being of citizens and communities. A potent example is the context of the recent COVID-19 (Coronavirus) pandemic, which combined many of the separate topics listed above.

In combination, the two conditions described in this section aim to maximize students' sense of relevance of the context to their current or future lives as adults, and improve the motivation and interest both of teachers and students. Hence, Civic Statistics contexts should be chosen which are meaningful and important in the sense that they are at the focus of public and political dialogue, of much interest to policy setting and to decision-makers at the national, regional, and local or community levels, and often discussed in the media.

13.4 How Do We Bring Meaningful Contexts and Statistics About Them into the Classroom?

As explained above, there are many meaningful and important contexts. Hence, teachers have much freedom to choose resources and topics in order to fit their and their students' interests and capabilities. *Please stop now and reflect on Thinking exercise #1:*

> **Thinking Exercise/Activity #1: What 'Teaching Resources' Are Suitable for Teaching About Civic Statistics?**
> In particular, focus your thinking on what *information sources* or materials can drive (or motivate) students' thinking and conversations around the 'need to know' of actors in real-world contexts.

Good datasets are essential for learning many statistical ideas. Yet, citizens, or social actors or decision makers, seldom see a raw dataset or need to analyze it by themselves (even though this is often possible, in the era of open data). Usually, citizens and decision makers alike are mostly *consumers* of statistical messages. The raw data, often, have already been analyzed by official statistics producers or by the media. It follows that using datasets, and asking students to analyze raw data may *not* be the preferred way to introduce and develop understanding of Civic Statistics. Students should not spend too much time on the mechanics of number-crunching. Instead, our goal is to develop students' understanding of the meaning of statistics that are reported to the public, and their ability to critically analyze as well as communicate about socially meaningful questions, relying on data-based arguments.

The goal described requires that we consider two questions:

1. *How are statistics reported to the general public?* Our answer: *mainly via text-based messages*, either written or spoken.
2. *Where can you find such text-based messages?* Our answer: There are multiple places or channels where statistical texts (written or spoken) are communicated to the public, such as:

   (a) Articles in the print and digital media
   (b) Press releases, reports, and other products of official statistics producers (these can be found on the websites official statistics agencies)
   (c) TV programs and websites of news channels (e.g., news reports, or interviews with experts or public officials). Copies of past programs can often be retrieved from the websites of such organizations, and some of them are uploaded to YouTube and other video websites
   (d) Posts on social media such as Facebook or Twitter (nowadays, most news organizations as well as official statistics agencies have official channels on social networks)
   (e) Blogs (written) and Podcasts (audio recordings) by commentators and social activists who address a range of civic issues

Materials from any of the types of channels listed above can be useful resources that students should learn to comprehend, analyze, and reason about—see subsequent sections for details. *Authentic sources*—whether *written texts* (as in an article or report) or *spoken texts* (as in a TV news broadcast, or an interview with a public figure or expert)—are the foundational elements which need to be brought into the classroom to enable learners to directly engage with real-world messages involving statistics and quantitative ideas about important contexts.

Presenting students with *authentic* texts (printed or spoken) from such resources carries a great advantage for teachers, for two reasons: the text eliminates or reduces the burden of explaining the social or economic context, and hyperlinks (clickable links) inside digital texts can point to original data sources such as reports from statistics producers or public bodies, or to additional data or even datasets and associated metadata (i.e., definitions of variables, data collection or sampling methods, etc.). And, as will be explained later, authentic texts can provide great opportunities for *question-posing* and designing instructional tasks.

It is further important to emphasize that the messages that teachers or students will find in channels such as those listed above (written or spoken) will contain mainly or only *texts*, i.e., most statistical ideas, findings, or projections, will be conveyed via words, or numbers embedded in words, not via graphical elements. Of course, some visual displays (e.g., infographics, tables, graphs, charts or dynamic visualizations) may accompany the text, but such displays are seldom the core of the statistical messages that the public encounters. The context and the societal issues which motivate the data will not be clear to students without *reading* or *listening*. If students need to get further background information about the civic issue involved, again, they will have to access and comprehend more text (e.g., on Wikipedia). Thus, *text comprehension* and *critical reading skills* are essential for understanding Civic Statistics.

13.5   Worthy Tasks and 'Opinion Questions' for Developing Critical Understanding of Civic Statistics

This section, and subsequent ones, build on the ideas in Sects. 13.2–13.4, and discuss principles that can guide the design of learning tasks related to contexts and critical understanding of Civic Statistics, offering some examples. To start, assume that you found useful textual sources regarding meaningful and important contexts which discuss Civic Statistics about topics that you or your students may care about. Now you face two different issues:

- What questions should *you* ask your students, or what tasks would *you* assign to your students, about the resource/article you found, in order to develop (or assess) their statistical literacy and understanding of Civic Statistics?
- What questions would you like *your students* to pose to the author/source of the article, or about articles or graphical displays they encounter in real-life? And what mindset or attitudes would you like *your students* to develop and take away from the instructional activities you designed for them?

This section seemingly focuses only on the first challenge listed above, which involves teaching-related issues, as this is the teacher's playing field. But, in fact, we aim to address the second challenge, because this is the goal of your educational work. This section thus focuses on *question-posing* and *task design*, which are a part of the art of teaching. The terms 'question' or 'task' should be taken broadly, to encompass the diverse queries, problems, projects and assignments given to students, whether in class or as homework.

Ainley et al. (2015) have argued for the use of tasks that have two characteristics, i.e., questions that have a clear *purpose* and that present an *engaging challenge* for the learners, whether or not they refer to a real-world application. More recently, Arnold and Franklin (2021) have expanded to four types of questions associated with the 'statistical problem-solving cycle' and differentiate between Interrogative questions, Investigative questions, Survey or data collection questions, and Analysis questions. However, this may be necessary but certainly is *not* sufficient, when dealing with Civic Statistics. After all, the statistical problem-solving cycle is usually not evident or fully relevant when dealing with Civic Statistics. This is in part because many Civic Statistics are collected on an ongoing basis or as part of a prolonged public process (i.e., for monitoring changes in key indicators related to social and economic phenomena as explained in Chaps. 2 and 3), not as part of a shorter (or one-shot) efforts, as are many regular surveys or empirical studies of a more modest scale which tend to be emphasized in introductory statistics classes.

Table 13.2 Five heuristics for designing opinion questions about Civic Statistics

Heuristic: Does the question or task ...
1. ... have an authentic context
2. ... reflect a possible genuine 'need to know' of a stakeholder in the given civic context, or be of some service to such an actor
3. ... *not* provide specific hints as to where in the text, table or graph to look, or what data or statistics to consider or use
4. ... call for a *judgment* or *opinion* (not a computed response) that connects with the given civic context
5. ... make it clear to students that they will have to *explain* and *justify* any opinion they present, and be alert to the need to reflect on all the information presented, before responding

Going beyond the Ainley et al. (2015) and Arnold and Franklin (2021) ideas, Table 13.2 presents a broader set of expectations or heuristics for designing a broader type of *opinion questions*, which are tasks that can encourage students' *reflection* and expression of *(possibly critical) opinions* regarding Civic Statistics and their *societal or organizational implications*. (These heuristics are elaborated in Sect. 13.6 below):

Before explaining the five heuristics in Table 13.2, let us first discuss the notion of 'opinions'. A key idea presented in this chapter, and earlier in Part I of this book, is that students should engage directly with the societal meaning or implications of the statistics and data they encounter. This implies that students have to be exposed to the interchanges and paths between *facts* about Civic Statistics (i.e., statistics or findings or data-based arguments or texts with statistical messages) and *opinions, deductions, and recommendations for action* about Civic Statistics (either ones that they will generate, or that actors in the public sphere communicate via various channels or texts).

Dealing with students' *opinions* may seem a novel idea because opinions are not usually part of instruction about mathematical subjects—though they are part of many other educational subjects! After all, opinions encountered in the real world may or may not be fully based on facts, and may be influenced by value judgments and subjective views. Further, opinions on complex subjects such as civic topics probably cannot be always classified as 'right' or 'wrong', and may have various degrees of reasonableness and logical consistency.

In Civic Statistics, dealing with opinions in addition to facts is essential and inevitable. Fred Mosteller, a renowned statistician, said, "Policy implies politics, and politics implies controversy, and the same data that some people use to support a policy are used by others to oppose it" (cited in Moore, 1998, p. 1255). If we want to prepare our students to engage as citizens with burning civic topics, they should be comfortable to generate fact-based opinions but also be able to think critically and consider the evidential basis for their own and others' opinions. This is especially important if a secondary goal is to understand the use (and misuse) of statistics in the civic sphere in the twenty-first century, where invented 'evidence' and biased use of data are common.

With the above in mind, Sect. 13.6 below discusses heuristics for the design of questions and tasks that can generate *opinions* about Civic Statistics topics. It is followed by an annotated example (Sect. 13.7), and a discussion of more types of critical 'worry questions' about statistical messages in general (Sect. 13.8).

13.6 More About Heuristics for Designing Opinion Questions

Table 13.2 presented five general heuristics for the design of tasks that can elicit open-ended opinions related to civic contexts. A brief format was used, so it is easy to employ the five heuristics as a check-list to evaluate the appropriateness of tasks and questions being considered for use in class. These heuristics are based in part on Gal (1998) and earlier sources, and the first two also based on Ograjenšek and Gal (2016).

1. Questions posed to students who learn Civic Statistics should emerge from or relate to *authentic contexts*, i.e., should not be 'contrived' or 'fictitious' or 'cleaned'.
2. The context and the questions about it should connect with or reflect a genuine '*need to know*'. That is, students should be presented with questions or tasks which seek an answer that *can be of some service to a stakeholder in the given civic context,* i.e., a policy-maker, public official, manager, activist, or any other actor operating within or interested in the given context.
3. A question or task should not provide specific hints as to where in the text, table or graph the student should look, or what data or statistics to consider or use. The idea is that the student will have to decide what parts of the text and inherent displays to examine, and how different aspects of the text, or data points in a graph or display, relate to each other.
4. A question or task should be phrased so (a) students realize that a *judgment* or *opinion* is called for, rather than a precise 'mathematical' or computed response in the form of a specific number, and (b) that a connection must be made between the opinion and the given authentic civic context.
5. An 'opinion' question or task should be phrased so students realize that they will be asked to *explain* and *justify* any opinion they present, and alert them to the need to examine all the information presented and *reflect* on it before responding, in order to formulate a reasoned opinion.

Rationale The five heuristics can be explained in several ways:

- We want students to think about the meaning and interpretation of any statistics within the social context; use their reasoning to examine the logic and support from data for any arguments presented in the text; reflect on causal factors, correlates or covariants or confounders, and alternative interpretations for the findings or data being discussed; and consider to what extent the implications or consequences of the findings being discussed appear sensible

- We want students to not immediately look only for formal statistical terms in the text but realize that many statistical ideas may be expressed in words in various ways. For example, the statistical idea of a 'correlation' can be expressed by many words or phrases, such as association, link, relationship, co-occurrence, influence, and many others
- We want students to be sensitive and open to ambiguities, inconsistencies, or improper uses of wording in what the text or statistics portray (e.g., does 'influence' imply that data really shows that there is a causal relationship between the variables? or that the writer/speaker just chose a word without thinking deeply about its statistical implications)

Of course, heuristics are just general guidelines and can be used in a flexible way. That said, opinion questions whose designs are based on these general heuristics can be powerful tools in connecting generic statistical content to civic contexts, as well as helping to develop students' ability to critically interpret Civic Statistics. *The most important heuristics are the first two:* Unless students are presented with a reasonably realistic context and a reasonable 'need to know', they may simply treat the question as a mathematical puzzle, not as an intellectual challenge. For Civic Statistics, we want students to bring into the task the full power of their knowledge about life and society, and their reasoning skills, and to be aware of, and be able to articulate, the assumptions that they have made and rely on as part of their reasoning. *Hence, please stop now and reflect on Thinking exercise #2:*

Thinking Exercise/Activity #2: How Do We Apply the Heuristics Summarized in Table 13.2 for Designing a Task About a Civic Issue?
Please design a task or a set of questions that can generate opinions and reflections about one of the topics described below. Make sure to apply the five heuristics explained above and listed in Table 13.2.

Topic 1—Health inequality: During the COVID-19 (Coronavirus) pandemic, in some countries, people from certain backgrounds or who live in certain communities (e.g., people from certain minority or social backgrounds, or who are in poverty), had quite different (usually higher) rates of infection or mortality and (lower) willingness to vaccinate. This led to articles and TV programs involving discussions and debates (with experts, public officials, politicians, or journalists), regarding the factors that cause such differences in rates, their implications in terms of equality and social justice, and their ramifications for social policy. So an important question is, in simple words: what should a country do about these differences? what investments or changes are needed? *Design an opinion question as explained above,*

(continued)

Thinking Exercise/Activity #2: How Do We Apply the Heuristics Summarized in Table 13.2 for Designing a Task About a Civic Issue? (continued)

> *that pertains to this topic and requires the use of public reports or media articles about this issue.*

Topic 2—Economic and social inequality: Read the Wikipedia article about 'Gender pay gap', which discusses salary (Wage) inequality among men and women, which was introduced as Example 2 in Chap. 3. This page exists in multiple languages. *Design an opinion question as explained above, that pertains to this topic and requires the use of public reports or media articles about this issue.* (Note: many countries publish annual data on this issue, so perhaps you can find local publications on this topic.).

Designing a task or opinion questions about differences between social groups (in this case, in infection or mortality rates, or economic outcomes of labor) is challenging, because of the many possible covariates or intervening variables, such as poverty or economic conditions, social norms, religious practices, age profiles, etc. Further, deeper issues need to be examined, such as whether people from different backgrounds or communities have equal access to healthcare, proper nutrition, living conditions, employment opportunities, and so forth. All this requires that students reflect on many factors and processes in the real world. (More ideas regarding the statistical reporting about the COVID-19 pandemic, and problems with group comparisons, can be found in Ancker, 2020; Ridgway, 2021; and Gal & Geiger, 2022).

However, we need to be careful because a social situation or civic context may not be equally familiar to all students, and they may have different levels of world knowledge or make different assumptions about it. This may cause different students to come up with different opinions based on the same source, and in fact can motivate rich discourse in the classroom. Hence, students' ideas and thinking processes about text interpretation, data analysis and interpretation can be revealed through follow-up questioning (in class), and the design of the task should make sure the students justify their opinions in effective ways. Nonetheless, such questions are both *feasible* (i.e., students can explore them by using published reports and articles, not by analyzing raw data) and *address meaning for society* (e.g., students can connect the statistics with and discuss implications for social policy).

13.7 An Example for a Task Involving Opinion Questions

Question-posing when developing statistical literacy about meaningful and important societal issues raises dilemmas and requires instructional decisions. To illustrate some of them, we now turn to examine in detail a single task, which also helps to highlight the differences between different kinds of questions that can be posed in class, and provides some additional scholarly background. The task described below is based on Gal and Trostianitser (2016), and involves understanding a seemingly simple data table showing *population projections* for two subgroups in a society. (Such a table in fact is seldom encountered by citizens learners 'as is', but is instead embedded in text, as in a newspaper article which discusses new population projections based on a press release of an official statistics agency).

As a brief background, many scholars have examined issues regarding reading and interpreting information in tables and graphs, given their key role in statistics. Curcio's (1987) well known framework has discussed three stages in graph comprehension, i.e., reading the data, reading between the data, and reading beyond the data. Friel et al. (2001) have outlined six related cognitive processes in this regard: reading, describing, interpreting, analysing, predicting and extrapolating data. Building on these and other sources, Kemp and Kisanne (2010) offered a five-step framework to guide class discussions:

1. GETTING STARTED: mediating the task to the learners, providing context.
2. WHAT do the numbers mean?
3. HOW do they change or differ (e.g., across subpopulations, or different years)?
4. WHERE are the differences or relationships?
5. WHY do the numbers change (or differ when comparing different groups or timepoints)?

Gal and Trostianitser (2016) have argued for the need to extend the five-step framework introduced by Kemp and Kisanne (2010; see also Prodromou, 2015) by adding a sixth step with questions about the *actual societal meaning or civic implications of the data*, as illustrated in Fig. 13.1. The rationale for adding such a step, in line with Chaps. 2 and 3 of this book, is that there is a need to enhance the linkage with the civic context, as a way to address questions of purpose and motivation when using data or products of official statistics agencies that involve statistics about society.

Figure 13.1 shows a real task given to my students in a first-year college course 'Introduction to Human Services' in a Department focused on preparing students to manage service operations in organizations in the public and private sectors in Israel, which is a country with much ethnic, religious, and social diversity. A key feature of the task was that it was presented as a *management simulation* related to understanding client diversity. Thus, students were not 'doing statistics' but had to operate in a tangible context in which they can be a real actor, not a passive or disinterested observer who was just given some data.

The data table in Fig. 13.1 is based on *population projections* published by the Israeli Central Bureau of Statistics. (Note: all national statistics agencies publish such projections; It should be easy to replace it with data relevant for your national context). Figure 13.1 shows anticipated changes in the demographic composition of the two largest social groups in Israeli, Jewish and Arab, over two time points. This

Managerial simulation

You are a new, motivated manager at [organization].

You received from your senior management the following table, which is based on new data from the Central Bureau of Statistics.

The table shows projections regarding demographic trends among certain social and age groups.

Your task: Please send your personal evaluation and opinions regarding the following 5 key questions:

Central Bureau of Statistics: Projections 2005 - 2030
Note: Figures are in Thousands

	Arabs		Jews		*2005*
Total (000)	%	Number (000)	%	Number (000)	Age
	59%	800	41%	2,284	0-24
	38%	512	48%	2,659	25-64
	3%	44	11%	629	+65
6,928 =	100%	1,356	100%	5,572	TOTAL

	Arabs		Jews		*2030*
Total (000)	%	Number (000)	%	Number (000)	Age
	47%	1,115	35%	2,737	0-24
	46%	1,082	51%	4,004	25-64
	7%	165	14%	1,129	+65
10,232=	100%	2,362	100%	7,870	TOTAL

Q1. What key trends or differences do you see between the social and age groups, for 2005?

Q2. What key trends or differences do you see between the social and age groups, for 2030?

Q3. What key trends or changes do you see between 2005 and 2030?

Q4. What reasons or factors may explain the projected changes between 2005 and 2030, regarding these social and age groups? list key ones.

Q5. Given these trends or changes, what are the implications or impact for long-range planning, and for needed managerial decisions in [organization]? Why?

Fig. 13.1 Sample task: table reading with opinion questions

table is couched in a rich social reality known to all students who undertook this task (40% of whom were from the Arab sector in Israel).

The data table in Fig. 13.1 is comprised only of counts (in thousands) and percentages, which are typical in demographic tables, and are the simplest possible statistics. Thus, the table should be accessible to all students from the middle school level to the college level, even without learning any statistics. However, although the table uses basic figures or what may be seen as rudimentary statistics, it in fact is not trivial to interpret as it shows rather complex patterns: due to its $2 \times 3 \times 2$ design (i.e., social group, age, year), it portrays a *multivariate civic phenomenon* and shows multiple *changes over time*, using a visualization that is more dense than typical one-way frequency distributions or even two-way cross-tabulations employed in learning introductory statistics. Overall, the data table in Fig. 13.1 offers a rich teaching opportunity, as it illustrates key features of Civic Statistics explained in Chap. 2, and has the potential to serve as a good resource for many observations (by the students) and critical questions (by the teacher and students), and can be the basis for a rich class discussion—depending on whether the teacher can pose suitable opinion questions.

Task Design Notice in Fig. 13.1 both the sequencing and the change in the nature of the questions being asked. Q1 to Q3 cover the first four steps in the Kemp and Kisanne (2010) model described above, and aim to scaffold the thinking process by breaking down for students the table analysis into steps, i.e., first asking about trends or changes in 2005 (top half of the table), then in 2030 (bottom half) and finally across the two timeframes (whole table). This approach to question-posing is used to ensure that students pay attention to the key variables and axes along which the data are organized, and can gradually build a picture of trends and changes within the data, from bivariate to multivariate. This approach is preferred to a generic question such as "what do you notice in the data?", which is sensible, but in a pilot stage proved confusing for many inexperienced students, who 'got lost' in a multi-variate three-way data table.

Where Are the Opinion Questions? Q4 and Q5 illustrate the five heuristics listed earlier and summarized in Table 13.1 for shaping 'opinion questions.' Q4 addresses the same goal as Step 5 proposed by Kemp and Kisanne (WHY do they change?) but uses a structured phrasing tailored to the specific context used here. Q5, however, adds a new layer and requires that students think about the actual societal, manage-rial, or economic *implications* of the data. Together, Q4 and Q5 take students from a mere analysis of how numbers change within the cells of a table, to engagement with a real-world context. Q4 and A5 are essential because they force students to think both about the social implications of the data as well as the underlying factors or causes (e.g., social, economic, or other) that affect the actual behaviors of large parts of the population. Thus, Q4 and Q5 are critical to students' deeper understanding of the projections and their meaning to society and policy.

Class Planning and Task Extension The example in Fig. 13.1 is of course limited by design, being based on a single table and not having information about the social context and variables involved (because the basic demographics were known to all students), nor about richer statistical issues. Nonetheless, the task demonstrates the use of open-ended questions that encourage students to generate an informed opinion based on given data, while making sure students attend to multiple aspects of the data, and connect statistics with social topics.

The interpretation of the three-way table shown in Fig. 13.1, and discussing correlates, causes, conclusions and implications, requires time and patience from the teacher and the students. The analysis may raise issues related to proportional changes, trends, and internal comparisons of counts or percents, and students may also need some help with terminology regarding the direction or magnitude of the observed changes and patterns, giving rise to a rich mathematical discourse.

Such tasks can be extended since both Q4 and Q5 bring into the class discussion new variables and civic issues (causal factors, correlates, consequences) and a richer multivariate network of interacting factors, each one of which can be further explored. For example, in response to Q4, students may explain that some population groups are projected to grow faster than others due to different birth rates, or that births now happen at older ages (associated with rising education levels for women). Such ideas can be further developed into follow-up tasks where students can be asked to seek additional information on those new variables, e.g., find press releases or reports from an official statistics agency about causal factors or correlates, or by exploring dynamic population pyramids where different modelling assumptions (for example about birth rates) can be made—see Chap. 5. Finally, such a task can be further extended by using richer textual resources (i.e., a newspaper article with embedded statistics, or the press releases on which it is based) covering a broader range of civic topics and statistical information that can give rise to more diverse types of questions and tasks.

13.8   Beyond Opinion Questions: Towards Critical 'Worry Questions'

This section continues to discuss the third issue of 'question posing' noted in Table 13.1. It goes beyond Sects. 13.6 and 13.7 which discussed general ideas regarding the shaping of questions which can tease out students' general opinions regarding statistics about specific civic issues. Students and (future) citizens need to develop a broader ability to critically evaluate quantitative and statistical messages to the public (Weiland, 2017, 2019). Such messages may be issued by many stakeholders (e.g., politicians, political action groups, civic leaders, journalists, business leaders, *etc.*) and they are influenced by political, commercial, social, or other agendas which may be absent when statistics are taught in the classroom. Depending on their needs and goals, such sources may not necessarily be motivated to present a balanced and objective report of findings or implications.

To be able to effectively engage and interpret information from such sources, students need to internalize and be able to use some critical questions, which are called 'worry questions', to differentiate them from the questions posed *to* the students in class. Worry questions are expected to be deployed whenever students or citizens see data claims, i.e., messages purporting to be based on data or on quantitative evidence. Ten examples for worry questions are offered in Table 13.3— but many more do exist!

The need to develop a broad ability to critically evaluate messages (including quantitative and statistical messages communicated via print/text only, even without any numerals or mathematical symbols), and worry about underlying motives and

Table 13.3 Ten examples for worry questions

1. Where did the data (on which this statement is based) come from? What kind of study was it, and is it reasonable in this context?

2. Was a sample used? How was it derived? How many people actually participated? Is the sample large enough? Did the sample include people/units which are representative of the population? Is the sample biased in some way? Overall, could this sample reasonably lead to valid inferences about the target population?

3. How reliable or accurate were the measures (tests, questionnaires, interviews) used to generate the reported data?

4. What is the shape of the underlying distribution of raw data (on which this summary statistic is based)? Does it matter how it is shaped?

5. Are the reported statistics appropriate for this kind of data, e.g., was an average used to summarize ordinal data; is a mode a reasonable summary? Could outliers distort the true picture?

6. Is a given graph or chart drawn appropriately? Does it distort or exaggerate trends in the data (e.g., the relative difference between groups)?

7. How were any probabilistic statements derived? Are there enough credible data to justify the estimate of likelihood given?

8. Overall, are the claims made here sensible and supported by the data? e.g., is correlation confused with causation, or a small difference made to loom large?

9. Should additional information be made available to enable me to evaluate the plausibility of these arguments? Is something missing? e.g., did the writer 'conveniently forget' to specify the base of a reported percentage change, or the actual sample size?

10. Are there alternative interpretations for the meaning of the findings or different explanations for what caused them, e.g., could an intervening variable affect the results? Are there additional or different civic implications that are not mentioned?

Adapted from Gal (2002)

intentions, has been a recurring theme in writings of many scholars interested in adults' basic skills (Frankenstein, 1989; Freire, 1972; Huff, 1954). For example, Paulos (1995) noted that originators of messages regarding diseases, accidents, or other human problems can make them appear more scary by choosing to report absolute numbers (e.g., "2500 people nationwide suffer from X"), or downplay them by using incidence rate (e.g., "only 1 in every 100,000 people suffer from X").

Given such considerations, we need to develop our students' *ability and willingness* to worry about the reasonableness of statistical and quantitative claims presented in the media and social networks, the validity of messages, the credibility of the evidence presented, and possible alternative interpretations of conclusions conveyed to them. When faced with arguments or messages involving Civic Statistics, we want people (and students) to have internalized worry questions, so they become habits of mind—immediate reactions whenever faced with arguments involving data. Weiland (2019) further discusses the connection between critical questions in mathematics and statistics education.

The answers students generate to questions such as those listed in Fig. 13.1 can support a critical evaluation of statistical messages and lead to the creation of more informed interpretations and judgments. This list can of course be modified and expanded, and some of its elements regrouped, depending on the life contexts and functional needs of different learners and teachers. Ridgway et al. (2016) illustrate a way in which learners can be encouraged to build on these ten 'worry questions' by deriving their own 'worry questions' from errors in political speeches that are reported by 'fact-checking' organisations. These organizations offer on their websites a rich source of analyses of statements about Civic Statistics, and students can be asked to analyse and categorise the mistakes made and compiled on these websites. Hopefully, students will use the practical experiences of working with expert critiques of authentic texts to internalize the 'worry questions' they develop.

13.9   Summary and Implications

The development of statistical literacy at the school and university levels alike is essential, if graduates are to function effectively in a world filled with rich Civic Statistics. This is the justification for the first of the six key recommendations emerging from the ProCivicStat project—see Chap. 4—which calls on educators to *Develop activities which promote engagement with social issues and develop learners' critical understanding of statistics about key civic phenomena.*

However, developing the ability to critically understand Civic Statistics poses multiple challenges. Hence, this chapter has examined selected issues and dilemmas in this regard. The chapter highlights that developing understanding of the *context* within which Civic Statistics are used (by various stakeholders) and generated (e.g., by official statistics providers, other data producers, or the media itself) is an essential component of teaching for statistical literacy in general and teaching about Civic Statistics in particular.

The use of rich and engaging contexts in the classroom has many advantages, in terms of students' motivation, development of core reasoning and argumentation skills, and deeper understanding of statistics and mathematics. However, working on 'meaningful and important' contexts is far from being simple for educators, if they are only focused on developing their students' technical mastery of statistical constructs and methods, or prefer to avoid sensitive social issues and hence choose to engage only neutral topics.

For this reason, the chapter posed four questions for educators to consider:

- What contexts are valuable (meaningful and important) for *my* students?
- How can contexts be meaningfully engaged with in *my* classroom (via the use of meaningful textual sources)?
- What tasks or questions can *I* pose about statistics in context, and how can questions and tasks be scaffolded so as to develop students' ability to express and justify *opinions* about Civic Statistics and about their social implications?
- What are the best *worry questions* for *my* students to internalise about statistical or data-based claims?

The chapter provided several examples for its core ideas. Other chapters in this book provide many more illustrations regarding contextualization, task design, question-posing, and teacher options. The arena of statistical literacy is much wider (See Gal, 2002; Gal & Ograjenšek, 2017; Watson, 2013; Weiland, 2017, 2019), and more issues need to be addressed when teaching for statistical literacy, including how to assess learners' knowledge (Ziegler & Garfield, 2018). Further, 'contexts' and 'opinion questions' were discussed here mainly in connection with findings based on datasets and surveys that are in typical use by statistics producers, but are of equal importance for critical understanding of messages and public communications related to chance, risk, and probability (See Gal, 2005).

The ideas in this chapter have many implications for the design of instruction about Civic Statistics and about statistics in general, in diverse teaching contexts, and can help to transform statistics teaching into a more active and engaging form of learning. The chapter implies that students should be asked to *read* and *engage* with meaningful texts about Civic Statistics topics. This in turn requires changes in how much time and effort are allocated to teaching core statistical ideas vs. discussing them *in context*, and designing instructional tasks that reflect a genuine 'need to know' and are motivating for students because of the chosen contexts and realistic and meaningful questions posed about them.

References

Ainley, J., Gould, R., & Pratt, D. (2015). Learning to reason from samples: Commentary from the perspectives of task design and the emergence of "big data". *Educational Studies in Mathematics, 88*(3), 405–412.

Ancker, J. (2020). The COVID-19 pandemic and the power of numbers. *Numeracy, 13*(2). Article 2. Retrieved October 1, 2020, from https://scholarcommons.usf.edu/numeracy/vol13/iss2/art2/

Arnold, P., & Franklin, C. (2021). What makes a good statistical question? *Journal of Statistics and Data Science Education, 29*(1), 122–130.

Budgett, S., & Rose, D. (2017). Developing statistical literacy in the final school year. *Statistics Education Research Journal, 16*(1), 139–162.

Chance, B. L., & Rossman, A. J. (2001). Sequencing topics in introductory statistics: A debate on what to teach when. *The American Statistician, 55*(2), 140–144.

Cobb, G. W. (2007). The introductory statistics course: A Ptolemaic curriculum? *Technology Innovations in Statistics Education, 1*(1).

Cobb, G. W., & Moore, D. S. (1997). Mathematics, statistics, and teaching. *The American mathematical monthly, 104*(9), 801–823.

Curcio, F. R. (1987). Comprehension of mathematical relationships expressed in graphs. *Journal for Research in Mathematics Education, 18*(5), 382–393.

du Feu, C. (2001). Naming and shaming. *Mathematics in School, 30*(3), 2–8.

Engel, J., Gal, I., & Ridgway, J. (2016, July). *Mathematical literacy and citizen engagement: The role of Civic Statistics.* Paper presented at the 13th international congress on mathematics education (ICME13), Hamburg, Germany.

Frankenstein, M. (1989). *Relearning mathematics: A different "R" –radical mathematics.* Free Association Books.

Freire, P. (1972). Education: Domestication or liberation? *Prospects, 2*(2), 173–181.

Friel, S. N., Curcio, F. R., & Bright, G. W. (2001). Making sense of graphs: Critical factors influencing comprehension and instructional applications. *Journal for Research in Mathematics Education, 32*(2), 124–158.

GAISE. (2016). *Guidelines for assessment and instruction in statistics education: College report.* American Statistical Association. Available from http://www.amstat.org/ASA/Education/Undergraduate-Educators

Gal, I. (1997). Numeracy: imperatives of a forgotten goal. In L. A. Steen (Ed.), *Why numbers count: Quantitative literacy for tomorrow's America* (pp. 36–44). The College Board.

Gal, I. (1998). Assessing statistical knowledge as it relates to students' interpretation of data. In S. Lajoie (Ed.), *Reflections on statistics: Learning, teaching, and assessment in grades K-12* (pp. 275–295). Lawrence Erlbaum. (peer-reviewed).

Gal, I. (2002). Adults' statistical literacy: Meanings, components, responsibilities. *International Statistical Review, 70*(*1*), 1–25.

Gal, I. (2005). Towards 'probability literacy' for all citizens. In G. Jones (Ed.), *Exploring probability in school: Challenges for teaching and learning* (pp. 43–71). Kluwer Academic.

Gal, I., & Geiger, V. (2022). Welcome to the era of vague news: a study of the demands of statistical and mathematical products in the COVID-19 pandemic media. *Educational Studies in Mathematics, 111*, 5–28. https://doi.org/10.1007/s10649-022-10151-7

Gal, I., Grotlüschen, A., Tout, D., & Kaiser, G. (2020). Numeracy, adult education, and vulnerable adults: A critical view of a neglected field. *ZDM Mathematics Education, 52*(*3*), 377–394.

Gal, I., & Ograjenšek, I. (2017). Official statistics and statistics education: Bridging the gap. *Journal of Official Statistics, 33*(1), 79–100.

Gal, I., & Trostianitser, A. (2016). Understanding basic demographic trends: The interplay between statistical literacy, table reading, & motivation. In *Proceedings of the International Association for Statistics Education (IASE)*. Available from https://iase-web.org/documents/papers/rt2016/Gal.pdf

Greatorex, J. (2014). Context in mathematics questions. *Research Matters: A Cambridge Assessment Publication, 17*, 18–23.

Haack, D. G. (1979). *Statistical literacy: A guide to interpretation*. Duxbury Press.

Huff, D. (1954). *How to lie with statistics*. Norton.

Kemp, M., & Kisanne, B. (2010). A five step framework for interpreting tables and graphs in their contexts. In C. Reading (Ed.), *Data and context in statistics education: Towards an evidence-based society. Proceedings of the 8th international conference on teaching statistics (ICOTS8)*. International Statistical Institute/IASE. http://iase-web.org/documents/papers/icots8/ICOTS8_7G3_kemp.pdf

Kilpatrick, J. (2001). Understanding mathematical literacy: The contribution of research. *Educational Studies in Mathematics, 47*(1), 101–116.

Malone, C. J., Gabrosek, J., Curtiss, P., & Race, M. (2012). Resequencing topics in an introductory applied statistics course. *The American Statistician, 64*(1), 52–58.

Moore, D. S. (1998). Statistics among the liberal arts. *Journal of the American Statistical Association, 93*(444), 1253–1259.

Nicholson, J., Ridgway, R., & Gal, I. (2017). Understanding statistics about society: Mapping the knowledge and skills needed to engage with Civic Statistics. In *Proceedings, 61st world statistics congress*. ISI. Available from https://isi-web.org/index.php/publications/proceedings.

Ograjenšek, I., & Gal, I. (2016). Enhancing statistics education by including qualitative research. *International Statistical Review, 84*(2), 165–178. https://doi.org/10.1111/insr.12158

Paulos, J. A. (1995). *A mathematician reads the newspaper*. Anchor Books/Doubleday.

ProCivicStat Partners. (2018, August). *Engaging Civic Statistics: A call for action and recommendations*. A product of the ProCivicStat project. Available from http://iase-web.org/islp/pcs

Prodromou, T. (2015). Students' emerging reasoning about data tables of large-scale data. *International Journal of Statistics and Probability, 4*(3), 181–197.

Ridgway, J. (2021). Covid and data science: Understanding R0 could change your life. *Teaching Statistics, 43*(1), 84–92.

Ridgway, J., Arnold, P., Moy, W., & Ridgway, R. (2016, July). Deriving heuristics from political speeches for understanding statistics about society. In J. Engel (Ed.), *Promoting understanding of statistics about society. Proceedings of the roundtable conference of the International Association of Statistics Education (IASE), Berlin, Germany*. Online: http://iase-web.org/documents/papers/rt2016/Ridgway.pdf

Schield, M. (2016). GAISE 2016 promotes statistical literacy. *Statistics Education Research Journal, 16*(1), 46–50.

Watson, J. M. (2000). Statistics in context. *The Mathematics Teacher, 93*(1), 54–58.

Watson, J. M. (2013). *Statistical literacy at school: Growth and goals* (2nd ed.). Routledge.

Weiland, T. (2017). Problematizing statistical literacy: An intersection of critical and statistical literacies. *Educational Studies in Mathematics, 96*(1), 33–47.

Weiland, T. (2019). Critical mathematics education and statistics education: possibilities for transforming the school mathematics curriculum. In G. Burrill & D. Ben-Zvi (Eds.), *Topics and trends in current statistics education research* (Chapter 18, pp. 391–411). ICME-13 Monographs. Springer. https://doi.org/10.1007/978-3-030-03472-6_18

West, J. D., & Bergstrom, C. T. (2020). *Calling bullshit: The art of scepticism in a data-driven world*. Penguin UK.

Ziegler, L., & Garfield, J. (2018). Developing a statistical literacy assessment for the modern introductory statistics course. *Statistics Education Research Journal, 17*(2), 161–178.

Chapter 14
Implementing Civic Statistics in Business Education: Technology in Small and Large Classrooms

Peter Kovacs (iD)**, Klara Kazar, and Eva Kuruczleki**

Abstract Introducing Civic Statistics is of high importance in business education as its multidisciplinary nature helps students to develop complex and critical thinking and also to link different areas of their studies. In this chapter we share our hands-on experiences on the implementation of Civic Statistics both in large and small classrooms and highlight the differences between the techniques and topics employed in different circumstances. The study materials developed include topics such as the ageing society, poverty and income inequality, social and business networks and even financial literacy, the implementation of which will be discussed in detail in this chapter. The challenges of introducing Civic Statistics in a small or a large classroom in business education are different, and both are described here. In general, we received positive feedback from students: the social themes explored facilitated increased engagement and participation, and students welcomed the topics and tools—even though they are rather unusual compared to their 'ordinary' statistics classes.

Keywords Business education · Large class · Small class · Student experience · Voting systems · Critical questions

14.1 Introduction

Developing citizens' and students' ability to understand complex, real social and economic phenomena and to interpret relationships among social and business data correctly has a key position in university education in general, and is of particular importance in business education. Students nowadays, in the "post-truth" era face an immense supply of raw data, and are ill-prepared to handle them efficiently and confidently. This can lead to many problems and malpractices both in their studies

P. Kovacs (✉) · K. Kazar · E. Kuruczleki
University of Szeged, Szeged, Hungary
e-mail: kovacs.peter@eco.u-szeged.hu; kazar.klara@eco.u-szeged.hu; kuruczleki.eva@eco.u-szeged.hu

345
J. Ridgway (ed.), *Statistics for Empowerment and Social Engagement*,
https://doi.org/10.1007/978-3-031-20748-8_14

and in their personal lives as consumers, from vulnerability to emotional appeals, through the lack of engagement and critical thinking, to the inadequacy in the skills required to interpret the data (Ridgway et al., 2017). Given the above, the ProCivicStat project has emphasized the importance of teaching Civic Statistics (CS). Part I of this book described the many features of Civic Statistics (Chap. 2), discussed and illustrated the 11 facets and tools (i.e., knowledge bases, skills, dispositions) needed to understand Civic Statistics (Chap. 3) and outlined general recommendations regarding teaching and assessment issues (Chap. 4).

This chapter focuses on introducing Civic Statistics into an academic curriculum, with a focus on programs oriented towards business or management. This is challenging not only because of various constraints and pressures in statistics classes, but also because students usually possess very limited prior knowledge on civic issues, and on Civic Statistics. Compared to regular statistics classes, Civic Statistics is a multidisciplinary area which requires a different way of thinking (Ridgway & Ridgway, 2019) and more preparation both from educators and students. Both parties need to learn how to link knowledge elements from different fields such as sociology and economics, and how to formulate questions that can be addressed using rich data sources.

This chapter deals with two general challenges that many teachers and universities face, namely introducing Civic Statistics into the curriculum of a regular statistics course at the university level and, as well, into a statistics course in a business school, where students' orientation and expectations have a unique focus, different to that in general introductory statistics courses. When teaching students in business or management-oriented programs, many students do not usually encounter civic issues in a statistics class or in a business context, even though there is a need for them to discuss social issues alongside business-related topics during classes. This is a common challenge most academic institutions face, since almost all universities in the world offer business education. This is a challenge not only at the level of tertiary education but also at the level of high schools offering business education; therefore this chapter can be of broad interest.

Current university students are members of Generation Y and Z, who share common characteristics: they are the most technologically literate generation, who cannot live their lives without IT tools or the Internet. They cannot be motivated in classes to learn statistics with tools they perceive to be obsolete, such as entirely paper-based analyses (even though learning some basics by hand is important to help students better understand the methodology behind some calculations); educators must embrace technological tools and interactive analyses in classes (Eckleberry-Hunt & Tucciarone, 2011; Reilly, 2012; Sox et al., 2014).

Using technology, IT and visualization tools in statistics classes provides an appropriate solution for teaching members of Gen Y and Z (Chance et al., 2007; Ridgway, 2016). Educators are facing new challenges on how to introduce new methodological tools in both economic and statistical education. In this chapter, we share our experiences implementing both new analytical methods as part of statistical courses in business and economics education, and of implementing Civic Statistics in both small and large classes.

In response to the challenges sketched above, our team (at the University of Szeged) developed new ideas and implemented lessons on diverse civic topics with a particular focus on business education. Examples include activities addressing poverty, income equality, ageing society, and social and business network analysis. A variety of technologies were employed, including an online voting game on financial literacy ('Are you better than your national average?'). A whole new course named *Data Collection and Analysis* was launched, oriented towards Civic Statistics. These and related initiatives were implemented in business education at both the undergraduate and postgraduate levels; materials were developed for use both in small seminar groups and in large classes for business students. In addition, we implemented some of these ideas with secondary school pupils, both in school and in summer camps.

We faced several challenges in developing new approaches for teaching about Civic Statistics. These included:

- Ensuring that students encountered a balanced and valuable mixture of statistical methods.
- Developing ways to use IT and learning technologies effectively.
- Providing sufficient social and economic content.
- Finding an appropriate place for Civic Statistics in the curriculum.
- Reflecting new educational goals in assessment systems.
- Preparing for the new topics—namely topics that had not been taught previously by the teachers.
- Assessing prior knowledge of students in the relevant societal topics.

The above challenges will be discussed in more detail in the later parts of this chapter. Our evaluation during and at the end of the revised or new courses shows that, initially, students faced difficulties using software and seeing the conceptual links between a given civic topic and their academic discipline. However, with the help of structured presentations and detailed discussions of the activities, students were able to discover and gain personal experiences and deeper knowledge about the given social topic and the societal context. These lessons help to facilitate more active student participation, and students enjoy this form of education.

This chapter builds on ideas and methods introduced in the previous parts of this book and summarizes the most important takeaway messages from the lessons learned at the University of Szeged concerning the implementation of Civic Statistics in business education programs. Below we illustrate some new activities used and their underlying principles, and discuss experiences regarding the implementation of selected topics in different teaching and learning environments. These include working with small and large classes, and the role of technology (software, Internet, datasets, online voting systems). The chapter concludes with an analysis of the differences between an ordinary statistics course and a Civic Statistics course, from both the educators' and the students' point of view.

14.2 The Importance and Challenge of Including Civic Statistics in Business Education

Traditional statistics classes at several universities are not dealing with real life processes; most of the data used during classes are generated artificially. However, using real world data must be an essential element of economic analysis if students are to better understand not only the methodology behind data collection and analyses but also real-world processes. Students need to learn how to explore the connections between data and real-life events. Teachers should also aim to immerse students in the data set, to increase their engagement with economic analysis (Brown, 2016). Even though students in business education encounter several semesters (at least two) of statistics, they barely see the world through statistical analyses. While regular statistics classes aim at teaching the theoretical background and methodology of analyses and how to conduct an analysis, Civic Statistics requires a deeper understanding into the sociological, demographic, or economic background of certain phenomena. This section offers examples from our experiences and provides insights into innovative approaches that can be included in statistics education, based on case studies of live courses designed to implement materials developed as part of the ProCivicStatistics project (PCS).

The goal of implementing Civic Statistics in business education is therefore two-fold: first, to create a bridge between economic issues and statistical analyses, and second to provide students with a deeper understanding of the societal and economic mechanisms, processes, or correlates behind the examined issues, which are essential for proper interpretation of the results of statistical findings. Through the introduction of Civic Statistics in business education, different areas of study become connected with the help of statistics; statistical analysis becomes no longer isolated from other subjects such as macro or microeconomics. Rather, students learn how to integrate their knowledge into a more complex web of economic analysis and can develop their critical thinking. And second, Civic Statistics can add much value through providing students with an expanded and deeper perception about their place in society, making them overall more responsible citizens.

The limitations of the curriculum is also a challenge in implementing Civic Statistics in business education: regular statistics courses have limited room for manoeuvre in modifying the syllabus of the courses and cannot give much space for Civic Statistics. However, through the introduction of a course which focuses entirely on the social and economic aspects of some critical social issues, students can acquire knowledge that complements their prior economic and statistical skills. That said, educators in business education must consider where to place such a course in the curriculum, taking into account students' prior knowledge: when designing a course on Civic Statistics. PCS study materials do not require notable prior mathematical and IT skills; yet students must possess some degree of preliminary knowledge in economics if they want to better understand Civic Statistics in business education.

14.3 An Implementation of CS: Building Modules into Existing Courses

For implementing Civic Statistics in business education, we followed two paths: first, we have developed four Civic Statistics teaching modules, which we have included in our already existing small and large statistics classes, and second, a separate course dedicated to teaching Civic Statistics has been developed. Therefore, Sect. 14.3 introduces and discusses the modules and our experiences of implementing CS in existing courses, while Sect. 14.4 describes the newly developed course *Data Collection and Analysis*, a course developed for teaching Civic Statistics in small classes.

14.3.1 Exploring Social Problems

We have developed four modules, which focused on four main social themes, which are: poverty and income inequality; ageing society; social and business networks; and last, but not least, financial literacy. These social and economic issues require various tools to explore them effectively. This provides an opportunity to balance the curriculum in terms of statistical concepts and techniques, exposure to different software packages and styles of working. Table 14.1 provides an illustration. A fuller (searchable) index of the content of every PCS teaching module (including the ones listed below) can be found here

Lessons on the topics of **poverty and income inequality** focus on the differences in the distribution of wealth among different nations and across time periods, trends and patterns of income distribution and poverty, the causes and reasons behind the

Table 14.1 Social themes and content of the teaching modules

Social theme	Content, tools and pedagogy
Poverty and income inequality	• Concepts (e.g. absolute and relative poverty, Gini index), measurement, analysis and interpretation of data, correlation analysis • Lectures and small group work • Visualization: Gapminder, Tableau
Ageing society	• Concepts (e.g. population pyramid, ageing), measurement, analysis and interpretation of data • Lectures, small group work and individual problem solving • Visualization: online population pyramids
Social and business networks	• Concepts (e.g. node, edge, complex systems), measurement, network analysis • Small group work and individual projects and presentations • Visualization: Gephi, ORA, Cytoscape
Financial literacy	• Concepts (e.g. inflation, diversification, interest), measurement • Lectures and small group work • Online voting systems

deepening gap between the rich and the poor, and the social and economic causes of such growing inequalities. The classes on poverty and inequality not only introduce the main notions and concepts to the students, but familiarize them with the variety of indicators and measurement methods relevant to inequalities, such as the ratio of people living below a given poverty threshold as a measure of poverty, or inflation-adjusted GDP per capita as a measure of wealth in countries. The processes associated with poverty and inequality can be best examined using time series and comparison of data, e.g. through correlation analysis to uncover whether certain countries show similar progress in reducing poverty or income inequality. Within the framework of PCS, lesson plans focusing on income inequality and poverty are utilizing such tools as *Gapminder* or *Tableau*, which are excellent for visualizing multivariate data.

Gapminder Online is a free online dynamic visualization tool which can be used to visualize five different variables on a single chart simultaneously while still keeping the visualisation simple enough so that students can easily understand social and economic progress. Chapter 8 provided an overview on the use of Gapminder for dynamic data visualization. Gapminder Offline is a publicly available desktop version of Gapminder Offline which does not require constant internet access and in which students can visualize their own data as well. Tableau Public is also a free visualization tool which—similarly to Gapminder Offline—allows us to utilize our own data—hence, when using Tableau and Gapminder Offline, students not only learn how to visualize and explore data but how to construct their own databases.

Figure 14.1 shows just one example of the use of Tableau for visualization on the topic of poverty and income inequality. It shows the Gini index for countries of the World on a heatmap. Darker green areas of the map refer to countries where the Gini index—and therefore income inequality as well—is lower, while the darker red areas are countries where the Gini index is higher, with one example highlighted. In 2016, the Gini index and with it, income inequality, was the highest in Brazil according to the World Bank estimates. Such a geographical layout is not only a visually pleasing way of showing data to students but is also an excellent method to make students link the data to their general knowledge of the World, e.g. linking income inequalities to the politics or economic issues of a country.

Ageing society is a serious issue facing modern societies. According to reports from the World Health Organisation (WHO), the percentage of the global population living above the age of 60 will increase to 22% by 2050 from 12% in 2015, and the number of people above the age of 80 years will more than triple from 125 to 434 million persons by 2050.[1] It is important for all citizens to engage with the topic of an ageing society; it is particularly important for students of economics because of the implications for (for example) pensions, tax policies, and retirement planning. Ageing puts a huge burden on the economy and economists of the future should be aware of the processes behind the changes. Ageing society can be best examined

---

[1] WHO (2018). Ageing and health. Online: https://www.who.int/news-room/fact-sheets/detail/ageing-and-health, downloaded: 8 January 2020

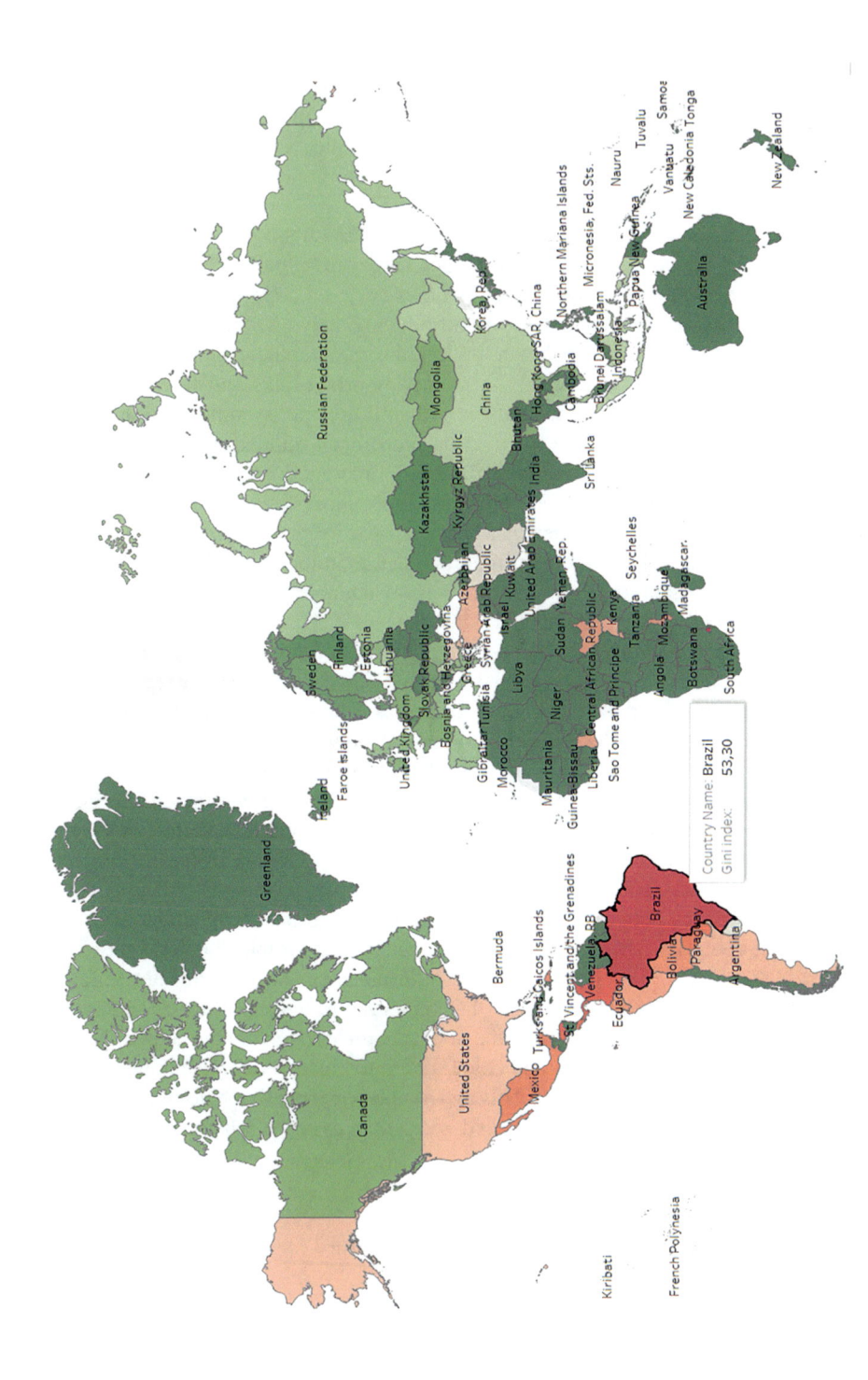

Fig. 14.1 Heatmap in Tableau visualizing the Gini index for 2016, data source: World Bank data

through population pyramids—examples can be accessed online or can be created with the help of such tools as Gapminder or Tableau. Examples of online population pyramids are provided on the World Life Expectancy website,[2] population pyramid net[3] Our World in Data[4] and elsewhere in this book. A population pyramid is shown in Chap. 8, along with descriptions of how to introduce students to modelling by changing the assumptions underpinning dynamic population pyramids and then examining the resulting predictions.

The topic of **social and business networks** focuses on the step-by-step introduction of students to network analysis and graph theory to help them better understand the links between agents of a network, or flows between countries or other entities forming a network. The advantage of introducing network analysis in business education is that students can better understand geographical and historical ties between countries; it is much easier to notice important links and flows when the network is visualized. Network analysis not only develops complex thinking in students, but can also sensitize them to be more open-minded when considering societal issues such as the state of refugees or international migration. Network analysis lessons within the PCS framework introduce students to basic notions around networks, such as the idea of a network, and its constituent elements; basic measures of networks help uncover important actors in the network. Students learn how to construct their own datasets in a form suitable for visualization, create visualizations, and analyze the networks themselves.

Network analysis is mainly carried out by using *Gephi*, open-source software for network visualization. The software is one of the most widely used software packages for graph and network visualization and exploration, and is available here.[5] Even though PCS lessons in the topic of networks and graphs have been created for Gephi, most of them can be further customized so that the given social and economic networks can be explored with the help of various other graph visualization and analysis software. As an example for graphs created in Gephi, Fig. 14.2 shows a graph on the topic of international migration and refugees made by one of the authors (EK) when a student. The graph visualises refugee flows (appearing as edges between the nodes of the graph) from their country of origin to the target countries (appearing as nodes on the graph) for the year 2015 based on United Nations data. To emphasize the possibilities for customizing networks in Gephi, the nodes of the network have different sizes to highlight the most popular target countries (the larger the size of the node, the greater the number of people who arrived in that country in 2015); and colours refer to clusters of nodes within which migration patterns can be detected. This means that countries that belong to the same cluster are such countries of origin and recipient countries which have stronger

---

[2]https://www.worldlifeexpectancy.com/world-population-pyramid

[3]https://www.populationpyramid.net/

[4]https://ourworldindata.org/global-population-pyramid

[5]https://gephi.org/

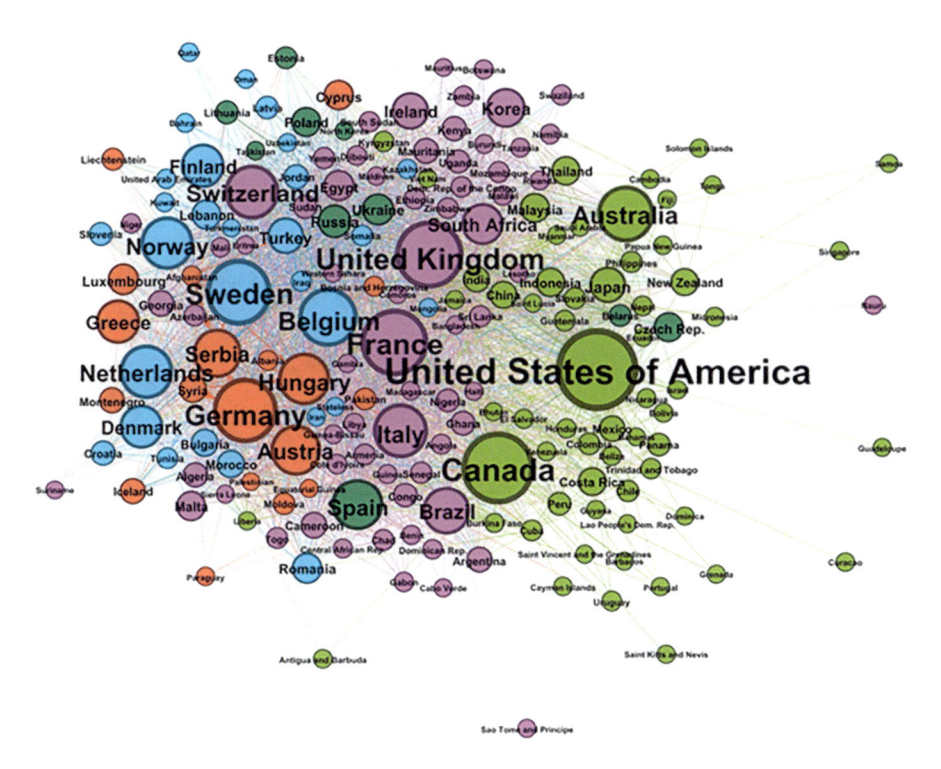

Fig. 14.2 Network of international refugee flows in 2015, data source: UN

migration flows between themselves than with the rest of the countries outside of their cluster.

Network analysis can not only be examined with the help of Gephi; *Tableau* can be useful as well, however to a different extent. Figure 14.3 illustrates refugee applications on a flow diagram or Sankey diagram, created as a dashboard in Tableau using the same UN refugee dataset as above, but in this case limiting the analysis to the top countries of origin (shown on the left side of the chart) and top asylum countries (right side). Such a diagram can also be helpful for the students in understanding flows in a much simpler context compared to a graph. However creating such a graph (or in this case, a Tableau dashboard in which the visualization was made) requires notable prior experience in Tableau, while creating a graph in Gephi is much easier even for a student who has no previous experience in the use of visualization tools. One common benefit of both, however, is that both Tableau and Gephi can handle geographical layouts, and these, combined with visualizing flows, can promote better understanding of social and economic phenomena—here international migration flows.

The fourth main module developed focuses on **financial literacy**. Financial literacy is *a combination of awareness, knowledge, skill, attitude and behaviour necessary to make sound financial decisions and ultimately achieve individual*

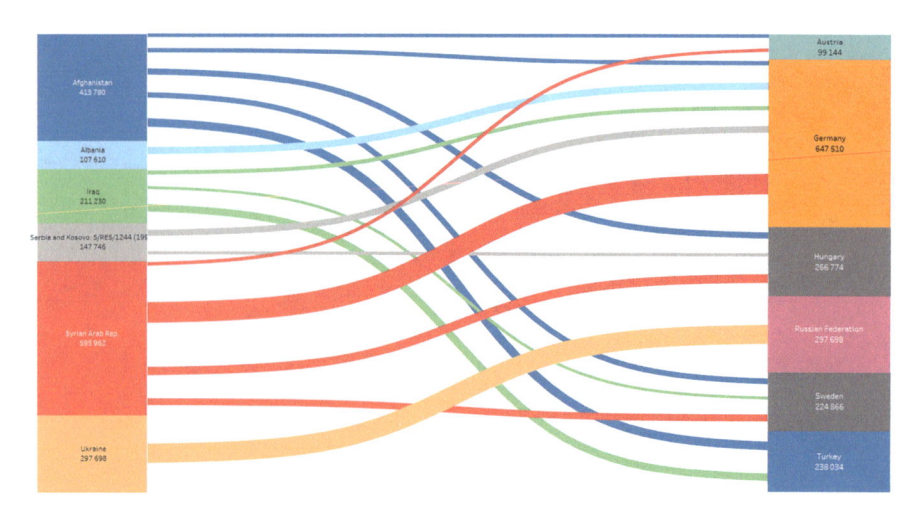

Fig. 14.3 Refugee applications in 2015–2017 by top countries of origin and top asylum countries, persons, data source: UN

financial wellbeing (OECD definition cited by Atkinson & Messy, 2012, p. 14). Following the 2008 financial crisis some blamed individuals for their poor financial decisions, which contributed to the crisis to the same extent as businesses' improper financial decisions (Klapper et al., 2012; Lusardi & Mitchell, 2014). Because of this, financial literacy research and financial education of individuals has been in the spotlight of many major international organizations, such as OECD, in the past decade. In business education it is equally as important for economics students to be aware of personal financial issues as well as general economics and finance, so that they can better understand financial processes from both the consumers' and companies' aspects.

The topic of financial literacy includes more discussions and far fewer visualizations; students are encouraged to think critically about their everyday finances and to test both their knowledge and attitudes. Online voting sites, such as VoxVote or Kahoot! served to support the ice-breaker for the topic: students filled out the same questionnaires as those used by OECD or Standard & Poor in their surveys, and can compare their results to either their national or the global average and discuss the differences in the results and the reason behind such differences.

The above four topics (poverty and income inequality, ageing society, social and business networks and financial literacy) serve as starting points in implementing Civic Statistics in business education. Depending on the previous knowledge and preparedness of the students and on the size of the classes, lesson plans can be tailored in different ways. Lessons on poverty and income inequality, ageing society and network analysis can function well in smaller classes, while quizzes and discussions on the topic of financial literacy can be both applied in smaller and larger classes, (most online voting sites do not have limitations on the number of participants in quizzes and polls) we have used quizzes with classes of 450 students.

14.3.2 Teaching Environments

Table 14.2 shows how teaching modules have been used with different student groups. Business education was the focus of our early development work; topics were first introduced to different sized groups of business students. Working in small classes has the advantage over large classes in that students can better collaborate with each other, and there is more room for conversations, use of interactive tools and group work. At the University of Szeged, Faculty of Economics and Business Administration, statistical education has been provided both in large and small classes: large classes of up to 450 students are aimed more at teaching the theoretical basics of statistics with less emphasis on the practical application of analytical tools in social and economic environments, while small classes of up to 30 students are aimed at teaching the practical application of statistical analyses, introducing some analytical methods and software, and developing students' critical thinking around data. Apart from economics students, through introductory statistics courses and high school programmes both law students and high school students have had the opportunity to learn about Civic Statistics. In the case of the law and high school students, courses were held in small groups, meaning that more discussions and debates were held on the topics of ageing society and financial literacy. These topics were chosen for these groups because of their implications in their everyday lives; high school students have just started managing their own finances and will soon leave their parents to continue their university studies, so they have to be aware of their finances way more than before. Law students upon becoming lawyers will have to be familiar with current demographic processes of our society and the world.

Civic Statistics has been implemented in both small and large classes in business education. In this environment, not all students own computers, however, more than 98% of students use smartphones with internet connections, and several of them use notebooks, or tablets to make notes during lectures. Most of the schools have Wi-Fi networks. These factors offer the opportunity to use online voting systems, online idea boxes, and data collection to encourage students' activities in classes. The

Table 14.2 Teaching modules introduced to different student groups

Program	Topics/Tools
Business program at bachelor level (small groups of 20–30 students in a special course after an introductory statistics course), IT	Ageing society Social and business networks CODAP, Tableau
Business program at bachelor level (large classes with 450 students in an introductory statistics course), IT	Ageing society Voting systems
Business programs at master level (small groups of 20–30 students in a special course), IT	Ageing society Poverty and income equality
Law programs (small groups of 20–30 students in an introductory statistics course), IT	Ageing society
Secondary school students (small groups of 20–30 students), IT	Financial literacy

implementation of Civic Statistics in large classes of up to 450 students served the purpose of introducing a topic and generating ideas; with the help of the voting sites used, students had the opportunity to engage and express themselves even in such large classes. For instance, at the beginning of the classes, we use warm-up questions. In the ageing society module can ask students for their perceptions about the age profiles of different countries. VoxVote can manage it either as a closed or an open question, and we can show the result immediately on a horizontal bar chart or on a word cloud. These systems provide immediate feedback, and engage students. They can also help develop critical thinking in students. For instance, we create activities on interpretations of different charts and tables in a quiz form. The open questions can help in formalizing critical questions.

Our experiences showed that sometimes students have a hard time expressing their ideas verbally in public even if they have valuable opinions to share, because of their fear of others' judgments. Through the introduction of the online voting sites, students feel more liberated and freer of the stress caused by speaking up in front of hundreds of their classmates.

After answering the questions about the teaching material we developed, students evaluated the online voting system through two questions. The opinions about using the online voting system were measured in a 5-point Likert scale (1—*I do not like the online voting system at all*, 5—*I like the online voting system very much*). 78% of the students (n = 189) gave 5 points as an evaluation, and only 9 students gave 3 or fewer points. The average evaluation score was 4.68 points (SD = 0.73 points), so students really liked getting questions through an online voting system. There was a closed question about the usage of the online voting system (*Shall we use this online voting system during the lectures?*) where 93% of the respondents (n = 183) voted yes; only 1 person voted no and 12 students responded *it does not matter* (7%).

In the following part of this chapter, we describe the introduction of a course called *Data Collection and Analysis* which has been developed primarily to test PCS materials, and has been further adapted to fit the needs of economics students. We also describe our experiences and takeaway lessons from implementing Civic Statistics in business education.

14.4   A New Course on Civic Statistics

The course *Data Collection and Analysis* has been developed on CS at the University of Szeged, Hungary, where students use both our and PCS partners' materials. The aim of the course is to bridge the gap between traditional statistics courses and social and economic issues, to show students how they can better analyze everyday phenomena using statistical analysis and visualisation tools and also to support the understanding of complex socio-economic phenomena through statistics. The course continues to run and evolve; it has been designed to run in the spring semesters of the academic year for a maximum of 30 students, making it a small class activity. Practical training, lab work and seminars are usually held in smaller groups of students at universities; in Hungarian high schools, one class is usually composed of 20–30 persons. Smaller groups enable the educators and the students to engage better with topics and facilitate better communication and collaboration in the group.

The reason behind launching a course for such a small group of students has been twofold: one reason has been the limitation of computer rooms—most computer rooms at universities contain around 30 or even fewer computers. The other reason is that most of the PCS materials work better in small classes because they focus more on the practical application of analyses, and because of the important role of discussions around certain topics. Economics students take their first statistics class in the third semester; this is a prerequisite to register for the *Data Collection and Analysis* course, which is optional. So students already possess some preliminary knowledge about statistics which provides a good foundation in understanding Civic Statistics.

14.4.1 Lesson Structure

Classes are designed to be 90 min long and to cover one or two Civic Statistics themes during one class, depending on the complexity of the analysis to be performed. The structure of a typical lecture is given in Table 14.3.

Every lesson begins with a short (10 min) introduction to the topic. This introduction can include: a short presentation from the teacher; a short video on the topic (many educational and thought-provoking videos are freely available online and can be used to start a conversation and to attract students' interest in the topic); or even a short quiz or game (gamification in many cases can help to break the ice and encourage students to participate more actively in class activities). Following the introduction, students can share their impressions about the topic, what preliminary knowledge or assumptions they have about a given social or economic topic, or they might even formulate their own questions about the topic (10 min). Encouraging them to formulate questions which later can be answered through data analysis can not only strengthen students' engagement in class but can also develop their critical and logical thinking.

Table 14.3 Lesson structure in Data Collection and Analysis course

Lesson element	Length (minutes)
Introduction to the topic: basic notions, videos on the topic, quizzes, etc.	10
Warming up discussion: exploring students' preliminary knowledge and assumptions about the phenomenon	10
Exploring datasets in the topic	20–30
Data analysis and visualization in the topic	30–40
Closing remarks, discussing main takeaways, eliciting the experiences of the students	10

The core element of the class is the analytical module, which is separated into two parts, the first focusing on exploring real datasets which can be both from official statistics institutions or could be other real data (e.g. from university surveys); the second part focuses on the practical use of this data, aiming at answering students' questions on the topic. This analytical module requires around 60 min of class time. The length of each part can vary, depending on the scale of the datasets to be explored, the difficulty of the analysis methods, and the complexity of the software. In this module the main focus is on active participation and enhanced cooperation between the students. Teachers can set group tasks so that students have to collaborate in solving problems or can set competitions to find the most creative solution to a given social or economic problem, or can hold debates on the topic. This part of the class not only improves their analytical thinking and skills, but through the group activities or interactive exercises their communication skills can further develop as well.

In the last 10 min of the class, students discuss what they have learned during class, and can share their positive or negative experiences concerning the exercises or their interest in the phenomenon itself. It is important to close every class with a discussion, so that students have an opportunity to share with others the main messages (or moral) that the topic has given them, and also to collect valuable comments on how to develop the upcoming classes so that they will better fit future students' aims and needs.

14.4.2 Course Design

The *Data Collection and Analysis* course is generally planned for 12 weeks of classes (twelve 90 min classes). The materials selected for the classes are all taken from the PCS Teaching Resources, which are available from the CivicStatMap.[6]

In business education it is crucial to select topics that are directly connected to the studies of the students. Teachers need to keep in mind when designing the course that classes should be planned to allow a progression from the easiest to the most complex analysis methods and topics; at the beginning of the course, it is important not to overload students with analyses that are too complex, or to address social issues that are too controversial, because these can deter students from participating in classes. PCS Teaching Materials provide lesson plans to support (in addition to the topics outlined here) investigations about migration and refugees, climate and environment, gender equity, education, health, statistical literacy, and human development. Topics in many cases can be selected around an overarching theme—for example, gender equity, education, health and income inequality, and poverty are all related to personal well-being. A different approach is to take a single theme

---

[6]https://rstudio.up.pt/shiny/users/pcs/civicstatmap/

Table 14.4 Sample curriculum for the *Data Collection and Analysis* course

Week	Topic	PCS teaching material	Software
1	Introduction, course requirements, assessment, warming up	5.202 Daily routine[a]	Online datasets
2	Interpretation practices	5.304 Interpretation practices[b]	–
3	Population and human development	5.102 World Population[c]	CODAP, iNZight
4	Human development, happiness	5.105 Human Development Index[d] 5.106 Happiness[e]	CODAP, iNZight
5	Ageing society	5.303 Ageing society[f]	Dynamic population pyramids
6	Introduction to Gapminder	5.301 Introduction to Gapminder[g]	Gapminder
7	Poverty and income inequality	5.302 Gapminder level 2[h] 5.201 Inequality[i]	Gapminder
8	Risk of poverty and social exclusion	5.302 Gapminder level 2 5.410 Risk of Poverty and Social Exclusion[j]	Gapminder, Tableau
9	Migration and refugees	5.405 Refugees[k]	Tableau
10	Migration and refugees	5.412 Refugees[l]	PowerBI
11	Introduction to networks and graphs	5.305 Networks level 1[m]	Gephi
12	Migration and refugees	5.306 Networks level 2[n]	Gephi

[a]https://rstudio.up.pt/shiny/users/pcs/civicstatmap/5.202_SV_RoutineDay_EN.pdf
[b]https://rstudio.up.pt/shiny/users/pcs/civicstatmap/5.304_TV_interpretation%20practices_EN.pdf
[c]https://rstudio.up.pt/shiny/users/pcs/civicstatmap/5.102_TV_world's%20population_EN.pdf
[d]https://rstudio.up.pt/shiny/users/pcs/civicstatmap/5.105_TV_HDI_EN.pdf
[e]https://rstudio.up.pt/shiny/users/pcs/civicstatmap/5.106_TV_Happiness_EN.pdf
[f]https://rstudio.up.pt/shiny/users/pcs/civicstatmap/5.303_TV_AgeingSociety_EN.pdf
[g]https://rstudio.up.pt/shiny/users/pcs/civicstatmap/5.301_TV_gapminder_level1_EN.pdf
[h]https://rstudio.up.pt/shiny/users/pcs/civicstatmap/5.302_TV_gapminder_level2_poverty_EN.pdf
[i]https://rstudio.up.pt/shiny/users/pcs/civicstatmap/5.201_TV_Inequality_EN.pdf
[j]https://rstudio.up.pt/shiny/users/pcs/civicstatmap/5.410_TV_Riskof%20Poverty%20or%20SocialExclusion_EN.pdf
[k]https://rstudio.up.pt/shiny/users/pcs/civicstatmap/5.405_TV_RefugeesUNHCR_EN.pdf
[l]https://rstudio.up.pt/shiny/users/pcs/civicstatmap/5.412_TV_RefugeesUNdata_EN.pdf
[m]https://rstudio.up.pt/shiny/users/pcs/civicstatmap/5.305_TV_Networks_Level1_EN.pdf
[n]https://rstudio.up.pt/shiny/users/pcs/civicstatmap/5.306_TV_Networks_Level2_EN.pdf

(e.g. gender equality), and to plan a sequence of explorations of increasing sophistication using multiple data sets.

Most of the PCS teaching materials address a given dataset that students can explore with the help of pre-specified software or analysis methods. However, teachers are encouraged to complement PCS materials with new datasets and to tailor the analysis methods to the students' needs or preliminary knowledge by e.g. choosing different software. Table 14.4 shows a sample syllabus for one semester of the Data Collection and Analysis course, illustrating the selected PCS materials to be discussed during the course and the software needed to solve the exercises.

The above sample syllabus set out in Table 14.4 can be separated into four main modules, each module focusing on a given social or economic phenomenon:

- **Weeks 1–2:** introductory module. Students are introduced to the aims of the course and learn about the requirements in terms of activities and assessment. Warming up activities, basic practice with interpreting different visualisations.
- **Weeks 3–5**: module on population and population projections. Students learn about and discuss population processes, the current state of our society, how human development has progressed over the years and what projections we have about our future, concerning aging societies and population growth. Students are introduced to *Codap* and *iNZight* and as well online population pyramid tools.
- **Weeks 6–8:** module on inequalities, poverty and social exclusion. Students learn about income differences all around the world, different measures of poverty and social exclusion, and they discuss how to act against poverty and what projections show about future development in poor countries. The two main software packages used in this module are *Gapminder* and *Tableau*, using both *Gapminder Online* and *Gapminder Offline* is recommended in classes.
- **Weeks 9–12:** module on migration and the state of refugees. The prior weeks on income inequalities lead to the question of why people leave their countries and migrate to others. This module seeks to answer this question by exploring UN refugee and international migration datasets through various analysis methods (using *Tableau*, *PowerBI* and *Gephi*). The second part of this module contains an introduction to networks and graphs, which make it easier for students to discover the political and geographical patterns associated with migration.

14.4.3   Options for Adapting and Expanding the Course Design and Activities

This sample syllabus is built along four main social topics which have important economic implications (for pensions, healthcare, gender pay gap, aid to countries in need. etc.) which students all encounter during their studies. These modules support better understanding of how social problems and processes can play out in global and national economic systems. This syllabus is not set in stone; modules can be modified according to the particular needs of students. In a small course it is possible to include a more extended project that has many advantages. To give an example, the material on Gender Equity[7] contains a 4-week project about the gender pay gap, culminating in a student presentation. This project is divided into four 90 min long

---

[7] https://rstudio.up.pt/shiny/users/pcs/civicstatmap/5.409_TV_Gender%20Equity_EN.pdf

sessions, during which students explore the topic of gender inequality and the gender pay gap, via rich data investigations. In summary:

- **Session 1:** introduction to topic, general discussion about the gender pay gap.
- **Session 2 and 3:** data analysis on the topic of the gender pay gap.
- **Session 4:** presentations and discussion of results.

Previous sections of this book introduced various tools, techniques and topics that can be further included in the course design. Chapters 5–12 each introduce different tools and datasets which can further enrich the syllabus. For example, the visualization tools introduced in Chap. 5 can complement the social themes introduced in the above syllabus (e.g. ageing society), and similarly, the data sources and visualizations on the topic of refugees in Chap. 6 can widen the range of datasets and tools that can be used during weeks 9–12 in the above-described syllabus. Moreover, educators are encouraged to relate such actual phenomena in the course structure such as climate change (see Chap. 11 about exploring climate change data) or even the "hottest" topic of the early 2020s, the COVID-19 pandemic (see Chap. 12 on civic statistics in the time of COVID-19).

This course can not only be implemented at the college and university level but can also be of interest to high school educators as well, because educating pupils about societal issues and data analysis techniques can be excellent preparation for their further studies in tertiary education. Pupils who learn about Civic Statistics during their high school years are not only going to be better equipped with the knowledge of statistical analysis and visualization tools but are also going to be more open and sensitive to important social and economic issues that are part of our everyday lives regardless of the profession one chooses. Therefore, we highly recommend adapting this course for use at high school level as well. The tools and topics introduced as part of the syllabus can be flexibly adapted to the needs of high school pupils and teachers, e.g. by including the visualization tools introduced in Chap. 9.

14.4.4 Evaluation

How can teachers evaluate the work and products of students who work on hands-on tasks or extended projects? This is a challenging topic that has been the subject of much scholarly work. Project based learning (PBL) is an educational approach which allows students to develop their skills through real life examples and at the same time promotes engagement in the classroom, and results in better educational outcomes compared to traditional learning environments (Krajcik & Blumenfeld, 2005). We can not only consider student engagement and learning activities but must think about how we can assess student performance. With PBL, assessment becomes not as straightforward as in the case of traditional teaching methods, because PBL teaching not only develops the theoretical knowledge of students, but endows them with complex analytical and critical skills, some of which we cannot measure with traditional tests. Therefore, this teaching approach is creating an opportunity for innovation in assessment methods, illustrated by the examples in Bergeron et al. (2019). In our course, we aimed at developing an appropriate assessment model, which is virtually inseparable from the learning activities, therefore not burdening students further with additional course requirements. Rather, we set out to promote active participation and to gather evidence about the development of the skills students have developed, and to reward not only the tangible elements of students' work (e.g. written materials), but also their personal contribution to the course..

In order to pass the *Data Collection and Analysis* course, students have to work on a project in groups of 4 or 5 during the whole semester, exploring their chosen social or economic phenomenon. This phenomenon can be one discussed during the semester or even something else they are interested in and is approved by the teacher. From the first class of the course, students are encouraged to work in teams both during the course and in their project work, to develop their cooperation and conflict resolution skills. In their project work, students have to be able to formulate questions (i.e. they have to decide what they want to research in their project; they are not working on pre-defined questions, so that they learn how to ask better questions when it comes to research) and solve these questions using the tools they meet during the semester.

Students have to form groups at the beginning of the semester and during the whole semester they are expected to work together on their project. They have to report on their progress three times during the semester:

- **Week 3:** submitting group members' names; the submitted group composition is regarded as final by this week, and cannot be changed during the semester. Students get 3 weeks to form a group and are not forced to do this during the first class, because as classes are quite large, they might not know each other, making group formulation problematic at the beginning. Teachers allow time for students to get to know each other, and make their own choices about group composition, to ensure better cooperation between group members.
- **Week 6:** submitting their chosen topic and initial questions. During the semester students are developing their skills in formulating better questions, but they have to be able to briefly outline what they want to research by the middle of the semester. Teachers can give them some guidance on narrowing down the topic and students can start looking for data when they have the preliminary research questions.
- **Week 9:** reporting the final research question they are about to answer in their project. This research question should be well focussed. As an example, "What is the state of poverty in Africa?" cannot be considered an appropriate research question as it is too broad and too general, however "How has the proportion of people living in extreme poverty in Sub-Saharan Africa changed over time?" can be considered a suitably specific research question. The course is designed for undergraduate students who might never have carried out a research project, so teachers need to be generous in critiquing their research questions and offer guidance in specifying at least the target group and sub-topic they are to examine.

Table 14.5 Requirements of Data Collection and Analysis course

Assessment component	Weight (%)
Class participation and work	**10**
Group project	**60**
– Suitability of research questions	20
– Accuracy of chosen data analysis methods	20
– Accuracy of chosen visualisations	20
Group presentation	**30**
– Every member takes part in the presentation	5
– The presentation is easy to understand	5
– Reasoning is accurate and well-founded	10
– Students can answer questions related to their research	10
Total	**100**

- **Last week or exam period:** presenting results of the group project. Students have to make a 15–20 min presentation about how they answered their research question and their results; these are then discussed with the whole class for 5–10 min. Teachers encourage other students to formulate questions for the presenters, this way preparing each other for future presentations and exam situations where they must be able to accept critical comments and reply to the questions from the audience.

Given the size of the class (maximum of 30 students) teachers can monitor the progress of each group through the semester continuously and can base their evaluation not only on the reports of the students and the group project but can also monitor how they have developed individually during the semester. Groups are evaluated along the following criteria set out in Table 14.5.

14.4.5 Feedback from Students

The end-of-class discussions served the purpose of collecting student feedback about the course. Table 14.6 summarizes this student feedback. Students faced many challenges during the course, but could overcome many of them by the end of the semester.

Students faced the challenge of how to formalize questions properly, but the group project and the in-class discussions helped them develop their skills in this area. Students were also unfamiliar with multivariate issues as part of traditional statistics classes; they have not faced multivariate data or analyses, but only rather simple analyses.

The main positive feedback received from the students is that with the help of the teacher and through the guidance provided by the teachers during the introductory parts of the course students could successfully explore a social or economic topic they have been unfamiliar with prior the course.

Table 14.6 Student feedback from Data Collection and Analysis course

Challenges for the students	• Formalizing appropriate questions • Handling multivariate data to address questions • Learning to use the software • Linking knowledge elements from different fields
Positive results/experiences—feedback from students	• Learning to formulate and answer questions about complex situations • More personal experiences and deeper knowledge about the topic and ways in which they can use evidence to engage with reality • Active student participation • The students enjoy this form of learning • "Unconventional" and "more modern" analysis and visualisation methods are popular among students
Negative results/experiences—feedback from students	Some students had difficulty understanding • The importance of the topic for their study (and/or) for themselves • The relationship between the topic and the need for civic engagement

Students were not rushed; the ambition was not to learn something as fast as they can, but rather to get a deeper understanding of how and why to use certain software or analysis tools. The end-of-class discussions and self-reflection provided for the students a great platform to summarize their thoughts and feelings about the class and they were generally grateful for this opportunity, because they felt that the course was designed really for them and with them, because (as stated earlier) introductory discussions served the purpose of fine-tuning the upcoming classes to student interests. The informal style of the course and the introduction of new methods and topics proved to be interesting for the students; those participated in the course generally reported enjoying this interactive form of learning adopted for the course.

Some negative feedback arrived from the students as well. Some of them reported having difficulties in understanding why a certain topic needed to be covered. For example, students found some topics irrelevant for their studies. Some students wanted to focus more on visualization and not social issues, and were sometimes less interested in some phenomena than in ways of representing it. Civic Statistics was at first a notion hard to understand for the students. They could not understand the difference between social statistics and Civic Statistics; this issue, however, could be resolved when the teacher had a clear vision of these differences and could explain it in detail for the students.

Despite the difficulties reported by some students, the course *Data Collection and Analysis* proved to be a course suitable in business education as it provided the participants with valuable insight to the economic implications of many social themes and as well giving students a more colourful and diverse analysis toolkit to complement their statistical skills.

14.5 General Conclusions: Experiences and Recommendations

14.5.1 Experiences

In teaching large classes, the main challenges teachers had to face related to course design, finding the right balance between substantive exploration of the topic and teaching analytic methods in sufficient breadth and depth. Including too few tools and methods might not provide students with enough new skills for their future and could also result in boredom during classes; however, teachers also had to avoid overloading students with new tools, because it takes some time to get to know how to use these tools. Here, lesson plans were selected to cover around 7–8 social topics and 4–5 tools during the semester, so that students have enough time to learn how to use these tools effectively to their own benefit.

Another challenge for teachers is motivating students during the course. Student initial responses to the unconventional content and teaching approaches were not always positive; as students had no significant prior knowledge of the social topics covered, they sometimes were not engaged from the outset, and did not participate fully in class activities. Teachers needed to find a way to break the ice and engage students' attention. Breaking the ice is probably the greatest challenge of the course, but after tackling this issue students showed much more willingness to participate actively on subsequent courses; this process can be further supported with the tasks introduced in Chap. 7 which we have found beneficial for student motivation. As a result of the introduction of interactive class activities and quizzes, students enjoyed the courses much better, collaborated more, and were more communicative during classes.

In large classes, speaking up and participating in the discussion is a challenge both for the teachers and the students. Teachers often have problems with facilitating discussion and engaging all of the students, while for students, speaking up and expressing their opinion in front of others can be stressful, especially with a younger audience, who are not often used to speaking in front of dozens or even hundreds of people. Therefore, the introduction of online quizzes, where all of the students could share their opinions anonymously, served as a good foundation for further discussion. The use of digital tools, especially mobile phones is generally not recommended in education; however our experiences with university students and high school students showed that members of generations Y and Z are not only accustomed to have their phones in their hands all the time, even in school, but welcome every opportunity to use them—even if for educational purposes. The notion that smartphones simply distract students from learning is wrong; if used well, they can not only help engage students in a topic but can also promote sharing opinions, leading to increased class participation.

In the case of Civic Statistics topics, teachers need to know about the social context, the relation between statistics and the social content, and possible civic engagement; hence at the very beginning of the courses more preparation was needed. The main challenges teachers and instructors faced during the courses were associated with finding an appropriate level of difficulty during the course, taking account of students' preliminary knowledge and interests, and constructing a course in which IT tools, statistical methods, social context and the importance of the topics covered are weighted appropriately. Teachers had to balance different course elements and stress the value of each element to the students to motivate them while learning to use new tools and discussing controversial topics.

14.5.2 Recommendations for Introducing Civic Statistics in Classes

In the previous sections of this chapter we have summarized our experiences from the implementation of Civic Statistics in different classes and the feedback received from students. Even though there was some negative feedback and difficulties experienced by both teachers and students, in general, the inclusion of civic statistics in either business education or as part of introductory statistics courses was found to be beneficial both at high school and university level.

Our recommendations for the implementation of Civic Statistics can be summarized in a few points:

- **Breaking the ice is key**: students, especially in large classes can be intimidated when it comes to speaking up in front of others.
- **Find the right balance, do not try to introduce too many societal topics and statistical tools at the same time**: the capacity of students to comprehend is limited. The aim of introducing Civic Statistics is to draw their attention to important topics and to develop their critical thinking. More generally, we aim to make students better informed and open to certain topics—so it is important not to overwhelm them with too many topics and tools during one course.
- **Find the right balance in the choice of software**: on one hand, we want to give students a feeling for what can be achieved using different packages, but on the other hand, changing from one tool to another too quickly can distract students and does not give them enough time to develop mastery over a given package.
- **Tailor the implementation to your students' needs and prior skills**: the modules, analysis tools and topics require different levels of prior knowledge on the usage of these tools and in the topics they discuss;therefore we highly recommend exploring your students' skills and also their needs in order to tailor the course to the students' knowledge and needs.
- **Do not forget the economic implications of the topics when introduced in business education**: even though the course we have described can be implemented in any field of education, as the topic of this chapter was the implementation of Civic Statistics in business education, when adopting any of the modules or even the entire course, teachers should not forget to link the topics

to students' original studies, this way ensuring that Civic Statistics becomes a valuable extension of their business-related studies.

- **Devote time in conversation with the students about the economic implications of social issues** to make explicit the relevance of each topic covered during the semester to their overall courses of study. For people new to teaching about Civic Statistics we do recommend that the first lesson is used to fine-tune the content for the semester. PCS Teaching Materials are extensive; teachers can ask students what they would be most interested in studying during the semester, to tailor the course to the group's personal needs and interests.
- **Start with relatively easier things and then proceed to more complex ones:** students learned how to discover connections between the variables and how to understand the complex background of many phenomena.

Statistics classes in business education are usually not focussed on real life problems and do not include real data. Implementing Civic Statistics in business education can sometimes be tough and challenging, and requires notable efforts from both students and teachers at the beginning, but can complement the statistical courses in such programmes nicely. A number of approaches can be taken to introducing Civic Statistics into teaching. We can expand existing statistics classes with just a handful of PCS modules and materials to engage students in certain topics, or to facilitate discussion in a large class, or we can implement the whole *Data Collection and Analysis* course, tailored to the needs and skills of students. In small classes, our experiences show that we can give students relevant complementary knowledge in societal issues which can not only help them in their further studies, but in the long run can open their eyes to real issues and problems, and make them more responsible citizens in their future life.

References

Atkinson, A., & Messy, F. (2012). *Measuring financial literacy: Results of the OECD/International Network on Financial Education (INFE) Pilot Study* (OECD Working Papers on Insurance and Private Pensions No. 15). OECD.

Bergeron, L., Schrader, D., & Williams, K. (2019). Guest editors' introduction: Unpacking the role of assessment in problem- and project-based learning. *Interdisciplinary Journal of Problem-Based Learning, 13*(2). https://doi.org/10.7771/1541-5015.1936

Brown, M. (2016). Engaging students in quantitative methods: Real questions, real data. In J. Engel (Ed.), *Promoting understanding of statistics about society. Proceedings of the roundtable conference of the International Association of Statistics Education (IASE)*. ISI/IASE.

Chance, B., Ben-Zvi, D., Garfield, J., & Medina, E. (2007). The role of technology in improving student learning of statistics. *Technology Innovations in Statistics Education, 1*(1), Article 2.

Eckleberry-Hunt, J., & Tucciarone, J. (2011). The challenges and opportunities of teaching "generation Y". *Journal of Graduate Medical Education, 3*(4), 458–461.

Klapper, L. F., Lusardi, A., & Panos, G. A. (2012). *Financial literacy and the financial crisis* (No. w17930). National Bureau of Economic Research.

Krajcik, J., & Blumenfeld, P. (2005). Project-based learning. In R. Sawyer (Ed.), *The Cambridge handbook of the learning sciences* (Cambridge handbooks in psychology) (pp. 317–334). Cambridge University Press. https://doi.org/10.1017/CBO9780511816833.020

Lusardi, A., & Mitchell, O. S. (2014). The economic importance of financial literacy: Theory and evidence. *Journal of Economic Literature, 52*(1), 5–44.

Reilly, P. (2012). Understanding and teaching generation Y. *English Teaching Forum, 50*(1), 2–11.

Ridgway, J. (2016). Implications of the data revolution for statistics education. *International Statistical Review, 84*(3), 528–549.

Ridgway, J., Nicholson, J., & Stern, D. (2017). Statistics education in a post-truth era. In *Teaching statistics in a data rich world proceedings of the satellite conference of the International Association for Statistical Education (IASE)*.

Ridgway, J., & Ridgway, R. (2019). Teaching for citizen empowerment and engagement. *Radical Statistics, 123*, 15–23.

Sox, C. B., Kline, S. F., & Crews, T. B. (2014). Identifying best practices, opportunities and barriers in meeting planning for Generation Y. *International Journal of Hospitality Management, 36*(January), 244–254.

Chapter 15
Civic Statistics for Prospective Teachers: Developing Content and Pedagogical Content Knowledge Through Project Work

Susanne Podworny ⓘ**, Daniel Frischemeier, and Rolf Biehler** ⓘ

Abstract This chapter presents and discusses the design of a course on Civic Statistics for pre-service mathematics teachers in their teacher education program. We developed this course because there is a need for all citizens of a modern country to understand data-based conclusions in the context of Civic Statistics. Suggestions for organizing a whole course and individual Civic Statistics activities are presented. At the beginning of such a course, the participants can be confronted with a first example of Civic Statistics and then, as though taking a step back, the participants' statistical knowledge can be refreshed in several sessions in order to carry out further Civic Statistics activities. A structure for Civic Statistics activities is presented on the one hand to introduce a design for implementing Civic Statistics content in classes following the principles of the Statistical Reasoning Learning Environment, and on the other for understanding the example lesson plans that can be found at CivicStatMap. We provide detailed examples of Civic Statistics activities organized both in short mini-projects and in a longer project. Teaching a course on Civic Statistics offers great potential for linking statistics contents with real and multivariate data in a wide range of academic disciplines. Specific learning goals for teaching Civic Statistics are also discussed.

Keywords Statistics education · Civic Statistics · SRLE · Critical thinking

S. Podworny (✉) · R. Biehler
Institute of Mathematics, Paderborn University, Paderborn, Germany
e-mail: podworny@math.upb.de; biehler@math.upb.de

D. Frischemeier
Faculty of Mathematics and Computer Science, University of Münster, Münster, Germany
e-mail: dafr@math.upb.de

J. Ridgway (ed.), *Statistics for Empowerment and Social Engagement*,
https://doi.org/10.1007/978-3-031-20748-8_15

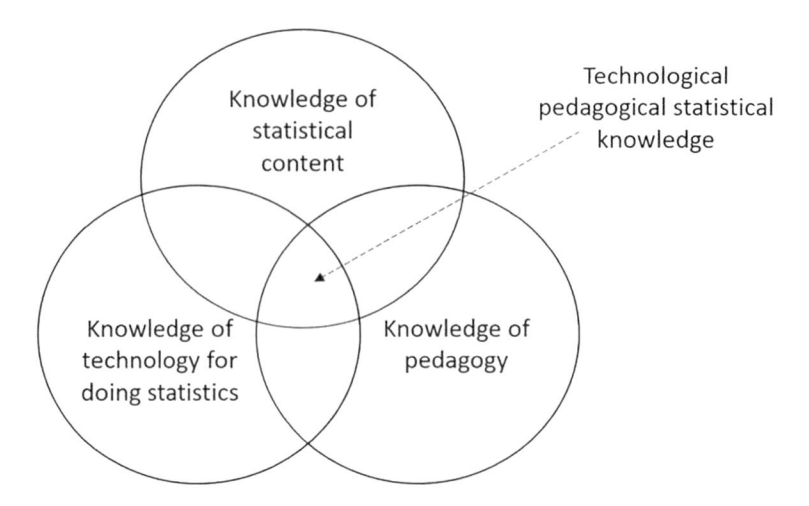

Fig. 15.1 Different knowledge aspects of statistics education (based on Groth, 2007 and Wassong & Biehler, 2010)

15.1 Introduction

Statistically literate citizens are a prerequisite for vibrant democracies (Engel, 2017). Being able to keep up with the flood of data information, dealing with problems like fabricated news in the media and on the internet, requires a confident handling of data and basic data competence. In Chap. 2, Engel and Ridgway describe how Civic Statistics can support statistical literacy and civic engagement. Nowadays, there is an increasing availability of open and big data (Teixeira, Campos, and Trostianitser offer examples in Chap. 6) e.g. on the websites of government statistics offices. Other websites, e.g. Our World in Data, offer transnational data, for example, on the COVID-19 pandemic. [1] For exploring such large and often messy data it is inevitably necessary to be able to use digital tools for data management and exploration. We refer to selected examples on how to use digital tools (such as educational software like *TinkerPlots*, *Fathom*, *CODAP*) to explore Civic Statistics data in Chap. 9. A broader overview of the use of digital tools in statistics education can be found in Biehler et al. (2013).

For developing statistical literacy and Civic Statistics competence in school, it is necessary to educate pre-service and in-service teachers appropriately. According to Mishra and Koehler (2006), we can distinguish between the different knowledge aspects of content, pedagogy, and technology. This approach has been put in concrete terms for statistics by Groth (2007) and refined by Wassong and Biehler (2010), see Fig. 15.1.

---

[1] https://ourworldindata.org/coronavirus

Since Civic Statistics itself is usually not a regular part of current statistics curricula, either at school nor university, we have designed and implemented as part on the work of the *ProCivicStat project* (PCS) and its *Call for Action* (ProCivicStat Partners, 2018) a course called "Statistical Literacy in Mathematics Classrooms" to develop the statistical content knowledge, the pedagogical and technological content knowledge, and, by combining them, the technological pedagogical content knowledge of future secondary school teachers.

Our course is implemented in the university programme for future mathematics teachers as an advanced non-obligatory course. All participants have acquired basic knowledge of elements of statistics and probability and the didactics of probability and statistics in an earlier compulsory course. The preceding course on elements of statistics and probability for pre-service junior high school teachers covers topics like data, data analysis with digital tools, distribution, variation, representation of data, and basic probability concepts, discrete probability, the law of large numbers, intuitive confidence intervals, and the simulation of probability models. The software used in the obligatory course was the German version [2] of Fathom. [3]

Civic Statistics topics are used as a motivation booster for learning statistical content knowledge by providing the immediate experience of the relevance of statistics and illustrating how statistical content knowledge and technological content knowledge open the door to a deeper understanding of complex issues that affect humanity. Multiple facets and skills are needed in order to engage with Civic Statistics as Gal, Nicholson, and Ridgway explained in Chap. 3. Many of these facets are not addressed in regular courses nor in teacher training. This chapter discusses how to deal with three separate challenges in statistics education:

1. How to teach Civic Statistics.
2. How to teach the pedagogy of teaching statistics to prospective teachers.
3. Doing both in a single course that will also spark learners' interest and motivation to teach (Civic) Statistics.

These challenges are not unique to our course nor to our university. Other educators may face them as well. There is almost no literature on or established approach to teaching Civic Statistics. This explains the experimental nature of our course. We had to develop new approaches and design new materials. Because of the experimental nature of the course we included some research and evaluation elements both in the course and in this chapter. Another approach to teaching Civic Statistics to preservice teachers is presented by Schiller and Engel in Chap. 16. However, Chap. 16 describes work with novices who presumably have never studied statistics, whereas we work with students with a stronger background in statistics. This has affected our goals and design decisions. Both Chaps. 15 and 16 complement each other and together present a range of ideas which should be of value to different audiences.

---

[2] https://www.stochastik-interaktiv.de/fathom/

[3] https://fathom.concord.org/

In our course, we followed the design based research approach and offered the class repeatedly the opportunity to test and improve its components. This chapter bridges the gap between the theoretical framework described in Part I of the book and its implementation in concrete teaching practice using tools and teaching designs discussed in Chap. 7 by Trostianitser, Teixeira, and Campos and in Chap. 9 by Frischemeier, Podworny and Biehler. Accordingly, this chapter is organized in eight sections. Section 15.2 elaborates on the goals and working style for a course on Civic Statistics. A classroom-tested structure for a course is considered in Sect. 15.3. Section 15.4 briefly presents the implementation of such a course. The PCS project team developed a design for mini-projects including lesson plans. We tested several lesson plans in our course and explain how to run a selected mini-project in Sect. 15.5 to encourage educators to design their own activities following this example. How to administer a larger activity is discussed in Sect. 15.6. In Sect. 15.7, we report some of our experiences when teaching a course on Civic Statistics. Finally, Sect. 15.8 summarizes key messages and gives recommendations on how to teach Civic Statistics.

15.2 Overview of Goals and Working Style of a Civic Statistics Course

In the following, we refer to a course consisting of 15 sessions of 90 min each. This was the situation we were faced with when designing our course "Statistical Literacy in Mathematics Classrooms", where we connect Civic Statistics issues that affect the well-being and quality of life of almost everyone with the learning of statistics in the course.

A fundamental role in the re-designed course are Civic Statistics activities that follow the principles of the Statistical Reasoning Learning Environment (SRLE) of Garfield and Ben-Zvi (2008).

SRLE principles, that are useful for a course on Civic Statistics are:

- Focusing on central statistical ideas (content).
- Using real and motivating data.
- Using classroom activities to develop students' statistical reasoning.
- Integrating the use of appropriate technological tools.
- Promoting classroom discourse.

We suggest using all these principles when designing a course on Civic Statistics.

SRLE has a double meaning in our approach: on the one hand, we use these guidelines to design activities for our participants (future secondary school teachers); on the other hand, in our course we also emphasize SRLE at a meta-level to provide our participants with guidelines on how to design teaching-learning environments themselves for their later professional lives in school.

Different working formats can be useful for enhancing the statistical content knowledge, technological content knowledge, pedagogical knowledge, and technological pedagogical statistical knowledge of future teachers. In our course, we designed sessions in which the lecturer coordinates the session and provides the participants with input concerning content knowledge and technological (pedagogical) content knowledge.

Other sessions were designed to test so-called mini-projects for one session based on SRLE, developed as lesson plans. In mini-projects, which are described in Sect. 15.4 in more detail, the participants work in pairs on a specific data set, using a specific digital tool. The use of mini-projects has two goals:

1. Participants work on mini-projects and solve the given tasks. In a course for teacher education this also means being able to adopt a learner perspective with respect to mini-projects.
2. The mini-project can be discussed from a teacher perspective in order to enhance pedagogical knowledge.

Additionally, a larger activity can be used to delve deeper into one topic—see details in Sect. 15.6. In our course, we chose the gender pay gap in Germany as a topic for a larger activity because this is an important topic in the German media every year and it is relevant in many other countries too. The German Federal Statistics Office provides a large multivariate data set with variables concerning German employees. Finding appropriate data on a meaningful topic can be a challenge (see Chap. 16), so the availability of the data set was another reason for choosing the gender pay gap as a topic.

It is also important to understand the reactions and impacts of the course on its participants. For our course, as accompanying research, we collected all the work notes and worksheets of the participants and also asked them to fill out reflection and feedback forms at the end of each session.

An overall learning goal for such a course is to foster understanding of statistical information about society. In Table 15.1, we present the learning goals of our course. We assume that these can be transferred to a different course with little effort.

15.3 Structure and Specific Content of the Course

The course structure we will describe here is based on our experiences during two actual courses that were offered. A teacher has to make different decisions when implementing Civic Statistics in a course. This includes decisions on datasets, technology, and student inquiry. All of this is connected to the design of the learning environment and to SRLE in our course.

In order to be able to pursue all the objectives set out in Table 15.1 in one course, we propose a course structure that includes different sessions. Related sessions are called a module. One module can introduce Civic Statistics and statistical literacy as one approach, another module can refresh (or establish) statistical and technological

Table 15.1 Learning goals

Learning goals for a course in Civic Statistics
in connection with the three overarching ideas (see Chap. 2)
Contexts and interpretations
• Introducing learners to selected fields related to Civic Statistics, e.g. economy, medicine, traffic, statistics about the world
• Introducing learners to the distinction between correlation and causality
• Fostering discussions about conclusions, implications, or consequences
The nature of statistics
• Exploring multivariate data sets based on suggested guiding questions and statistical questions formulated by participants themselves
• Deepening knowledge about reading and interpreting summary statistics and graphical displays (also in the sense of reading beyond data as defined by Friel et al., 2001)
• Deepening understanding of statistical concepts and constructs such as correlation and causality and Simpson's paradox
Rich, new, or uncommon methods or representations
• Introducing different technological tools for viewing or analyzing data
• Discussing innovative or complex visual data displays (like bubble charts in *Gapminder*)

Table 15.2 A proposed course structure

Module	Content
1	Introduction
2	Refreshing statistical and technological content knowledge
3	Several mini-projects on Civic Statistics
4	One (or more) larger activity
5	Concluding session

content knowledge; a third module can include working on and pedagogically discussing mini-projects. Based on our previous experience, we propose the course structure in Table 15.2.

The modules in Table 15.2 may have different lengths. Depending on the knowledge of the participants, the given numbers of sessions can be adapted by other course designers. In our course, we were faced with the need to refresh the statistical and technological content knowledge of the participants in more depth than expected when we carried out the course the first time (maybe this was due to the fact that the compulsory course the participants attended had taken place several semesters before). This resulted in four sessions for module 2. When working on the mini-projects with future mathematics teachers, we wanted: on the one hand to have them explore the activities from the perspective of a learner in order to foster a pedagogical discussion on concrete learning goals and design ideas for implementing the mini-projects in a secondary school classroom; and on the other hand, we aimed at presenting different topics, and, what is also very important for future teachers, at presenting different tools and web-applets that are freely available. Our selection of topics and tools can be seen in Table 15.3. An explanation of the

Table 15.3 Structure and content of our course as a model for other Civic Statistics courses

Number of sessions	Module	Content/example	Tool
1	Introduction	Wealth distribution in the world as a "teaser"	Graph
4	Refreshing statistical and technological content knowledge	Different data sets & examples	*Fathom*
5	Several mini-project on Civic Statistics	Statistics about the world Medicine Inequality in the world Traffic Daily life	*CODAP* *Fathom* *Gapminder* Web applets
4	One (or more) larger activity	Gender pay gap in Germany	*Fathom*
1	Concluding session		

rationales and design ideas of the different modules follows after Table 15.3 and gives suggestions for other courses.

Module 1: Introduction
The first module consists of one session. We suggest confronting the participants with a Civic Statistics activity and a rich visualization at a very early stage as a teaser for Civic Statistics. Our example was the regional composition of global wealth using data from the Global Wealth Report (Keating et al., 2013, p13).

Module 2: Refreshing Statistical and Technological Content Knowledge
Depending on the learners' knowledge, we suggest a brief revision of:

- Reading data in multivariate tables.
- The meaning of different referencing formats (percentages presented in rows, columns, cells).
- Group comparisons.
- Correlation & causation.
- Simpson's paradox.

Additionally, the technological knowledge required for a certain tool may be refreshed. For a selection of appropriate tools see Chap. 8 (*Gapminder*), Chap. 9 (*Fathom*, *TinkerPlots*, and *CODAP*), Chap. 10 (*iNZight*), and Chap. 11 (*R*).

Module 3: Several Mini-projects on Civic Statistics
A selection of contexts of public interest concerning the social and economic well-being of citizens (for examples see Chap. 2) are used in this module. Different data sets and visualization tools should be used for a variety of activities. The mini-projects aim at empowering learners to "understand statistics about society in order to support their informed participation in public discourse and evidence-informed decision processes" (Chap. 2, p. 4).

We used the following mini-projects:

- Statistics about the world with the data analysis tool *CODAP*.
- The situation of German hospitals in rural areas with a data set from the German Federal Statistics Office and the data analysis tool *Fathom*.
- Inequality in the world with the visualization tool *Gapminder*.
- German accident statistics with a free web applet from the German Federal Statistics Office.
- Daily routines of US citizens based on a free web applet from the New York Times. [4]

Several of these, as well as many other mini-projects, and additional material like our course structure can be found as classroom-tested material on our website CivicStatMap. [5]

Module 4: A Larger Project in Civic Statistics
Learners should work in more detail on one larger activity, similar to authentic project work. We propose allocating at least four sessions. Our example was exploring the gender pay gap situation in Germany with the use of *Fathom*. More details can be found in Sect. 15.6 of this chapter.

Module 5: Concluding Session
In the final session, a summing-up and a final reflection can take place.

15.4   Implementing Civic Statistic Activities: Mini-projects

There are many ways to implement the SRLE principles (discussed in Sect. 15.2) and address the learning goals (listed in Sect. 15.2). In this chapter, we discuss in detail two related but separate options, using mini-projects (this section) and using a larger activity (see Sect. 15.6). Other instructors can adapt these ideas for their own purposes and/or with their own current data sources. SRLE principles provide an appropriate framework for designing Civic Statistics activities for implementation in high school, at college level, or in teacher education. For implementing Civic Statistics activities like the ones proposed in this section some statistical content knowledge is needed as well as technological content knowledge for doing statistics with a certain tool. Either a learner has pre-knowledge in these domains, or a module on instructing or refreshing such knowledge should be preceded as proposed in our course structure (see Table 15.3).

---

[4] The New York Times' tool is no longer available, but the same data is freely available at https://flowingdata.com/2017/10/19/american-daily-routine/.

[5] https://rstudio.up.pt/shiny/users/pcs/civicstatmap.

Table 15.4 Structure for mini-projects

Phase of a mini-project	Brief description
Phase 1. Introduction	Address features of Civic Statistics (Chap. 3) concerning *context and interpretation* of the concrete mini-project's topic, starting with an eye catcher
Phase 2. What is it about & Why is it important?	Address the nature of the statistics and background information on the mini-project's topic; introduce the context of the topic
Phase 3. Why does it matter & How is it measured?	Show how the topic can relate to people's lives. How could the corresponding underlying phenomenon be explored, empirically?
Phase 4. Data & list of variables	Introduce the background of the data, their origin, and how they fit in with the topic; explore the meta-data—exactly how are these variables measured?
Phase 5. Task & analysis	Pose a leading question concerning the topic and give students time to explore the data
Phase 6. Discussion	Discuss in a whole group the findings and relate them to people's lives

15.5 How to Administer a Mini-project

Mini-projects aim at a Civic Statistics activity for one session of 90 min with the goals and working style sketched in Sect. 15.2.

There are essentially two parts in a mini-project. First, information about the context and the data is provided, and then statistical explorations are carried out based on questions provided by the instructor, in addition to participants' own ones.

We suggest a fixed structure for any mini-project as in Table 15.4.

The structure provided by Table 15.4 may be used by educators from several fields like social science, and geography. In maths, mini-projects could be based on questions involving specific statistical content. A list of data sets and a description of appropriate data analysis tools can be found in Chaps. 6 and 8 of this book. Applications of these materials and this approach for a wide range of subjects are described by Engel, Louie, and Nicholson in Chap. 18.

15.5.1 A Lesson Plan for the Mini-project

Mini-projects have been assembled as lesson plans to support teachers who want to carry out a Civic Statistics activity in their class.

In our course, we developed and tested several lesson plans. In this section, we present a sample lesson plan on the topic of inequality in the world using *Gapminder* as a tool to exemplify the stages of such a mini-project (Table 15.4). The corresponding lesson plan can be seen in Fig. 15.2 and can be found at

Co-funded by the
Erasmus+ Programme
of the European Union

Pro Civic Stat

Promoting Civic Engagement via Exploration of Evidence:
Challenges for Statistics Education

Inequalities in the world - Get to know the earth better

More than 7 billion people now live on Earth. The number is still growing every day. The gap between rich and poor and between prosperity and poverty is also widening.

The Oxfam report, for example, once again highlights the enormous discrepancy between rich and poor. One is the following press release:
https://www.oxfam.org/en/pressroom/pressreleases/2018-01-22/richest-1-percent-bagged-82-percent-wealth-created-last-year

Richest 1 percent bagged 82 percent of wealth created last year - poorest half of humanity got nothing

Published: 22 January 2018

Eighty two percent of the wealth generated last year went to the richest one percent of the global population, while the 3.7 billion people who make up the poorest half of the world saw no increase in their wealth, according to a new Oxfam report released today. The report is being launched as political and business elites gather for the World Economic Forum in Davos, Switzerland.

'Reward Work, Not Wealth' reveals how the global economy enables a wealthy elite to accumulate vast fortunes while hundreds of millions of people are struggling to survive on poverty pay.

- *Billionaire wealth has risen by an annual average of 13 percent since 2010 – six times faster than the wages of ordinary workers, which have risen by a yearly average of just 2 percent. The number of billionaires rose at an unprecedented rate of one every two days between March 2016 and March 2017.*
- *It takes just four days for a CEO from one of the top five global fashion brands to earn what a Bangladeshi garment worker will earn in her lifetime. In the US, it takes slightly over one working day for a CEO to earn what an ordinary worker makes in a year.*
- *It would cost $2.2 billion a year to increase the wages of all 2.5 million Vietnamese garment workers to a living wage. This is about a third of the amount paid out to wealthy shareholders by the top 5 companies in the garment sector in 2016.*

[...]

How can the inequalities be explained? How can we better understand the world?

With the help of statistics we can explore some patterns that appear in the growing world population and get an insight into what some of these patterns could mean to us. The data analysis tool Gapminder (http://www.gapminder.org), developed by the Swede Hans Rosling, uses interactive bubble diagrams to visualize global statistics and data collection and tries to make them easier to understand through its visualizations.

Source: https://www.oxfam.org/en/pressroom/pressreleases/2018-01-22/richest-1-percent-bagged-82-percent-wealth-created-last-year

1

Co-funded by the
Erasmus+ Programme
of the European Union

Pro Civic Stat

Promoting Civic Engagement via Exploration of Evidence:
Challenges for Statistics Education

Uncovering and recognizing inequalities in the world

ProCivicStat © - Worksheet. S.201

Daniel Frischemeier | Susanne Podworny | Rolf Biehler
dafr@math.upb.de | podworny@math.upb.de | biehler@math.upb.de
Paderborn University, Germany

1

Fig. 15.2 The first two pages of the lesson plan for the mini-project "Uncovering and recognizing inequalities in the world"

Artist: Macha Selbach, copyright reserved by Ludwigsburg University of Education for Erasmus + ProCivicStat

Fig. 15.3 The introductory cartoon for the mini-project "Uncovering and recognizing inequalities in the world"

CivicStatMap. [6] This lesson plan is available in English, German, Hungarian, and Portuguese.

15.5.1.1 Phase 1: Introduction

A mini-project may start with an eye-catcher to illustrate the content of the session. Maybe learners are not familiar with the topic or with the underlying problem. A picture at the beginning of a mini-project can serve as a way into the content and make learners aware of the underlying problem. We chose to start with cartoons because they are cognitively demanding and activating and can arouse learners' interest (Cho & Lawrence, 2014).

As an example, Fig. 15.2 shows the cartoon used for mini-project on inequalities in the world, a larger version of the cartoon can be seen in Fig. 15.3.

---

[6] See lesson plan "Uncovering and recognizing inequalities in the world" under the "Lesson plans" section on the ProCivicStat webpage at http://iase-web.org/islp/pcs or use the CivicStatMap tool there. Note that there is a student and a teacher version.

Depending on the learners' knowledge the introductory cartoon can be used for a classroom discussion making learners aware of inequality as a socially relevant topic. We suggest limiting the discussion to ten minutes.

15.5.1.2   Phase 2: "What Is the Topic of the Mini-project?" and "Why Is It Important?"

The problem to be discussed in the mini-project is introduced next including background information about the context. Civic Statistics problems have their root in specific contexts (e.g. economics, medicine, sociology) and require reflection on the meaning and implications of data and analyses for society. Therefore, it is essential for teachers to ensure that students understand and relate to the context. This is a challenge particularly for mathematics teachers who are not usually trained to moderate discussions on controversial issues in the classroom. However, this is unavoidable when using real and multivariate data. A recent media report or newspaper article related to the topic can be used to indicate the importance of the topic. The selection of reports and sources should be made appropriate to the learner group. A summary might be more suitable for younger learners but reading and discussing authentic sources can be appropriate for older learners.

In our sample mini-project, we have selected a short excerpt from the Oxfam report as shown in Fig. 15.4. Oxfam [7] is a confederation of independent organizations focusing on uncovering and working against global inequality and poverty. The main message of the excerpt and the examples are discussed with the learners. In our course, we asked an open question "What do you think?" and later "What do you understand? What don't you understand?"—and a brief discussion arose about whether the report might be true and how much a CEO might earn. The discussion was quite short. We see the reason for this in the fact that it was still a mathematics course and the participants wanted to get to what they saw as the "real problem"— i.e. the data analysis.

15.5.1.3   Phase 3: "Why Does It Matter?" and "How Is It Measured?"

Many social phenomena are very complex. By using authentic multivariate data-bases on a particular subject, learners will have a better understanding of the reality they live in. Multivariate data allow the investigation of a variety of factors or variables that may influence an observed phenomenon.

Civic Statistics content relies on civic concepts, like poverty, for example. Such a civic concept has several facets and needs to be explained. In our course, we encouraged our participants to do a keyword search for poverty and how it is measured. Wikipedia and a page from the German Federal Ministry for Economic

---

[7] www.oxfam.org

Inequalities in the world - Get to know the earth better

More than 7 billion people now live on earth. The number is still growing every day. The gap between rich and poor and between prosperity and poverty is also widening.

The Oxfam report highlights the enormous discrepancy between rich and poor.

Richest 1 percent bagged 82 percent of wealth created last year - poorest half of humanity got nothing

Published: 22 January 2018

Eighty-two percent of the wealth generated last year went to the richest one percent of the global population, while the 3.7 billion people who make up the poorest half of the world saw no increase in their wealth, according to a new Oxfam report released today. The report is being launched as political and business elites gather for the World Economic Forum in Davos, Switzerland.

https://www.oxfam.org/en/research/reward-work-not-wealth reveals how the global economy enables a wealthy elite to accumulate vast fortunes while hundreds of millions of people are struggling to survive on poverty pay.

- ***Billionaire wealth has risen*** *by an annual average of 13 percent since 2010 – six times faster than the wages of ordinary workers, which have risen by a yearly average of just 2 percent. The number of billionaires rose at an unprecedented rate of one every two days between March 2016 and March 2017.*
- ***It takes just four days*** *for a CEO from one of the top five global fashion brands to earn what a Bangladeshi garment worker will earn in her lifetime. In the US, it takes slightly over one working day for a CEO to earn what an ordinary worker makes in a year.*
- ***It would cost $2.2 billion a year*** *to increase the wages of all 2.5 million Vietnamese garment workers to a living wage. This is about a third of the amount paid out to wealthy shareholders by the top 5 companies in the garment sector in 2016.*

(...)

Fig. 15.4 The introductory text for the mini-project "Uncovering and recognizing inequalities in the world"

Cooperation and Development [8] were finally selected for discussion. We followed the definition of the World Bank [9] which defines extreme poverty as living on less

---

[8] https://www.bmz.de/de/service/glossar/A/armut.html

[9] https://www.worldbank.org/en/topic/poverty

> **How can the inequalities be explained? How can we better understand the world?**
> With the help of statistics, we can explore some patterns that appear in the growing world population and get an insight into what some of these patterns could mean to us. The data analysis tool Gapminder (http://www.gapminder.org), developed by the Swede Hans Rosling, uses interactive bubble diagrams to visualize global statistics and data collection and tries to make them easier to understand through its visualizations.

Fig. 15.5 Introducing *Gapminder* for the mini-project "Uncovering and recognizing inequalities in the world"

than US\$1.90 per day, and moderate poverty as less than US\$ 3.10 per day. This is a definition on absolute numbers. In contrast, the German poverty line refers to people living in relative poverty. The *poor* are people in Germany who earn less than 40% of the median income. For some participants, it seemed to be a new insight that measuring poverty is not easy, and is measured differently in different countries.

In our mini-project, we briefly introduced the notion that statistics can help in uncovering inequalities and that software like *Gapminder* can be used as a support as expressed in the text in Fig. 15.5, because *Gapminder* already includes the measurement and comparison of different concepts like poverty, and appropriate data has already been collected. This makes *Gapminder* a very good exploration tool for examining statistical and historical data about the development of the countries of the world (Kovacs, Kazar, and Kuruczleki give more details on using *Gapminder* in class—see Chap. 8). *Gapminder* has several features and one of them uses a bubble visualization tool that can lead to a better understanding of social and economic phenomena.

15.5.1.4 Phase 4: Data and List of Variables

With reference to a specific context the underlying data are of central importance. It is therefore essential to understand the metadata—where are the data from, and exactly what is being measured? In *Gapminder*, the data source of every variable can be found by clicking on the variable's question mark.

Because there are several concepts like poverty, income, birth rate, etc. implemented in *Gapminder* we decided not to explain each one before the analysis. Instead, we set learners the task of understanding each concept when it is used in the exploration.

Considering the datasets in *Gapminder*, there are more than 500 indicators organized into several main categories. The *Gapminder* documentation [10] describes

---

[10] https://www.gapminder.org/data/documentation/

the methods, sources, and data used. The data itself are made available via Excel files, and can be downloaded.

If a data set is provided within the mini-project, we recommend that students be given a list of variables with short explanations for each variable.

In the case of *Gapminder*, a list of variables can be found [11] where each variable is described and linked to its source.

15.5.1.5   Phase 5: Task and Analysis

We suggest posing a leading question to guide the analysis accompanied by several sub-questions to structure the data analysis. The first sub-question should make learners think about the context before they start on the data analysis. A next sub-question asks about what learners have not understood in the data. This can be clarified at a very early stage together with other students or by the teacher and is especially necessary when working with a complex software package like *Gapminder*. Next, several sub-questions follow from guided to more open questions and aim at several aspects concerning the leading question. For example, we set tasks like "Explore whether there is a relationship between *life expectancy* and *income per capita*". Additionally, it might be fruitful to let learners pose and answer their own questions so that questions arising individually can be answered during the analysis. In the end, conclusions based on the findings concerning the leading question should be summarized. Each analysis should end with a critical reflection on the findings and the data and what the findings mean for one's own life.

In our sample mini-project, we pose as a leading question *What insight into the world's inequality can you gain from this data and using the Gapminder tool?* We emphasize the importance of learners posing their own questions concerning the content of our mini-projects and focus therefore on this part of the mini-projects.

Sub-questions for the participants in the mini-project on inequality can be found in Fig. 15.6.

An additional aspect when working on the mini-projects can be to use not just the given materials such as the data and the tool. Other sources of information may also be used when questions arise. In the example of the mini-project on inequality, this could be done, for example, by using the links in *Gapminder* to get further information about the data sources and backgrounds. Also, a keyword search in current newspaper reports on the relevant content, here *inequality*, is a strategy that can also be addressed in a mini-project, for example as a task for homework.

---

[11] https://www.gapminder.org/data/

1. Who do you think could be interested in this data?
2. Which variables are used in the tool? Is there anything you don't know about the concept or context of this data? Are unfamiliar technical terms used (statistical terms, operationalization of variables, data quality, etc.)? Ask 2-3 questions to help you better understand this data and answer them here.
3. The main question of this data set is: What insight into the world's inequality can you gain from this data and using the Gapminder tool? Try to find an answer to this question using suitable graphical representations and statistical calculations. The following aspects can be taken into account:

   – First, explain exactly what the variables of the following tasks mean.
   – Explore whether there is a relationship between life expectancy and income per capita (GDP/capita in $/year adjusted for inflation & prices). What do you notice?
   – Explore whether there is a relationship between CO_2 emissions (CO_2 per capita, metric tons per person) and per capita income (income per person, GDP/capita in $/year adjusted for inflation & prices). What do you notice?
   – Can you see a pattern or trend in the former two explorations from 1950 to the most recent date (2018)? If so, which ones?

4. Ask your own statistical questions (at least three) about the world population, then answer them using the data set and the tool.
5. What can be said about your insights into the world based on the data? Summarize your findings in writing, including suitable graphs.
6. Now take a critical stance. At which point can you critically question the data, your analyses or your evaluations? What implications do the findings have for you?

Fig. 15.6 Questions for the mini-project "Uncovering and recognizing inequalities in the world"

15.5.1.6 Phase 6: Discussing Findings in a Plenary

The final step of a mini-project should be a whole-class discussion. Selected findings concerning the leading question are presented. Additional sources of information can be discussed and questions that have arisen clarified. If there is enough time, selected self-generated questions and corresponding explorations can be presented. The benefit of this for learners can be for them to recognize once again the multivariate nature of the data. Third, a discussion on the aspect of *engagement and action* (cf. the conceptual model for Civic Statistics, Chap. 2) should conclude the session. The final question of the mini-project can be a starting point for such a discussion, while the relevance for society and social policies as well as learners' attitudes can be discussed in a final stage too, by referring back to the first question of the analysis.

Table 15.5 Structure for a larger activity

Phase of the project	Brief description
Introduction	Discuss background information, read and discuss newspaper/media articles related to the topic, discuss concepts like adjusted and unadjusted pay gap, introduce the data with its variables Scope: at least 1 session
Data analysis	Use a familiar tool for data analysis, give hints on how to explore the data from several perspectives, prepare results in a presentation Scope: at least 2 sessions
Presentation	Present and discuss findings and relate to people's lives Scope: at least 1 session

In our course, the plenary session at the end of the mini-project consisted of three short presentations by participants and a short discussion on them. The first participant presented selected findings on the given questions/tasks (No. 3 in Fig. 15.6). The other two presented additional findings related to two self-formulated questions (No. 4 in Fig. 15.6). A very short discussion (due to time restrictions) on the implications for everyone in the room concluded the activity.

With respect to our course, we discussed possible application scenarios for school lessons for this mini-project, together with difficulties that might be expected to arise for students.

15.6 How to Conduct a Larger Project in Civic Statistics

A larger activity is meant to delve deeper into a certain topic for a few hours. Several aspects can be explored to get a better understanding of the multivariate phenomena associated with Civic Statistics and to acquire knowledge on relevant content as well as deepening central statistical ideas.

We suggest a fixed structure of several sessions for a larger activity as in Table 15.5.

We present "gender pay gap in Germany" as an example of a larger project to show how to design and run such an activity. A brief overview [12] of the German gender pay gap project and student worksheets can be found at CivicStatMap that is similar to the following description from our course.

We chose the topic of gender pay gap because in Germany, as well as in other countries, the pay gap between men and women is an annually recurring topic in the media. Our example of a larger activity on the gender pay gap in Germany is the highlight of the course and consists of four sessions (each 90 min). Every year, German newspapers report about the gender pay gap in Germany pointing out that

---

[12] See "Overview for project: Gender Pay Gap" under the "Lesson plans" section on the ProCivicStat webpage at http://iase-web.org/islp/pcs.

men earn about 23% more on average than women. Young adults, like the participants of our course, should acquire deeper knowledge on this topic. The goal was to identify additional factors (e.g. age or profession) that influence the pay gap by analysing official data from the German Federal Statistics Office.

Data on the gender pay gap is available for many other countries as well, e.g. from national statistical offices, from Eurostat, or OECD which reports annually on the gender pay gap in many countries. We encourage all readers to look for national data.

15.6.1 Introductory Session for a Larger Project

For the first session, select an actual newspaper article to introduce the topic and discuss it with the participants. Second, present the data and the background information about the data. The data for a large activity should originate from official sources (e.g. national statistics offices, Eurostat, etc.). In our case we use a sample of the income structure survey by the German Federal Statistics Office of all German employees, which contains about 60,000 cases with variables such as gender, wage per month, region, type of employment, age, etc.

A reading and research assignment for the gender pay gap in Germany includes background information on the context, and on the data, and relates to recent media articles. Participants familiarise themselves with the topic based on the literature provided and internet research. The dossier [13] "Pay Inequality between Women and Men in Germany" from the Federal Ministry for Family Affairs, Senior Citizens, Women and Young People is given to the participants together with the metadata for the variables. In this dossier, participants get some information about the situation of pay inequality from the perspective of the Federal Ministry and learn about the definition and distinction between the adjusted and unadjusted gender pay gap. Besides this, they are already reading about the first partial explanations of wage inequality between female and male employees in Germany—for example, women are missing in certain professions with higher average salaries, or missing at the top of the career ladder, or interrupt and/or reduce their working time for family reasons. If these explanations are taken into account, there still remains a (smaller) difference between men and women, which is the adjusted pay gap. Both the partial explanations and the adjusted pay gap are significant and give directions for possible social changes to further reduce the gender pay gap. The analysis of the data also serves to help understand how the partial explanations come about.

The metadata on the income structure survey provide information on the survey procedure and the individual variables that have been surveyed, so that students can

---

[13] https://www.bmfsfj.de/blob/94442/efbd528467e361882848c23486fcc8d8/pay-ine-quality-data.pdf

A) The following questions should be answered in writing in about five sentences.
  - What is the unadjusted gender pay gap?
  - What is the adjusted gender pay gap?
  - What causes are listed for the gender pay gap in Germany in the dossier "Pay Inequality between Women and Men in Germany"?

B) Read the metadata on the income structure earnings survey and familiarise yourself with the data set! The questions are for your orientation and do not have to be answered in writing.
  - How was the data collected?
  - Which variables does the data set contain?
  - How are the variables operationalized?

C) How is the gender pay gap in Germany portrayed in the media? Collect three different newspaper/internet articles and briefly summarize the core message for each article.

Fig. 15.7 Tasks for the introductory session on the gender pay gap project

start exploring the data in the next session. Tasks for the reading assignment can be seen in Fig. 15.7.

15.6.2 Data Analysis Sessions for a Larger Project

In the next (at least) two sessions, the participants are introduced to the data set and a data analysis tool. Doing data explorations, interpreting data and combining all findings in a presentation are important ingredients for these sessions.

The task for the gender pay gap data analysis with a sample topic (here: age) can be seen in Fig. 15.8. From our past experiences we know that exploring a large multivariate data set, creating meaningful representations in *Fathom* and applying useful functions are a challenging task for the participants. For this reason, we structured the task and gave additional assistance for the use of *Fathom*. The task requires a variable (age) to function as a starting point for the analysis. Several additional recommendations are given to guide the analysis. To include other variables in the analysis, we suggested generating and answering additional questions. Other suggestions offer assistance with *Fathom*. Students' findings have to be presented in the last session, so a proposal for structuring the presentation ends the task.

Corresponding worksheets for the different topics can be found at CivicStatMap.

We suggest dividing participants into groups of 3–4 for the data exploration. Each group explores the data according to a research question they have chosen themselves. The following variables can be used as a starting point for exploring different influences on the pay gap between men and women:

Task

Investigate the influence of age on the differences in earnings between women and men. Investigate the data set from this perspective and work out to what extent differences in earnings are caused by age. Also, examine which other factors related to this aspect influence the differences in earnings.

Create various graphs and concise descriptions that you can present to your classmates in a PowerPoint presentation.

Additional help
  — Formulate question(s). For example, to what extent is there a noticeable relationship between gender and the two variables of age and hourly wage? The articles read last week can help you to find additional questions.
  — Assistance for the research using Fathom: identify characteristics relevant to your topic using the list of variables. Create different representations in Fathom to find out with which representation you can   best   answer   your   questions. Useful functions can be: the filter function (filters can be activated and defined by right-clicking on the graph), converting the distribution form to boxplot, trying out different class divisions in histograms, creating axis links, categorising numerical characteristics by means of the transform command,...

Presentation

You should present your results to your course members using presentation software. The presentation should have the following structure:

1. Introduction
2. A short introduction of the relevant variables
3. Presentation of the questions
4. Presentation of the meaningful graphs to answer the questions, each with a description ("What is shown in the graphs?") and interpretation ("What does this mean in relation to my question?")
5. Discussion/Questions from the plenum

Fig. 15.8 Tasks for the work sessions on the gender pay gap project

- Age. [14]
- Economy branch. [15]

---

[14] See "Gender Pay Gap in Germany: Aspect Age" under the "Lesson plans" section on the ProCivicStat webpage at http://iase-web.org/islp/pcs

[15] See "Gender Pay Gap in Germany: Aspect Economy branch" under the "Lesson plans" section on the ProCivicStat webpage at http://iase-web.org/islp/pcs

- Region. [16]
- Job position. [17]
- Occupation group. [18]

The adjusted pay gap investigation considers many of these factors simultaneously. This makes the gender pay gap a truly multivariate issue. By identifying different factors and setting them as a starting point for data analysis, we simplify the task for the learners. This enables the participants to better understand partial explanations better and gives them easier access to data analysis. Later on, they can address the multivariate character of the data.

15.6.3 Presentation Session for a Larger Project

The presentation of findings is an important aspect of the larger activity. Here the participants have to use and focus on central statistical ideas to create meaningful visualizations, short descriptions and interpretations in order to communicate their findings to their classmates. We suggest that, in a final session, the results, conclusions and open questions are compiled to create a more holistic picture of the situation of the context of the activity, i.e. understanding the gender pay gap in Germany. A concluding discussion of overarching aspects of the activity should conclude the activity.

15.7 Experiences from Our Course

The teaching of Civic Statistics in a university course was quite a challenge for us because of its multifaceted nature, as outlined by the 11 aspects of engagement and action, knowledge and enabling process—illustrated above and in Chap. 3. Having participants engage with real and multivariate data and explorations of socially meaningful issues involves several potential benefits and several challenges. Some are discussed in this section.

We asked our participants at the end of each Civic Statistics mini-project and after the larger project activity to reflect on the activity by submitting a brief evaluation form. A simple formative evaluation tool with the task of rating three statements ("I have understood today's activity very well", "I liked the content of today's activity

---

[16] See "Gender Pay Gap in Germany: Aspect Region" under the "Lesson plans" section on the ProCivicStat webpage at http://iase-web.org/islp/pcs

[17] See "Gender Pay Gap in Germany: Aspect Job position" under the "Lesson plans" section on the ProCivicStat webpage at http://iase-web.org/islp/pcs

[18] See "Gender Pay Gap in Germany: Aspect Occupation group" under the "Lesson plans" section on the ProCivicStat webpage at http://iase-web.org/islp/pcs

On a scale from 1 (does not apply at all) to 7 (fully applies), rate the following statement: "I have understood today's activities very well."

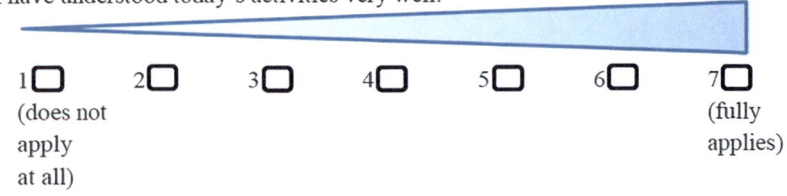

1 ☐   2 ☐   3 ☐   4 ☐   5 ☐   6 ☐   7 ☐
(does not apply at all)   (fully applies)

Fig. 15.9 Scale for cognitive self-assessment

Table 15.6 Evaluation of sessions 6–14 in the winter semester 2017/2018 (for n = 11 participants)

Session	Self-assessment (mean)	Affective attitude (mean)	Potential for classroom use (mean)
6	6	6.3	5.9
7	6.5	4.2	4
8	5.8	5.2	4.4
9	6.6	5.6	5
10	6.2	5	3.6
11–14	5.9	5.9	4.9

very much", "The contents of today's activity have a great potential for classroom use") was administered. This was a self-assessment of a small number of participants and was not intended as a systematic study. The evaluations show how teachers can gauge not only students' reactions to Civic Statistics tasks as learners, but also, because they are prospective teachers, how they view the educational value of the tasks. We share the impressions of our participants here, as it may prepare readers to what may transpire when they try similar activities. The mini-projects and the gender pay gap activity were evaluated by all participants (n = 11).

The three statements were rated on a 7 point Lickert scale. The first statement concerning a cognitive self-assessment can be seen in Fig. 15.9.

The second statement "I liked the contents of today's activity very much" concerned the affective attitude of the participants and the third statement "The content of today's activity has a great potential for classrooms use" reflected participants' opinions about the potential of the activity for classroom use. The results of the evaluation are displayed in Table 15.6.

The 11 participants rated their understanding of the different activities quite highly. The lowest rating for the mini-project about inequalities in the world in Session 8 was mainly explained by the participants in terms of the language barrier because English was not their native language. The highest ratings were given to the mini-project about the situation of hospitals in Germany in Session 7 and to the German accident statistics in Session 9. Both sessions included data with only a few variables.

The participants had the strongest affective response to Session 6, which explored statistics about the world (with the use of *CODAP*), and to the gender pay gap activity (Sessions 11–14). The mini-project about the situation of hospitals in Session 7 was approved the least with a mean of 4.2, which is still a good rating.

The highest potential for classroom use is seen by the participants in the mini-project on statistics about the world in Session 6 and, with some distance from the mini-project about German accident statistics in Session 9. Four participants wrote in their explanation that the accident statistics are very well suited as an introduction to statistics. Both, the hospital situation (Session 7) in Germany and the daily routines of US citizens in Session 10 were explained by many participants as not suitable or interesting for German high school students and therefore had quite low ratings for potential classroom use. The gender pay gap activity was evaluated positively throughout.

Overall, the analysis of the evaluation shows that the 11 participants showed a thoroughly positive attitude towards the mini-projects and the gender pay gap activity.

15.8   Conclusions and Recommendations

The following section is based on our experiences in both implementations of the course. Interpreting Civic Statistics graphs based on real and multivariate data was a complex activity that involved many challenges. Participants experienced problems in interpreting a complex Civic Statistics graph in the first session, perhaps because we needed almost all of the time to describe and interpret the introductory graph. We had estimated that this would take only about 30 min. But, after refreshing their knowledge in the second module, it became clear that the participants were quite capable of exploring Civic Statistics issues in real multivariate data and using digital tools in activities in every session. The positive affective attitude of the participants concerning the mini-projects (see Table 15.6) was frequently followed by additional explanations like "The use of real data was motivating for me" or "I like working with today's tools very much!".

The use of educational software like *Fathom* for the data analysis of multivariate data, as in the gender pay gap activity, allowed participants to deal with complex data and use the data to answer their own questions. Project-based work on Civic Statistics content fostered high motivation and led to interesting results and more differentiated dispositions on the part of participants. For example, most of our participants were not familiar with the terms *unadjusted* and *adjusted gender pay gap* at the beginning of the course (we asked that as a question at the beginning). At the end of the gender pay gap activity they discussed very intensively how to deal with the newly gained insights and what should be changed in society to reduce the gap.

Table 15.7 Take-away messages from our experience: What to consider when designing a course for future secondary school teachers

No.	Recommendation
1	Identify the teacher professional knowledge you want to develop and take this into close consideration when selecting your activities and tasks
2	It is important to refresh participants' knowledge on statistics and technology at the start
3	Find appropriate examples and data for different statistical activities in the CivicStatMap
4	Use SRLE principles for designing the mini-projects and also for implementing the lesson plans in the classroom
5	Use activities like the mini-projects for providing participants with the opportunity to work on well-organized small activities with different contexts, data, and digital tools
6	Issues and concepts like poverty, unemployment etc. are complex and need a lot of attention. Mathematics teachers need to read around the topic before they teach it, so they are prepared for a range of ideas (and know about other data sources)
7	Use larger activities like the gender pay gap activity in which all competencies already gained can be applied, further elaborated, and integrated
8	Support participants in generating statistical research questions by providing a selection of "guiding" questions for their analysis during the activities
9	Support participants with technical issues when they use *Fathom* or other statistical tools. Provide them with short manuals for specific and basic commands (e.g. the filter function)
10	Schedule enough time to discuss the potential for use of the activities in the classrooms

Based on our experience, Table 15.7 lists ten recommendations regarding issues that other course designers may want to consider when designing their own course involving Civic Statistics activities.

This chapter presented a design for carrying out Civic Statistics based on mini-projects and larger activities. This, together with Chap. 16, shows how Civic Statistics can be used in a course in teacher training. The main findings are that students in teacher education are quite capable of exploring Civic Statistics issues using real and multivariate data and utilizing digital tools while working on these activities (this is reinforced by the presentations discussed in Chap. 16, where the participants show a high level of commitment to project-based independent work). Here, the evaluations show the positive attitudes of the participants towards the contexts and the potential of the different activities for use in the classroom. However, there are also challenges. Essential challenges are the use of the statistics content and the corresponding link to Civic Statistics. It is a major task to find authentic data which can illustrate core statistical ideas, such as Simpson's paradox, and where students can learn fundamental statistical ideas (such as correlation).

Using real and multivariate data on socially relevant issues in the classroom is the concern of this book. Nevertheless, time and space in the mathematics or social science curriculum are limited, and introducing Civic Statistics content might be seen as a burden on curriculum time. The use of mini-projects or a larger activity as proposed above shows a way to integrate statistics content in a Civic Statistics context by using elements of the Statistical Reasoning Learning Environment of

Garfield and Ben-Zvi (2008) in a project-based environment and over a short period of time.

Further development or integration of individual (mini-)projects in mathematics classes or in other subjects (e.g. politics, social sciences, geography—see Chap. 18 for examples) is possible and desirable using the suggested structure presented in Sect. 15.5.

All in all, working with Civic Statistics makes it not only necessary to deal with statistics content but also motivates learners to do so. A course focusing on Civic Statistics should, therefore, be an essential component of statistics education in schools and universities.

References

Biehler, R., Ben-Zvi, D., Bakker, A., & Makar, K. (2013). Technology for enhancing statistical reasoning at the school level. In M. A. Clements, A. J. Bishop, C. Keitel-Kreidt, J. Kilpatrick, & F. K.-S. Leung (Eds.), *Third international handbook of mathematics education* (pp. 643–689). Springer.

Cho, H., & Lawrence, G. D. (2014). Cartoons in middle school classrooms. *Mathematics Teaching in the Middle School, 20*(5), 304–307.

Engel, J. (2017). Statistical literacy for active citizenship: A call for data science education. *Statistics Education Research Journal, 16*(1), 44–49.

Friel, S. N., Curcio, F. R., & Bright, G. W. (2001). Making sense of graphs: Critical factors influencing comprehension and instructional implications. *Journal for Research in Mathematics Education, 32*(2), 124–158.

Garfield, J., & Ben-Zvi, D. (2008). *Developing students' statistical reasoning. Connecting research and teaching practice*. Springer.

Groth, R. E. (2007). Toward a conceptualization of statistical knowledge for teaching. *Journal for Research in Mathematics Education, 38*(5), 427–437.

Keating, G., O'Sullivan, M., Shorrocks, A., Davies, J. B., Lluberas, R., & Koutsoukis, A. (2013). *Global wealth report 2013.*. Credit Suisse Research Institute.

Mishra, P., & Koehler, M. (2006). Technological pedagogical content knowledge: A framework for teacher knowledge. *The Teachers College Record, 108*(6), 1017–1054.

ProCivicStat Partners. (2018). *Engaging civic statistics: A call for action and recommendations*. A product of the ProCivicStat project. Online: http://iase-web.org/islp/pcs

Wassong, T., & Biehler, R. (2010). A model for teacher knowledge as a basis for online courses for professional development of statistics teacher. In C. Reading (Ed.), *Data and context in statistics education: Towards an evidence-based society. Proceedings of the eighth international conference on teaching statistics, Ljubljana, Slovenia*. International Statistical Institute.

Chapter 16
Implementing Civic Statistics in Mathematics Teacher Education

Achim Schiller and Joachim Engel ⓘ

Abstract This chapter describes and reflects on a course for prospective secondary school mathematics teachers designed to provide improved skills and confidence in understanding statistics about trends and current or projected changes in society. It outlines a new type of introductory statistics course which focuses on Civic Statistics. The course aims at developing statistical content knowledge with regard to Civic Statistics, critical thinking, cross-disciplinarity, contextual knowledge as well as subject-matter related pedagogical competencies, and technological competencies. A specific challenge is to get students majoring in mathematics engaged with socio-politically sensitive and controversial issues, and to get them to reflect about these topics from an instructional and educational perspective. A distinct part of the course is a unit called "Critical questioning of data-based statements in the media" which focuses on deconstructing media headlines by evaluating claims using the original data and information about the research design. The course design is based on principles associated with the Statistical Reasoning Learning Environment (Garfield & Ben-Zvi. Teaching Statistics 31(3):72–77, 2009) as well as the recommendations of the ProCivicStat Partners (Engaging civic statistics: A call for action and recommendations. A product of the ProCivicStat Project. https://iase-web.org/islp/pcs, 2018), and is characterised by the use of authentic multivariate data for Civic Statistics in teaching.

Keywords Civic statistics · Teacher preparation · SRLE · Assessment · Professional development · Critical thinking

A. Schiller · J. Engel (✉)
Ludwigsburg University of Education, Ludwigsburg, Germany
e-mail: engel@ph-ludwigsburg.de

© Springer Nature Switzerland AG 2022
J. Ridgway (ed.), *Statistics for Empowerment and Social Engagement*,
https://doi.org/10.1007/978-3-031-20748-8_16

16.1 Introduction

Few high school teachers in mathematics or social science receive any training on how to teach statistics. As a result, when reaching the statistics parts of a national curriculum, teachers stay within their comfort zone and overemphasise a narrow range of statistical techniques and computations (mathematics) or fail to engage with statistical ideas at all (social science). In particular, they pay too little attention to working with and understanding multivariate data that are characteristic of social trends, or to the analysis and interpretation of and communication about the meaning of such data (Batanero et al., 2011; Hannigan et al., 2013; Ridgway, 2015). Hence this chapter addresses issues of teacher preparation and professional development. This chapter describes and reflects on a new type of course, designed for prospective secondary school teachers to provide skills and confidence in understanding statistics about trends, gaps and current or projected changes in society, based on the conceptual framework of Civic Statistics described in Part I of this book. The course faces the three-fold challenge of combining statistical and socio-political learning with providing a background in the pedagogy of teaching statistics. It has been tested with students preparing to be mathematics secondary teachers who have not taken a statistics class before. Therefore, the course does not assume any knowledge in statistics beyond high school, hence may also be suitable for students majoring in fields other than mathematics. In contrast, in Chap. 15 Podworny, Frischemeier and Biehler describe a course in Civic Statistics designed for prospective secondary mathematics teachers who *have* attended a university level class in statistics and probability previously. While providing an account of the whole course, we focus in this chapter on a topic of general educational interest: the critical reception and deconstruction of statistical messages in the media. We did not find a learning unit that takes into account the needs of today's informed society by combining statistical and socio-political learning with critical thinking as part of mathematics teacher preparation, on which we could build. Therefore, this chapter describes the design of an innovative experimental course.

In this chapter, after introducing the "autonomous citizen" as a desirable model ("Mündigkeit") in Sect. 16.2, we report on the goals (Sect. 16.3), pedagogy (Sect. 16.4) and content (Sect. 16.5) of a course on Civic Statistics for 2nd year students preparing to be secondary school mathematics teachers. A focus is on two distinct elements of the course: the module about critical reflection on data-based statements in the media (Sect. 16.6) and assessment via a video project (Sect. 16.7). The final section concludes with a summary of key messages taken from teaching this course.

16.2   Background: The Autonomous Citizen

In today's society, as highlighted in Part I of this book, knowledge, information and communication are essential components of almost all areas of everyday life. The evaluation of data-based information and the resulting decisions are essential. However, our society is far from being homogeneous with respect to the quality and trustworthiness of received and perceived information. There is a huge gap between knowledge and ignorance, and between judgement and prejudice, which makes our societies vulnerable to populism. The best remedy for unconscious acceptance and obtuseness is an enlightened, critical citizenry who "dares to think for themselves" (Kant), are in charge of themselves and act independently. The German word "Mündigkeit" summarises a collection of qualities that enable an individual to adapt to social demands for personal responsibility (Dammer & Wortmann, 2014). *Mündigkeit* [1] or personal autonomy requires maturity, includes self-determination that goes beyond dependence on experts (Böhme, 2010), and is a central goal of schooling, as expressed in many preambles to public policy statements on the goals of education. *Mündigkeit* requires maturity, knowledge and critical thinking. In the twenty-first century, this also includes statistical thinking.

In order to articulate knowledge, to support positions with evidence, to test conjectures or to estimate probabilities in situations of uncertainty and risk, the capacity to explore and understand data is indispensable. In order for people to obtain information and to evaluate its quality so as to be able to develop sound and independent opinions, media literacy is also required. Precisely because people in their private and public lives are repeatedly challenged to make decisions that go beyond their area of actual knowledge and experience, it is important for them to learn how to obtain the necessary information, to ask questions, in order to better understand issues and to make evidence-informed decisions (Lengnink et al., 2013).

Therefore, *autonomous* citizens also need a sense of orientation in view of the complexity of the modern data-based information jungle, along with some basic knowledge about the mechanisms of opinion formation in a democratic state (Gramm, 2010). Autonomous citizens are aware that images, political views, opinions, assessments and judgements are essentially influenced by the media. This implies that not only in pictorial reports, but also in headlines and written or spoken news, emotional evaluations are often communicated in addition to the bare facts, which are more or less unconsciously received by the audience or readership.

Citizen rarely access original data sources. As a result of widespread access to social media everyone is able to disseminate images, political views, opinions, assessments and judgements, regardless of whether they are based on facts or not. So-called *alternative facts* (translation: lies by politicians) and *fake news*

---

[1] For purposes of readability in the following the term "personal autonomy" for "Mündigkeit" and "*autonomous*" for "mündig" will be used, although the German terms are somewhat broader in meaning.

(translation: politicians' attempts to discredit authentic sources) are threats to an open and free society.

In public discourse, statements are increasingly backed up with data in order to reinforce them. This also increases the demands on autonomous citizens to make sense of and deconstruct data-based statements. Himmelmann (2011) lists the following skills, among others, as democratic competences: information reception, understanding, interpreting, reasoning, reflecting and evaluating. He explicitly includes the handling of statistics and graphs. In today's information society, therefore, personal *autonomy* includes increasingly dealing with information and reasoning involving statistically backed arguments. Enlightened citizens need statistical competences in order to be able to evaluate statistical information critically. These competences are as essential as maturity, freedom and independence, personal responsibility, the use of reason, and the ability to judge and reflect, if citizens are to participate in democratic decision-making processes.

> Personal *autonomy* includes dealing with information and reasoning involving statistically backed arguments. Enlightened citizens need statistical competences in order to be able to evaluate statistical information critically.

16.3 Goals of the Course

This chapter describes and reflects on a course for prospective secondary school mathematics teachers designed to provide improved skills and confidence in understanding statistics about trends and current or projected changes in society. The course aims at developing statistical and pedagogical content knowledge with regard to Civic Statistics, critical thinking, and cross-disciplinary context knowledge as well as subject-matter related pedagogical competences and technological competences. The overriding goal of the course is for students to learn how to process and reflect on statistical information about topics relevant for society and to develop their capacity for evidence-informed decision making as responsible citizens—in short, to foster their skills in Civic Statistics. A particular challenge is to get students majoring in mathematics to engage in socio-politically sensitive and controversial issues and reflect on these topics from an instructional and educational perspective.

As future teachers, the students should reflect on the use of the materials and the potential of using multivariate socially relevant data in secondary education. A strong interest in socially relevant topics (economic inequality, migration, climate change) and in particular their use in mathematics teaching cannot be assumed and must first be aroused. Mathematics teaching should take on the task of conveying the technical basics and their implementation for the verification of data-based statements. Key components include:

- *Reading and interpreting parameters in socially relevant contexts:* The students know the concepts underpinning common parameters (e.g., arithmetic mean or median, dispersion, correlation), their definition and properties, know about their strengths and weaknesses as measures, and thus can assess conclusions based on these indicators within the social context.
- *Reading and interpreting statistical representations in socially relevant contexts:* Students know the strengths and weaknesses of common statistical representations and are able to assess possible conclusions while taking into account possible misleading representations and are also able to apply these competences to dynamic interactive representations.
- *Understanding concepts associated with socially relevant indicators:* In order to be able to assess and evaluate developments within society, knowledge of socially relevant indicators is essential, especially if there are different operationalizations possible, as in the definition and measurement of (say) *poverty* or *unemployment.*
- *Getting to know important statistical concepts:* Using motivating examples, students learn important statistical concepts for evaluating data-based statements, illustrated by "correlation is not causality", "percentages of what?", as well as possible sources of error and knowledge of their importance within data-based argumentations.
- *Evaluating and reflecting on the data:* Important for an evidence-based assessment are key non-technical questions such as: Whose story is told here? By whom and why is it told? What evidence is presented? Is the source credible?
- *Evaluating statistical conclusions:* By means of a critical review of the conclusions, students evaluate the adequacy of the underlying model, review the possibility of other, alternative explanations for the observed phenomena and decide whether the conclusions obtained are consistent with the evidence.
- *Asking relevant statistical questions:* An important competence for statistically literate citizens is to ask relevant statistical questions. Civic Statistics issues rarely have a clear cut yes-or-no answer. Often times asking good questions within the investigative process may be more conducive to success than obtaining quick answers.
- *Researching relevant information:* The students know which information concerning statistics or data-based statements is relevant for an evidence-informed evaluation and are able to research more information with the help of technical support.
- *Reflecting on the use of technology and media:* The students reflect on the added value of technology and other media as tools to communicate statistical information to the public.
- *Communicating statistical concepts and results to non-experts in a clear and understandable way:* Communication about socially relevant subjects in schools or public discourses may necessitate breaking ideas down into their basic elements (didactic reductions).

Table 16.1 Goals of the course in their relation to the tools and facets of Civic Statistics

Meaning for Society and policy
• Read and interpret parameters in socially relevant contexts
• Read and interpret statistical representations in socially relevant contexts
• Understand concepts associated with socially relevant indicators
Knowledge
• Get to know important statistical concepts
• Evaluate and reflect on the data
• Evaluate statistical conclusions
• Ask relevant statistical questions
Enabling processes
• Research relevant information
• Reflect on the use of technology and media
• Communicate statistical concepts and results to non-experts in a clear and understandable way

These goals relate closely to the framework for Civic Statistics described by Gal, Nicholson, and Ridgway in Chap. 3. Table 16.1 illustrates how the goals of this course correspond to the tools and facets set out in Chap. 3 needed so that students (and citizen in general) can critically understand statistics about society.

16.4 Pedagogical Approach

The pedagogical approach taken when designing the course applies the concept of the Statistical Reasoning Learning Environment (SRLE, Garfield & Ben-Zvi, 2009) to teaching the key conceptual ideas and recommendations for Civic Statistics introduced and discussed in Chaps. 2–4. The SRLE approach can be characterised as research in which the design of educational materials (e.g., computer tools, learning activities, or a professional development programme) is a crucial part of the research. The design of learning environments is interwoven with the testing or developing of theory (Bakker & van Eerde, 2015, p. 430). Design experiments are extended, iterative, interventionist and theory-oriented undertakings whose "theories" do real work in practical educational contexts (Cobb et al., 2003). A learner-centred approach is adopted that offers students a variety of opportunities to think, argue and reflect. Such a learning environment helps learners to develop a deeper understanding of statistics by promoting statistical thinking and statistical reasoning.

The key recommendations of ProCivicStat conceived by the ProCivicStat Partners (2018) and further set out in Chap. 4 are aimed at statistical education in schools and universities and correspond to the core points of SRLE, with a distinct focus on socio-political considerations and content. We refer here to the first five Recommendations in Chap. 4 which are about teaching and learning, while Recommendation 6 deals with systemic changes in educational institutions.

Table 16.2 Comparison of PCS and SRLE recommendations

Pro Civic Stat	SRLE
PCS Recommendation 1: Develop activities which promote engagement with societal issues and develop learners' critical understanding of statistics about key civic phenomena	SRLE 1: Focus on developing central statistical ideas rather than on presenting sets of tools and procedures
PCS Recommendation 2: Use relevant data and texts, and highlight the multivariate, dynamic and aggregated nature of social phenomena	SRLE 2: Use real and motivating data sets to engage students in making and testing conjectures
PCS Recommendation 3: Embrace technologies that enable rich visualizations and interactions with data about relevant social phenomena	SRLE 4: Integrate the use of appropriate technological tools that allow students to test their conjectures, explore and analyse data, and develop their statistical reasoning
PCS Recommendation 4: Adopt teaching methods to develop skills of critical interpretation applicable to a wide variety of data and textual sources	SRLE 3: Use classroom activities to support the development of students' reasoning SRLE 5: Promote classroom discourse that includes statistical arguments and sustained exchanges that focus on significant statistical ideas
PCS Recommendation 5: Implement assessments which examine the ability to investigate and critically understand data, statistics findings and messages about key social phenomena	SRLE 6: Use assessment to learn what students know and to monitor the development of their statistical learning, as well as to evaluate instructional plans and progress

Key features are: (1) statistical topics addressing the specific characteristics of data about society, (2) use of versatile digital technologies, (3) promotion of critical evaluation and (4) alternative evaluation approaches.

In the following, the five key recommendations of PCS (see Chap. 4) are related to the six characteristics of a SRLE (see Table 16.2):

These Recommendations can be amplified further

• *Develop activities which promote engagement with social issues and develop learners' critical understanding of statistics about key civic phenomena (PCS Recommendation 1) and focus on developing central statistical ideas (content; SRLE 1):* People need to acquire competences with statistics in order to be able to deal critically with socially relevant phenomena. In particular, central statistical ideas such as distribution and variability should be understood by all students, including how they relate to each other, if students are to achieve a deeper understanding that facilitates application in other contexts. In particular, activities based on socially relevant issues require a broad spectrum of statistical competences, for example to enable citizens to understand the role of statistical evidence in decision-making on public policy.

- *Use real and motivating data (SRLE 2) or relevant data and texts, and highlight the multivariate, dynamic and aggregated nature of social phenomena (PCS Recommendation 2):* Students are motivated by interesting subject areas and bring some knowledge (and assumptions) before the actual analysis begins. Understanding social phenomena and making decisions about them requires dealing with multivariate data. Activities should therefore consider data from important providers, and multiple and novel data sources should be used to triangulate problems. To develop metacognition, students can be asked to reflect on the characteristics of data used in different subject areas, and in a variety of political arguments.
- *Integrate appropriate technological tools (SRLE 4) enabling rich visualizations and interactions with data about relevant social phenomena (PCS Recommendation 3):* There is a variety of technological tools to help learners develop understanding and reasoning. They relieve students from cognitive overload associated with detailed calculations so that they can concentrate on more important tasks such as selecting methods or presenting, evaluating and discussing the results. Relevant and innovative software should include dynamic and interactive data visualizations that encourage learners to use a variety of tools.
- *Teaching methods should develop skills in critical interpretation of a wide variety of data and text sources (PCS Recommendation 4) for example develop students' statistical reasoning (SRLE 3) and promote classroom discourse (SRLE 5):* An important component is the use of carefully designed activities that promote learning through collaboration, interaction, discussion, and interesting problems. Discussions are a central part of the learning environment. Students should ask each other questions and, if possible, answer the questions among themselves. Questions should encourage new conjectures and independent thinking. The activities focus on the development of competences in the field of statistical reasoning. Different teaching methods should be used, with a focus on asking appropriate questions, searching for answers and interpretations in a reasoned way, using appropriate analysis methods. The aim is to develop skills in critical interpretation and to stimulate communication on social issues, including through narrative reports. Through early argumentation with non-linear, multivariate data, modelling competences can also be developed so that students can recognise the respective strengths and weaknesses of modelling in social contexts.
- *Use alternative assessments (SRLE 6) that examine the ability to investigate and critically understand data, statistics findings and messages about key social phenomena (PCS Recommendation 5):* The use of different forms for the assessment of statistical competences makes it possible to focus on the understanding of basic ideas. In addition, assessments are an important orientation for learners in their progress. Therefore, for example, the ability to relate data analysis to societal and policy relevance should be assessed.

16.5 Content and Structure of the Course

From the PCS recommendations and the characteristics of SRLE as well as from the goals of the course, we developed the following structure for a typical 90 min session (with the exception of the sessions described in Sect. 16.6 which followed a different structure). Usually at the beginning of a session, the statistical knowledge necessary is introduced or refreshed in order to provide an appropriate knowledge base among the students. When a new socio-political topic is introduced, the instructor presents basic background information which is supplemented by a short video, a cartoon or a short text. Details and more background information about the societal topic are provided through the worksheets or lesson plans. In addition, the worksheets contain information about relevant variables (including their operationalization and measurement) and a link to an electronic *CODAP* worksheet containing a comprehensive dataset. A list of tasks guides the students through their investigations and data analysis. Students work in teams of two or three. A question and answer period and class discussion follow before the instructor summarizes the session. Table 16.3 gives an overview of the session structure.

ProCivicStat developed around 40 detailed lesson plans or worksheets (all plans are available as student and as teacher version in English, and several are also translated into German, Hungarian and Portuguese) which are freely available under "Lesson Plans" through the ProCivicStat website https://iase-web.org/islp/pcs or use the CivicStatMap tool there. Figure 16.1 shows the cover and list of tasks for one of the worksheets.[2] Using the freely available software *CODAP* (described by Frischemeier, Podworny and Biehler in Chap. 9) or *Gapminder*, students analyse multivariate datasets by answering questions on the worksheets while consolidating the previously introduced content. Depending on the needs of the respective learning groups, the teacher supports, advises or holds back. Individual groups engage with

Table 16.3 Structure of a typical 90-min class session

	What	Who	Media/ tools	How long (in minutes)
1	Statistical concepts Intro to *CODAP*, *Gapminder* Intro to social context	Instructor	Blackboard apps, videos	20–25
2	Discussion, questions	Whole class		5–10
3	Data exploration	Teams of 2–3 students	Worksheets; *CODAP*, *Gapminder*	45–50
4	Discussion, questions	Whole class		15–20
5	Summary	Instructor		5

---

[2] See lesson plan 5.105 *Human Development Index* https://iase-web.org/islp/pcs or use CivicStatMap tool there.

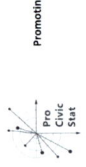

Fig. 16.1 Cover and list of tasks for one of the worksheets

Table 16.4 Possible statistical topics and concepts

Topic	Concepts
Location parameters	Mean, median, percentiles
Dispersion parameters	Interquartile range, variance, standard deviation, range
Data visualisation	Boxplot, histogram, comparing distributions
Measurement	Operationalization of variables
Bivariate data	scatter plot, correlation, regression line
Multivariate data	Confounders, Simpson's paradox
Visualisation of multivariate data	Scatterplot matrix, *Gapminder* bubble charts

Table 16.5 A list of socio-political topics addressed in the course

Theme	Lead question
Income distributions in Europe[a]	*Why are there in some countries large discrepancies between the rich and the poor while in other countries the income distribution is more equal?*
Exploring the World with Data[b]	*What insights about the state of the world and the differences in living conditions in different regions can you gain from this dataset?*
Human Development Index[c]	*What insights about the quality of life in various countries of the world can you gain from this dataset?*
World Happiness Report[d]	*What are the main differences between countries with respect to happiness?*
Racism in European Football[e]	*Are players with darker skin tone in four European football leagues more likely to receive a red or yellow card than lighter skinned players?*

[a]See lesson plan 5.101 *Some so rich, others so poor -. income inequalities in Europe*
[b]See lesson plan 5.102 *How can we describe the state of the world's population?*
[c]See lesson plan 5.105 *Human Development Index: Can you compare countries?*
[d]See lesson plan 5.106: *World Happiness Report: How happy are we?*
[e]See lesson plan 5.103: *Is there racial bias in European football?*
All lesson plans available under "Lesson Plans" from https://iase-web.org/islp/pcs or use the CivicStatMap tool there

the instructor according to their needs. At the end of the session there is a short summary of the students' findings including discussion and evaluation.

Table 16.4 gives an overview of the statistical content being addressed, which covers standard elements of descriptive statistics, data visualisations and an introduction to dealing with multivariate data.

During the four iterations of the course, we experimented with various socio-political topics; the number of topics covered in class varied between 2 and 3. Table 16.5 contains a list of the topics addressed, including a lead question to investigate.

16.6   The Module: Critical Questioning of Data-Based Statements

While there is a rich literature on pedagogical principles for teaching statistics (e.g. GAISE College Report, 2016; Garfield & Ben-Zvi, 2009) and some of the statistical topics we dealt with are generic (location and dispersion parameters, boxplots, regression and correlation), in the following we focus on some distinct features of the course in more detail: the analysis and re-construction of journalistic products or *Critical Questioning of Data-based Statements* (CQS) because it shows in a specific way the interrelationship between statistics, important social issues and critical thinking (Schiller & Engel, 2018). This module covers about two 90-min sessions of class time. It is specifically directed towards understanding and reflecting on how quantitative information is communicated in the media. The structure of the CQS module is based on the procedures for producing and communicating data-based statements as well as comprehending and dealing with data-based statements (see Fig. 16.2). The upper half of the figure shows a common sequence of steps for generating a headline from the data-based information of a (scientific) study that is of general public interest. The figure illustrates a typical pathway showing how results from social studies or other investigations of public interest enter into our media, and shows how, at interfaces between production and communication of data-based statements, subjective decisions influence the transmission of information. Such subjective decisions and interpretations can lead to a situation where the statements in the journalistic product no longer correspond to the conclusions backed by the underlying studies (resulting in false or even fake news). This is a general problem which is demonstrated to the students throughout the CQS module.

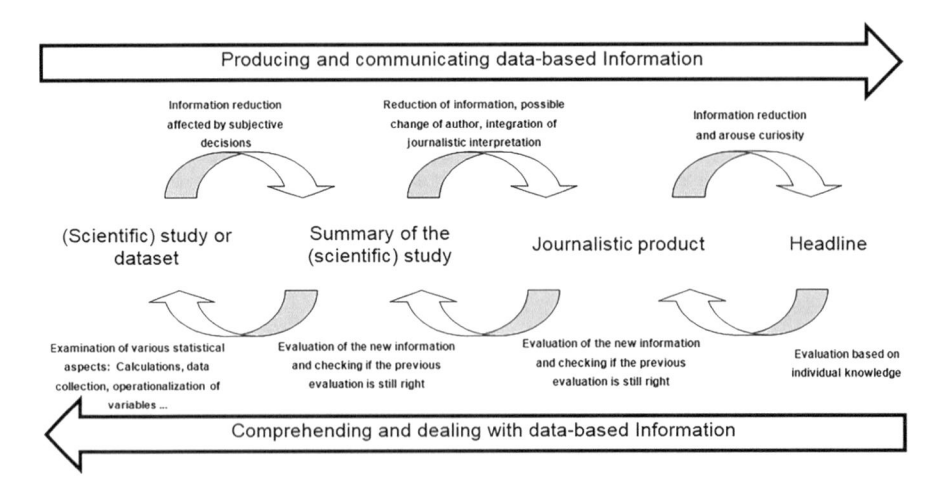

Fig. 16.2 Framework for critical questioning of data-based statements

We start with the results of a scientific investigation based on data that has already been collected and analysed by some statistical methods. The selection of which procedures are carried out has a subjective element, and thus influences the results and possible interpretations. The ensuing results and conclusions are also based on subjective decisions. Results usually contain a lot of information, and highlights are presented in abstracts and conclusions. In journalistic products, information can be further condensed to reduce the original study to a basic message, perhaps omitting essential information on the basis of subjective decisions in order to make the message more comprehensible and thus more accessible to the general public. Journalistic interpretations and evaluations can also be incorporated into the product. As a rule, the choice of headline is based on the target group of the medium. In principle, the initial information is reduced at each interface.

The lower half of Fig. 16.2 shows a typical process of comprehending and dealing with data-based statements. First, a headline draws attention to a topic. The headline is subjectively evaluated on the basis of the reader's own knowledge. If the corresponding journalistic product is picked up, a new overall assessment of the topic is made, based on the additional information within the journalistic product. In some cases, objective evaluations may be blurred by prejudices and one-sided prior information. Source references may be used to obtain further information and to check the statements of the journalistic product. By resorting to the underlying data set and the available metadata, the reported conclusion of the study may be re-examined, the quality of the data collection can be assessed and the operationalisation of the variables can be evaluated.

The CQS module tries to replicate exactly these two information flows. The intention is to raise students' awareness that subjective influences affect both the production of statements and their interpretation. Accordingly, the CQS module consists of two parts: comprehending and dealing with data-based statements (Part 1); and producing and communicating data-based statements (Part 2). Since comprehending and dealing with data takes place more frequently in everyday life and is fundamental to the formation of individual opinions, the major focus of the CQS module is on this part. The structure of the respective parts of the CQS module is based on the process shown in Fig. 16.2.

16.6.1 Part 1: Comprehending and Dealing with Data-Based Statements

In this part of the CQS module, which consists of three working steps, data-based statements from the media are to be analysed step by step (e.g., their significance) using the corresponding sources (articles and data sets) on socially relevant topics (PCS recommendation 1, SRLE 2). The students should also be able to identify the difference between opinion-making and propaganda and neutral information (PCS recommendation 4). In Chap. 13, Gal provides many examples of "opinion questions" and, in particular Sect. 13.7. gives a list of "worry questions" that help students to adopt a critical stance.

In the first step, data-based statements in the form of headlines on various topics (e.g. obesity) are to be assessed with regard to their significance. In the first phase, students are individually confronted with the authentic headlines from current newspapers, e.g.: "*So dick war die Menschheit noch nie. Erstmals leben mehr Fettleibige als Untergewichtige*"—"Humanity has never been so fat; for the first time the number of obese people; outnumbers the underweight" (ZEIT Online), "*Virus has killed one million worldwide*" (New York Times), "*Lab-grown food will soon destroy farming—and save the planet*" (The Guardian). They identify terms, phrases, and details of the study that need definition or clarification (e.g., when are people "fat", "obese", or "underweight"? How were these variables operationalised? and how were the data collected?). They consider the informative value of the headline and identify additional information that may be needed to evaluate its veracity. To explore students' affective involvement with the topic, they describe whether the headline has negative, neutral or positive connotations for them. The students' results are discussed in the plenary that concludes this phase (SRLE 5). This gives the group an overview of what further information is considered necessary and how differently the significance and connotations of the data-based statement can be perceived.

In the second step, the students receive the journalistic products associated with the respective headlines and are to use these, now in partner work, to reflect on their results from the first step (PCS recommendation 4, SRLE 3). Have the connotations changed? Are the terms used in the headline now unambiguous? What other information is contained in the article? Have new questions arisen? Has the perceived importance of the message changed as a result of the additional information? Students are asked to invent an alternative headline for the article. With the exception of the alternative headline, which will be used in the second part of the module, the results are again discussed in a plenary session. The aim of the discussion is to give the students an overview of different (if available) views and evaluations within the group (SRLE 5).

Computers with internet access are required for the third step, as the students work with various software tools and multivariate data sets and may have to research further information (PCS recommendation 3, SRLE 4). With the help of the data sets and the corresponding metadata, to which the journalistic products and the headline refer, their data-based statements are re-evaluated (PCS recommendation 2, SRLE 2). In addition, the quality of the data collection is assessed and their own questions raised in the course of the discussions are addressed (PCS recommendation 4). The students combine graphical and numerical representations to support their assessments (e.g., Fig. 16.3 shows that in each world region the number of obese men has increased between 1975 and 2016).

Using the results of their own analyses (e.g., by means of comparing distributions; SRLE 1), the students are asked to reflect again on their assessment and evaluation of the conclusions drawn in the newspaper article as well as their perceived connotations. During the discussion in the plenary, the students now

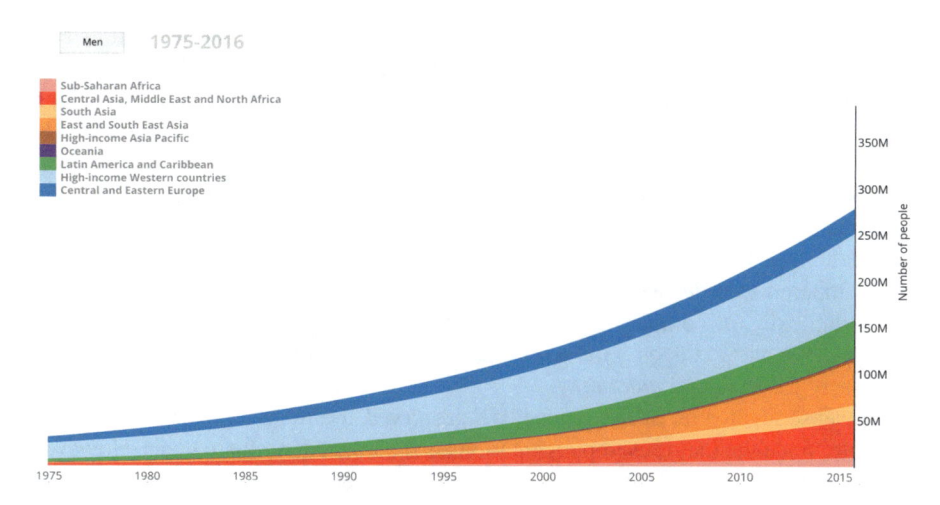

Fig. 16.3 Number of obese men (BMI > 30) in millions worldwide from 1975 to 2016, broken down by world region. Source: http://ncdrisc.org/obesity-population-stacked.html

justify their assessment of the article using their analyses and argue whether they deem the original headline to still be appropriate and whether meaningful evidence-based conclusions can be drawn (SRLE 5).

At the end of the first part of the CQS module, the students work out categories relevant for an evaluation of data-based statements in the media. To this end they reflect on their experiences in earlier steps and create a list of questions involving unclear terms and missing information in the media report (e.g., How is obesity defined? What does BMI measure? Are the data representative for the claimed population?). These categories are related to the fundamental statistical ideas of Burrill and Biehler (2011): (1) data collection, (2) operationalization of variables, (3) context knowledge, (4) graphical or other representations and (5) statistical calculations. To guide the students, the instructor takes a suitable selection from the student's question list, structured in several groups or categories (according to the five statistical ideas of Burrill and Biehler) and asks the students to assign the remaining issues of their list into these groups. For this activity, working in small groups of students is recommended, followed by a plenary discussion which ends in a general description of categories.

16.6.2 Part 2: Producing and Communicating Data-Based Statements

In the second part of the module, students gain experience in the production and communication of data-based statements. They are given the task of writing a half-page article including a headline on the basis of aggregated data from a published study. Subsequently, the students compare their results with each other and discuss differences and similarities. The next step is to compare the students' products with several real newspaper articles (PCS Recommendation 2). In this way, students become aware of how prior knowledge and subjective decisions influence the selection and presentation of data-based statements. In addition, the discussions in the plenary session help to identify ways of distinguishing between purely statistical information and an opinion underpinned by statistical information (PCS Recommendation 4). The alternative headlines formulated by the students from the first part are compared in order to identify differences and similarities, in order to highlight the complexity in comparing, verifying and evaluating statements from different sources. We view this as an essential activity for developing the critical thinking necessary for *personal autonomy*.

In subsequent runs of the course, we preserved the main structure of the CQS module, since the previous implementations had achieved our main goals. However, to be more focused on the chosen topic, the number of articles was reduced. By working on only one article (*obesity*) and the corresponding additional material, in subsequent runs of the course the time saved was used for more discussion and more in-depth data analysis. The original idea of diversity by choosing different focal points within the supplementary material was rejected in order that all students could work on the same topic with shared contextual knowledge. *Obesity* was chosen because the website provides informative additional graphical representations with web applications, and the topic met with great interest from students. Furthermore, the freely available data has a rich structure suitable for exploration without being too overwhelming. In addition, various data sets were downloaded for implementation in *CODAP* in order to get a better overview of annual changes and trends, for example to compare changes in the *Mean BMI* of women in neighbouring countries. The very different curves of three neighbouring countries can be seen in Fig. 16.4. The development in Switzerland is intriguing and could be investigated further. This development is quite different from the German curve, which is more in line with the Europe-wide and worldwide trend. The representations used by the students can only be the beginning of a deeper investigation, but should show in which different directions research can be done. The students also questioned different definitions of obesity.

16.7 Assessment: The Video Project

Both, the SRLE and the PCS recommendations propose alternative assessments for evaluating the extent to which students have acquired the desired competences (PCS Recommendation 5, SRLE 6). In our course, we chose to assess student learning via a video production instead of the more traditional paper or oral presentation.

The students are asked to address an interesting statistical question relevant to society based on data and to present their results in a video (approx. 10 min). Teams of two or three students, after consultation with the instructor, work on a Civic

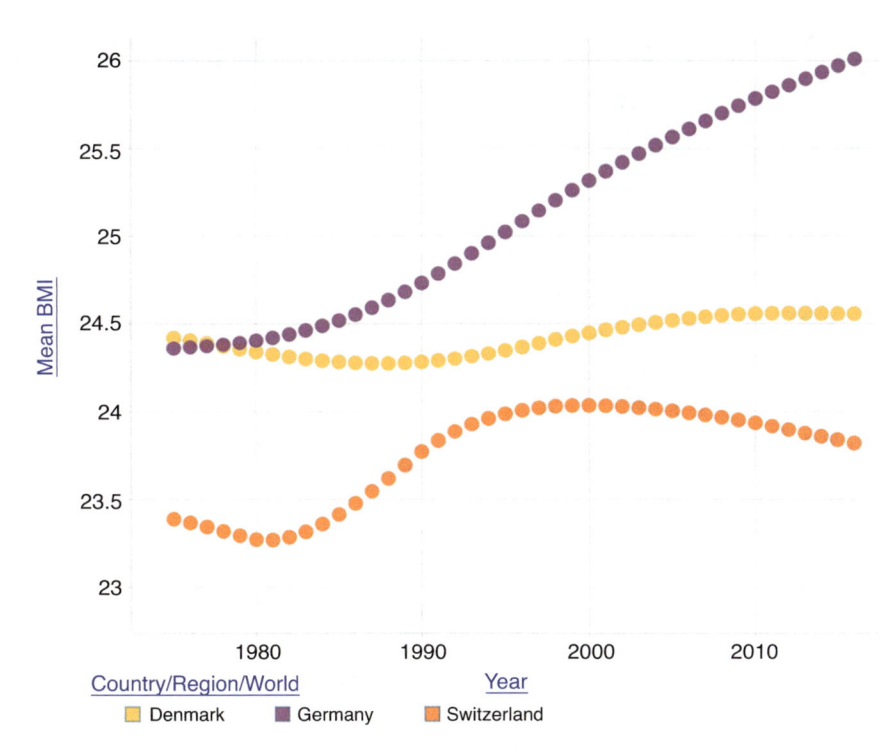

Fig. 16.4 Different development of the mean BMI of women 1975–2016 in Germany, Denmark and Switzerland (created with *CODAP*)

Statistics topic of their own choice. During the process of the video production, the instructor is available for consultation and feedback to provide formative assessment, while the end product of the video together with additional homework assignments during the course serves as a summative evaluation determining the students' grades.

Producing the video requires the students to search for a suitable data set and to identify questions to address the chosen topic and its relevance, followed by data visualisations, analyses, and final conclusions. The videos include an introduction to the social context and a characterisation of the data, e.g., by describing the data source, data collection methods employed, and explaining the variables involved, so that the viewer receives an overview of the topic and an impression of the quality of the data set. The data analysis around the chosen questions is carried out with the help of software, notably *CODAP, iNZight, Excel* or *Gapminder*. The students document interesting discoveries within the data (e.g., conspicuous patterns) and explain them by placing them in context. Based on relevant calculations and graphical representations, students draw (hopefully) well-founded conclusions. The procedure follows the PPDAC cycle (Wild & Pfannkuch, 1999), except that the Plan and Data steps are replaced by finding a suitable data set on the internet. A critical review, limitations of the conclusions and possible subsequent questions are addressed at the end of the video.

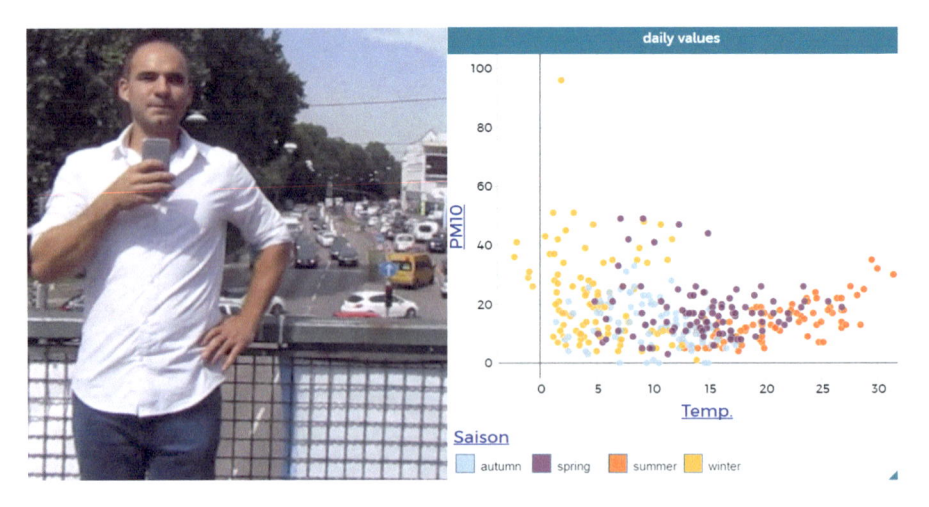

Fig. 16.5 Snapshot from a student video about fine dust pollution in the city of Stuttgart, together with some data analytic displays (created with CODAP)

As an example, Fig. 16.5 gives a snapshot from a student video analysing episodes of fine dust pollution in the city of Stuttgart. To produce the video, most student teams used just the software available on their personal computers (Windows *Movie Maker 2012*, screen capture), freeware such as *Captura 8.0*, *VSDC Free Video Editor* or programs such as *Moovly* or *DaVinci Resolve*.

For evaluating the videos, two instructors independently assigned a score (total sum 100) along seven criteria: motivation for the study (15); commenting on data quality and provenance (5); correctness of calculations (5); quality of visualisations (15); quality of data analysis, modelling, confounders, etc. (30); interpretation (15); and critical review and limitations (15).

16.8 Reflections and Lessons Learnt from the Course

The course in the format outlined above was conducted four times by two different instructors. The concept of the course was developed on a theory-driven basis (SRLE and PCS recommendations) and changed iteratively on the basis of student feedback, and review of students' products and evaluations by the instructors, following the schema of design-based research. In addition to assessing students' statistical skills and their attitudes towards statistics before and after the course (for more detailed results, see Schiller, 2020), students were also asked for feedback and evaluations directly after each unit (see also Frischemeier et al., 2018). Students rated statements on cognitive self-assessment, affective attitude and the didactic potential of the materials on a 7-point Likert scale and with open questions to gather more detailed feedback (see also the evaluation reported by Podworny, Frischemeier and Biehler in Chap. 15).

16.8.1 *Reflections on the CQS Module*

In general, most students were well motivated to work on the CQS module as confirmed by positive feedback. The analysis of the evaluation forms showed that the selection of topics in the various worksheets and the CQS module was largely motivating for the students confirming the didactic potential of the CQS module.

The discussion about the headlines in plenary sessions worked well; ambiguities within the headlines were examined. The choice of the topics in the first cycle of the course (poverty, inflation and obesity) engaged the interest of the students and was motivating for them. The work with the newspaper articles also went as planned. Many questions related to more in-depth information were raised by the students, indicating true intrinsic motivation to examine the evidence underpinning these headlines. However, to have even more focused discussions, we reduced the number of articles for later iterations of the course at the cost of less variety in the choice of topics.

Working with the supplementary materials (websites, data sets, apps) was received differently by different students, and caused some challenges. The work with predominantly text-based material (topic: *poverty*) tended to be demotivating for some students (notably with mathematics majors). The topic *inflation* tended to be overtaxing, as not all students were able to cope with the independent linking of the various formats (app, data table, texts). While focusing on the topic of *increasing obesity*, the students were able to analyse the data provided online, using seven different interactive and dynamic web applications. Choosing the right web application for the respective problem created some interesting challenges, in addition to interpreting the results.

The discussions in the plenary about the written headlines or articles written by the students also showed that in the large group again only a few students actively participated. For this reason, initial discussions were held in small groups in the following runs of the course. The different student headlines provided the desired diversity for comparison with published articles; this made it easier to discuss the issue of different journalists using different sources when writing about the same issue. The students thus learned to differentiate between statistical information and opinions which are underpinned by statistical information.

16.8.2 *Reflections on the Video Project*

Through the videos the students demonstrated that they were able to connect the presentation of statistical results in the form of graphs and numerical summaries with socially relevant topics and to reflect critically on the limitations of their conclusions. The tools and statistical methods applied were not particularly sophisticated (comparing distributions, boxplots, subgroup analyses, searching for relevant third variables, scatter plots with some curve fitting etc.). Students were highly motivated despite a heavy workload to learn about video technology on top of all the statistical and the contextual challenges. On the feedback forms most students described the video production as a fun activity, but also as challenging, because enhancing their media competences required many hours of work. Finding a relevant and feasible topic for the video project was not always easy for the students. Besides being of relevance for society and Civic Statistics, it was essential to find rich, meaningful and accessible datasets that could be downloaded from a website and imported into familiar software (*CODAP*, *iNZight*). A second challenge was for some of the students to identify meaningful statistical questions and a suitable interpretation of the obtained results and conclusions.

As instructors, we learnt that for a successful video project it is important to restrict the investigation to a well-defined, precise question and to have a reasonably rich data set with information related to the question under investigation. An ideal data set has between 5 and 20 variables of mixed types (numeric and categorical), and between 200 and 2000 cases. By the time they began work on the video projects, our students had no difficulties handling the data analysis software they chose (*CODAP*, *Excel*, *Gapminder* or *iNZight*). The statistical methods applied did not go beyond an elementary level, yet the conclusions were reason-based.

16.9   General Conclusion and Lessons Learnt

The course was aimed at students training to become teachers of mathematics, with the specific goal of integrating broader topics of societal relevance into learning statistical content. Even though the majority of students had learned some statistics during their high school years, they were barely able to apply this knowledge to everyday life as evidenced by a competence test given at the beginning of the course (see Schiller, 2020). This was also noticeable when students were asked to interpret statistical results or to invent their own meaningful statistical questions. To integrate broader civic topics into the mathematics classroom proved at the same time a motivation for the majority of students and a big challenge. The numerous discussions within the CQS module and the video production both promoted students' ability to communicate statistical concepts and results. However, some students had difficulty understanding important statistical concepts such as correlation and causality. Statistical ideas were introduced and explored when immediately needed, and students' statistical development was not guided by a systematic syllabus of a traditional statistics class. Students became aware of the fact that important socially relevant indicators such as unemployment or poverty can be defined differently, but not all students were aware of its implications for society. Students were quickly at ease with the technology and digital tools used in the course (software for data exploration as well as video technology) and its use for fostering learning. While recognizing the value of applying statistical thinking to wider societal questions as an important goal of school education, some students hesitated to embrace the integration of Civic Statistics as a goal of mathematics education.

Some take-away messages for the instructor of this course are:

- It is essential to find a balance between teaching important statistical concepts and teaching a critical attitude towards statistics. This is central for applying statistical considerations in real-life, everyday situations, and in evidence-based evaluations of issues affecting society.
- In this type of course, students learn statistical concepts from applying them in the search for solutions in concrete situations, not from following a systematic statistics syllabus. Therefore, the instructor may limit the statistical inputs to some more basic information and provide time for the students to explore the data sets themselves and to discuss their explorations together.
- Many of the students' analyses are based on common sense, sometimes coloured with some misconceptions. Therefore, the instructor needs to listen carefully to the students' reasoning and intervene to clear up misunderstandings.
- A challenging and interesting topic of relevance for the students' life and for society is crucial for motivating the students. Topics such as personal happiness, human development, health, income inequalities, racism, natural disasters, and crime (see PCS website or CivicStatMap[3]) proved to enhance students' interest in exploring data, learning basic statistical concepts and relating the conclusions to the context.
- The use of real and relevant data sets in the teaching of statistics not only ensures a more realistic learning of statistical skills, but also makes them more applicable in situations in everyday life.
- Videos offer opportunities for team work and are a source for motivation, and enhance media literacy. Yet the processes of creating videos are time consuming, both for students and instructor. If used as a student project, it is important to focus on a specific topic investigating a single precise question. Videos can be used for formative and summative assessment.

This innovative course connecting introductory statistics with socio-political topics and a critical reception of media reports puts specific demands on students as well as on the instructor. Carefully planned and implemented, it addresses an important aim of general education, namely to help students develop as autonomous citizens.

References

Bakker, A., & van Eerde, D. (2015). An introduction to design-based research with an example from statistics education. In A. Bikner-Ahsbahs, C. Knipping, & N. Presmeg (Eds.), *Approaches to qualitative research in mathematics education. Examples of methodology and methods* (pp. 429–466). Springer. https://doi.org/10.1007/978-94-017-9181-6_16

Batanero, C., Burrill, G., & Reading, C. (Eds.). (2011). *Teaching statistics in school mathematics— Challenges for teaching and teacher education: A Joint ICMI/IASE Study.* Springer.

---

[3] https://iase-web.org/islp/pcs , https://rstudio.up.pt/shiny/users/pcs/civicstatmap/

Böhme, G. (2010). Der mündige Patient. In G. Böhme (Ed.), *Der mündige Mensch. Denkmodelle der Philosophie, Geschichte, Medizin und Rechtswissenschaft* (pp. 143–155). WBG— Wissenschaftliche Buchgesellschaft.

Burrill, G., & Biehler, R. (2011). Fundamental statistical ideas in the school curriculum and in training teachers. In C. Batanero, G. Burrill, & C. Reading (Eds.), *Teaching statistics in school mathematics—Challenges for teaching and teacher education: A joint ICMI/IASE study* (pp. 57–69). Springer.

Cobb, P., Confrey, J., diSessa, A., Lehrer, R., & Schauble, L. (2003). Design experiments in educational research. *Educational Researcher, 32*(1), 9–13. https://doi.org/10.3102/0013189X032001009

CODAP, Common Online Data Analysis Platform [Computer software]. (2014). The Concord Consortium.

Dammer, K. -H., & Wortmann, E. (2014). *Mündigkeit. Didaktische, bildungstheoretische und politische Überlegungen zu einem schwierigen Begriff.* Didactica nova, Bd. 23. Schneider-Verlag Hohengehren.

Frischemeier, D., Podworny, S., & Biehler, R. (2018). Activities for promoting Civic statistical knowledge of preservice teachers. In P. Kovács (Ed.), *Proceedings of challenges and innovations in statistics education multiplier conference of ProCivicStat.* University of Szeged. http://eco.u-szeged.hu/download.php?docID=73886

GAISE College Report ASA Revision Committee. (2016). *Guidelines for assessment and instruction in statistics education college report 2016.* American Statistical Association. https://www.amstat.org/asa/education/Guidelines-for-Assessment-and-Instruction-in-Statistics-Education-Reports.aspx

Garfield, J., & Ben-Zvi, D. (2009). Helping students develop statistical reasoning: implementing a statistical reasoning learning environment. *Teaching Statistics, 31*(3), 72–77. https://doi.org/10.1111/j.1467-9639.2009.00363.x

Gramm, C. (2010). *Schlüsselqualifikationen für Staatsbürger. Politik verstehen—Demokratie bejahen.* Olzog.

Hannigan, A., Gill, O., & Leavy, A. M. (2013). An investigation of prospective secondary mathematics teachers' conceptual knowledge of and attitudes towards statistics. *Journal of Mathematics Teacher Education, 16*(6), 427–449. https://doi.org/10.1007/s10857-013-9246-3

Himmelmann, G. (2011). Demokratische Handlungskompetenz. Standards für Mündigkeit. In W. Beutel & P. Fauser (Eds.), *Demokratiepädagogik. Lernen für die Zivilgesellschaft (Reihe Politik und Bildung)* (Vol. 43, 2nd ed., pp. 42–70) Wochenschau-Verlag.

Lengnink, K., Meyerhöfer, W., & Vohns, A. (2013). Mathematische Bildung als staatsbürgerliche Erziehung? *Der Mathematikunterricht, 59*(4), 2–7.

ProCivicStat Partners. (2018). *Engaging civic statistics: A call for action and recommendations. A product of the ProCivicStat Project.* https://iase-web.org/islp/pcs

Ridgway, J. (2015). Implications of the data revolution for statistics education. *International Statistical Review, 84*(3), 528–549.

Schiller, A. (2020). *Mathematische Bildung und Demokratie: Statistical Literacy als eine Basiskompetenz zivilgesellschaftlicher Partizipation—Entwicklung und Evaluation einer statistischen Lerneinheit zur Förderung von Mündigkeit* (Doctoral Dissertation). Ludwigsburg University of Education. https://phblopus.phlb.de/frontdoor/deliver/index/docId/679/file/Mathematische_Bildung_Diss_Achim_Schiller.pdf

Schiller, A., & Engel, J. (2018). The importance of statistical literacy for democracy—civic education through statistics. In P. Kovacs (Ed.), *Proceedings of challenges and innovations in statistics education multiplier conference of ProCivicStat.* University of Szeged. http://eco.u-szeged.hu/download.php?docID=73883

Wild, C. J., & Pfannkuch, M. (1999). Statistical thinking in empirical enquiry. *International Statistical Review, 67*, 223–265.

Chapter 17
Civic Statistics at School: Reasoning with Real Data in the Classroom

Christoph Wassner and Andreas Proemmel

Abstract It is a fundamental philosophy of this book that data literacy must become an integral part of general education. To achieve this, more attention at school level must be given to skills in reasoning with real data, with a particular emphasis on key societal issues. With this aim in mind, this chapter describes the authors' work in the ProCivicStat project, in which they designed, implemented and evaluated learning units for the upper secondary level at the high schools where they teach. In addition to sharing experiences, the authors offer conceptual, as well as process- and curriculum-oriented considerations, suggestions, and recommendations for the teaching and learning of Civic Statistics at the secondary level, taking into account didactic principles and the special educational demands involved.

Keywords Statistical education · Data education · Secondary level · Project work · Real-world problem solving · Interdisciplinary teaching · Statistics curriculum

17.1 Fundamental Considerations for Statistical Education at School Level

Students may come into contact with statistical thinking at a very early age, without even knowing it explicitly. Already at the earliest stage of education, children develop skills related to data handling, finding patterns, and collecting information. For example, when electing a class representative, the voting process is only accepted unanimously if the statistical counting procedure is transparent, e.g. by using a tally sheet. The further development of so-called statistical or data literacy is traditionally taught in the field of mathematics, where the contents for dealing with data and statistics are more or less extensively integrated into the courses. There is,

C. Wassner (✉)
Martin-Behaim-Gymnasium Nürnberg, Nuremberg, Germany
e-mail: wassner@martin-behaim-gymnasium.de

A. Proemmel
Gymnasium Ernestinum Gotha, Gotha, Germany

© Springer Nature Switzerland AG 2022
J. Ridgway (ed.), *Statistics for Empowerment and Social Engagement*,
https://doi.org/10.1007/978-3-031-20748-8_17

however, a general tendency to give too little attention to the fact that data and statistics are of very substantial importance. This is especially true nowadays, when data is used in almost all industries and has become a very big business, along with the ever-growing power of computers and data storage facilities, and the increased use of social media and online tools. This is discussed in detail in Part I of the book.

In this chapter, we—as math teachers who are particularly engaged in teaching statistics—report on attempts to implement the framework and ideas from the *ProCivicStat* project (PCS) in the classroom. It is our intention to support the general aim to improve statistical literacy in children and students at school and recommend doing so via the "PCS approach", which utilizes real data sets and relevant social issues.

In many countries, much development has gone into increasing data skills at the school level in recent years. What these proposals often lack, however, is up-to-date relevance regarding major socio-political issues and topics such as climate, poverty, racism, migration, pandemics, and so on. Statistics, however, is a subject that is needed in the here and now—in everyday life—and it is in this context that we should teach the subject to our students.

It is possible that some will think it too high a demand for math teachers to deal with rich contexts as well as complex data sets, if the core task is still to teach probabilistic models. "For educational purposes, statistics needs to be defined by the ends it pursues rather than the means statisticians have most often used to pursue them in the past." (Wild et al., 2018, p. 5). Strictly speaking, much of what is mentioned in the context of Civic Statistics is not traditional statistics (as a sub-area of mathematics), but rather belongs to subjects such as politics, social studies, economics, and geography. Moreover, the indispensable use of information and communications technology (ICT) also refers more to computer science than to mathematics.

On closer examination, it becomes obvious that teaching statistics according to the PCS approach cannot be achieved within the framework of teaching mathematics (statistics) alone, but rather seems to be more of an interdisciplinary task. This notion is supported by a general trend in schools today to take an interdisciplinary approach to teaching, instead of strictly separating subjects. Another prominent example is what we currently refer to as "media literacy education" (Abreu et al., 2017).

Our contribution in this book, as teachers of mathematics and computer science, is to transform ideas taken from the PCS approach into practicable learning units which can be implemented in secondary classrooms. We have tested the practical aspect of this endeavor in initial classroom experiments, and the findings of these attempts will be reported in the last part of this chapter.

Before providing a detailed presentation of our concept for teaching Civic Statistics, classroom resources and results from teaching experiments, we will discuss several general aspects of didactic research, which are—from our point of view—of special importance for this type of teaching.

17.1.1 *Reality and Drawbacks of the School Curricula*

Competences like "[...] determine absolute and relative frequencies for data from statistical surveys and flexibly use different representations for the latter, present data prepared in this way in a graphically structured way also using a computer program and discuss the advantages and disadvantages of different presentations." (from the current curriculum of the Bavarian Gymnasium, Grade 6 Mathematics) indicate the didactic potential of Exploratory Data Analysis (EDA) (Tukey, 1977). EDA should be perceived as an interactive process in which detours and wrong turns are understood as learning opportunities. In this light, the exploratory analysis of data requires unique autonomous forms of learning and working. The special importance of graphical representations for EDA indicates a further dimension of didactic interest. Consequently, graphic representations are considered tools for insight, not only as a means with which to present results (Biehler, 1982, 1999).

Since the National Council of Teachers of Mathematics (NCTM) announced trend-setting recommendations for the teaching of mathematics from preschool through to twelfth grade, *data and chance* has generally been established as one of five strands of mathematical content that span the entire curricula of primary and secondary education. The main learning objectives in the field of data and chance have been comprehensively formulated again and again, so that a consensus is emerging on the minimum standard of skills that students should achieve by the end of their school education. NCTM (2000) argued that students should be taught to make sense of information in a critical manner. Many countries now emphasise the importance of dealing with data within the school mathematics curriculum (for instance in Germany, see the working group "Stochastik in der Schule" of Gesellschaft für Didaktik der Mathematik, 2002).[1]

In today's school mathematics curricula, we still often find a combined strand, *Data Analysis and Probability*. Absurdly, probability theory is the main focus, and it is taught much more frequently than "real" statistics, even though statistical topics have a much greater potential to support interesting, everyday school mathematics. In most real-life situations we do not have exact knowledge about the composition of a population and have to infer properties about the population on the basis of a selection (a random sample). Sampling implies variability and uncertainty, and this is exactly what is interesting about statistical questions, which differ from the usual deductive type of mathematics.

It is still the case that too few high- and middle- school mathematics teachers (or science and social science teachers) receive any solid training in statistics or on how to teach statistics; thus they do not feel qualified to teach it. For the most part, traditional school courses and textbooks do not link data analysis to societal contexts and issues (see ProCivicStat Report 2018,[2] points 13 and 14). Teaching Civic Statistics does not seem to fit traditional notions of what should be covered in

---

[1] https://didaktik-der-mathematik.de/ak/stochastik/
[2] http://iase-web.org/islp/pcs/ProCivicStat Partners (2018).

high-school, where the subject of statistics is mainly subsumed within the teaching of mathematics (Callingham & Watson, 2017). In our opinion, it should be the other way around—the mathematics (statistics) should be chosen to fit the context, rather than contexts being chosen to illustrate the mathematics (statistics). Wild et al. (2018) argue "Similar to physics [...], statistics attempts to turn data into real-world insights and presses mathematics into service wherever it can help." As a result, the usual reduction of "data and chance" to a set of mathematical exercises must be reconsidered, and there is an urgent need to give more prominence to dealing with real societal data within the context of the school curriculum.

17.1.2   The Role of Modelling the Real World

In the sense of the phenomenology of mathematical concepts suggested by Hans Freudenthal "... our mathematical concepts, structures, ideas have been invented as tools to organise the phenomena of the physical, social and mental world". (Freudenthal, 1983, p. ix). If one regards data as "numbers about phenomena", mathematizing consists of illuminating and interpreting the situation (e.g. Fischbein, 1975). Current didactic discussions in mathematics emphasize the *relevance to reality* and the *modelling character of mathematics* (for an overview: Blum et al., 2007). Reality-based modelling should, of course, be a goal of mathematics education in general, but this is most relevant to stochastics. "... today more than ever we have to look critically at our stochastic approaches and results, ... and regard them more as decision-making aids than as decisions" (Schupp, 2004, p. 6; translated from German by the authors). In addition to the overall contribution to the teaching of mathematics, stochastics offers "specific opportunities for reflection which general schooling cannot do without" (ibid. p.12).

Regarding teaching practice on the subject of "data", this perspective means that an *authentic situation*, which has not been invented by the teacher, and which is as interesting and relevant as possible for the learners, is taken as a starting point (see Gal in Chap. 13). Similarly, in "situated learning" (e.g. Anderson et al., 1996), the focus should be on a credible relation to reality and the constructivist activity that results (e.g. Reich, 2007). In line with this idea of learning, Civic Statistics issues are situated in an information space that is both complex and multifaceted, rather than restricted and simplified (see ProCivicStat Report, 2018, point 13).

A critical role is played by the students' *dispositions*, i.e. their willingness to engage in evidence-based findings in order to determine what is true (see facet 3 in the Conceptual Framework for Civic Statistics, described in Chap. 3). Overcoming the "why should I care?" attitude of students by finding topics that are of real interest to them is a crucial factor for successful teaching. From educational psychology, we know that there is a robust propensity for people to understand their social environment (Wentzel & Wigfield, 2009). We can absolutely affirm this finding from our teaching experience: current, up-to-date, burning social issues, in particular, can arouse high levels of interest among students.

The importance of creating links between the real world and the world of mathematics is crucial for the successful learning of statistics, even more than in all other areas of school mathematics. In Chap. 3, Gal, Nicholson, and Ridgway argue that educational resources and class activities need to have a direct and clear connection with an actual societal issue. Thus, the interpretation of statistical results also benefits from and depends on the students' *contextual civic knowledge* (see facet 8). The deeper this contextual knowledge is, the more meaningful and influential students' conclusions are regarding societal discussions. However, a student does not usually acquire this knowledge in math class, but rather in classes that teach social sciences, politics, economics or ethics, which again tends to support the argument advocating the interdisciplinary nature of (civic) statistics. Challenging dubious claims (for example, by politicians) via evidence-based *critical evaluation and reflection* (facet 2) provides students with very special learning opportunities.

Here, two important didactic models are considered, which are directly relevant to the idea of teaching Civic Statistics. A well-established approach is the PPDAC Investigative cycle (Wild & Pfannkuch, 1999). PPDAC maps five stages a person goes through when solving a real-world problem using data: Problem, Plan, Data, Analysis, and Conclusion. In educational practice, PPDAC usually refers to data collected by the learners themselves. However, the PCS-approach assumes that the educated citizen must learn to deal with real and complex data. This requires people to engage with data that they did not personally collect. In contrast, data sets traditionally used for teaching in schools tend to be smaller and are often collected by the students themselves. We suggest broadening the PPDAC, namely the Plan and Data stage, to apply to situations where learners use existing public data rather than collecting their own. We will further discuss these viewpoints when describing the way our teaching is structured (see Sect. 17.2.4).

A second model is the well-known *cycle of mathematical modelling* (e.g. Blum et al., 2007), which focuses on the relationship between the "real world" and "mathematics", and is generally applicable when modelling mathematical content. We propose an adaptation of this cycle to identify learning activities a student should engage with when reasoning about data (Fig. 17.1).

In practice, various steps of the *PPDAC-cycle* (or the mathematical modelling cycle) are repeated over and over again until the results are satisfactory, or until there are some steps that initially present learners with impassable hurdles. In this case, they must take a "detour" that only the teacher can show them. Biehler and Ben-Zvi's metaphor of a journey well illustrates this concept (Biehler et al., 2013, p. 678): "We compare statistical reasoning metaphorically with travelling from particular points (statements) to other destinations (conclusions based on data) while remaining aware of the environment (e.g., uncertainty, variation, lurking variables). Our travelling is never-ending: reaching a conclusion can raise further questions; conflicting conclusions can raise doubts, caveats, or even rebuttals. In short, inquiry involves a lot of metaphorical travelling—not only from A to B, but also backwards, forwards, and going round in circles."

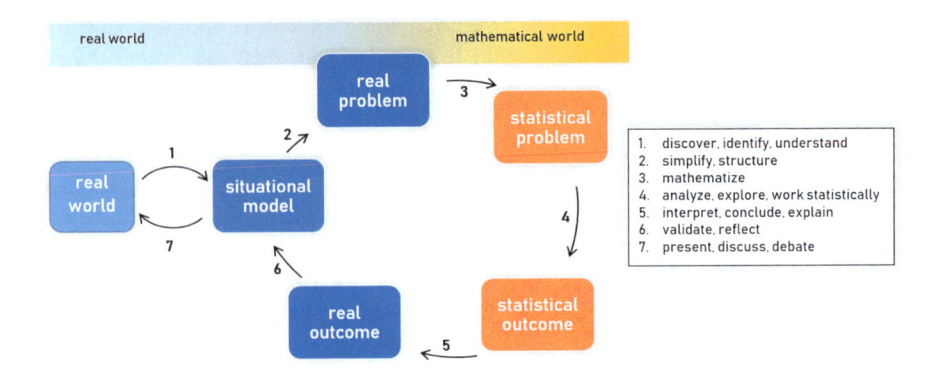

Fig. 17.1 Proposal of an adaptation for data-oriented statistics in the mathematical modelling cycle (Blum et al., 2007)

17.1.3 The Role of ICT

The increasing presence of computers in teaching practice has naturally meant far-reaching changes for modern school teaching. In addition to the usual ICT-based tools deployed in other areas of school mathematics, statistics teaching makes use of ICT in: the search for relevant data; acquisition or generation of data; exploration, analysis and visualization of data; the drawing of conclusions from data and their descriptive presentation; as well as in the implementation of demonstrations and simulations for the exploration of probabilistic models (Biehler et al., 2013; Batanero et al., 2016; also see the Civic Statistics Conceptual Framework, facet 9).

ICT, as in any other subject, can also help achieve a certain degree of self-reliance in the student's work. Moreover, if we return to the metaphor of travelling, "... the role of a computer tool is to make travelling (whichever way) easier and faster, inevitably with some "black box" effects: when travelling by plane or train we see fewer details along the road than when walking or cycling" (Biehler et al., 2013, p. 678). Students become "apprentices" in the world of information and data. This involves interacting with a rich technological environment. In doing so, teaching goals at the secondary level should go beyond inculcating knowledge of procedures on the computer (e.g. creating statistical charts with a particular software package). The competence demanded of students is to apply ICT-tools sensibly in a situational context. Biehler et al. (2013, p. 650) use the term *embedded microworlds* as a notion that comprises exploratory interactive experiments, visualization, simulations and applets which can be used (at a lower level) as a ready-made blackbox, but can even be modified (at the highest level) according to the students' own needs by means of their knowledge of the software.

Teachers must develop competences in order to be able to adapt these microworlds to their teaching. However, there are many barriers that must first be overcome. Teachers must learn to handle the ICT-tools and learn how to organize a classroom for ICT-based tasks. Other challenges arise in the classroom, such as learning how to shift fluidly between whole class and individual computer work, and how to manage the students' multiple approaches to tasks. "Working with computers adds a layer of complexity to organizing learning. With landscape-type software especially, teachers often feel uncomfortable with the many options and the variety of plots and conclusions that students might create or reach. This emphasizes the importance of supporting their professional development, and in some cases, helping them to find ways to limit possibilities and steer students along some trajectory." (Biehler et al., 2013, p. 682).

There is a wide range of software and digital tools that support teaching and learning. In our teaching units we use the dynamic data software *Fathom*, which is now freely available in Germany.[3] *Fathom* was developed specifically for doing and teaching statistics at secondary and tertiary levels. The software supports data analysis as well as modelling and simulation, both visually and computationally. In this chapter, we concentrate on the essential elements of data analysis. A striking advantage of *Fathom*, compared to conceptually similar programs, is its intuitive interface. It encourages dragging operations and facilitates dynamic handling—for example, changing data in one display affects related representations and measures in real time. Furthermore, we see an advantage over internet-based online tools in the fact that it is still not the case that internet access is always available in schools. The functionality of *Fathom* covers all aspects of school statistics (a detailed description is given by Frischemeier, Podworny and Biehler in Chap. 9).

17.2 Teaching Civic Statistics at the Secondary Level

In this section, we describe a strategy for teaching Civic Statistics. The conceptual framework described in Part 1 of the book, together with selected outcomes of the PCS-project, served as a starting point to develop practical teaching sequences. This strategy is intended to stimulate a critical analysis and revisions of the current classroom reality in statistics. We address several preconditions with regard to competencies, teaching methods, and motivation. Then, we describe in detail the content, design, and sequential arrangement of the learning units, and formulate learning objectives.

17.2.1 Competency Conditions

Math teachers often find that their students have barely acquired the necessary technical competences to deal with data within lessons. Process-oriented modelling

---

[3] https://www.stochastik-interaktiv.de/fathom

competencies—such as the PPDAC cycle discussed above—are often not sufficiently established, let alone fluent skills in dealing with ICT-based tools for data analysis. We share this view with many fellow teachers who consider the curriculum content in the area of statistics to be unsatisfactory, and not at all in line with current recommendations (e.g. ProCivicStat Report, 2018,[4] part 4). On the one hand, a common situation is when the enhancement of basic skills in data analysis is necessary for students to be able to deal with statistical issues at a greater depth. On the other hand, due to tight time constraints this type of enhancing repetitive training is not planned for in the curricula. Therefore, it has to be as short and effective as possible.

17.2.2 Pedagogical Conditions

In addition to basic technical skills, pedagogical changes are often necessary for the successful teaching of Civic Statistics. We suggest an orientation to modern teaching methods, embracing open, student-oriented and student-active, real life-oriented, and activity-based learning methods. Some characteristics of these methods include:

- Project-oriented learning: learning organized in project groups.
- An open time structure, as far as is possible, and process-oriented learning.
- Interest-oriented learning, taking account of students' ages and interests, and students' gradual increased participation in decision-making.
- Action- and situation-oriented learning: current, relevant, and stimulating situations in which problems and barriers can be experienced, leading to committed action.
- Communication orientation: communication and interaction as integral competences.

17.2.3 Motivational Conditions

We regard project-based work over several school hours in small groups to be an effective working method. A decisive factor for successful progress in project work is the learners' interest and motivation (also see Chap. 7). We consider the following conditions to be critical in the selection of topics:

- General relevance in terms of a current focus in the media.
- Availability of controversial statements and discussions on the subject, e.g. media reports.

---

[4] http://iase-web.org/islp/pcs/ProCivicStat Partners (2018).

- Topics of particular concern to the learners, because they relate to populations directly relevant to them (e.g. men/women in Germany).
- Topics that serve as "eye openers", since statements (such as "men earn more than women") may be new to the students.

17.2.4 Content Design and Sequential Arrangement of Training Units

The training we propose is based on teaching ideas and materials from Prömmel et al. (2010)[5] and Biehler et al. (2011) for secondary level classrooms. The training units were designed as part of the support materials for the data-analysis software package *Fathom 2* for German-speaking countries. The training units started in a web-based environment, notably *eFathom*.[6] Work on these online tutorials should be carried out by the students outside of the classroom, at a pace that is convenient for them. We advocate a *flipped classroom* approach, which is appropriate for enhancing the basic skills which we outline below. Table 17.1 shows the contents and sequence of the training units using this flipped classroom approach.

The flipped classroom intentionally shifts instruction to a learner-centered model, in which the class time is used to engage in data analysis topics in greater depth with the guidance of the teacher. By outsourcing the acquisition of basic skills, the teachers' role shifts from that of instructor to that of a learning guide (e.g. Bergmann & Sams, 2012). In addition to the effect on cognitive learning performance, the flipped classroom seems to also have a positive influence on affective learning outcomes. In didactic research across all subjects and forms of training, it has been shown that learners' motivation can be improved by the use of the flipped classroom (Abeysekera & Dawson, 2015).

Please note that the essential contents of each unit require about one hour of homework time, followed by further review through applications and exercises in the form of one-and-a-half-hour classroom activities. In total, four such units have been planned and implemented. The goal of this training is for the students to become familiar with the basic components of descriptive statistics and statistical data analysis, as well as the essential functionality of *Fathom*. Furthermore, students should be enabled to use their acquired skills to carry out more detailed investigations of civic statistical issues on the basis of real data sets, which is almost impossible without establishing a certain basic level of competence with statistical techniques.

Besides the fundamental ideas of statistics such as variation, distribution, and the important role of graphical or other representations, the importance of skills in

---

[5] https://kobra.uni-kassel.de/handle/123456789/2007011016602 (in German).

[6] In German: http://euler.math.upb.de/eFathom/; for alternative use in English: "*Fathom* tutorials" and "*Fathom* movies" https://fathom.concord.org/help/HelpFiles/index.html

Table 17.1 Overview of the contents of the basic training units using the flipped classroom concept

Unit	Time (expected)	Unit content	Location/Media
1	60 min	A first statistical analysis: data collection, table, graph, evaluation table, scatter diagram, arithmetic mean	home/online *e-Fathom*
	90 min	Application and practice examples with *Fathom* (working in pairs)	classroom/worksheets *Fathom 2*
2	60 min	Distinction of numerical and categorical variables and specific features; adjustment of data and different visualizations; display of data as a histogram and interpretation; absolute and relative frequencies; measures for location and spread (mean vs. median), summary statistics and boxplots	home/online-work *e-Fathom*
	90 min	Application and practice examples with *Fathom* (working in pairs)	Classroom/worksheets *Fathom 2*
3	60 min	Group comparison (categorization) and visualization (e.g. multi-field table, split chart, stacked/grouped bar or column chart, etc.)	Home/online (e.g. via Learning Management System)
	90 min	Application and practice examples with *Fathom* (working in pairs)	Classroom/worksheets *Fathom 2*
4	60 min	Relationship between two numerical variables; correlation and trend lines; line fitting	Home/online-work (e.g. via Learning Management System)
	90 min	Application and practice examples with *Fathom* (working in pairs); final "challenge" (final self-test)	Classroom/worksheets *Fathom 2*

dealing with multivariate and aggregated data are emphasized as key features of Civic Statistics (e.g. Burrill & Biehler, 2011; ProCivicStat Report, 2018, point 8). Most interesting for beginners in the world of data are bivariate situations where one variable is categorical. The corresponding terms are referred to as *grouping* or categorization, and the statistical activities of group comparison are often perceived as "the heart of statistics" (Konold & Higgins, 2003, p. 206; for a detailed discussion of corresponding educational research, see Biehler et al., 2018, p. 163 f.).

Categorization (putting things into classes or categories based on their similarities) enables humans to organize the world around them, thus simplifying it. This is a fundamental activity which people constantly engage in, e.g. when they interpret and evaluate information, when they recognize concrete objects or understand abstract ideas, when they make decisions or when they deal with risk, generally, in all forms of interaction with the environment (Martignon et al., 2011). Categorization is a basic concept of our thinking (Anderson, 1991; Jordan & Russell, 1999).

The idea of comparing—say, boys and girls, older and younger people—on different attributes is often raised even by young pupils. Thus, it is quite natural

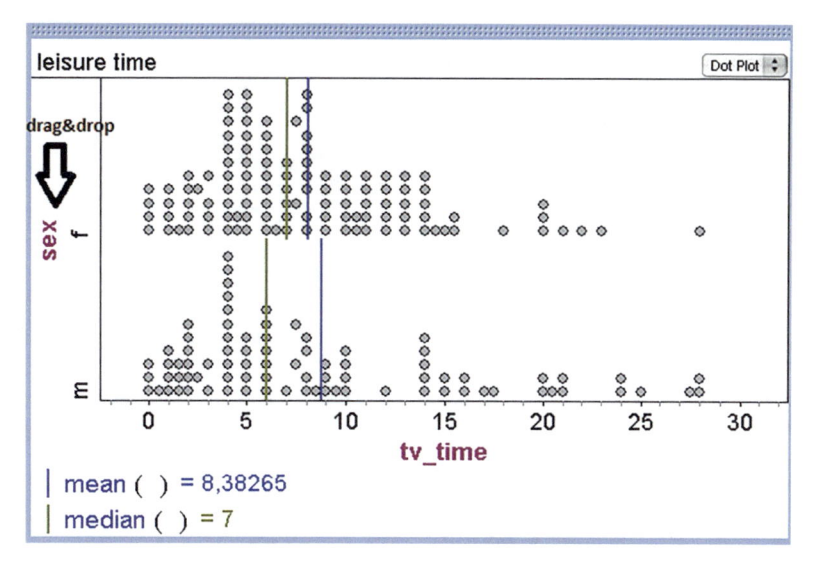

Fig. 17.2 Grouping within a dot plot diagram with drag-and-drop, grouping variable: sex (Fathom, 2018)

that initial statistical activities also deal with grouping. The most natural question here is: "Is there a difference between ... and ...?" (boys and girls, young and old, rich and poor, today and in the past, industrialized and developing countries, and so on ...). Curiosity alone makes pupils want to investigate such questions, and even more so if they are members of a subgroup in the comparison. So this is a great starting point for intrinsically motivated learning.

Technically speaking, students now learn to represent relationships in different ways, depending on the nature of the variables themselves—for example, if both variables are categorical using contingency tables or trees. If one variable is categorical and the other is numerical (e.g. gender and body height), then the task is to compare different distributions. With dynamic visualization software (like *Fathom*) grouping is very easy to handle. The grouping variable is simply dragged onto the "free" axis of an already created chart or table, which *Fathom* automatically divides by categories. Figure 17.2 shows a dot plot representation of pupils' answers to the question "How many hours do you watch TV a week?" grouped by sex. In principle, this simple but fundamental procedure of grouping is possible within all types of charts.

If the other variable is also categorical, then contingency tables can be created in the same simple way by dragging the variables into the evaluation table. Figure 17.3 shows an example of a contingency table with the variables "Owns a computer?" (yes/no) and sex.

If both variables are numerical, the relationship between the variables is usually visualized via a scatter diagram, such as Fig. 17.4 which shows the relationship between total leisure time *netto_time* and the time spent on the computer

Fig. 17.3 Contingency table, variables: owns computer/sex (Fathom, 2018)

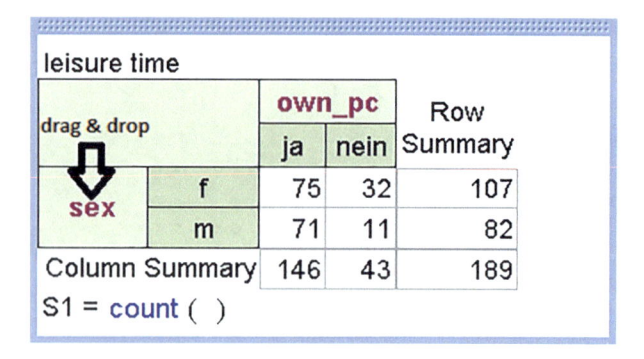

Fig. 17.4 Scatter diagram, variables: leisure time in total/time spent on a computer in hours per week (Fathom, 2018)

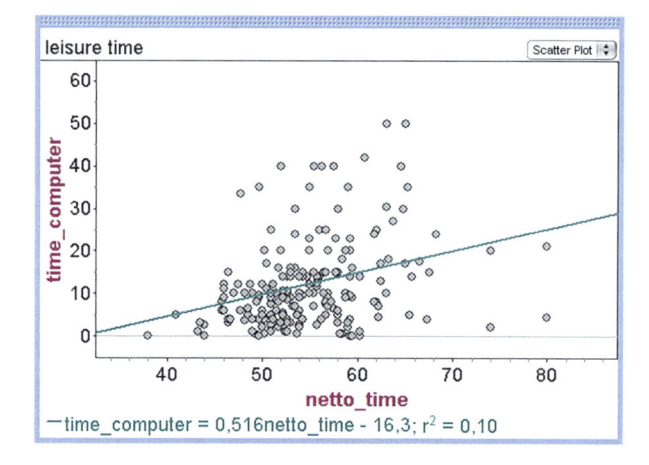

time_computer. However, reasoning about covariation and association is likely to be more difficult to grasp for beginners because it combines two basic ideas: "data and chance" and "relation and function" (for a detailed discussion of the corresponding educational research see Biehler et al., 2018, p. 173 f.). Nevertheless, the relationship between two numerical variables is of such fundamental interest that one cannot do without it in an introduction to data exploration. Besides the representation as a scatterplot, *Fathom* offers the possibility of modelling a functional relationship between two numerical variables by fitting curves to the data.

17.2.5 Content Design and Sequential Arrangement of Project-Based Units

The skills obtained in the basic training are intended to be applied by the students who conduct their own Civic Statistics project with a socially relevant topic and with the help of easy-to-use data analysis software tools like *Fathom*. A useful aid for structuring the project work is, of course, the PPDAC-model (Wild & Pfannkuch,

1999). As mentioned, this model documents the major steps a person would take in carrying out a statistical inquiry, with modifications for public rather than self-collected data. The first step is to identify a topic that is related to a relevant, real-world **problem** (PPDAC). A better term for "problem" might be "knowledge-deficit" or "understanding-deficit" (Wild et al., 2018). For the identification of topics suitable for teaching purposes, PCS provides the "CivicStatMap"[7] tool, a way to access teaching materials quickly by aspects such as language, education level, social theme (topic), and appropriate ICT-tools.

For example, one topic selected by our students for project work was *income inequality*, which we will discuss in further detail below. Table 17.2 presents an overview of the contents and sequence of 6–7 learning units, of 90 min each, including references to PPDAC stages and typical task activities.

The initiation of project work with students is a crucial phase. Students' curiosity to investigate a topic often comes from the media, such as in the following example: "What is *Equal Pay Day*?"—There is a story behind the answer to this question, which can easily be found with an online search:

> Every year there is the so-called Equal Pay Day, an international day of action for equal payment between women and men (see Fig. 17.5), which aims to draw attention to the existing gender-specific income differences in different countries (known as the "Gender Pay Gap" or "GPG"). It symbolizes the date, how much longer than a year the "average woman" must work in order to earn what the "average man" has earned in the previous year. The calculation of the Equal Pay Day depends on the GPG measured as the average difference between women's and men's wages. In this regard, Equal Pay Day reflects the respective pay gap.

Perhaps some students still do not understand why this is an important issue therefore, it should be emphasized:

> Equal pay for equal work is a demand that is in accordance with the third article of the German Constitutional Act. Section two of this act reads: "Men and women have equal rights. The State shall promote the effective implementation of equality between women and men at work to eliminate existing disadvantages."

An online-search of media reports leads to quite controversial statements about the GPG. For instance on the one hand the weekly German newspaper "Die Zeit" writes:

> Salary differences are particularly high in Germany [. . .] As the EU Commission announced in Brussels, the Federal Republic of Germany ranks 26th out of 28 EU countries with a difference of 22 percent [income difference between women and men].[8]

---

[7] http://iase-web.org/islp/pcs (see CivicStatMap).

[8] source: ZEIT online, nov. 20, 2017, translated from German by the authors, https://www.zeit.de/wirtschaft/2017-11/gender-pay-gap-lohn-deutschland-schlusslicht-europa

Table 17.2 Overview of project sequence and contents on the topic "The Gender Pay Gap"

Time (units of 90 min each)	Unit contents	Media	Stage (typical activities)
2	Introduction to the social topic The Gender Pay Gap (GPG) and to the historical and current discussion about the GPG; Identifying specific research questions; Searching for data sources; Obtaining public data; Becoming familiar with the data (variables); Forming work groups	Online-search; media-reports; *Pay inequality between women and men in Germany* report; worksheet (adaption of CivicStatMap material 5.211)[a]; Data-set of the Earnings Structure Survey with metadata (i.e. a list of variables, together with detailed descriptions)	Problem-Plan-Data (search, check, discover, read, ask, wonder, identify, predict, organize …)
2–3	Working in groups: Investigating specific research questions; applying statistical reasoning (visualization, aggregation, group comparison, association between variables) by using software; formulating findings, drawing conclusions, interpretations, answering questions, and forming new/unanswered questions; Preparation of a presentation with software and practising for the presentation	Data-set with metadata; list of research questions; *Fathom 2* software package and presentation software	Analysis-Conclusion (investigate, analyze, explore, visualize, summarize, evaluate, reason, infer, interpret, explain, conclude, decide, reflect, formulate, recommend, persuade …)
2	Presentation by each group (ca. 10-15 min); peer-discussion and feedback; teachers' feedback	Presentation software; Written text	Presentation-Discussion (present, communicate, discuss, argue, debate, give feedback, review …)

[a]http://iase-web.org/islp/pcs (see Sample lesson plans: 5.211_OV_OverviewGenderPayGap.pdf)

However, in a press release issued by the German Federal Statistics Office in March 2017, we are presented with rather different information:

> [. . .] three-quarters of the gender pay gap [is] attributable to structural differences [. . .] The Federal Statistics Office (Destatis) also reports on the occasion of Equal Pay Day on

Fig. 17.5 Equal Pay Day in Berlin (BPW Germany, 2016-03-18 https://www.flickr.com/photos/bpwgermany/26175596082/in/album-72157666292076870, copyright: CC BY-ND 2.0)

18 March 2017 that nearly three-quarters of the unadjusted gender pay gap could be attributed to structural differences.[9]

As these two examples show, controversial reporting raises questions of whether the story is partly inaccurately or even incorrectly presented in the media, and whether it is even possible to discover "the real truth". Put in more general terms, the question is: *What is the problem here and how can we better understand it?* In this early stage, the problem is typically vague. The first step is about trying to find very *specific questions*, which we should be able to answer using accessible public data. "Arriving at useful questions that can realistically be answered using statistical data always involves a lot of hard thinking and often a lot of hard preparatory work. Statistics education research says little about this . . ." (Wild et al., 2018, p. 11).

In this respect, different degrees of openness may be appropriate depending on the competence and autonomy of learners—from completely open questions to the pre-setting of some relevant questions by the teacher. Thus, it remains a didactic-pedagogical decision for the teacher with consideration of the learning group. In our opinion, it is reasonable that high-school teachers will provide some basic structure in the form of prepared data records, thought-provoking articles, media-based claims, or explanations of special terminology related to the topic, in order to help students find relevant questions for investigation (for an overview of research in relation to posing and refining statistical questions, see Watson et al. 2018; see, in particular, Gal's Sects. 13.5–13.8 in Chap. 13).

For the GPG topic, we describe ideas and resources from the PCS project (see ProCivicStat lesson plans 5.205 to 5.211[10]). First, the students were introduced to the historical and current discussion about the GPG through a report entitled *Pay inequality between women and men in Germany* from the Federal Ministry for

---

[9]Source: DESTATIS, press release No. 094, 14 March 2017, translated from German by the authors https://www.destatis.de/DE/Presse/Pressemitteilungen/2017/03/PD17_094_621.html

[10]http://iase-web.org/islp/pcs (see Sample lesson plans).

Family Affairs, Senior Citizens, Women and Youth, 2009.[11] This report allowed students to familiarize themselves with the situation of pay inequality and learn about the definitions and distinctions between adjusted and unadjusted GPG. In addition, the report contains some causes of wage inequality between female and male employees in Germany, which the students could then explore in more detail. Examples of focussed questions on the subject are formulated, e.g.: "What is the adjusted GPG?"; "What causes (aspects) can be listed for the GPG?"; "To what extent are these causes (aspects) really responsible for income differences?"; etc.

In the implementation of the (PPDAC) **plan** and **data** stages, the learner has to decide how to answer the question(s) developed in the previous stage. Since Civic Statistics is rarely about collecting one's own data, but rather is about using external data sources, students should ask questions such as: "Which organization would keep data on this?"; "What kind of data are needed to answer the questions?"; "How reputable is the data source?"; "Does the government or local authority release data sets on this topic?"; "Which data source could possibly be classified as the most trustworthy source?"; "Is the data recent and freely accessible?"; etc. We have to realize here, of course, that secondary level students have very little knowledge about real data sources and their quality. Therefore, it is reasonable at this point for teachers to help students search for suitable public data sets to a greater or lesser extent – again, depending on the students' self-reliance, as in the formulation of the research questions. The dataset (and associated metadata) we used with our students is from the Federal Statistics Office of Germany, taken from an official earnings structure survey. The metadata document on the earnings structure survey provides information on the survey procedure and the individual variables that have been surveyed.[12] The task in this step is for students to familiarize themselves with the data set and its variables, identifying characteristics relevant to different aspects and questions using the variable list. The students should assume that multiple factors have an influence on the GPG, including age, region, economic status, job position, and occupation group. Students are asked "Are these characteristics included in the data set?"; "What are the typical values?"; "Is data categorical or numerical?"; etc.

Now the basics are in place for the students to demonstrate their investigative skills in the (PPDAC) **analysis** stage. Our students carried out data analysis with *Fathom 2*, which was also used previously for training. Whatever the ICT tool, however, the analysis stage should always emphasize teaching and learning a conceptual understanding of analytical techniques and the ability to interpret the output of software packages. Learners must learn how to make sense of what the data means in the context of the questions.

The first step is to become more familiar with the data, often by "eyeballing" it in a graph or table, which requires a certain basic understanding of the idea of variation

---

[11] https://www.bmfsfj.de/blob/94442/efbd528467e361882848c23486fcc8d8/pay-ine-quality-data.pdf

[12] for more information about the dataset and metadata document see http://iase-web.org/islp/pcs (Sample lesson plans: 5.211_OV_OverviewGenderPayGap.pdf).

and distribution. Reasoning related to distribution often benefits from viewing data in different visualizations that "do the best job of telling the story sharply and fairly" (Konold & Higgins, 2003). On the one hand, this means technically knowing how to create tables, charts, graphs, etc. by using ICT-tools; on the other hand, how to read and reason about tables, charts, graphs, etc.

Continuing with the analysis, it is often necessary to summarize or reduce the data. This process encourages students to see the aggregate characteristics of a distribution, which are not evident in any of the individual cases (Konold & Higgins, 2003). Reasoning related to distribution is viewed as a meta-concept and involves reasoning about features such as centre, spread, shape, density, skewness, outliers, etc. It is worth emphasizing, once again, that an essential aspect of the analysis stage consists of comparing groups and the idea of the association between two variables, which we have already discussed in detail in the presentation of training units (see Sect. 17.2.4). The students can discover, for instance, that the difference in earnings is associated with variables like *profession group*, *economic status*, *performance group*, *age* and *region*. A special role is also played by factors such as *level of employment* (full-time, part-time, marginally employed) and *interruption in employment*.

In the (PPDAC) **conclusion** stage, the students use the results from the analysis to answer the questions from the problem stage. They have to decide how to formulate the results and communicate them to others, and they are often able to form new questions which could be answered in the next PPDAC cycle. This stage arguably involves the most important critical thinking skills: data interpretation skills enable students to reflect critically on the claims made by others, such as politicians, other opinion-leaders, or the media—in election campaigns, in adverts, in the workplace, etc.

Developing this ability is the core goal of the Civic Statistics approach. The overall objectives are the ability to recognize some topic's current relevance for society and social policy, and to form an opinion, which is grounded in concrete evidence, about what could and should be done to address policy issues (see Chap. 3 of this book, facet 1).

17.2.6 *Learning Objectives*

In this part of the chapter, we describe some key activities that students engage with during the course. Developing fluency in engaging in these activities is, in our opinion, a core goal for statistics education:

> 1. Students *discover causes* for the inequality of pay between male and female employees, including less obvious causes.

(continued)

2. Students *become familiar with terms* in the context of Gender Pay Gap and can distinguish between the adjusted and unadjusted GPG.

3. Students *discuss (often passionately) differences and causes* of GPG.

4. Students *explore and reason about the data* based on questions arising from the materials.

5. Students *explore and reason about the data* according to their own questions or hypotheses.

6. Students *explore and reason about the data* using techniques of exploratory data analysis via ICT-based tools to pursue objectives 4 and 5.

7. Students *critically interpret* the results on the topic, *reflect* on media discussions about the topic, and can thus *uncover inaccurate reporting*.

8. Students *draw conclusions* based on the outcomes of their investigations, and *justify* them with statistical statements and visualizations.

9. Students *prepare their results* (text, posters, software-based presentation, etc.), so that they can *present* them to their classmates in a clear and persuasive way.

10. Students *discuss their current findings* in a plenary session and may *find further questions* on the topic.

If the project is to be treated as interdisciplinary (e.g. mathematics with social science subjects), splitting the learning objectives between the two subjects is also very practical. For example, a discussion of social issues is essential within social science subjects, while statistical analysis can be the main focus of mathematics classes. In this sense, learning objectives 1–3 would be more related to the context knowledge, while objectives 4–6 are typically part of statistical or mathematical knowledge. Objectives 7–10 relate to learning outcomes of the project work and address cross-curricular competencies such as critical thinking, creativity, verbal and writing skills, etc. Other cross-curricular key competencies are generally addressed by this kind of project-based learning, such as communication, use of ICT and effective work methods, cooperation, social and civic competence, and cultural awareness.

17.2.7 Special Learning Opportunities

The special nature of Civic Statistics lies in the extraordinary opportunities that arise for mathematics teaching. Learners are given room to express their curiosity and make discoveries; they can choose their own learning paths and create their own outcomes. The pay gap difference between women and men can be measured in different ways: according to hourly, monthly or annual income or income over the individuals' entire working life; gross or net income can be considered; individual groups may be the focus, e.g. only full-time employees or certain professional

Table 17.3 Characteristics of the classes taught in Civic Statistics

	Thuringian classes	Bavarian classes
Course type and main subject	Regular classes/computer science	Seminar course/computer science
Grade level	11/upper secondary	11/upper secondary
Number of project groups (members of each group)	5 (3 students each)	5 (2 students each) and 1 (3 students)
Duration of training (units of 90 min)	5	4 (classroom) and about 4×1 h of homework
Project work (units of 90 min)	6	7
Student output	Presenting a report using appropriate media	
Method of assessment	Teachers' feedback and peers' feedback	

groups. The number of combinations of the individual variables is almost unlimited. There is no "correct" result or "right" answer. In this sense, the students' results are likely to be different and may also deviate significantly from the teachers' expected conclusions, which is rarely the case in mathematics lessons.

17.3 Results and Conclusions from Practical Lessons

In this section, we would like to briefly present some of the results of the first teaching experiments using the Civic Statistics approach. Classes from high schools ("Gymnasium") in two German federal states were taught by the authors. Here, in addition to examples of students' work in terms of achieving desired competencies, procedural and curricular aspects of teaching Civic Statistics are discussed. We have to emphasize that we did not conduct a quasi-experimental teaching study with a well-defined research design. We also did not conduct a quantitative assessment to test learning success. The following describes our personal teaching experiences on project work in the Civic Statistics context. We report "lessons learned", give tips for further projects, and highlight some of the difficulties we encountered.

We had slightly different course conditions (summarized in Table 17.3); however these did not lead to substantial differences in terms of outcome. There were some differences in group sizes and in the type of basic training which was provided (with or without the flipped classroom concept). Furthermore, the Bavarian students were taught in a special course, the content of which can be designed more flexibly than in regular classes (see further details in Sect. 17.3.3).

17.3.1 Competence-Related Findings

Of course, an essential question is whether the formulated learning objectives can actually be achieved by most students, in particular objectives 7–9 in the earlier list.

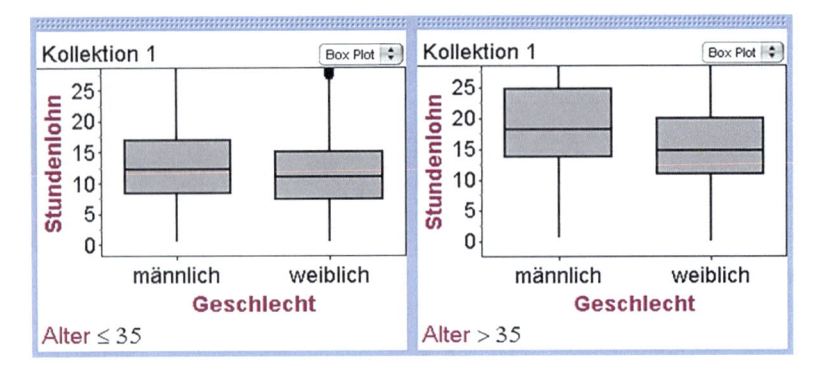

Fig. 17.6 A boxplot visualization from students' presentation, aspect "age" (Fathom, 2018).

Kollektion 1		Geschlecht		Row
		männlich	weiblich	Summary
	Angelernte_Arbeitskräfte_einfache_Tätigkeiten	59	41	100
	Leitende Stellung	64	36	100
Leistungsgruppe	Schwierige Tätigkeiten	57	43	100
	Sehr_schwierige_kompl_Tätigkeiten	56	44	100
	Ungelernte_Arbeitskräft_einfache_Tätigkeiten	45	55	100
	Column Summary	56	44	100

S1 = round (rowproportion•100)

Fig. 17.7 Contingency table from the students' presentation, aspect "job position" (Fathom, 2018)

Our classroom experiences support the view that these competences can be reached by 11th graders, who have acquired descriptive statistics skills within conventional mathematics curricula together with training of the type presented above. The following examples of students' statements (translated from the original German by the authors) on the visualizations they created for their presentations illustrate that the learners were able to acquire competencies aligned with our learning objectives (see Sect. 17.2.6).

Daniel P. and Daniel V. (see Fig. 17.6): "Afterwards, we dealt with the question of whether the GPG depends on the age of the employees. This thesis was confirmed by comparing two box plots (age < 35 and age > 35), which shows that men receive a higher salary than women with increasing age."

Anwar and Nikolas (see Fig. 17.7): "The aspect of the occupational level affects the GPG! According to our statistics, women are more likely to be found in lower occupational levels than in management positions."

Lara, Fatih and Max (see Fig. 17.8): "The best-paid professions are mainly occupied by men. Women mostly work in jobs that are less challenging, and have the lowest hourly wages. This is also why, with increasing age, the average income of men increases faster than that of women. Comparing the slope of the median-median functions shows this."

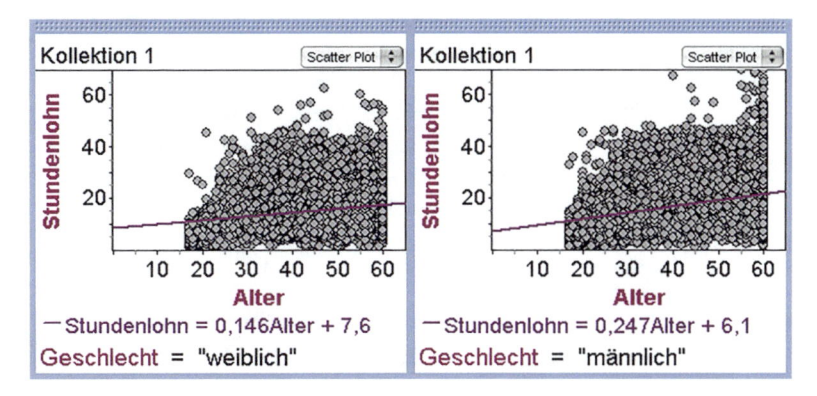

Fig. 17.8 Scatter plot visualization with trend lines from the students' presentation, aspect "age" (Fathom, 2018)

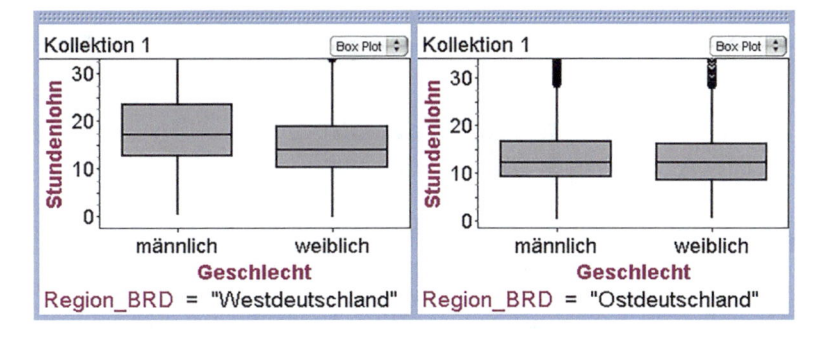

Fig. 17.9 A boxplot visualization from the students' presentation, aspect "region" (Fathom, 2018).

Frederik and Aland (see Fig. 17.9): "The GPG is much smaller in the new federal states than in the old ones [author's note: "old" refers to West German and "new" to East German federal states after the fall of the Wall]. The GPG problem is barely visible in East Germany. However, women in West Germany earn on average a bit more than men in East Germany."

Another example shows that students were also able to identify factors that have an influence on gender differences in payment, which are more difficult to detect. For instance, the fact that the GPG becomes apparent only with increasing age was clarified by students modifying a scatter plot of the relationship between payment and age (see Fig. 17.10).

A modification with the *transform()*-command in *Fathom* allows for the individual construction of categories for single variables (in this case, for age groups). One project group, which looked more closely at certain occupational groups, illustrated an interesting aspect: men are paid higher salaries even in fields in which women tend to dominate, such as *education and teaching*. They defined their own salary categories for this (see Fig. 17.11): In the lowest category (up to 10 € per hour), a

Fig. 17.10 Grouped scatter plot visualization from the students' presentation, aspect "region" (Fathom, 2018)

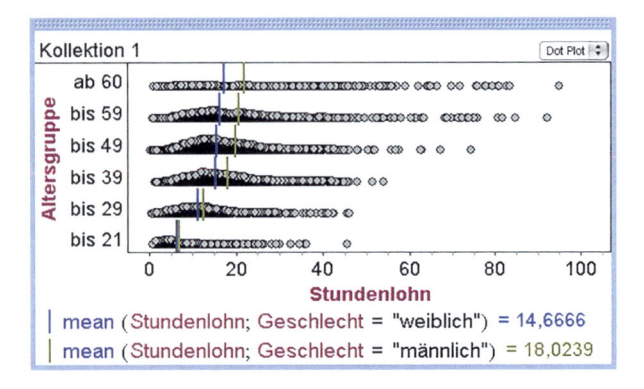

Fig. 17.11 Contingency table from the students' presentation; the focus is on the occupational group "education and teaching", aspects "gender" and "salary groups" (Fathom, 2018)

Kollektion 1

		Geschlecht		Row Summary
		männlich	weiblich	
Lohngruppe	bis 10 €	45	55	100
	bis 20 €	54	46	100
	bis 30 €	63	37	100
	bis 40 €	82	18	100
	bis 50 €	89	11	100
Column Summary		56	44	100

S1 = round (rowproportion•100)

total of 55% were women; in the highest category (over 40 € per hour), a total of 89% were men.

An important component of achieving competencies in reasoning about data is the intention to present and discuss results, preferably in a *peer-feedback* session (the last unit of the project work). The quintessential process in project work is for students to defend their own conclusions based on their own statistical investigations with real data, rather than just to reproduce or evaluate others' claims. To be able to reflect on different strategies and outcomes in context with more complex non-mathematical problem situations requires sophisticated metacognitive skills (Schoenfeld, 2016), and to discuss them with sound arguments calls on the highest levels of mathematical competence at the end of the lower secondary education period (cf. models for competence levels for mathematical education, Blum et al., 2013).

In our classes, we witnessed lively discussions on whether meaningful cause-and-effect relationships had been identified and coherent conclusions drawn. Students' own findings in relation to actual media discussions and statements were put to the test. Another important point is that students were made aware of the fact that clear evidence is often denied even by prominent persons (on issues that range from discrimination to climate change to the dangers of a virus pandemic). For example, *Time Magazine* reports that according to an online poll of over 8000 American adults in 2019, "still nearly half of men believe that the [gender] pay gap is made up to serve a political purpose, rather than being a legitimate issue".[13]

Apart from achieving learning objectives, perhaps the most important aspect is that learners can reach a level of competence that is increasingly relevant in today's world: it is not enough to simply make claims about societal issues; they must be supported by real data. Learners need to achieve essential competences in "data literacy" if they are to distinguish clearly between a personal opinion and a substantiated conclusion based on evidence (Suarez-Alvarez, 2021). From this perspective, learning Civic Statistics is empowering for everyday life.

17.3.2 Process-Related Findings

The process-oriented view focuses on the question of characteristics related to the teaching and learning processes. What potential does the teaching of Civic Statistics offer in this respect? Observing the learning processes of our students, typical characteristics can be found which are usually referred to via terms such as *independent, self-determined, self-directed*, or *self-regulated learning*. In other words, there is a clear emphasis on the *constructive* part of the teaching and learning processes. A key point is, of course, the project-oriented style of teaching and learning. Projects provide the opportunity to develop a wide range of competences, notably methodological, personal, communicative, and practical. It is very learner focussed, and overcomes the classic restriction to 45- or 90-min teaching units.

The following observations on processes while working on the GPG project are likely to characterise similar projects where students work with relevant and interesting social topics:

- Topics currently being discussed in the media make it meaningful, and also easier for learners to access relevant content.
- Such topics stimulate a lot of activity and provide an opportunity for inquiry-based learning, because they challenge the students to make conjectures and validate them.
- The course is designed to make learners aware of their learning strategies. They need to think about their approaches to learning from data and discuss their strategies. They reflect not only *what* is learned, but also *why* and *how* it is learned, developing their metacognitive skills.
- The working method creates positive social experiences. Students can challenge, support, and encourage each other when dealing with the topic by exchanging

---

[13] Source: Time Magazine, April 2, 2019, https://time.com/5562171/pay-gap-survey-equal-pay-day/?utm_medium=socialflowtw & utm_source=twitter.com & utm_campaign=time & xid=time_socialflow_twitter

individual ideas and insights, and designing formulations and visualizations for their presentation.

- The learners can experience situations in which they are responsible for their own learning because they have to make most of the decisions in the project themselves.
- The teacher has a supportive (rather than directive) role in this teaching and learning process. This openness and the variety of possible outcomes facilitates a natural differentiation – making it easier to provide individualized learning. This gives teachers more opportunities to deal with heterogeneity in the classroom.

Of course, as in any kind of teaching and learning processes, there are challenges and obstacles:

- Too much openness in the choice of topics, materials, or questions usually does not lead to meaningful results. If there is no solid didactic preparation, projects can become chaotic events. While some groups managed to organize themselves well, others could not really cope with the openness and needed organizational help from the teacher.
- We found some cognitive overload, due to the complexity of the topics, causing students to avoid more elaborate and difficult reasoning. This, of course, does not encourage critical thinking.
- As in all cases of collaboration, we have to reckon with process irregularities in the groups, due to mismanagement of time, poor communication, unequal distribution of tasks, lack of responsibility of certain group members, etc.
- Student performance is usually evaluated. The type of assessment is an integral part of school teaching and must be clearly defined, but the work presented is difficult to grade. This is a matter for further reflection.

17.3.3   Curriculum-Related Findings

Not only in Germany, but also in many other countries, the majority of high school students only have limited statistical expertise. Process-oriented skills are also hard to find, as are skills in handling ICT-based tools for data analysis. Statistics is probably the most taught adjunct subject in the academic world. There is almost no academic or scientific discipline that can do without statistics. But in nearly all countries, statistics is not a separate subject taught in secondary level education, but a subject that is taught within math classes (Burrill & Biehler, 2011). In Germany, for example, the regular high school mathematics curricula offers few opportunities for more demanding statistical thinking in the sense of reasoning about data. One explanation for this general neglect of statistical thinking content within the mathematics curricula may be tensions between mathematics and basic statistical ideas, e.g. Gal (in Petocz et al., 2018, p. 96):

The development of statistical literacy, although important from a societal perspective, is facing many obstacles as it does not have a natural place in the curriculum or in the mind and schedules of many teachers (such as those who teach traditional introductory statistics at the college or high school levels).

With our experience as math teachers, we affirm that there is still a strong need for further improvement and innovation in statistics school practice and curricula (for an overview of innovative ideas and revisions, see Pfannkuch, 2018). In addition, because mathematical and statistical thinking often differ in their essential characteristics, there is an urgent need for further discussion on expanding the teaching of statistics to other subjects (e.g. computer sciences and social sciences). These ideas are further elaborated by Engel, Louie, and Nicholson in Chap. 18.

Here, we used a special form of course organization to teach Civic Statistics, in which the emphasis is on developing process skills (such as scientific or statistical thinking) rather than focussing on content knowledge or specific procedural skills. In German high schools, there are so-called *seminar courses* (literally translated from the German "Seminarkurs") in upper secondary level education (e.g. in Bavaria: "W-Seminar", the "W" stands for "wissenschaftlich" = "scientific"). One aim of the W-seminar course is to introduce scientific ideas and to teach general scientific working methods. The seminar courses are intended to prepare students for scientific or professional work. Education in dealing with social data fits very well with these goals.

The project work on the Gender Pay Gap of the Nuremberg students was part of a seminar course "World of Data", which had a quite extensive time-frame of 2 h per week over 3 semesters (Wassner et al., 2018). With this scope, it is obvious that the course was not only related to mathematics, but also interdisciplinary content from computer science, social science, and economics. Ethical aspects of extensive data collection were discussed, such as the misuse of social data, violation of personal rights, (excessive or illegal) observation of people, and data protection. Each student had to pick a topic within the main theme "Data", as the basis for a paper of 10–15 pages that meets appropriate academic standards; each student then gave a final presentation of their work. To give an example, one student's work dealt with data analysis on a typical Civic Statistics topic: "*Influences on life expectancy in Germany since the 1800s*". The student writes in the introduction to his paper:

Around the year 1800, the life expectancy in Germany was 38.4 years. One hundred years later it was 44, and after another 100 years, the life expectancy was 78. Life expectancy is influenced by many different factors, which have a varying impact on the phenomenon. I will evaluate these factors empirically using trustworthy data sets and assess which of these factors have a significant effect on life expectancy. [...] By identifying the reasons for increased life expectancy in Germany, we may learn from history how life expectancy can be further increased.

Such an interdisciplinary course under the keyword "Data" may not be integrated in current curriculum frameworks in the short-term, but it is worth thinking about the idea regarding further statistical education. Our first attempt at a "Data" seminar over a longer period of time and at the school-level was very promising. We recommend that it should become an integral part of general school education.

17.4   Conclusions

Reasoning about real data at the school level is essential in order to lay the foundation for our students to cope with complicated information and growing amounts of data in today's world. Successful teaching adopting a Civic Statistics approach in secondary education is possible. Our first attempts and outcomes illustrate the achievability of competences and learning objectives, which have been formulated in detail in this chapter, despite the challenges and difficulties involved in the process, which must be taken into account.

In terms of preparedness, the students should already be able to cope with a certain degree of self-directed learning at about the ninth grade level. As the teaching of statistics within the school framework can vary significantly from country to country (or even from teacher to teacher), we highly recommend developing and further honing the basics of statistics knowledge before Civic Statistics issues are addressed in class. Teaching Civic Statistics has great significance for the teaching of mathematics, in light of its relevance to reality. Teaching and learning processes can be described as open, self-regulating, activating, creative, productive, and social. The teacher is perceived more as a guide and advisor than as an instructor.

Other teaching methods, beyond the usual subject-oriented organization of learning at school, are very useful for Civic Statistics, i.e. interdisciplinary project-oriented forms or even self-contained multidisciplinary courses on a major key topic in the sense of the data seminars presented here. Teaching Civic Statistics is a prime example of interdisciplinary teaching. Data analysis connects mathematics with social issues related to subjects such as social sciences, economics, geography, history, ethics, use of ICT to computer science, and more. We need more innovative ideas for the future of statistical education, e.g. team teaching and the development of interdisciplinary curricula to create a new balance between curriculum, teaching practice, teacher professionalism, subject expertise, social environment, and reality of life, if we are to improve the quality of education in modern information societies.

References

Abeysekera, L., & Dawson, P. (2015). Motivation and cognitive load in the flipped classroom: Definition, rationale and a call for research. *Higher Education Research and Development, 34*(1), 1–14.

Abreu, B. D. S., Mihailidis, P., Lee, A. Y. L., & Melki, J. (2017). *International handbook of media literacy education* (1st ed.). Routledge.

AK Stochastik in der Schule der Gesellschaft für Didaktik der Mathematik (GDM). (2002). Empfehlungen zu Zielen und zur Gestaltung des Stochastikunterrichts. In: Toepell, M. (Hrsg.). *Mitteilungen der Gesellschaft für Didaktik der Mathematik*, Dez. 2002. Universität Leipzig.

Anderson, J. R. (1991). The adaptive nature of human categorization. *Psychological Review, 98*, 409–429.

Anderson, J. R., Reder, L. M., & Simon, H. A. (1996). Situated learning and education. *Educational Researcher, 25*(4), 5–11.

Batanero, C., Chernoff, E. J., Engel, J., Lee, H. S., & Sánchez, E. (2016). *Research on teaching and learning probability. ICME-13 topical surveys.* Springer.

Bergmann, J., & Sams, A. (2012). *Flip your classroom: Reach every student in every class every day.* International Society for Technology in Education.

Biehler, R. (1982). *Explorative Datenanalyse – eine Untersuchung aus der Perspektive einer deskriptiv-empirischen Wissenschaftstheorie.* IDM Materialien und Studien, Band 24, Universität Bielefeld.

Biehler, R. (1999). Auf Entdeckungsreise in Daten. *Mathematik lehren, 97,* 4–5.

Biehler, R., Hofmann, T., Maxara, C. & Prömmel, A. (2011). *Daten und Zufall mit Fathom – Unterrichtsideen für die SI und SII mit Software-Einführung* [translated from German: Data and chance with Fathom - teaching ideas for secondary education with software introduction]. Schroedel.

Biehler, R., Ben-Zvi, D., Bakker, A., & Makar, K. (2013). Technology for enhancing statistical reasoning at the school level. In M. A. Clements et al. (Eds.), *Third international handbook of mathematics education* (pp. 643–690). Springer.

Biehler, R., Frischemeier, D., Reading, C., & Shaughnessy, J. M. (2018). Reasoning about data. In D. Ben-Zvi, K. Makar, & J. Garfield (Eds.), *International handbook of research in statistics education* (pp. 139–192). Springer.

Blum, W., Galbraith, P., Henn, H.-W., & Niss, M. (Eds.) (2007). *Modelling and applications in mathematics education.* New ICMI Study Series, vol. 10. Springer.

Blum, W., Roppelt, A., & Müller, M. (2013). Kompetenzstufenmodelle für das Fach Mathematik. In H. A. Pant, P. Stanat, et al. (Eds.), *IQB-Ländervergleich 2012. Mathematische und naturwissenschaftliche Kompetenzen am Ende der Sekundarstufe* (Vol. I, pp. 61–73). Waxmann.

Burrill, G. & Biehler, R. (2011). Fundamental statistical ideas in the school curriculum and in training teachers. In: Batanero, C., Burrill G., Reading C. (Eds.). *Teaching statistics in school mathematics - Challenges for teaching and teacher education.* New ICMI Study Series, vol. 14, 57-69. Springer.

Callingham, R., & Watson, J. M. (2017). The development of statistical literacy at school. *Statistics Education Research Journal, 17*(1), 181–201.

Fathom. (2018). *Fathom Dynamic Data Software 2.4.* The Concord Consortium. https://fathom.concord.org

Fischbein, E. (1975). *The intuitive sources of probabilistic thinking in children.* D. Reidel.

Freudenthal, H. (1983). *Didactical phenomenology of mathematical structures.* D. Reidel.

Jordan, M. I. & Russell, S. (1999). Categorization. In: *The MIT encyclopedia of the cognitive sciences* (pp. 104-106). The MIT Press.

Konold, C., & Higgins, T. L. (2003). *Reasoning about data. A research companion to principles and standards for school mathematics* (pp. 193–215). National Council of Teachers of Mathematics.

Martignon, L., Katsikopoulos, K. V., & Woike, J. (2011). Categorization with limited resources: A family of simple heuristics. In G. Gigerenzer, R. Hertwig, & T. Pachur (Eds.), *Heuristics: The foundations of adaptive behavior* (pp. 319–332). Oxford University Press.

National Council of Teachers of Mathematics. (2000). *Principles and Standards for School Mathematics.* NCTM.

Petocz, P., Reid, A., & Gal, I. (2018). Statistics education research. In D. Ben-Zvi, K. Makar, & J. Garfield (Eds.), *International handbook of research in statistics education* (pp. 71–99). Springer.

Pfannkuch, M. (2018). Reimagining curriculum approaches. In D. Ben-Zvi, K. Makar, & J. Garfield (Eds.), *International handbook of research in statistics education* (pp. 387–413). Springer.

ProCivicStat Partners. (2018). *Engaging civic statistics: A call for action and recommendations. A product of the ProCivicStat project.* http://iase-web.org/islp/pcs

Prömmel, A., Göckede, B., et al. (2010). Beschreibende Statistik mit Fathom. In R. Biehler (Ed.), *Kasseler Online-Schriften zur Didaktik der Stochastik (KaDiSto)* (Vol. 8). Universität Kassel. https://kobra.uni-kassel.de/handle/123456789/2007011016602

Reich, K. (2007). Interactive constructivism in education. *Education and Culture, 23*(1), 7–26.

Schoenfeld, A. (2016). Learning to think mathematically: Problem solving, metacognition, and sense making in mathematics (Reprint). *Journal of Education, 196*, 1–38. https://doi.org/10.1177/002205741619600202

Schupp, H. (2004). Allgemeinbildender Stochastikunterricht. *Stochastik in der Schule, 24*(3), 4–13.

Suarez-Alvarez, J. (2021). Are 15-year-olds prepared to deal with fake news and misinformation? *PISA in Focus*, 113, OECD Publishing.

Tukey, J. (1977). *Exploratory data analysis* (1st ed.). Pearson.

Wassner, C., Podworny, S., & Biehler, R. (2018). Reale Datenkompetenz im Unterricht fördern. In Fachgruppe Didaktik der Mathematik der Universität Paderborn (Ed.), *Beiträge zum Mathematikunterricht 2018*, Band IV, 1923-1926. WTM-Verlag.

Watson, J., Fitzallen, N., Fielding-Wells, J., & Madden, S. (2018). The practice of statistics? In D. Ben-Zvi, K. Makar, & J. Garfield (Eds.), *International handbook of research in statistics education* (pp. 105–137). Springer.

Wentzel, K. R., & Wigfield, A. (2009). *Handbook of motivation at school*. Educational psychology handbook series. Routledge.

Wild, C. J., & Pfannkuch, M. (1999). Statistical thinking in empirical enquiry. *International Statistical Review, 67*(3), 223–265.

Wild, C. J., Utts, J. M., & Horton, N. J. (2018). What is statistics? In D. Ben-Zvi, K. Makar, & J. Garfield (Eds.), *International handbook of research in statistics education* (pp. 5–36). Springer.

Chapter 18
Preparing for a Data-Rich World: Civic Statistics Across the Curriculum

Joachim Engel ⓘ, James Nicholson, and Josephine Louie

Abstract Civic Statistics by its nature is highly interdisciplinary. From a cross-curricular perspective, teaching and learning Civic Statistics faces specific challenges related to the preparation of teachers and the design of instruction. This chapter presents examples of how Civic Statistics resources and concepts can be used in different courses and subject areas. Because topical issues and current data are central to these resources, we recognise that the original ProCivicStat resources will become outdated in time. We offer some guidance about developing Civic Statistics resources of your own.

Keywords Civic Statistics · Cross-disciplinary teaching · Teacher preparation · Curriculum

18.1 Background and Introduction

In many countries school curricula introduce statistics mainly within mathematics, with limited exposure to real data, and rarely use data to address questions of importance in the real world. Where statistics is embedded within mathematics, teachers are often not very comfortable in pedagogical situations where there is not a clear method and a 'right answer' to problems (Batanero et al., 2011). However, Civic Statistics is too important to be restricted to a single field of knowledge. Similar to school media curricula (or media or digital literacy curricula, as they are

J. Engel (✉)
Ludwigsburg University of Education, Ludwigsburg, Germany
e-mail: engel@ph-ludwigsburg.de

J. Nicholson
University of Durham, Durham, UK
e-mail: j.r.nicholson53@gmail.com

J. Louie
Education Development Center, Waltham, Massachusetts, USA
e-mail: jlouie@edc.org

J. Ridgway (ed.), *Statistics for Empowerment and Social Engagement*,
https://doi.org/10.1007/978-3-031-20748-8_18

called in the United States), Civic Statistics involves cross-curricular knowledge and practices, including media competencies, quantitative reasoning, and critical thinking skills (see also Chap. 3) and more general "21st century skills" (OECD, 2018). Its features, tools and facets were introduced in Chaps. 2 and 3, which highlight the comprehensive scope of skills, dispositions and the knowledge base needed to be able to make sense of data about society.

> Civic Statistics is too important to be restricted to a single field of knowledge. It should also be taught in other courses and PCS resources can help.

Courses in Civic Statistics can be developed at the college level and made available across multiple degree programmes. The curriculum pressures at the secondary school level may make it difficult to implement an entire course in Civic Statistics; however, the curriculum resources developed by ProCivicStat (PCS) can be used as stand-alone activities that are suitable for inclusion in existing courses. Opportunities for incorporating Civic Statistics resources exist in geography, history, citizenship/civics, politics, economics, sociology, biology, physics and many other subject areas. The following list is not intended to be exhaustive but may help to illustrate the range of subjects and areas of focus that provide opportunities for including Civic Statistics across the school curriculum (subject names will vary in different countries).

Biology: Monitoring and sustaining the environment; feeding the human race; tracking and maintaining public health.

Business and Economics: Business impacts on the environment; impacts of globalisation on local and regional economic opportunities; economic inequality; the gender pay gap; trends in the concentration of wealth (see Kovacs et al. in Chap. 14).

Citizenship/Civics: This is the curriculum area where Civic Statistics could be viewed as an integral component already. Possible topics include civic participation, quality of democracy, understanding the electoral process and a full range of Civic Statistics themes like the effects of migration on voting patterns, public beliefs about social welfare policies, racial and ethnic disparities in policing, etc.

Geography: Impacts of climate change (see Guimarães et al. in Chap. 11) on human poverty and migration; urbanisation and hunger; modelling the spread of disease, ageing societies, etc.

Media studies: Media use by youth; how the media influences social and political events; how information and disinformation spreads through social networks, etc.

In addition, when identifying a topic that is of interest to multiple teachers and their students, there are opportunities for creating alliances, cross-subject cooperation and—if the situation allows—team-teaching. Interactive data visualisations can allow students to explore complex data and describe relationships they can see—using the data to 'tell stories' (Pfannkuch et al., 2010). Describing the stories in the data naturally leads students to ask questions about the reasons for these relationships. In theory, PCS resources could be used in a coordinated fashion across multiple subject areas to help students understand the diverse disciplinary concepts and contexts that are needed to make sense of data. Although timetabling constraints at the secondary school level often make team teaching across more than one subject difficult to implement, such an arrangement would be an opportune way for students to explore the full richness of PCS resources.

The next section provides an overview of past and current efforts to support the learning and teaching of statistics in general (not merely Civic Statistics) in interdisciplinary ways. We then follow with examples of PCS resources that can be used in different subject areas from high school to college. A subsequent section offers suggestions on how to start developing your own Civic Statistics resources if the existing resources do not address a topic you would like to explore with your students. The chapter then concludes with a few summary thoughts on the interdisciplinary promise of Civic Statistics.

18.2 Interdisciplinary Teaching of Statistics: Promises and Challenges

18.2.1 The Rationale for Teaching Statistics Across the Curriculum

For decades, educators and scholars have argued that statistics and data analysis should be taught using cross-curricular approaches starting in early school years and continuing through higher education. Participants of the 1992 IASE Roundtable conference *Introducing Data Analysis in the Schools: Who Should Teach It and How?* pointed out that data analysis should be taught across the curriculum with contributions from teachers in all disciplines (Pereira-Mendoza, 1993). These arguments arise from the recognition that drawing meaning from data is an inherently interdisciplinary activity. Cobb and Moore (1997) described statistics as a field that incorporates ideas and tools to help people work with and make sense of data, which are not simply numbers but "numbers with a context" (p. 801). Making sense of data therefore requires efforts not only to identify quantitative relationships and patterns in data, but also to understand the contexts from which the data were collected and the substantive content to which the data refer. For example, analysing and interpreting Gross Domestic Product (GDP) data for OECD countries over time requires an understanding of both the (contested) concept of GDP and knowledge of how economists measure GDP, as well as the economic conditions of these countries.

> Educators and researchers argue that statistics should be taught using cross-curricular approaches, because making sense of data requires an understanding of the contexts from which the data were collected.

Table 18.1 Three potential instructional formats for cross-curricular teaching of statistics

Possible cross-curricular formats
1. Integrating other disciplines into the teaching of statistics
2. Integrating statistics into the teaching of other disciplines
3. Coordinating the teaching of statistics with other disciplines

As another example, interpreting the incidence of extreme weather events in a local region requires knowledge of how scientists define extreme weather as well as historical weather patterns in that region. Because data analysis and interpretation require knowledge of not only statistical concepts and tools but also the social, scientific, or other disciplinary ideas associated with the data, scholars have advocated that students learn statistics in interdisciplinary ways. Educators and researchers have explored and recommended a variety of promising approaches, including: integrating the learning of other subjects into statistics teaching (e.g., Carter & Nicholson, 2016; Day, 2013; Dierker et al., 2012; Leonard, 2010); teaching statistics across the curriculum—as part of literacy, science, the social sciences, and other subjects (e.g., Pereira-Mendoza, 1993; Howery & Rodriguez, 2006; Remsburg et al., 2014; Usiskin, 2015); and supporting efforts by teachers to coordinate and collaborate in the teaching of data analysis and interpretation across multiple subjects (e.g., Vahey et al., 2010). These three formats are summarized in Table 18.1, and examples of each approach are discussed in the following section.

18.2.2 Examples of Cross-Curricular Teaching Efforts

Integrating Other Disciplines into the Teaching of Mathematics and Statistics For many years, efforts have occurred across the globe to integrate into statistics courses both real data and content from relevant disciplines to help students interpret and make sense of patterns in real data. As a university-level example, statistics education faculty in Spain have helped prospective teachers prepare to teach high school statistics with projects examining topics such as international life expectancy and gender inequality using data from the United Nations (Gea et al., 2016). At the secondary level, Nicholson and researchers in the U.K. worked in a multi-year collaboration to develop and study statistics curriculum materials that use multivariate social science data to explore topics such as substance use, public health outcomes, and educational disparities among youth (see Ridgway et al., 2008; Nicholson et al., 2011). Scholars in the Philippines have similarly developed materials to help students build both statistical literacy and greater understanding of youth development patterns through a statistics course designed for the national high school curriculum, using national and international datasets with variables on youth employment, health, digital media use, and other topics (Reston et al., 2016).

Working in the U.S. with students as early as the fifth grade, mathematics educators such as Eric Gutstein, Bob Peterson, and their colleagues have developed and taught mathematics lessons that promote the learning of statistical concepts while expressly examining issues of social and economic inequality within the U.S. and across the globe (Gutstein & Peterson, 2013). In these lessons, they have had students explore data and topics such as the distribution of wealth in society (e.g., Hersh & Peterson, 2013; Langyel, 2013); racial patterns in U.S. home purchase prices and home mortgage lending rates (Gutstein, 2003, 2013); racial profiling by police (Gutstein, 2013; Himmelstein, 2013); urban school overcrowding (Turner & Font Strawhun, 2013); and large-scale standardized test scores by students' demographic character- istics (Gutstein, 2003). These educators have explicitly created space for students to discuss and investigate the social and political questions that arise from the observed data patterns and to consider civic actions that may address social injustices. In the process, they have described higher levels of engagement and motivation for statistics learning among students, more positive dispositions toward quantitative studies, and stronger statistical and mathematical reasoning—all while serving students from traditionally marginalized and underserved groups (Gutstein, 2003; Peterson, 2013).

In line with this work, the *Strengthening Data Literacy across the Curriculum* project has developed prototype statistics modules with a social justice focus for U.S. students who must take a fourth year of mathematics in high school and who are not eligible for or interested in taking an advanced-level course (Louie et al., 2021). One module focuses on income inequality and another focuses on immigration. Both modules are designed as three-week long sets of applied data investigations in which students examine person-level microdata from the U.S. decennial census and the annual American Community Survey to answer questions such as: How have incomes for higher- and lower-income individuals changed over time? Does educa- tion explain the wage gap between males and females? Are immigrants as likely as the native born to be participating in the labour force, after adjusting for education? Students conduct their investigations using the Common Online Data Analysis Platform (*CODAP*—see also Frischemeier et al. in Chap. 9), an open-source set of tools that supports data visualization and conceptual understanding of statistical ideas. Students in classrooms that have used the modules (who have been predom- inantly from racial and ethnic minority as well as low-income groups) have shown statistically significant growth in their interest in statistics and data analysis, as well as in their understanding of core statistical concepts, as measured through surveys and assessments administered pre- and post-module implementation (Louie et al., 2022).

The journal *Teaching Statistics* has published a number of articles where social issues are in many ways the primary focus, with statistics being used to illuminate those issues: McCune and Tunstall (2019) look at a metric for measuring partisan gerrymandering which threatens democratic values in a host of countries; Poling and Weiland (2020) explore how spatial data can inform understanding of inequalities across multiple aspects of a citizen's existence; Byun and Croucher (2018) outline ways in which the failure of jurors (ordinary citizens) to be able to reason with probability and with statistical data can, and has, led to severe miscarriages of justice. These and other articles such as Nicholson et al. (2013) can be used as background reading to promote debate on value systems using data-driven arguments.

Integrating Statistics into the Teaching of Other Disciplines Scholars and educators have also endeavoured for many years to incorporate the learning of statistics and quantitative reasoning in other subject areas. In a national effort that lasted over a decade in the UK, the Quantitative Step Change (or Q-Step) programme funded multiple universities and centres to promote statistics and quantitative data skills among undergraduate students in the social sciences and humanities (Carter & Nicholson, 2016). To engage students in quantitative data analysis, faculty members designed courses in which students choose questions that match their disciplinary interests and learn to work with and analyse real data to address these questions (Brown, 2016; Buckley et al., 2015). Concerted efforts to strengthen statistical and quantitative literacy using problem-based learning approaches and real-world datasets have also been occurring widely in a diversity of fields and countries around the world, such as in sociology departments in the U.S. (e.g., Burdette & McLoughlin, 2010); management and business programmes in Israel (Gal & Trostianitser, 2016) and Hungary (Kazar, 2016); college courses for communications majors in Portugal (Silvestre & Meireles, 2017); and biology courses for first-year biology majors in Mexico (Navarro-Alberto & Barrientos-Medina, 2017).

At the primary school level, Peterson (2013) provides an example of how he incorporated statistics and quantitative reasoning into an American history lesson in a fifth grade classroom. In response to a question by students about how many U.S. presidents have owned slaves, he initiated a project for students to find the answer using historical texts. He asked students to compile data, and using tables and charts, to generate and present new knowledge from the data—such as the proportion of all U.S. presidents who have owned slaves, and the proportion of years in U.S. history when a president owned slaves. Students engaged in this quantitative work while also discussing larger themes of the history unit, including the reliability of existing historical sources and the information that such sources may include or exclude, to inform their understanding of the past and present. As another example, educators in a Canadian girls' private school describe how they organized an annual Social Justice Data Fair, where students from grades 1–12 presented findings on topics and questions that they had generated (Alexander & Munk, 2013). Projects included investigations of species extinction patterns in the face of global climate change; results of an audit that students conducted of the types of waste generated by their school; rates of suicide in different countries; and the relationship between national GDP and carbon dioxide emissions. These types of projects could be explored further in science, health, or social studies classes.

Coordinating the Teaching of Statistics with Other Disciplines Although it may require more flexible or less traditional educational environments to execute, an interdisciplinary approach towards statistics learning can also occur when educators from different disciplines coordinate instruction. Examples can be found in the United States, where university faculty have collaborated across departments to build introductory statistics courses that incorporate the data and disciplinary content of multiple subject areas to serve students across disciplinary departments (e.g., Ravenscroft & Chen, 2017; Wolfe, 1993; Lesser & Nordenhaug, 2004). Scholars in Germany have created a high school course that sits outside other traditional subjects, where students learn statistics through project-based activities analysing national income and economic data (see Proemmel and Wassner in Chap. 17). Researchers in Belgium and Brazil have engaged students, teachers, and community members in out-of-school citizen science projects that involve the collection and analysis of local environmental data to build awareness of community resources and challenges and to spur potential social action (see Francois and Monteiro in Chap. 20).

As an example of a unique cross-disciplinary collaboration in the middle grades, a team of US researchers worked with teachers in schools to coordinate the learning of quantitative data literacy skills across four curriculum areas: social studies, mathematics, science, and English language arts (Vahey et al., 2010). The *Thinking with Data* project developed four two-week learning modules designed to be implemented sequentially by teachers in each of the four subject areas for a common group of seventh-grade students. The overarching topic of the modules was world water use, and each module was designed to support or build on previous units. Teaching began with the social studies module, where students examined water use patterns among countries in the Middle East and considered ways of distributing water equitably in the region. In the mathematics module that followed, students engaged in proportional reasoning to devise measures of water distribution that could be considered fair. In the subsequent science module, students examined data on water quality and salinity in the region and implications for agriculture and plant growth. In the culminating English language arts module, students drew on their prior data work to write essays arguing for specific water distribution proposals. The modules were tested in a quasi-experimental study involving two middle schools that used team-teaching approaches; results indicate that project students outperformed comparison students on data literacy as well as mathematics and science assessments. Based on teacher reports, the project had a particularly beneficial impact on students' persuasive writing in English language arts (Vahey et al., 2010).

18.2.3 Challenges to Cross-Curricular Statistics Teaching

The examples of interdisciplinary approaches toward statistics learning described above have taken place in the face of numerous obstacles. Barriers that researchers have identified toward interdisciplinary instruction include concerns among teachers that they do not have the expertise, time, resources, or organizational support to plan and implement instruction that includes content outside their own discipline (Johnston & Tsai, 2018; Weinberg & McMeeking, 2017). In addition, the teaching of statistics at the primary and secondary levels is most often done by teachers of mathematics, and research suggests that many mathematics teachers themselves—let alone teachers from other disciplines—are not adequately prepared to teach statistics or required data-related skills effectively (Engel et al., 2016; Franklin et al., 2015). Many mathematics teachers who are tasked with teaching statistical and other data-related concepts often lack both the content and pedagogical knowledge for supporting deep understandings of core statistical concepts and ways of thinking with data (Batanero et al. 2011; Hannigan et al., 2013) (see also Podworny et al. in Chap. 15, and Schiller and Engel in Chap. 16).

As an illustration of some of the hurdles involved, researchers in Canada found that a small group of middle-school mathematics teachers who used rich statistical tasks with students during instruction focused on the procedural aspects of the mathematics involved and did not highlight connections among statistical ideas nor the contextual, interdisciplinary links that the tasks afforded (Savard & Manuel, 2016).

> Although many challenges exist for cross-curricular teaching of statistics, it is important to find ways to do so, particularly at the primary and secondary levels.

Despite these challenges, there is wide recognition that cross-curricular approaches toward statistics instruction are needed to prepare students for an increasingly data-rich world, and to support the functioning of healthy democratic societies where citizens must make sense of increasing troves of data to inform social and scientific policy-making. More work is needed to build interdisciplinary statistics learning opportunities, particularly at the primary and secondary levels where there is wide agreement that statistics learning must be strengthened. The next section points to resource ideas for those who are inspired to build or expand on existing opportunities in their settings.

18.3   Using Existing PCS Resources Across the Curriculum

ProCivicStat developed around 40 detailed lesson plans (all plans are available as student and as teacher version in English, and several are also translated into German, Hungarian and Portuguese) which are freely available under "Lesson Plans" through the ProCivicStat website https://iase-web.org/islp/pcs or use the CivicStatMap tool there.

Each lesson plan contains detailed information about the contextual topic with references to more background information, information about the data source, metadata, list of variables and measurement issues leading to a series of concrete tasks to be worked on with various technological tools. Links to the original data, in selected cases supported via electronic worksheets containing the data, are also provided.

Vital for teaching Civic Statistics is that the issues to be investigated address important current topics with up-to-date data. While ProCivicStat also developed a syllabus for a complete course on Civic Statistics, most of these teaching materials have been designed to be useful also as stand-alone activities which delve in depth into a topic in social studies, health, geography, civics etc. promoting enquiry-based learning. In what follows, we showcase some examples for enriching teaching through these materials. Our materials are designed for high school and college students (some are suitable for students with modest academic attainments). They do not constitute a detailed master plan for your teaching, and need to be adapted to the specific teaching contexts and academic level of your students.

> Vital for teaching Civic Statistics is that the issues to be investigated address important current topics with up-to-date data.
> The PCS website provides ample examples.

Discussing the whole range of teaching units is beyond the scope of this chapter; the following are just brief exemplary illustrations of the potential of our materials where we highlight some key ideas. While the Examples 1–4 were designed and field-tested from the perspective of integrating other disciplines into the teaching of statistics, the last two examples were devised for a political science course that included reasoning with statistical evidence. Depending on what your curriculum allows, your student's knowledge in statistics and their interest in political topics, we believe that after some adaptation each of the following examples can be used to follow either one of the three approaches set out in Table 18.1.

In Chap. 5, Ridgway et al. describe in some detail what data visualisation has to offer in making Civic Statistics ideas accessible to students, even at an early age. In Chap. 6, Teixeira et al. discuss the promises and challenges of dealing with real-life authentic data, which can give students an opportunity to learn skills in a realistic and relevant context. We will not rehearse again the arguments made in these chapters, but will provide illustrative examples of activities suitable for use with secondary school pupils. For each example we identify curriculum areas where the materials would have immediate relevance; the description of the resource offers some elaboration of how it might be used in the different areas.

18.3.1 Example 1: Human Development and World Happiness[1]

Human Development and World Happiness	
What?	Investigating human development and world happiness index
Goals	• Reflect on quality of life and how it can be measured
	• Learn about living conditions across the globe
Statistical topics	Multivariate data, comparing distributions, confounders, trends, linear regression, sub-group analyses, indices
Disciplines	Civics, Economics, Geography, Politics
Level	Grade 11 and higher
Prerequisites	Boxplots, location parameter, scatterplots
Digital tools	CODAP, iNZight
Duration	5–7 lessons of 50 min each

We all strive for a life of fulfilment and happiness for ourselves, our people and the whole human family. But how can you measure quantities such as *quality of life* or people's *happiness*? Economic wealth alone, on an aggregated level of national averages measured by the gross domestic product (GDP) is a poor measure. As an alternative the Human Development Index (HDI) is a summary measure of average achievement of countries in several key dimensions of human development such as a long and healthy life, access to education, and a decent standard of living. The HDI is used by the United Nations Development Programme and was created to emphasize that people and their capabilities should be the ultimate criteria for assessing the development of a country, not economic growth alone. The HDI can also be used to question national policy choices, asking how two countries with the same level of GNP per capita can end up with different human development outcomes. These contrasts can stimulate debate about government policy priorities. A good starting point for teaching is the animated OECD Better-Life-Index,[2] a measure different from HDI. Students are challenged to explore their own priorities for a good quality of life; they assign their own weights to the components of this index to compare countries. Next, students download the HDI data,[3] which contains 21 variables for each of 195 countries, and explore relations between variables such as health (*life expectancy, physicians per 1000 inhabitants, fertility rate, health expenditures*), education (*school enrolment*), economic wealth and its distribution (measured by various indicators such as the Gini coefficient or income deciles) and how these indicators relate to the HDI. As another example, the World Happiness Report 2020,[4] published annually by the United Nations Sustainable Development

---

[1] See lesson plans 5.105 *Human Development Index: Can you compare countries?* and 5.106: *World Happiness Report: How happy are we?,* available from https://iase-web.org/islp/pcs or use CivicStatMap tool there.

[2] http://www.oecdbetterlifeindex.org

[3] http://hdr.undp.org/en/data

[4] https://worldhappiness.report/ed/2020/

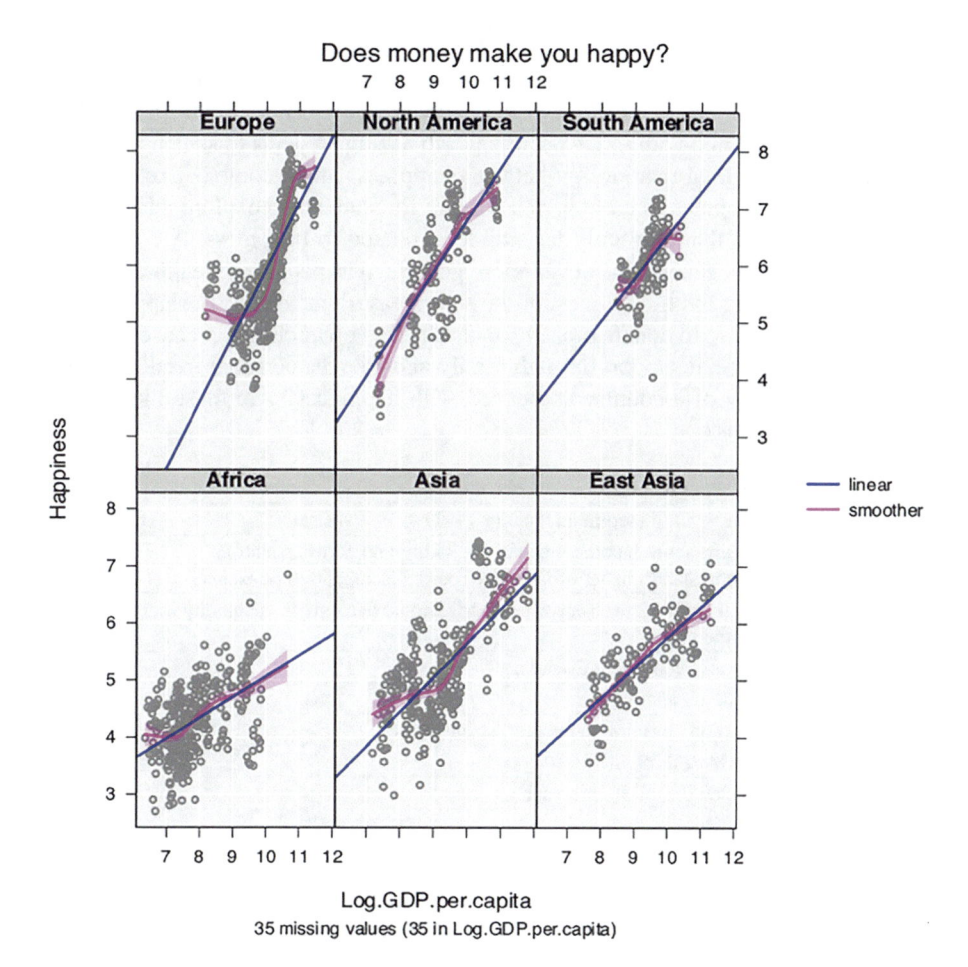

Fig. 18.1 Scatterplots of Happiness versus log (per capita GDP), for six regions of the world, with linear regression line and nonparametric smoother (created with iNZight, https://www.stat.auckland.ac.nz/~wild/iNZight/)

Solutions Network, is conducted to capture global happiness. It ranks countries by their happiness levels, based on comprehensive survey data from 155 countries around the globe; it continues to gain global recognition as governments, organizations and civil society increasingly use happiness indicators to inform their policy-making decisions. To measure happiness, the survey asks individuals for a self-assessment by responding to the following question: *Please imagine a ladder, with steps numbered from 0 at the bottom to 10 at the top. The top of the ladder represents the best possible life for you and the bottom of the ladder represents the worst possible life for you. On which step of the ladder would you say you personally feel you stand at this time?*

Notice that the data are national averages, not data from individuals, presented separately for each year from 2008 to 2016 (so each country will have 9 data points, except where there are missing values). On the basis of our materials, interesting questions to investigate include: *If you think money causes happiness, what should the relationship be between income and happiness?* Before studying the actual data, (see Fig. 18.1, created with *iNZight*), it is worth asking students to sketch what they imagine the functional relationship between happiness and income is like.

The World Happiness dataset is rich enough for students to explore relationships between variables that may only be indirectly related to happiness. Are people in poorer countries as generous (or even more generous) as people in wealthier parts of the world (inviting the tricky question how to measure generosity)? Happy people may be more willing to donate money for charity and other common causes. How is people's health, social support through family and friends, personal freedom, or the democratic quality of a country associated with happiness? Are these likely to be causal relationships?

Some so rich, others so poor	
What?	Investigating income inequality worldwide
Goals	• Learn about income inequalities within and across countries • Understand impact of large economic discrepancies on society
Statistical topics	Multivariate data, comparing distributions, percentiles, inequality indices, trends in time series
Disciplines	Civics, Economics, Sociology
Level	Grade 10 and higher
Prerequisites	Boxplots, location parameter, scatterplots
Digital tools	CODAP, iNZight
Duration	4–6 lessons of 50 min each

18.3.2   Example 2: Some So Rich, Others So Poor[5]

"All human beings are born free and equal in dignity and rights", states Article 1 of the Universal Declaration of Human Rights[6]). How much do our societies live up to this commitment? Do people from all walks of life really have equal access to the benefits offered by the modern state—like education, health care, social services etc.? The 2017 world economic forum at Davos, a gathering not known for social romanticism or revolutionary rhetoric, stated: *"Income inequality specifically is one of the most visible aspects of a broader and more complex issue, one that entails inequality of opportunity and extends to gender, ethnicity, disability, and age, among others. .... This affects all countries around the world. In developed and*

---

[5]See lesson plan 5.101 *Some so rich, others so poor* and 5.107 *Income inequality revisited*, available from https://iase-web.org/islp/pcs or use CivicStatMap tool there.

[6]https://www.un.org/en/universal-declaration-human-rights/

developing countries alike, the poorest half of the population often controls less than 10% of its wealth."[7]

The inherent dangers of neglecting inequality are obvious. People, especially young people, excluded from the mainstream, can end up feeling disenfranchised and their marginalization breeds new conflicts in society. It has been argued that this in turn reduces the sustainability of economic growth, weakens social cohesion and security, encourages inequitable access to, and use of, global commons such as the earth's shared natural resources, undermines our democracies, and cripples our hopes for sustainable development and peaceful societies. Several of our materials address the issue of economic inequality. They invite students to pose and investigate a number of important questions, e.g.: *Why do some countries have large discrepancies between the rich and the poor while in other countries the income distribution is more equal? What are common characteristics of countries that have a large discrepancy between rich and poor?*

To get young students motivated to investigate economic inequality, it is important to have them reflect on their own values and views about the distribution of income and wealth in society. Questions like *"Think about the 10% of people who earn most money in our country, and the 10% of people who earn least. How big do YOU think the difference in earnings should be?"* then *"What do you think is the case?"* can be good starting points, to be discussed before looking at data. The OECD website Compare Your income[8] helps students view their own economic situation in a global context and to reflect on which world they would want to live in. This can be explored by asking students a question like *"If you had the choice: would you rather live in a moderately wealthy country where everybody earns about the same or in a much wealthier country with large discrepancies between the rich and the not so well-off? What pros and cons do you see in each respective option?"*

Another website illustrating and exploring economic inequality on a global as well as on a country-by-country level is the world inequality data base.[9]

An exploration of data with the software CODAP supports an investigation of the relative incomes of the 10% lowest earning workers (D1) and the 10% highest earning workers (D10). Figure 18.2 displays a scatterplot of D10 versus D1 for selected years between 1980 and 2015 for 32 countries across all continents. Each dot represents a country. The inverse relationship is obvious: the more the 10% highest earners get from the "total cake" the less remains for the remaining 90% - with implications for the 10% lowest earners.

A reasonable indicator for disparity (and an alternative for the more sophisticated Gini coefficient) is the quotient of certain income shares, e.g., D10 divided by D1. This indicator measures the factor by which the 10% highest earners exceed the income of the 10% lowest earners. Figure 18.3 shows the time series of D10/D1 for four selected countries: Brazil, United States, Russia and Norway. While in Brazil

---

[7] http://widgets.weforum.org/outlook15/01.html

[8] https://www.compareyourincome.org

[9] https://wid.world

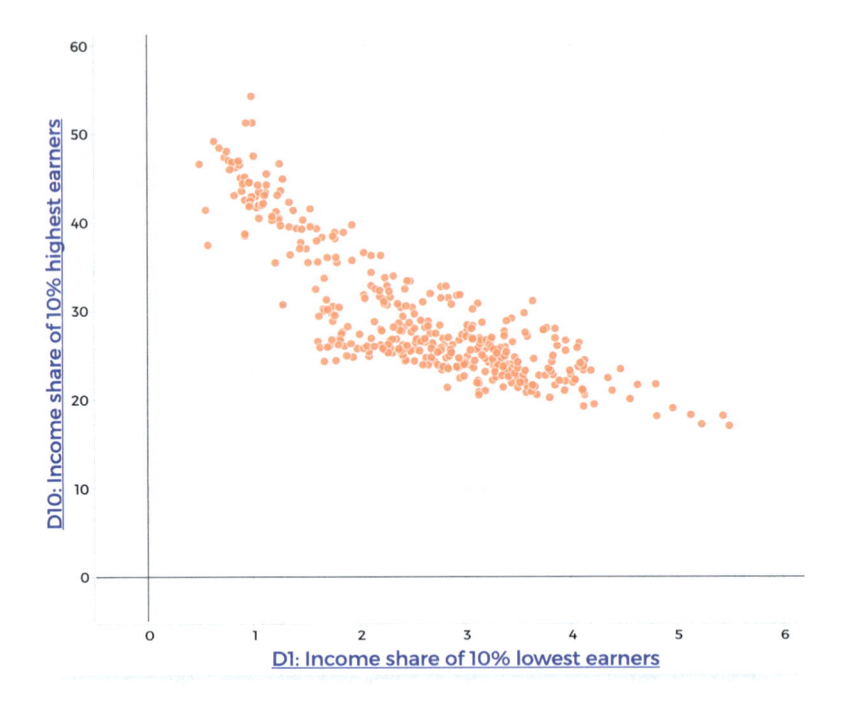

Fig. 18.2 Income share of total income for the 10% highest earning workers versus income share for the 10% lowest earning workers. The scales represent percentages of total income, and are different by a factor of 10 (created with CODAP, https://concord.org)

Fig. 18.3 Time series of the variable D10/D1 for Brazil, United States, Russia and Norway (created with CODAP, https://concord.org)

this factor ranged between 35 and 50 from 2004 to 2018, in Norway the salary of the highest earners has "only" been around seven times as much as the income of the 10% lowest earners (and has remained quite consistent at that level for a number of years).

18.3.3   Example 3: Gender Pay Gap, or Do Women Earn as Much as Men?[10]

Gender Pay Gap or Do women earn as much as men?	
What?	Investigating income of men and women across various subgroups
Goals	• Learn about gender inequality across the globe • Understand adjusted and raw pay gap
Statistical topics	Multivariate data, comparing distributions, data visualizations of confounders
Disciplines	Civics, Economics, Sociology
Level	Grade 9 and higher
Prerequisites	Boxplots, location parameter, scatterplots
Digital tools	Gapminder, CODAP
Duration	2–4 lessons of 50 min each

A heated topic among students in high school as well as in college is the topic of fairness among the sexes. In all countries around the world the average earnings of the male population exceeds the income of the female population. But is it just the sex of a person, or are other cultural and workplace-related variables accountable for the gender pay gap (GPG), such as branch of employment, years of tenure, education, and levels of labour force participation (where female workers are more likely than male workers to reduce their paid working hours to raise and care for family members)? To determine how big this gap is, a distinction is made between the adjusted and the unadjusted wage gap. The unadjusted or raw GPG does not take into account differences in personal and workplace characteristics between men and women. Part of the raw pay gap can be attributed to the fact that women, for instance, tend to engage more often in part-time work and tend to work in lower-paid branches. Datasets of national income can be found at many countries' statistics offices—so for your own teaching you can have a look there. The data can be used to verify the gap and to check how much some other variables contribute to the pay gap.

Chapter 15 reports on design ideas to implement activities with regard to the Gender Pay Gap in teacher education and in Chap. 17 Proemmel and Wassner report on their experiences taking this topic into the classrooms of upper secondary schools. Why does the gender pay gap (GPG)—defined as the difference between

---

[10] See lesson plans 5.205–5.211 on *Gender Pay Gap* and 5.409 on *Gender Equity,* available from https://iase-web.org/islp/pcs or use CivicStatMap tool there.

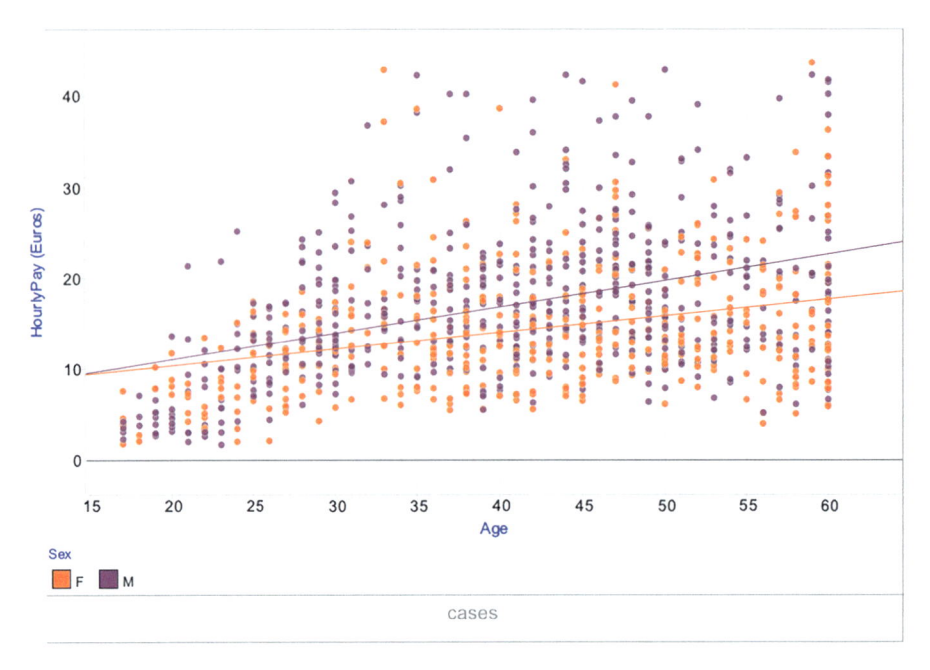

Fig. 18.4 Scatterplot of hourly pay versus age plus linear regression lines for a random sample of 1000 German employees (created with CODAP, https://concord.org)

male and female earnings as a percentage of male earnings—vary so much between different countries? For example, Estonia and Lithuania are neighbouring countries of similar size and geography and share a similar twentieth-century history, yet the GPG is 28.3% in the former and 12.5% in the latter. Also, Canada and Denmark are two liberal democracies in the western hemisphere where GPG figures (18.7% and 5.3%, respectively) differ markedly. Maybe variables other than gender influence earnings. Questions can be posed like: *Is the pay gap dependent on the age of employees?* Figure 18.4 displays a scatterplot (created with CODAP) of *Hourly Pay* against *Age*, including regression lines, separate for men and women, for a random sample of 1000 employees from a German income survey. While both sexes start off at about equal rates of pay, by age 60 there is a Gender Pay Gap of about 27%.

We have presented a reasonable amount of detail on these three examples, but now outline three additional examples to illustrate the range of opportunities available.

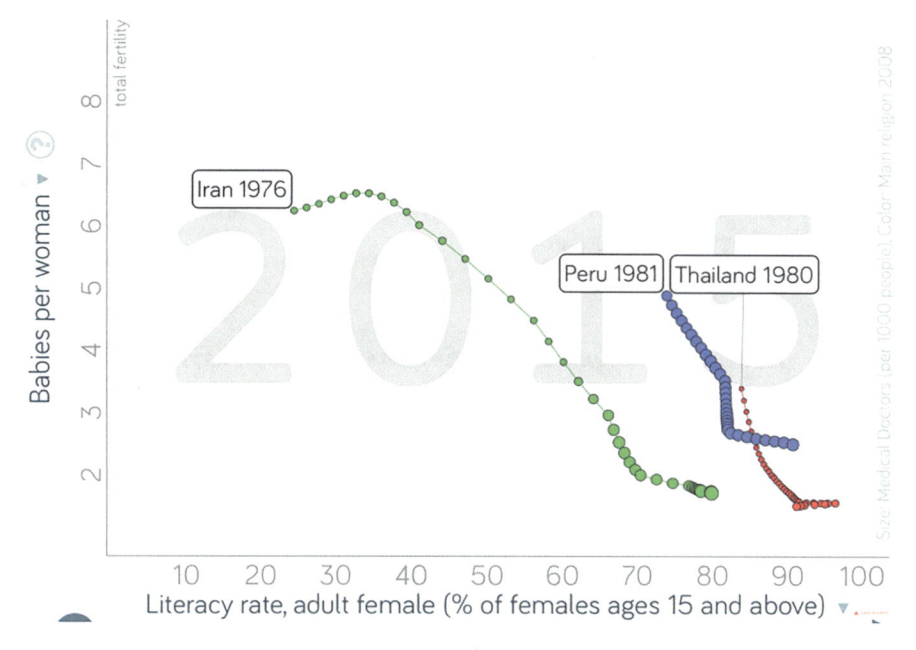

Fig. 18.5   Graphical representation of the variables *literacy rate of women* and *average number of babies per woman* (source: www.gapminder.org). Gapminder is licenced under CC by 4.0

18.3.4   Example 4: Do More Years of School among Women Impact the Birth Rate?[11]

Some so rich, others so poor	
What?	Female education and reproduction rate
Goals	• Learn about factors influencing birth rates • Understand the role of education for female liberation
Statistical topics	Visualisation, trends over time, confounders
Disciplines	Biology, Geography
Level	Grade 10 and higher
Prerequisites	Location parameter, scatterplots
Digital tools	Gapminder, CODAP
Duration	3–5 lessons of 50 min each

Studying demographic change about aging societies and world population growth can be used to initiate many discussions. For example, consider the relationship between literacy and fertility rates among women (including its evolution over the years, see Fig. 18.5, created with *Gapminder*). Each dot represents one data point per

---

[11] This example refers to data from lesson plan 5.105 on *the Human Development Index* to be investigated with *CODAP* or directly with *Gapminder,* available from https://iase-web.org/islp/pcs or use CivicStatMap tool there.

year for the three countries shown. The point size is proportional to the number of physicians per thousand inhabitants.

The striking decline in birth rate with increasing female literacy is mediated by several influential confounding variables which may be explored further with the data provided. Students could be asked to explore (confirm or refute) the association between *female literacy rate* and *birth rate* with data from other countries. Are there other variables (like number of physicians, GDP, female participation in labour market etc.) that serve as mediators?

18.3.5   Example 5: What Is Causing the Earth to Warm Up?[12]

Climate Change	
What?	Exploration of historic climate data and sea levels
Goals	• Learn about human-caused factors associated with global warming • Understand impact of global warming
Statistical topics	Visualisation, trends over time series
Disciplines	Geography, Earth Sciences
Level	Grade 10 and higher
Prerequisites	Scatterplots
Digital tools	CODAP, iNZight, Apps from the web
Duration	3–5 lessons of 50 min each

Global warming and climate change—at least since destructive hurricanes, scorching summer heat and mild winters have been piling up—are topics of intense debate. Students could be asked to find evidence about the influence of global warming, e.g., declining polar ice caps, rising sea levels, different sorts of extreme weather (for visualising climate change data, see Guimarães et al. in Chap. 11). The year 2019 was the fifth in a series of exceptionally warm years. It was the hottest year in Europe since weather records were made. This conclusion was confirmed by the Copernicus Climate Change Service (C3S), which published its findings[13] on January 8, 2020.

The earth has warmed since 1880. Based on research by NASA's Goddard Institute for Space Studies, Fig. 18.6 visualizes the evidence for this warming trend.

However, there are different opinions about the causes of this development, and different science disciplines can offer different perspectives. What actually warms the earth? Can changes in temperature be attributed to changes in the Earth's orbit, the sun, volcanoes, deforestation, or ozone pollution?

---

[12] See lesson plan 5.115 "Climate Change", available from https://iase-web.org/islp/pcs or use CivicStatMap tool there.

[13] https://climate.copernicus.eu/press-releases

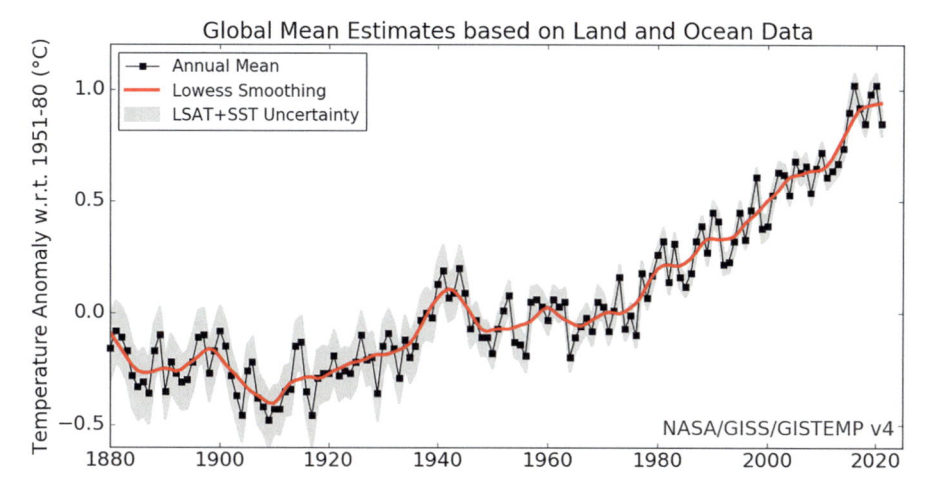

Fig. 18.6 Land-ocean temperature index, 1880 to present, with base period 1951–1980. The solid black line is the global annual mean and the solid red line is the 5-year lowess smoothed line. The gray shading represents the total annual uncertainty at a 95% confidence level (GISTEMP Team, 2022; Lenssen et al., 2019, source: https://data.giss.nasa.gov/gistemp/)

18.3.6   Example 6: What Makes a Vibrant Democracy?[14]

Civil Society Participation	
What?	Quality of democracy, citizen participation
Goals	• Learn about core elements of democracy • Understand role of citizen role in vivid democracy
Statistical topics	Trends in time series, measurement and indices
Disciplines	Civics, Sociology, History, Politics
Level	Grade 11 and higher
Prerequisites	Boxplots, location parameter, scatterplots
Digital tools	Gapminder
Duration	4–6 lessons of 50 min each

Democracy does not just mean participation in an electoral process every 4 years. Active citizen engagement and participation in public decision processes are essential for the effective functioning of democracy, the legitimacy of government, the successful implementation of policy and the achievement of positive social outcomes. How much room and encouragement do various political systems provide for its members to be involved in public affairs? Fortunately, there are various indices developed by political scientists to measure the quality of democracy and civil participation. Here we refer to the civil society participation index,[15] created by

---

[14] See lesson plan 5.114 *Quality of Democracy,* available from https://iase-web.org/islp/pcs

[15] https://www.idea.int/gsod-indices/dataset-resources

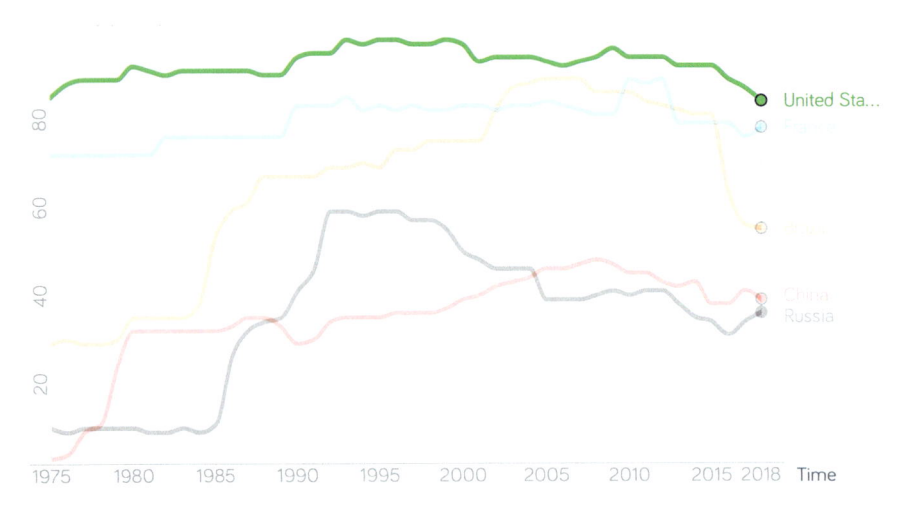

Fig. 18.7 Civil society participation index between 1975 and 2018 for five selected countries (source: www.gapminder.org)

the Stockholm-based International Institute for Democracy and Electoral Assistance (International IDEA). The measurement of civil society participation relies on three indicators which result from country experts assessing the extent to which the population is engaged in civil society activities. The link gives details of the methodology used. For example, one indicator is measured by responses to the question: *Are major civil society organizations routinely consulted by policymakers on policies relevant to their members?* Figure 18.7 displays time series of this indicator for Russia, China, Brazil, France and United States, obtained through the platform *Gapminder*. These time series can promote a variety of explorations and discussions. For example, students could be asked to associate trends in these curves with specific historical and political events in these countries, or be asked whether they would have expected to see an increase in the index for Russia over the period 2015–2018.

The examples above illustrate some of the uses of Civic Statistics teaching units in cross-curricular settings. The depository of freely available ProCivicStat materials includes lesson plans on a wide variety of topics. Generic tasks that apply to all examples include defining and exploring measures, aggregating and disaggregating data, finding or inventing good visual displays, visualising data distributions and exploring relations between variables. To various degrees, these units provoke critical thinking about data quality, require students to relate the visualisations and numerical analyses to the context, and raise awareness of possible confounding third variables.

18.4 How to Start Developing Civic Statistics Resources of Your Own

In time, the data used in existing ProCivicStat resources will become outdated. Then you may want to search for more current data sources, and use these to refresh the tasks. However, if none of the existing ProCivicStat resources address the topics you identify, then you should consider developing your own resources. This section is not intended to be prescriptive as to how to do this, but merely illustrative of some potential approaches, and provides some details based on personal experiences to exemplify the process.

All of the ProCivicStat curriculum tasks follow a broadly similar structure where there is an introduction to a broader context addressing an issue of high relevance for society, and a clear articulation of what the focus of the task is going to be. Statistics is used as a tool for enlightenment, not taught for its own sake. The purpose is to gain deeper insight into some context. The contextual problem and its implications for the world are the driving motivation to apply familiar, or acquire new, statistical ideas for better understanding of the issue at stake. The interplay between context and statistical exploration provides two important experiences for students: they get a deeper and more profound understanding of the context, and at the same time they gain first-hand experience appreciating the power and usefulness of statistical thinking and methods.

It is important to identify specific questions that can be addressed based on quantitative evidence using statistical thinking and reasoning. A statistical exploration requires trustworthy data that inform central aspects of the problem. Authentic data with a context and purpose are integrated, fostering active learning, using technology to explore concepts and analyse data, and using assessments to improve and evaluate student learning. Lessons should provide a description of the data to be used, including metadata for the variables in the data set, along with any supplementary information needed to explain new ideas (e.g., how *happiness* is measured). The tasks start with closed questions to ensure that students can find their way around the dataset and then move to more open activities where students make decisions about how to approach the problem. We give some recommendations for the design of activities here, and elaborate on them below. Further recommendations and guidelines on designing your class activities are given in other chapters of this book, especially in Chaps. 4, 7, 15 and 16.

> **Nine recommendations for designing your own Civic Statistics material**
> With your target learner group in mind, specify prerequisites and learning goals
> Identify a suitable topic of relevance to society to be explored with data
> Sensitize and motivate your students; relate the topic to personal experiences
>
> (continued)

Search for background material (Cartoons, YouTube Videos, texts, media reports) to generate interest and provide information

Search for rich, relevant data sets (including metadata) and texts

Choose suitable digital tools for data visualization and exploration

Design activities, with closed and open assignments, enticing critical thinking

Ask for a summary and critical review—which must include an account of strengths and limitations of conclusions drawn

Use alternate forms of assessment to improve and evaluate student learning

18.4.1 With Your Target Group in Mind, Specify Prerequisites and Learning Goals

Each teaching activity is an intentional intervention directed towards a distinct group of learners guided by specific goals. Civic Statistics focuses on burning issues that affect the economic or social well-being and living conditions of human beings. Data visualisations and statistical representations are used as tools to get a deeper insight into the issues involved. Also, vice versa, the societal theme serves as a motivation booster to learn new concepts and techniques for data visualisation and statistical analyses. It provides a valuable experience: statistical knowledge is useful for deeper understanding, and the relevance of the topic enhances the motivation to acquire new statistical knowledge. When planning a Civic Statistics activity, it is essential to be aware of the target group (age, cognitive prerequisites) and to specify concrete learning goals.

18.4.2 Identify a Suitable Topic of Relevance to Society to Be Explored with Data

Civic Statistics is about evidence-based understanding of the socio-political, economic and ecological dimensions of the world around us. The origin and destination of any Civic Statistics activity is a topic that focuses on a common social good, the well-being and health of people or their civil liberties and rights. An important educational goal is to develop students' positive dispositions towards appreciating the potential value of quantitative evidence and towards engaging with the world. The school curriculum offers plenty of topics across many disciplines which can be explored with data, thus allowing an evidence-based foundation for deeper understanding, reasoning and decision-making. Students could be invited to propose and investigate an issue of great meaning and importance to themselves and their community, or they can be offered a choice from among a range of questions or issues to study. Statistics as a discipline is valuable because it can empower people to address real-world problems and enable engagement with complex social phenomena. It also provides useful tools for identifying false claims and invented data, disseminated through unchecked journalism or social media. These ideas have relevance across a wide range of curriculum areas.

18.4.3   Sensitize and Motivate Your Students, Relate the Topic to Personal Experience

The integral design of tasks connecting real-life problems with data exploration gives students the opportunity to gain a rich experience where statistical knowledge and statistical reasoning really matters, helps in understanding phenomena about important issues, guides in the assessment of risks, and helps in one's own decision-making. However, addressing authentic issues in the classroom requires careful thought and preparation. Teachers must allocate sufficient time to solicit students' ideas for investigation and to connect them with appropriate datasets and tools for exploring them, or to help students make connections with important issues that are newer or more distant to them. To help students relate to a topic, consider finding ways to make the topic personal for them. For example, if the topic is climate change, you can have your students explore their individual ecological footprint,[16] which is a measure of how much area of biologically productive land and water an individual requires to produce all the resources he or she consumes and to absorb the waste he or she generates. If the topic addresses the quality of human development you may start by asking: *What makes a good and happy life for you? Discuss and rank the value of the following commodities for you: community & friends; income; health; personal safety; access to cultural life and education.*

18.4.4   Use Introductory Material (Cartoons, YouTube Videos, Texts, Media Reports) to Generate Interest and Provide Information

Engaging students in complex contexts can require a considerable investment in time, especially if it is not an area in which you have particular experience or expertise. There is a plethora of publicly available web-based resources you could consider using. One current example is the inequalities resource[17] created by the

---

[16]https://www.footprintcalculator.org

[17]https://inequality.org

Institute for Policy Studies in the United States, where income, where income and wealth inequality by race and sex are explored, as well as the relationship between economic inequality and health. Texts, cartoons, audio recordings or videos (e.g., *YouTube*) and other multi-media applets are important sources to motivate students and provide information. One approach is to look for a starting point to set the scene, which might be media reports which cover more than one aspect of a context, or to use a resource such as *Stats and Stories*,[18] which has a large set of podcasts exploring quantitative ideas in our daily lives and in journalism, or the weekly New York Times *What is going on in this graph* challenge.[19]

18.4.5 Search for Rich, Relevant Data Sets and Written Texts with Statistical Content

Civic Statistics contexts are at the focus of public and political dialogue, of much interest to policy-makers at the national, regional, and local levels, and are often discussed in the media. Depending on your specific topic you may decide to focus more on written texts with statistical messages, the exploration of authentic data, or both. Text-based messages can be found in articles in the print and digital media, in press releases and other products of official statistics producers (e.g., the websites of official statistics agencies) or non-government organisations, in TV programs and websites of news channels. There, the data are already analysed by statistics producers or by the media—see Gal in Chap. 13. You may also decide to ask students to analyse data sets to develop a deeper understanding of Civic Statistics. Another possible approach is to start with text messages in the media, and deconstruct the conclusions by exploring the relevant data yourself to come to a critical appraisal of the original text. This approach is described by Schiller and Engel in Chap. 16.

Finding appropriate data can be quite a challenge, despite the availability and accessibility of large data repositories (see Chap. 6 for the survey by Teixeira, Campos, & Trostianitser). Understanding social phenomena, and thinking through the implications of possible policy decisions in the social arena requires an understanding of and ability to work with multivariate data.

The data set should be rich enough to allow for exploration and discovery, but still manageable for your students and the software you use. The appropriate level of complexity of data should be chosen according to the experience of your students and the capacity of your software. Many datasets from the internet have to be curated before they are ready for import in visualization and analysis software. Also, it is important to provide metadata (how was the data collected and by whom, exactly how were the variables measured, and constructs operationalized?). Rich and useful sources can be found through major data providers such as Eurostat, UN, OECD or

---

[18] https://www.npr.org/podcasts/530134710/stats-stories

[19] https://www.nytimes.com/column/whats-going-on-in-this-graph

portals like Gapminder, IPUMS or OurWorldinData.[20] The United Nations provides plenty of information and data about its sustainable development goals.[21] National statistics offices provide press releases and media reports in text formats, as do nongovernment organizations which monitor international civil rights compliances or environment and health issues (*Germanwatch,*[22] etc.).

18.4.6 Choose Suitable Digital Tools for Data Visualization and Exploration

The scope of available digital tools ranges from data visualization software to software for teaching statistics to professional tools for doing statistics. Biehler et al. (2013) provide an overview on digital tools in statistics education. Pros and cons of these tools are discussed in detail in Chaps. 8–11. Gapminder, OurWorldinData, SMART Centre displays or dynamic population pyramids, usually require no more than some basic knowledge of descriptive statistics to explore the data that are provided by the software. These are innovative products for visual representation of multivariate data, and may provide more insight into patterns in the data than any numerical analysis. Without requiring much formal and technical introduction, they facilitate the discovery of patterns in data and lead to important statistical activities such as the search for explanatory confounding variables.

Products such as *Fathom*, *CODAP* or *iNZight* are designed as educational tools for data analysis without requiring any programming skills beyond using a formula editor. These tools support a broad range of data moves (Erickson et al., 2019), such as transforming or defining new variables. The browser-based software *CODAP* in particular has simple-to-use features for restructuring data and for subsetting—both useful functions when the data are multivariate (although *CODAP* slows down considerably if the number of cases exceeds several thousand). Generic activities that can help students see patterns in data include:

• Comparing distributions, e.g. studying population pyramids animated as a function of time
• Aggregating data, e.g. summarizing climate data by calculating average monthly temperatures across several years
• Disaggregating and investigating subpopulations, e.g. comparing income of men and women conditioned on their educational level, occupation and years of tenure
• Creating new variables, e.g. defining the ratio of income shares of the 10% highest earners to the 10% lowest earners
• Restructuring data, e.g. reorganizing data about Covid-19 cases according to severity (mild—moderate—serious—fatal), the prevalence of risk factors (diabetes, smoking, heart disease, age), hospitalisation (no, yes)

(continued)

---

[20] https://ourworldindata.org

[21] https://www.un.org/sustainabledevelopment

[22] https://germanwatch.org/en

> • Searching for explanatory third variables, e.g. the high correlation between life expectancy and gross national product per person could be explained by the number of physicians per 1000 people in the population
> • Modelling functional relationships, e.g. identifying seasonal components and finding trends in atmospheric CO_2 content

However, the capacity of many educational tools for handling large datasets is quite limited. For investigating very large data sets, you will have to resort to professional packages (such as *JMP*, *R*, *Jupyter Notebooks*), which require deep knowledge of statistics (in order to understand options and default settings!) as well as programming skills.

18.4.7 Design Activities with Closed and Open Tasks to Promote Critical Thinking

Activities in Civic Statistics are rather different from standard courses in statistics, research methods or social statistics, and aim to develop skills in statistical reasoning. Recommended learning and teaching strategies include:

> • Employ a variety of teaching strategies, with an emphasis on active learning approaches where learners formalise questions, find evidence and choose appropriate methods of analysis
> • Develop skills of critical interpretation via analyses of a wide variety of sources (including newspaper articles and unsubstantiated claims)
> • Encourage students to communicate about social issues by creating narrative accounts of complex situations, based on multiple sources of statistical evidence
> • Introduce reasoning with multivariate data, relevant to important social issues, early in the course, including data with non-linear relationships among variables
> • Develop modelling skills so that learners bring an awareness of the strengths and weaknesses of tools used to model social situations
> • Engage students with the variety of ways that evidence is used to support theory in different academic disciplines
> • Encourage student enquiry about data sources, and reflections on the likely reliability of data
> • Emphasise the importance of metadata - defining measures and operationalizing variables

18.4.8 Ask for a Summary and Critical Review

Civic Statistics issues rarely have a clear cut yes-or-no answer. Any conclusion is based on assumptions, and could be modified in light of additional pieces of evidence. Often times asking good questions within the investigative process may be more productive than finding quick answers. The generation of a good question is a fundamental issue in statistics education and within the investigative data analysis cycle PPDAC (Problem, Plan, Data, Analysis, Conclusion) of Wild and Pfannkuch

(1999). In Chap. 13, Gal addresses this topic in detail, and offers examples and principles for creating 'opinion questions' for students. A *good* investigative question is one that allows for rich exploration of the data in hand, discovery, and thinking statistically. A good investigative question allows students to engage in interesting work and has an element of open-endedness (Arnold, 2013). The question is likely to draw on data that will be available within the time frame of the investigation and is specific, so that it is answerable from data. Posing a good investigative question is certainly not a trivial task, but it is of high relevance for analysis and conclusions. This holds in particular when drawing conclusions about causal relationships (especially if based on observational data). Conclusions gain in strength and validity if data analytic approaches support the assertions. At the end of the assignments, students should be encouraged to return to their focal question(s). By conducting a critical review of the conclusions, students evaluate the adequacy of the underlying arguments, review the possibility of alternative explanations for the observed phenomenon, state limitations of their conclusions and whether the conclusions obtained are consistent with the evidence.

18.4.9 Use Alternate Forms of Assessment to Improve and Evaluate Student Learning

The assessments that learners face during and at the end of any course are the strongest guide for learners about what is to be learned, and the extent to which they are making progress. Using formative and summative assessments to improve and evaluate student learning should ensure that students build the ability to draw from their data analyses implications *for society and policy*. In Chap. 4, Gal et al. discuss general ideas for assessment specifically related to Civic Statistics, and introduce a radar plot tool to analyse the demands of Civic Statistics tasks. PCS Recommendation 5 in Sect. 4.5 argues for the need for a variety of assessments and evaluation processes to examine and to promote students' ability to investigate and critically understand data in a social context. We recommend forms of assessments which examine the ability to investigate and critically understand data, statistical findings and messages about key social phenomena such as project work or portfolios, creating videos (see Schiller and Engel in Chap. 16), presentations or other non-traditional media, either as individuals or in groups.

18.5 Summary

Civic Statistics by its nature is highly interdisciplinary. At its centre are issues of public interest that concern the social and economic well-being of all citizens and the functioning of democracy. Engaging with Civic Statistics requires skills and content knowledge that do not fall under a single subject area and require interdisciplinary learning approaches to acquire. Making sense of data about society occurs in geography, history, social studies, economics as well as in biology and many more fields. Mathematics provides important analytical tools, methods, and representations for exploring and drawing conclusions from data. Disciplinary content knowledge helps people situate data in relevant contexts and to draw social meaning from numerical patterns and trends.

Whatever your goal is—such as integrating civic issues into teaching statistics, introducing statistical concepts in teaching social studies, or coordinating the teaching of statistics with another subject—there will be challenges. Success in the teaching and learning of Civic Statistics will require teamwork and the contributions of experts from different fields. Carefully planned and implemented, Civic Statistics holds great promise for inspiring and enlivening statistics education. It can motivate students to learn statistical concepts by highlighting the relevance of statistics, and by illustrating how statistical content knowledge is key to a deeper understanding of complex issues that affect humanity.

References

Alexander, B., & Munk, M. (2013). A social justice data fair. In E. Gutstein & B. Peterson (Eds.), *Rethinking mathematics: Teaching social justice by the numbers* (2nd ed., pp. 243–247). Rethinking Schools.

Arnold, P. M. (2013). *Statistical investigative questions - An enquiry into posing and answering investigative questions from existing data.* [Doctoral dissertation, The University of Auckland]. https://researchspace.auckland.ac.nz/handle/2292/21305

Batanero, C., Burrill, G., & Reading, C. (2011). Overview. In C. Batanero, G. Burrill, & C. Reading (Eds.), *Teaching statistics in school - Mathematics challenges for teaching and teacher education: A joint ICMI/IASE study* (pp. 407–418). Springer Science+Business Media B.V. https://doi.org/10.1007/978-94-007-1131-0

Biehler, R., Ben-Zvi, D., Bakker, A., & Makar, K. (2013). Technology for enhancing statistical reasoning at the school level. In M. A. Clements, A. J. Bishop, C. Keitel-Kreidt, J. Kilpatrick, & F. K.-S. Leung (Eds.), *Third international handbook of mathematics education* (pp. 643–689). Springer Science + Business Media.

Brown, M. (2016). Engaging students in quantitative methods: Real questions, real data. In J. Engel (Ed.), *Promoting understanding of statistics about society: Proceedings of the Roundtable Conference of the International Association of Statistics Education (IASE)*, Berlin.

Buckley, J., Brown, M., Thomson, S., Olsen, W., & Carter, J. (2015). Embedding quantitative skills into the social science curriculum: Case studies from Manchester. *International Journal of Social Research Methodology, 18*(5), 495–510.

Burdette, A. M., & McLoughlin, K. (2010). Using census data in the classroom to increase quantitative literacy and promote critical sociological thinking. *Teaching Sociology, 38*(3), 247–257.

Byun, K. J., & Croucher, J. S. (2018). Teaching statistics through the law. *Teaching Statistics, 40*(2), 46–50.

Carter, J., & Nicholson, J. (2016). Teaching statistical literacy by getting students to use real world data: 40 years worth of experience in 40 minutes. In J. Engel (Ed.), *Promoting understanding of statistics about society: Proceedings of the Roundtable Conference of the International Association of Statistics Education (IASE)*, Berlin.

Cobb, G. W., & Moore, D. S. (1997). Mathematics, statistics, and teaching. *The American Mathematical Monthly, 104*(9), 801–823.

Day, L. (2013). Using statistics to explore cross-curricular and social issues opportunities. *The Australian Mathematics Teacher, 59*(4), 3–7.

Dierker, L., Kaparakis, E., Rose, J., Selya, A., & Beveridge, D. (2012). Strength in numbers: A multidisciplinary, project-based course in introductory statistics. *Strength in Numbers, 12*(2), 12.

Engel, J., Gal, I., & Ridgway, J. (2016). Mathematical literacy and citizen engagement: The role of Civic Statistics. Presented at the *13th International Conference on Mathematical Education*, Hamburg.

Erickson, T., Wilkerson, M., Finzer, W., & Reichsman, F. (2019). Data moves. *Technology Innovations in Statistics Education, 12*(1).

Franklin, C., Bargagliotti, A. E., Case, C. A., Kader, G. D., Scheaffer, R. L., & Spangler, D. A. (2015). *Statistical education of teachers*. American Statistical Association. http://www.amstat.org/asa/files/pdfs/EDU-SET.pdf

Gal, I., & Trostianitser, A. (2016). Understanding basic demographic trends: Connecting table reading, task design, and context. In J. Engel (Ed.), *Promoting understanding of statistics about society: Proceedings of the Roundtable Conference of the International Association of Statistics Education (IASE)*, Berlin.

Gea, M., Lopez-Martin, M., Batanero, C., & Arteaga, P. (2016). Using United Nations data in the training of teachers to teach statistics. In J. Engel (Ed.), *Promoting understanding of statistics about society: Proceedings of the Roundtable Conference of the International Association of Statistics Education (IASE)*, Berlin.

GISTEMP Team. (2022). *GISS Surface Temperature Analysis (GISTEMP), version 4*. NASA Goddard Institute for Space Studies. Dataset accessed 2022-02-21 at https://data.giss.nasa.gov/gistemp/

Gutstein, E. (2003). Teaching and learning mathematics for social justice in an urban, Latino school. *Journal for Research in Mathematics Education, 34*, 37–73.

Gutstein, E. (2013). Driving while black or brown: A math project about racial profiling. In E. Gutstein & B. Peterson (Eds.), *Rethinking mathematics: Teaching social justice by the numbers* (2nd ed., pp. 16–18). Rethinking Schools.

Gutstein, E., & Peterson, B. (Eds.). (2013). *Rethinking mathematics: Teaching social justice by the numbers* (2nd ed.). Rethinking Schools.

Hannigan, A., Gill, O., & Leavy, A. M. (2013). An investigation of prospective secondary mathematics teachers' conceptual knowledge of and attitudes towards statistics. *Journal of Mathematics Teacher Education, 16*(6), 427–449. https://doi.org/10.1007/s10857-013-9246-3

Hersh, S., & Peterson, B. (2013). Poverty and world wealth: Recognizing inequality. In E. Gutstein & B. Peterson (Eds.), *Rethinking mathematics: Teaching social justice by the numbers* (2nd ed., pp. 89–92). Rethinking Schools.

Himmelstein, K. (2013). Racism and stop and frisk. In E. Gutstein & B. Peterson (Eds.), *Rethinking mathematics: Teaching social justice by the numbers* (2nd ed., pp. 122–128). Rethinking Schools.

Howery, C. B., & Rodriguez, H. (2006). Integrating data analysis (IDA): Working with sociology departments to address the quantitative literacy gap. *Teaching Sociology, 34*(1), 23–38.

Johnston, W., & Tsai, T. (2018). *The prevalence of collaboration among American teachers: National findings from the American teacher panel*. RAND Corporation. https://doi.org/10.7249/RR2217

Kazar, K. (2016). Using statistical datasets for describing poverty and income inequality. In J. Engel (Ed.), *Promoting understanding of statistics about society: Proceedings of the Roundtable Conference of the International Association of Statistics Education (IASE)*, Berlin

Langyel, M. (2013). Unequal distribution of U.S. wealth: Recognizing inequality, part two. In E. Gutstein & B. Peterson (Eds.), *Rethinking mathematics: Teaching social justice by the numbers* (2nd ed., pp. 93–94). Rethinking Schools.

Lenssen, N., Schmidt, G., Hansen, J., Menne, M., Persin, A., Ruedy, R., & Zyss, D. (2019). Improvements in the GISTEMP uncertainty model. *Journal of Geophysical Research – Atmospheres, 124*(12), 6307–6326. https://doi.org/10.1029/2018JD029522

Leonard, J. (2010). Using U.S. census data to teach mathematics for social justice. *Middle School Journal, 42*(1), 38–44. https://doi.org/10.1080/00940771.2010.11461749

Lesser, L., & Nordenhaug, E. (2004). Ethical statistics and statistical ethics: Making an interdisciplinary module. *Journal of Statistics Education, 12*(3), jse.amstat.org/v12n3/lesser.html.

Louie, J., Roy, S., Chance, B., Stiles, J., & Fagan, E. (2021). Promoting interest and skills in statistical and multivariable thinking with social justice data investigations. *Proceedings of the International Association for Statistical Education (IASE) 2021 Satellite Conference*, Online Conference. http://iaseweb.org/documents/papers/sat2021/IASE2021%20Satellite%20133_LOUIE.pdf?1649974212

Louie, J., Stiles, J., Fagan, E., Chance, B., & Roy, S. (2022). Building toward critical data literacy with investigations of income inequality. *Educational Technology & Society, 25*(4), 142–163. https://drive.google.com/file/d/1JJsKkvtm8Lp1VolrSssHNfX5aIi2K6Z/view

McCune, D., & Tunstall, S. L. (2019). Calculated democracy—Explorations in gerrymandering. *Teaching Statistics, 41*, 47–53. https://doi.org/10.1111/test.12181

Navarro-Alberto, J. A., & Barrientos-Medina, R. C. (2017). The power of balancing in a data-rich material world: Teaching introductory mathematics and statistics to biology students. In A. Molnar (Ed.), *Teaching Statistics in a Data Rich World: Proceedings of the Satellite Conference of the International Association for Statistical Education (IASE)*. Rabat.

Nicholson, J., Ridgway, J., & McCusker, S. (2011). Visualise then conceptualise. *Social Science Teacher, 40*(3), 8–13.

Nicholson, J., Ridgway, J., & McCusker, S. (2013). Health, wealth and lifestyle choices - Provoking discussion on public spending. *Teaching Citizenship, 36*, 23–27.

OECD. (2018). *The future of education and skills 2030: The future we want*. https://www.oecd.org/education/2030/E2030%20Position%20Paper%20(05.04.2018).pdf

Pereira-Mendoza, L. (1993). Introducing data analysis in the schools: Who should teach it and how? *Proceedings of the International Statistics Institute Round Table Conference*. Lennoxville, August 10–14, 1992.

Peterson, B. (2013). Teaching math across the curriculum. In E. Gutstein & B. Peterson (Eds.), *Rethinking mathematics: Teaching social justice by the numbers* (2nd ed., pp. 9–15). Rethinking Schools.

Pfannkuch, M., Regan, M., Wild, C., & Horton, N. J. (2010). Telling data stories: Essential dialogues for comparative reasoning. *Journal of Statistics Education, 18*(1) www.amstat.org/publications/jse/v18n1/pfannkuch.pdf

Poling, L., & Weiland, T. (2020). Using an interactive platform to recognize the intersection of social and spatial inequalities. *Teaching Statistics, 42*, 108–116. https://doi.org/10.1111/test.12234

Ravenscroft, B., & Chen, V. (2017). Balancing act: Creating a multidisciplinary blended introductory statistics course. *Balancing Act, 10*(1), 15.

Remsburg, A., Harris, M., & Batzli, J. (2014). Research and teaching: Statistics across the curriculum using an iterative, interactive approach in an inquiry-based lab sequence. *Journal of College Science Teaching, 044*(02). https://doi.org/10.2505/4/jcst14_044_02_72

Reston, E., Piramide, J., & Loquias, C. (2016). Promoting statistical literacy and understanding of youth population dynamics in a new statistics and probability course for senior high school. In J. Engel (Ed.), *Promoting understanding of statistics about society: Proceedings of the Roundtable Conference of the International Association of Statistics Education (IASE)*, Berlin.

Ridgway, J., Nicholson, J, & McCusker, S. (2008). Alcohol and a mash-up: Understanding student understanding. *ENAC biannual conference*, Berlin.

Savard, A., & Manuel, D. (2016). Teaching statistics: Creating an intersection for intra and interdisciplinarity. *Statistics Education Research Journal, 15*(2), 239–256.

Silvestre, C., & Meireles, A. (2017). Towards a statistically literate communication professionals. In A. Molnar (Ed.), *Teaching Statistics in a Data Rich World: Proceedings of the Satellite conference of the International Association for Statistical Education (IASE)*, Rabat.

Turner, E., & Font Strawhun, T. (2013). With math, it's like you have more defense. In I. E. Gutstein & B. Peterson (Eds.), *Rethinking mathematics: Teaching social justice by the numbers* (2nd ed.). Rethinking Schools.

Usiskin, Z. (2015). The relationships between statistics and other subjects in the K-12 curriculum. *Chance, 28*(3), 4–18.

Vahey, P., Rafanan, K., Swan, K., van't Hooft, M. A., Annette Kratcoski, R., Stanford, T., & Patton, C. (2010). *Thinking with data: A cross-disciplinary approach to teaching data literacy and proportionality.* American Educational Research Association Annual Meeting, Denver, CO. http://www.academia.edu/download/30714030/AERA_2010_TWD_Math_Vahey.pdf

Weinberg, A. E., & McMeeking, L. B. S. (2017). Toward meaningful interdisciplinary education: High school teachers' views of mathematics and science integration. *School Science and Mathematics, 117*(5), 204–213. https://doi.org/10.1111/ssm.12224

Wild, C., & Pfannkuch, M. (1999). Statistical thinking in empirical enquiry. *International Statistical Review, 67*(3), 223–248.

Wolfe, C. R. (1993). Quantitative reasoning across a college curriculum. *College Teaching, 41*(1), 3–7.

Chapter 19
Dynamic, Interactive Trees and Icon Arrays for Visualizing Risks in Civic Statistics

Laura Martignon ⓘ**, Daniel Frischemeier, Michelle McDowell, and Christoph Till**

To remember simplified pictures is better than to forget accurate figures. Neurath 1973, 223)

Abstract Through our lives we face risks which may appear scary and threatening. Estimating risks is often experienced as difficult. This is important when we make decisions about how to take actions and order our lives. In many cases risks can be measured based on statistical evidence. However, such measures may be difficult to grasp. Sometimes the difficulties are intrinsic and sometimes the difficulties may be inherent in the representations and formalisms used to represent them. In this chapter we describe particular practices for understanding features of civic statistics and for communicating risks and uncertainties visually, using simple, transparent representations, which foster intuition and are easily grasped. These tools become handy for modelling risky situations and making decisions that can lead to better informed action. Children should acquire basic skills for dealing with risks and in this chapter we intend to show that this can be done in a playful way and that primary school students can acquire the first elements of risk literacy.

Keywords Civic statistics · Risk · Uncertainty · Conditional probabilities · Risk reduction · Natural frequencies · Icon arrays

---

L. Martignon (✉)
Institute for Mathematics and Computing, Ludwigsburg University of Education, Ludwigsburg, Germany
e-mail: martignon@ph-ludwigsburg.de

D. Frischemeier
University of Münster, Münster, Germany
e-mail: dafr@math.upb.de

M. McDowell
University of Potsdam, Potsdam, Germany
e-mail: mcdowell@fgw-brandenburg.de

C. Till
Eichwald-Realschule, Sachsenheim, Sachsenheim, Germany

19.1 Introduction and Motivation

Owing to the amount of quantitative information to be dealt with on a daily basis, people need to acquire basic numeracy and quantitative skills at an early stage in their lives. However, mere numeracy is not enough. To illustrate a typical problem using the Covid pandemic as an example, consider that a person's Covid-19 test is negative and she is told that the false negative rate of the test is 2%—is she really not infected? And what does it mean, that the test's sensitivity is 98%? Answers to these types of questions have become crucial for citizens all over the world to know and understand during 2020, as this book is being written. But it is not just the Covid 19 pandemic which prompts our need to understand and assess information about tests or symptoms. For instance, when a woman is told that regular screening reduces the risk of breast cancer by 20%, what should she do? Or, citing a famous example of David Spiegelhalter, if we are told that eating bacon sandwiches increases our risk of getting bowel cancer by 20%, how seriously should we make an effort to avoid eating bacon sandwiches? As we will illustrate in this chapter, there are simple tools and principles for modelling and analyzing risks and uncertainties which can be acquired early in school.

As we learned in Chap. 3, engaging with Civic Statistics requires understanding and possession of 11 facets and tools. This chapter connects with and elaborates on issues related to two of these facets, regarding understanding probability and risk (Facet 4) and representations (Facet 5). We link both of them to the notion of risk literacy, which concerns people's disposition to identify, model, and evaluate risks and to trade off benefits against risks when important resources are at stake. Thus, risk literacy is more useful in everyday life than the abstract notions of probability taught in regular statistics or mathematics classes. Risk literacy is essential to enable understanding of uncertainties and risks that emerge in various areas of individual, social and economic life encompassed by Civic Statistics. Risk literacy also enables informed decisions (at the individual or societal level), particularly when resources like health, food, money, and time are at stake in order to avoid losses that can have critical or even fatal consequences.

Risks have been around through all eras of human history. In fact, life used to be far riskier for the whole of humankind even a few centuries ago, as the first chapter of the book Homo Deus by Yuval Harari describes at length (Harari, 2016). The concept of risk is only about 800 years old and emerged as insurances became popular. It developed in parallel with the first official insurance contracts between shipping companies transporting goods and wares, and the craftsmen in Renaissance Italy, who produced them (Scheller, 2017). The mathematical tools for analysing risks were developed during the late Renaissance and the Enlightenment, and the first analytical treatment of risks and so-called life contingencies was written by the British mathematician Augustus de Morgan in 1838 (de Morgan, 1838).

The development of a formal theory of risk and uncertainty took off with de Morgan's text. Today risk analysis is a flourishing field that overlaps with mathematics, finance and economics. It is not the purpose of this chapter to present formal results from risk analysis. The purpose is to treat elementary but relevant properties of those risks people face in their daily lives, mainly with regard to their health, and address frequent problems they encounter when trying to assess them. We know well that medical treatments have potential risks as well as potential benefits. Being able to trade these against each other is important. Just to mention an example of crucial relevance while this book is written, in the case of vaccines, the benefits involve many dimensions for others as well as for ourselves, while the risks seem difficult to assess. It is well known that the communication of these risks can be made opaque and difficult, or transparent and easy to grasp (Kurz-Milcke et al., 2008).

This chapter discusses specific *representations and visualizations related to risk*, because in all their aspects and varieties, representations are a central way for communicating statistical and probabilistic information—hence are a key issue faced by Civic Statistics. Educators often talk about 'misleading graphs' or other forms of bad representations that may create a distorted or biased view of patterns in data (Spiegelhalter, 2019). In this chapter we focused more on the opposite, i.e., on adequate or effective representations which can help people understand data in general, and visualize levels of risk in particular. To illustrate all of the above, the chapter will discuss specific graphical and analogue representations related to health and health-related risks. These representations, such as the one presented in Fig. 19.2, are promoted by the Harding Center for Risk Literacy.[1] Gigerenzer (2002) documents how few people understand fundamental concepts such as the base rate of a disease, the sensitivity of a test, its specificity or its predictive value. Elementary distinctions, such as that between absolute and relative risks are also far from being understood by the general public. Such issues can be helped, to some extent, by the use of appropriate representations. Civic Statistics aims to foster the understanding of statistics about health, society, politics etc. and to support young people on their way to becoming informed and enlightened citizens; understanding risks and representations are key concepts that can help future citizens.

As a motivating example for this chapter, we illustrate the use of a *Fact Box* produced by the Harding Center to communicate risks about medical interventions to the public (McDowell et al., 2016). These Fact Boxes have inspired insurance companies to work with the Harding Center to better communicate risks to their customers. The aim of the Fact Box in Fig. 19.1 is to communicate the risk reduction in breast cancer caused by regular screening, using an icon array.

This Fact Box makes good use of icon arrays, following Otto Neurath (see Chaps. 5 and 20). The icon array on the left shows icons for 1000 women who do not undergo screening, coded as: having died from breast cancer; having died from any cancer (including breast cancer); and survivors. Five women die from breast cancer. On the right side we see outcomes for 1000 women who undergo screening regularly, coded in the same way. Here, four women die of breast cancer, meaning that the absolute risk reduction by performing screening regularly for breast cancer is 1 per 1000. The distinction between absolute and relative risk is critically important

---

[1] https://www.hardingcenter.de/en

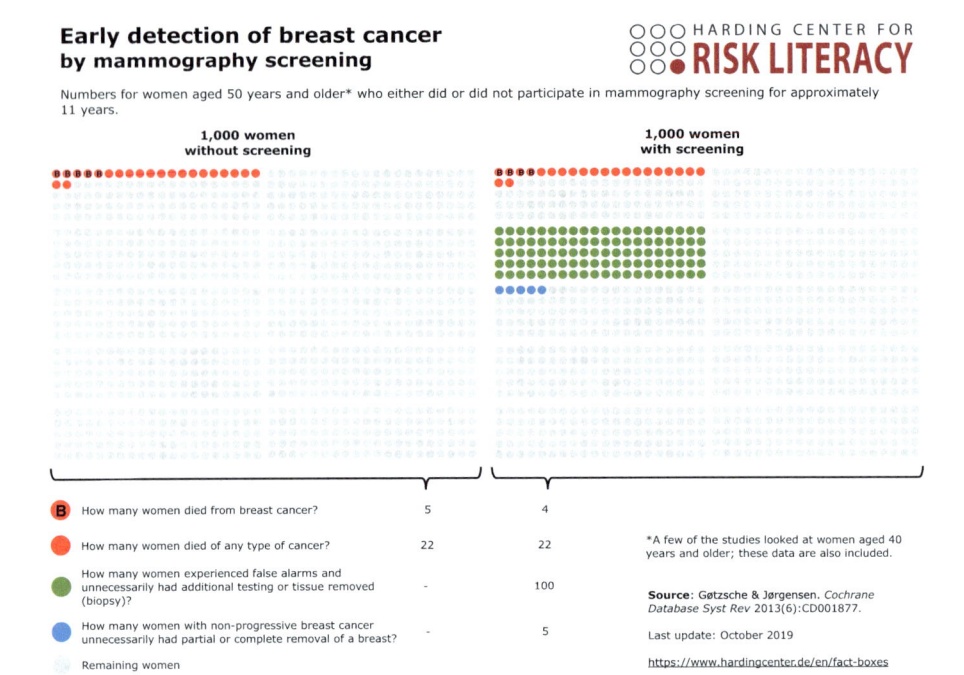

Fig. 19.1 A fact box for communicating information on the risk reduction caused by regular screening

too—for people making decisions about whether to undergo some form of treatment (here, screening). A risk reduction for breast cancer of 20% for women as a result of screening sounds dramatic, and a justification for action. However, a risk reduction of 1 in 1000 is far less impressive. This example shows how icon arrays can be the basis for decision making in a way that is not only different to analyses based on frequency distributions which are taught in statistics classes, but which is also far more effective for communicating levels of probability and risk.

A second example is presented in Fig. 19.2, produced at the Winton Centre for the Risk and Evidence Communication at the University of Cambridge. This graphic has been published in the Sun newspaper and has been presented by CNN, for describing benefits and harms associated with the AstraZeneca vaccine.

Icon arrays, like those presented in Figs. 19.1 and 19.2, are a form of graphical representation inspired by Neurath's Isotypes, that adhere to principles for the design of risk communications (Trevena et al., 2013). An icon array is a form of pictograph or graphical representation that uses matrices of circles, squares, matchstick figures, faces, or other symbols to represent statistical information. Arrays are usually constructed in blocks, say, of 10, 20, 25, 50, 100 or 1000 icons where each icon represents an individual in a population. Icons are then distinguished by color, shading, shape or form to indicate differences in the characteristics of the population, such as the presence (or absence) of a risk factor or the occurrence of an event (e.g.,

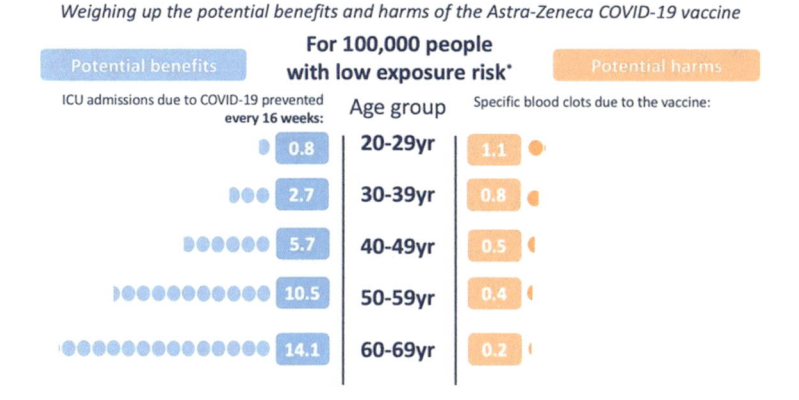

Fig. 19.2 An illustration based on the use of Icon Arrays for describing benefits and harms of the Astra-Zeneca vaccine (https://wintoncentre.maths.cam.ac.uk/news/communicating-potential-bene fits-and-harms-astra-zeneca-covid-19-vaccine/)

experiencing a side-effect) according to the frequency or probability of that risk factor or event.

Icon arrays are helpful for communicating risk information because they draw on people's natural disposition to count (Dehaene, 1996), while also facilitating the visual comparison of proportions (Brase, 2009). Further, the one-to-one match between individual and icon has been proposed to invite identification with the individuals represented in the graphic to a greater extent than other graphical formats (Kurz-Milcke et al., 2011). Some features of icon arrays characterize their function and strength:

Part-to-Whole Relationships

- Icon arrays depict part-to-whole relationships, thereby facilitating understanding of proportions (Ancker et al., 2006). An improved understanding of quantitative proportions is associated with automatic visual area processing and the visual salience of the numerator and denominator in a ratio, when depicted in icon format.

Arrangement of Icon Arrays

- Icons representing a sub-population of individuals can be arranged sequentially (grouped together or sorted) or randomly (scattered among the population at large). The arrangement can promote understanding of different aspects of the data. Randomly arranged icon arrays can convey the concept of chance or randomness (Ancker et al., 2011). However, in random-arrangement icon arrays, the proportion of individuals affected is harder to judge, because area judgment is not easy to do when icons are scattered (Ancker et al., 2006). Sorting icons becomes a first statistical activity (see next section).

Representational Appeal

- Icons represent items capturing characteristic aspects of the represented items, and thus are able to be interpreted without the need for text descriptions.

We will now start by describing Risk Literacy as a construct and then pass on to introducing representational tools for facilitating basic aspects of risk literacy.

19.2   Risk Literacy as a Construct

Risk literacy is a construct made up of four components or levels as illustrated in Fig. 19.3 (adapted from Martignon & Hoffrage, 2019; see also Martignon & Laskey, 2019):

1. Detecting risk and uncertainty
2. Analysing and representing risk and modelling risky situations
3. Dealing with trade-offs by reflecting on and comparing alternatives
4. Making decisions and acting

We describe these components briefly:

- The first component depends on a psychological disposition or 'readiness'—one of the eleven components of the conceptual model of Civic Statistics (see Chap. 3, Fig. 3.1)—to be sensitive to situations where risk plays an important role.
- The second component consists of analyzing, modelling and representing risky situations; this requires basic instruction. Analyzing, modelling and representing

Fig. 19.3 Scaffolding risk literacy by means of four components

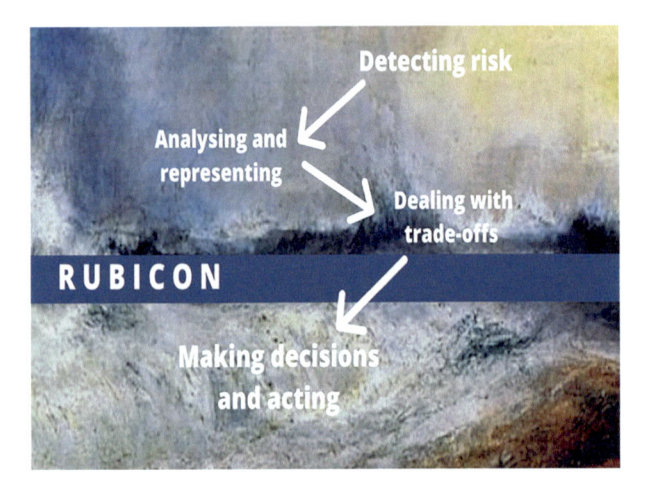

is facilitated by tools developed from elementary probability and statistical literacy teaching for estimating key features of risky situations. Models are used for estimating predictive values of tests or symptoms, as well as associated risk reductions or enhancements, for example. Familiarity with these tools, however, have to be acquired; later we show that appropriate skills can be developed, at an early age. The third component of Risk Literacy builds on the first two and requires the ability to compare alternatives and deal with trade-offs. Many risky situations are also associated with possible benefits. Riding a bicycle without a helmet can be experienced as more pleasurable than riding with a helmet, but the risk of injury when falling is quite large (see Fig. 19.16). And investments are typical actions which require weighing risks versus benefits. Making decisions thus often requires conscious deliberation, (note, however, the extensive research that shows how simple heuristics based on features of situations (see Component II) may lead to successful and robust decisions e.g. Gigerenzer & Gaissmaier, 2011; Martignon & Laskey, 2019)

- The fourth component involves decision making as the result of a conscious or deliberative process based on features characterizing situations under conditions of risk or uncertainty

The present chapter focuses mainly on the second component of Risk Literacy. It describes ways in which the environment can facilitate the process of analyzing features of risky situations, like symptoms and tests, by representing information on these features in accessible, transparent formats. It also proposes how these basic elements of Risk Literacy can be implemented in classrooms. Our treatment of risk communication builds on the tenets of ecological rationality, which emphasize the interaction between mind (e.g., internal representations) and environment (e.g., external representations). In modern times, shaping the environment means finding representational tools that are easily grasped and interpreted by the public. Today this requires making sensible use of digital technologies.

19.3 Modelling Risks and Uncertainty in the Health Domain

The era of Covid-19 has pointed to the necessity of understanding and trusting scientific research and its assessments of risks and uncertainties. Covid-19 has shocked the world, clearly reminding humans of the crucial truth that health is their one fundamental resource. However, individuals face decisions about their health and that of their children not only during this particularly dark period of the Covid-19 pandemic, but also throughout their lives.

Here are some illustrative decision questions:

- If I have a positive antibody test, can I go partying?
- Should young children be vaccinated against rubella?
- Should women undergo routine breast-screening?

In general, people have trouble making these decisions, which often require a basic understanding of statistical statements involving risks. A comprehensive review of the work of Kahneman and Tversky in the 1980s and 90s on fallible heuristics is offered by Gilovich et al. (2002). A reaction to that research was the effort to determine which factors of the representation of information caused the fallacies and biases discovered by the school of Kahneman and Tversky. During the nineties, Gigerenzer and his school looked into these "ecological" factors, which influence inferences under uncertainty (e.g. Gigerenzer & Hoffrage, 1995).

A plethora of empirical results on the topic led to work directed at supporting communication between patients and doctors. In Gigerenzer et al. (2007), doctors and patients make sense of health statistics by presenting probabilistic information in novel formats. A very recent study by Binder et al. (2021) demonstrates once again that doctors understand and perform Bayesian updating much better when data are presented by means of natural frequencies. The insights of these studies constitute an important element of this chapter.

Key recommendations arising from this research are to use frequency statements instead of single-event probabilities, to communicate absolute risks rather than relative risk, and natural frequencies rather than conditional probabilities (see also Garcia-Retamero et al., 2010; Paling, 2003: Kurz-Milcke et al., 2008; Schapira & Van Ruiswyk, 2000). A glance at medical brochures for doctor-patient interaction shows that transparent communication is the exception rather than the norm. A prerequisite to decisions about medical procedures or treatments is an ethical requirement to inform patients about the *benefits and harms of interventions* in a format they can understand. Without it, shared decision-making and informed consent are impossible. But what makes the information about medical tests, incidence of diseases, risk enhancement due to bad habits and risk reduction due to good habits transparent and accessible?

In order to enhance the public's understanding of risks two remedies are immediately at hand: one is to improve the way information on risks is communicated and the other is to develop and encourage programs for fostering risk literacy at an early stage, namely in school (Martignon & Hoffrage, 2019).

To illustrate how to improve the communication of medical evidence so as to make it more transparent and accessible, let's first look at how information is typically communicated and why many people have trouble interpreting that evidence. In a typical medical situation, physicians must reason from evidence, like symptoms and test results. This evidence can support and corroborate a hypothesis, such as whether or not a patient has a disease. A formal way of treating this inference is to consider the following two elements: (1) the *prior* probability that the disease (here denoted by D) is present; and (2) probabilities or likelihoods that the evidence (denoted as E) would be observed if the disease was present or absent. In the case of evidence from a test, the doctor may observe a positive result. For making an inference the physician should use her prior probability and test likelihoods to calculate the so-called *posterior* probability that the disease is indeed present given the positive test result. The corresponding formula is called *Bayes' Rule*, and was first formulated by the mathematician, philosopher and minister Thomas Bayes in the eighteenth century.

$$P(D|E) = \frac{P(E|D)P(D)}{P(E|D)P(D) + P(E|\overline{D})P(\overline{D})}$$

The formula shows how to solve this evidential reasoning problem: P(D|E) or the probability that the patient has the disease given that they tested positive on the test. However, people are notoriously bad at manipulating probabilities, as a plethora of empirical studies have shown (Eddy, 1982; Gigerenzer & Hoffrage, 1995). In Eddy's classical study on doctors' estimate of the probability that a certain disease is present, given that a test of the disease is positive, he discovered that his participants made mistakes based on misconceptions. The so-called predictive value of the test was estimated as being close to the chances of the test detecting the disease. Thus, if a test had a probability of 95% of detecting the disease, Eddy's participants estimated that the actual chances of having the disease, given a positive test, was a value quite close to 95%. What surprised Eddy was that the doctors' estimates of P(D|E), i.e., the chances of being ill with the disease, given that the test is positive, remained quite close to the inverse probability P(E|D), i.e., the test is positive given that they have the disease, also called sensitivity of the test. Further, they made this error even when the base rate of the disease was very small. As the base rate is found in the numerator, it has a big influence on the result. Therefore, when the disease is very rare, the posterior probability, namely the test's positive predictive value (PPV), tends to be small. This discovery led to a sequence of important replications with the same discouraging results. The key factor that makes this kind of reasoning difficult—even for experts, as Gigerenzer and Hoffrage (1995) pointed out—seems to be the abstract, symbolic format of the 'probabilistic' information used for inference. In the next section, we will present representations and visual aids that simplify the understanding of that same information (again, focussing mainly on examples from medicine).

19.4   Iconic and En-Active Representations

We make judgments on situations or phenomena based on features we extract from them, and it is crucial that we can assess the reliability of these features. When judging the weather for instance, and wondering whether it will rain, we extract features from the sky above us: is it cloudy, or does the sun shine? Recently the discoveries of neuroscientists have begun to explain how neural assemblies in our brains function as "classification machines" under uncertainty (Amari, 1977;

Fig. 19.4 Fairy tale creatures with and without crowns

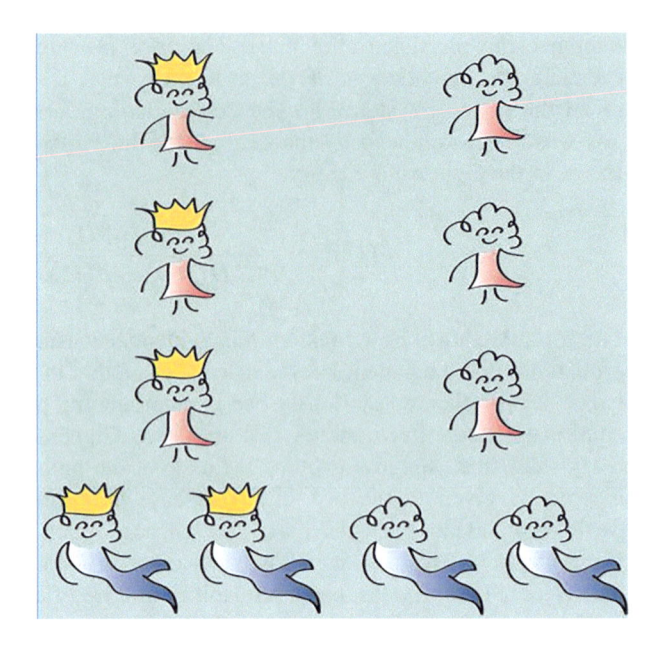

Braitenberg & Schütz, 1991): If a child looks pale his mother will tend to classify him as "ill" and make the decision that he should stay home the next day; the same is true if the child has fever. These features are, in general, not completely diagnostic which is why Bayes' theorem is so helpful. Going back to our example above, a child might be pale because he is just frightened, for instance. Besides, more than one feature is usually necessary for a medical diagnosis: situations are judged based on several aspects, symptoms, tests. When under time pressure, decision-making is often carried out by means of a simple tallying of features or a lexicographic treatment of features one at a time, ranked according to their reliability measures (Martignon et al., 2008). How early can we start training our disposition to assess the predictive value of individual features? The following icon array (see Fig. 19.4) has been presented to children aged 7 years old They are able to assess whether the feature "wears a crown" is predictive of "being a princess".

Such representations are already used for instruction of children in primary school in some schools in Baden Württemberg. Insurance companies in Germany and in Italy use such representations for workshops in schools, where risk literacy concepts are introduced both in primary and secondary school. In England, materials based on such representations have been used for school instruction (see Gage & Spiegelhalter, 2016). The representations usually taught in sixth class in Germany, Italy and other European countries are pie charts, simple scales and tables; percentages are taught in sixth and seventh class. All of these representations clearly require competencies beyond counting. In contrast, icon arrays present information in a transparent way. We return to this theme later.

Children can learn effectively when they use their hands and play with materials. Can enactive representations foster fourth graders' intuitions on Bayesian reasoning

Fig. 19.5 Tinker Cubes for enactive representations for treating risks in primary school classrooms

and risk? A study involving 244 students from 12 grade 4 classes (see Till & Sprösser, 2020) investigated the effect of enactive representations for representing probabilistic information and also for dealing with trade-offs in risky situations. For instance, in a training lesson the following problem was posed; "In a school yard there are 2 girls—one with long hair and one with short hair. There are also 8 boys— 2 with long hair and 6 with short hair. Assuming I tell you that I talked with one of these children and the child had long hair, would you bet it was a girl?"

The students used colored Tinker Cubes to encode the features *boy, girl, long hair* and *short hair* and modeled the situation. By adjoining cubes on top of each other, students were able to represent compounded features (i.e., long-haired boy). In Fig. 19.5, blue cubes represent boys and red cubes represent girls. Green cubes represent short hair, and yellow cubes represent long hair.

If I talk to a child at random in the playground, the chance that the child is a girl is 2 out of 10 (prior probability or base rate) and changes to 1 out of 3 (posterior probability) in the light of new evidence ('... the one I talked to had long hair ...'). By looking at the front row of the tinker towers the answer is quite clear. Although girls usually have long hair, in this situation the person talked to is more likely to be a boy since 2 out of 3 children with long hair are boys. In this intervention study based on displaying the numerical information in terms of natural frequencies, icon arrays and colorful tinker-cubes, the school students successfully mastered Bayesian tasks. Furthermore, the intervention could show how they playfully modeled risky situations. Till's investigation shows that children can acquire the first elements of risk literacy in fourth class, if instruction is aided by activities supported with appropriate materials. For instance, a 1-h training session with Tinker Cubes was shown to significantly improve test scores for Bayesian tasks. Till and Sprösser (2020) report that these increases depend heavily on whether the test item refers to subsets of the sets of test items. If so, the students do much better. We believe and propose here that highlighting the subset-relationships within icon arrays, described in detail below, can also make a big contribution to promoting Bayesian reasoning. In fact, we propose the use of multiple representations for fostering elementary Bayesian reasoning.

Fig. 19.6 100 people tested as to whether they are HIV positive; unstructured data

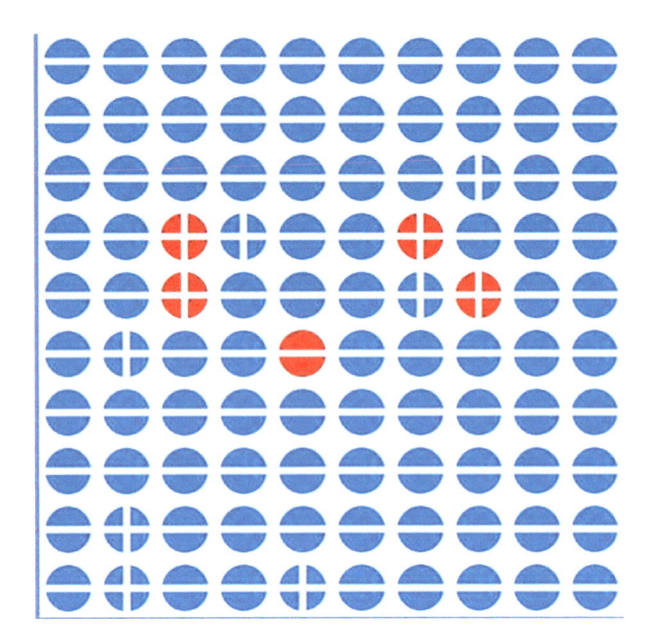

The next example of the use of icon arrays (used in secondary school) demonstrates that sorting within icon arrays is useful. Consider a population of 100 people who were tested as to whether they are HIV positive. The possible outcomes are:

- no disease and tested negative

- no disease and tested positive

- disease is present but test is negative

- disease is present and test is positive

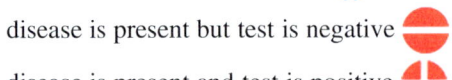

We present several icon arrays to illustrate different ways to display the data (see Figs. 19.6 and 19.7). The first icon array shows the data randomly, for example by simply recording results as patients take the test.

19.5   Design Ideas for Instruction Based on Icon Arrays, Risks and Uncertainty in a Civic Statistics Context

In the following sections we will describe design characteristics for the successful implementation of icon arrays and transform these into trees with natural frequencies, as a way to communicate and represent relative and absolute risks in the classroom. Ours is just *one* example, especially conceived for school children; we will cite other such implementations in the course of the next sections. The

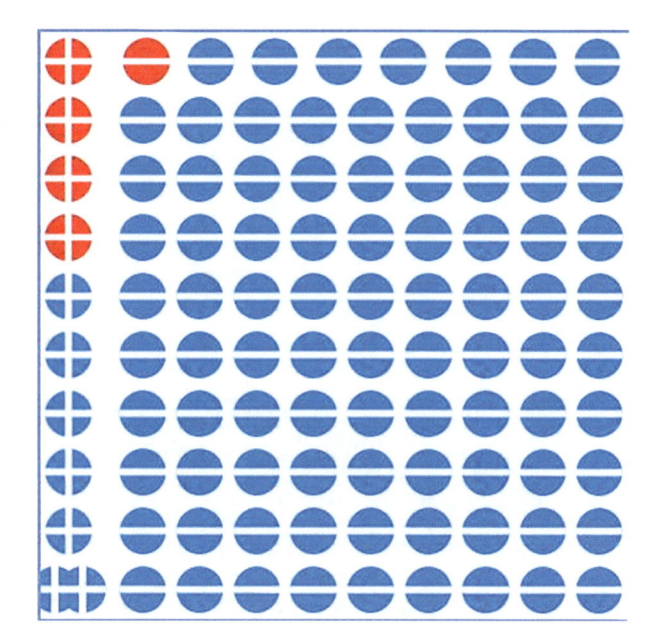

Fig. 19.7 Shows data from the same 100 people, grouping those who test positive, together by using a button at the bottom of the array

implementation we will describe is by means of dynamic, interactive icon arrays on the webpage "worth the risk?" presented in Sect. 19.5.1. We will then show how to make the transition from the dynamic, interactive icon arrays to trees and double trees, similar in their structure to the typical trees and double trees used for teaching probabilities. The dynamic features of the webpage "worth the risk?" can also support learners when making the transition from very simple statistical settings to more complex and realistic ones.

19.5.1 Dynamic, Interactive Icon Arrays: The Website "Worth the Risk?"

By providing a toolbox of visual methods and metrics, Tim Erickson and Laura Martignon created a digital tool-box for presenting risk-related information in school in a variety of ways. It has been successfully used in school during the last months (Martignon & Hoffrage, 2019). This section is devoted to its description. The reader can reach this web page called "Worth the risk?" by means of the QR Code (Fig. 19.8) below.[2]

The first page provides links to topics covered, and is shown in Fig. 19.9.

---

[2]https://www.eeps.com/projects/wwg/wwg-en.html

Fig. 19.8 QR-Code for the
dynamic web page "worth
the risk?"

Fig. 19.9 The cover page of the Website "Worth the risk?"

Resources are designed to support instruction of children and adults to become informed and competent when

- dealing both with the sensitivity or specificity of a test
- dealing with positive/negative predictive value of a test and how they depend on base rates
- understanding base rates

- understanding relative and absolute risks
- understanding the subtleties of features' conjunctions

To summarise, the resource is designed to make the teaching and training of risk literacy easy and transparent, by offering multiple complementary and interactive perspectives on the interplay between key parameters. Icon arrays are excellent tools for representing information but their effectiveness can be enhanced: they can be made dynamic and interactive. Dynamic displays of icon arrays can be designed in a way that fosters elements of Civic Statistics, statistical literacy in general, and risk literacy in particular. Such interactive displays for adults have been introduced, for instance, by Garcia-Retamero et al. (2012). Hans-Jörg Neth and his colleagues at the psychology Department of the University of Konstanz have also produced dynamic pages for adults, where graphs and scales for representing features and their properties are dynamic and interactive.[3] Chapter 12 offers further references to other web pages for adults dedicated to the reliability of tests:[4,5] our dynamic web page is designed for school children of different ages.

Clicking on any of the three sections, leads to pages where a variety of contexts are presented. For instance, in *The explanatory power of features* one can choose between contexts—one is *Pets and bells*, which is quite appropriate for children of fourth class—and see a display like the following (see Fig. 19.10).

The intention of this representation is to explain the relevance of parameters regarding the feature "Wears a bell". The natural question is: "If a pet is wearing a bell, is it likely to be a cat?" The task is to judge the predictive value of this feature for the category *Cats*. Children are instructed to click the button "group bells together", at the left side under the picture (Fig. 19.11). They can see how the pets are regrouped so that those with the feature "bell" are visually separated. It is now clear that "bell" is not a good way to identify cats.

The importance of base rates can also be easily illustrated, through the use of the sliders placed under the array. For instance, maintaining the total number of pets equal to 10 one can enhance the base rate of "cats" keeping the sensitivity of "bell" constant (Fig. 19.12).

The rate of cats wearing bells has remained the same but the number of cats is now 6. Here, wearing a bell now becomes moderately predictive for the category "cats"—so the "bell" test now has a greater PPV.

The next instructional step deals with another statistical format, which allows a better grasp of features and their reliability: trees and doubletrees. Trees are hierarchical directed graphs that can represent how a category of items/individuals is partitioned by one or more features in a sequence of steps or levels. They are among the oldest visual aids for knowledge representation.

---

[3] http://riskyr.org
[4] https://qz.com/1848674/how-to-interpret-the-specificity-sensitivity-of-antibody-tests/
[5] https://kennis-research.shinyapps.io/Bayes-App/

Fig. 19.10 A
representation of 10 pets,
cats and dogs, with and
without a bell

Clicking on the "tree" button on the top of the array in the dynamic web page changes the page and exhibits a doubletree like the following (see Fig. 19.13).

The doubletree in Fig. 19.13 exhibits two inference directions: one is causal, the other is diagnostic. Assume children think that "wearing a bell" is more characteristic of cats than of dogs: The first level of the tree on top exhibits the numbers corresponding to pets, while the second level corresponds to the feature analyzed, namely the bell. Here the cause for wearing a bell is being a pet. The other tree from the bottom looks at the feature and exhibits the narrative about the diagnosticity, or predictive value of the feature.

The doubletree is a simple and transparent way of approaching Bayesian reasoning. Studies by Christoph Wassner (2004), clearly demonstrated the effectiveness of such doubletrees for fostering successful Bayesian reasoning in the classroom. He worked with ninth grade students in Germany. It was precisely that work which motivated the design of doubletrees for the Worth the risk? website.

Other options are available on the website (see Fig. 19.14).

The *options* button opens up the possibility of choosing between three levels of stochastic precision, illustrated in Fig. 19.15. They present information which corresponds to three competency levels:

Fig. 19.11 Clicking *Group bells together* leads to a sorted icon array

The three levels correspond to three different school epochs: end of primary school, eighth grade and tenth grade. Young children in fourth class can reason in a proto-Bayesian way based on the information provided by icon arrays such as those shown in Figs. 19.10 and 19.11 (Gigerenzer et al., 2020; Martignon & Hoffrage, 2019). Later on, once they have acquired knowledge and proficiency with percentages, the measures determining feature predictive value are added at the second level. Later the concept of random sampling is added thus fostering the understanding of more realistic situations.

In the same section (*The explanatory power of features*) an example directly concerned with health is treated along the same lines: populations of patients testing positive or negative, who either have, or have not contracted HIV.

The second section in "Worth the risk?" is dedicated to risk variation, be it its reduction or increase. It is well known that treatment benefits and harms are often communicated in terms of relative risk reductions and increases, and that these are frequently misunderstood both by doctors and patients. The relevant factor for

Fig. 19.12 In this display
the number of pets remains
10 but the base rate of cats is
now "6 out of 10"

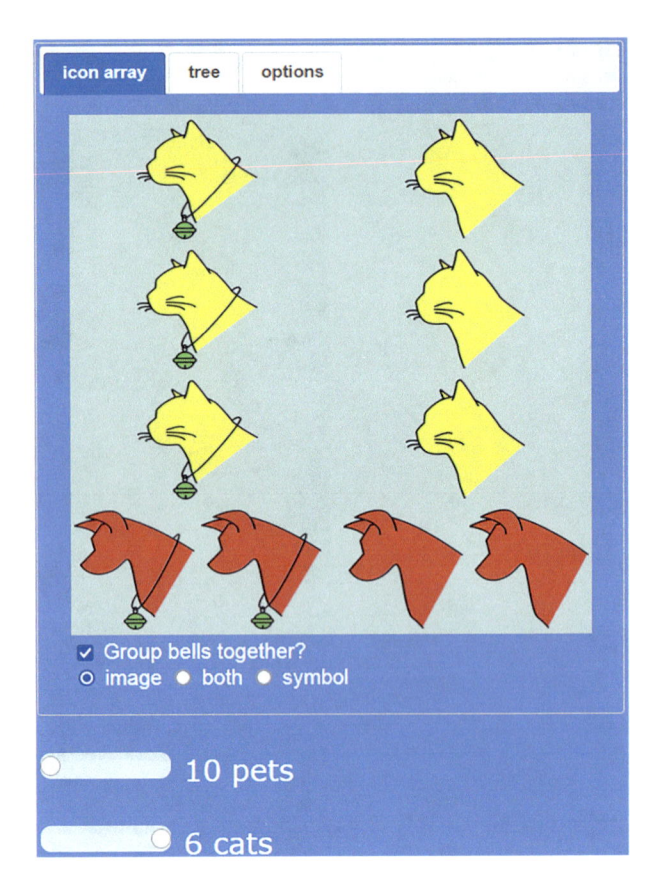

improving understanding of such risk information is to also communicate the
baseline risk.

The Webpage "Worth the risk?", also illustrates the subtleties connected with risk
reductions and increases in transparent ways that are easy to grasp. Figure 19.16
shows 20 boys who have had a bike accident, ten of which are wearing a helmet. The
faces with a pad and a black eye represent boys with severe injury caused by the bike
accident.

Simply sorting the icon array by grouping helmets together allows an easy grasp
of the risk reduction provided by helmets (Fig. 19.17).

The absolute risk reduction is from 6 out of 10 to 2 out of 10, which corresponds
to a relative reduction of 66%. A doubletree synthesizes the situation (see
Fig. 19.18).

The doubletree is organized according to two features, namely wearing or not
wearing a helmet and having or not having an injury. The relevant question that can
be asked concerns the risk reduction—from 6 out of 10 to 2 out of 10, which is
illustrated by the nodes corresponding to injuries at the center level and the branches
connecting them with the nodes at the top level. Changes in the population size and

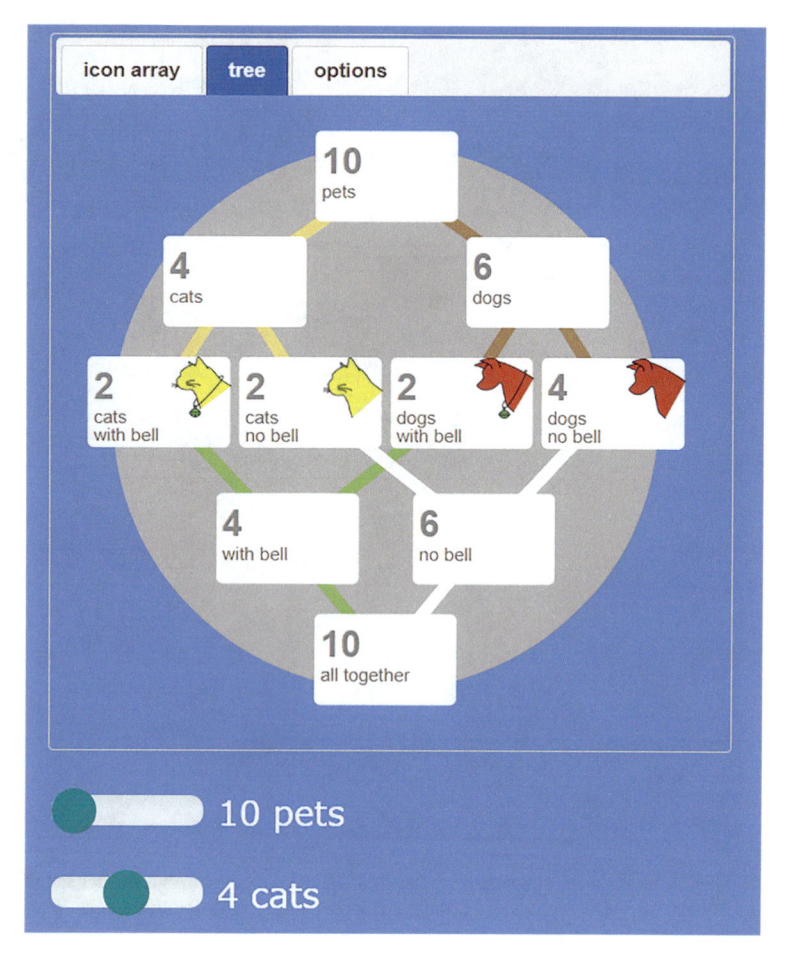

Fig. 19.13 A doubletree representing information about pets and bells hierarchically both in the causal and diagnostic direction

Fig. 19.14 The button *options*

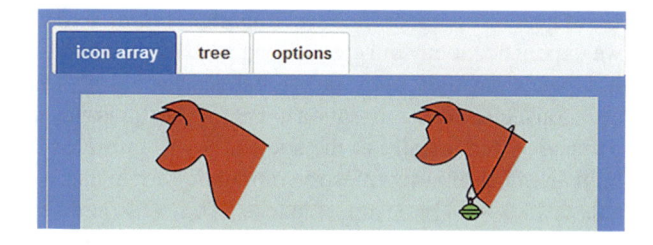

in the baselines of the category can easily be performed by using the corresponding buttons and sliders. Here again, there are three possible levels of stochastic precision activated by the button "Options" and selecting one of three levels.

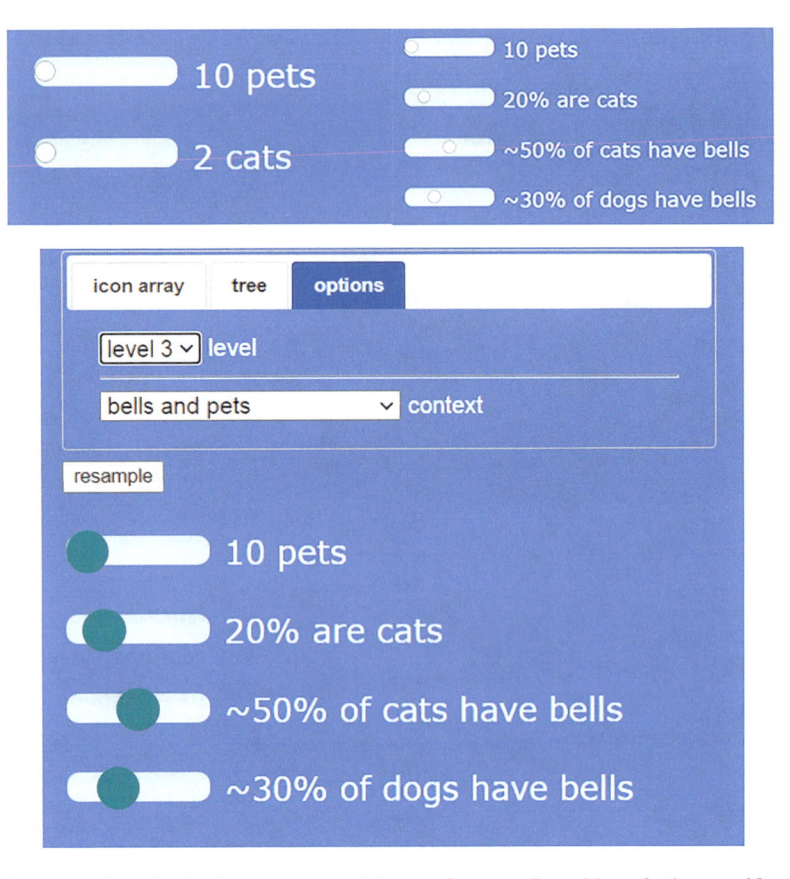

Fig. 19.15 The three levels of stochastic precision: static proportion without further specifications, static proportion with specifications, randomly extracted sample with specifications

19.6 Concluding Remarks

Good health is perhaps the most important resource in the life of individuals. Yet, as we experience today during the long global confrontation with the Covid pandemic, it depends not only upon individual actions but also upon collective and political decisions. Informed consent on collective health issues thus becomes a purpose to be pursued systematically at the societal level. Informed consent about risks requires both an effort of authorities to communicate relevant information in an understandable fashion, and basic competencies in citizens for discerning this information. Otto Neurath was a pioneer in developing information formats (his Isotypes) which communicate information clearly, and can foster informed consent at the societal level.

A variety of icon arrays have been developed from Neurath's Isotypes, and share with them the ideal of simplicity and transparency. The aim is to support the

Fig. 19.16 An icon array exhibiting 20 boys having a bike accident, ten of them wearing helmets

understanding of features describing risk, their likelihood and the strength of association between different features and risk. Combining icon arrays with double trees transmits structural properties of inferential reasoning under uncertainty. If children and youngsters learn to assess the positive and negative predictive values of tests, symptoms and treatments while in school, they will be prepared to face the collective challenges of pandemics and diseases. Because these crises affect societies across the world and because they can only be faced by means of wise political decisions which in turn impact on the actions of citizens, the methodologies presented here provide direct routes to promoting Civic Statistics.

Fig. 19.17 Sorted icon
array illustrating the relative
risk reduction caused by
wearing a helmet

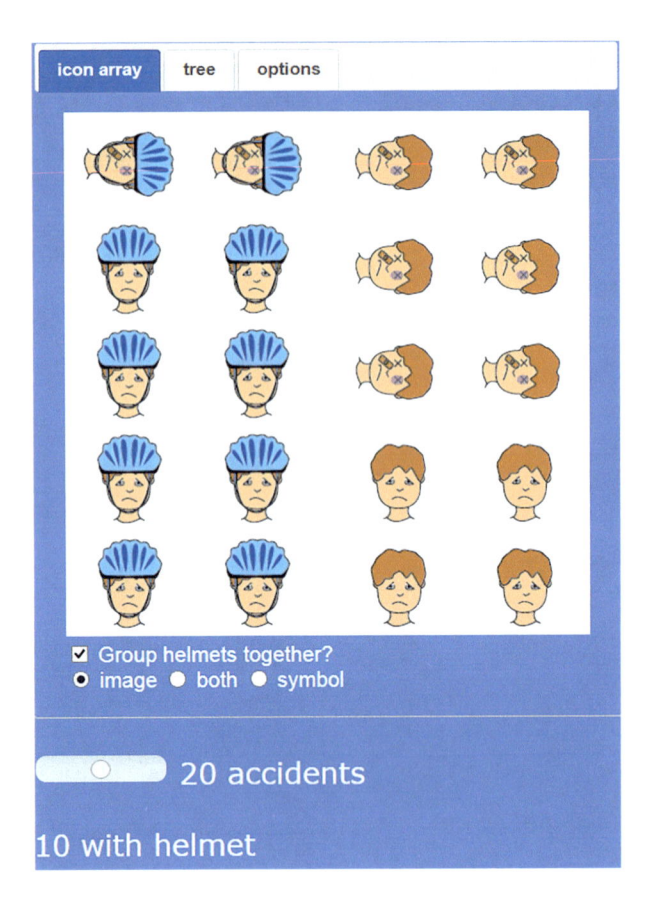

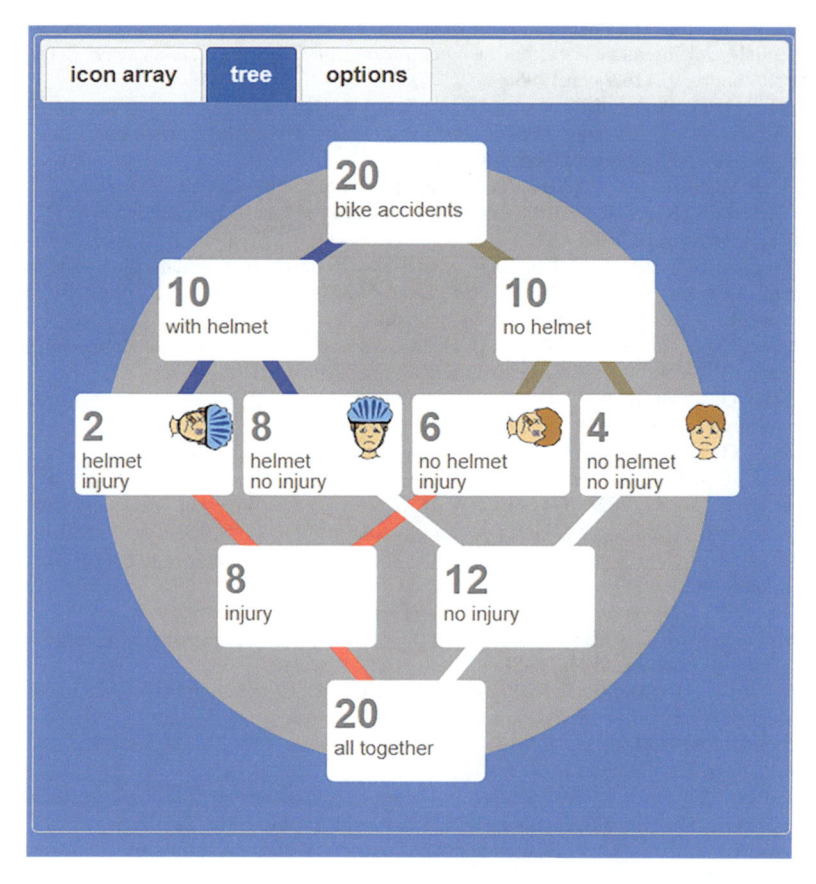

Fig. 19.18 A doubletree representing the risk reduction of having an injury associated with wearing a helmet when having a bike accident

References

Amari, S. I. (1977). Neural theory of association and concept-formation. *Biological Cybernetics, 26*, 175–185.

Ancker, J. S., et al. (2006). Design features of graphs in health risk communication: A systematic review. *Journal of the American Medical Informatics Association, 13*(6), 608–618.

Ancker, J. S., et al. (2011). Effect of arrangement of stick figures on estimates of proportion in risk graphics. *Medical Decision Making, 31*(1), 143–150. https://doi.org/10.1177/0272989x10369006

Binder, K. et al. (2021). Natural frequency trees improve diagnostic efficiency in Bayesian reasoning. *Advances in Health Sciences Education.* Online first.

Braitenberg, V., & Schütz, A. (1991). *Anatomy of the cortex: Statistics and geometry* (p. 249 S). Springer.

Brase, G. L. (2009). Pictorial representations in statistical reasoning. *Applied Cognitive Psychology, 23*, 369–381.

De Morgan, A. (1838). *An essay on probabilities, and their application to life contingencies and insurance offices.* Longmans.

Dehaene, S. (1996). The organization of brain activations in number comparison: event-related potentials and the additive-factors method. *Journal of Cognitive Neuroscience, 8*(1), 47–68. https://doi.org/10.1162/jocn.1996.8.1.47

Eddy, D. (1982). Probabilistic reasoning in clinical medicine: Problems and opportunities. In P. Slovic & A. Tversky (Eds.), *Judgment under uncertainty: Heuristics and biases* (pp. 249–267). Cambridge University Press.

Gage, J., & Spiegelhalter, D. (2016). *Teaching probability*. Cambridge University Press.

Garcia-Retamero, R., et al. (2010). Do icon arrays help reduce denominator neglect? *Medical Decision Making, 30*, 672–684.

Garcia-Retamero, R., et al. (2012). Using visual aids to improve communication of risks about health: A review. *ScientificWorldJournal, 2012*, 562637. https://doi.org/10.1100/2012/562637

Gigerenzer, G. (2002). *Reckoning with risk*. Penguin.

Gigerenzer, G., & Gaissmaier, W. (2011). Heuristic decision making. *Annual Review of Psychology, 62*, 451–484. https://doi.org/10.1146/annurev-psych-120709-145346

Gigerenzer, G., & Hoffrage, U. (1995). How to improve Bayesian reasoning without instruction: Frequency formats. *Psychological Review, 102*, 684–704.

Gigerenzer, G., et al. (2007). Helping doctors and patients make sense of health statistics. *Psychological Science in the Public Interest, 8*, 53–96.

Gigerenzer, G. et al. (2020, October 29). Do children have Bayesian intuitions? *Journal of Experimental Psychology: General Advance*. doi:https://doi.org/10.1037/xge0000979

Gilovich, T., et al. (2002). *Heuristics and biases: The psychology of intuitive judgment*. Cambridge University Press.

Harari, Y. (2016). *Homo Deus: A brief history of tomorrow*. Harvill & Secker.

Kurz-Milcke, E., et al. (2008). Transparency in risk communication. *Annals of the New York Academy of Sciences, 1128*, 18–28.

Kurz-Milcke, E., Gigerenzer, G., Martignon, L., et al. (2011). Risiken durchschauen: Grafische und analoge Werkzeuge. *Stochastik in der Schule, 31*(1), 8–16.

Martignon, L., & Hoffrage, U. (2019). *Wer wagt, gewinnt? Wie Sie die Risikokompetenz von Kindern und Jugendlichen fördern können*. Hogrefe.

Martignon, L., & Laskey, K. (2019). Statistical literacy for classification under risk: An educational perspective. *AStA Wirtschafts- und Sozialstatistisches Archiv, 13*(3), 269–278.

Martignon, L., et al. (2008). Categorization with limited resources: A family of simple heuristics. *Journal of Mathematical Psychology, 52*(6), 352–361.

McDowell, M., Rebitschek, F. G., Gigerenzer, G., Wegwarth, O., et al. (2016). A simple tool for communicating the benefits and harms of health interventions: A guide for creating a fact box. *MDM Policy and Practice, 1*(1), 2381468316665365. https://doi.org/10.1177/2381468316665365

Neurath, O. (1933/1973). Museums of the future. In M. Neurath, and R. Cohen (eds.) *Empiricism and sociology*, D. Reidel Publishing Company, 220.

Paling, J. (2003). Strategies to help patients understand risks. *BMJ, 327*(7417), 745–748. https://doi.org/10.1136/bmj.327.7417.745

Schapira, M., & Van Ruiswyk, J. (2000). The effect of an illustrated pamphlet decision-aid on the use of prostate cancer screening tests. *Journal of Family Practice, 49*(5), 418–424.

Scheller, B. (2017). Geburt des Risikos: Kontingenz und kaufmännische Praxis im Mittelalter. *Historische Zeitschrift, 304*(2), 305–331.

Spiegelhalter, D. (2019). *The art of statistics: Learning from data*. Penguin Random House.

Till, Ch., & Sprösser, U. (2020). Frequency formats: How primary school stochastics profits from cognitive psychology. *Frontiers: Psychology and Mathematics Education*. doi: https://doi.org/10.3389/feduc.2020.00073.

Trevena, L. J., et al. (2013). Presenting quantitative information about decision outcomes: A risk communication primer for patient decision aid developers. *BMC Medical Informatics and Decision Making, 13*(2), 7. https://doi.org/10.1186/1472-6947-13-S2-S

Wassner, C. (2004). *Förderung Bayesianischen Denkens-Kognitionspsychologische Grundlagen und didaktische Analysen*. Franzbecker.

Chapter 20
Reflections on Civic Statistics: A Triangulation of Citizen, State and Statistics: Past, Present and Future

Karen François ⓘ and Carlos Monteiro

Abstract The chapter aims to develop four lines of discussion on people's relationships with statistics. A first line problematizes historical aspects related to the origins of statistics and its relationship with people's lives. A second line discusses social aspects which enable people's empowerment through the use of statistics. In the third line we address elements of the cognitive, socio-cultural, and affective dimensions of critical issues associated with people interpreting statistical data. In the fourth line, we present three examples of educational projects that involve teachers, students, and communities with the aim of employing Civic Statistics to initiate social actions. These projects are related to environmental themes and use Civic Statistics as a tool to empower people to achieve cultural changes in their social contexts.

Keywords Belgium contexts · Brazilian contexts · Critical perspective · Freire · Indigenous teachers · Neurath · Quetelet

20.1 Introduction

In this chapter we will explore four lines of connection between citizens and statistics: a historical one, a social one, a critical one and implications for education. These discussion lines refer to specific socio-historical trajectories linked to contexts of construction and use of knowledge related to statistics. However, in pursuing these lines it is not our intention to be exhaustive, nor to state that these are the only lines of enquiry.

K. François (✉)
Centre for Logic and Philosophy of Science (CLPS) of the Vrije Universiteit Brussel (VUB),
Brussels, Belgium
e-mail: Karen.Francois@vub.be

C. Monteiro
Centro de Educação/Edumatec/UFPE Avenida Acadêmico Hélio Ramos s/n, Cidade
Universitária, Recife, PE, Brazil
e-mail: carlos.fmonteiro@ufpe.br

© Springer Nature Switzerland AG 2022
J. Ridgway (ed.), *Statistics for Empowerment and Social Engagement*,
https://doi.org/10.1007/978-3-031-20748-8_20

With the historical perspective we will emphasise the original connection between the development of statistics and the state, the civic state. Originally statistics (as a narrative) was related to demographic information to describe the state, the power of the state, and the economic and political situation of the state. By the end of the nineteenth century, the close and direct relation between these civic aspects and statistics faded away as mathematical (or inferential) statistics became more and more practiced as a method in the social and behavioral sciences. The nature of statistics changed with the rise of probability-based inferential methods to become a general methodological tool for scientific inquiry. In social sciences, the method was applied to describe human practices in an attempt to grasp essential knowledge—as natural sciences had been doing for decades. In this first line, the historical one, we will explain the original connection between civics and statistics and explain that statistics was mostly 'about the people'.

It was at the same time, the end of the nineteenth century to the beginning of the twentieth century, that philosophers addressed the issue of raising people's awareness and understanding of data relevant to social issues and governance. Informed people are better equipped to take part in society as fully informed critical citizens. Statistical information developed as a discipline and was no longer accessible for lay people. It was Neurath's concern—one of the members of the *Wiener Kreis*—to bring information to the people and to connect statistics to citizens. This social perspective we will explore in the second line of enquiry, i.e. the connection between civics and statistics as 'statistics for the people'.

A discussion about social and cultural aspects related to statistics will almost always be a partial one because specific issues have certainly played different roles in different parts of the world. For example, in order to understand the social role of statistics we need to consider that the knowledge and uses of statistics were historically developed in countries in the northern hemisphere to meet their particular social and economic needs. Therefore, it is necessary to bear in mind that countries with different and specific social and cultural needs have been the recipients of knowledge and practices applied in their own specific contexts which were in fact only meeting the interests of the people who had created them. On the one hand, statistics served to homogenise procedures that disregarded different cultural contexts. On the other hand, it may have served to deepen the differences between countries, especially between those classified as 'developed' and 'underdeveloped'.

An interesting example refers to the term *Civic Statistics* itself. When statistical educators in Brazil have access to this book, it is likely that the title itself may raise questions, since in the context of Brazil the word "civic" (Brazilian Portuguese) is loaded with meanings for people who are critical of the repression and censorship during the Brazilian military dictatorship (1964–1985). At that time there was a school subject called *Moral and Civic Education* that addressed citizen participation based on disciplinary values and rules. Therefore, for most Brazilian educators the word *civic* will have negative connotations. However, for a minority of educators the same word might sound positive, nostalgia for a time when citizens were obedient. The purpose of this example was to argue that statistics as an area of knowledge, as a social tool, has an influence on socio-cultural contexts.

In a third line we explore the critical aspect of reading statistics. Statistical information is open to interpretation, especially when it comes to the visual representation of statistical data.

In a fourth line we will translate the theoretical ideas into ways that can be implemented in (teacher) education. For this purpose, we will provide three examples from different contexts: one example from the Dutch-speaking part of Belgium (Flanders) and two from a Brazilian context to illustrate how statistics educators deal with Civic Statistics in a given context. The three examples are related to the topic of the environment and have mobilised teachers, students, and communities to utilise statistics to empower them and lead to social and cultural changes.

Referring to the project in the Dutch-speaking part of Belgium, we show how nowadays people can be involved in statistics by being motivated to collect data. The project in question was called *CurieuzeNeuzen Vlaanderen*, a citizen science project in which 20,000 citizens measured the air quality near their own homes during May 2018. This project involved all citizens in collecting data about air pollution and was initiated by a primary school that had started an initiative on collecting data on air pollution. In the Brazilian context, we discuss two educational projects that address the relationship between the environment, statistical literacy, and cultural aspects. One project was developed with indigenous Xukuru do Ororubá teachers, while another ongoing project is addressing the issue of sensitive coexistence with the environment in a semi-arid region of Brazil.

20.2   A Historical Line: The Origin of Statistics, Statistics About People

Looking back at the origin of statistics, a connection between civics, the state, the citizen and statistics is already traceable in the word itself. An etymological analysis of the word indicates that the word *statistics* derives from the Latin word *status* which has a double meaning (Carvalho, 2001). *Status* can be *the state* but also a description of *the situation of the state*. The word *statistics* first appears, in this latter meaning, in French and in Latin, at the end of the seventeenth century. The French word *statistiques* was used in a publication that reported on the economic situation (goods, charges, debts, etc.) of the French region of Burgundy (Bracke, 2008). The word *state* in English can mean a *political state* (e.g. The United States of America), but it can also mean *a condition* or *a state of things* (e.g. *the state of affairs* or *a state of mind*). Both meanings come together when the state is described in terms such as geographical extent, or population size.

Statistics was initially developed as an official resource which enabled the government to present or make public its social and economic outcomes, and during the Industrial Revolution, statistics became a vital resource for capitalists who needed to analyse income. This was a common practice even used before the term *statistics* was coined. Governments, emperors, leaders used data collection and registration to collect taxes and to recruit soldiers. To do that they needed 'statistical' information.

According to Carvalho, statistics was introduced as an academic field in 1748 by the German professor Gottfried Achenwall. The term became more widespread during the eighteenth century through the work of Achenwall, who is counted among the inventors of statistics (Willcox, 1938). Achenwall, who used the word statistics himself, referred to the Italian word *statista*, which means *statesman*. During his professorship at the University of Göttingen, Germany (1748–1772), Achenwall set up a course in statistics to introduce a general outline of contemporary affairs and of the national fabric in the widest sense. The new subject was also called *Staatswissenschaft*—political science (Hull, 1914).

Indeed, until the nineteenth century the meaning of statistics was restricted to information about states. European states, such as France, the United Kingdom and The Netherlands, collected demographic information related to different aspects of the population (baptisms, marriages, deaths, etc.). In Germany, the concept of *Staatenkunde* (*theory of the state* or *the art of government*) was used to describe the country and its society, in order to have solid information about the power and the 'strength' of a state, as a basis for governing a country. *Staatenkunde* was both a narrative and an administrative discipline consisting of descriptions, numbers, and figures. It took some time to overcome skepticism about the use of numbers and figures to describe the nature of the state. Initially, integrating probability calculus, to make universal statements based on a limited number of observations, did not really flourish in statistics (Stamhuis, 1992). It was in the first half of the nineteenth century that statistics evolved in the direction of political arithmetic. Statistics increasingly came to be understood as a science that calculated and represented patterns from many quantifiable observations about society. Statistics thus was first and foremost 'social statistics' because it was connected to information related to the population, the nature, the politics and the economy of the state. In Chap. 2, Engel and Ridgway refer to the Royal Statistical Society (founded in 1834) and the diverse backgrounds of the members. The first statisticians were concerned with social issues and their aim was to develop and apply new methods to understand the world.

Carvalho (2001) argues that statistics gradually moved away from the status of official resources generated by governments. She also points out that systematic approaches based on probabilistic theoretical perspectives promoted the development of inferential statistics which significantly broadened their area of application. This was the first step in the direction of the use of statistics in order to gain more abstract and more certain knowledge. Although statistics is unlikely to reach the level of abstraction that mathematics provides, statistics has provided a proper way of dealing with uncertainty. Statistics became recognised as a separate field only in the twentieth century (Stigler, 2000). This development was spurred on by the developments of scientists in other disciplines, e.g. biologists, doctors, economists, psychologists. Important examples are Karl Pearson's contribution from eugenics and biometrics (estimation theory, hypothesis testing, etc.), and Ronald Fisher's agricultural laboratory (analysis of variance (ANOVA) etc.). From that time, statistics became a branch of applied mathematics (Desrosières, 1998). Around 1900, encyclopaedias characterised statistics as both a descriptive and a mathematical discipline. Moreover, it was at this point no longer exclusively related to political and social phenomena, but it was a key component of a scientific method designed to secure or evaluate the validity of scientific claims in any research domain. The evolution of the concept of statistics was a gradual process, and different meanings—*Staatenkunde*, social statistics, mathematical statistics—coexisted. They sometimes even coincided, as was the case with the Belgian Adolphe Quetelet (1796–1874), who was at the same time state statistician, social scientist and probability theorist (François & Bracke, 2006).

The basic idea of modern science as developed by Descartes (1628 reprinted 1966) implies the application of mathematics to all sciences. The failure to investigate social sciences by a mathematical, deductive method contributed to the development of statistics by social scientists (Leti, 2000). Although mathematical theories of statistics and probability made significant progress, the statistical approach to a problem was still considered a confession of ignorance. Kline (1985) defines the difference between statistics and mathematics based on this criterion of certainty. Mathematics has to do with certainty, while statistics is a way to handle uncertainty. Whereas the former predicts what must happen in an individual case, the latter can tell us what happens to large groups but does not provide definite predictions about any one given case (Kline, 1985).

Stigler (2000) describes how the methods of probability theory were developed for measuring uncertainty. Today, modern statistics provides a quantitative technology for empirical sciences. It is a tool based on the logic and the methodology of measuring uncertainty and trying to explain the consequences of that uncertainty in the planning and interpretations of observation.

Quetelet (1796–1874), scientist, mathematician, statistician and sociologist, revived the idea that statistical methods might produce significant laws for social sciences to reach a higher degree of objectivity. Political arithmetic and probability provide the opportunity to detect causal relations between variables, to test the reliability of observations and to generate universal knowledge based on partial observations. He introduced the statistical method in his social-scientific research to objectify relations between variables in people and society. Quetelet developed the Body Mass Index (BMI) not as a value-laden and normative instrument to differentiate between the healthy and problematic weight of people, but as a mere description of human bodies. He founded a new science on this; originally called 'social mechanics' and from 1835 onward *social physics* as originally introduced by Auguste Comte (Quetelet, 1835). The name makes an association with natural science. The same way physics was looking for the laws of nature, social statistics and social physics were investigating the laws of society (Leti, 2000).

Florence Nightingale (1820–1910) is called one of the most enthusiastic statisticians to apply the laws Quetelet discovered (Porter, 1986). In Chap. 5, Ridgway, Campos, Nicholson, and Teixeira show how she integrated statistics into administration and the reporting of the death of soldiers to describe (and subsequently reduce) military mortality rates. Some disciplines are challenged by small sample surveys as is the case in medical science, where it is common to have very small test cases. As a result of the revelation and the developments of mathematician (and beer brewer of Guinness beer) William Sealy Gosset (1876–1937) a statistical method called 'Student's *t*-test' and the accompanying *t*-distribution tables were developed between 1904 and 1905 (Barnard et al., 1990: 16). The paper was published in 1907 under the pseudonym 'Student' in an agreement with Guinness, because Gosset was employed by the brewery at that time. The ban forbidding staff to use their own name was common, and secrecy was widely practiced in industrial circles in the UK. The newly developed *t*-test enabled researchers (and beer brewers) to make intelligent decisions and it became one of the cornerstones of modern statistics (Cals & Winkens, 2018).

New methods were being created to gain more certain knowledge, not only in natural science—that relies on mathematics—but also in the social and political sciences. This development of statistics from a purely descriptive and narrative account of national and democratic affairs to a specific research field of applied mathematics had an impact on the curricula of mathematics and statistics education at the different faculties at universities. Originally, as a discipline relevant to adminstration, statistics was taught in faculties of law (Ottaviani, 1991: 245). Until the nineteenth century, statisticians in Belgium were mostly lawyers. It was a compulsory part of the curriculum for a law degree from the very foundation (1817) of Ghent and Liège Universities (both state universities). Most lecturers were recruited from Germany because of their familiarity with descriptive *Staatenkunde*. The lectures provided an insight into the relationship between the state and its population. Topics like political organisation, geographic development, agriculture, economy, and population were main subjects in the curriculum. During the nineteenth century the subject of whether statistics should form a part of the curriculum of different faculties (of law, the arts, science, etc.) was subject to critical discussion. The field was added to the curriculum but then also removed—because of rising criticism in Parliament about the high cost of gathering official statistics.

It was only in the twentieth century that statistics as a descriptive and mathematical discipline found its way into the curricula of various faculties. Note that statistics disappeared from the curricula in the arts and philosophy and law faculties—where it had initially appeared. Right up to today, if students want to avoid statistics in the curriculum, they mostly take the option of law or history; all other options have statistics in the curriculum. From the twentieth century on, statistics has been taught as a methodological discipline for future social scientists, psychologists, and economists. At the same time, it has become the subject of a science itself. It has been during the same period that awareness has been raised of the importance for the broader public of understanding statistics. In the following line of investigation, we will elaborate on this social program.

20.3 A Social Line: Statistics for the People as a Means of Empowering People

In this section we still give some historical information about the intention of bringing statistics to all members of society. The idea of educating people and bringing information to them is not all that new. During the Enlightenment, philosophers such as Condorcet (1743–1794), Wollstonecraft (1759–1797), amongst others, were concerned about people's education. After the French Revolution (1789) and mainly during the nineteenth century Zoë (1806–1854) and Isabelle (1839–1905) Gatti de Gamond (mother and daughter from a liberal and free-thinking background) started to organise primary and secondary education for girls. And by the end of nineteenth century women could enter university. Growing attention was paid to education for people and to making statistics available to people so as to inform them and thus enable them to take part in society. Therefore, we now go back to the beginning of the twentieth century, to the time when statistics was rapidly developing, and mathematical statistics became applied to many scientific practices.

It was the concern of Otto Neurath (1882–1945) and his wife Maria Reidemeister (1898–1986) to make data with societal and political relevance available to everyone. It should enhance people's understanding of numerical information, one of the conditions for becoming a critical citizen. Otto Neurath, influenced by Ernst Mach, French conventionalism (e.g. Duhem) and by Marxism was concerned with social programs in addition to the foundation of mathematics, physicalism, and the unity of science.

Chapters 5 and 19 refer to the work of Neurath although from the perspective of the visual representation of data. We will concentrate here on the philosophical and historical perspective to explain civic concern during the period that positivism flourished in Europe. Otto Neurath was a member of The Vienna Circle, a group of philosophers that adhered to the project of the unity of science; the idea of reducing all sciences to a common (physicalist) language. This idea of reductionism was central to the logical positivists' program and developed by Carnap in his *The Unity of Science* (1934). As Carnap expressed the idea: "[S]cience is a unity, [...] all empirical statements can be expressed in a single language, all states of affairs are of one kind and are known by the same method" (Carnap, 1934: 32). The concept of reductionism was further developed by Oppenheim & Putnam (1958). In *Unity of Science as a Working Hypothesis* (Oppenheim & Putnam, 1958) they proposed the idea not to reduce the scientific languages to one single language (i.e. physics) but to reduce all sciences to the basic science of (mathematical) physics. Note that this working hypothesis was not the work of the members of The Vienna Circle, it was a further development of the idea of a single language for all sciences.

The Vienna Circle also had an ethical-political agenda as well as is shown in the Manifesto: "The representatives of the scientific world-conception resolutely stand on the ground of simple human experience. They confidently approach the task of removing metaphysical and theological debris of millennia. Or, as some have it: returning, after a metaphysical interlude, to a unified picture of this world which had,

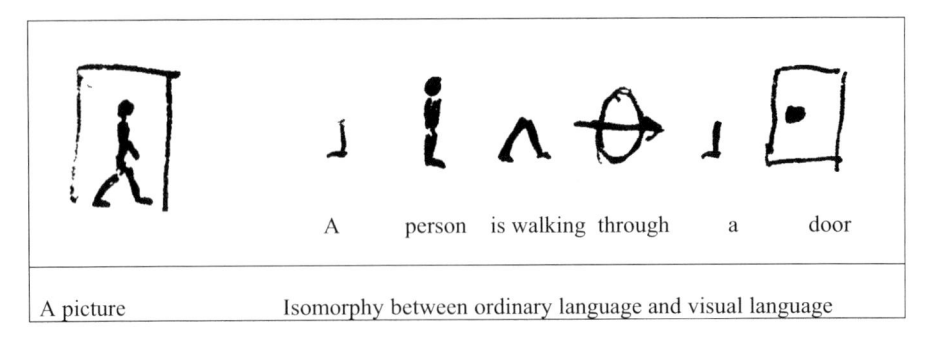

Fig. 20.1 The principle of visual representation as drawn by Neurath (Nemeth & Stadler, 1996: 330)

in a sense, been at the basis of magical beliefs, free from theology, in the earliest times." (Neurath & Cohen, 1973, p. 317). The ethical-political agenda can be understood as part of The Vienna Circle project. It was the time when philosophers concentrated on the big question of the foundation of mathematics and of all the sciences. Investigations came from different philosophical directions ranging from phenomenology, with the emphasis on experiences and the Lifeworld (Husserl, Brouwer), to Logic (Frege, Carnap). The metaphysical project led at the same time to philosophers raising awareness about educating people. The following quotation makes clear that the scientific world-conception goes hand in hand with the concern to use scientific advances for the improvement of people's lives. "We witness the spirit of the scientific world-conception penetrating in growing measure the forms of personal and public life, in education, upbringing, architecture, and the shaping of economic and social life according to rational principles. The scientific world-conception serves life, and life receives it." (Neurath & Cohen, 1973, pp. 317–318).

Indeed, the focus of the Neuraths (Otto & Maria) was on visualizing data to improve the way people understand and interpret the world based on data. They developed ISOTYPE—the International System Of Typographic Picture Education (Lehrer & Marek, 1997; Nemeth & Stadler, 1996). The basic principle of visual representation is drawing a picture that almost *shows* its meaning. The picture or the diagram offers the possibility of seeing everything *at a glance* (Fig. 20.1 left side). Visual representation is thus not isomorphy between ordinary language and the visual language, which latter is almost like solving a puzzle—as is shown below in Fig. 20.1 right side. The social implication of the replacement of a *literal* translation (or the iconographic representation) by a simple *picture* is that most people can now easily grasp sometimes complex information.

The Neuraths started their project to set up a museum in order to share the knowledge and the universal ISOTYPE language with all members of society. A first project was the Museum of City Planning (Museum für Siedlung und Städtebau), followed by a second project, the Museum of Economy and Society (Gesellschaft- und Wirtschaftsmuseum). These museums were meant as places for the education of the general public to allow a full-blown participation by all citizens in society. We see in this attempt a first project that could be called *Civic Statistics* in order to bring all members of society into contact with statistics in an alternative educational way. The Neuraths believed that the representation of knowledge through pictures should play an increasing role in the future. Indeed, ISOTYPE charts and picture language became an important tool for skillfully and simply communicating economic arguments, developments in history, and relative statistics about many contemporary and historical political societal activities (Van Bendegem et al., 2010). The picture language ISOTYPE has also made its mark on education. Although there was no direct influence of the ethical-political part of the Neuraths' project, the concern to enable people to become fully informed and critical citizens is entirely consistent with contemporary views of the importance of statistical literacy—exemplified by the International Statistical Literacy Project' (https://iase-web.org/islp/).

Neurath's work does not aim at statistical literacy per se but educating people about the true state of society. To achieve this, he used pictorial representations of statistical information. Nowadays statistical educators and researchers are challenged to enable students to understand basic information about what is happening in the world, also directly related to themselves. This has become even more sensitive during the past decade where big data and being part of a big data generation are central issues of living in a postmodern information society. The accessibility of (statistical) information, or competence at higher levels of statistical literacy became explicitly connected to an ethical dimension from 1993 by the Wallman (1993) presidential statement and it is still a central topic in Garfield & Ben-Zvi's (2008) notion of statistical thinking, which involves a deep understanding of the theories underlying statistical processes and methods. These descriptions of statistical literacy are still relevant because of the connection between the technical and the ethical-political aspects that even nowadays are very important in a society that is characterised by big data practices. Belonging to a big data society has consequences at different levels. It has become a part of the personal lives of (young) people using social media and as consumers in a big data society. People are taking part in big data practices, on the one hand by generating data (e.g. through their purchasing behaviour); on the other hand, by ways in which their behaviour is driven by the same big data. Big data society also has consequences for scientific practices. Data-ethics (Floridi & Taddeo, 2016) as well as the field of critical data-studies (Kitchin, 2014) are in full development, and have identified a vast array of concrete ethical risks. These include concerns over the correctness, fairness, accountability, and intelligibility of decisions that are informed by the analysis of data. There are additional concerns over the impact that such processes have on the fundamental rights of data subjects (e.g. privacy, autonomy, the right to self-determination and the right not to be measured). The development of a critical research agenda on contemporary data practices is a new challenge for critical statistical literacy.

20.4 A Critical Line: People's Reading and Interpretation of Statistics

The term 'critical' can have multiple meanings depending on the theoretical and argumentative context in which it is used. Weiland (2017) argues that in the context of statistical literacy, the term 'critical' can have at least two meanings as discussed by Gutstein et al. (1997). A first meaning can be related to critical thinking, as in making sense of problems, creating arguments, making conjectures or critiquing the reasoning of others. Another meaning refers to a broad sense in which an issue can be analysed from multiple perspectives, questioning one's subjectivity and the context one is situated in.

Monteiro (2005) developed a concept of *critical sense* for the interpretation of statistical data that is related to how a person can mobilise and balance factors that interact in a reading context (Gal, 2002). Critical sense is related to a process in which the person who interprets has an important role.

Monteiro (2005) argues that in order for a person to interpret statistical data, he/she needs to mobilise his/her statistical and mathematical knowledge, for example, those associated with numerical and quantitative relationships, measurement and geometry. However, it is also necessary that the person contextualise the statistical data by making reference to their formal knowledge in different areas (e.g. geography, health care, sociology) and their opinions (e.g. personal views on politics, economics and other social issues). The activity of interpretation is not only related to the cognitive dimension. A person also mobilises affective aspects, which can express themselves in their scepticism, sarcasm, anger, or hope. The person can also give examples based on personal experiences which are used to explain her/his interpretation of statistical data. Therefore, *critical sense* also comprises the sensitivity of readers towards examining their own ideas, beliefs, emotions, feelings, conceptions, interests, and conjectures about the data being interpreted.

The term *sense* is used to emphasise this broader dimension of *critical*, in which the interpretation of statistical data is viewed as a crucial process related to a self-evaluation of the interpreter who needs to *balance* the knowledge and experiences *mobilised*. The reader needs to take a critical approach to the whole process, including him/herself. Based on this perspective of *critical*, we will discuss in the next subsections some studies related to three aspects of critical sense: knowledge and the contextual and affective dimensions.

20.4.1 'Critical Sense' Related to People's Knowledge

Human cognition is a complex phenomenon involving several factors related, for example, to the individual's interaction with the environment, which can be amplified using mediators (Vygotsky, 1978). Statistics and its resources, such as graphical representations, can be approached as mediators which are not only a way to display statistical data, but they can also promote reflections for understanding social situations.

Thus, the interpretation of statistical data is not only a data decoding action, in which a person understands information in a mechanical stimulus-responses situation. For example, in order to interpret, people need to question data displayed in graphical representation (e.g. diSessa et al., 1991; Swatton & Taylor, 1994; Ainley et al., 2001; Roth & Bowen, 2001; Arcavi, 2003). These questions are related to the complex range of elements connected with the interpretation of statistical data. For example, McKnight (1990) assessed individual competencies in the critical evaluation of graphical arguments using survey procedures. She argued that high-school participants did not find it difficult to *observe facts* and *relationships* in graphical data. However, the *interpretation of relationships* and *evaluation of the value* of the graphical data seemed complex and problematic tasks. McKnight et al. (1990) recognise that such complex tasks must be investigated with qualitative data from interviews in order to have details of the participants' interpretation. They find it difficult to label as 'erroneous' certain participants' answers which are linked to personal beliefs, which in turn are influenced by cognitive factors (Philipp, 2007).

McKnight's work influenced other studies which investigated the interpretation of statistical data in assessment tasks composed of three levels of questions (Friel et al., 2001). The *elementary* question level requires the extraction of information from the data (*reading the data*). The *intermediate* question level needs the reader to find relationships in the data (*reading between the data*). An *overall* question level requires moving beyond the data (*reading beyond the data*). Therefore, to be critical about data demands that a person develop cognitive understanding which promotes a broader questioning interpretation.

Watson (1997) argues that a critical interpretation also depends on people's cognitive knowledge about statistics. She suggests a three-tiered hierarchy for assessing students' statistical literacy based on authentic material collected from the media. The classification is based on how students understand statistical data. Tier 1 is classified as students with a basic understanding of statistical terminology. In tier 2 students' understanding of statistical terminology is embedded in wider social discussion. The highest level is tier 3, in which students are able to question unrealistic claims made by the media or others, and their questioning attitude can apply more sophisticated concepts to contradict claims made without proper statistical foundation. Watson states that at the highest level of the statistical thinking hierarchy, students have the confidence to challenge what they read in the media. She highlights the tendency in the media for claims to be made without proper statistical foundation, either inadvertently or sometimes deliberately. Therefore, whether there is an intention to mislead or just insufficient information, students need to be made aware that they must constantly question conclusions. Watson argues that the purpose of this type of assessing interpretative task is to discover if students can move to higher levels of cognitive functioning than are generally required to perform computation. Watson's study emphasises that students' statistical knowledge can enable them to make critical or skeptical interpretations of statistical data.

20.4.2   'Critical Sense' Related to People's Social Context

The critical dimension has important bases in statistical and mathematical knowledge; nevertheless, to interpret statistical data critically it is necessary to relate statistics knowledge to a wider understanding of the world. Freire (1972/1990) developed a critical educative perspective in which he argues that social and economic relations are considered forms of exploitation by the oppressors of the oppressed. This situation causes dehumanization, a distortion of the vocation to become more fully human. Freire developed an original concept of *critical consciousness*, which is an aspect that each individual must develop in order to perceive social, political and economic contradictions and to act consciously and creatively against oppressors' versions of reality.

Freire *op. cit.* emphasised that education is not a neutral process in which we can isolate concepts and the cognitive processes of learning and teaching. For instance, police officers and teachers, curricula, teaching methods and theoretical perspectives are aspects that correspond implicitly and explicitly to a dominant ideology. He argues that traditional education can be seen as *banking education* because it is similar to a deposit bank procedure in which students are depositaries and the teacher is the depositor. Thus, depositing teachers *fill* students with content that is disconnected from reality, from the totality of factors that engendered them and that could give them meaning; the discourses are emptied of concreteness and become alienated and alienating verbiage (Freire, 1993).

As we have argued in this chapter, statistics is a particular type of human knowledge which began to be built on the needs of social and cultural practices. However, Freire (1992/2003) warns of the fact that in banking education, the knowledge of mathematics (and statistics) is supposedly approached in a neutral way, without explaining the social and political aspects involved. These approaches can be a useful way of disguising the important role of statistics in constructing social knowledge.

Education should encourage people to have authentic reflections that consider their concrete relationships with the social world. Consciousness and the world are simultaneous: consciousness does not precede the world nor follow it (Freire, 1972/1990). As an alternative, the author proposes a *problematising education*, in which teachers and students develop their power to perceive critically the way they exist in the world with which they interact and in which they find themselves; they come to see the world not as a static reality, but as a reality in process, in transformation.

A problematising education considers dialogue as an indispensable action. Only dialogue, which requires critical thinking, can generate critical thinking (Freire, 1992/2003). There is no communication without dialogue. There is no authentic education without communication. Freire (1972/1990) suggested that resources external to the school (for example, articles, interviews and graphs from newspapers and magazines) can be important starting points for "dialogue processes". This emphasis that Freire placed on material from the media as a starting point seems important, as bringing, for example, a statistical graph into the classroom as a pedagogical approach would not be enough to develop a critical sense. It would be necessary to create strategies that lead students to enter into dialogue and problematise with their fellows in order to understand the statistical data in context. These reflections should be the basis for the development of interpretations that allow the development of a critical consciousness.

Contemporary society has challenged educators to enable citizens to be aware of statistical data presented by the media which contains inaccuracies or has technical limitations (Gal, 2002, Monteiro & Ainley, 2004). This statistical data is disseminated in the context of news, which in general is intentional, uses argumentative strategies that emphasise or disguise aspects of information. Misinformation is related to misleading information created or disseminated without manipulative or malicious intent. Misinformation is information that is false, but which the person who is disseminating it believes to be true (Ireton & Posetti, 2018). Tandoc et al. (2018) analysed 34 academic articles, published between 2003 and 2017, and they identified types of misinformation, such as: satire, parody, propaganda and advertising. These ways of presenting news demand critical reading by people because journalists try to persuade people and use argumentation by which certain conclusions are established that are of interest to particular people, groups or companies. However, a great current challenge is to analyse and identify disinformation, which is not verifiable information in the public interest; it does not meet minimal standards to deserve the label of news (Ireton & Posetti, 2018). 'Disinformation' refers to deliberate and orchestrated attempts to confuse or manipulate people by delivering dishonest information to them. Disinformation is dangerous for society because it is organised, well resourced and reinforced by automated technology. Disinformation is false, and the person who is disseminating it knows it is false. It is a deliberate, intentional lie, and points to people being actively disinformed by malicious actors.

Disinformation is particularly dangerous when it is produced and disseminated to populations with only basic levels of education and, therefore, with little or no statistical literacy. In Brazil and in several countries in Latin America, illiteracy rates have decreased significantly in recent decades, accompanied by the expansion of access to basic schooling. However, access was not accompanied to the same degree by the provision of what Freire calls *problematising education. Banking education* is still predominant by which students learn to use codes and reproduce ready-made and frequently repeated knowledge without meaning for their own real-life situations.

This has led to a high rate of functional illiteracy among the Brazilian population (Catelli, 2018). Allied to this situation, in Brazil there is widespread access by the population to smartphones and consequently to messenger apps. The use of these communication resources has increased the possibilities for communication between people but has also made it possible for inexperienced users of technology to have frequent and quick access to disinformation. This spread of disinformation includes statistical data, graphs and infographics related to, for example, false data on voting intentions for particular candidates in elections or the economic index. When interpreting statistical data, readers then need to adopt a critical reading of those data, try to contextualise them, and to read them in connection to the reality of their own lives.

20.4.3 'Critical Sense' Related to People's Affective Dimension

Monteiro (2005) also argues that affective aspects are important for the critical dimension, as the interpretation of statistical data is a dynamic process in which people can mobilise their emotions, feelings, and beliefs. Philipp (2007) defines *affect* as "a disposition or tendency or an emotion or feeling attached to an idea or object" (p. 259). According to this conceptualisation, affect involves the following three aspects: *emotions* (feelings or states of consciousness); *attitudes* (manners of acting, feeling or thinking that show one's disposition or opinion), and *beliefs* (understandings, premises, or propositions about the world that are thought to be true). These three aspects of affect are not completely dissociated from cognition, while belief is more cognitively influenced than emotions and attitudes are.

Studies in statistics education which address affective aspects are not common (Zieffler et al., 2011) and they have mainly focused on attitudes towards statistics (e.g., Gordon, 2004; Estrada et al., 2011; Martins, 2018).

In the context of our discussion of critical sense related to the interpretations of statistical data, we used the term *affective expression* (Monteiro, 2005), considering the complexity of the human affective dimension. We also considered the fact that in research situations it is likely that we can only have access to certain indications of the affective elements of the person who is interpreting. *Affective expression* can be conceptualised as an exhibition of aspects related to emotions, attitudes, or beliefs (Philipp, 2007) during the process of interpreting data.

Monteiro & Ainley (2007) discussed aspects of the interpretation of statistical graphs among primary school student teachers. They chose graphs published in international magazines and a local government document, which were related to familiar topics and which seemed to present accessible levels of statistical relationships and which were free from technical errors or misleading elements. Figure 20.2 presents an example, a graph about road accidents.

Figure 20.2 was initially presented to participants as a questionnaire task. In a second stage, some volunteers took part in an interview in which questions about the graph were posed to give opportunities for participants to respond in ways which might be similar to reading contexts (Gal, 2002). As part of the data analyses, the excerpts were quantified in order to give us an idea of the occurrence of *affective expressions* related to the different subcategories and the different backgrounds of the undergraduate students we examined. The following excerpt is from the interview with Hillary, a 35-year-old postgraduate certificate of education student with a degree in music.

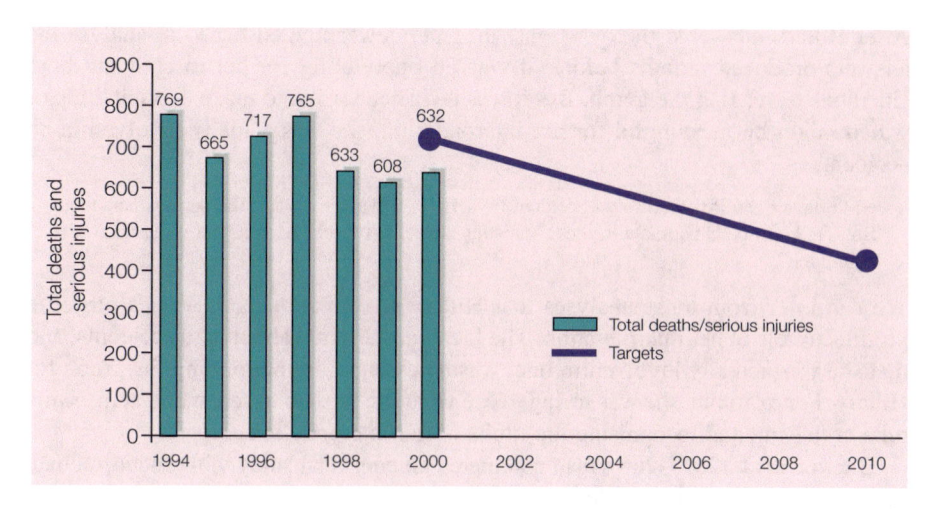

Fig. 20.2 Road accident graphs task (Warwickshire County Council, 2001)

Researcher: *If the target for 2000–2010. . . there is a target there. . . What do you think the pattern would be from 2010 for 2020?*

H: 20 . . . All right . . . hum . . . I think provided that technology doesn't take over people's well being . . . Then. . . I think the pattern should decline. But there are so many other things that might influence that pattern, like population rates . . . and . . . It is difficult to say . . . it is really difficult . . . it is hard question that . . . But I think . . . I think it would be a decline. I think there will always be a decline, because it is such important issue . . . And then . . . There obviously . . . it always has been history of some kind of decline. But obviously things come along the way that interrupt the flow . . . obviously here (pointing to 1997 figure on the graph) there is . . . more deaths on the roads. There are reasons . . . Well, I don't know. It is hard to say whether it's death and injuries. (. . .) But obviously that was addressed, because there was a big drop there (1997–98). So, I think there's always a kind of picture of a decline, or an attempt for a decline. With something as serious you know . . . as this issue.

Hillary's interpretation seemed to be a journey through symbolic space (Carraher et al., 1995) in which she was projecting feelings about the figures. She was looking carefully at the graph but was also expressing her desire to see safer roads with lower levels of accidents. Her speech suggested that the data mobilised a strong feeling: . . . *It is difficult to say . . . it is really difficult . . . it is hard question that.* When she was encouraged to try to give a specific figure, Hillary managed to *guess* an answer that seems to be based on the graph but takes into consideration such aspects as the *hope* that was implicitly present in the interpretation.

R: "If [you] could say a rate as well?"

H: "Rate? . . . Do you want that I say what I think that death and injury rate might be . . .? Right. So if it's starting at 500 which is obviously that's what they're hoping . . . I don't think it's actually going to hit the bottom. I think there is always going to be deaths and serious injury on the road. I don't think you ever avoid that happening, but it might be . . . For instance, a target . . . realistic might be straight from 500 to . . . say 300 . . . Yeah, it seems a realistic target".

After Hillary answered the questions, the interviewer invited her to re-analyse the answers produced months before. It was an opportunity for her to compare both situations of reading the graph. But it was a chance for her to make explicit a factor which might be meaningful for her interpretation: she was actually involved in an accident.

> H: "I have been involved in an accident myself … It wasn't a particular serious accident. But, … I can perhaps relate to these statistics more … I think. I can actually see what it's telling me".

We can infer from these analyses that Hillary's motivations and wishes played a prominent role in her interpretation. The fact that she cared about road accidents, and that she was actually involved in one, was an essential in interpreting the graph for Hillary. For example, she was trying to see what she wished to see, while at the same time criticising and recognising the limits of her interpretation.

Queiroz et al. (2017) have also conducted an empirical study with undergraduate pedagogy and statistics students, which aimed to explore and identify affective expression as part of the process of interpretation during different statistical tasks in order to understand the interrelations of affective expression in situations of data interpretation. The research tasks presented data concerning controversial contemporary issues, and our intention was to present tasks that would encourage personal expressions during data interpretation. We expected that the different curricular background (pedagogy/statistics) would influence how the participants interpreted and expressed their affect in relation to the data. Regarding students' previous academic experiences in the curriculum of their degree course, we should point out that the pedagogy students had participated in a university course where affectivity is discussed explicitly, while the statistics students had attended various related disciplines of data analysis but had not taken courses involving subjects related to affectivity. However, we cannot say that these aspects had an influence on the data found in our research. There is no specific type of affective expression that characterises a group of students. In affective expressions linked to the task data, both statistics and pedagogy students continually displayed their affectivity with regard to the research tasks.

People's cognitive, contextual and affective aspects can enable them to be critical towards statistical data. The consideration of these factors associated with who is interpreting the data seems to be a perspective that places people in a leading role in their relationship with statistics, and thus can promote the empowerment of people as citizens.

Weiland (2017) analyses the barriers to and possibilities for implementing critical statistical literacy in the school curriculum. As the context is central for statistics (Groth, 2013), the teaching and learning of statistics establishes relationships to contextual knowledge. This can be a barrier to developing a critical statistical literacy perspective, because generally teachers use neutral or trivial examples to teach statistical concepts and procedures. In order to overcome this obstacle, statistics education must take socio-political contexts into account. However, pre-service and in-service teacher education usually do not provide opportunities for mathematics teachers who teach statistics to learn how to consider such complex contexts. Therefore, in addition to improving their statistical knowledge, teachers need to develop their critical knowledge of controversial socio-cultural issues, to be aware of different resources, to learn how to create lessons that provide critical statistics education, and to know how to deal with their own possible uncomfortable feelings and those of students and parents facing these issues. Weiland (2017) suggests that to overcome these barriers, a concerted effort by different agents will be necessary, in order to explore the potential transdisciplinary nature of statistics, offering "opportunities to tackle complex socio-political issues in conjunction with learning powerful statistical concepts and practices in an effort to be able to read and write both the word and world with statistics as critical citizens" (Weiland, 2017, p. 45).

The discussion of critical dimensions developed in this section relates directly to facets of Civic Statistics set out in Chap. 3. The critical perspective is associated with the social implications of statistics (Facet 1), the need to question and reflect, and critically evaluate statistical data (Facet 2), the consideration of affective elements (Facet 3), and contextual civic knowledge (Facet 8).

20.5 Implications for Education

In this section we present three examples of how Civic Statistics can be used and developed in situations in which people immersed in a given socio-cultural context act as protagonists, so that they become aware of their political role in strengthening their local communities. The examples are taken from contrasting regions—we consider both a Flemish and a Brazilian perspective. We decided to do so in order to broaden the Eurocentric scope in the debate and in the development of Civic Statistics. Europe is a forerunner in connecting science and the citizen. Many projects are financed by the European Union to foster city science initiatives. One important example is the HORIZON 2020 Research and Innovation Programme (https://ec.europa.eu/programmes/horizon2020/en/h2020-sections-projects) where people are involved in all aspects of the research.

Citizen science has become a worldwide movement to give leverage to democracy and sustainability based on participative citizenship. Some examples are given by Zejnilović and Campos in Chap. 21. Beside activities supported by the European Union, it is useful to look beyond the pioneers of citizen science initiatives to point out similar projects and initiatives from developing countries. The authors are based in Europe and Brazil and rely on many years of collaboration exploring how diverse regions can enrich each other (Monteiro et al., 2013).

We present three projects that relate to aspects of the investigative cycle (Wild & Pfannkuch, 1999); one in Flanders involving urban populations who collected and analysed data on air pollution; one in the Brazilian northeast with indigenous teachers addressing water resources in the territory of the Xukuru do Ororubá people; and the third with teachers who offer contextualised education on 'coexistence with a semi-arid region'. The Brazilian projects were not developed explicitly as 'Civic Statistics' but are coherent with the themes in this book in that they challenge the current purposes and nature of statistics education and, offer an alternative framework. The ramifications of the experiences of these projects are not limited to just using, teaching or learning statistics, but involve repositioning the relationships between 'statistics' and 'citizens' so that people can act and transform social and cultural situations. It is our ambition that these actions have more wide-reaching repercussions and serve to empower citizen to use practices that can be transferred to other issues.

20.5.1 Air Quality in Flanders

In this example we show how people can be involved in statistics by engaging with them to collect data. The project exemplifies Civic Statistics in action; it was been developed to enhance people's awareness of pollution (civic aspect) that can be measured (statistical aspect) by people themselves (educational aspect). The statistics are embedded in a societal context and in a rich text; and there are clear consequences for society. Within this conceptual framework, people with little or no statistical background are working with multivariate, aggregated, and dynamic data. Further, the project is characterised by innovative methods since the data collection method was organised as a means of raising political awareness amongst citizens.

Although the main target of this project was not primarily to collect data but rather to involve people in a project that centers on the current political debate on climate change—a debate that moves most people to take up a position and to change their personal lives. The critical aspect goes beyond what citizens 'see, read or hear' in public discourses (as mentioned in Chap. 3 by Engel and Ridgway). Instead, citizens are involved in the project as 'researchers' who collect the data. *Doing research*, in a way, is an inherent critical position, it is looking for evidence-based positions and arguments. An educational aspect is part of the project as people were instructed on how to measure the mean concentration of nitrogen dioxide (NO2) in the ambient air. This is a nice way to bring science down to earth as the project did.

The project called *CurieuzeNeuzen Vlaanderen* is a citizens science project in which 20,000 citizens measured the air quality near their own home during May 2018. The name *CurieuzeNeuzen Vlaanderen*, literally translated, means *CuriousNoses Flanders* and refers to *being curious* or *having a nose for*. The aim of the project was to acquire a detailed geographical map with statistical data on the air quality in Flanders. The project was carried out both in cities as well as in the countryside and all the materials were provide by the Flemish Environment Agency, the main sponsor of the project. Participants were asked to install a (standardised) measurement device on a street facing a window in the place they lived. The device

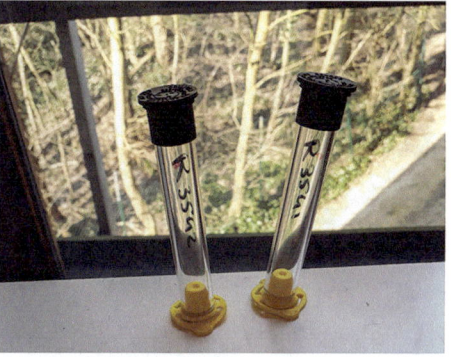

Fig. 20.3 A measurement device on a street-facing window: a window sign (on the left) and two sampling tubes that are attached on the inside (on the right) (Curieuzeneuzen, 2021)

consisted of a V-shaped window sign that could easily be stuck on the window. Data collecting tubes were connected to the inside of the V-sign (Fig. 20.3).

The diffusion tubes determined the mean concentration of NO_2 in the ambient air as an important indicator of traffic pollution. Data collection was organised during May 2018 and more than 99% of the participants returned the test tubes to the lab to be analysed. Not all the tubes could be used for the research; some of them were invalid because of cobwebs found in the tubes. 96% of the test tubes were determined to be valid for further analysis and NO_2 reading. An overview of the project can be consulted at the project webpage.[1]

The project was judged to be successful in involving people in collecting data and making them aware of political issues such as climate change and air pollution. One of the outcomes of the project was an informative map of air quality in Flanders. However the project also formulated more issues that the investigators learned from this ground-breaking project: people care about air; people can be involved in collecting big data, people are curious about measures; people can be involved in science (citizen science) and in statistics (Civic Statistics). Although this is an interesting example, it is, however, not without its problems. Sensitive information can have a negative impact for some partners (e.g. people wanting to sell their house on a busy street might want to suppress information about air pollution). However, all the information was made public on the website of the main sponsor, the Flemish government, to inform all people.

The project became popular and many more projects have been set up to collect data on air pollution. Data have been collected using strawberries, white bedsheets and students' T-shirts. Although the *CuriousNoses Flanders* project was set up for the general public without direct implications for education, the idea has been taken up by some schools which started similar projects. At this level, the project became meaningful for institutional education. Chapter 4 provides more illustrations for

---

[1] https://curieuzeneuzen.be/home-en/

Fig. 20.4 The Ket & Co primary school, Molenbeek, Brussels (credits P. Allo)

activities pertaining to Civic Statistics. With the example of the Brussels primary school below, we provide an additional example of how to integrate a Civic Statistics project for the general public into the curriculum and into classroom teaching practices.

Ket & Co is a project based on a Brussels primary school. Here we report on a project where primary school children collect statistical data. White T-shirts were used, hanging outside on a school fence to measure the air quality of the pupils' school environment. The educational project involved not only the collection of data but the whole cycle of data collection, analysis and interpretation. Statistics education studies (Wild & Pfannkuch, 1999) have suggested that in order to understand statistics in general (and specifically the statistical cycle), it is necessary to be involved in activities related to the whole statistical cycle (Fig. 20.4).

The picture illustrates a project where young pupils are involved in science, in statistics and in data collection from the early school years. Also here, we see a first stepping stone towards Civic Statistics from the early school years.

20.5.2   *Water Resources in the Xukuru Do Ororubá Territory*

Although Brazil was officially discovered (invaded) in 1500, before that over 1000 ethnic groups were living in their territories, all with cultural differences and speaking their own languages (Rodrigues, 2005). The last Brazilian census indicated that there are still 155,000 speakers of 188 living indigenous languages (IBGE, 2012).

The Brazilian *Indians* became full citizens only after the promulgation of the Brazilian constitution in 1988, as a result of struggles by the indigenous movement over a number of decades. Although they had legal citizenship, many indigenous communities continued to be excluded from decision making, and their cultures marginalised by being incorporated into the dominant culture (D'Ambrosio, 2007). In order for the local cultures of the different indigenous peoples to be valued it was necessary to fight for the introduction of an indigenous school education (Decreto n° 26, 1991) which had specific curricular guidelines (MEC, 1998). An important principle of pedagogical approaches in indigenous schools is critical inter-culturality, which is conceptualised as a dialogic process in constant transformation that occurs through interactions between different people and/or groups from specific cultures (Nascimento et al., 2016).

Oliveira (2016) developed a survey in collaboration with indigenous teachers from the *Xukuru do Ororubá* people. They are a population of more than 12,000 indigenous people (Leal & Andrade, 2013) who live in 24 villages in an indigenous territory of 27,555 ha (276 km^2) demarcated in 2001 (Silva & Garcia, 2019). There are 41 schools in their territory, in which 221 teachers and assistants are involved in teaching activities (Silva, 2017). Almost all the schools are small with one or two classrooms. The classroom groups for the initial years are called *multiseriate* because they bring together students of two or more school years in the same group (Janata & Anhaia, 2015). In these groups the teacher teaches all school subjects.

The research aimed to analyse aspects of teaching and learning processes in statistical education, relating them to the context of the life of Xukuru do Ororubá communities (Oliveira et al., 2018). The study involved the analysis of curricular documents, semi-structured interviews and the development of a collaborative teacher education process exploring statistical literacy (Gal, 2002) and the investigative cycle (Wild & Pfannkuch, 1999; Rumsey, 2002; Cazorla & Santana, 2010).

The analyses of interviews provide evidence that the participants had had little or no access to pedagogical approaches to the teaching of statistics during their undergraduate study program. Only two teachers stated that during their college pre-service program they attended a mathematics education course which addressed some aspects of the teaching of statistics. However, courses were not conducted from an inter-cultural perspective. The analysis of the curriculum guide-line documents for indigenous school education indicated that there are no topics on statistics.

The collaborative group consisted of 11 indigenous teachers who work in multi-grade classes which comprised students from the first to the fifth years of elementary school. The participants were aged between 24 and 50 years old. All teachers have degrees in pedagogy but only one has a post-graduation specialisation certificate in school management. During the collaborative group meetings teachers reflected on theoretical aspects and statistical concepts. Each teacher also proposed a pedagogical project related to the investigative cycle to be developed with their students. As part of the planning processes, they discussed a common main theme for all projects, and they decided to approach the water resources in the Xukuru do Ororubá territory. The teachers found the water issues important as a way of relating the investigative cycle to problematising and raising awareness about access, use and the preservation of water, as well as the real problems that their villages were facing, such as supply shortages and water pollution.

The teachers' proposals had an interdisciplinary perspective which associated the statistics topics with other curricular subjects, such as natural sciences, geography, and history. The project also aimed to analyse the realities of each village and to address specific elements of the Xukuru culture. For example, the Xukuru Indians still preserve some elements of their ancestral religion, in which water is associated with deities. The proposal suggested the use of a pedagogical project in statistics as an intercultural tool, as it can enhance the relationship between knowledge of curriculum content and the experiences and local challenges of indigenous communities.

The pedagogical projects based on the investigative cycle provided teaching experiences for teachers who until the beginning of the research project had had little or no contact with approaches to statistics education. Students were able to experience the stages of the investigative cycle (Cazorla & Santana, 2010) linked to local realities: i.e. the formulation of research questions, contextualisation of the problem situation within their village, definition of the population to be investigated, the planning of data collection, data collection, data treatment, the analysis, interpretation and communication of the results. In addition, the analyses of activities suggested that they demonstrated having a reasonable numerical sense, estimating quantities, and the ability to represent data through pie charts and bar graphs. However, the analyses also indicated the need to teach specific statistical concepts related to handling data—those related to the organisation and systematisation of information, the use of scale in bar graphs and proportion in sector graphs.

This project calls on most of the facets and skills described in Chap. 3 (but not statistics and risk (Facet 4), discussion of official statistics (Facet 7), or the use of Information and Communication Technologies—(Facet 9).

20.5.3 Coexisting with a Semi-Arid Region

The Brazilian semi-arid region covers 1,128,697 km^2 (Sudene, 2018), corresponding to 13.2% of the national territory; it has a population of 27,870,241 inhabitants. The Caatinga biome covers an area of 912,529 km^2 (Silva et al., 2017), which has enormous endemic biodiversity, with unique characteristics exclusive to Brazil (Ribeiro et al., 2016). The name Caatinga means *white forest* in the Tupi-Guarani language. Among other characteristics, it has a shallow soil, with outcrops of rock and stony ground, having a climate that has high annual average temperatures (27 °C) and a high evapotranspiration rate (3000 mm per year). Rainfall is concentrated in 3–5 months, varying (on average) between 270 and 800 mm per year, irregularly distributed in time and space (Lima et al., 2011). The combination of these elements causes a daily percentage of water deficit equal to or greater than 60%, considering all days of the year (Sudene, 2018) (Fig. 20.5).

Fig. 20.5 The semi-arid region of Brazil (Sudene, 2018)

From the sixteenth century onwards, European colonisers introduced inappropriate economic and cultural practices to Brazilian semi-arid regions, such as agriculture based on deforestation on the banks of water sources, burning, and exotic crop plantation. These cultivation techniques are still causing environmental degradation, including the process of desertification. Over centuries, the semi-arid characteristics associated with climate and soil have been treated as problems to be confronted.

The long periods of severe drought caused tragedies for populations of the semi-arid region because they were involved in economic activities which depended on seasonal rains. The social and economic vulnerabilities of people were opportunities for corrupt politicians to take advantage of, sponsored by regional and local oligarchies (Costa, 2017). In this situation, families were coerced to give up their rights of a free and democratic vote, electing people from the same political group and therefore maintaining degrading social and economic conditions for the majority of the population.

From the 1960s, the region experienced significant changes in its infrastructure and in the growth of some economic sectors (Silva, 2006). However, as this modernisation was not accompanied by a policy that supported populations excluded from the new production models, it resulted in an increase in poverty, and emigration to the large cities on the northeast coast, or to northern and southern regions (Costa, 2017).

Since the 1990s, non-governmental organisations such as rural unions, farmers' associations, production cooperatives, social movements and other civil sectors have mobilised opinion towards proposing *coexistence with the semi-arid region* (ASA, 2009). From the 2000s some public policies began to consider this perspective and economic potential linked to respect for semi-arid biodiversity, the diverse culture of populations, the sustainability of water resources, agro-ecological practices, coexistence technologies and food sovereignty. Discussions and actions developed in northern Brazil are also connected to other Latin America initiatives through shared platforms (Plataforma Semiáridos de América Latina, 2020): *Dry Corridor* in Central America (Nicaragua, Guatemala, El Salvador, and Honduras), and *Chaco Region* (Argentina, Bolivia, and Paraguay).

A group of educators from different organisations also formed the *Educational Network of the Brazilian Semi-Arid Region* (RESAB) to formulate new conceptions and construct other meanings from everyday experiences in semi-arid territories based on political dialogue with teachers, school managers and other educational agents (Araújo et al., 2017). RESAB has developed a perspective called *Contextualised Education for Coexistence with the Brazilian Semi-arid* (ECSAB), which seeks to break with the narratives historically presented as universal, based on scientific perspectives that disregarded local cultural aspects (Reis, 2020). This contextualised education can be an empowerment tool for populations in semi-arid regions because it takes account of their socio-cultural issues, and it is actually developed and implemented in their territories.

François et al. (2015) argue that the government's inadequate response to populations requiring an education that respects their cultural identities could be partly explained by their denying epistemological constraints and imposing political hegemony. In order to seek an educational approach which takes into consideration important socio-cultural aspects it is useful in the implementation of education programs to discuss the notion of power. It is important to understand and to analyse the politics of knowledge and how it operates in schooling processes. Therefore, school programs that are developed and implemented in specific contexts turn out to be tools of power (François et al., 2014).

Cavalcante and Monteiro (2021) are developing a study that investigates how teacher education that addresses statistical literacy, with a perspective on contextualised education, can enhance statistical knowledge, resignifying it so that teaching statistics problematises and strengthens the perspective of coexistence with semi-arid regions. The research field is taking place in the semi-arid *Paraiban Cariri* region, in which there are experiences of continuing teacher education based on ECSAB.

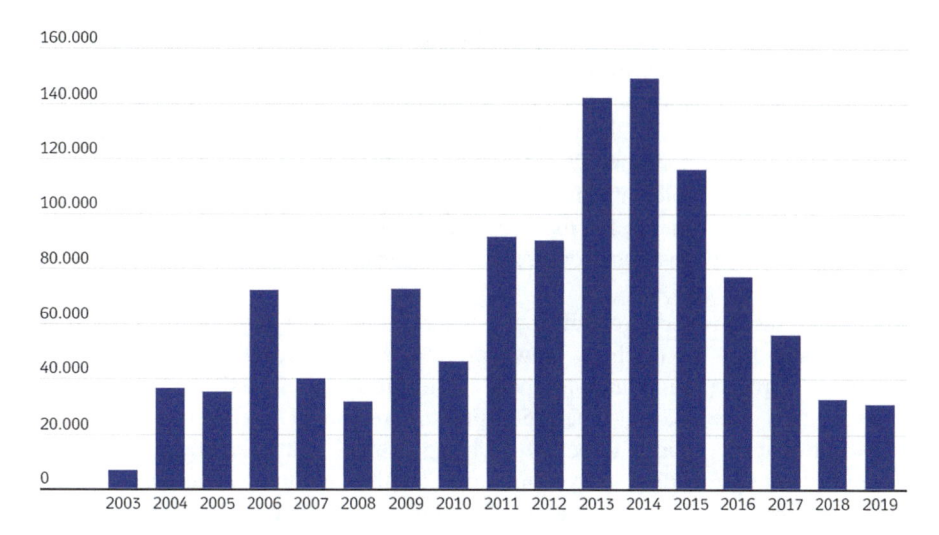

Fig. 20.6 Number of cisterns constructed with financial support by the federal government (Madeiro, 2020)

The study is characterised as an action research procedure (Tripp, 2005) with the participation of final-years elementary school teachers. The first stage will involve assessing teachers' knowledge of and experiences with statistical literacy, the teaching of statistics and the challenges of coexistence with semi-arid regions. For this stage it was originally planned to carry out observations of the teachers' pedagogical practice in local urban and rural schools. However, due to the Covid-19 pandemic, this procedure will not be possible. It will be conducted through semi-structured interviews which will include, it is proposed, the interpretation of graphs, infographics, tables, and texts with statistical data related to the cultural, economic, social, political and geographic aspects of the semi-arid region. Figure 20.6 is an example of a task, a bar graph that presents a historical series with the number of cisterns built in the northeast region with federal funds since the program was created.

During the interviews, questions will be asked about Fig. 20.6, such as:

- What message could be conveyed by this graph?
- Did you already know about the information presented?
- Did any of the information surprise you? Why did it surprise you?
- What can you say about the period presented?
- Does this graph reach its aim? What is missing? What is unnecessary?
- How would you calculate the total number of cisterns built?
- How would you calculate the annual average construction of cisterns?
- Is the average the best option to understand the data distribution?
- Is the graph a continuous series? Why?
- If you were to use this graph in your classroom, what would you change?
- What situations could be problematised on the basis of the graph?

The analysis of the data produced by the interviews will also be important because it will provide elements for developing statistical literacy activities oriented towards the contextualised education perspective for the second stage of the project. The activities will be based on the investigative cycle in statistics (Wild & Pfannkuch, 1999; Guimarães & Gitirana, 2013), while emphasising critical reflection (Freire, 1972/1990), and problematising the data. It is expected that this approach can facilitate teacher education for the construction of statistical literacy which relates knowledge and disposition components to each other, as well as enhancing contextualised education.

For instance, it is very probable that teachers know about the concept of statistical average, and how to teach it. However, the teacher education workshops will incorporate processes in which teachers can resignify this statistics topic and relate it to the perspective of coexistence with semi-arid regions. Therefore, problematising statistical concepts related to actual data (e.g. annual rainfall average, water consumption, family planning, increasing desertification and the Human Development Index) can resignify not only knowledge elements of statistical literacy, but also mobilise affective aspects, such as preoccupation with, and indignation at, the social context. The workshops with the teachers will be filmed, and a questionnaire will also be applied at the end of the activities, in order to obtain more analytical elements in relation to the teacher education process experienced.

This project is currently under development, and the authors are considering taking into account other aspects of the Civic Statistics conceptual framework, such as probability elements related to semi-arid phenomena (Facet 4) and ICT elements (Facet 9).

20.6   Discussion

In this chapter, our reflections focused on the socio-historical construction of statistics and its social and cultural repercussions. The understanding and use of statistics were approached as a complex process that involved aspects of different contexts in which knowledge was systematised and continues to be developed. In addition, we discussed the need to focus and reflect on a person's active role as a citizen. In this sense, the use and development of Civic Statistics requires a critical sense to be developed by each individual so that he/she can become aware and balance the various aspects involved. In our discussions of examples, we were able to reflect on these aspects in the context of experiences with different actors who can play an important role regarding environmental issues. From the critical sense perspective, the individual has a role in analysing the data and balancing the various aspects involved. This role can be evidenced by the social groups involved in the projects discussed.

In the example of a project developed in Flanders, the prospect of engaging the population made it possible to reflect on the pollution situation and think about possible ways to control it. In this project there was an exploration of creative aspects that involved the use of unconventional resources, not restricted to traditional procedures within classrooms. The experiences involved recreational activities that related to aspects of people's daily lives, such as the use of personal objects (e.g. T-shirts) that served as instruments to collect data. This educational approach explicitly listed aspects of people's affective dimension which may have been an important element for people's critical sense, as it mobilised far more than just cognitive elements. The project also shows that Civic Statistics can be carried out by everyone, ranging from adult citizen to pupils in institutional education. The power of this project is the way in which a general project on citizen science was integrated into the curriculum and the classroom context of institutional education. This relates to one of the facets of Civic Statistics, being related to wider society in a multivariable way. It shows how 'school' statistics can be related to society and how young pupils can be educated in a critical way to provide them with the tools necessary to take part in a democratic society as a critical citizen.

In the case of the project developed with the indigenous people, they had, over the past decades, already built up a recognition of themselves as individuals belonging to a group which has its own cultural and political issues. The experience with indigenous schools has enabled indigenous teachers to introduce ways of using the investigative cycle for issues in their communities. This experience would certainly need to be continued so that pedagogical activities could be explored and developed with the investigative cycle that could better explain the intercultural aspects of the realities experienced by indigenous students and their villages. In addition, it could lead to greater discussions, consciousness, and a critical analysis of reality. In this case, the perspective of Civic Statistics may in future give greater empowerment to the participants in similar projects. An important aspect would be to deepen statistical concepts in order to encourage teachers to establish the relationships between statistical data on water issues better. Thus, it would be interesting if the relationships between statistical concepts and practices (Facets 4, 5, 6, 8 and 10) on the one hand and key concepts from the political and social sciences (Facets 1, 2, and 7) on the other could be made explicit in such a way that those specific communities would be able to understand the social situations they are experiencing better.

In the discussion of the project under development with the populations of the semi-arid region, statistical literacy and the perspective of Civic Statistics may contribute to educational actions that can enhance the recognition of issues related to living in a region that has its own natural and cultural characteristics.

These projects have potential to be adapted to other socio-cultural contexts, and they present ways to develop critical statistical literacy approaches (Weiland, 2017) which can provide opportunities for reflecting on and making sense of complex and controversial socio-political issues, such as systematic racism, sexism and classism. According to this perspective, critical statistics can be a lens which enables people to read the world, identifying and questioning social structures and discourses reinforced by statistical data-based arguments. "Statistics investigations do not only need to be used to destabilise but can also be used to produce new structures and discourses as well, using statistical investigations to alleviate and resolve sociopolitical issues of injustice" (Weiland, 2017, p. 42).

The reflections and actions of these projects will not transform situations in themselves, but they can be a starting point for other actions that lead to organised interventions that can more profoundly transform social and cultural realities. Reflecting on the movement to bring science to the people and to collaborate with people in the construction of knowledge, Civic Statistics is a necessary condition for and at the forefront of this democratising process. Citizens can take part in a democratic process only in so far as they are well informed. The media play a crucial role in this process and indeed a large number of arguments in the democratic decision-making process is data-based. An information (and data-based information) democratic society requires what Schiller & Engel (2018) call *Mündigkeit*, an attitude and a competence that needs to be developed by civic education. Following the arguments of Schiller & Engel (2018), *Mündigkeit* is inconceivable without Civic Statistics and so is democracy inconceivable without Civic Statistics. This explains the obvious need for Civic Statistics training in education, in teacher training and in lifelong learning projects.

There are limited studies that examine the impact of citizen science and Civic Statistics. A systematic review of the effects on learning and scientific literacy (Aristeidou & Herodotou, 2020) shows evidence for the cultivation on citizens' knowledge and skills. At the same time, they point to unexplored areas and the need for experimental and long-term studies in both formal and informal education settings. Therefore, we suggest further research on the projects of Civic Statistics and citizen science so as to have better empirical evidence of the impact and the power of these projects. Leading questions will address (1) changes that have been brought about by the projects and (2) changes in attitudes and beliefs about statistics associated with participation in the projects.

References

Ainley, J., Pratt, D., & Nardi, E. (2001). Normalising: Children's activity to construct meanings for trend. *Educational Studies in Mathematics, 45*(1–3), 131–146.

Araújo, A. M. R. B., Melo, L. F., Campos, W. D. B., Melo, R. R., & Araújo, A. E. (2017). Rede de educação do semiárido brasileiro: vivências a partir da experiência local. *Proceedings of 2nd Seminário Nacional de Educação em Agroecologia (SNEA): Resistências e Lutas pela Democracia*, Cadernos de Agroecologia 12(1), 1–9.

Arcavi, A. (2003). The role of visual representation in the learning of mathematics. *Educational Studies in Mathematics, 52*, 215–241.

Aristeidou, M., & Herodotou, C. (2020). Online citizen science: A systematic review of effects on learning and scientific literacy. *Citizen Science: Theory and Practice, 5*(1), 11. https://doi.org/10.5334/cstp.224

ASA. (2009, September 30). *Sobre nós: história.* https://www.asabrasil.org.br/sobre-nos/historia

Barnard, G. A., Plackett, R. L., & Pearson, E. S. (1990). *'Student'. A statistical biography of William Sealy Gosset.* Oxford University Press.

Bracke, N. (2008). *Een monument voor het land. Overheidsstatistiek in België, 1795-1870.* [A monument for the country. Official statistics in Belgium, 1795-1870]. Academia Press.

Cals, J., & Winkens, B. (2018). De Student-t-toets is een biertoets [The Student t-test is a beer test]. *Nederlands Tijdschrift Geneeskunde 162*(3204). Dutch.

Carnap, R. (1934). *The unity of science*. Kegan Paul, Trench, Trubner, and Co.

Carraher, D., Schliemann, A., & Nemirovsky, R. (1995). Graphing from everyday experience. *Hands On!, 18*(2), 7–9.

Carvalho, C. F. (2001). *Interacções entre pares: contributos para a promoção do desenvolvimento lógico e do desempenho estatístico no 7° ano de escolaridade* [Doctoral thesis, University of Lisbon]. ISPA Repository. http://repositorio.ispa.pt/handle/10400.12/1624.

Catelli, R. (2018). Made to measure: Using INAF to check literacy levels. *Journal AED: Adult Education and Development, 85*, 80–83.

Cavalcante, N. I. S., & Monteiro, C. (2021). Letramento estatístico para empoderar a convivência com o Semiárido. In C. Monteiro & L. Carvalho (Org.), *Temas emergentes em Letramento Estatístico* (pp. 148–162). Universitária UFPE.

Cazorla, I., & Santana, E. (2010). *Do tratamento da informação ao letramento estatístico*. Litterarum.

Costa, T. P. (2017). A Convivência com o Semiárido como Paradigma Sustentável na Perspectiva do Bem Viver. *REVASF, 7*(12), 79–100.

Curieuzeneuzen. (2021). *Curieuze Neuzen Vlaanderen*. Retreived March 18 at https://curieuzeneuzen.be/home-en/

D'Ambrosio, U. (2007). *Etnomatemática: elo entre as tradições e a modernidade* (2ª ed.). Autêntica.

Decreto n° 26, de 4 de fevereiro de 1991. (1991). *Dispõe Sobre A Educação Indígena no Brasil*. Brasília.

Descartes, R. (1966). *Regulae ad directionem ingenii (avec la collaboration de Giovanni Crapulii)*. Nijhoff. (Original work from 1628).

Desrosières, A. (1998). *The politics of large numbers. A history of statistical reasoning*. Harvard University Press.

diSessa, A., Hammer, D., Sherin, B., & Kolpakowski, T. (1991). Inventing graphing: Meta-representational expertise in children. *The Journal of Mathematical Behavior, 10*(2), 117–160.

Estrada, A., Batanero, C., & Lancaster, S. (2011). Teachers' attitudes towards statistics. In C. Batanero, G. Burrill, & C. Reading (Eds.), *Teaching statistics in school mathematics – challenges for teaching and teacher education* (pp. 163–174). Springer.

Floridi, L., & Taddeo, M. (2016). What is data-ethics? *Philosophical Transactions of the Royal Society A: Mathematical, Physical and Engineering Sciences, 374*(2083), 1–5.

François, K. & Bracke, N. (2006). Teaching statistics in a critical way: Historical, philosophical and political aspects of statistics. In A. Rossman & B. Chance (eds.). *Proceedings of the 7th International Conference on Teaching Statistics (ICOTS-7) Working Cooperatively in Statistics Education. Session 8D: History and the teaching of Statistics* (pp. 1–6). Salvador, Bahia, July 2–7. https://iase-web.org/documents/papers/icots7/8D2_FRAN.pdf

François, K., Coessens, K., & Van Bendegem, J. P. (2014). The liberating power of mathematics. In P. Smeyers (Ed.) *Proceedings of the 2014 conference of the research community philosophy and history of the discipline of education* (pp. 72–83).

François, K., Monteiro, C., Carvalho, L., & Vandendriessche, E. (2015). Politics of ethnomathematics: An epistemological, political and educational perspective. In S. Mukhopadhyay, & B. Greer (Eds.) *Proceedings of 8th Mathematics Education and Society Conference* (pp. 492–504).

Freire, P. (1990). *Pedagogy of the oppressed*. Penguin. (Original work published 1972).

Freire, P. (1993). *Pedagogy of the city*. Continuum.

Freire, P. (2003). *Pedagogy of hope*. Continuum (Original work published 1992).

Friel, S., Curcio, F., & Bright, G. (2001). Making sense of graphs: critical factors influencing comprehension and instructional implications. *Journal for Research in Mathematics Education, 32*(2), 124–158.

Gal, I. (2002). Adult statistical literacy: Meanings, components, responsibilities. *International Statistical Review, 70*(1), 1–25.

Garfield, J. B., & Ben-Zvi, D. (2008). *Developing students' statistical reasoning: Connecting research and teaching practice*. Springer.

Gordon, S. (2004). Understanding students' experiences of statistics in a service course. *Statistics Education Research Journal, 3*(1), 40–59.

Groth, R. E. (2013). Characterizing key developmental understandings and pedagogically powerful ideas within a statistical knowledge for teaching framework. *Mathematical Thinking and Learning, 15*(2), 121–145.

Guimarães, G. L., & Gitirana, V. (2013). Estatística no Ensino Fundamental: A pesquisa como eixo estruturador. In R. E. Borba & C. E. Monteiro (Eds.), *Processos de ensino e aprendizagem em Educação Matemática* (pp. 93–132). Universitária UFPE.

Gutstein, E., Lipman, P., Hernandez, P., & de los Reyes, R. (1997). Culturally relevant mathematics teaching in a Mexican American context. *Journal for Research in Mathematics Education, 28*(6), 709–737.

Hull, C. H. (1914). The service of statistics to history. *Publications of the American Statistical Association, 14*(105), 30–39.

Instituto Brasileiro de Geografia e Estatística. (2012 April 19). *Indígena - Censo 2010*. Instituto Brasileiro de Geografia e Estatística – IBGE. https://indigenas.ibge.gov.br/apresentacao-indigenas.html

Ireton, C., & Posetti, J. (2018). *Journalism, fake news & disinformation: Handbook for journalism education and training*. UNESCO Publishing.

Janata, N. E., & Anhaia, E. M. (2015). Escolas/Classes Multisseriadas do Campo: Reflexões para a formação docente. *Educação & Realidade, 40*(3), 685–704. https://doi.org/10.1590/2175-623645783

Kitchin, R. (2014). *The data revolution: Big data, open data, data infrastructures and their consequences*. Sage.

Kline, M. (1985). *Mathematics for the nonmathematician*. Dover.

Leal, C., & Andrade, L. (2013). Guerreiras: A força da mulher indígena. .

Lehrer, K., & Marek, J. C. (Eds.). (1997). *Austrian philosophy past and present. Essays in honor of Rudolf Haller* (Vol. 190). Boston studies in the philosophy of science. Kluwer.

Leti, G. (2000). The birth of statistics and the Origins of the New Natural Sciences. *Metron, 58*(3–4), 185–211.

Lima, R. C. C., Cavalcante, A. M. B., & Perez-Marin, A. M. (2011). *Desertificação e mudanças climáticas no semiárido brasileiro*. INSA-PB.

Madeiro, C. (2020). *Sob Bolsonaro, programa construiu menor número de cisternas de sua história*. Politica. Retreived September 30 at https://noticias.uol.com.br/politica/ultimas-noticias/2020/02/12/bolsonaro-menor-numero-cisternas-desde-origem-programa.htm?cmpid=copiaecola

Martins, M. N. P. (2018). Atitudes face à estatística e escolhas de gráficos por professores dos anos iniciais do Ensino Fundamental. *Repositório da Universidade de Lisboa*. https://repositorio.ul.pt/handle/10451/36928.

McKnight, C. (1990). Critical evaluation of quantitative arguments. In G. Klum (Ed.), *Assessing higher-order thinking in mathematics* (pp. 169–185). American Association for the Advancement of Science.

McKnight, C., Kallman, C. & Fisher, M. (1990). Task analyses of critical evaluations of quantitative arguments: first steps in critical interpretation of graphically presented data. In *Proceedings of Annual Meeting of American Educational Research Association*, Boston (pp. 1–22).

Ministério da Educação. (1998). *Referencial Curricular Nacional para as escolas indígenas - RCNEI*. MEC.

Monteiro, C. (2005). *Investigating critical sense in the interpretation of media graphs* [PhD thesis, The University of Warwick]. University of Warwick publications services and WRAP. http://wrap.warwick.ac.uk/73122/

Monteiro, C., & Ainley, J. (2004). Exploring the complexity of the interpretation of media graphs. In O. McNamara & R. Barwell (Eds.), *Research in mathematics education* (Vol. 6, pp. 115–128). BSRLM.

Monteiro, C., & Ainley, J. (2007). Investigating the interpretation of media graphs among student teachers. *International Electronic Journal of Mathematics Education, 2*, 187–207.

Monteiro, C., Carvalho, L., & François, K. (2013). The teaching of mathematics in rural schools in Brazil: What teachers say. In M. Berger, K. Brodie, & V. Frith et al. (Eds.). *Proceedings of the Seventh International Conference on Mathematics Education and Society*. Vols. 1 and 2, Book Series: Mathematics Education and Society (pp. 400–409). Cape Town, APR 02–07, 2013.

Nascimento, R. N. F., Quadros, M. T., & Fialho, V. (2016). Interculturalidade Enquanto Prática na Educação Escolar Indígena. *Anthropologica, 27*(20), 87–217.

Nemeth, E., & Stadler, F. (Eds.). (1996). *Encyclopedia and utopia: The life and work of Otto Neurath (1882–1945)* (Vol. 4, Vienna Circle Institute Yearbook). Kluwer.

Neurath, M., & Cohen, R. S. (Eds.). (1973). *Otto Neurath: Empiricism and sociology: Vol. 1. Vienna circle collection*. Reidel.

Oliveira, S. A. P. (2016). *Educação estatística em escolas do povo Xukuru do Ororubá.* [Master Dissertation, The Federal University of Pernambuco]. Attena UFPE digital repository. https://repositorio.ufpe.br/handle/123456789/18717

Oliveira, S., Carvalho, L., Monteiro, C., & François, K. (2018). Collaboration with Xukuru teachers: Reflecting about statistics education at indigenous schools. *Revista de Educação Matemática e Tecnológica Iberoamericana – EM TEIA, 9*(2), 1–15. https://doi.org/10.36397/emteia.v9i2.237665

Oppenheim, P., & Putnam, H. (1958). *Unity of science as a working hypothesis. Minnesota studies in the philosophy of science* (Vol. 2). University of Minnesota Press.

Ottaviani, M. G. (1991). A history of the teaching of statistics in higher education in Europe and the United States, 1600 to 1915. In R. Morris (Ed.), *Studies in mathematics education. The teaching of statistics* (Vol. 7, pp. 243–252). UNESCO.

Philipp, R. A. (2007). Mathematics teachers' beliefs and affect. In F. K. Lester Jr. (Ed.), *Second handbook of research on mathematics teaching and learning* (pp. 257–315). NCTM.

Plataforma Semiáridos América Latina (2020, April 21). *Un ambicioso plan pro semiáridos en alianza con fida*. https://www.semiaridos.org/noticias/un-ambicioso-plan-pro-semiaridos-en-alianza-con-fida/

Porter, T. M. (1986). *The rise of statistical thinking 1820–1900*. Princeton University Press.

Queiroz, T., Monteiro, C., Carvalho, L., & François, K. (2017). Interpretation of statistical data: The importance of affective expressions. *Statistics Education Research Journal, 16*(1).

Quetelet, A. (1835). *Sur l'homme et le développement de ses facultés ou Essai de physique sociale*. Bachelier.

Reis, E. S. (2020). Educação contextualizada e educação glocal: pertencimento na mundialização ou formação para uma cidadania planetária. *ComSertões, 8*, 55–65. https://doi.org/10.36943/comsertoes.v8i1.8720

Ribeiro, K., Sousa-Neto, E. R., Carvalho Junior, J. A., Lima, J. R. S., Menezes, R. S. C., Duarte-Neto, P. J., Guerra, G. S., & Ometto, J. P. H. B. (2016). Land cover changes and greenhouse gas emissions in two different soil covers in the Brazilian Caatinga. *Science of the Total Environment, 571*, 1048–1057.

Rodrigues, A. D. (2005). Sobre as línguas indígenas e sua pesquisa no Brasil. *Ciência e Cultura, 57*(2), 35–38.

Roth, W., & Bowen, G. (2001). Professionals read graphs: A semiotic analysis. *Journal for Research in Mathematics Education, 32*(2), 159–194.

Rumsey, D. J. (2002). Statistical literacy as a goal for introductory statistics courses. *Journal of Statistics Education, 10*(3). https://doi.org/10.1080/10691898.2002.11910678

Schiller, A. & Engel, J. (2018). The importance of statistical literacy for democracy – A civic-education through statistics. In P. Kovács (ed.) Challenges and innovations in statistics education. *Proceedings of Challenges and Innovations in Statistics Education Multiplier Conference of ProCivicStat*. University of Szeged, ISBN 978-963-306-575-4.

Silva, R. M. A. (2006). Entre o Combate e a Convivência com o Semiárido: transições paradigmáticas e sustentabilidade do desenvolvimento. [Doctoral thesis, Universidade de Brasília]. Repositório institucional da UnB. https://repositorio.unb.br/handle/10482/2309

Silva, E. (2017). *Xukuru: memórias e história dos índios da serra do Ororubá (Pesqueira/PE), 1950–1988* (2nd ed.). UFPE.

Silva, E., & Garcia, A. D. V. (2019). Discutindo os protagonismos indígenas na aula de história. *Fronteiras: Revista Catarinense de História, 34*, 61–75. https://doi.org/10.36661/2238-9717. 2019n3201107

Silva, J. M. C., Leal, I. R., & Tabarelli, M. (2017). *Caatinga: The largest dry forest region in South America*. Springer. https://doi.org/10.1007/978-3-319-68339-3

Stamhuis, I. H. (1992). De 'probabilistic revolution' in de wetenschappen. *Gewina, 15*, 141–152.

Stigler, S. M. (2000). *The history of statistics. The measurement of uncertainty before 1900*. Belknap Harvard.

Sudene. (2018 April 2). N*ova delimitação Semiárido. Ministério da Integração Nacional, Superintendência do Desenvolvimento do Nordeste*. https://www.gov.br/sudene/pt-br/centrais-de-conteudo/relao-de-municpios-semirido-pdf.

Swatton, P., & Taylor, R. (1994). Pupil performance in graphical tasks and its relationship to the ability to handle variables. *British Educational Research Journal, 20*(2), 227–243.

Tandoc, E., Jr., Lim, W. Z., & Ling, R. (2018). Defining 'fake news': A typology of scholarly definitions. *Digital Journalism, 6*(2). https://doi.org/10.1080/21670811.2017.1360143

Tripp, D. (2005). Action research: A methodological introduction. *Educação e Pesquisa, 31*(3), 443–466. https://doi.org/10.1590/S1517-97022005000300009

Van Bendegem, J. P., François, K., & Coessens, K. (2010). The good, the beautiful and the literate: Making statistics accessible for action. In P. Smeyers & M. Depaepe (Eds.), *Educational research. The ethics and aesthetics of statistics* (pp. 145–160). Springer.

Vygotsky, L. S. (1978). *Mind in society: The development of higher psychological processes*. Harvard University Press.

Wallman, K. (1993). Enhancing statistical literacy: Enriching our society. *Journal of the American Statistical Association, 88*(421), 1–8.

Warwickshire County Council. (2001). *Quality of life in Warwickshire*. Warwickshire County Council.

Watson, J. (1997). Assessing statistical literacy through the use of media surveys. In I. Gal & J. Garfield (Eds.), *The assessment challenge in statistics education* (pp. 107–121). IOS and Press International Statistical Institute.

Weiland, T. (2017). Problematizing statistical literacy: An intersection of critical and statistical literacies. *Educational Studies in Mathematics, 96*(1), 33–47. https://doi.org/10.1007/s10649-017-9764-5

Wild, C. J., & Pfannkuch, M. (1999). Statistical thinking in empirical enquiry. *International Statistics Review, 67*(3), 223–265. https://doi.org/10.1111/j.1751-5823.1999.tb00442.x

Willcox, W. F. (1938). The founder of statistics. *Revue de l'Institut International de Statistique/ Review of the International Statistical Institute, 5*(4), 321–328. https://doi.org/10.2307/1400906

Zieffler, A., Garfield, J., Delmas, R., Le, L., Isaak, R., Bjornsdottir, A., & Park, J. (2011). Publishing in SERJ: An analysis of papers from 2002–2009. *Statistics Education Research Journal, 10*(2), 5–26.

Chapter 21
Project-Based Learning with a Social Impact: Connecting Data Science Movements, Civic Statistics, and Service-Learning

Leid Zejnilović ⓘ **and Pedro Campos**

Abstract Ever since there has been an organized collection and use of data for informing decision making, there has been a debate about the extent to which these data have been put to the best use for improving social welfare in terms of general well-being of a community or an entire society. This chapter offers a contribution to that debate, showing how different facets of civic statistics can be translated into action that delivers social impact. We first introduce data movements and how they emerged as a response to the unmet need for data science services to scale social impact of nonprofit and governmental organizations. These movements focused on feasible hands-on projects which are simultaneously educational, impactful, and scalable. Their success is notable, and their operational model applicable in the context of formal educational organizations, as we show using two exemplary cases. The cases offer insights about how organizations can engage with society through civic action and applied data science to create new academic and training programs. Our intention is to share the lessons learned from the data movements and their interactions with educational institutions, also in the context of service-learning, to inspire others to create exciting, engaging educational programs with lasting social impact.

Keywords Project based learning · Data science for social good · DSSG · Data science · Machine learning · Data movements

L. Zejnilović (✉)
Nova School of Business and Economics, Nova University of Lisbon, Carcavelos, Portugal
e-mail: leid.zejnilovic@novasbe.pt

P. Campos
LIAAD-INESC TEC and University of Porto, Porto, Portugal
e-mail: pedro.campos@ine.pt

© Springer Nature Switzerland AG 2022
J. Ridgway (ed.), *Statistics for Empowerment and Social Engagement*,
https://doi.org/10.1007/978-3-031-20748-8_21

21.1   Introduction

How we teach statistics and analytics to new generations matters. It always did. But we never had such capacities as we do today to collect data, derive information out of the data, and put the derived information to a good use. Take mobile positioning data, for example. A few columns with information about longitude and latitude, time stamps, and the devices' unique identifiers for all the mobile devices in a region collected every few minutes could bring immense value. From that data we could derive information about mobility patterns, groupings of people, and time spending per person or for groups. Such information could, for example, inform city planners to discover the habits of the citizens, healthcare management in the context of disease spread, the tourism and hospitality industry in terms of investment potentials, or transportation companies to optimize service delivery. Until recently, we did not have the capacity to store that much mobile positioning data, process them in near-real time, and act upon the information generated. What is the implication of that new capacity on how and what we teach the new generations of students, and how can we improve existing practices? In short, there is a lot more we can do with data in almost every aspect of human life, and we can bring that diversity into our classrooms. The key arguments promoted in this chapter are that: (1) education should be closer to the real-world and unresolved, often unstructured and messy problems with social impact; (2) the students should directly be involved in solving such problems and interact with problem owners; (3) good and responsible use of data and information should be taught as part of the value system that guides decisions; and (4) students should be empowered to readily take up exciting challenges as they complete education. In simple terms, we should nurture the education that maximizes the positive social impact we produce with statistics, data science,[1] or artificial intelligence. These arguments and objectives are perhaps not new, but there are new opportunities to act upon them and improve what we as educators, practitioners, or citizens do to fulfil them. Arguably, formal education at all levels has not yet picked up sufficiently to gain from these opportunities. But as we show here, there are increasingly many opportunities and tools to accelerate the adoption and make the education process more effective and enjoyable for the teachers, learners, and the society. Before we delve into these opportunities, let us consider what history can teach us about the use of data for social good and why that topic is so important today.

Ever since there has been an organized collection and use of data for informing decision making, there has been a debate about the extent to which these data have been put to the best use for improving social welfare in terms of general well-being of a community or an entire society. The source of the problem is that different agents have different motivations and competences when it comes to collecting, processing, and acting upon data. Often, those who own and can access the data are

---

[1]Data science is the field of study that combines mathematics, statistics, programming skills, and domain knowledge to solve complex problems.

not necessarily the ones who can maximize their use. To better understand how the problem manifests itself, let us consider an example from the nineteenth century borrowed from a paper by Lynn McDonald (2001) about the early origins of evidence-based nursing. There, we find a quote from a letter to Benjamin Jowett, written by Florence Nightingale in 1891, where she laments the failure to take the advantage of data collected by government departments for decision making of societal interest:

> Our chief point was that the enormous amount of statistics at this moment available at their disposal (or in their pigeon holes which means not at their disposal) is almost absolutely useless. Why? Because the Cabinet ministers: their subordinates, the large majority of whom have received a university education, have received no education whatever on the point upon which all legislation and all administration must—to be progressive and not vibratory— ultimately be based. We do not want a great arithmetical law; we want to know what we are doing in things which must be tested by results.

Note that Nightingale was a pioneer of evidence-based nursing, and the first female fellow of the Royal Statistical Society, the organization that was established to advance the use of data for society (Ashby, 2019). One way to interpret the situation described in the quote above is to speculate that once government agencies collect data, there is little or no interest to explore the use of these data past their agencies' immediate needs and goals, effectively limiting the value that could be created with the data. But visionaries, like Florence Nightingale, seem to not easily accept the status quo. Perhaps Florence was intrinsically motivated to act as she did, but we wonder what is it that educational systems can do to imprint the importance of sharing data and acting upon them to inform and guide action, especially when that is in common interest to the general population?

It is important to raise this question as many would find the situation from the late nineteenth century quite relevant even today. However, there is a big difference between the time Nightingale writes about and present time: the interest in evidence-based decision-making has never been as high as it is today. This interest is propelled by an unprecedented amount of data being generated and systematically collected, affordable and constantly growing computational power, and increasingly sophisticated machine learning algorithms. The benefits of the newfound capacity to use data to guide and even autonomously make decisions at scale were first appropriated by profit-driven entities, like Yahoo, Google, Amazon, Facebook, and others (Agrawal et al., 2016; Davenport & Harris, 2005). As these entities sought to improve that capacity to gain competitive advantage and make profit, more people became aware of the usefulness of statistics, data science and the application of machine learning for solving pressing issues in our society, instigating stronger interest among public administration organizations to explore ways to improve decision-making (Catlett & Ghani, 2015).

The surge of interest for tackling social issues with evidence-based decision making based on credible data and bolstered with scientific methods has motivated different forms of action. One such form of action, elaborated on in this chapter, is manifested as the rise of what we refer to as *data movements*. Data movements are formal and informal communities of skilled individuals who work on improving the sharing and the use of data, on developing and implementing hands-on projects with social impact organizations, and who educate others to continue and extend that work. Here, we show how these movements quickly adapt through a learning-by-doing process, and how as they evolve, they deploy (and embody expertise in) what is presented in Chap. 3 as the facets of Civic Statistics. The second form of action is the one where the awareness, interest in, and drive for social impact is integrated into formal educational programs. This is of relevance for the chapter, as one of the main objectives of Civic Statistics is the empowerment of students to engage with society through statistics and, as Nightingale did, tackle social issues and improve decision-making at all levels, from the personal, through local, national, and international levels.

Hence, the purpose of this chapter is threefold. Firstly, it aims to contribute to the understanding of the relationship between Civic Statistics and the data movements. Data movements often have a strong but informal educational component. Their actions, projects, and programs can inform but also be integrated in the formal educational offering in the schools at all education levels. That information would be of great value to the institutions that are aligned with the core values of Civic Statistics, as we elaborate in the next sections. Secondly, this chapter offers insights which we hope will raise awareness and inspire others to consider new ways to engage with society through applied data science, in the context of education, civic action, or personal direct engagement with non-profit organizations. Thirdly, connecting these insights with the service-learning literature, we may expect that the positive consequence of such engagement is that people who take part in it are more likely to become active citizens (Doehler, 2018).

In the following sections, we first briefly describe how some of the major data movements came to exist, and what they are doing to transform non-profit and governmental organizations and foster the use of data science for achieving social impact. Next, we analyse the educational modus operandi of one of these data movements, followed by a discussion about the relationship between data movements and Civic Statistics. We then provide an example of how an educational institution adopted and adapted the lessons learned by the data movement for designing a unique project-based learning specialization as part of a new Master program in Business Analytics. Finally, we conclude this chapter with a discussion on how other educators can make use of the knowledge generated by the data movements and the early adopters of that knowledge, and the commonalities and differences of these approaches compared to what we know from the service-learning literature.

21.2 The Rise of the Communities of Data Science for Social Impact

Several global communities have emerged over the past decade to foster the use of data science for creating measurable social impact, like DataKind,[2] Data Science for Social Good,[3] GovLab,[4] AI for Good,[5] Data.org,[6] and others. These grassroot initiatives came to exist led by what Verba et al. (1995) refer to as *a good cause* to be involved in: help non-profit and governmental organizations improve their impact with data, by helping them to understand their performance, make better decisions, become more efficient with their existing resources, and understand how and where to expand their activities. The origins of these communities are different. A few started from universities as projects led by one or more faculties, like Data Science for Social Good, GovLab and Data Collaboratives, or AI for Good. Some, like DataKind, started as spontaneous ideas that attracted the interest of people, and around which sizable communities were built and maintained over time. Others, such as Data.org, are a result of premeditated action of influential individuals or groups to enact a change.

Regardless of their origins, the proposition these organizations made is simple and very appealing—make an impact by solving a real-world problem with data, and by doing that, develop skills of those in charge to adopt, adapt, and further develop the solutions. By helping the adoption of data science in non-profit and governmental organizations, the data movements hoped to see the productivity gains that learning-by-doing mechanism (Arrow, 1962) would eventually create. That proposition and aspiration has proven to be extremely attractive. Thousands of data scientists, ranging from students with affinity towards machine learning, self-taught data scientists, to senior experts in machine learning and consultancy from all over the world have offered help and invested their leisure time to be part of what has been perceived as a game-changer for our society. As an exemplar, we choose the story of the beginning of DataKind.

In October 2020, during a webinar,[7] Jake Porway told a story how his blog post (Porway, 2011), written while he was still a data scientist at The New York Times R & D Lab, transformed his life. He felt inspired at a conference, listening to a speaker holding a hard disk and saying that she has all the data from the health clinics in Uganda on a drive, but she does not know what can be done with it. Jake later saw a data scientist talking to her, and in 15 min explaining which questions she can ask and how to answer them, practically opening her eyes to the world of possibilities

---

[2]https://www.datakind.org/

[3]https://www.datascienceforsocialgood.org/

[4]https://datacollaboratives.org/ and https://www.thegovlab.org/

[5]https://ai4good.org/

[6]http://data.org/

[7]The webinar was part of DSSG Iberia Summit, available on YouTube: https://youtu.be/WTj8x_SWpGM

she was not aware of. A short conversation between a problem holder and expert knowledge holder may have created a tremendous impact. That revelation left a strong imprint on Jake, a Ph.D. in Machine Learning. He thought of a sentence he heard, how helping solve pressing social issues is a better use of the advanced skills he and others like him hold than nudging people to click on ads. Hence, his blog post made a proposition to create something like "data without borders", for data scientists like him to meet and consult non-profit and other organizations that may create social impact. Within weeks there were thousands of people signing-up to meet and help, technology influencers spreading the idea on their social networks, and everyone pushed to create a movement. Fast forward a decade, and DataKind, as the organization was named, is a global organization, formally established as a non-profit association, with funding to facilitate the execution of applied projects that reach the implementation phase, and with many volunteers working with non-profit and governmental organizations to increase the adoption of data science. Their activities include: (1) community events, where problem holders ask experts for advice, (2) Data Dives, where over a short-period of time group of volunteers do initial data analysis and prototyping, and (3) Data Corps, long-term projects conducted by pro-bono data scientists and DataKind partners.

Let us take a moment here, to recall from the Introduction Nightingale's comment about the (useless) data in "pigeonholes", and compare it with Jake's story about the data from health clinics in Uganda. The grand difference in the latter story is the action of those with data to proactively seek external expertise to explore the use of their data beyond the original reasons to collect them. The unorthodoxy of that exploration, making an open call at a large conference, was effective to help Jake realize the scale of the problem and to act towards providing systematic help to more organizations who are in a similar situation.

Another movement, Data Science for Social Good (DSSG) had a rather different beginning. In 2012, after serving as a chief scientist in what Domingos (2015) refers to as one of the largest ever data-driven presidential campaigns (Obama for America, 2012), Rayid Ghani moved to the University of Chicago to use his skills for making a social impact. There, he and his colleagues launched the Data Science for Social Good Summer Fellowship with generous support from the Eric and Wendy Schmidt Foundation. The first enactment of the fellowship programme was held in 2013, repeating annually ever since at several locations in the USA and Europe. The characteristic property of this 12-week fellowship is the focus on solving problems that matter, which both present a reasonable challenge to a group of excellent fellows and guarantee a commitment from the partner organization that has an interest in solving the problem. By the end of the fellowship, the fellows and partners usually develop a testable prototype of a machine learning system, an understanding of how to scope and develop data science projects, and a good sense of what the application of data science in the real world looks like and how it can be managed. As it was the case of DataKind, the fellowships attracted a huge interest, with about a thousand of applicants annually, and the program had an acceptance rate of about five percent. Fast forward about a decade since the first fellowship; now DSSG is formally

Table 21.1 Learning activities of the Data for social impact movements

Example of the learning activity	Example of how educational institutions can adapt the learning activity to their needs (We invite you to think of other ways these examples could help you enrich your classes and inspire new generations)
Data Kind's Community events are occasional networking events, where experts meet problem holders, to identify potentials for the application of data science in an informal environment	Engaging students to interact with problem holders but also experts, and learn about solving real-world problems, so that they could reflect how the knowledge they have or are acquiring can be put to good use
Data Kind's Data Corps is a program where pro-bono data scientists are partnered with social change organizations (e.g., NGOs, community hospitals) to mentor them over a long time to transform their work	Partnering pro-bono data scientists and students, again in the context of a real-world problem, so that students can learn new things but also build an awareness of the challenges on a path to a problem solution, mentored by professionals
DSSG Summer Fellowship is a 12-week long integrated project-based learning event, where the fellows work on a scalable real-world project with social impact, and while doing it, learn new, and improve their existing, skills mentored by experienced professionals	Creating programs that have real-world problem solving as a backbone, building on top of that some educational content that equips the students with the knowledge for this and other problems where they can apply the learning
Data.org organizes grant-awarding competitions like the Inclusive Growth and Recovery Challenge to push the knowledge and application boundaries, build solutions and develop organizational capacity	Challenging students to tackle problems with societal impact in a form of an institution-wide competition, giving public recognition to the winning team
NYU GovLab started data collaboratives, building shared data sources to enable more and richer applications of data science	Developing tutorials and courses about the importance of shared data sources, the associated risks and opportunities, and understanding the value of shared and linked data for problem solving and societal resilience

established as a foundation, with many projects conducted across the globe, and a large alumni community.

Common to these two initiatives, but also to other data for social impact movements, is the project-based learning component; the focus on real world projects as part of the aspiration to bring about structural changes to the social impact organizations. These movements are organized communities which mobilise resources and take direct action to achieve their objectives (Moro, 2010), which are effective civic actions. Table 21.1 serves to help in the understanding of what the organizations like DataKind or DSSG are doing, and challenges the readers to think how they could adapt or integrate some of these activities into their environment to enrich what we do in other programs, schools, or universities.

Let us, in the next section, take a deeper look into a non-degree granting educational program by one of these data movements, Data Science for Social Good.

21.3 DSSG Summer Fellowship: A Project-Based Learning Data Science Program

21.3.1 What Is DSSG Summer Fellowship?

The Data Science for Social Good (DSSG) Summer Fellowship follows the integrated project-based learning approach. It typically brings graduate students, 20–40 fellows selected from a pool of about 1000 candidates, with backgrounds in computational and quantitative disciplines including computer science, statistics, math, engineering, psychology, sociology, economics, and public policy. The fellows work in small, cross-disciplinary teams on social good projects spanning education, health, energy, transportation, criminal justice, social services, economic development, and international development in collaboration with global government agencies and non-profits (DSSG, 2020). This work is done under close and hands-on mentorship from full-time, dedicated data science mentors as well as dedicated project managers with industry experience. The process, ideally, results in a cohort of highly trained fellows, improved data science capacity in the participating social good organizations, and high-quality data science tools that are ready for field trial at the end of the program. To achieve such an outcome, beyond the project work, the summer program features a series of workshops, tutorials, and ethics discussion groups based on data science for a social good curriculum designed to train the fellows in doing practical data science and artificial intelligence for social impact. DSSG may be seen as an approach to learning (and working with) data science. The example of DSSG aims to show initiatives can be scaled from a single problem to a broad project (see Chap. 16, where authors refer to the use of projects in the teaching of mathematics). We believe this example illustrates how ideas emphasized both in regular curricula and in other chapters in the book—such as modeling, teamwork, exploratory data analysis, and representations—can be taken to a higher level, and how this can also help to see how 'data science' and statistics can be introduced and made to serve the common good.

21.3.2 DSSG and Project Based Learning

Project-based learning is the guiding principle of the fellowship, as reflected in key properties typical for such learning (Society for Research into Higher Education, & Adderley 1975; Blumenfeld et al., 1991; Kokotsaki et al., 2016). The fellows are dealing with real-world problems, work goes on for considerable time and is done in teams, teaching staff are involved in an advisory role, there are direct and frequent interactions with project partners, the solutions of parts of a problem is often set by the fellows, and the final output is a testable model, an end product. The fellowship also promotes interdisciplinary work on data science and statistical studies, a well-recognized necessity for the era of big data (e.g., ASA, 2014). With numerous iterations over the years, a very comprehensive and focused DSSG Summer Fellowship curriculum has been developed and shared as an open-source *GitHub* repository.[8] Besides the common base of any data science curriculum, there are additional curricular units covering topics typical of social sciences, as well as ethics, privacy, and confidentiality issues. These additions were made as the fellowship is focused on social impact problems that require such knowledge.

Considering the list of skills needed for a data scientist who wants to work in social impact, compiled by the DSSG community (see Appendix A), one may perceive it as quite daunting. But the combination of the project-based learning approach and carefully designed lectures makes the task of equipping a cohort of motivated individuals with the foundation for the acquisition of these skills feasible over a relatively short amount of time. That is precisely why project-based learning is essential, to provide the context that renders having all the different skills essential. Note that for the fellowship, a threshold skills level is required of all accepted fellows and includes moderate programming skills, some understanding of machine learning algorithms and of the modelling process. Such a threshold ensures balanced progress of all the teams, and feasibility of the program goals.

The curriculum is designed to support the development and handover of the prototype of a system that embeds machine learning models. The project development consists of four general stages: (1) project definition and data discovery; (2) code pipeline development; (3) communication and transition planning; (4) presentations and transition. The first stage is critical, as it serves to frame the problem and map it from its operational context to the domain of machine learning; it is essential to assess the feasibility and potential impact of the project from the outset. Although the fellowship planning team spends about 7 months enticing potential partners' interest, doing initial scoping, and verifying the existence of useful data, the fellowship usually starts at a point where the fellows are required to complete the project scoping. By doing so, they experience the messiness of the real-world, the difficulties of getting access to data, legal hurdles and considerations, and the process of articulating the problem in a written document to converge on shared conceptions and expectations with the project partners.

Another advantage of project-based learning is the opportunity for the fellows to engage in deep conversations with the partner about the future use of the system that they committed to co-design and then test at the end of the program. During that process, all sides can build a better understanding of the tool that needs to be made, and to benchmark against that understanding at every stage of the project development. Most importantly, during project scoping, the fellows engage in deliberation about ethical aspects of the data collection and the proposed solutions, data privacy, fairness, and issues common to machine learning algorithms like interpretability of the outputs and understanding and explaining the machine learning models. Some examples of project scoping are available in the DSSG Hitchhikers Guide.[9]

---

[8] https://github.com/dssg/hitchhikers-guide

[9] https://dssg.github.io/hitchhikers-guide/curriculum/scoping/overview/

It is during this phase that most of the preparatory lectures are delivered as practical classes. These include programming for data analysis with best practices for collaborative work, open-source databases and SQL, security and practices aiming to preserve data privacy, soft skills for working with partners, the machine learning pipeline, project deliverables, and ethics. Most of the classes are relevant for immediate actions that teams need to undertake, reinforcing the stickiness of the knowledge transferred. A sample of the curriculum, with a timeline of when to introduce what, is provided in Appendix B.

At the second stage of project development—code pipeline development—the fellows get to work with messy and complex data, common to most data science projects. At this stage, it is expected that they deepen their understanding of the processes that generated the data, perform exploratory data analysis, and prepare the data for the modelling stage. While data science projects are most commonly associated with the application of machine learning algorithms, the data preparation—or Extract, Transform, and Load (ETL)—process is arguably equally important. In many courses the students receive curated data to reduce complexity and reach the intended point faster. The reality of ETL, however, is burdened with many imperfections that invoke decisions which may influence the quality of the outcomes and may often have ethical implications. For example, the data may have many missing values regarding families with economic difficulties; excluding observations related to that sub-population during training may introduce bias into the resulting model.

21.3.3 The (Data Science) Project Pipeline

Over 8 weeks, the fellows are expected to build a functional project code pipeline (see Fig. 21.1), automating the whole process from the data preparation (or ETL), over model development, to presenting the model outputs in a suitable form, whilst carefully registering all decision choices to enable reproducible results. Each layer (or stage) of the pipeline is a program, a computer code that receives input information (e.g., data or a model) and executes operations to transform the input into a suitable output for the next stage. The ETL stage of the pipeline is a program or a collection of smaller programs that perform data collection from different sources, data quality verification, and transformation of the data into a single table or a form suitable (output) for the modelling stage. The output contains the original features (properties, variables) and engineered features (e.g., calculated values, transformed variables), and has the form that corresponds to the type of analysis intended, like prediction, explanation, recommendation, or optimization. In the modelling stage, the program contains the specification of all the machine learning algorithms, the variation of their parameters that should be used to train a set of models, how the data set is divided for training, validation, and testing, and which are the metrics that should be produced to compare different models. The result of this process is a set of models stored on a file system in a suitable format (e.g., as a python's pickle file—.

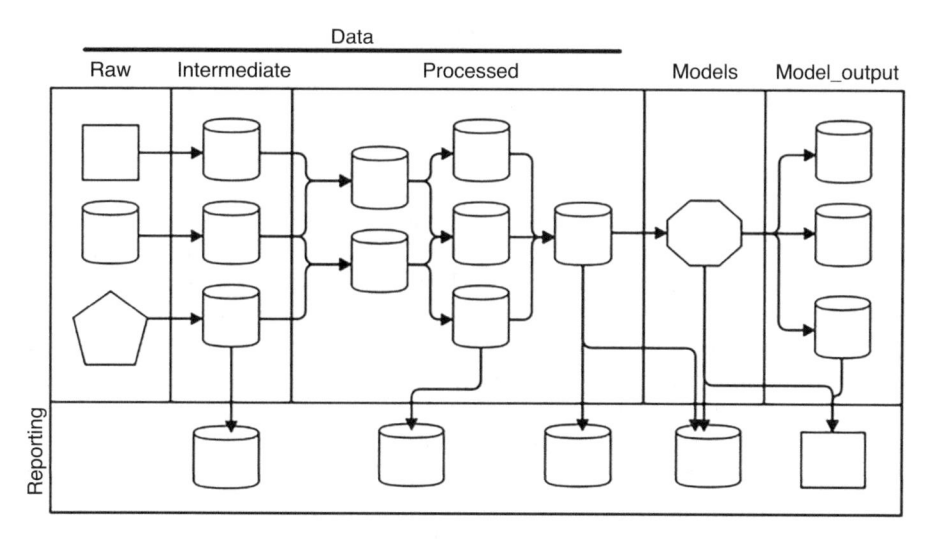

Fig. 21.1 Project pipeline, graphic representation. Adapted from: DSSG Hitchikers' Guide

pkl, or open neural network exchange format—.onnx) along with information about models and parameters used for their training. The model output layer stores the models' performance matrix, models selection, and the model predictions. The advantages of having a well-designed project pipeline include easier debugging, quality assurance, maintenance of the final product and its future improvement. For example, if one of the data sources changes, it is easy to fix that part of the pipeline with minor changes and little or no impact on other parts; or, when doing model re-training, in the modelling part of the pipeline, one can easily add a new algorithm and its parameters to the list of the machine learning algorithms. Finally, such a design enables reproducible outcomes and a performance comparison of multiple models against metrics of interest when deciding on the optimal solution.

During the fellowship, the fellows typically build the entire project pipeline, to experience decision making about the cohorts, units of analysis, outcomes, features to generate, model training, evaluation, and how to audit the results. Over the years, the DSSG community has understood that there are patterns of errors that new and even some experienced data scientists make when making those decisions, which could be avoided with proper guidance. That understanding motivated the development of a set of open-source tools that are freely available on the DSSG github repository. Triage,[10] an end-to-end predictive risk modelling system, is an example of the toolkit developed by the community. While Triage is not used during the fellowship, for educational reasons, it offers a handy checklist of design elements for the development of the project pipeline.

An advantage of having several teams working on projects during the program is the opportunity to subject design choices to scrutiny with respect to potential ethical

---

[10]https://dssg.github.io/triage/

consequences in different contexts. Through guided group discussions, the fellows share their views and exchange thoughts about this important matter and discuss potential remedies. These discussions include deliberations about whether using features (predictive variables) like race or economic conditions introduces biases, or how end users will use the tool, and how different design choices might contribute to better quality decision making by the action takers, in terms of effectiveness, fairness, or ethics. Also, the fellows engage intensively in discussing with project partners about the metrics that they will use. For example, in a project with the Portuguese Public Employment Services (PES), the objective was to predict the risk of a registrant becoming long-term unemployed, staying unemployed for 12 months or more. Two metrics were considered for model selection, *precision* (of the identified positive how many were indeed positive) and *recall* (of all positive how many were identified) at k% of the unemployed population. Optimizing at k% of a population, as explained by Ghani and Schierholz (2020), is a common metric when there are internal resource constraints. At PES, there is a limit on how many services can be given to the citizens at a given time. That means that in the model selection, if one takes precision@k% as the selection metric, the choice falls on the model that, when all the cases are scored and ranked with respect to the risk, has the best precision at the top k% of the population. What are the consequences of the choice of metrics? Choosing recall means that we give preferences to finding more people, and that the possible cost of erroneously selecting also non-positive cases is not as important as finding positive cases. But in the case of the public employment services project, it was considered more important that among those that receive the services there are as many individuals that are likely to be long-term unemployed as possible (precision). In other words, to have as many as possible individuals who really need help among those to whom the help is offered.

The modelling and the model output presentation usually finishes sometimes close to the end of the fellowship. The third stage of the DSSG summer fellowship—communication and transition planning—usually starts in parallel to the second stage, halfway through the fellowship. Most of the technically oriented fellows benefit from external training about articulating the complex work being done during the summer so that it is comprehensible to a general audience. Around the 9th week, the fellows, along with the project partner, start planning the transition process that happens in the last week of the project. The official closure of the fellowship is marked by a public ceremony, during which the fellows give short oral presentations of each project, followed by a poster and networking session.

21.3.4 Fellowship Trends and Outcomes

As the reader may deduce from the descriptions above, the fellowship is quite intensive and a laborious endeavour for all the stakeholders. It requires careful planning before, and close coordination during, the summer. But the richness of the experience offers a unique opportunity for multidisciplinary learning for everyone involved. By going through the process, the non-profit and governmental organizations learn how to plan and execute data science projects and obtain valuable pilot projects to test. The fellows learn the same, but also obtain additional advanced training in cloud computing, programming, databases, machine learning, presentation and public speaking, managing relationships with partners, and teamwork—all through a practical experience of a completed project. DSSG thus offers project-based learning, and teamwork with the ability to bring together different skills to solve a specific and real problem for a community that needs help. The combination of the project-based learning approach and carefully designed lectures provides enough skills for the students to acquire competences over a relatively short amount of time. And that is precisely why project-based learning is essential.

Iterating the fellowship over the years, two important trends were observable. The first trend was the growth of the number of applicants, indicating a stable demand for the project-based learning proposition of the fellowship. The feedback collected from the fellows was consistent; project-based hands-on learning and the opportunity to make an impact on society with data science are the principal drivers for applying and spending their time in the fellowship. The second trend is the growth of the number of academic institutions interested in hosting the fellowship, indicating the potential for scaling up the impact. However, academic institutions are rooted in the practices of academic degree-granting programs with credit transfer systems in place. Hence, they are hardly the easiest choice for programs like the DSSG fellowship. The financial burden and practice orientation with unclear opportunities for research opportunities often renders the initial enthusiasm for the program ephemeral among university professors. The latter issue, of uncertainty regarding scientific and research opportunities of the projects, has been identified as one of the earliest and strongest sources of criticism of project-based learning in academic institutions (Heitmann, 1996).

We provide an example of how to integrate the lessons from programs like the DSSG Summer Fellowship into an educational institution in Sect. 21.4. But first we will analyse the relationship between this program and Civic Statistics in more detail.

21.4 The Relationship Between Civic Statistics and Data Movements Through the Case of DSSG Summer Fellowship

One of the main objectives of Civic Statistics is the empowerment of students to engage with society through statistics and, as Nightingale did, tackle social issues to achieve a lasting impact. In support of such empowerment, The GAISE Report (2016) argued that statistics should be taught as an investigative process of problem-solving and decision-making, providing students with complex multivariable models and statistical learning experiences. Furthermore, to enhance the learning, teaching should be accompanied by cases based on real data with a context and purpose, fostering active learning and the use of technology to explore concepts and analyse the data.

A prerequisite for meaningful and effective teaching of Civic Statistics is that examples and activities used in the classroom are set in realistic social contexts (see Chap. 3). There are many exemplary cases of such a practice. Take for example the National Action Civics Collaborative program which aims to improve youth civic engagement through the "Action Civics"[11] initiative (Center for Universal Education at the Brookings Institution, 2017). This initiative nurtures a student-centered, project-based approach to civics education. Students develop personal agency and civic knowledge by acting toward solving real-world problems in their own lives and their communities. Dewar et al. (2011), describe an approach to incorporating a civic engagement component into a quantitative literacy (QL) course and the resulting gains in student learning. Extended group projects involved local community issues that students could investigate using the mathematical topics of the course. Compared to students enrolled in a standard QL course, the civic engagement component was associated with increased awareness of community issues, higher levels of confidence in their ability to respond to mathematical situations using course material, and students reporting learning non-mathematical skills. Another complementary literature stream, of service-learning corroborates those findings, and suggests a growing interest of educational institutions to integrate project-based learning that includes civic action within courses or groups of courses, as there is evidence of multiple positive effects on students and the society (Doehler, 2018). Service-learning is in fact an educational method which combines learning objectives with services to contribute with positive impact on the community (Knapp & Fisher, 2010), hence very relevant for and closely related with Civic Statistics.

To explore the link between data movements and Civic Statistics, let us consider the above described Data Science for Social Good Summer Fellowship program. It is an exemplary case of data movements which exhibits strong alignment with Civic Statistics over multiple dimensions. Consider, for example, one of the dimensions introduced in the conceptual model for Civic Statistics (Chap. 3), Engagement & Action. It refers to teaching that addresses the meaning for society and policy, and requires students to engage in critical evaluation and reflection. DSSG focuses on real-world projects as part of the aspiration to bring about a structural change to the social impact organizations. The projects where students work with data to improve or transform how services or help are delivered, like improving the provision of free legal aid for citizens in Uganda, or improving public employment services decision-making in Portugal, perfectly embody Civic Statistics objectives. Over the entire fellowship, the fellows are invited to not only develop a tool, but also to reflect upon the design choices and possible implications on the beneficiaries.

---

[11] https://actioncivicscollaborative.org/

Table 21.2 Correspondence between the Civic Statistics' recommendations and the characteristics of the DSSG summer fellowship

	Civic statistics' recommendations	DSSG summer fellowship
#1	Develop activities that promote engagement with societal issues and develop learners' critical understanding of statistics about key civic phenomena	Yes. Participants work directly with institutions on problems with social impact
#2	Use relevant data and texts, and highlight the multivariate, dynamic, and aggregated nature of social phenomena	Yes. Each project is scoped to be sufficiently complex to require the application of advanced methods and to be embedded in a complex social context, with messy and large datasets that reflect the common challenges for data scientists in their future jobs in social impact organizations
#3	Embrace technologies that enable rich visualizations and interactions with data about relevant social phenomena	Yes. Participants use data analytics/machine learning tools to visualize data, extract information, and do post hoc analysis regarding bias and fairness
#4	Adopt teaching methods to develop critical interpretation skills applicable to a wide variety of data and textual sources	Yes. Each group of fellows work on different problems, often requiring very different approaches and methods, and regularly exchange experiences for each project development stage
#5	Implement assessments that examine the ability to investigate and critically understand data, statistics findings, and messages about key social phenomena	Yes. Project partners provide a formal assessment of the project outcome and the interactions during the project. Additionally, there are continuous internal assessments in the form of feedback on each project stage's results, feedback from external experts, and, most importantly, continuous assessment of the results by the project partners
#6	Engage stakeholders at all levels in the process of systemic change designed to promote the understanding of Civic Statistics	Yes. All stakeholders are heavily engaged in project scoping, development, model performance evaluation, implementation, and impact assessment

The DSSG's project-based learning approach is aligned with the recommendations defined as a future agenda for action to promote understanding of Civic Statistics, as elaborated in Chap. 4. In Table 21.2, we offer a brief comparison of the characteristics of the DSSG summer fellowship against these recommendations.

If we accept that there is a practical value of the programs like the DSSG summer fellowship, that it is closely aligned with the Civic Statistics as a concept, to what extent is the fellowship concept transferable to formal educational programs? We answer this question by means of an example of such a transfer that occurred in Portugal. The example is provided to demonstrate the opportunity for educational institutions to learn from data movements, but also to highlight the hurdles that arise when adapting learning initiatives from the outside into regular programs.

21.5 A Master Program with Program-Oriented Project-Based Learning

In 2018, the management of Nova School of Business and Economics (Nova SBE) started developing a curriculum for the Master in Business Analytics program. Positive experience with the DSSG Summer Fellowship inspired the school to co-create the program with the DSSG Foundation. The key challenge was to make the lessons from the fellowship permeate into an official academic program. The program was launched in September 2020, and one of major influences of the fellowship was a project-based learning specialization. In this section, we elaborate about the above-mentioned challenge and how it was resolved.

21.5.1 Bringing Management and Economics Closer to Data Science

As technology made it to the core of most leading businesses today, and machine learning offered an opportunity for achieving scale and convenience of service delivery, the rules of competition fundamentally changed (Ianisti & Lakhani, 2020). That triggered schools of business and economics across the globe to start entering what has been considered the turf of schools of engineering and information technology—machine learning and in general terms, data science. To distinguish themselves, business schools frame data-science-related programs as 'business analytics', emphasizing the nominal and practical distinction. Although it is plausible that some see boundaries between engineering and social science disciplines are blurring, they each have distinctive characteristics. The engineering side of data science is about developing tools, new algorithms, and methods. The social science side of data science is about the implications of those tools and the knowledge that engineers create on how we organize work, how we create and maintain effective organizations, the effect on individuals and the workforce, and how to make a functional and humane society. At Nova School of Business and Economics (Nova SBE), there was an understanding that the impact of data science and machine learning is likely to be transformative for society at an unprecedented scale. Hence, the school was eager to host the DSSG summer fellowship and run two editions, in 2017 and 2018, as experimental programs to internalize the knowledge, expand the understanding of the field, and extend its offer in a meaningful way.

To enable the effects of the fellowship and the shift towards data science to be felt at the institutional level, Nova SBE made three important steps. Firstly, it experimented with the introduction of courses like programming into undergraduate and Master programs, and programming, data curation, data visualization, and machine learning into the Master degree granting programs, as a specialization. These courses quickly entered the list of most popular courses. Secondly, it created a Data Science Knowledge Centre to concentrate the initiatives under a single umbrella and leverage the administrative investment to scale the activities. And thirdly, arguably the boldest step, was that the school embraced the proposal to develop a project-based learning program that adapts the summer fellowship approach to the degree-granting program.

21.5.2 Adapting DSSG Summer Fellowship to an Accredited Degree-Granting Program

Let us focus on the third step, describing how the adaptation from DSSG summer fellowship to a degree-granting program was operationalized. Project-based learning is a recurring idea whenever there is a discussion about curriculum that promotes motivation and thinking (Blumenfeld et al., 1991). It is particularly relevant for the teaching of data science, where the complexities associated with the development and implementation of machine learning models to inform or make decisions are unlikely to be effectively transmitted via traditional teaching formats (Rodolfa et al., 2019). The choice Nova SBE made for the project-based specialization is an adaptation of the concept that Morgan (1983) refers to as Project Orientation, where the entire curriculum philosophy of a programme of study revolves around a project that is conducted in parallel to the courses and spans the entire duration of the program. To the best of our knowledge, there is no similar academic program that starts with a project scoping, has credit based and transferable courses, places an emphasis on a project developed in a long-term team, with a committed partner that enters into the partnership with an intention to implement the project outcomes, and that is supported by technical mentors and project managers from the very beginning. There are good reasons for that; such a configuration adds to the complexity of the program, with coordination and material costs of an already costly and complex academic program. In addition, many academic institutions are balancing two important objectives, to educate (teaching) and to produce knowledge (research), which places an additional burden on the teaching staff. However, if carefully managed to the end, the benefits of the project-oriented program can outweigh material and other costs. It can result in a gratifying experience for the students and prepare them to be effective on their job, which is a major objective for our higher education institution.

It is common knowledge that most pre-experience students exiting schools are viewed as lacking experience. As Balzotti and Rawlins (2016) report, students often have difficulties applying the learning from a course into their other activities. The project-based learning approach offers an opportunity to immediately apply the learning from the courses by solving a practical problem, and in that way reinforcing and extending the knowledge acquired. In addition, they gain all the other skills typically acquired during the DSSG summer fellowship—understanding of the complexities of real-world projects and how to deal with them, maintaining functional relationships with project partners, working in teams over an extended period, communication and presentation skills, and if successful, the students have a chance to pilot test the end product they develop, the model. Since the project work lasts for about 12 to 16 months, almost the entire time to complete the Master degree program, there is sufficient time to build a prototype, design and implement a pilot test, and analyse the results of the system in use—an invaluable skill for entry into the modern age workforce.

The integration of this type of project-based learning into university courses is a challenging task. That is why most of the existing applications of project-based learning are located within a single course or a Master degree requirement like internships or capstone projects (Hydorn, 2007). The program-oriented project-based learning, as we refer to it in this text, is conceptualized as a specialization within a new Master in Business Analytics. The local accreditation institution imposed certain requirements for a program to be officially recognized and offered on the market, which includes the number of credit points allocated to obligatory courses, electives, modules, and minimal project time. The obligatory courses are, as in the fellowship or other data science programs, those that equip candidates from both engineering and social science backgrounds with skills to collect, process, and visualize data, work with databases, and engage in statistical thinking and data-driven decision-making, machine learning, ethics, governance of organizational data, impact evaluation, and project management. The advantage of being in a school of business and economics is the abundance of elective courses which allow students to deepen their understanding of the operational context and choose topics of their interest, like healthcare, finance, policy, innovation, strategy, leadership, econometrics, and others. In the project-based specialization, it is suggested that the elective courses are project-related. A drawback of a business school is the lack of deep technical courses, which is why the Master program is offered jointly with the School of Science and Technology of Nova University of Lisbon, which adds more technical courses to the portfolio. The Master in Business Analytics program can be either taken in a traditional form of courses that are followed by the final project, or as the program-oriented PBL specialization.

This specialization is a three-way partnership, among the students, educators, and the partner. An important advantage is that the program brings the additional capacity to operationalize complex projects and build research upon them. It has a potential to solve one of the limitations of the DSSG Summer fellowship which stops after 12 weeks, leaving the project partner to find funds or internally conduct the testing and further tuning and development. With up to 16 months available for the project, although part time work, there is a possibility to complete the full cycle of prototyping, testing, and implementation, and to observe measurable impact.

The critical challenge for running program-oriented project-based learning was the internal capacity for initiating and conducting activities regarding the three stages presented in Fig. 21.2. Running the DSSG summer fellowship was an excellent opportunity for building that capacity, and a deliberate effort was made to internalize the project scoping and management skills. Having highly trained and effective personnel brings the weight needed for having a good program. By limiting the number of the available project-based learning spots and the number of projects—up

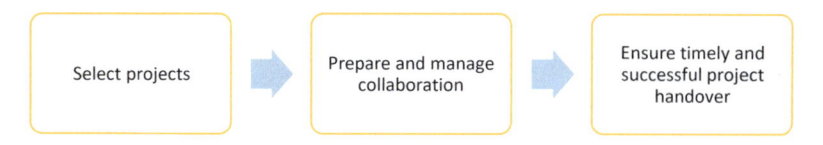

Fig. 21.2 Key stages of the full-program project-based learning (PBL)

to 20 students, with 4 students per team—and partnering with a large consultancy house for part-time project management and technical guidance, the challenge of running such a complex program has been made less burdensome.

The selection of the projects was completed on a partnership basis, as experimental projects by private, governmental, and non-profit organizations who agreed to support projects with data, personnel to hold regular meetings, and who were committed to test the prototype if verifiable and promising results are achieved. In addition, some partners agreed to sponsor the projects i.e., to cover some of the costs.

The Data Science Knowledge Centre has been an instrumental enabler of the project-based learning, as it hosts a team of trained personnel working full-time on projects associated with the centre. That way, they could also help in the stages depicted in Fig. 21.2, as their side task. The first cohort of the program started in the fall 2020. While it is too early to evaluate it, the program is an example of an academic institution internalizing the learnings from a data movement—Data Science for Social Good—and an experimentation with alternative approaches to teaching data science with an impact.

21.6 Conclusions and Recommendations

The example elaborated in the previous section demonstrates how a collaboration between an academic institution and a data movement can not only advance purposeful project-based interactions with society but can also help partners internalize practical data-science related skills and transfer relevant knowledge onto their other activities, like educational programs. The emphasis in this chapter is on collaborations that create social impact, as they are harder to start and maintain over time, unlike industry-academia relationships which are lucrative and desirable for all parties involved (Blumenthal et al., 1996). Although project-based collaborations among educational institutions and society are not rare, they are very much needed for a technology such as artificial intelligence if its benefits are to be materialized.

How can educational institutions like high-schools or universities contribute to the adoption of artificial intelligence and data-driven decision-making for social impact? To answer this question, let us consider three key functions of the institutions of higher education: (1) education, (2) knowledge production (research); (3) knowledge dissemination. Table 21.3 shows how interactions with data movements can contribute to improving these educational institutions' functions. The last column is a bridge illustrating alignment with Civic Statistics recommendations.

Table 21.3 Potential interactions between educational institutions and data for social impact movements

Type of academic activity	Example(s)	Collaboration with data movement	Potential output/benefits for the educational institution	Potential output/benefits for the data movements	Alignment with Civic Statistics Recommendations (see Table 21.2)
Education—courses	Social Impact assessment of data science projects; Data collaboratives	Proposal of courses, Participation in construction of syllabi, provision of lecturers or guest lectures	New courses in academic environments (high-schools or universities)	Raised awareness of social issues; educating potential volunteers, staff, and promotion of the movements' goals	#1
Education—teaching material	Content for teaching, case studies, relevant unresolved problems, methods, data	Execution of joint hands-on projects, identification and writing of case studies, development of new methods, collection and preparation of data	Relevant teaching material	Multiplication of impact through sharing; further development of the best practices; systematic preparation and use of didactic material	#1
Education—tools	Software packages (e.g. Triage, Aequitas, etc.); Frameworks	Co-development or adaptation of tools used by either of the parties for education	Tools used in practice that can help in enhancing the knowledge transfer to the students	As developers, further testing and adoption of the tool; as users, better tools to solve problems	#3
Research—topics	Identifying unresolved pressing problems	Engaging in joint problem solving and brainstorming	New and relevant problems with social impact, potentials for new and impactful research	New solutions and knowledge how to solve problems	#1
Research—data	Data from projects e.g. data from healthcare clinics in Uganda	Joint work on data collection, sharing agreements, and making data available and used for research	New data for research	New research and insights about the problems and solutions	#2
Research—example studies	A researcher with a theory may need a context	Collaborative studies with partners	Evidence for theories, knowledge creation	Knowledge and solutions to problems	#1, #2, #5

	and experimental playground				
Knowledge dissemination —meetings	Theoretical and practical contributions shared on community meetings	Joint events, or participation in meetings	Raising awareness regarding the knowledge created	New insights and learning	#5, #6
Knowledge dissemination —application/impact	Application of a theory, or a framework for problem solving	Making tools or knowledge available and applying it in practice	Enhancing impact of knowledge/research	Better knowledge about problems and solutions and more effective work	#5, #6

Many of the data movements' activities, mentioned in this chapter, can easily fit into typical educational programs with some effort and to the benefit of all the parties involved. The example of Nova SBE shows that the learning can be taken as far as informing the delivery format of a degree granting program. The important takeaway message of this chapter is that by leveraging civic action to use statistics, data science, and advanced machine learning for social impact, educational institutions may multiply positive effects and contribute to both more effective learning and better civic engagement. The civic action may be taken through the data movements, to promote awareness, interest in, and drive for social impact. It can also be taken by applying the concept of civic statistics in education, which has as one of the main objectives to empower the students to engage with society through the use of statistics and help solving burning social issues.

Often, and also notable in this chapter, we see different scholarly communities developing complementary and sometimes overlapping knowledge. It is critical, therefore, to unlock knowledge flows among these communities and amplify what is presumed to be the common objective. This chapter is an attempt to connect data movements and civic statistics, but also link in service-learning literature. Focusing on the latter, service-learning literature offers rich evidence that students involved in learning through services to community become more competent, skilful, active, and arguably more responsible citizens (e.g., McCarthy & Tucker, 1999; Blouin & Perry, 2009). That dimension is clearly aligned with both the activities of the above introduced Data Movements and Civic Statistics. One of the key points that distinguishes service-learning is what Furco (1996) refers to as active reflections along the service process, and a balance between the service and learning outcomes. The focus on social and community problems strongly links service-learning to civic action and civic statistics. Many authors define service-learning as course based (e.g., McCarthy & Tucker, 1999), and the models of integrating it in a course may vary from pure service-learning, through blends of non-service disciplinary content, to service internships (Hydorn, 2007). Narrowing the definition to the level of a course, in addition to the emphasis on the learning reflections and balancing of the service and learning outcomes gives the much-needed clarity of the concept and distinction from the other forms of experiential learning. Blouin & Perry (2009) suggest that service-learning as a form of experiential learning rests upon the idea of three stakeholders or beneficiaries, the students, universities, and the communities. Albeit, as they find, the impact on the communities is hindered by the poor fit of the course and the organizational objectives, and lack of communication between the instructor and the organizations. We see that among the activities organized by data movements, program-oriented project-based learning as implemented by Nova SBE is closest to solving those constraints, by introducing the orchestrator, or project manager, and careful project scoping that occurs before the program. Professionalization of the project management is costly, but brings the much-needed guidance to students' and consistency in orchestrating the work, especially given that the projects span multiple courses and semesters. Also, by doing so, students gain experiences that are similar to the situations in their future work environment.

This chapter proposes that there is a strong relationship between data movements, civic statistics, and service-learning, although they are better described as complementary. We offered examples and insights about the similarities and possible learning points from these literature streams and communities, hoping to unlock the knowledge flows among these communities and amplify the effects of the efforts invested to make a stronger social impact. And as the final takeaway, there is an abundance of tools, data, cases, and partnerships that data movements diligently work to create and establish, that many educators can access for free and consider using for teaching and learning purposes.

Appendix A: The List of Skills Required for Doing Data Science for Social Good, as Listed On DSSG Hitchhikers guide

Skills/Knowledge of	Function—to be able to
Programming	Write the code that instructs computers what to do
Computer Science	Understand the data structures and algorithms
Mathematics	Translate problems into mathematical terms
Statistics	Measure and understand how to deal with uncertainty
Machine Learning	Building models that predict or explain and learn over time
Social Sciences	Know how and when to claim causality, design and analyse experiments
Problem and Project Scoping	Translate ambiguous descriptions into meaningful goals, identify actions that make those goals achievable, the information that is required for taking action, and how data and analytics can help generating that information
Project Management	Make sure that a useful and high-quality solution is delivered to the partner on time.
Privacy and security	Keep private data of people and their needs confidential and secure
Ethics, fairness, bias, and transparency	Understand how the project may impact people's lives and manage negative impact, consider how the outcomes could be misused, analyse biases in the data and analysis and their implications, and make the work interpretable and transparent to the users and those who are impacted by it.
Communications	Communicate what is the work and how is it done to a broad audience
Social issues	Understand the issue that is being tackled in its present context and how it came to exist, and how the solution could be implemented effectively given the context.

Appendix B: An Example of the DSSG Summer Fellowship Curriculum (2019); Source DSSG. https://dssg.github.io/hitchhikers-guide/curriculum/sample/

Every week	Fellowship-wide Check-in (15–30 min in the morning)	*Short updates from every team*	*Deep dives— 2 teams every week*		• Code Review • External Talk • Ethics Discussions
Week 1	Software installation and check logins	• Prpject Scoping • How does a project go over the summer	• Technical Environment Setup, cmd line, workflow • git • Interacting with project partners	• Python for Data Analysis • ML Pipeline • Communications for the summer	Databases and SQL
Week 2	• Data Maturity Assessment • DSSG Project Deliverables • Ethics Overview	• more dbs and ETL Working in a team	• Good software practices • No deep dive—partner session	Data Exploration (two sessions)— viz., pandas, sql, spatial	
Week 3	• Policy Problem templates • Machine Learning Overview—formulation and validation	Intro to Social Sciences	• sql • Record linkage	• ML overview—validation • case study from previous dssg	
Week 4	• Machine Learning overview—methods • Non-technical session—elective	Causal Inference with Observational Data	Feature Engineering	• ML overview—methods • User interfaces and usability	
Week 5	Text Analysis	ML Pipelines—Deeper Dive	Feature Engineering workshop	Optimization	
week 6	• Model Validation • Model Interpretation	Communications—speaking	Audition and Overview of post modeling	Bias and Fairness	

(continued)

Week 7	Post-modeling Analysis	Causal Inference—experiments	Case Study	Post-Modeling Analysis	
Week 8	Recap of what needs to be done for the rest of the summer	Experimental design	technical session—elective		
Week 9	Recap of what needs to be done	Social Science methods	technical session—elective		
Week 10	Bias and Fairness in ML	Communications—writing	Image/Video analysis	Network Analysis	

References

Agrawal, A., Gans, J., & Goldfarb, A. (2016). The simple economics of machine intelligence. *Harvard Business Review*. Retrieved from https://hbr.org/2016/11/the-simple-economics-of-machine-intelligence

Arrow, K. J. (1962). The economic implications of learning by doing. *The Review of Economic Studies, 29*(3), 155–173.

ASA. (2014). *Curriculum guidelines for undergraduate programs in statistical science*. Retrieved July 13, 2021 from https://www.amstat.org/asa/files/pdfs/EDU-guidelines2014-11-15.pdf

Ashby, D. (2019). Pigeonholes and mustard seeds: growing capacity to use data for society. *Journal of the Royal Statistical Society. Series A: Statistics in Society, 182*(4), 1121–1137. https://doi.org/10.1111/rssa.12483

Balzotti, J., & Rawlins, J. D. (2016). Client-based pedagogy meets workplace simulation: developing social processes in the Arisoph Case Study. *IEEE Transactions on Professional Communication, 59*(2), 140–152. https://doi.org/10.1109/TPC.2016.2561082

Blouin, D. D., & Perry, E. M. (2009). Whom does service learning really serve? Community-based organizations' perspectives on service learning. *Teaching Sociology, 37*(2), 120–135. https://doi.org/10.1177/0092055X0903700201

Blumenfeld, P. C., Soloway, E., Marx, R. W., Krajcik, J. S., Guzdial, M., & Palincsar, A. (1991). Motivating project-based learning: sustaining the doing, supporting the learning. *Educational Psychologist, 26*(3–4), 369–398. https://doi.org/10.1080/00461520.1991.9653139

Blumenthal, D., Causino, N., Campbell, E., & Louis, K. S. (1996). Relationships between academic institutions and industry in the life sciences — An industry survey. *New England Journal of Medicine, 334*(6), 368–374. https://doi.org/10.1056/nejm199602083340606

Catlett, C., & Ghani, R. (2015). Big data for social good. *Big Data, 3*(1), 1–2. https://doi.org/10.1089/big.2015.1530

Center for Universal Education at the Brookings Institution. (2017). *Measuring global citizenship education: A collection of practices and tools.*

Davenport, T. H., & Harris, J. G. (2005). Automated decision making comes of age. *MIT Sloan Management Review*, (Summer).

Dewar, J., Larson, S., & Zachariah, T. (2011). Group projects and civic engagement in a quantitative literacy course. *PRIMUS, 21*(7), 606–637. https://doi.org/10.1080/10511970903579048

Doehler, K. (2018). Successful service-learning for statistics students studying survey sampling. *Statistics Education Research Journal, 17*(2), 82–103.

Domingos, P. (2015). *The master algorithm: how the quest for the ultimate learning machine will remake our world*. Basic Books.

DSSG. (2020). *DSSG summer fellowship*. Retrieved December 1, 2020, from https://www.dssgfellowship.org/

Furco, A. (1996). Service-learning: A balanced approach to experiential education. In *Expanding boundaries: Serving and learning*. Cooperative Education Association, Beltsville, MD.

GAISE College Report ASA Revision Committee (2016). *Guidelines for Assessment and Instruction in Statistics Education College Report 2016*. American Statistical Association. Online: https://www.amstat.org/asa/education/Guidelines-for-Assessment-and-Instruction-in-Statistics-Education-Reports.aspx

Ghani, R., & Schierholz, M. (2020). Chapter 7: Machine learning. In I. Foster, R. Ghani, R. S. Jarmin, F. Kreuter, & J. Lane (Eds.), *Big data and social science> data science methods and tools for research and practice*. Chapman and Hall/CRC.

Heitmann, G. (1996). Project-oriented study and project-organized curricula: A brief review of intentions and solutions. *European Journal of Engineering Education, 21*(2), 121–131. https://doi.org/10.1080/03043799608923395

Hydorn, D. L. (2007). Community service-learning in statistics: Course design and assessment. *Journal of Statistics Education, 15*(2), 1–8.

Ianisti, M., & Lakhani, K. R. (2020). Competing in the age of AI. *Harvard Business Review*, Jan–Feb.

Knapp, T. D., & Fisher, B. J. (2010). The effectiveness of service-learning: It's not always what you think. *The Journal of Experimental Education, 33*(3), 208–224.

Kokotsaki, D., Menzies, V., & Wiggins, A. (2016). Project-based learning: A review of the literature. *Improving Schools, 19*(3), 267–277. https://doi.org/10.1177/1365480216659733

McCarthy, A. M., & Tucker, M. L. (1999). Student attitudes toward service-learning: Implications for implementation. *Journal of Management Education, 23*(5), 554–573. https://doi.org/10.1177/105256299902300511

McDonald, L. (2001). Florence Nightingale and the early origins of evidence-based nursing. *Evidence-Based Nursing, 4*(3), 68–69. https://doi.org/10.1136/ebn.4.3.68

Morgan, A. (1983). Theoretical aspects of project-based learning in higher education. *British Journal of Educational Technology, 14*(1), 66–78. https://doi.org/10.1111/j.1467-8535.1983.tb00450.x

Moro, G. (2010). Civic action. In H. K. Anheier & S. Toepler (Eds.), *International encyclopedia of civil society*. https://doi.org/10.1007/978-0-387-93996-4_128

Porway, J. (2011). *Doing good with data – Data without borders*. Retrieved from https://www.datakind.org/blog/doing-good-with-data-data-without-borders/

Rodolfa, K. T., de Unanue, A., Gee, M., & Ghani, R. (2019). *A clinical approach to training effective data scientists*. ArXiv.

Society for Research into Higher Education, and, & Adderley, K. (1975). *Project methods in higher education*. Society for Research into Higher Education.

Verba, S., Lehman Schlozman, K., & Brady, H. E. (1995). *Voice and equality: Civic voluntarism in American politics*. Harvard University Press.

Chapter 22
Data Science, Statistics, and Civic Statistics: Education for a Fast Changing World

Jim Ridgway (ID), **Pedro Campos, and Rolf Biehler** (ID)

> *The field of Statistics is at a crossroads: we either flourish by embracing and leading Data Science or we decline and become irrelevant. In the long run, to thrive, we must redefine, broaden, and transform the field of Statistics.*
> National Science Foundation (2019, P. 5)

Abstract What is the relationship between data science, statistics, and Civic Statistics? Are they symbiotic, or are they in conflict? A graphic on the homepage of the American Statistical Association (https://www.amstat.org/ASA/about/home.aspx?hkey=6a706b5c-e60b-496b-b0c6-195c953ffdbc) reads *BIGTENT statistics+data science*, indicating their intended direction of travel—statistics and data science need to live together. Products of data science (including social media) have transformed modern life. We outline the idea of disruptive socio-technical systems (DST)—new social practices that have been made possible by innovative technologies, and which have profound social consequences—and we point to some examples of technologies that are, or have capacity to facilitate DST.

Civic Statistics aims to address pressing social issues, and data science has created new concerns and also new approaches to work on social issues. Here, we argue that this should go beyond simply addressing known problems, and should include empowering citizens to engage in discussions about our possible futures, including the regulation of potential and actual DST.

J. Ridgway (✉)
School of Education, University of Durham, Durham, UK
e-mail: jim.ridgway@durham.ac.uk

P. Campos
LIAAD-INESC TEC and University of Porto, Porto, Portugal
e-mail: pedro.campos@ine.pt

R. Biehler
Institute of Mathematics, Paderborn University, Paderborn, Germany
e-mail: biehler@math.upb.de

© Springer Nature Switzerland AG 2022
J. Ridgway (ed.), *Statistics for Empowerment and Social Engagement*,
https://doi.org/10.1007/978-3-031-20748-8_22

These are exciting times; there are new approaches to knowing about and understanding the world, many of them associated with data science, and students need to engage with these important epistemological issues as a key element in Civic Statistics skills.

Here, we relate features of data science to features of Civic Statistics, and to dimensions of knowledge relevant to Civic Statistics. From the viewpoint of Civic Statistics, we argue that we have a responsibility to prepare students for their roles as *spectators* (understanding the nature and potential of data science products in creating DST), and as *referees* (having a political voice about which DST are acceptable and unacceptable), and as *players* (engaging with data science for their own and others' benefit). We elaborate on the skills needed for these roles. We argue that citizens should use ideas and tools from data science to improve their lives and their environments.

Keywords Data science · Disruptive technologies · Machine learning · Curriculum reform · Participatory science · Citizen science

22.1   Introduction

The definition of *data science* is contested; here we define data science to be the collection of methods and processes that led to the development of the artefacts, tools and processes in the bullet list in Sect. 22.2. We could explore the relationship between data science and statistics—describing things they have in common, ways in which the disciplines diverge, and so on. However, both statistics and data science are evolving rapidly, and such discussions would quickly become obsolete. Any examination of statistics teaching should take to heart the warning from the National Science Foundation (2019) used to introduce this chapter: we either flourish by embracing and leading data science or we decline and become irrelevant. The American Statistical Society advocated the idea of a BIGTENT that incorporated both statistics and data science. They see living and growing together as an appropriate way forward; we endorse this view.

The rationale underpinning our advocacy of Civic Statistics is that education should prepare students to function as empowered citizens. This requires: an understanding of emerging elements that are shaping the world; the ability to contribute to decisions about what *should be*; and agency in shaping *what can be*.

Data science is having a significant impact on the modern world. Data science will continue to change patterns of human activity, and to use and invent novel ways to access, analyse and act on data. Any discussion of Civic Statistics must embrace the concepts, philosophies and products of data science, because they are having a profound effect on our lives.

We begin with an exploration of the nature of disruptive technologies. We point to examples of modern technologies that have shaped human behaviour, such as the web, and pattern recognition, to illustrate the scale of the impact of data science on society. Data science is also intellectually disruptive; it raises questions about discovery methods, explanation, and ways to make decisions. We explore some of these themes.

22.2 Disruptive Technologies and Civic Statistics

It is easy to see computers as the embodiment of *disruptive technology* i.e. of technologies that transform the ways we work and live—however, it is too simple to think of technologies themselves as being disruptive. Disruption is a function of the way something is used, not of the object or technology itself. A better (but clumsier) phrase might be *disruptive socio-technical systems* (DST)—capturing the idea that patterns of human behaviour have changed because we use some tools in novel ways. A current example is working from home; the technologies (*Zoom*, laptops) that enable large numbers of people to work from home have been available for a long time, yet—pre-Covid-19—most people travelled to work. During Covid-19, there was a dramatic increase in home working, even in situations where face-to-face contact has been deemed to be critically important, such as in higher education. So the technology itself did not create the change in patterns of human activity; rather, the technologies facilitated changes that were suddenly seen to be desirable for other reasons. It may well be impossible to predict the consequences of DST; in the case of technologies that facilitate home working, their use might be much reduced if Covid-19 is eradicated, and people resume their earlier work patterns. However, experiences of home working might lead to home working becoming a major part of working life, and people insisting on urban renewal, demanding better social facilities closer to their homes, and/or to environmental renewal as people travel less, and pollute less, ... and/or many other scenarios.

Civic Statistics (in our definition) aims to use knowledge about statistics for public good, and to use social issues as a focus to broaden and enrich statistics teaching. Social issues are not static—addressing poverty in 1940s Europe presented different challenges to addressing poverty in 2020s Europe. The ways in which societies function change over time—sometimes in dramatic ways via disasters such as disease, fire, famine, wars, or flood, and sometimes in less dramatic (but profound) ways by adopting new technologies. The adoption of particular technologies is not inevitable; choices are often involved, and citizens can have a voice in these choices (as well as making personal decisions to adopt—or not).

Technologies underpin DST, and many technologies have had a dramatic impact on our world. The agricultural revolution resulted in a surplus of food that allowed the human population to expand dramatically. The printing press led to the dissemination of ideas (e.g. on theology) which provoked wars within and between countries, and also paved the way for mass education; developments in transport have led to profound changes in patterns of human mobility. Automation has always had a dramatic effect on patterns of employment; examples include migration to cities (associated with mass production in the industrial revolution) and—in recent times—robots replacing about half of the workforce in the car industry. DST are characterised by unintended consequences. For example, increasing use of robotics in developed countries could have unintended consequences for developing ones; if automation results in very low manufacturing costs, and developed countries repatriate manufacturing, there will be profound economic effects on developing countries.

Two striking features of the modern world have been the speed of adoption of new devices and new ways of doing things, and the very modest extent of discussion and debate about whether new technologies should be adopted or banned (perhaps reflecting the adoption of DST in earlier eras without discussion).

Examples of technologies that are, or have the potential to be DST, include:

- Immediate access to both factual and procedural knowledge via *Wikipedia* and *YouTube*
- Changes in patterns of human communication (including targeted marketing and on-line fraud) mediated via email, *Instagram*, *WeChat*, *Grindr*, *Facebook*, *Zoom* and *Skype*
- Industrial robots
- The Internet of Things (IoT)—smart refrigerators, TVs, cars, and domestic robots
- Cryptocurrencies
- Emotion detectors for classrooms and cars
- Detection of disease outbreaks via analysis of *Google* search data
- Predicting crime and recommending custodial sentences
- Recommender systems for media (e.g. *Netflix*) and warehouses (*Amazon*)
- Pattern recognition (conceived broadly) and detecting abnormal patterns (e.g. in shipping or air traffic; identifying fake videos) such as:

  – speech recognition and language translation
  – recognition of individuals via face, fingerprint, voice, gait, or patterns of key presses

- Tracking of individuals (e.g. via phone, fitness tracker or credit card use)
- Automated analyses of spatial data (e.g. using AI to identify dwellings in remote areas as part of anti malaria campaigns)
- Autonomous vehicles and weapons systems
- 'Deep fake' videos
- Playing complex games better than any human (e.g. chess, Go)
- Virtual, augmented, and mixed reality devices (VR, AR, MR)
- Gene editing
- Brain-driven prosthetics and computer-brain interfaces

The list provides vivid examples of three key Civic Statistics features (see Engel and Ridgway in Chap. 2): *novel data sources* (e.g. location data, video clips) *and techniques* (e.g. face recognition, autonomous vehicles), *varied data collection methods* (e.g. home-based spy devices such as *Alexa*, sensors, satellite detection of shipping movements); and *measures and operationalisation* (e.g. detecting 'emotion'; predicting recidivism). In terms of dimensions of knowledge (see Gal, Nicholson and Ridgway in Chap. 3), it is clear that these examples require robust quantitative skills (*quantitative core*) and fluency with ICT (*ICT and search*). Most important, all these applications have major *implications and consequences for society*. Many of the examples here can provide the basis for discussions about current, observable, consequences for society. Further, they can provide the basis for discussions with students about potential future implications for society—for example, the potential of tracking technologies for social control.

If our goals are to encourage citizens to contribute actively to decisions about which technologies should be adopted, and how, and also to think creatively about the affordances of different technological developments, how might this be addressed in a Civics Statistics classroom? One approach to fostering *meaning for society and policy* is to ask students about the affordances of one or more of the innovative technologies in the list, then to ask them to explore *what-if* scenarios, around these affordances. For example, suppose as a response to Covid-19, a track-and-trace technology is developed which allows governments to know the contacts, proximity, and context of every encounter between every citizen. How might this be used for social good? How might the technology be abused?

Technologies are never neutral—their use bestows advantages on some sectors of society, and often disadvantages others. For example, the advantages of car ownership are enjoyed largely by relatively affluent people in a certain age range; disadvantages fall on people who live by busy roads (and others). There *have* been some near-universal benefits of some technologies—billions of people now have Internet access, are living longer, and are in better health than previous generations (see Rosling et al., 2018). However, some technologies may have near-universal negative consequences: generating electricity by burning fossil fuels now poses a threat to the entire biosphere; technologies for mass surveillance are available; nuclear weapons pose an existential threat to humanity. The fact that the technologies that have been, and continue to be, invented are having a profound effect on human lives means that any discussion of Civic Statistics should explore the concepts, philosophies and products of data science.

We will consider the knowledge required to function at different levels of engagement with data science, notably, as: *spectators*—which simply requires an understanding of what is going on around; *referees*—where students are empowered to make reasoned political judgements about the sorts of courses of action they would like to see followed in circumstances where the products of data science are likely to have social impact; and as *players*—where students are empowered to act, for example by analysing evidence using data science tools, presenting evidence in an accessible form, or via advocacy or direct engagement in participatory science (readers will note that this is very different from the distinction between producers and consumers commonly applied to statistics and social media). Students should have experiences (and develop competences) in each of these roles.

From the viewpoint of student *spectators,* it is important for students to know that disruptive technologies will continue to be invented, and that it will be impossible to un-invent them once they have been invented—and that these technologies are often adopted on a very large scale, before human systems have had time to adapt—an essential characteristic of DST. Spectators also need to be aware of the range of applications that have been created, and the promises and potential perils of their use. In the context of data science, examples include the uses and abuses of social media, advantages and disadvantages of cryptocurrencies, the IoT, deep fake videos, and

Virtual, Augmented and Mixed Reality devices. Spectators are often directly influenced by DST—as the discussion of *referees* will illustrate.

Referees need a wide range of skills, to inform their political judgments about the uses of disruptive technologies. Referees need to consider the intended and potentially unintended consequences of new technologies, and to be able to identify (and make value judgements about) groups that will benefit from, and be disadvantaged by, disruptive technologies. For example, using location data for 'track and trace' during epidemics, along with anonymised location data to understand the transmission processes is likely to be beneficial; tracking the movements of all citizens for purposes of political control is more problematic. To give a concrete example: anyone in China who buys a new mobile phone or SIM card must have their face scanned. The Chinese government says this is to protect legitimate users in cyberspace; critics say this is part of national surveillance of all citizens—in a country where human rights violations occur on an industrial scale. The Financial Times[1] (FT) reported (2 Dec 2019) that 'Chinese companies are shaping new facial recognition and surveillance standards in the UN'. The same article reported that Chinese surveillance systems have been adopted by 67 countries, and that the government of Zimbabwe will send data on millions of African faces to the Chinese company Cloudwalk to enable it to train face recognition technology.

The vulnerability of Global Positioning Systems (GPS) provides another example; GPS are easy to hack, and there is no back-up in place. This poses a threat to all systems that depend on GPS, such as aircraft navigation systems.[2] Automated systems for decision making are another cause for serious concern–the title of O'Neil's, 2016 book *Weapons of Math Destruction* gives a flavour. O'Neil offers many examples where human-designed algorithms lead to injustices, as well as examples where the model underlying the decision is opaque (as in the case of machine generated algorithms). Students should be made aware that, in general, whenever automated decision making is employed, it is important to think through issues of fairness (as well as to evaluate its performance). A vivid example is the allocation of grades used to determine university admissions in 2020 to UK students.[3] In the UK, students are assessed on individual subjects (English, French, Art etc.). In normal circumstances, every student takes a written examination that is set and graded externally. Because of Covid-19, this did not happen, so grades were allocated on the basis of teacher assessment, subject to statistical moderation. The government was concerned about 'grade inflation'—so teacher grades had to be moderated; a simple regression model which included the past performance of the school was used. It is reasonable to predict that, for large samples, the distribution of grades from 1 year to the next would be similar, and so students in schools where examination grades are historically low could reasonably be expected to perform less

---

[1] https://www.ft.com/content/c3555a3c-0d3e-11ea-b2d6-9bf4d1957a67

[2] https://www.scientificamerican.com/article/gps-is-easy-to-hack-and-the-u-s-has-no-backup/

[3] https://www.theguardian.com/education/2020/aug/17/uk-exams-debacle-how-did-results-end-up-chaos

well, on average, than students in schools where examination grades are historically high. However, any attempt to use small samples (small schools, or courses with few students) to moderate grades is likely to be highly inaccurate, for obvious reasons. More important, at the level of the individual student, there may be serious injustices; a high-attaining student could have their grades reduced (and their application to the university of their choice rejected) simply on the basis of the past performance of other students in their school. There was a huge backlash from students to the grades awarded (even though grades *were* higher overall than in previous years). The UK government decided to scrap the model, and accept (high) teacher grades—incidentally causing problems for universities (who were instructed to accept all students who met their entrance requirements). This example illustrates the need to examine the consequences of different rule systems. In this case, the algorithm was a simple regression model available for inspection in the public domain. However, in some models (such as neural networks), it can be the case that no-one knows what the rule system actually *is*. Here we have described just two data science examples (face recognition; automated decision making) where citizens should engage as referees. Any one of the topics described earlier could be the basis for *referee* activities in class.

What of *players*? The growth in the use of mobile devices, such as smartphones and activity trackers which contain a variety of sensors, has provided opportunities to gather data from a large number of sources on a wide range of topics. There is a growing movement to democratise the creation and analysis of data (especially data relevant to Civic Statistics), often as part of civic campaigning—this has been labelled *public participation, citizen science, crowd sensing* (and the related *crowd mapping*) and *participatory sensing*. An early paper by Burke et al. (2006) describes the use of participatory sensing (PS), and offers illustrative examples of the use of PS in public health, urban planning, management of natural resources, cultural identity and creative expression—see also Gould (2017) for an integration of participatory sensing into a data science course. Other examples where PS has been used include monitoring local air pollution and other environmental hazards (see examples from François and Monteiro in Chap. 20), and managing epidemics. Applications of crowd mapping include creating maps of crime, natural disasters, wars, and famine (e.g. via Ushahidi)[4] based on data collected from a large number of people. PS enables citizens to engage as *players* in campaigns that affect their lives. Detailed examples and links to websites and resources are provided by Zejnilović and Campos in Chap. 21. The European Union has initiated a project to encourage citizens to share their data.[5] This online platform serves as a Knowledge Hub, to support the mainstreaming of citizen science, and build on the growing impact of citizens participating in research across the full range of scientific inquiry. One of the main goals of this platform is public engagement, through data production and analysis. Citizen scientists may, if they wish, participate in multiple stages of the

---

[4] https://www.ushahidi.com/about

[5] https://en.wikipedia.org/wiki/Ushahidi

scientific process, including developing the research question, designing the method, gathering and analysing data, and communicating the results.

Citizen science can provide topics for projects at school level including optional activities for students outside their classrooms. These projects are often related to the science curriculum, and are not necessarily related to statistics or data science education as such. To develop skills as *players*, experiences with PS can be built into students' educational activities. A pioneering project in this respect is the Introduction to Data Science (IDS) project. Gould et al. (2016) describe their Mobilize IDS curriculum, which uses PS as part of the cycle of data investigation. Campaigns include Mobilize Snack, which sets out to describe student snacks in terms of, *inter alia,* what was eaten, healthiness, cost, location, and circumstances of eating (e.g. with whom?); and Mobilize Trash, which aims to reduce reliance on landfill. Usually, a PS campaign begins by choosing a topic, and setting out to understand it better. Decisions have to be made about what to measure, and how to measure it (this can include accessing relevant open data sources). There is then a data collection phase; observations are collected via 'trigger events' rather than via random sampling. For example, in the Mobilize Snack campaign, a recording is triggered whenever a participant eats a snack. In the Mobilize Trash campaign, recording is triggered whenever a student discards something. An interesting feature of IDS is the variety of data types that are captured. For example, in the Trash campaign, students record: the type of bin the discarded item was placed in; the nature of the discarded item; the activity that generated the item; and where the item was discarded (all categorical variables); the number of recycling bins visible from the location where the item was discarded; the number of trash bins visible; and the number of compost bins visible (all numerical variables); photographs of items (images); date; time; and location; and also text—here, an open-ended description of the item.

Sagy et al. (2019) extend these arguments in favour of CS, and describe the benefits of CS to different stakeholders, including scientists and non-scientists, and statistics and science educators.

22.3 Disruptive Thinking: Critical Evaluation and Reflection on Data Science and Ways of Knowing and Acting

> Competent statisticians will be front line troops in our war for survival—but how do we get them? I think there is now a wide readiness to agree that what we want are neither mere theorem provers nor mere users of a cookbook. A proper balance of theory and practice is needed and, more important, statisticians must learn to be good scientists, a talent which has to be acquired by experience and example.

George E. P. Box, "Science and Statistics" (CATS, 1994, p. vi) quoted in Horton and Hardin (2018).

Box talks about *our war for survival.* We are living in interesting times; the problems faced by previous generations have not gone away, but we now face existential threats such as nuclear war, global warming, pollution, and the militarisation of space. We argued earlier that data science uses a very wide range of data sources, and is associated with new approaches for data analysis. However, some advocates of data science argue for a rethink about the whole enterprise of science and technology—so if we are to take Box's exhortation seriously, everyone concerned with statistics needs to rethink their ideas about science. In this section, we explore some of these ideas, and argue that some of the dimensions of knowledge we deemed necessary for Civic Statistics in Chap. 3 that may seem familiar (*models, patterns and representations*; and *methodology and enquiry processes*) are not as straightforward as they first appear.

22.3.1 On Modelling

All models are wrong, but some are useful. (Box & Draper, 1987, p. 424).

All models simplify reality, and the usefulness of a model depends on the match between the phenomenon being modelled, the model, and on the uses made of the model. There are two distinct purposes underpinning modelling—prediction and explanation. Models can be found that do either, both, or neither. For example, one can predict astronomical events such as phases of the moon and seasons, yet hold an Earth-centred view of the universe (prediction with the wrong explanation). A heliocentric theory of the solar system both predicts and explains the phenomena. Chaos theory (used to model dynamic systems such as weather and cardiac arrhythmias for example) provides models which, in some states, exhibit disorder and seemingly random patterns yet which are completely deterministic, governed by a set of simple equations. The behaviour of these models is often very sensitive to initial conditions. An extraordinary claim associated with Chaos theory is that the flutter of a butterfly wing in one part of the world can cause a typhoon in another. This *is* hyperbole; however, very small changes in the initial states in a model of a weather system can lead to very big differences in predicted outcomes, so, in some model states, if a weather model were rerun with tiny changes in the starting conditions, results from the two simulations would diverge exponentially over time. In meteorology it is useful to explore the theoretical effects of small changes in the current state of the model on its predictions, to determine whether weather systems are in predictable or chaotic states. In the study of arrhythmias, it is useful to know about the medical interventions that can stabilize the electrical functioning of a heart when it is in a chaotic state. So Chaos theory provides an example where a model (say of the weather) in some states has explanatory power but no predictive power.

There are examples in science and data science of models that make robust predictions, but do not offer full explanations of the phenomena. Newton's laws of motion are three equations that model existing empirical results, and support prediction of future events—for example providing all the mathematics needed to support a Moon landing—but are incomplete as explanations of the phenomena (what *is* gravity?).

Now consider the problem of categorising an image as either a cat or a dog. A number of cases (each labelled *cat* or *dog*) can be presented to a neural net which finds a combination of features that lead to good discrimination between images of cats and dogs. The model has no underlying theory about the natures of cats or dogs. Anderson (2008) argued that science should be based entirely on identifying patterns in data, via machine learning. He famously declared the death of theory, as follows: 'Out with every theory of human behaviour, from linguistics to sociology. Forget taxonomy, ontology, and psychology. Who knows why people do what they do? The point is they do it, and we can track and measure it with unprecedented fidelity. With enough data, the numbers speak for themselves'.

Data science (by incorporating machine learning) emerged in response to massive increases in computing power, access to new sorts of data, and the invention of new mathematical (and physical) tools. (These have created DST in science itself— genome mapping, and gene editing are examples). However, being able to predict events does not mean that explanation ceases to be a desirable feature of a model. The world of business furnishes a plethora of examples where attention to data (e.g. profitability, sales growth) and not to the whole market environment has led to disaster. Examples include: Kodak, which in 1976 sold 85% of all film cameras and 90% of all film sold in the US, went bankrupt in 2012[6] (despite the digital camera being invented by a Kodak engineer); and manufacturers of mainframe computers such as Control Data Corporation and IBM failing to see the emergence of mini- and personal computers. In many areas of science (such as modelling global warming) empirical generalisation from old data simply won't work—models of interacting systems are essential.

We have pointed out that both science and data science use some models that are atheoretical. What of models with explanatory power? These abound in science. In machine learning, we can point to models that do have an explanatory function— classification and regression trees (CART) provide an example. In the early days of AI, diagnostic systems were sometimes associated with explanatory systems. For example, in the 1970s, *MYCIN* was created to diagnose bacterial infections, and could identify the rules it had used to come to a specific diagnosis. Explanation was made easier because *MYCIN* was written in *LISP*—a list processing language whose functioning could be interrogated. The decision rules had been hand-crafted by clinicians and computer scientists working together; then, it was deemed important for users of decision aids (such as *MYCIN*) to understand the basis for the decisions made by the automated system. This need to understand the functioning of auto- mated decision systems is now more important than ever (we return to this theme later). Consequently, a good deal of work is being conducted to create 'Explainable

---

[6]https://petapixel.com/2018/06/14/a-brief-history-of-kodak-the-camera-giants-rise-and-fall/

AI[7]—using AI to explain the workings of AI systems to human decision makers (see also Berthold et al., 2010).

The process of modelling benefits from knowledge of a wide range of ways to model—if the only tool you have is a hammer, most problems look like nails. Breiman (2001) argued for the use of a wider range of models in statistics. He pointed to two cultures of data analysis, and argued that the majority of statisticians use relatively simple models (such as regression) where outputs depend on a small collection of inputs that can be described in words; the aim is to create models that have both predictive and explanatory properties. He described these as analytic models. In contrast, at the time Breiman was writing, only a minority of statisticians used algorithmic modelling (common in computer science), where AI techniques such as neural nets and boosted decision trees are used to map inputs and outputs. Here, taking the example of neural nets, there need be little attempt to specify the exact nature of the inputs, or the mathematical functions that relate inputs to outputs. Henceforth, we will refer to these as machine learning (ML) models. Natural language processing (e.g. *Google translate*) provides a vivid example where ML models have had great success in a domain characterised by decades of patchy success using analytic methods. A major contribution of data science to science has been the creation of new sorts of models, and new approaches to model evaluation— these are used increasingly by statisticians. Both analytic and ML models have been used successfully. It is worth exploring some strengths and weaknesses of each.

22.3.1.1 Challenges for Machine Learning Models

Machine learning is often considered as part of statistics and as part of computer science; the border lines and interfaces are blurred. ML can be interpreted as an extension of multivariate statistical models, where the function that maps multivariate input onto the output can best be described as a black box algorithm. The specific perspective of statistics on ML is concerned with inference and uncertainty; for instance, when uncertainty and variability are quantified in the cases where the training data can be regarded as a random sample from the population of interest.

A major challenge facing ML models is the choice of training data—the outputs depend entirely on the training data set (for example, the particular breeds of cats and dogs shown, and the angles from which they are viewed). ML models are strong on '*what was* in data set X', and can often be good on 'discrimination' in a new data set Y. In order to check the robustness of a model, validation on a new data set from the target population is required.

Future predictions from the model are likely to be valid only if applied to the population from which the training and validation data were taken. However, this restriction is often not communicated, and the producers of models may not be aware of them. Sometimes restrictions show up when the model is applied to a (plausibly)

---

[7] https://www.darpa.mil/program/explainable-artificial-intelligence

similar but (actually) different target population. This can lead to pernicious errors when these models are used for e.g. face recognition, if the training set does not represent the whole population of interest.

Further, ML models have nothing to say per se about '*what ought to be*' or '*what will be*'. Consider job selection or sentencing in court. Suppose we use a sample of all the employees in the most successful 100 companies nation-wide, where most chief executives are old white males. Should we then look for old white males when hiring a new CEO? Suppose we find that white criminals sent to gaol are more likely to reoffend than black criminals sent to goal—should white criminals be given longer sentences?

Students should be encouraged to ask about the match between the training set and the current population—were relevant sub-samples included? Are there reasons to believe that things have changed over time? (thereby invalidating the model). And—at least as important—are the criteria for success the correct ones? In the case of identifying diseases, they probably are. In the case of assessing risk of disease, there may well be problems if the standardising sample does not represent the population as a whole, or if the population is segmented in important ways. Some failures using AI methods arose because data provenance and methods were not subjected to the sorts of critical analysis that characterises statistical thinking (see Friedrich et al., 2020).

There are also important issues around model validation. Is it appropriate to simply count the number of correct and incorrect classifications a system makes? A critical issue here is the performance of the system in dealing with different subgroups of the data. For example, a system for detecting dangerous objects in suitcases might be claimed to classify suitcases correctly in 99.99% of cases, in realistic settings. However, a rule 'every suitcase is OK' would easily hit this level of accuracy. Performance needs to be judged on the basis of every core group being classified; here safe and dangerous suitcases, but elsewhere, classification of women and men, or people from different ethnic or cultural groups. This need to disaggregate data, and to examine the performance of subgroups is a recurring theme in this book; visualisations in Chaps. 5 and 10 show the importance of disaggregation ('facetting') if data are to be understood.

A further major problem with ML models can be the absence of any explanatory power (discussed above). Indeed, one of the problems in dealing with machine learning models instead of "classical" statistical approaches, is that most work as a "black box" where even its designers cannot explain why a model arrived at a specific decision. For some tasks (such as face recognition) this is unnecessary. For other applications—such as recommending sentencing in criminal cases—it is essential because the legal system must be seen to be based on both morality and equity. Similarly, when considering 'systems problems'—such as those in ecology involving feedback loops—the opacity of ML models, and the inability to explore alternative courses of action, renders them unusable if decisions about actions are to be made by humans.

These problems are not confined to ML models. Indeed, a major contribution to science from data science has been a heightened awareness of sampling issues and generalisation. For example, Perez (2019) points out that the dummies used to establish car safety are based on male bodies; women are more likely than men to die when involved in comparable car crashes. She claims that drug trials often exclude women, on the grounds that varying hormone levels add noise to the experimental data. Murgia (2017) estimates that more than 80% of the genome data that underpins genetic medicine comes from Caucasians (and a further 14% from Asians); it is possible that recommended medical interventions may be ineffective and perhaps dangerous when applied to (say) Africans.

Let us return to the problem of sampling in ML. As a principle, training data for machine learning tasks should be representative of the target population. However, consider the study of fraud detection in the financial transactions of bank clients. If you take a sample of financial transactions to analyse fraud, it will be highly probable that your samples contain no fraudulent records at all. Oversampling (deliberately including a disproportionately larger number of examples of representatives of key sub-populations—here, fraudulent transactions) and undersampling (deliberately restricting the number of examples of representatives of some sub-populations—here, non-fraudulent transactions) are helpful, as they can be used to adjust the class distribution of a data set (i.e. the ratio between the different classes/categories represented).

22.3.1.2 Challenges for Analytic Models

As with ML models, analytic models are not without their problems. Most obviously, it is very difficult to address some classification problems using analytic models—for example, if one set out to use a regression model to identify potentially dangerous objects in suitcases, or human faces, it would be impossible to define the predictor variables. However, recently, there have been challenges to the scientific underpinnings of entire academic disciplines which use analytic models. Peer-reviewed publication in reputable scientific journals does not guarantee that research has been done competently. The Open Science Collaboration (2015) set out to replicate 100 'well-known' results in psychology, and failed, in the majority of cases. A pervasive problem *(methodology and enquiry processes, quantitative core)* was that relatively small sample sizes were being used to detect weak effects. As a consequence, false positive results were found, and published, and (because negative results from small samples are rarely published) went unchallenged. Further, Ioannidis (2005) maps out a number of poor research practices in medical science that led to the publication of misleading results in a paper entitled *Why most published research findings are false*. He argues that over-analysis often leads to faulty conclusions—for example by conducting multiple *post-hoc* comparisons based on (say) ethnicity, location, age, and sex and concluding that (say) Indian, northern, young, males are more prone to some disease ($p < 0.01$) than other groups. In ecology, there are concerns that relatively recent data on (say) the distribution of birds defines their 'natural' or 'preferred' habitat—ignoring data from earlier times where there was less intensive agriculture, which showed quite different spatial distributions. These failures are signs that academic disciplines can become paradigm-bound—locked into a narrow set of data gathering tools and ways of representing and modelling data—and that some refreshing new approaches may be needed.

22.3.1.3 Revisiting Models, Patterns and Representations

From the viewpoint of modelling, data science has contributed some important classes of models. Challenges that were insoluble before (such as language translation and automated face recognition) have now been met, and are part of the everyday experiences of many people (e.g. mobile phone users). Some failures of data science (such as mis-classifying whole groups of people) highlighted some important problems with conventional science, notably, the dangers of poor sampling, and overgeneralisation. There is an increasing number of ways to model phenomena, and students and citizens need to be aware of these opportunities. They also need to be aware of the whole process of modelling, model evaluation, and Box and Draper's (1987) caution about the uses and possible abuse of models.

Ridgway (1998) identified three distinct classes of model—analytic, systems and macrosystemic (In Breiman's (2001) terms, these are all 'analytic' models). In analytic models (found in school physics), a more complex problem can be broken down into simple problems, and the solutions to the simple problems can be aggregated into a solution to the complex problem—the combined gas laws provide an example. In systems models (such as those found in school biology) feedback is an essential component of the model—homeostasis provides an example. Macrosystemic models are systems models where the system itself undergoes change. Macrosystemic models can be divided into two groups—models where the changes in the system are relatively predictable (e.g. ecological restoration; the life cycle of the butterfly) or relatively unpredictable (such as the impact of a pandemic, or climate change, where—for example—few models predicted that major forest fires would occur in Alaska and Siberia and would contribute to increased carbon emissions). Unstable macrosystemic change will always be a feature of complex systems because humans will always seek to understand, then 'game' systems. For example, if sentiment analysis identifies specific words that predict stock exchange movements, it is likely that traders will create bots to flood social media with these words before their large trades.

The UN Sustainable Development Goals (SDG) offer a dramatic illustration of the difficulty of modelling and changing complex systems. The 17 SDG are associated with 169 targets. However, these targets can be in conflict with each other. For example, good nutrition requires access to food and clean water. Food production depends on an adequate supply of water of appropriate quality. However, increasing food production can increase land and water degradation. Fu et al. (2019) offer some guidance on unravelling these complexities.

Complex problems are associated with multiple data sources, and will require the use of a variety of analytical tools, and models at a variety of levels. Civic Statistics should raise awareness of these levels. Civic Statistics needs to embrace the insights, tools and models of both statistics and data science.

22.4   Education for a Fast Changing World

In Chap. 2, Engel and Ridgway described some important features of Civic Statistics; it is now clear that the examples considered under *novel data sources and techniques* and *varied data collection methods* discussed under the heading of *Unfamiliar Methods and Representations*, need to be broadened to embrace sources and methods from data science. Under the heading of *Contexts and Interpretations, implications and consequences for society* we need to consider the variety of potential futures made possible by data science and the artefacts that have been created. In Chap. 3, Gal, Nicholson, and Ridgway described *Engagement and Action*; it is clear that participatory science adds a set of important tools with the potential to increase citizen empowerment. Earlier, we offered a classification of *spectators*, *referees*, and *players*. Students should be expected to adopt all of these roles at different times in their lives.

Spectators need a mind-set such that they continue to update their knowledge about developments relevant to Civic Statistics (*dispositions*) at the level of understanding how new tools and devices derived from data science (such as the Internet of Things) can affect them directly—for example, by harvesting data about their activities that could be used by others to shape their subsequent behaviour. Spectators need to be able to evaluate the benefits and potential costs of engaging with different sorts of technology, as they emerge (*meaning for society and policy*). Their skill set should include:

- Awareness of the politics of technology: technologies are never neutral (e.g. cars cannot be driven by the very young or very old, nor by the poor; access to the internet facilitates home learning during a pandemic, but is not universally available)
- Ability to identify groups who might benefit from, or be disadvantaged by, emerging technologies. Engaging with moral issues (e.g. the dangers of the Panopticon—the ability of states to identify and observe citizens without their consent, as they go about their daily lives)
- Ability to explore possible unintended consequences (e.g. cyberbullying via social media) via 'what if' games

Referees need a critical awareness of developments, (*novel data sources and techniques*; *varied data collection methods*) and a mind-set (*dispositions*) to speculate about the impact that emerging technologies (new sorts of data, new tools, new techniques) might have on society at local, national and global levels (*meaning for society and policy, critical evaluation and reflection*). Referees should engage in political processes to shape the ways that new technologies are used (in as far as this is possible).

In addition to the skills of *spectators,* if we are to develop informed *referees,* it will be necessary to inculcate:

- A sophisticated view of the status of knowledge claims, and a list of key questions to ask about different sorts of evidence and different sorts of analysis (see Gal's Chap. 13)
- The ability to explore possible unintended consequences and to speculate about ways in which they might be mitigated
- Understanding about the characteristics of different sorts of models, the limits of modelling, and the principles of model validation
- Understanding the principles underpinning different techniques (e.g. neural nets) and a willingness to explore emerging techniques
- Knowledge that models can be unstable for a variety of reasons (e.g. insufficient data to produce robust parameters; sample bias)
- Knowledge that systems can be unstable for a variety of reasons (e.g. the world can change)

Players need a wide variety of skills, in addition to the skills of *referees.* If we are to develop *players* we need to teach the skills associated with Box's idea of *being a good scientist.* This requires considerable sophistication in approaches to understanding and interacting with the world. Components include:

- Modelling skills (conceived broadly), and in particular experiences of using a wide variety of tools. In the context of statistics education and Civic Statistics, this means embracing Breiman's (2001) exhortation to work with (what we would now call) data science tools. We can point to a variety of sources of ideas for reforming the statistics curriculum, such as those mapped out by the National Science Foundation (2019), and in Biehler and Schulte (2018), and De Veaux et al. (2017), and Nolan and Temple Lang (2010)
- Wrestling with epistemological issues: the nature of knowledge as conceived in different academic disciplines—how it is created, shared, learned, and used (and by whom, and for what purposes)
- Engagement with citizen science
- An awareness of the nature of DST, and the motivation to maximise the benefits of emerging technologies for humankind

Citizen scientists are *players*; student citizen scientists may become future data scientists, as they engage in developing research questions, designing methods, gathering and analysing data, and communicating results.

22.5 Conclusions

Data science is a driving force creating DST, and is shaping human experiences in radical ways by the creation of new tools, which may have unintended long-term social consequences. Students need to be aware of these developments, both for their personal welfare (as *spectators*), and as citizens (*referees*) who have a voice in the uses of novel technologies, and as users of tools for personal and environmental change (as *players*).

Data science is associated with epistemological turmoil. There has been a call for 'the death of theory', a crisis of replication in conventional science and concerns that many published results are unreliable, awareness that some applied science practices are based on datasets that are not representative of the populations to which results are generalised, and concerns about the use of opaque decision making models. Some of these problems arise because researchers failed to act on key statistical ideas such as attention to sample composition, sample size, and the dangers of inappropriate procedures such as data dredging. This turmoil is a healthy development which is likely to lead to better science. These epistemological issues are central to Civic Statistics—students should understand the nature and robustness of evidence claims that underpin decision making on social issues.

Data science is associated with accessing and analysing a very wide variety of data sources, and inventing novel methods for analysis. It is also associated with action and creating products that work. Students need to engage with these new developments—participatory science can be a useful introduction, if students are to become *players*. In any event, they should be exposed to a wider variety of models than those experienced on conventional introductory statistics courses.

We began by quoting a 2019 report from the National Science Foundation. . . . *we either flourish by embracing and leading Data Science or we decline and become irrelevant. In the long run, to thrive, we must redefine, broaden, and transform the field of Statistics.* Early turf wars between disciplines about which is the pre-eminent discipline in reasoning with data have given way to syntheses and synergies, encapsulated by the ASA notion of the BIGTENT. From the viewpoint of Civic Statistics, if we are to address pressing social issues, we need to take a radical view of the nature of discovering and knowing, informed by current advances (wherever they occur). We have a responsibility to prepare students for their roles as spectators, referees, and players. More generally, we need to shape the discipline of statistics in such a way that it co-evolves with data science and science, and promotes human well-being.

References

Anderson, C. (2008). The end of theory: The data deluge makes the scientific method obsolete. *Wired Magazine*. https://www.wired.com/2008/06/pb-theory/

Berthold, M. R., Borgelt, C., Höppner, F., & Klawonn, F. (2010). *Guide to intelligent data analysis—How to intelligently make sense of real data.* Springer. https://doi.org/10.1007/978-1-84882-260-3

Biehler, R., & Schulte, C. (2018). Perspectives for an interdisciplinary data science curriculum at German secondary schools. In R. Biehler, L. Budde, D. Frischemeier, B. Heinemann, S. Podworny, C. Schulte, & T. Wassong (Eds.), *Paderborn symposium on data science* education at school level 2017: The collected extended abstracts (pp. 2–14). Universitätsbibliothek Paderborn.

Box, G., & Draper, N. (1987). Empirical model-building and response surfaces. Wiley.

Breiman, L. (2001). Statistical modeling: The two cultures (with comments and a rejoinder by the author). Statistical Science, 16(3), 199–231.

Burke, J. A., Estrin, D., Hansen, M., Parker, A., Ramanathan, N., Reddy, S., & Srivastava, M. B. (2006). Participatory sensing. Center for Embedded Network Sensing. https://escholarship.org/uc/item/19h777qd

De Veaux, R. D., Agarwal, M., Averett, M., Baumer, B. S., Bray, A., Bressoud, T. C., & Kim, A. Y. (2017). Curriculum guidelines for undergraduate programs in data science. Annual Review of Statistics and Its Application, 4, 15–30. https://doi.org/10.1146/annurev-statistics-060116-053930

Friedrich, S., Antes, G., Behr, S., Binder, H., Brannath, W., Dumpert, F., Ickstadt, K., Kestler, H., Lederer, J., Leitgöb, H., Pauly, M., Steland, A., Wilhelm, A., & Friede, T. (2020). Is there a role for statistics in artificial intelligence? Advances in Data Analysis and Classification, 1–24. https://arxiv.org/abs/2009.09070

Fu, B., Wang, S., Zhang, J., Hou, Z., & Li, J. (2019). Unravelling the complexity in achieving the 17 sustainable-development goals. National Science Review, 6(3), 386–388. https://doi.org/10.1093/nsr/nwz038

Gould, R. (2017). Data literacy is statistical literacy. Statistics Education Research Journal, 16(1), 22–25.

Gould, R., Machado, S., Ong, C., Johnson, T., Molyneux, J., Nolen, S., Tangmunarunkit, H., Trusela, L., & Zanontian, L. (2016). Teaching data science to secondary students: The MOBILIZE introduction to data science curriculum. In J. Engel (Ed.), Promoting understanding of statistics about society. Proceedings of the roundtable conference of the International Association of Statistics Education (IASE), Berlin, Germany. https://www.iase-web.org/documents/papers/rt2016/Gould.pdf

Horton, N., & Hardin, J. (2018). Challenges and opportunities for statistics and data science undergraduate major and minor degree programs. In M. A. Sorto, A. White, & L. Guyot (Eds.), Looking back, looking forward. International Statistical Institute. https://iase-web.org/icots/10/proceedings/pdfs/ICOTS10_3A3.pdf

Ioannidis, J. (2005). Why most published research findings are false. PLoS Medicine, 2(8), e124. https://doi.org/10.1371/journal.pmed.0020124

Murgia, M. (2017, Oct 1). The data flow that can be deadly. Financial Times, 10.

National Science Foundation. (2019). Statistics at a crossroads: Who is for the challenge? https://www.amstat.org/asa/files/pdfs/POL-Statistics%20at%20a%20Crossroads%20Report.pdf

Nolan, D., & Temple Lang, D. (2010). Computing in the statistics curricula. The American Statistician, 64, 97–107. https://doi.org/10.1198/tast.2010.09132

O'Neil, C. (2016). Weapons of math destruction: How big data increases inequality & threatens democracy. Crown Publishing Group.

Open Science Collaboration. (2015). Estimating the reproducibility of psychological science. Science, 348(6251). https://doi.org/10.1126/science.aac4716

Perez, C. (2019). Invisible women: Exposing data bias in a world designed for men. Penguin Books.

Ridgway, J. (1998). The modelling of systems and macro-systemic change—lessons for evaluation from epidemiology and ecology. National Institute for Science Education Monograph 8. University of Wisconsin-Madison. http://archive.wceruw.org/nise/Publications/Research_Monographs/Vol8.pdf

Rosling, H., Rosling, O., & Rosling-Ronnlund, A. (2018). Factfulness. Hodder and Stoughton.

Sagy, O., Golumbic, Y. N., Ben-Horin Abramsky, H., Benichou, M., Atias, O., Manor Braham, H., Baram-Tsabari, A., Kali, Y., Ben-Zvi, D., Hod, Y., & Angel, D. (2019). Citizen science: An opportunity for learning in the networked society. In Y. Kali, A. Baram-Tsabari, & A. M. Schejter (Eds.), Learning in a networked society: Spontaneous and designed technology enhanced learning communities (pp. 97–115). Springer. https://doi.org/10.1007/978-3-030-14610-8_6

Chapter 23
Civic Statistics in Context: Mapping the Global Evidence Ecosystem

Jim Ridgway (ID) **and Rosie Ridgway**

> *It was the best of times, it was the worst of times, it was the age of wisdom, it was the age of foolishness, it was the epoch of belief, it was the epoch of incredulity, it was the season of light, it was the season of darkness, it was the spring of hope, it was the winter of despair.* Dickens (1859)

Abstract Human knowledge is not a coherent body of carefully structured knowledge, created by an expert group, and made accessible to others. Rather, it should be thought of as a dynamic ecosystem made up of creators and consumers connected in complex ways. Here, we identify some of the elements in this ecosystem, and map some of their relationships with Civic Statistics. Civic Statistics embraces many of the ideas of the Enlightenment—notably that human happiness can be increased by knowledge, evidence and wise actions. Many actors in the evidence ecosystem share Enlightenment views, but may have honest disagreements about evidence; other actors reject the Enlightenment view entirely. Here, we argue that students should see the evidence they encounter in their daily lives (and in class) in the context of an evidence ecosystem, comprising agents whose ambitions range from benign to malevolent. As educators, we should look for ways to develop student resilience—in particular to make them more resistant to polluting elements in the evidence ecosystem. This is clearly a political stance—not a stance on either right wing or left wing politics, but rather a stance on Enlightenment vs counter-Enlightenment positions. Students need to be aware of the web of creation and destruction that underpins knowledge building, and of the tensions between the Enlightenment and the counter-Enlightenment movements. We offer some practical suggestions for educational practices.

Keywords Ecosystem · Democracy · Pollution · Enlightenment · Evidence

J. Ridgway (✉) · R. Ridgway
School of Education, University of Durham, Durham, UK
e-mail: jim.ridgway@durham.ac.uk; r.a.ridgway@durham.ac.uk

© Springer Nature Switzerland AG 2022
J. Ridgway (ed.), *Statistics for Empowerment and Social Engagement*,
https://doi.org/10.1007/978-3-031-20748-8_23

23.1   Data, Information, Evidence

Dickens' *A Tale of Two Cities* was set in an era where parts of Europe were in turmoil; revolutionary events in one country looked set to spill across the continent. His opening sentence is reminiscent of current global events: life is getting better for humanity as whole; life expectancy is increasing along with the quality of people's lives; there is greater access to health care and education; it is reasonable to claim that this is an era of wisdom, belief, light and hope (see Rosling et al., 2019). In contrast, life is not getting better for everyone; many regions are damaged by wars, diseases, and corrupt politicians. Climate change and pandemics pose existential threats to humanity. So one can point to foolishness, incredulity, darkness and despair.

The vision of the Enlightenment was that knowledge would provide a pathway from darkness to light—to liberation and an increase in human happiness. Science would deliver universal benefits; informed citizens would contribute to debate, and politicians would make evidence-informed decisions. This optimism is reflected in a recent publication from the United Nations[1] (UN) entitled *A World that Counts— mobilizing the data revolution for sustainable development*. It asserted (p. 2): *Data are the lifeblood of decision-making and the raw material for accountability. Without high-quality data providing the right information on the right things at the right time; designing, monitoring and evaluating effective policies becomes almost impossible.* This is not a new idea; James Madison (1825),[2] a key author of the United States Constitution, wrote *Government, without popular information, or the means of acquiring it, is but a Prologue to a Farce or a Tragedy; or, perhaps, both* and *. . .the advancement and diffusion of knowledge* is *the only Guardian of true liberty.*

However, data are neither facts nor truth. They do not provide objective representations of the world. They might arise opportunistically, or as a result of conscious decisions to explore some issue, by someone. They have often been cleaned in some way, and are made available in particular forms. Data emerge from and are entangled in a web of culture, politics, power and money. Data only become information after processing and interpretation, and only become new knowledge when integrated into a larger semantic network, i.e. when they are re-entangled into the web of knowledge. Evidence-*based* decision making is an unfortunate phrase; decisions need to be informed by evidence, but not governed by it. In the words of Tom Eliot:

Where is the wisdom we have lost in knowledge?
Where is the knowledge we have lost in information?
    Eliot (1969)
By way of balance, but less poetically, we might also ask:

---

[1] http://www.undatarevolution.org/wp-content/uploads/2014/11/A-World-That-Counts.pdf
[2] https://www.justice.gov/oip/blog/foia-post-2008-celebrating-james-madison-and-freedom-infor mation-act

What is knowledge without information?
What is wisdom without knowledge?

23.2 On the Evidence Ecosystem

Ecosystems can provide a starting point for thinking about the creation and uses of information in our data-rich world. One useful aspect of the analogy is the idea that there are many systems which must be understood in their own right (coral reefs have an ecology that is different to the ecology of prairies) yet which are interconnected in a grander scale of things. So academic research and government policy are distinct systems, but have interconnections. Another is the idea of dependencies—there are identifiable food chains in ecosystems. In food chains, agents at different layers can make use of different resources—so rabbits can be nourished by grass, but foxes cannot. In information systems, end users do not need to be able to digest raw data—but they do need resources in a form which they can use.

In the evidence ecosystem there are data gatherers who provide information which is used (or not) by media and politicians. Some of the dependencies in natural ecosystems are predatory—with animals eating each other; others are symbiotic, where collaboration is mutually beneficial to each participant, for example cattle egrets and cattle. In the evidence ecosystem, politicians and the media often enjoy a symbiotic relationship. In some cases, different organisms can be dependent on each other for survival (for example, most land plants fix carbon from the air, but depend on mycorrhizal fungi for help extracting minerals and water from the ground). In the evidence ecosystem, we see that government depends on evidence about the economy; government agencies collecting economic information depend on government funding. Another useful idea is that ecosystems can undergo dramatic changes—sometimes in unpredictable ways—for example if a new species is introduced (such as rats to an ecology with ground-nesting birds) the ecology can be changed in dramatic ways. The evidence ecosystem is characterised by disruptive technologies (see Ridgway, Campos and Biehler, Chap. 22 in this book)—television, computers replacing type setting, the internet, *Google*, *Twitter*, and cybercrime, provide examples. A particularly important idea is the role of pollution—toxic elements must be kept within bounds for systems to survive. However, this is not a simple idea: for example, oxygen is essential for some functions, but becomes toxic at certain levels; animal waste can be a valuable nutrient or a pollutant, depending on its concentration. In the context of evidence ecosystems, we can identify some obvious pollutants in the form of deliberate lies; however, it may be the case that too much unprocessed data might have similar effects. For example, the World Health Organisation (2020)[3] referred to the information flow around the outbreak of the coronavirus as *a massive*

---

[3] https://www.who.int/docs/default-source/coronaviruse/situation-reports/20200202-sitrep-13-ncov-v3.pdf

Table 23.1 Features of ecosystems exemplified

Ecosystem feature	Natural ecosystem examples	Evidence ecosystem examples
Sub-systems need to be understood in their own right	Coral reefs, prairies	Political systems, the internet
Sub-systems are connected	Deforestation influences global warming which influences coral reefs	Criminal activity can create wealth which can be used for political influence
Food chains	Rabbits eat grass, foxes eat rabbits	National Statistics Offices gather data, governments use NSO
Symbiotic relationships	Cattle and egrets	Politicians and media
Subject to rapid dramatic change	Introduction of rats to islands	The internet
Pollution	Plastics at sea	Conspiracy theories
Concentration levels can be critical	Animal waste as fertiliser or toxin	Medical advice can be precise or an 'infodemic'

'infodemic'—an overabundance of information—some accurate and some not— that makes it hard for people to find trustworthy sources and reliable guidance when they need it. Table 23.1 maps some features of ecosystems, and offers examples from the natural world, and from the evidence ecosystem.

Individuals, civic statistics curricula, schools and universities, media and politicians are all elements in a complex web where life-changing decisions are made, justified by different sorts of stories—some grounded in evidence, and some not. In the next section, we map some of the elements in the evidence ecosystem.

23.3   Elements in the Evidence Ecosystem

We can identify different phases in the creation, consumption and use of information. Information is created by a large number of agencies, as we have seen throughout this volume. These range across a spectrum from sources which set out to collect and distribute robust and authentic information (such as official statistics offices and researchers), to agencies which set out to misinform (such as some subversive government agencies, and bloggers who will use any tactic to encourage traffic to their websites). The motivation for creating information can range from professional duty, altruism, through politics, financial reward and a desire for attention, affirmation or emotional leverage. Information is distributed across a range of types of media, including video, print and the internet. Recipients can be mass audiences, people in information 'bubbles' who attend to just a small set of information sources that are compatible with and reinforce their existing beliefs, or people targeted on the basis of a profile determined by information about them on-line, and their internet use. How is information used? It may be passed on via social networks, rejected because it does not fit pre-existing beliefs, accepted because it reinforces current beliefs, or evaluated carefully.

We can identify a number of agencies which play a role in the evidence ecosystem. Few agencies fit into exactly one category; here we present an oversimplified view which we believe has some heuristic merit. This section identifies elements in the evidence ecosystem, and describes their roles in both the evidence ecosystem, and current or potential roles in Civic Statistics. Tables 23.2, 23.3 and 23.4 provides a summary describing agents working at global (macro), inter/national (meso) and sub/national or sector (micro) levels of the ecosystem.

23.3.1 Governments

National governments are important elements in the evidence ecosystem. They are amongst the largest creators and consumers of curated data, determining what is created and how it is used. Government influences on the evidence ecosystem can range from the benign (such as conducting a census, and making data publicly available) through to the nefarious (such as establishing a national panopticon based on face and gait recognition, and analyses of social media, in order to monitor all citizens). They determine the actual elements of each country's evidence ecosystem, including the size and nature of the 'black evidence ecosystem' (by deciding which agencies to protect from scrutiny, such as government itself, law firms and banks), the extent of press freedom, and the nature of the social media accessible to citizens.

As well as having a major influence on the evidence ecosystem in their own country, many governments have global reach, an influence beyond their own borders. This might be blatant—such as funding groups to engage in cyber warfare or large scale fraud, or may be less obvious. Less obvious influences can be tolerance for secretive practices by corporations based at home, defending the practices abroad of untaxed and unaccountable social media and IT companies, and accepting and hiding large scale investments based on corrupt practices in other countries.

23.3.2 Politicians and Political Leaders

Everyone is entitled to their own opinions, but no-one is entitled to their own facts.

News items often focus on the latest claims and actions by politicians. Politicians vary a great deal in their use of evidence and in their scale of influence, from global leaders in the form of presidents and prime ministers to national, and local agenda setting. Politicians also influence the moral tone of debate. The Washington Post Fact Checker team analysed claims made by President Trump in his first 100 days in

Table 23.2 Agents in the evidence ecosystem (I): roles and relevance to Civic Statistics

Agency	Role in the Evidence Ecosystem	Relevance to Civic Statistics Education
Governments		
Government	Decide what data are gathered and disseminated; use evidence as they see fit. May regulate some aspects of the ecosystem. Can be benign or pollutant	Set national agenda for education policy, education funding, teacher education, involved in decision making about curriculum content and assessment
Politicians		
Politicians	Information consumers and distributors in the form of making data claims	Set national agenda, are a target for education about statistics 'basics'
Print and video media		
Television, newspapers e.g. Fox News, BBC, FT, YouTube	Information producer: Primary sources of evidence, usually with some degree of critical commentary	Illustrate the need to teach students to understand and deconstruct arguments
Social media		
The internet e.g. Facebook, Twitter, YouTube	Information producer, information distribution platform, information monitor: Primary sources of evidence, often without critical commentary. Facilitates information bubbles, and conspiracy theories. A serious threat to the evidence ecosystem	See print and video media. Illustrate the need to teach awareness for citizen engagement with information flows and the need to triangulate sources
Cyber warriors		
Military Intelligence e.g. US cybersecurity and infrastructure security agency	Information distributor and information monitor: Disseminate information (false and true) in foreign countries to achieve their own ends	Provide examples for analysis
Private companies e.g. Cambridge Analytica	Information distributor and information monitor: Present messages tailored to the perceived needs of specific individuals	Provide examples of profiling, and case studies for ethics
Agencies countering threats e.g. military intelligence, hybridco	Information distributor and information monitor: Offer advice to government on countering threats	Provide examples of positive (and negative) uses of data science; illustrates basics of evidence for government
People's intelligence agencies e.g. Bellingcat	Information monitor: Synthesise social media, satellite data and databases to identify bad behaviour and bad actors	Illustrate uses of data science and citizen empowerment

Table 23.3 Agents in the evidence ecosystem (II): roles and relevance to Civic Statistics

Agency	Role in the evidence ecosystem	Relevance to civic statistics education
Survey data collectors and distributors		
National Statistics Offices	Information producer, information distribution platform, information monitor: Gather data; provide data and reports	Provide data sources for analysis. Create resources that can be used for teaching such as visualisations, and descriptions of methodology
Transnational organisations (NGOs) e.g. OECD, Eurostat, World Bank, United Nations	Information producer, information distribution platform, information monitor: Provide data; active in finding solutions to global problems; create resources for policy makers	Create resources, interactive visualisations, teaching materials (especially good on indicator systems and metadata)
Sensor data collectors and distributors		
Science laboratories e.g. NASA	Information producer information monitor: Collect and distribute sensor data e.g. from satellites	Create resources such as sensor data (pollution, ice area) with a spatial dimension. Illustrate the political dimensions of evidence, when closed down by governments
NGOs e.g. Africa Regional Data Cube[a]	Information producer, information distribution platform, information monitor: Create and distribute GIS data cubes addressing a wide range of topics	Illustration of mixed data sources for government and public use, and for education
Unaccountable data collectors and distributors		
Corporations and governments e.g. Amazon, Google, Facebook, credit card agencies, retail outlets, and government agencies	Gather novel types of data on an industrial scale, some in the public domain, some not. Very high pollution potential	Give access to novel forms of data. Case histories for discussions on novel methodologies, data types and ethics

[a] https://www.who.int/docs/default-source/coronaviruse/situation-reports/20200202-sitrep-13-ncov-v3.pdf

office.[4] They counted 492 false claims. Of these, 107 were made in prepared speeches (their tally over the whole presidency was 30,573 false claims). Donald Trump's 2020 presidential campaign identified the free press as 'the enemy'—an echo of the phrase *enemy of the people* that has been used at least since Roman times, and *inter alia* by Robespierre, Goebbels, Lenin, Stalin, and Mao to justify extreme measures against political opponents. Trump's campaign set out to raise funds to be targeted on discrediting specific journalists in reputable media outlets (Guardian,

---

[4] https://www.washingtonpost.com/graphics/politics/trump-claims/

Table 23.4 Agents in the evidence ecosystem (III): roles and relevance to Civic Statistics

Agency	Role in the evidence ecosystem	Relevance to civic statistics education
Knowledge creators and curators		
Universities	Create theories and models of phenomena, and new data and new mathematics	Provide data, theories, models, and tools for analysis
Curators e.g. Open Data Institute, Cochrane and Campbell collaborations; Google Scholar	Promote open data. Summarise large bodies of research; create evidence to support action; facilitate access to evidence	Assemble resources to support critical evaluation of different sorts of research methodology. Create tools to empower students
Data scientists	Create new sorts of data, new ways to analyse data, and new ways to make decisions. Potential to pollute the ecosystem by introducing non-transparent algorithms for decision making	Create new sorts of data, new ways to analyse data, and new ways to make decisions. Needs awareness of the dangers of non-transparent algorithms for decision making
Advocacy agencies		
Advocacy groups e.g. United Nations; Amnesty International; Aid Charities	Use data to provoke (often global) action and to monitor outcomes	Create resources; illustrate the enlightenment in action. Offer interesting examples of complex systems models, and predictive modelling
Fact checkers		
Honest fact Checkers e.g. *Africacheck, Fullfact, Politifact*	Check and evaluate statements by politicians, claims on the web; identify hate speech, obscenity etc.	Provide case studies of different sorts of deceptions; provide some tutorial materials; illustrations of AI in action
Dishonest fact Checkers e.g. *factcheckUK*	Present false claims as checked 'facts'. Aim to pollute the ecosystem	Encourages 'criticality'
Investigative journalists		
Investigative Journalists e.g. the International Consortium of Investigative Journalists	Gather and publish evidence to expose corrupt and illegal practices	Show the ways that evidence is hidden, and can be uncovered. Gives insight into the 'black evidence ecosystem', and its role influencing governance, globally
Educators		
Agencies engaged in both formal and informal education e.g. UN, OECD, NYT, CDC	Aim to educate interested adults about both statistical ideas and substantive knowledge	Vital contributors to adult education. Useful sources of interactive data visualisations, and large carefully curated data sets

7 Sept 2019[5]). Having lost the 2020 presidential election, Trump made extraordinary claims about the probity of the election process. In the UK, prime minister Johnson used the term 'people vs parliament'. Lies, and attacks on the free press and the whole democratic process all pollute the evidence ecosystem. Citizens should be encouraged to engage in critical evaluation of claims, but the misuse of this can result in cynicism, confusion and doubt. Fear, confusion and lies as well as attacks on the free press and democratic institutions pollute the evidence ecosystem.

23.3.3   Print and Video Media

This is perhaps the most visible and accessible element in the data ecology. The category covers a broad spectrum from polemic outlets to agencies attempting to provide a balanced view of events. Audience is a critical consideration; it is easy to understand pressures to make a story more dramatic and vivid than the data allow. There is also a problem with the statistical expertise of journalists; many have few quantitative skills, and so are unable to critique the quality of evidence offered (for instance, by politicians) or to access and understand relevant data. A review of 4285 statistical references in news reporting across a wide range of media types (Cushion et al., 2017) concluded *While we found that statistics were often referenced in news coverage, their role in storytelling was often vague, patchy and imprecise.* (p. 1198).

Data journalism has been an important development, wherein support is provided to journalists for all phases of their work involving data. Sites such as https:// datajournalism.com/ set out to support responsible, evidence based journalism. There is advice on data visualisation and mapping, and courses on such things as countering hate speech, and effective approaches to searching the internet. *The Data Journalism Handbooks,*[6] produced by the European Journalism Centre and the Google News Initiative set out to support journalists in adopting a constructive and critical approach to data—by not assuming that data are 'given' and uncontested, but rather adopting the critical stance advocated in Chap. 3. *The Data Journalism Handbook 2*, for example, offers guidance on: assembling data—particularly for countries where it is difficult to access, such as in China and Cuba; different ways of working with data via algorithms; information on the use of a variety of digital tools—for example, tools that can be applied to text and social media; ways to present data, including data visualisation, and via interactive web pages; ways to explore content going viral; approaches to misinformation; and ways to assess user responses.

---

[5] https://www.theguardian.com/us-news/2019/sep/07/donald-trump-war-on-the-media-oppo-research

[6] https://datajournalism.com/read/handbook/two

The United Nations has also created a handbook[7] for journalism education and training on fake news and disinformation. In addition, *First Draft*—a group based at Harvard[8]—hosts a 'global verification and collaborative investigation network'. The group provides resources for online training of different groups such as journalists, academics and technology companies. This includes cross-checking platforms (e.g. in Europe, Nigeria and Australia) designed to adapt to different threats to authentic information.

Forbes Magazine adopted a robust approach to people who have told lies on behalf of a politician. An editorial states[9]: *Hire any of Trump's fellow fabulists* [names of people who had worked for Trump and who had made misleading statements on his behalf had been named earlier in the article], *and Forbes will assume that everything your company or firm talks about is a lie. We're going to scrutinize, double-check, investigate with the same skepticism we'd approach a Trump tweet. Want to ensure the world's biggest business media brand approaches you as a potential funnel of disinformation? Then hire away.*

There has been a great deal of debate around the notion of *free press and media*. Just as freedom of speech does *not* encompass shouting 'fire' in a cinema, there have been concerns about the deliberate dissemination of lies, and the responsibility of media in not reporting, or curtailing the spread of lies. A dramatic example[10] was major television networks (e.g. CNN, MSNBC, and ABC) in the USA deciding to stop broadcasting an on-going speech by the president: *"Here we are again in the unusual position of not only interrupting the president of the United States, but correcting the president of the United States,"* Brian Williams says on @MSNBC moments into the president's statement tonight.

This raises important issues about media regulation—who should be responsible for monitoring and addressing pollution in the evidence ecosystem? It is entirely appropriate for media outlets to correct false statements, but what about blocking speech itself? We discuss this in the next section on social media.

23.3.4   Social Media

Social media such as *Facebook, YouTube, WhatsApp, Messenger, WeChat, Instagram, QQW, Tumblr, Qzone, Tik Tok, Twitter* facilitate communication between citizens, with little moderation of content. This can have positive benefits—for example, by holding people accountable for their actions (e.g. by posting video of events) and negative effects—for example, by spreading conspiracy theories.

---

[7] https://unesdoc.unesco.org/ark:/48223/pf0000265552

[8] https://firstdraftnews.org/

[9] https://www.forbes.com/sites/randalllane/2021/01/07/a-truth-reckoning-why-were-holding-those-who-lied-for-trump-accountable/

[10] https://www.theguardian.com/us-news/2020/nov/05/tv-news-cut-away-trump-election-lies

The ways we each see our individual identity and group affiliations (our social selves) colour the ways we access and share information—for example by retweeting or forwarding news stories. We have emotional responses to information. The death of Kobe Bryant illustrates the importance of emotional responses in communication. Early in 2020, Bryant, a (retired) distinguished American basketball player, was killed with his daughter and seven others in a helicopter crash. In the week following the crash, there were 208 million relevant interactions with social media (more than the sum of interactions relevant to the outbreak of coronavirus (66 million), Trump's first impeachment trial (59 million), the Super Bowl (50 million), and the Grammys (12 million)). There were about 97,000 relevant stories—about half the number associated with the coronavirus.[11]

Cognitive aspects of accessing information are self-evident. Accessing information is not a passive process; we choose what to attend to, and make decisions about how much effort to allocate to evaluating and acting on the evidence we see (Kahneman, 2012). Choices around exposure to different data sources are coloured by frameworks of belief, loyalties and personal identities. Information that challenges firmly held beliefs is likely to be subject to more rigorous examination (or simply rejected) than information that is coherent with our beliefs. Cognitive biases may be accelerated by the echo chamber effect of social media. There is evidence of a trend where more people are choosing to live in 'information bubbles' and distrust non-preferred sources—for example, a 2020 poll by PEW[12] in the USA found that 75% of conservative Republicans trust Fox News and 67% distrust CNN; 77% of liberal Democrats distrust Fox News and 70% trust CNN.

People do not necessarily make active choices to live in information bubbles; the technologies themselves help users find content similar to the content they chose to access on earlier occasions—so the technology that supports 'if you liked this video, try this one' works for both *Bambi* and *QAnon*. More problematic are Google algorithms that underpin Google search. If you type in *climate change is* Google will offer: *disrupting the planet*; *is not man made*; *is a hoax*; depending on your search history.

In Chap. 22, Ridgway, Campos and Biehler explored ideas around disruptive socio-technical systems. They argued that it is not the technologies themselves that are disruptive, but that technologies can facilitate new patterns of human interaction, and can enable actions that were difficult or impossible without technology. Social media provide a prime example. A Nextflix documentary drama entitled *The Social Dilemma*[13] examines the practices of big tech companies, and makes extensive use of interviews with former employees and executives of *Instagram*, *Twitter* etc. some

---

[11] https://www.axios.com/newsletters/axios-media-trends-cf1f7b04-8fca-4de3-8a9d-6f8e212d2 6a4.html?utm_source=newsletter&utm_medium=email&utm_campaign=newsletter_ axiosmediatrends&stream=top

[12] https://www.journalism.org/2020/01/24/u-s-media-polarization-and-the-2020-election-a-nation-divided/?utm_source=newsletter&utm_medium=email&utm_campaign=newsletter_axiosam& stream=top

[13] https://www.netflix.com/gb/title/81254224

of whom created familiar tools such as *YouTube's* recommendation algorithm, and the *like* button. Many of the interviewees express regret about the ways that the tools they created have subsequently been used to 'erode the fabric of society'. These erosions include large negative effects on the mental health of young people and, indeed, on democracy itself. Social media obviously build upon human needs for social contact. The film points to design features based on psychological research which manipulate users' attention (often towards advertising) and which reward continued use via intermittent reinforcement. Returning to the theme of Chap. 22, social media in their present forms emerged in a particular social and economic climate—notably unregulated free-market capitalism (*if you are not paying for it you are the product*[14]). In a different political, social and economic climate it is unlikely that social media would have developed in exactly the same way.

There have been attempts by some owners of social media platforms to introduce some form of fact checking to messages on their platforms. At the time of writing, available evidence[15] showed that *Facebook's* introduction of labels to dubious claims had very little effect on the frequency of resharing; *Twitter's* more aggressive approach had more (but still rather limited) success. However, a critical incident in 2020 brought the tensions between enabling free speech and deterring misinformation to the centre of political debate. This was the decision by *Twitter* to ban President Trump in the aftermath of riots inside the Capitol Building. Angela Merkel and others argued strongly that the managers of social platforms should not have the right to curtail free speech. Bruno Le Maire, the French Finance Minister, argued[16] *Digital regulation should not be done by the digital oligarchy itself . . . Regulation of the digital arena is a matter for the sovereign people, governments and the judiciary.*

23.3.5 Cyber Warriors

International politics has always been about exerting influence. Tools include military might, economics—including control of energy and natural resources, espionage, and bribery. Relatively recently, 'information' has been added to this list. This includes direct action by military intelligence to access information or to disrupt IT systems (for example by introducing malware), and also to exert political influence by targeted use of social media. Profiling voters (both by political parties inside a country, and by foreigners) and tailoring messages specifically for individuals has been made much easier by the internet; these messages are not available for public

---

[14] https://www.forbes.com/sites/marketshare/2012/03/05/if-youre-not-paying-for-it-you-become-the-product/

[15] https://www.politico.com/story/2017/09/11/facebook-fake-news-fact-checks-242567

[16] https://www.francetvinfo.fr/monde/usa/presidentielle/donald-trump/bruno-le-maire-choque-que-ce-soit-twitter-qui-ferme-le-compte-de-donald-trump_4252977.html

scrutiny. There has been a great deal of discussion about real and imagined influences on elections via campaigns of information and misinformation, via financial support for particular political parties from foreign states, and via bribery of individuals. Interesting accounts of deliberate efforts to pollute the evidence ecosystem are offered by MacLachlan[17] (2019) in a Transparency International Report entitled *Corruption as Statecraft: using corrupt practices as foreign policy tools.*

It is worth distinguishing between mis-information and dis-information. The former covers activities such as forwarding content without checking its veracity—for example, a news clip video of a flood that was actually archive footage. The latter is information that the author knows to be wrong, and is distributed with the intention to deceive. Wardle and Derakhshan, (Wardle & Derakhshan, 2017)[18] add on mal-information, which is information that is correct, but which is distributed with the intention of causing harm. Examples include Hillary Clinton's leaked emails, or compromising photographs.

Of course, military intelligence also concerns itself with thwarting the efforts of foreign states. In addition to nations using their security services defensively as well as offensively, we can point to *The European Centre of Excellence for Countering Hybrid Threats*[19]—an initiative supported by the European Union and the North Atlantic Treaty Organisation to provide advice to countries on countering threats to national security posed by foreign powers that seek to interfere with internal decision making at state, institutional or local levels. These threats can be (mis)information, economic, military or political. Advice includes methods to identify vulnerabilities and risks, and to build resilience.

Bellingcat[20] is an example of a cyber warrior group of direct interest to Civic Statistics. Eliot Higgins, its founder, pioneered new ways to synthesise satellite data, social media posts and confidential databases (e.g. purchased illegally from Russian civil servants) to conduct impressive detective work. This includes discovering the identity of the Russian agents responsible for murder and attempted murder in the UK, and providing evidence against war criminals in Syria. One key message from this work is to see what can be achieved by synthesising data resources (here, for the good). A second message is that individuals can play a big role in international affairs.

We now move to consider agencies which have a more obvious role in the creation and curation of evidence—with benign intent, in most cases. Table 23.3 provides a summary.

---

[17] https://ti-defence.org/publications/corruption-as-statescraft/

[18] https://money.cnn.com/2017/11/03/media/claire-wardle-fake-news-reliable-sources-podcast/index.html

[19] https://www.hybridcoe.fi/

[20] https://www.bellingcat.com/

23.3.6 Survey Data Collectors and Distributors

Throughout the book we have used, and advocated the use of, large-scale data sets from reputable sources: these include National Statistics Offices, and international organisations such as the Organisation for Economic Co-operation and Development, Eurostat, and the World Bank. The scale of data collection is impressive, as is the attention to methodological issues, and the availability of fine grained and clear descriptions of metadata. Until relatively recently, access to these large data sets was restricted; now a great deal of data can be downloaded by anyone with computer access. There have been two other major developments. First is that many organisations have created educational materials—ranging from interactive elements that can be explored on their websites, through to materials designed for use in schools and universities. Second is a movement to create documents designed to be useful to policy makers, available in the public domain.

23.3.7 Sensor Data Collectors and Distributors

The US National Aeronautics and Space Administration (NASA) provides an interesting case history in organisational evolution. As well as having a responsibility for the civilian space programme, they now make huge amounts of data from satellites freely available via their Earth Observatory.[21] These include video of spectacular events such as volcanoes, and remote sensing of data such as temperature, light, infrared, sonar, gravity, and concentrations of different chemicals. NASA also provides teaching materials for teachers and students,[22] and supports citizen science.

A wide range of agencies (e.g. universities, NSOs) use sensors to collect data on a very wide range of subjects—for example Eurostat's surveys of land cover and usage.[23] A particularly interesting development from the viewpoint of Civic Statistics is the emergence of citizen sensing—engaging communities in fieldwork to collect data directly relevant to their interests and their environments (for example, monitoring pollution, or conducting surveys of flora and fauna, in order for citizens to improve the quality of their lives.[24]

---

[21] https://earthobservatory.nasa.gov

[22] https://www.nasa.gov/stem

[23] https://ec.europa.eu/eurostat/web/lucas

[24] https://citizensense.net/

23.3.8 'Invisible' Unaccountable Data Collectors and Distributors

Less traditional data collectors and distributors include: *Google, Amazon,* and *Facebook*, credit card agencies, travel card agencies, household devices that make use of the Internet of Things, *Alexa* and *Siri*. It is not always clear what data is collected, nor how data are stored, distributed and used. A controversial development is giving private companies access to large volumes of data—for example *Google* acquiring the personal health data from millions of people.[25] The role of the algorithms used in *Google's* search engine which act to offer users data sources likely to reinforce, rather than challenge, their beliefs was discussed earlier.

Table 23.4 summarises the roles and relevance of a third group agents in the information ecosystem.

23.3.9 Knowledge Creators and Curators

Universities (and other research agencies) play an important role in generating data, information, evidence, and stories about the world. Large databases of research such as *Scopus, PubMed* and *Google Scholar* are available which can be searched, and from which papers can be downloaded. This democratisation of science is a welcome development, and facilitates the spread of evidence and ideas. Academics progress in their careers by conducting research which is published in academic journals, and which is judged to be valuable by their peers (this process is summarised in the phrase "publish or perish"). It is unlikely that there was ever a 'golden age of science' where the entire scientific community was populated by altruistic persons bent on discovery, without thought for personal gain. However, the scientific community as a whole places value on honesty and due diligence, exemplified by practices such as peer-reviewing papers before publication. An alarming recent development has been the emergence of 'predatory journals' which publish the work of academics (for payment) without subjecting them to review. Worse, articles in these predatory journals can be found on widely used databases; the consequences are that database users might base their conclusions from a literature search that includes poorly conducted studies or even fabricated results. *Nature* reports a study[26] by Macháček and Srholec (2021) which found that 2.8% of the articles in a 2 year period on *Scopus* were from predatory journals. Providers of major databases are now aware of this problem, and are taking some actions to preserve

---

[25] https://www.wsj.com/articles/google-s-secret-project-nightingale-gathers-personal-health-data-on-millions-of-americans-11573496790

[26] https://www.nature.com/articles/d41586-021-00239-0?utm_source=Nature+Briefing&utm_campaign=0da5e44231-briefing-dy-20210209&utm_medium=email&utm_term=0_c9dfd39373-0da5e44231-45576630

the quality of the information available. It is clear that the critical evaluation and reflection that are the focus of facet 2 in Chap. 3 are necessary at every level of statistical competence.

An extraordinary recent development has been the dramatic increase in the politicisation of science. *Nature* is arguably the most prestigious and influential scientific journal in the world. On October 2020 it published an editorial entitled *Why Nature supports Joe Biden for US president.*[27] This is a remarkable polemic, which uses phrases such as *Trump's disregard for evidence and the truth*; *relentlessly attacked … science agencies;* and *politicize government agencies and purge them of scientific expertise.*

Open Data Advocates such as the Open Data Institute[28] (ODI) argue for the importance of open data, and advocate (and support) the use of open data to effect positive change. This involves addressing ethical issues around data collection, ensuring equity of access, and active engagement with people and organisations affected by the data. The ODI manifesto focuses on: developing and protecting open data infrastructures within societies; developing individual data literacy; using data in innovative ways; facilitating equality of access to data; ethical use of data; and promoting active engagement with data when addressing problems.

Websites devoted to the support of evidence informed practice include the Cochrane Library[29] for health studies which has assembled syntheses of research across the whole spectrum of medicine, and is used by (amongst others) the UK National Institute for Health and Care Evidence (NICE) in making decisions about which drugs can be licenced as part of the National Health Service. Similarly, the Campbell Collaboration[30] provides syntheses of research in social science. A third example is a resource for educators—the Teaching and Learning Toolkit[31] synthesises evidence in a way that makes it easy for practitioners in schools to see the effectiveness and cost of different interventions, and the strength of the supporting evidence.

Further welcome developments have been the creation of tools that facilitate literature searches, such as *Google Scholar*[32] and *Microsoft Academic*[33] other sites that offer clear advice on how to evaluate the quality of different sorts of study, such as the Critical Appraisal Skills Programme checklists.[34]

---

[27] https://www.nature.com/articles/d41586-020-02852-x?utm_source=Nature+Briefing&utm_campaign=7f2b123fc5-briefing-dy-20201014&utm_medium=email&utm_term=0_c9dfd39373-7f2b123fc5-45576630

[28] https://theodi.org/

[29] https://www.cochrane.org/

[30] https://campbellcollaboration.org/

[31] https://educationendowmentfoundation.org.uk/evidence-summaries/teaching-learning-toolkit/

[32] https://scholar.google.com

[33] https://academic.microsoft.com/home

[34] https://casp-uk.net/casp-tools-checklists/

Data science is creating new sorts of data, and new analytic tools. Decision making algorithms are being created, that can be problematic (see Ridgway, Campos and Biehler in Chap. 22) for a fuller discussion.

23.3.10 Advocacy Agencies

Many organisations gather data with a view to action. They create indicators, and aim to hold actors (such as governments) accountable. The United Nations Sustainable Development Goals[35] provide an example. There are 17 goals that include: Goal 1—*ending poverty in all forms, everywhere*; Goal 2—*ending hunger, achieving food security and improved nutrition, and promoting sustainable agriculture*; and Goal 16—*promoting peaceful and inclusive societies with access to justice for all, and with accountable and inclusive institutions at all levels*. Within these Goals are Targets; for example Target 16.10 is *Ensure public access to information and protect fundamental freedoms, in accordance with national legislation and international agreements*. Within Targets are Indicators. The relevant Indicators for Target 16.10 are: 16.10.1 *Number of verified cases of killing, kidnapping, enforced disappearance, arbitrary detention and torture of journalists, associated media personnel, trade unionists and human rights advocates in the previous 12 months* and 16.10.2 *Number of countries that adopt and implement constitutional, statutory and/or policy guarantees for public access to information.*

Other important advocacy agencies include International Aid agencies. These agencies are directly concerned with humanitarian issues, such as predicting and managing epidemics, supporting victims of floods and other natural disasters, and identifying and confronting corruption. This work calls directly on statistical skills such as predictive modelling (for example, using hydrological models to predict 'what next' in Region B in the aftermath of extreme weather events in Region A).

23.3.11 Fact Checking Organisations

There has been a gratifying growth in organisations concerned with fact checking, along with international developments to support the whole process. Agencies include *Chequeado*[36] in Argentina, *AfricaCheck*,[37] *Politifact*[38] in the USA, and *Full Fact*[39] in the UK. Their activities include checking facts in published print

---

[35] https://sustainabledevelopment.un.org/

[36] https://chequeado.com/

[37] https://africacheck.org/about-us

[38] https://www.politifact.com/

[39] https://fullfact.org/

media, social media, and in streaming media (e.g. TV debates). An interesting and important development is the move towards developing tools for automating the process of fact checking. Timing is important; a lie can race around the world whilst a factual correction is still in its starting blocks.

Full Fact aims to give journalists and fact checkers tools for automated fact checking that work in real time.[40] The Full Fact tool has two main components, *Live* and *Trends*. *Live* identifies claims in TV subtitles, and checks them against the Full Fact database; if items are found, these are displayed. If not, it fact checks using reliable relevant data, if they are available. AI approaches are being explored, cautiously. *Trends* records every repetition of a claim that Full Fact has identified as being wrong, and where it came from, in order to track those who are persistently disseminating misleading claims.

Google Fact Check Explorer[41] is designed to allow users to browse and search for fact checks, for example, of a politician's statement.

The *Factmata*[42] API claims to be able to assess web content in terms of its quality and credibility, as well as detecting hate speech, obscenity, threats, sexism and political bias.

Facebook is putting mechanisms in place to address false news. These include: using feedback from users, and from fact checkers; linking fact checkers' analyses to false news via links to 'related stories'; notifying people when they have shared false news; offering guidance ('ten top tips') to users on how to spot false news; and taking some action against repeat offenders, such as reducing their ability to advertise. Google has banned around 200 publishers from its AdSense advertising network on the basis of judgements about the veracity of content. However, the efficacy of these measures is unproven.

The *Partnership on AI* comprises over 100 partners (the BBC, Amazon, Apple, Google, Amnesty International, Baidu...) and sets out to promote dialogue and research into the uses of AI in society. One aspect of their work is the Deepfake Detection Challenge (DFDC). This encourages competition and collaboration amongst people involved in the development of technologies that can help detect manipulated media. Participants are encouraged to develop techniques that reliably distinguish authentic and manipulated data in a Deepfake dataset available on Kaggle. Open submissions are eligible for prizes (and, by definition, will be available to journalists and fact checking organisations in their work).

It is reasonable to encourage the widespread use of fact checking tools, however, such tools can be but part of a solution to countering false news. Earlier, we pointed to the problems associated with any time gap between the false story and the rebuttal. Credibility is a further problem—if users don't trust the fact checkers (for example, Republicans' distrust of the Washington Post fact checker), they will not disbelieve

---

[40] https://fullfact.org/automated

[41] https://toolbox.google.com/factcheck/explorer

[42] https://factmata.com/api.html

the false stories. A long-standing issue is 'all publicity is good publicity'—the extent to which negative fact checks reinforce or deflate false news needs to be explored.

In a similar vein, simply believing a 'fact check' is not without problems. In the UK, the Conservative Party rebranded its twitter account as *factcheckUK* during a television debate between rival politicians, and posted false claims as 'checked facts'.

23.3.12 Investigative Journalists and Leakers

The International Consortium of Investigative Journalists (ICIJ) is a network of over 250 journalists working in more than 70 countries. It is an independent group committed to exposing *inter alia* corruption, government abuses of citizens, illegal actions of the global elite, and powerful corporations. A number of major sources of leaked data can be accessed online. For example, *Wikileaks,*[43] the *Panama Papers*[44] and the *FinCEN*[45] files. *Wikileaks*, for example, demonstrated the scale of data gathered about citizens without their permission by both states and media companies. The *Panama Papers* comprise a leak of 11.5 million files from Mossack Fonseca, one of the world's biggest offshore law firms, with data on over 200,000 companies (over 100,000 of which are based in the British Virgin Islands). Journalists compiled lists of international criminals, leading politicians, and banks involved in illegal activities (a number of banks have subsequently been heavily fined). The ICIJ investigations have revealed the scale of the extent to which kleptocratic individuals have been able to move large amounts of money ($100 bn) around the world, hiding information about ownership. The Financial Crimes Enforcement Network monitors bank compliance with laws on financial crime, on behalf of the US Treasury. ICIJ analysed these *FinCEN* files and revealed money laundering on a *very* large scale (see our earlier definition of 'large') in which major financial institutions in the USA, the EU and (especially) the UK were complicit.[46] Investigative journalists are ideally placed to help maintain the evidence ecosystem; they can speak truth to citizens about power and corruption in a way that few other agents can.

23.3.13 Educators

In the context of the evidence ecosystem, we should accept a broad definition of the term *educators*. Obvious agents are schools and universities. In this book we have

---

[43] https://wikileaks.org/

[44] https://www.icij.org/tags/panama-papers/s/

[45] https://www.icij.org/tags/fincen-files/

[46] https://www.bbc.co.uk/news/uk-54226107

pointed to the limitations of many current curricula in meeting the pressing needs to create statistically literate citizens, and have offered some ways forward both conceptually (via a new conceptual framework), and practically via teaching materials. A very wide range of agencies provide tutorial materials, such as: newspapers (e.g. the New York Times); data visualisation advocates (e.g. *Datawrapper and Flowing Data)*; and agencies such as Eurostat, the World Bank. OECD, and Centres for Disease Control and Prevention.[47]

23.4 The Evidence Ecosystem as a Context for Civic Statistics

In the Introduction to this chapter, we used a quotation from James Madison (1825) *...the advancement and diffusion of knowledge* is *the only Guardian of true liberty*. In the previous section, we described the work of investigative journalists uncovering corrupt practices such as money laundering. In this section, we offer pointers to resources to support classroom activities, based on these themes of democracy and corruption, by considering approaches to measuring 'democracy' and 'perceptions of corruption'. Both of these challenges raise fundamental statistical issues that are central to Civic Statistics, and can also introduce students to some broad issues surrounding the idea of an evidence ecosystem.

23.4.1 Measuring 'Democracy'

Faced with the results of a single survey (say about universal suffrage (voting rights)), we could ask about how the survey was conducted, the sampling frame, the range of issues considered (who can vote? what is needed to vote?—such as high levels of literacy, or access to transport to a voting station etc.) and ways that data were analysed. Things get more complicated as the question gets bigger—and *how do we measure democracy* is a big question! Students can be asked to list the components of democracy, how they might be quantified, how data might be accessed, and then decisions need to be made about ways to combine these components (these key activities for designing measures, and creating indicator systems relate to themes discussed in Chap. 3 under the headings of *Critical Evaluation, Methodology*, and *Models, Patterns and Representations*). There are too many challenges here for students on introductory courses, but this context can provide an introduction to key ideas in measurement. A different approach is to use some of the carefully developed indicators available in the public domain. The *Gapminder* foundation hosts a spreadsheet which presents a number of indices (based on

---

[47] https://wwwn.cdc.gov/nchs/nhanes/tutorials/default.aspx

60 indicators, many of them relevant to Civic Statistics) created by the Intelligence Unit of *The Economist.*[48] The headline indicator is the *Democracy Index*, based on 60 different aspects of societies that are relevant to democracy, such as perception of human rights protection, universal suffrage, voter participation, and citizens' freedom to form organizations (such as trade unions) and political parties. The *Democracy Index* comprises the *Electoral Pluralism Index*, the *Government Index*, the *Political Participation Index*, the *Political Culture Index*, and the *Civil Liberty Index*.

Data are available by country, region, and aggregated for the whole world, over time. Figure 23.1 shows Democracy Indices for 167 countries, in 2019, via a colour-coded map. A 12-year time-series can be produced for any country via the pull-down menu, or by clicking on the map. Here, the *Democracy Index* for Russia has been chosen. The display shows a transition from *Hybrid regime* to *Authoritarian regime* over time.

Each of the sub-indices of the *Democracy Indicator* is made up of further indices—the *Civil Liberties Index*[49] is derived from 17 variables; here we show just 11 variables (with some minor editing) directly relevant to Civic Statistics.

1. Is there a free electronic media?
2. Is there a free print media?
3. Is there freedom of expression and protest (bar only generally accepted restrictions, such as banning advocacy of violence)?
4. Is media coverage robust? Is there open and free discussion of public issues, with a reasonable diversity of opinions?
5. Are there political restrictions on access to the Internet?
6. Are citizens free to form professional organisations and trade unions?
7. Do institutions provide citizens with the opportunity to petition government to redress grievances?
9. The degree to which the judiciary is independent of government influence. Consider the views of international legal and judicial watchdogs. Have the courts ever issued an important judgement against the government, or a senior government official?
10. The degree of religious tolerance and freedom of religious expression. Are all religions permitted to operate freely, or are some restricted? Is the right to worship permitted both publicly and privately? Do some religious groups feel intimidated by others, even if the law requires equality and protection?
16. There is no significant discrimination on the basis of people's race, colour or religious beliefs
17. Extent to which the government invokes new risks and threats as an excuse for curbing civil liberties.

---

[48] https://infographics.economist.com/2018/DemocracyIndex/

[49] https://docs.google.com/spreadsheets/d/1d0noZrwAWxNBTDSfDgG06_aLGWUz4 R6fgDhRaUZbDzE/edit#gid=935776888

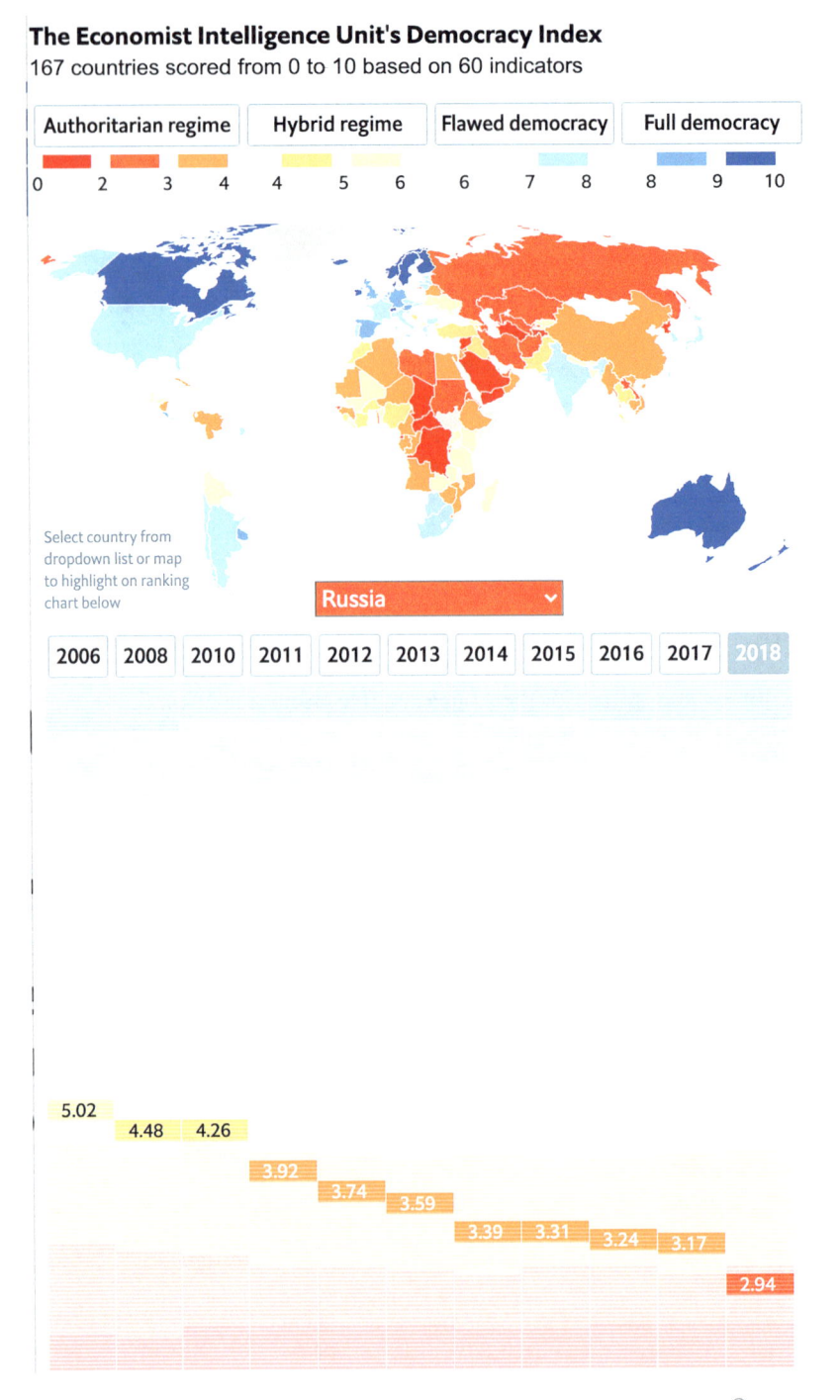

Fig. 23.1 Democracy Indicators for 167 countries, and World Trends Over Time. © Reused with permission of the Economist Intelligence Unit

Data are available in spreadsheet form, so students can be invited to look at trends over time in different countries, for single measures. They can also combine different measures to create new composite indicators (for example creating a *Discrimination Index*, by combining variables 10 and 16) and can explore topics such as transforming variables, and weighting variables in different combinations (so what happens to the *Discrimination Index* when variables 10 and 16 are given different weights?).

23.4.2 Assessing Perceptions of Corruption

Transparency International (TI)[50] is an independent, non-partisan group which aims to enable citizens to live their lives in societies free of corruption. Amongst other activities, they publish a *Corruption Perceptions Index*[51] which analyses public sector corruption in 180 countries; a graphical display is shown in Fig. 23.2. Data are derived from 13 data sets (not created nor gathered by TI) including data from the World Bank, and the World Economic Forum. Measures include bribery, diversion of public funds, the effective prosecution of corruption, access to information, and legal protection for whistle blowers and journalists. It does not include tax fraud, money laundering, or illicit flows of money.

These data can be the basis for student activities. Any of the activities associated with *Measuring democracy* could be done here. Students can be asked to analyse longitudinal data. Is corruption decreasing in the majority of countries? (answer: no). Are countries with good corruption scores (such as Western democracies) necessarily free of corruption? (no: transnational corruption is often facilitated by such countries—TI argues that countries which are the beneficiaries of money derived from corrupt practices have a responsibility to be open about money flows and ownership).

23.5 Civic Statistics in the Context of the Evidence Ecosystem

Engaging with evidence is not simply a cognitive process; it has emotional, social and cultural aspects. News reports do not simply provide information; they draw attention to important issues, and show dramatic scenes being acted out—such as warfare and natural disasters, along with personal triumphs and tragedies. Authors and actors strive to have their versions heard and actioned, and we engage emotionally. We are aware of our social identities—and pay more attention to things of direct

---

[50] https://www.transparency.org/

[51] https://www.transparency.org/cpi2019

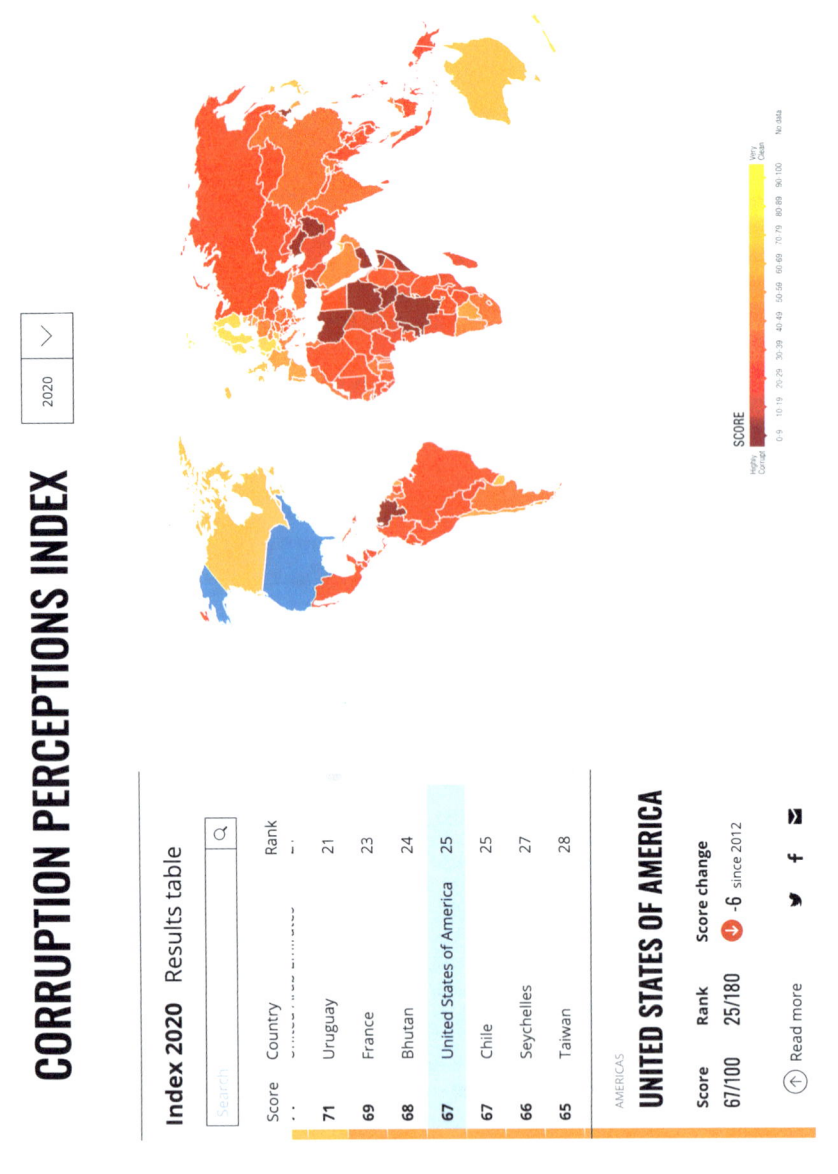

Fig. 23.2 Perception of Corruption in 180 Countries. This work from Transparency International (2020) is licenced under CC BY-ND 4.0

relevance to us. We are likely to accept assertions that reinforce our current beliefs and cultural values ("this politician has reduced unemployment" or "that politician has made things worse for poor people"). This is an issue for class discussion.

The evidence ecosystem will never be without some pollution. There are two factors that determine survival in any ecosystem; first is the extent of the pollution; second is the resilience of the species. A great deal of attention is being devoted in Western democracies to addressing the pollution in the evidence system (both to increase it for political purposes, and to decrease it for moral ones). This is a societal issue, and beyond the reach of educators. Too little attention has been devoted to building resilience; we can be active, here. Students need to be aware of the broad context in which evidence is created and valorised. This requires some understanding of the functioning of the evidence ecosystem, and some understanding of the interactions between producers, researchers, civil society, policy makers, and themselves as citizens.

Students can be asked questions which provoke reflection about the evidence ecosystem. For example:

- How can you turn <this example of deliberate deception> into a comedic routine (e.g. Sarah Cooper's videos using Trump's voice[52])
- If you had $1Billion to spend, how would you use it to; pollute the evidence ecosystem? Improve the hygiene of the evidence ecosystem?
- What are the advantages and disadvantages of an independent statistics office?
- What are the potential advantages and disadvantages of developing AI to monitor posts on social media?
- Write down 10 different uses of satellite data
- Find evidence of the dangers faced by investigative journalists in your country
- What are the advantages and disadvantages of using a search engine designed to offer a spectrum of opinions on contentious topics?
- Should the internet be regulated? If so, by whom and how?
- Describe your uses of the internet. What do you do when you feel an emotional response to something? How does the internet affect you socially? How do you search (do you use different information sources)? What information do you share? Do you fact-check before sharing?

We can be confident that developing understanding and acting in appropriate ways will be an on-going activity—the evidence ecosystem is evolving rapidly, and this will always be the case.

It is easy to point to examples where the quality of evidence is dubious, where evidence has been presented in misleading ways, and where powerful people use fabricated data as a warrant for their actions. However, cynicism about the use of evidence is dangerous. Cynicism encourages disengagement from evidence and informed action, and encourages judgements to be based on tribal loyalty rather than evidence, which can lead to an increasingly polarized society. In situations

---

[52] https://www.youtube.com/watch?v=bPLE34EemoE

where data are presented in a misleading way, students should be encouraged to re-present it in more appropriate ways; in situations where data are dubious (or fabricated) students should be encouraged to find relevant data from authoritative sources.

Resilience requires critical thinking and rationality; however, no-one has the capacity to check every evidence claim they encounter. Students can be encouraged to discuss the idea of 'trustworthiness'—how can one decide which information sources deserve a lower threshold of critical analysis than others? Why do some people believe that (say) evidence from Amnesty International is more trustworthy than evidence from some governments? Can these reasons (such as history of accuracy; motivation to mislead) be generalised to other sources they encounter?

23.6   A Brief Conclusion

Knowledge and beliefs are fluid, and have no fixed location. They are constructed and modified by a range of actors with different motives, and skills. Formal education typically embraces Enlightenment ideals, and often fails to take account of counter-Enlightenment views, and ignores the broad context of the evidence ecosystem. It is important to draw students' attention to the richness of the evidence ecosystem, and to the rival philosophies concerning the nature and functions of knowledge. It is important to encourage students to reflect on their own uses of knowledge both inside and outside the classroom, in order to make them more resilient in the face of polluting elements in the evidence ecosystem, and to enable them to benefit from the tremendous opportunities the evidence ecosystem holds to help humanity inhabit Dickens' *season of light*, rather than his *season of darkness.*

A Post-Script for This Chapter, and the Whole Book
In an enlightened society, citizens have access to information, can express their views openly, and can contribute to governance. This works only insofar as people feel empowered, and engage with evidence and ideas. The primary aim of Civic Statistics is to facilitate this process, not simply at the level of promoting appropriate skills of analysis, but also by inculcating confidence, and a willingness to engage. In this volume, we set out to make a contribution to statistics education by focusing on issues of social concern; this fundamental idea of using authentic data to address social problems is shared with a number of agencies and actors, and we believe that engagement with organisations and communities that share these values will be mutually beneficial.

Throughout, we have advocated the use of evidence to inform decision-making, and to lead to better actions. We have argued for the use of evidence as an integral part of decision making. We have argued for the need to interpret quantitative evidence in the context of broad knowledge schemas—evidence is part of a rich process of interpretation and understanding, and can support decision making. When we encourage our students to pursue understanding by exploring empirical evidence, we should bear in mind the words of T.S. Eliot—to paraphrase—information is not knowledge, and knowledge is not wisdom.

There is a battle for the soul of society, where proponents of informed democracy across the political spectrum are challenged by people (across the political spectrum) who believe in power and personal gain, no matter what the social cost. Technology offers some partial defences, but the most effective strategies for preserving things of value will always reside in shaping the ways that people interact with technologies. Citizens need to feel empowered, and have skills in critiquing interpreting evidence. For educators, there is a real opportunity to make use of new and exciting resources to both educate and empower. These are not easy ideas to communicate to our students—teaching to inculcate things that are 'correct' is far easier than teaching to develop nuanced judgement.

References

Cushion, S., Lewis, J., & Callaghan, R. (2017). Data journalism, impartiality and statistical claims. *Journalism Practice, 11*(10), 1198–1215. https://doi.org/10.1080/17512786.2016.1256789

Dickens, C. (1859). *A tale of two cities*. Penguin.

Eliot, T. (1969). *The complete poems and plays of TS. Eliot*. Faber and Faber.

Kahneman, D. (2012). *Thinking, fast and slow*. Penguin.

Macháček, V., & Srholec, M. (2021). Predatory publishing in Scopus: Evidence on cross-country differences. *Scientometrics, 126*, 1897–1921. https://doi.org/10.1007/s11192-020-03852-4

Rosling, H., Rosling, O., & Rosling-Ronnlund, A. (2019). *Factfulness: Ten reasons we're wrong about the world - and why things are better than you think*. Hodder and Stoughton.

Wardle, C., & Derakhshan, H. (2017). *Information disorder: Toward an interdisciplinary framework for research and policy making*. Council of Europe.

Index

Printed in the United States
by Baker & Taylor Publisher Services